THE COMPLETE ILLUSTRATED HISTORY OF

KNIGHTS& CRUSADES

BATTLES • CHIVALRY • CAMPAIGNS • WEAPONS • TOURNAMENTS

CHARLES PHILLIPS
CONSULTANT: DR CRAIG TAYLOR

HERMES
HOUSE

This edition is published by Hermes House,
an imprint of Anness Publishing Ltd,
Hermes House,
88–89 Blackfriars Road,
London SE1 8HA
tel. 020 7401 2077; fax 020 7633 9499

www.hermeshouse.com; www.annesspublishing.com

Anness Publishing has a new picture agency outlet for images for
publishing, promotions or advertising. Please visit our website
www.practicalpictures.com for more information.

Publisher: Joanna Lorenz
Editorial Director: Helen Sudell
Executive Editor: Joanne Rippin
Designer: Nigel Partridge
Artworks: Simon Smith
Production Controller: Wendy Lawson

ETHICAL TRADING POLICY

At Anness Publishing we believe that business should be conducted
in an ethical and ecologically sustainable way, with respect for the
environment and a proper regard to the replacement of the natural
resources we employ.

As a publisher, we use a lot of wood pulp in high-quality paper for
printing, and that wood commonly comes from spruce trees. We
are therefore currently growing more than 750,000 trees in three
Scottish forest plantations. The forests we manage contain more
than 3.5 times the number of trees employed each year in making
paper for the books we manufacture.

Because of this ongoing ecological investment programme, you, as
our customer, can have the pleasure and reassurance of knowing
that a tree is being cultivated on your behalf to naturally replace the
materials used to make the book you are holding. For further
information, go to www.annesspublishing.com/trees

PUBLISHER'S NOTE

Although the information in this book is believed to be accurate
and true at the time of going to press, neither the authors nor the
publisher can accept any legal responsibility or liability for any
errors or omissions that may have been made.

Previously published as two separate volumes: *The Complete
Illustrated History of Knights and the Golden Age of Chivalry*
and *A Complete Illustrated History of the Crusades and the
Crusader Knights*.

CONTENTS

Introduction 8

THE WORLD OF THE MEDIEVAL KNIGHT 16
Timeline of Medieval Chivalry 18

THE ORIGINS OF KNIGHTHOOD 20
The World Before Knights 22
Feudal Warriors 24
A Christian Empire in Europe 26
Paragon of Chivalry 28
The Emperor's Cavalry 30
A Time of Unrest 32
Alfred the Great and English Militias 34
The Rise of the Normans 36
The First Knights 38

HOLY WAR 40
Fighting a Holy War 42
Defenders of the Faith 44
Muslim Empires 46
Christians in the East 48
The Power of the Papacy 50
The Holy City of Jerusalem 52
The Penitential Journey 54
Crusader Pilgrims 56

BECOMING A KNIGHT 58
Acquiring Courtesy 60
At a Knight's Right Hand 62
'Arise, Sir Knight' 64
'Be Thou a Knight!' 66

The Meaning of Knighting 68
'Hotspur' 70
How to Be a Knight 72

THE KNIGHT AT HOME 74
A Lord in His Manor 76
Keeper of the Peace 78
Castles and Manor Houses 80
Knights at Leisure 82
Marriages and Alliances 84
Life in a Knightly Brotherhood 86

A KNIGHT AT ARMS 88
The Mounted Warrior 90
The Armoured Knight 92
A Knight's Role in Battle 94
Coeur de Lion 96
The Spectacle of War 98
The Age of Siege Warfare 100
Pillaging and Burning 102
'The Black Douglas' 104
The Business of War 106
Chivalry in Warfare 108

THE FIRST AND SECOND CRUSADES 110
Timeline of the First Crusades 112

A CALL TO ARMS 114
Constantinople Under Threat 116
Righteous Warfare 118
God Wills It! God Wills It! 120

The Quest for Glory 122
Walking to the Holy Land 124

THE JOURNEY TO PALESTINE 126
More Than the Stars of Heaven 128
Princes on Crusade 130
The Crusaders in Constantinople 132
The Siege of Nicaea 134
Men of Iron 136
Defender of Jerusalem 138
The March Across Anatolia 140

BOUND FOR JERUSALEM 142
The Siege of Antioch 144
The Fall of Antioch 146
Miracles at Antioch 148
The Prince of Antioch 150
The Way to the Holy City 152
Robert of Jerusalem 154
Jerusalem! Jerusalem! 156
The Holy City Captured 158
After the Victory 160

THE LAND OVERSEAS 162
The Kingdoms of Palestine 164
The Foundation of Outremer 166
Government of the Crusader States 168
Life in the Crusader States 170
Prince of Galilee 172
Krak des Chevaliers 174
By Sea from Italy 176

(continued overleaf)

MUSLIM RESURGENCE AND THE
SECOND CRUSADE 178
The Field of Blood 180
The Capture of Edessa 182
Soldiers of Islam 184
Call to a Second Crusade 186
Crusaders Set Out 188
Disaster at Dorylaeum 190
The Council of Acre 192
Despair and Recriminations 194
Nur ed-Din and a Unified Syria 196
The Battle for Egypt 198
The Chivalrous Infidel 200
Crusaders Destroyed 202
Jerusalem Recaptured 204

THE LATER AND EUROPEAN
CRUSADES 206
Timeline of the Later Crusades 208

RICHARD THE LIONHEART AND THE
THIRD CRUSADE 210
The Catholic Expansion 212
Once More to Jerusalem 214
Kings of Europe Take the Cross 216
Barbarossa's Crusade 218
In Sicily and Cyprus 220
A Sick Winter 222
The Capture of Acre 224
Atrocity at Acre? 226
Richard's March to Jaffa 228
An Uncertain Future 230

The Treaty of Jaffa 232
After the Third Crusade 234

CRUSADES OF THE EARLY 13TH
CENTURY 236
Fighting for Venice 238
On to Constantinople 240
The Sack of Constantinople 242
A New View of Crusading 244
The Children's Crusades 246
The Fifth Crusade 248
Jerusalem Regained 250
Kingdom of Jerusalem Rebuilt 252

CRUSADES OF THE MID-13TH TO
15TH CENTURIES 254
Crusade in Egypt 256
A King's Ransom 258
The Eighth Crusade 260
Saint Louis 262
The Ninth Crusade 264
The Fall of Tripoli and Acre 266
The Attack on Alexandria 268
Peter I of Cyprus 270
Crusade to Mahdia 272
Defeat at Nicopolis 274
The End of Byzantium 276
The Conqueror 278
The Miracle of Belgrade 280

THE WARRIOR MONKS 282
Knights of St John 284

Hospitallers Save Rhodes 286
Suleyman Takes Rhodes 288
Knights of the Temple of Solomon 290
Knights Templar in the Field 292
Templar Builders 294
Downfall of the Templars 296
Teutonic Knights 298
Warriors of the Reconquista 300
Knights of St Thomas 302
The Order of St Lazarus 304

THE EUROPEAN CRUSADES 306
The Reconquista 308
The Spanish Crusade of 1212 310
The Conquest of Granada 312
The Albigensian Crusade 314
Massacre of the Cathars 316
The Cathar Inquisition 318
The Baltic Crusades 320
In Prussia and Lithuania 322
Crusades against the Hussites 324
Crusades in Italy 326

THE GLORY OF CHIVALRY 328
Timeline of Chivalry 330

THE GOLDEN AGE OF THE
CHIVALRIC KNIGHT 332
A Knight Loyal and Brave 334
Crusader King 336
The Gentle Qualities of a Knight 338
'The Most Courteous Knight Alive' 340

A Christian Warrior 342
Tales of War and Love 344
Noble Warfare 346
A Knight Fearless and Blameless 348
Brotherhood of Arms 350
King of Chivalry 352
Orders of Chivalry 354
The Black Prince 356

KNIGHT OF THE TOURNEY 358
Martial Games 360
Prowess on Display 362
Heralds and Challenges 364
A Sea of Colours 366
Queen of the Tournament 368
War and Peace 370
Death and Danger 372
'The Greatest Knight That Ever
 Lived' 374
Rules of the Game 376
Protection in the Lists 378
Brothers in Arms 380
Knights of Good Standing 382

LEGENDARY KNIGHTS 384
Timeline of Legendary Knights 386

KNIGHTLY HEROES OF THE BIBLICAL
AND CLASSICAL WORLDS 388
God's Soldiers 390
Heroes of Ancient Greece 392
The Adventures of Alexander 394

Knight of Rome 396
Sir Orfeo 398

KING ARTHUR AND THE KNIGHTS OF
THE ROUND TABLE 400
Lord of Camelot 402
A King Betrayed 404
King Arthur's Squire and Seneschal 406
The Married Knight Errant 408
The Holy Knight 410
A Mystical Journey 412
The Flawed Knight 414
The Perfect Knight 416
A Knight Strong as the Sun 418
A Villain at Camelot 420

KNIGHTS IN HISTORY 422
Christian Knights in Battle 424
In Search of Glory 426
Rebel Lords 428
German Knight at Court 430
El Cid 432
Defender of Jerusalem 434
German Crusader 436
The Romance of Coeur de Lion 438
Adventures in Love and on
 Crusade 440
Scotland's Greatest Knight 442
Defender of French Chivalry 444
The Eagle of Brittany 446
Hero in the Lists 448
The 'English Achilles' 450

KNIGHTLY LOVERS AT COURT 452
Games of Love 454
In a Lady's Service 456
Knights Errant 458
The Glories of Chivalric Love 460
Orlando in Love 462
When a Christian Loved a Pagan 464
Into the Otherworld 466
Brave Knights and Phantom Ladies 468

SAINTS AND OUTLAWS 470
The Ideal Christian Knight 472
Patron Saints at War 474
Holy Warrior 476
Outlaw Knights 478
The Scourge of the Vikings 480
Robber Knights 482
Knights of the Forest 484

DECLINE AND LEGACY OF
KNIGHTHOOD 486
Timeline of Decline and Legacy 488

THE END OF AN ERA 490
The Changing Face of Warfare 492
The Cannon and the Musket 494
Paid to Fight 496
The Last Days of Chivalry 498
The Enduring Romance of Knighthood 500
The Legacy of Crusading 502

Index and Acknowledgements 506

INTRODUCTION

They bear weapons suitable for war, they have the cross of Christ on their right shoulder or between their shoulders, and with a unified voice they give issue to the cry, "God wills it! God wills it! God wills it!" This was the description – according to an anonymous chronicle of the First Crusade, the *Gesta Francorum* ('Deeds of the Franks') of *c.*1100 – given to the Norman lord Bohemond of Taranto when he asked for information about the army marching across Europe in 1096, bound for the Holy Land. The army had arisen in response to a call from Pope Urban II, in November 1095, for the fighting men of Europe to hurry to the aid of Christians in the East, who were being persecuted by Muslim Seljuk Turks, and to liberate the sacred places of Jerusalem. Bohemond was inspired to follow them.Pope Urban's sermon at Clermont was one of the most powerful and influential in history. Its depiction of the humiliation of Christians by Turks and the

▼ *Fighting in the name and under the cross of Christ. Godfrey of Bouillon was the first ruler of the Latin Kingdom of Jerusalem.*

▲ *The Third Crusade (1189–92) achieved the Muslim surrender of Acre to King Philip II of France and Richard the Lionheart.*

Muslim possession of Jerusalem – represented as the taking 'into slavery of the Holy City of Christ' – inspired an outpouring of religious anger and energy sufficient to mobilize Christians in their thousands to leave their homes and march across continents risking all for Christ and the Church. Particularly persuasive was Urban's promise that participation made personal salvation almost certain – he said, according to an account of his speech by Robert the Monk: 'Take on this journey for the remission of sins, in confidence of the undying glory of God's kingdom.'

The speech launched the popular movement of pilgrims and soldiers described above – known as the People's Crusade by historians – and a second wave of armies led by leading nobles and minor royalty, called the Princes' Crusade, in which Bohemond of Taranto took part. These two waves of people converged on Constantinople, capital of the Christian Byzantine Empire, where they arrived between August 1096 and May 1097. A little over two years later, in July 1099,

after many gruelling marches, desperate sieges and brutal battles, and reportedly having been helped at Antioch by heavenly armies led by St George, the survivors of these crusader forces succeeded in capturing Jerusalem from Fatimid Muslims amid scenes of deplorable ferocity yet nevertheless in the belief that they were doing God's will. The crusade leaders reported to the pope: 'The Lord … made a gift to us of the city, along with his foes … in the portico of Solomon and in his Temple, our men rode in the blood of the Saracens even up to the knees of their horses.'

TWO CENTURIES, NINE CRUSADES

These events were celebrated as a glorious triumph in Europe and led to the establishment of a Christian Kingdom of Jerusalem in Palestine and Syria that survived in various forms until 1291. They inspired a whole series of crusading expeditions not only to the Holy Land but also to north Africa and within Europe itself.

Traditionally historians identified nine crusades. According to this reckoning, the First Crusade of 1095–99, which ended with the taking of Jerusalem and the establishment of the Kingdom of Jerusalem, was followed by a second (1147–49), called by Pope Eugenius III (ruled 1145–53) in response to the capture by Muslim forces of Christian-held Edessa. Led by King Louis VII of France and Conrad III of Germany, it ended dismally in a humiliating failure to take Damascus.

The Third Crusade (1189–92) was called in 1187 by Pope Gregory VIII (ruled October–December 1187) following the devastating defeat of the army of the Kingdom of Jerusalem by Muslim general Saladin at the Battle of the Horns of Hattin in July 1187 and Saladin's subsequent capture of Jerusalem. The crusade was led by Holy Roman Emperor Frederick I, King Philip II of France and

▲ *In the encounters between Christian crusaders and their Muslim enemies, both sides called on God to support their cause.*

King Richard I Coeur de Lion ('the Lion Hearted') of England. Frederick died en route, Philip and Richard were delayed in Sicily and Cyprus and then quarrelled, and although King Richard performed a number of heroic acts and won a great victory over Saladin in the Battle of Arsuf, the crusade ended in a negotiated settlement without the hoped-for recapture of the city of Jerusalem.

The Fourth Crusade (1202–04) was called by Pope Innocent III (ruled 1198–1216), with the aim of attacking the Holy Land by way of Egypt, but it fell under the control of the city of Venice, which provided the fleet for the crusader army, and diverted to attack the Christian city of Zara and then the Byzantine capital, Constantinople. The Fifth Crusade (1217–21) attacked Egypt and succeeded in capturing the port of Damietta, but then made an unwise attempt to attack Cairo that ended in defeat by the Egyptian sultan al-Kamil, bringing a humiliating end to what had been a promising campaign. In the course of this crusade, the papal legate Pelagius was offered possession of Jerusalem – indeed, the return to the borders of the Latin Kingdom of Jerusalem as

they had stood before the disastrous defeat at the Battle of the Horns of Hattin – but declined on the grounds that the Holy City must be won by the sword and not by negotiation with the infidel.

The Sixth Crusade (1228–29) was led by Holy Roman Emperor Frederick II while he was excommunicated following a quarrel with the pope and it was remarkably successful: through diplomacy rather than military might, he regained posses-

▼ *In November 1095, in the market place of Clermont, Pope Urban II makes the call to arms that results in the First Crusade.*

sion of Jerusalem, Nazareth and Bethlehem. The Seventh Crusade (1248–54) was led by King Louis IX of France in response to the fall of Jerusalem to the Khwarezmian Turks in 1244. Once again attacking Egypt and capturing Damietta, it again ended in failure for the Christians. Louis was captured and ransomed at enormous expense, after which he travelled to Acre in Palestine and remained there for some years.

The Eighth Crusade (1270) was again led by Louis IX. It set out for Syria but diverted to attack Tunis, where Louis died either of bubonic plague or dysentery and where the crusade came to nothing. The Ninth Crusade (1271–72) consisted of a campaign to the Holy Land led by the future King Edward I of England, in the course of which he made a few minor territorial gains – and famously survived an assassination attempt.

OTHER CRUSADES

The labelling of the nine crusades is arbitrary. There were not only a large number of other smaller crusades between those summarized above, but also many other campaigns that were promoted as crusades with the grant of indulgences after 1271 – at least until the Battle of Lepanto in 1571, between the Christian 'Holy League' (of the papal states, Spain, Venice, Genoa, the Duchy of Savoy and the Knights of Malta) and the fleet of the Ottoman empire, if not even later.

Moreover, the nine crusades in the traditional list include: one (the Fourth) that got no farther than Constantinople, two (the Fifth and the Seventh) directed not at the Holy Land but at Egypt, and one (the Eighth) that diverted to Tunisia and ran out of steam there. There were also many other crusades in Europe that do not make it into the traditional list. These were fought in Spain and Portugal against Muslims, in the Baltic region against pagans, in southern France and Bohemia against Christians declared heretics by the Catholic Church, and in Italy against enemies of the papacy.

As a result of these complications, modern historians question the traditional numbering. Some identify the Sixth Crusade (1228–29), the campaign by Holy Roman Emperor Frederick II, on

▼ *The reputation of Richard Coeur de Lion, one of the leaders of the Third Crusade, made much of his ferocity. Stories were told of the crusader king's fondness not only for killing but also for eating Saracens.*

which he regained possession of Jerusalem and Bethlehem through diplomacy, as part of the Fifth Crusade (1217–21), the campaign to Egypt under the command of papal legate Pelagius – for Frederick was pledged to join the Fifth Crusade but did not arrive despite the fact that a German army was in Egypt awaiting his command. Some see the Ninth Crusade (1271–72), on which the future King Edward I of England campaigned briefly in the Holy Land, as part of the Eighth Crusade (1270), the all-too-brief campaign during which King Louis IX of France died during the siege of Tunis.

Historians therefore also disagree as to the total number of crusades. In the 18th century some counted eight crusades while some insisted there were just five (the First, Second, Third, Fifth and Seventh). Many modern historians also limit the numbered crusades to just five, but usually number only the first five from the traditional list and then describe the rest by name.

In this book, for reasons of clarity and ease of comparison with other reference sources, we will follow the traditional numbering from the First to Ninth Crusades and refer to other campaigns by

▲ *Louis IX's ships on the Nile battle against the Saracens during the Seventh Crusade.*

name (usually that of the destination or leader) and date. Minor (unnumbered) crusades to the Holy Land or those aimed at restoring Christian power in the Holy Land are treated in the progression of the main narrative, but the crusades directed against Muslims in the Iberian Peninsula, against pagans and heretic Christians in central and northern Europe and Bohemia and against enemies of the Church in Italy are treated in a separate chapter.

BROTHERS IN ARMS

In the aftermath of the success of the First Crusade, the monastic order of the Knights Hospitaller of St John of Jerusalem was established in Jerusalem. It had responsibility for the defence of the Holy Land and had grown from a hospice (guesthouse) or hospital for pilgrims to Jerusalem. The brotherhood was recognized in 1113 by Pope Paschal II (ruled 1099–1118) as the Hospitallers of St John of Jerusalem. This was followed shortly afterwards by the establishment of the order of the Poor Knights of Christ and the Temple of Solomon – later known as

▲ *The Knights of St John defend the island of Rhodes against Ottoman attack in 1480.*

the Knights Templar, recognized in 1129 at the Council of Troyes and confirmed by Pope Innocent III in 1139. More brotherhoods followed, including the Teutonic Knights and the Knights of St Lazarus.

These monastic military brotherhoods won a reputation for great bravery and ferocity in defence of the Christian settlements in the Kingdom of Jerusalem, where they built and garrisoned many great castles. Later, the Knights Templar were charged with heresy and suppressed by the Catholic Church in the early 14th century, and most of their very considerable assets were passed to the Knights Hospitaller, who went on to win wide acclaim and admiration for their heroics in defending first Rhodes and then Malta against the Ottoman Turks. The warrior brotherhoods were an institution intimately connected with the crusading spirit and unique to the culture of chivalry.

ROMANCE OF CHIVALRY
By the 14th century the events of the First Crusade were a distant, romanticized memory. In this later era kings, princes

and gentlemen soldiers looked back on the knights of the 11th century – and the knights' imagined precursors in earlier years – as embodiments of military and even of religious perfection.

In August 1346 Edward Prince of Wales, the recently knighted 15-year-old son of King Edward III of England, covered himself in glory at the Battle of Crécy as he helped the English army to a famous victory over a French force that outnumbered them by three times.

One among as many as 30,000 casualties in the French army was King John of Bohemia, a major figure of 14th-century European chivalry who had insisted on proceeding into the thick of the battle with his men at arms despite the fact that he was almost completely blind. His corpse was found on the battlefield the next day surrounded by the bodies of his men, who

▼ *The Battle of Crécy. According to one account, Prince Edward was forced to his knees in the mêlée and was only saved from capture by Sir Richard Fitzsimon.*

had died defending him and had tied the reins of their bridles to each other so that they would not be driven apart in the mêlée of the conflict.

After the battle, Prince Edward (later known as the 'Black Prince', probably because he fought in black armour) paid tribute to King John, who had been killed fighting the Prince and his men, by adopting John's personal crest of an ostrich feather and his motto *Ich dien* (a short version of German *Ich diene*, 'I serve'). In adapted form this crest and motto remains that of the Prince of Wales to this day. Returning to England in October 1347, after besieging and capturing Calais and negotiating a truce, King Edward and the Black Prince celebrated Christmas at Guildford then held a great series of chivalric tournaments in 1348.

At one tournament, in Windsor, the king founded the Most Noble Order of the Garter, dedicated to the Virgin Mary and St George and conceived as a 'Round Table' of knights in tribute to the mythical chivalric warriors of King Arthur.

The founder members of the Order of the Garter were mostly veterans of Crécy and cherished companions and opponents of King Edward and the Black Prince at chivalric tournaments. One later but celebrated story explaining the origin of the Order's badge (a garter) and motto *Honi soit qui mal y pense* ('Shame come to him who thinks evil of it') was that it arose from an act of gallantry performed by the king when he swept up the garter that had fallen from the leg of his mistress the Countess of Salisbury and put it on his own leg with those words.

This sequence of events, from the Battle of Crécy to the foundation of the Order of the Garter, captures a great deal of the romance of medieval knighthood and encompasses many of the most glamorous aspects of its code of chivalry: triumph in battle for a newly made knight – often called 'winning his spurs'; King John's determination to seek glory as a warrior; the devoted service – even unto death – of his men at arms; the Black Prince's generosity in victory; the siege and capture of a foreign city; jousting in tournaments before admiring ladies of the court; the foundation of an order of knights in celebration of the legends of King Arthur and the knights of the Round Table, but also

▲ *By the reign of Edward III of England (left), the cult of St George (right) as patron of knights was well established. George was originally an Eastern Orthodox saint.*

as a mark of religious devotion to the Virgin Mary and St George; and the gallantry of a knight, in this case King Edward, towards his lady. Yet it presents only one face of medieval chivalry, which

in the course of about 500 years across many countries had many varied aspects.

At one time historians tended to treat the medieval institution of knighthood as if it were unchanging from the time of its development under the Normans in England during the second half of the 11th century, throughout the medieval period. However, it is important to emphasize that knighthood and knights' understanding of chivalry changed over the 250 or so years from the late 11th century to the mid-14th century and again over the next 200 to 250 years from the time of King Edward III of England to the last flowerings of chivalry in the later 16th and early 17th century. One key change was that knighthood became more exclusive: at one time a brotherhood of warriors to which the greatest martial figures could be raised, it became associated with inherited rank, and increasingly limited only to the descendants of knights.

A MOUNTED WARRIOR

In origin the knight was a mounted warrior. The word for knight in French (*chevalier*), Spanish (*caballero*) and

▼ *Edward III made St George the patron of the Order of the Garter.*

German (*ritter*) means in every case 'horse-man'. The knight had a relationship of near-religious intensity with his weapons (principally his lance and sword) and with his horse. In chivalric chansons ('songs') and romances, from which we learn so much of knights' received wisdom about chivalric warfare, King Arthur had his revered sword Excalibur, and Roland (leading knight of the Frankish king Charlemagne) fought with a magnificent weapon named Durandel. The chanson hero Renaud of Montauban had his famous magical horse Bayard, which could grow bigger or smaller to accommodate riders of different sizes, and the Spanish war captain Don Rodrigo Diaz de Vivar ('El Cid') had his extraordinary steed Bavieca, which refused ever to take another rider after Don Rodrigo's death.

However, the knights who rode as 'soldiers of Christ' to the Holy Land on crusade and those who jousted in the lists to win the favour of their lady were more than just mounted warriors. They certainly honoured bravery and courage, and praised prowess in battle (or in the lists at

▲ *The Arthurian knight Sir Galahad was more spiritual aspirant than bloodthirsty warrior. In the Grail cycle of legends, Galahad was praised as innocent and pure.*

▼ *Loyalty and honour often led to death. Knights drew inspiration from Roland, who fought to the end to prevent his sword Durandel falling into the hands of Saracens.*

chivalric tournaments). But they also aspired to a range of qualities such as Christian faith, courtesy, generosity, loyalty and moderation that were connected to a world of social and religious obligations rather than to life in the saddle.

AT YOUR SERVICE

The English word 'knight' is derived from the Anglo-Saxon *cniht*, meaning servant or young man, and service was a key element in the medieval institution of knighthood and the accompanying code of chivalry. Knight service was the name for the land-holding arrangement within the feudal system, under which knights were given the right to hold land in return for serving as a mounted soldier, usually for 40 days a year. The knight provided this obligation of military service to his suzerain (superior within the feudal system) or the king, to whom, initially at least, the land ultimately belonged.

◄ *Sir Lancelot, first knight of Arthur's round table, seen here capturing the castle Dolorous Garde, had all the qualities of the perfect knight, but his adultery with Guinevere was a grave failing.*

kings Charles Martel and Charlemagne. But these Macedonian, Roman or Frankish warriors were not knights in the way of the medieval knights, such as the mid-14th-century English knight Sir John Chandos, renowned for his diplomacy as well as his martial spirit and hailed in the chronicles of Froissart as 'the most courteous knight alive'. Or of 15th–16th century French knight Pierre de Terrail, Seigneur de Bayard, who was known for his spotless honour and carefree manner and was declared *Le chevalier sans peur et sans reproche* ('The fearless and blameless knight'), Or indeed of great knights in the chivalric literature, such as Roland, or the figures of the Arthurian tradition such as Lancelot or Percival.

▼ *French knight Bertrand du Guesclin was famous for rising from relatively humble origins to achieve high office.*

As the social and religious institution of knighthood developed, however, knightly service acquired other important aspects: service to Christ by fighting for the Christian faith; service to the weak and vulnerable by enforcing the peace; service to the knight's lady by winning honour either in combat at a tournament or by embarking on a journey of challenges as a 'knight errant'.

CHIVALRIC CODE

The medieval knight's devotion to service, and to the ethical and spiritual aspects of the chivalric code, made him different from a mounted soldier of earlier ages. We shall see that the medieval knights had precursors in the aristocratic elite of the hetairoi (companions) who rode into battle with spear and sword alongside the 4th-century BC Macedonian king and general Alexander the Great; they had forerunners also in the cavalry of the Parthian and Roman empires, and in the mounted warriors of the great Frankish

INSPIRATION TO CHIVALRY

Literary representations of knightly virtue were essential to the development of the institution of knighthood. Great deeds of knights were presented by poets and chroniclers as an inspiration to further great deeds of chivalry. The Spanish law codes *Las Siete Partidas*, promulgated in the mid-13th century by Alfonso 'the Wise' of Castile, declared that 'accounts of brave feats of arms should be declaimed before knights while they ate', to promote deeds of chivalry by generating a desire to outdo great deeds of the past.

Figures such as the 12th-century French poet and writer of romances Chrétien de Troyes, the author of five Arthurian romances and the writer who introduced Sir Lancelot into the cycle, played a key role in formulating prevailing images of knighthood. The most important patrons for Chrétien de Troyes and other poets of the time were lords such as Henry I, Count of Champagne (husband of Marie de Champagne, and thus son-in-law of Henry II of England's crusader armies has an undeniable heroic element. A good number of those who participated may have merely professed to be taking the cross for religious reasons while secretly hoping to find land, wealth or simply adventure. But another large contingent of crusaders genuinely committed themselves to crusading for religious reasons, and for these people, taking the cross was an act of self-denial, of committing to a larger cause.

This book celebrates the world of the medieval knight, his golden age but also his decline, and examines the knight as a symbol, a literary figure and a heroic ideal. The archetype of the knight lives on through the continuing popularity of chivalric romances – particularly of the Arthurian tradition – and beyond into the age of adventure movies and computer games. He has survived as an inspirational figure; an embodiment of the noble virtues of bravery, strength of character and simplicity of spirit.

wife Eleanor of Aquitaine), and Philip, Count of Flanders. These powerful figures were not only supporters of the arts, but financers and patrons of the chivalric sport of tourneying.

Chivalric literature and tournaments developed side by side with martial prowess. Inside noble courts, castles and, later, manor houses, knights and their retainers, exhausted after a physically demanding day of jousting in the lists, would settle down in the evening to listen to tales of chivalry. The audience had a taste for tales of arms in various settings, whether the Arthurian court, the Holy Land towns familiar to Crusaders, the classical world of Alexander the Great or Hector of Troy, or the battles against hordes of Saracens (Muslim warriors) fought by Charlemagne and his knights.

CONTINUING RESONANCE

The accounts of the crusades and of the exploits of knights that inspired generations in the Middle Ages retain an appeal today. The extraordinary enterprise of the

▲ *In tournaments knights proved their martial skills before appreciative courtiers. They fought first with lances, then swords.*

▼ *Early artillery cannon were difficult to load and inaccurate but still had a devastating effect against armoured knights.*

PART ONE

THE WORLD OF THE MEDIEVAL KNIGHT

The knight who won glory charging with couched lance on the battlefield or jousting in the lists at tournament had usually undergone a rigorous training, learning courtesy and the ways of war over many years as a page in a noble household and a squire in the service of a knight. As a result his skills as warrior and horseman were beyond question, and he understood his duties. In times of both war and peace, his principal task was to serve: to fight in the company of his feudal lord, to protect the Church by guarding the vulnerable and keeping the peace, and if by good fortune he were tied to the service of a noble lady, to honour her by feats of arms and knight errantry. Knightly service was a matter of great pride: a squire might have to wait many years to be knighted, but from the moment he was made a knight he would be driven by the desire to prove himself worthy of the honour.

▲ *In 1450, during the course of the Hundred Years War, the English surrendered Cherbourg to the French.*

▶ *The siege of the castle of Jean de Derval during the Hundred Years' War (1337–1453) between France and England. On the right of the picture, French knight and national hero Bertrand du Guesclin sits on a white horse; on the left, in front of his tent, Louis d'Anjou receives a royal order.*

TIMELINE OF MEDIEVAL CHIVALRY

732AD In the Battle of Poitiers (Tours), western France, a Frankish army commanded by Charles Martel defeats a Muslim force of the Umayyad Caliphate in Spain, ending a series of Muslim raids northwards into France.

768–814 Charlemagne reigns as King of the Franks. He is later celebrated as a great Christian king and exemplar of medieval chivalric values.

778 A Frankish army commanded by Charlemagne is defeated by Muslim or Basque raiders in a skirmish in the Pass of Roncesvalles in the Pyrenees mountains. Charlemagne's knight Roland is killed.

842 'War games' at Strasbourg to celebrate the alliance of Charlemagne's grandsons, Louis the German and Charles the Bald, are a forerunner of the tournament.

911 Viking chief Rollo or Robert is granted land in western France by King Charles II. His descendants, the Normans, establish an early form of knighthood and a feudal society in Normandy.

955 King Otto I of the Germans uses heavy cavalry to defeat the Magyars in the Battle of Augsburg, a victory celebrated by contemporaries as a great triumph for Christian knights.

1066 The Normans invade England and defeat King Harold at the Battle of Hastings. William, Duke of Normandy, becomes King William I of England and imports a feudal society and the Norman form of knighthood.

1095 Pope Urban II calls the knights of Christendom to liberate Jerusalem from Muslims, launching the First Crusade.

1099 The First Crusade ends in triumph as Christian knights capture Jerusalem. In its aftermath the religious brotherhoods of the Knights Templar and the Knights Hospitaller are founded.

1100–35 From the time of Henry I of England (r.1100–35) onwards, kings use paid soldiers as well as knights performing feudal service. They accept 'scutage'

▲ *A battle scene at the walls of Jerusalem.*

(payment) in lieu of feudal military service, and use the money to pay soldiers.

1128 The Council of Troyes approves the rule of the military brotherhood of the Knights Templar.

1130 Pope Innocent II bans tournaments.

*c.***1130** The earliest of the *chansons de geste, The Song of Roland* was written by this date, but may have been in circulation as early as 1050.

1135–39 Geoffrey of Monmouth's *History of the Kings of Britain* establishes Arthurian legend. Arthur was celebrated in Welsh poems as early as the 6th century AD.

1139 Pope Innocent II condemns 'the deadly art, which God hates, of crossbowmen and archers'.

1140 Roger II, Norman King of Sicily, forbids the knighting of men who are liable to disturb the peace.

1142 The Spanish *Song of My Cid* is written down, but has been current in oral form for decades.

1147 Troops setting out on the Second Crusade stop in Portugal and capture Lisbon from its Muslim rulers.

1147–49 The Second Crusade is a failure.

1152 A German decree excludes peasants from being knights.

*c.***1160** Benoit de Sainte-Maure writes *The Romance of Troy*, establishing a genre, the *romans d'antiquités*, of poems of the feudal age featuring classical warriors.

*c.***1160** The French romance *Floire and Blancheflor* tells of the love between a Saracen knight and a Christian lady.

1170–91 French poet Chrétien de Troyes writes five Arthurian romances. They introduce the character of Sir Perceval and the theme of the quest for the Holy Grail.

1186 Holy Roman Emperor Frederick I bans the sons of peasants and the sons of priests from being knighted.

1189–92 The Third Crusade. Also known as the Kings' Crusade: Kings Richard I of England and Philip II of France and Holy Roman Emperor Frederick I all take part.

1194 King Richard I of England defies the papal ban and introduces a licensing system under which tournaments can be legally held in England.

*c.***1200** Norman poet Alexander of Bernay writes *The Alexander Romance*, about the Macedonian king Alexander the Great.

*c.***1200** The great German epic poem *The Song of the Nibelungs* is written.

*c.***1200–1220** German poet Wolfram von Eschenbach writes his masterpiece *Parzival*, a version of the Sir Perceval story.

1202–04 The Fourth Crusade attacks Zara (Hungary) and Constantinople.

1209–1229 The Catholic Church fights the Albigensian Crusade against the heretical Cathars of Occitania (southern France).

1212 The Children's Crusade. A tiny minority reach the Holy Land.

*c.***1215** German poet Gottfried von Strassburg writes *Tristan und Isolt*, a version of the story of Arthurian knight Tristan and Irish princess Iseult.

1217–21 The Fifth Crusade attacks Muslim Egypt but ends in failure.

1223 A 'Round Table' tournament at which knights act out the parts of King Arthur and his knights is held by John of Ibelin, Lord of Beirut, in Cyprus.

c.1225 French poem *The Order of Chivalry* describes an idealized knighting ceremony.

c.1225 Anglo-Norman poem *The History of William Marshal* celebrates the life of the great English knight (1146–1219).

1228–29 Largely through diplomacy rather than fighting, Holy Roman Emperor Frederick II gains Jerusalem, Nazareth and Bethlehem on the Sixth Crusade.

1235 The Cortes of Catalonia declares that only the sons of knights can be knighted.

1248–54 The Seventh Crusade, led by Louis IX of France, attacks Egypt.

c.1250 The Anglo-Norman *Romance of Richard Coeur de Lion* is written. Just 50 years after his death in 1199 , Richard I of England is a figure of legend.

c.1260 *The Golden Legend* by Jacobus de Voragine popularizes the story of St George and the dragon.

1270 Louis IX leads the Eighth Crusade against Muslim North Africa. He dies in Tunis and the crusade fails.

1271–72 Prince Edward of England leads the Ninth Crusade but achieves little.

1265 Majorcan poet and philosopher Ramon Llull writes the *Book of the Order of Chivalry*, a handbook for knights.

1278 A lavish Arthurian tournament is held at Le Hem, Picardy. It is described in the poem *The Book of Le Hem* by Anglo-Norman trouvère Sarrasin.

1285–1314 King Philip IV of France (r.1285–1314) has a considerable part of his army in paid rather than feudal service.

1303 The Catalan Company founded by Italian adventurer Roger de Flor is among the first groups of mercenary knights.

1312 The *chanson de geste*, *A Peacock's Vows* introduces the 'Nine Worthies' of chivalry. These are: three biblical figures – Joshua, David and Judas Maccabeus; three classical warriors – Hector of Troy, Alexander the Great and Julius Caesar; and three of the Christian era – Arthur, Charlemagne and Godfrey of Bouillon.

1316 The papal ban on tournaments is lifted by Pope John XXII.

1325 King Charles of Hungary establishes the Order of St George.

1326 The city of Florence acquires two cannon for its defences. This is the first known record of artillery guns in Europe.

c.1330 The first plate armour suits appear.

1332 King Alfonso XI of Castile and Leon (r.1312–50) establishes the Order of the Sash brotherhood of knights.

c.1335 The chivalric Order of St Catherine is formed in the Dauphiné, France.

1337–1453 The armies in the Hundred Years War contain many paid soldiers. They are mainly infantry and bowmen rather than knights, although Charles VII of France has 1500 cavalry on fixed pay.

23 Apr 1348 King Edward III of England and his son form the chivalric order of the Most Noble Order of the Garter.

c.1350 French knight Geoffroi de Charny writes the *Book of Chivalry*.

c.1350 Another company of mercenary knights, the Grand Company, is formed.

1351 In the celebrated 'Combat of Thirty', two teams of thirty knights joust in Brittany.

1352 The French chivalric order, The Order of the Star is formed.

1356 The English defeat the French at Poitiers; in this victory, and at Crécy, knights are deployed to fight on foot.

1364 At the Battle of Auray English knight Sir John Chandos captures the great French knight Bertrand du Guesclin.

▼ *The battle of Crécy, 1346, with Edward the Black Prince in the centre.*

1367 Chandos, and Edward the Black Prince, take du Guesclin captive a second time. He is ransomed for 100,000 francs.

1369–1400 French poet and historian Jean Froissart writes his *Chronicles*, one of the most important sources on chivalry.

1382–87 Provençal writer Honoré Bonet composes *The Tree of Battles*.

1390 In the Jousts of St Inglevert in northern France four French knights occupy the lists for 30 days and fight all-comers.

1399 French knight Marshal de Boucicaut founds the order of the Enterprise of the Green Shield of the White Lady, with 12 members, sworn to protect women.

c.1400 The tilt or central barrier on the tournament lists is in common use from about this date.

1430 Philip the Good, Duke of Burgundy, establishes the chivalric Order of the Golden Fleece.

1434 Duarte, King of Portugal, writes *The Art of Good Horsemanship*, a manual on jousting and managing horses.

c.1450 René I of Naples, known as René d'Anjou, writes *The Book of Tournaments*.

c.1450 The first state infantry regiments are formed in France, part of a general movement at the time towards the establishment of professional standing armies.

1485 Sir Thomas Malory's *Le Morte d'Arthur*, one of the great English sources for the Arthurian tradition, is published.

1495 Matteo Maria Boiardo's *Orlando Innamorato* ('Roland in Love') is published.

1513–18 Italian courtier and diplomat Baldassare Castiglione writes *The Courtier*, a guide to being a gentleman, part of a movement away from chivalry to courtesy.

1515 French knight Pierre de Terrail, also known as the Chevalier de Bayard, knights his king, Francis I, after the Battle of Marignano.

1516 Lodovico Ariosto's *Orlando Furioso* ('Roland Maddened') is published.

1520 Kings Francis I of France and Henry VIII of England host the Field of the Cloth of Gold. Entertainments included jousting and wrestling and feasting.

1559 King Henry II of France sustains a fatal injury while jousting in Paris.

CHAPTER ONE

THE ORIGINS OF KNIGHTHOOD

In 732AD near Tours in what is now western France, the army of the Franks, commanded by the redoubtable Charles Martel, won a famous victory over a great Muslim force commanded by Abdul Rahman Al Ghafiqi. The Muslim army, with its powerful cavalry, was carrying out the largest in a series of northward invasions from the Umayyad Caliphate, an Islamic territory established in what is now Spain after an invasion from north Africa in 711. After this defeat, the Muslims abandoned all hope of invading northern Europe and settled in the Iberian peninsula, where their descendants lived until 1492.

The Battle of Tours has also been celebrated as a key stage in the history of chivalry, because it helped to establish the power of the Franks, whose heavy cavalry would be such an effective military tool in the hands of Charlemagne, King of the Franks 768–814, and because its demonstration of the steadfast bravery of Christian warriors fighting a great Islamic army struck a strong chord with audiences of the crusading era in the 11th century and afterwards.

Yet the Battle of Tours was not won by the Frankish cavalry. Charles Martel ordered his cavalry to dismount and fight alongside his infantry in a square. There, as footsoldiers, they stood firm in the face of repeated charges by the Islamic cavalry – in the words of the Muslim Mozarabic Chronicle 'unmoving as a solid wall, holding fast like a great ice block'.

▲ *Emperor Charlemagne leads his knights into battle in Agolant, Spain.*

◄ *The Battle of Tours in AD732 was a defining moment in European history, and can perhaps be seen as the conception of knighthood.*

THE WORLD BEFORE KNIGHTS

EARLY MOUNTED WARRIORS

Knights of the Middle Ages were not the first warriors to ride into battle on horseback, nor were their predecessors the mounted cavalry of the Franks. The use of horses in war extends back thousands of years, almost into prehistory.

PRECURSORS OF THE CAVALRY

People may have tamed and begun to ride the horse as long ago as 4000BC. We know that as far back as the 2nd millennium BC warriors fought in horse-drawn chariots: the Indo-Iranian nomads who overran the ancient civilization of northern India and Pakistan in c.1500BC fought with war chariots and iron weapons. The use of the war chariot was invented in the homeland of the Indo-Iranian peoples, probably the steppes of Central Asia, and they spread its use as they fanned out in at least two waves of migration from their original

▼ *Between the 9th and 7th centuries BC, the Assyrian cavalry were famed for their speed and strength in combat. They were armed with bows and arrows and spears.*

homeland in c.1500BC and c.800BC. The chariots were adopted in the Assyrian, Babylonian and ancient Egyptian empires.

In the 9th century BC the Assyrian army had a powerful cavalry. The Assyrian mounted warriors fought principally with bows, and arrows, although they also carried shields and swords. They rode without the benefit of saddles, stirrups or spurs. The warriors needed to be highly skilled riders because handling weapons while moving at speed on horseback was an extremely demanding task. They rode in pairs, taking it in turns to hold the reins of both horses, while the other prepared his bow and fired an arrow.

From the 5th to 3rd century BC the Scythians – originally another group of Indo-Iranian steppe nomads – were famed for their prowess as mounted warriors. Like the Assyrians, they rode bareback, fighting with bows and arrows. The Scythians were truly bloodthirsty fighters who beheaded and scalped any warriors they caught, scraped out the skulls and used the hollowed bone as a drinking cup.

▲ *With the help of his cavalry squadrons, the Macedonian king Alexander – known to history as 'the Great' – built a vast empire.*

ALEXANDER'S COMPANIONS

The armies of ancient Greece relied principally on infantry, but cavalry was a key part of the army of Alexander the Great, the 4th-century BC Macedonian king. He achieved extraordinary conquests and would later become a celebrated figure in medieval chivalric romances.

Alexander's cavalry was strikingly similar to the cadre of noble knights who fought alongside their lord in the Middle Ages. The main component of cavalry in Alexander's army was an aristocratic elite called the *hetairoi* (companions), equipped with a long spear for mounted combat and a slashing sword and a straight sword to use if they were forced to dismount. They also wore a helmet and a linen or bronze cuirass (protective jacket).

Alexander rode into battle at the head of his companions when they charged. He would use his infantry to immobilize the enemy and then attack with the companions on the enemy's right flank or from behind, while another lesser group of cavalry attacked on the left.

THE CATAPHRACT

The mounted soldiers of the Parthian empire, at its height in the 1st century BC, struck fear into the hearts of their enemies, including the armies of Ancient Rome. The mounted Parthian warriors rode armoured steeds and were famous for firing arrows over their shoulders as they rode away – a tactic known ever afterwards as the 'Parthian shot'. The Parthians – and their successors, the Seleucid and Sassanid empires of Iran – also used small units of armed cavalry fighting with lances, a formation called *kataphraktos* ('protected by a barrier') in Greek, and which came to be more commonly known as the 'cataphract'.

The Roman army also had cavalry. In the early years of the Roman republic, the cavalry was filled by wealthy landowners, the *equites*, who could afford a horse as well as the necessary weapons, but increasingly the *equites* became an elite social group and the cavalry was filled with foreign fighters from the tribes of the Iberians, Gauls and Numidians (Berber tribesmen from northern Africa). For a long period the Roman cavalry was used mainly for scouting and skirmishing rather than as an arm of the military in battle. However, during the Battle of Carrhae

▲ *The ancient Roman army combined the speed of lance-bearing horsemen with the tenacity of legionary footsoldiers.*

(modern Harran, Turkey) in 53BC, where Roman general Crassus was humiliatingly defeated by the Parthian general Spahbod Surena, the Romans saw how effectively large groups of cavalry – especially lance-bearing cataphracts – could be used in war. Thereafter they used more cavalry with better-trained men and began to deploy cataphracts of their own.

GOTHIC HORSEMEN

As the Roman Empire collapsed in the west in the 5th century AD, a number of Germanic tribes prospered in Europe. The Goths and Vandals who sacked Rome used powerful cavalry. A little earlier, at the Battle of Adrianople (modern Edirne, Turkey) in AD378, the Gothic cavalry had imposed a devastating defeat on the Roman army. This battle is traditionally seen as one of the first great triumphs for heavy cavalry and also as the conflict that initiated the final collapse of the Roman Empire in the west.

In the eastern Roman Empire, based on Constantinople (modern Istanbul), heavy cavalry became an important part of the imperial army. Under the command of Flavius Belisarius, 6th-century general to

▼ *Mounted warriors in the Persian army sat on large, coloured blankets. They did not wear armour or carry shields.*

Byzantine Emperor Justinian I, bands of heavy cavalry were a powerful weapon, fighting with javelins, bows and arrows.

In Europe, too, the use of armed cavalry spread. The Franks, a Germanic tribe who took control of most of the former Roman colony of Gaul and who would serve as highly effective mounted warriors under Charlemagne, initially fought on foot. They learned the use of cavalry from the Goths and many years later would pass it on to the Vikings – whose descendants, the Normans, were such accomplished practitioners of cavalry warfare.

By the time of the Battle of Tours in 732 the Franks were beginning to ride horses to war. The horses they used were little better than carthorses and their principal effectiveness was as beasts of burden rather than fighting animals. Wealthier Franks would ride horses to battle, then dismount to fight. They would be fresher for battle than their enemies, who might have marched for many days to reach the battlefield.

FEUDAL WARRIORS

THE RISE OF THE FRANKS AND THE EARLY FEUDAL SYSTEM

The nobles who fought in the heavy cavalry of Charlemagne, King of the Franks (r. 768–814), served their monarch in times of war in a way that prefigured the bonds of medieval knights to their lord. The Frankish nobles were tied to their lord by an early form of the feudal system, in which they were granted land in return for military service.

THE EMERGENCE OF THE FRANKS

The Franks were a federation of Germanic tribes, first known in history as settlers on the east bank of the Lower Rhine river in the 3rd century AD. They gained former Roman territories in what is now Belgium in the mid-4th century, and some of their leaders became allies of Rome, acting as guards of the empire's frontiers. They were already known as redoubtable warriors, and many of them served as auxiliaries in the Roman army.

▼ *The baptism of King Clovis by Bishop Remigius of Reims in 496 began the Franks' long association with the Catholic Church. The 6th-century historian Gregory of Tours likened Clovis to the biblical King David as father of his people and faith.*

▲ *Pepin III, son of Charles Martel and father of Charlemagne, was crowned by Pope Boniface I in 751. He was the first Frankish king to receive papal blessing.*

During the 5th century, as Rome's hold on its empire in Europe grew weaker, the Franks took control of north-eastern parts of the former Roman colony of Gaul (modern France). Clovis I (r. 481–511), king of the Salian Franks, one branch of the Frankish federation, conquered the rival groups, uniting all the Franks as he built an empire encompassing all of Gaul, save Burgundy and what is now Provence. He founded the Merovingian line of kings (named after his grandfather Merovech) that ruled until the rise of the Carolingian kings of the Franks in 751.

A CATHOLIC PRINCE

Clovis I also began the Franks' long association with the Catholic Church, converting to Catholic Christianity on his marriage to a Catholic Burgundian princess, Clotilde. At this time many other Germanic tribes had converted to the Arian form of Christianity (named after 4th-century theologian, Arius), which held that Christ was a created being rather than an equal presence with God the Father from the beginning of all things. Arianism was generally viewed as a heresy. However, the Franks, following the example of their leader, converted in large numbers from their pagan beliefs to Catholicism. Because

he united the Frankish tribes and the territories of Gaul, Clovis is often celebrated as the founder of France.

Following his death in 511, however, inheritance disputes broke up the Frankish empire into a number of competing kingdoms. The authority of the Merovingian kings withered and then power resided increasingly in the hand of the *Major Palatii* ('Mayor of the Palace') in each kingdom. This position had arisen from one current in the Roman Empire, that of *Major Domus* ('Household Supervisor') appointed by landowners to manage a number of estates.

RENEWED EXPANSION OF THE FRANKS

In the late 7th century, Pépin, Mayor of the Palace in the Frankish kingdom of Austrasia (the north-east part of the former empire), embarked on a campaign

---

COMMENDATION

A vassal swore loyalty in a special ceremony called the 'commendation'. The vassal knelt and put both his hands in those of the lord as he swore the oath of fealty, promising to be loyal to the lord and to provide military or other service, such as farming land. The lord kissed his vassal and pulled him to his feet. He handed him a symbol of the agreement – sometimes a piece of earth. The vassal was granted the lord's protection – an important consideration at a time when central authority was often weak and raiders such as the Vikings were at large. In early times the vassal might become part of the lord's retinue, but by the 9th century the oath required the vassal to provide mounted military service with lance, shield and sword.

▲ *The Frankish empire, initially won on the battlefield, was subsequently fractured by war. Charlemagne's grandson Lothair I was crowned emperor by Pope Paschal I in 823, and expected to inherit, but military defeats forced him to share power with his brothers.*

of territorial expansion. He took control of the neighbouring kingdom of Neustria (the north-west part of the former empire) and defeated the Frisians to the north of Austrasia. On Pépin's death in 714, his illegitimate son, Charles, succeeded as mayor and continued Frankish expansion. His military exploits won him a resounding reputation as Charles Martel ('the Hammer'). It was he who in 732 stopped the northward expansion of Islamic warriors at the bruising Battle of Tours.

VASSALAGE AND EARLY FORMS OF FEUDALISM

The principle in Frankish territories was that every free Frank was required to fight for the king. In addition Frankish kings kept groups of sworn warriors, called *antrustiones,* or vassals. These men swore loyalty to the ruler and promised him military service; in return they could expect to be equipped and fed, and would receive a share of war plunder. This arrangement had grown out of the *comitatus*, a group of sworn warriors serving and fighting for a leader in Germanic tribes. The antrustiones were given leading administrative positions as a *comes* (count) and military positions as a *dux* (duke).

In the 8th century, trade and an economy based on money had broken down in the Frankish territories, and wealth was measured in land. The principal landholders were the king, the Church and Frankish lords, to whom the king delegated control of sections of territory. The kings parcelled out land in the form of a benefice, a grant of full ownership for the lifetime of the recipient.

Under the Frankish kings the granting of benefices came to be associated with vassalage in the form of the fiefdom: the land given to the vassal remained the king's but rights over it were granted to the vassals in return for an oath of lifelong loyalty to the lord and the promise of military service.

The fiefdom tied to sworn military service became the basis of the feudal system that structured early medieval society. The lord–vassal relationship could be found at all social levels: between the king and his leading counts and dukes; between these men and the tenants on their land; and equally further down between the holder of a small fief and the vassals who held sections of his smallholding.

It became customary for the holders of fiefdoms to be able to bequeath them to their sons, and the holding of land in the form of the inheritable fiefdom allowed noble families to gradually build up considerable territories and pass them on after death. Some families became so powerful that they could begin to challenge the authority of the king. The right of holders of fiefdoms to pass the land on to their sons was accepted, but not legal until Charlemagne's grandson, King Charles the Bald, decreed that if a count died when the king was away on campaign, the count's son could inherit.

▼ *Charles Martel was impressed by Muslim horsemen at the Battle of Tours. He set about strengthening the Frankish cavalry, taking Church land and distributing it among his sworn followers to increase the number of landowners wealthy enough to equip themselves as mounted warriors.*

A CHRISTIAN EMPIRE IN EUROPE

THE HOLY ROMAN EMPIRE OF CHARLEMAGNE

Charles Martel's descendants – notably his grandson, Charles I, King of the Franks from AD768 – created a great empire that encompassed much of western and central Europe. They allied themselves with the Christian Church, and accepted the blessing of the pope in Rome on their rule, and through their conquests spread the faith, imposing Christianity on pagan tribes such as the Saxons in what is now northern Germany.

The Frankish armies built their success on the exploits of a highly mobile, well-equipped cavalry. Charles I was known as Charles the Great, in Latin *Carolus Magnus* and therefore as Charlemagne.

THE CAROLINGIAN DYNASTY

Charles Martel had ruled as king in all but name: he was Mayor of the Palace, and nominally subject to the Merovingian kings, descendants of Clovis I. In 751, however, Martel's son Pépin the Short ousted the last of the Merovingians, Childeric III, and became king in his own right. He founded the Carolingian dynasty (named from the Latin form of Charles, *Carolus*, in honour of his father Charles Martel and his son, Charlemagne).

Pépin was anointed twice, first by the Christian missionary St Boniface and then in 754, together with his two sons Carloman and Charlemagne, by Pope Stephen II in a magnificent ceremony at the Saint Denis Basilica in Paris. Pépin defeated the Lombards of northern Italy, and gave territories he had won to the papacy. He also brought Aquitaine (southwestern France) into the Frankish realm. He was succeeded by his sons in 768, but when Carloman died in 771, Charlemagne ruled alone.

CHRISTIAN WARRIORS

One of Charlemagne's first campaigns was to invade once more the kingdom of the Lombards in northern Italy, where

▲ *The papacy supported the rise of Frankish power. Charlemagne seized control in northern Italy in 774 and had his rule blessed by Pope Adrian I in Milan.*

Carloman's widow had fled seeking help. Charlemagne defeated and deposed the Lombard king, Desiderius, and seized the crown for himself in 774. He took possession of his nephews, who had a claim to power via their father, and they subsequently disappeared – presumably disposed of. He appointed Frankish lords to key positions in the Lombards' territory. In the course of this campaign he celebrated Easter in Rome with the pope and reaffirmed the alliance between the Franks and the papacy.

The association of Frankish rule with the Catholic Church was a crucial element in the development of knighthood. The mounted warriors of Charlemagne's army fought in the name of Christ. The Church developed theories under which violence could be seen as holy if committed in a sacred cause.

FIGHTING FOR CHRIST

Charlemagne saw it as a king's duty to spread the Christian faith. He rode into battle with an elite cadre of mounted warriors to fight for the Cross. In 772 he launched an attack on the pagan Saxons, a fiercely independent Germanic group, rivals to the Franks, in an attempt to bring them within his Christian realm. The Saxons proved to be of stern stuff: Charlemagne's onslaught against them lasted on and off for 32 years, until 804. He led no fewer than 18 campaigns himself at the head of his elite unit of soldiers.

He must have thought he was close to his goal when he oversaw a series of mass baptisms of Saxons in 775–77, but despite signing a treaty of allegiance in 777 the Saxons rebelled again, and Charlemagne unleashed a terrible punishment in the mass execution in 782 of no fewer than 4,500 Saxons. In the course of his reign he succeeded in bending all the other Germanic tribes to his will – defeating the Bavarians, the Frisians, the Alemanni and the Thuringians.

DEFEAT AND CHRISTIANIZATION OF THE AVARS

In the late 790s Charlemagne launched an onslaught on the Avars, a nomadic tribe from Asia who had settled in what is now Hungary and had launched raids into the eastern part of the Frankish realm. (The Avars were called 'Huns' by Charlemagne's biographer Einhard.) Charlemagne personally led a devastating rout of the Avars in 790–91. Further campaigns led by Charlemagne's second son Pépin (known as Pépin of Italy) and Duke Eric of Friull defeated the Avars decisively, and their leaders submitted, swearing fealty to Charlemagne as his vassals and accepting his Christian faith.

THE WESTERN ROMAN EMPIRE REVIVED

Charlemagne set out at first to maintain good relations with both the pope in Rome and the rulers of the Byzantine or eastern Roman empire in Constantinople. He was in Rome once more in 781, for the anointing of his sons Pépin and Louis as kings of the Lombards and of the

▼ *Christian warriors led by Charlemagne were overcome by Muslims in the Battle of Roncesvalles in Spain (778). The defeat was treated elegiacally in the* Song of Roland.

Aquitanians respectively. He recognized the Byzantine empress Irene – and the two rulers even entered into negotiations for the arranged marriage of Charlemagne's daughter Rotrude to Irene's son (the future Byzantine emperor Constantine VI) but the negotiations failed and the arrangement was broken off.

In 799 he gave refuge to Pope Leo III who had fled a revolt by Italian nobles; Charlemagne had him escorted safely back

▲ *The chapel of Charlemagne's imperial palace, built in c.790, survives as part of Aachen Cathedral (now in Germany).*

to Rome. The following year, Charlemagne visited Rome and Leo crowned him 'August Emperor'. This was an attempt to revive the Roman Empire in the west as a Christian realm.

It was a challenge to the Byzantine Empire, for nominally the popes and the Franks were subjects of the eastern empire, and the Byzantine emperor was seen as the ruler of all Christians. Briefly it seemed possible that the two halves of the empire might be reunited: Charlemagne proposed marriage to Empress Irene, but the negotiations failed and she died in 802. Subsequently there was a stand-off, and then the two sides fought an intermittent war over Byzantine-held territories in Italy. Finally in 812 Byzantine emperor Michael I recognized Charlemagne as emperor under the title of *Imperator Romanorum gubernans imperium* ('Emperor governing the lands of the Romans'). The following year Charlemagne declared his son Louis to be co-emperor and his chosen successor. Charlemagne himself died in 814.

PARAGON OF CHIVALRY

CHARLEMAGNE THE GREAT

In medieval Europe Charlemagne was seen as the model Christian king or emperor. A superb military tactician, he marshalled large armies and made effective use of the power of mounted warriors with his cavalry. He rode into battle with his elite cadre of mounted warriors, in whom medieval knights saw their forerunners. He was a Christian warrior, who fought to spread the faith of Christ: all the peoples he defeated accepted Christianity as part of their submission. Centuries later, he was celebrated as a chivalric hero in *chansons de geste* (chivalric poems) and a perfect knight, perhaps history's first great exemplar of the chivalric code.

CHARLEMAGNE'S FAITH

In his early campaign of AD774 against the Lombards, when he deposed the Lombard king Desiderius, took the crown for himself, eliminated his brother's sons as

▼ *Charlemagne attends Mass while on campaign. The wars he waged against pagan Germanic tribes were fought in Christ's name to spread the Gospel.*

potential rivals and renewed the Franks' alliance with the pope, Charlemagne demonstrated several of his key qualities: strategic intelligence, decisiveness, military force, and an element of ruthlessness in negating the claim to power of his nephews. The events of 774 also demonstrated his combination of political manoeuvring and religious faith – for while his alliance with the papacy was politically expedient, his commitment to the Christian faith was genuine.

Charlemagne was driven by a desire for power, but he believed himself to be doing God's will. He did not accept that the pope had any sovereignty over him: in his laws he described himself as *Imperator a Deo Coronatus* ('Emperor Crowned by God'), indicating that he was subject only to God.

AT COURT AND AS A PATRON

Not least among the qualities that contributed to Charlemagne's enduring reputation in the Middle Ages was his commitment to the Church and to learning. He was a great patron of the Church and of education and oversaw a revival of

art and learning known to history as the 'Carolingian Renaissance'.

He gathered many of the great minds of contemporary Europe at his court in Aachen, among them the Anglo-Saxon monk Alcuin who reorganized education within Charlemagne's vast realms. Alcuin reintroduced the study of the seven liberal arts of music, astronomy, geometry, logic, arithmetic, grammar and rhetoric, which had been studied in ancient Rome.

Another key figure among the courtiers at Aachen was the monk Einhard, originally a pupil of Alcuin, who wrote a biography of the emperor. From Einhard's account, we know that Charlemagne was well-built and unusually tall – his height was noted to be seven times the length of his feet. He had large eyes and nose, a full head of grey hair and a cheerful face. He walked purposefully and spoke with a higher voice than an observer might expect. From other sources we know that although he had rough manners, he enjoyed debating with the learned men he had gathered around him and was always keen to learn.

A FAMOUS DEFEAT IN SPAIN

Under Charlemagne, the Frankish army was a military machine of awesome effectiveness. Yet one of the great *chansons de geste* that celebrated medieval chivalric heroes focused on a rare defeat for this warrior king.

This setback took place in the Pyrenees mountains in 778. Charlemagne had invaded northern Spain at the urging of some Muslim emissaries whose request for help against the Umayyad emir of Córdoba had appealed to him as an opportunity to add lustre to his military reputation while also expanding the reach of Christianity into largely Muslim Spain. The campaign, during which he besieged and failed to capture Zaragoza, was not a success, but worse was to follow – for, as

▲ *Charlemagne refused to accept that his power was dependent upon papal approval. To emphasize this, he used the words 'Emperor Crowned by God' in his laws.*

he led his army back through the Pyrenees, they were ambushed by Basque fighters (perhaps in alliance with Muslim warriors) and many in Charlemagne's army were killed. One of these was Hroudland or Roland, Warden of the border territories with Brittany, and the warrior who gave his name to the 11th-century epic poem the *Chanson de Roland* (the *Song of Roland*), a masterpiece of medieval literature that makes a great celebration of this defeat.

CHARLEMAGNE THE WARRIOR

We know plenty about Charlemagne's campaigns, his political manoeuvring and his commitment to education, but we have little certain information about him as a warrior. Yet this aspect of his life was important in the Middle Ages, when he was revered as a knight, and in works such as the *Song of Roland* his relationship with his elite companions in his cavalry was presented as the epitome of chivalry, the perfection of chivalric relationship between a lord and his knights.

We do, however, have a description of Charlemagne dressed for battle. Notker of St Gall, a 9th-century Benedictine monk at the Abbey of St Gall (at modern St Gallen, Switzerland), left in his work *Gesta Caroli Magni* (*Life of Charlemagne*) a description of the king equipped for the battlefield. It refers to him as 'the Iron King': saying that his armour consisted of an iron helm, with sleeves of iron armour and a chain mail tunic; his upper legs also were covered with chain mail, with iron greaves on the lower leg.

KING WITH KNIGHTLY VIRTUES

Totila, King of the Ostrogoths in the mid-6th century, was celebrated as a great early precursor of chivalry in much the same way as Charlemagne was seen as an early example of the ideal knight. In the 540s Totila recaptured for the Goths most of central and southern Italy, which had been taken by the Byzantine or eastern Roman Empire. In near contemporary accounts, Totila was celebrated for his humanity and fairness in dealing with defeated enemies – later important chivalric virtues. He was also a great mounted warrior and a figure of heroic appearance. The 6th-century Byzantine historian Procopius described Totila's magnificent attire: gold armour, with adornments hanging from the cheek pieces, and a purple helmet and lance. He also praised the king's horsemanship and weapon-handling: in front of the armies arrayed on the field of battle, he danced on his horse and was able to throw and catch his spear while parading on horseback. Totila's name was Baduila, but chronicles suggest he fought under the name Totila.

▼ *On 21 March 543 Totila paid a visit at Monte Cassino to Benedict of Nursia, founder of the Benedictine monastic rule. Three years later, Totila took Rome.*

THE EMPEROR'S CAVALRY
MOUNTED WARRIORS IN THE CAROLINGIAN ARMY

Charlemagne's triumphant military success depended on his use of very large, well-equipped and superbly disciplined armies. They contained a large contingent of light cavalry and a smaller elite section of heavy cavalry. Some estimates of the number of mounted warriors in the Frankish army go as high as 35,000 men. Charlemagne issued detailed edicts laying out requirements for how the armies should be raised, equipped and supplied with food and weapons.

A MILITARY MACHINE

Charlemagne was a great tactician, but a major part of his armies' effectiveness depended on organization. Many of his army manoeuvres were only possible because his military machine was so big and so well organized that he was able to keep two or more large armies in the field at once.

As well as fighting on more than one front at once, his armies could undertake long-range campaigns of conquest – beyond the river Rhine, across the Alps in

▼ *A bearded, regal Charlemagne elevates a warrior to the cavalry. The illustration is from the 14th century and is coloured by notions of chivalry from this later age.*

Italy, in the far west of Brittany and once even across the Pyrenees in northern Spain (although this campaign was the scene of the celebrated failure in the Pass of Roncesvalles). In battle Charlemagne's armies were large enough to split into separate units. It was a favourite tactic of his – used in 778 in Spain, in 787 in Bavaria and in 791 in Pannonia – to outflank the enemy with columns of troops.

Charlemagne did not usually wage war during the winter. His custom was to gather his army at Easter, prior to embarking on campaigns in the summer months. Sometimes, however, he remained in the territory he was intent on subjugating for

▲ *Wearing the typical conical helmets of the day, mounted warriors in Charlemagne's army follow the baggage train on campaign.*

the winter break. In 776, for example, he defeated the Saxons at Lippespringe and forcibly baptized them, but they rose up in revolt, throwing off the Christian faith which they had accepted, almost at once. That winter he kept his court in Saxony – and, unusually, he kept up regular raids against Saxon targets during the winter months.

RAISING AN ARMY

Each count was held responsible for bringing with him all the warriors who were his vassals – save four, whom he could leave behind to guard his property and protect his wife. Bishops and abbots also had to give military service, with all their vassals – although they, too, could leave a pair of warriors to protect their possessions. A royal vassal at court did not have to perform military service, but he was responsible for ensuring that all his vassals joined up.

During the course of Charlemagne's reign, selective service became accepted: three vassals might join together to equip a fourth, who would go on campaign. One of the emperor's edicts, issued in Saxony in 806, required five Saxons to equip a sixth to fight for the king in a projected Spanish campaign, and for two more men to equip another warrior to serve in Bohemia.

Charlemagne's armies were always well supplied, and his campaigns were usually well planned. He ordered his mounted warriors to bring three months' worth of food and six months' worth of military clothing and weapons. The decree even specified that these three months would begin when the army assembled on campaign rather than when the warriors embarked from their homes. Herds of livestock for food were part of an army's baggage train.

During the Saxon campaigns the troops were well enough equipped to build bridges and forts; the army had collapsible boats for crossing the river Ebro on the Spanish campaign of 778 and carried a moveable bridge for its 792 campaign against the Avars. When he had forces fighting simultaneously in Hungary and Saxony he tried – though without success – to dig a canal between the Danube and the Rhine.

▼ Charlemagne's forces fight at Pamplona, Spain, during the ill-fated campaign that ended in defeat in the Pass of Roncesvalles.

▲ Fighting beneath a heavenly apparition of the Cross, Charlemagne's cavalry and the sheer might of his army defeat the pagan Avars, who were superbly skilled horsemen themselves, near the river Danube in 791.

FORTS AND PLUNDER

In conquered territories he ordered the building of permanent garrisoned fortifications – forerunners of the castles built by medieval knights. Plundering enemy riches was an accepted part of campaigning. The campaign against the Avars in 790–91 produced so much booty that 15 wagons were needed to carry it back to the court at Aachen.

Discipline was strict. Drunkenness was officially forbidden. There was a stiff fine for those who failed to attend when required. Desertion was punished with seizing all of a warrior's property followed by execution.

EQUIPMENT AND WEAPONS

Charlemagne laid down strict requirements for the military equipment his troops should have. In 792 his edict required mounted warriors to have a lance, a shield and both long and short swords, in addition to a horse. In 802 the warriors were ordered to bring body armour as well. In 805 he decreed that each mounted soldier in possession of at

least 300 acres (121 hectares) had to bring a *byrnie* (tunic of chain mail). The decree also stated that warriors who had chain mail armour but did not bring it to battle risked punishment by losing their fiefdom.

A typical mounted warrior in one of Charlemagne's armies had a chain mail tunic that extended down to his knees and was slit at the side to allow greater ease of movement. Some had a scale overshirt instead – a jacket of leather or fabric with metal or horn pieces attached to it. The warrior wore a conical helmet and carried a round shield with a spike in the centre, so that it could be used as a thrusting weapon as well as for defence. He had a long lance, used for thrusting – in this era, groups of mounted warriors did not yet charge with couched lance. His sword had a rounded end, and was effective for cutting but not for stabbing.

A TIME OF UNREST

THE PROTECTIVE ROLE OF MOUNTED WARRIORS IN AN UNRULY WORLD

In the years after Charlemagne's death in 814 his empire swiftly disintegrated in power struggles among his sons and their descendants. At the same time his former territories were assailed by violent raiders: from the north, Vikings came by sea and river in their longships; from the east, the reckless Magyars came on horseback; from the south and west (from North Africa and the Iberian Peninsula) came fierce Islamic raiders. It was a lawless time, seemingly lacking effective central authority.

Monasteries and churches were as much the raiders' targets as palaces and farms, and churchmen as well as lords looked to mounted warriors for protection. This led to the first idealizations of the warrior-horsemen as defenders of the Church and of right against lawless pagans. It was a key stage in the progression from the mounted warrior of Charlemagne's army to the knight of the 11th and 12th centuries, who was seen as a *miles Christi* ('soldier of Christ').

▼ *Viking attacks by sea were hard to defend against because their swift, powerful ships swept in, looted and departed before local defences could be organized.*

THE FIRST TRUE CAVALRY ENGAGEMENTS

Charlemagne's son Louis the Pious reigned for 26 years, 814–40. Early in his reign he attempted to settle the question of the succession among his descendants, but not to their satisfaction: he was twice deposed in major revolts by his sons, then subsequently reinstalled. After his death his three surviving sons fought amongst themselves, then divided the empire into three under the Treaty of Verdun (843). The former East Frankish kingdom became Francia Orientalis and was taken by Louis the German; the West Frankish kingdom became Francia Occidentalis, and was given to Charles the Bald. A central strip called Francia Media and the title of emperor was given to Lothair. (Francia Occidentalis and Francia Orientalis were later the basis of the countries of France and Germany respectively.)

These wars saw the first true mounted warrior engagements as cavalries from opposing armies met in full charge. By this stage the stirrup had been widely adopted, but the mounted warriors had not yet developed the technique of charging with couched lance.

A NEW WARRIOR CLASS

Power struggles continued for decades. All the time the authority and influence of the royal house grew weaker; meanwhile, Magyars and Vikings struck repeatedly. The most effective resistance came from local lords, whose power grew steadily as they built a large territorial holding, often through the grant by weak kings of hereditary fiefdoms. These lords in turn granted fiefdoms to their warrior supporters. An elite class of landholding warrior-knights began to develop.

These warriors' principal loyalty was to their lord rather than the king. In 792–93 Charlemagne had been able to impose an oath of loyalty to the king on all royal vassals and required the vassals to make their vassals swear it also. But as royal authority collapsed, and counts became more powerful as they accumulated land, it began to be accepted that vassals would fight for their lord against the king.

VIKING RAIDS AND CONSOLIDATING LOCAL POWER

From the 830s through to 910 Viking raids were a persistent threat to the western Frankish lands. They hit coastal targets

▲ *The Magyar mounted warriors were expert at ambushing troops, and often pretended to retreat before turning suddenly on their pursuers.*

as well as any settlements that could be reached by river. In c.840 they raided Nourmoutier, Utrecht and Antwerp; in 841 they razed Rouen; in 843 they attacked Nantes and sailed up the river Loire. By the 850s they had set up camps on the Seine, Loire and Garonne. In 847, 861 and 865 they attacked Paris.

Frankish kings relied on local counts and dukes to repel the threat. Charles the Bald of the western Frankish kingdom (r. 844–70) made fiefdoms hereditary as a means of maintaining the loyalty of local lords who had proved their worth in countering the Vikings. Local lords who benefited in this way included Baldwin 'Iron-Arm' who made his name combating the Vikings in Flanders and was made *margrave* (ruler) of Flanders by Charles the Bald in 864. Similarly Richard the Justiciar, who defeated the Vikings in Burgundy in 888 and relieved the Viking siege of Chartres in 911, was established as the first margrave of Burgundy.

Raids on the western Frankish kingdom largely came to an end after the early 10th century, when a settlement of Vikings was established by Charles III the Simple in what became Normandy, as a buffer zone to protect against future raiding.

MAGYAR HORSEMEN

The Magyars were warlike descendants of nomadic people originally from the region of the Ural Mountains, who had settled in what is now Ukraine in c.830. They began launching mounted raids on the eastern Frankish territories in 862.

They were superb horsemen and archers, who fought mainly with bows and arrows but also with lassos and javelins. They would pour into an area, looting widely, then disappear just as quickly. Otto I (r. 936–73) of the eastern Frankish kingdom (around this time generally described as Germany) ended the Magyar threat once and for all at the Battle of Ausgburg in 955 (see box).

WAR BY SEA

For much of the 9th century, Islamic raiders dominated the Mediterranean. They captured Bari in Italy, the island of Crete and part of Sicily (where they developed Palermo as a great cosmopolitan city). They established bases in what is now southern France, including Farakshanit (Fraxinet) near modern St Tropez, and raided up the river Rhone as far as Upper and Lower Burgundy.

The Europeans called them infidels (people of no faith) or Saracens from the Arabic word *sharqiyin* ('Easterners'). In southern France feudal lords defended local populations against the raiders, and achieved increasing independence from Frankish or Byzantine authority in building fortifications to hold the raiders at bay.

ALFRED THE GREAT AND ENGLISH MILITIAS

KNIGHTHOOD IN ENGLAND BEFORE THE NORMAN CONQUEST

Alfred of Wessex (r. 871–99) is the only king in English history to be honoured with the epithet 'the Great'. As with Charlemagne in Europe, Alfred has been revered by later generations in England as a great warrior monarch, military reformer, administrator, lawgiver and educator. Like Charlemagne, Alfred was a close ally of the Church, and celebrated as a defender and promoter of the Christian faith against pagan enemies. Throughout the age of chivalry he was celebrated as a pioneer of knightly virtues such as bravery, charity and magnanimity, as a giver of laws, and as an inspirational example of a king and general who achieved victory when all seemed lost.

MILITARY REFORMS

In 871 Anglo-Saxon England appeared to be at the mercy of Danish Vikings: a great Viking army had landed in 865 and won control of York, Northumbria and East

Anglia. Alfred, still a prince, led the armies of his brother King Aethelred of Wessex in a stirring victory over the Danes on the Ridgeway at Ashdown in Berkshire on 8 January 871. However, the Danes quickly regrouped afterwards and won important victories. Alfred meanwhile acceded to the throne on the death of Aethelred.

Alfred bought peace by bribing the invaders, but the Vikings, after conquering the Anglo-Saxon kingdom of Mercia, attacked again in 877, penetrating far into Wessex. Alfred fought back, initially conducting a guerrilla war from a base deep in the impenetrable wetlands of Somerset, then the following year leading a West Saxon army to another great victory over the Danes, in the Battle of Edington on Salisbury Plain. Alfred's men harried the Danes for more than 15 miles (24km) back to the invaders' base at Chippenham, which surrendered after a siege of 14 days. Alfred later freed London from the Danes.

The Viking leader Guthrum and his army pledged not to attack Wessex, but the invaders remained in England, established in the eastern region of the country, between the rivers Thames and Tees, in the area known as the Danelaw. Alfred set about improving his kingdom's defences and the effectiveness of its army. He split the *fyrd* (militia) into two, and thereafter ensured that one half was always ready for action while the other half rested at home. He adopted the tactics of the invaders, introducing mobile groups of mounted warriors as part of the army.

◄ *King Alfred discusses his new ship design with associates. The heavy boats, when made, ran aground on their first use.*

► *This iron ceremonial helmet was buried with an Anglo-Saxon chief at Sutton Hoo, Suffolk, in the 7th century. The Anglo-Saxon warriors were footsoldiers, but their army did use Celtic-British cavalry units.*

▲ *Alfred is a great figure in the traditions of English law as well as in the country's military history. His Book of Laws was based on three Saxon law codes.*

Alfred also revamped the navy and introduced a heavier, 60-oar boat that he had designed. Most importantly, he ordered the building of a string of defensive forts, or burghs, around his kingdom. He decreed that there should be a fort within 20 miles of every settlement. Some of the burghs were newly built, others were based on old Roman or Iron Age forts; some were small, others appear to have been planned from the start as fortified towns.

▲ *The two sides of a silver penny issued by King Alfred in c.880.*

NECESSARY KNOWLEDGE

Alfred believed that the violent visitations of the Vikings were God's judgement on an ignorant people, and saw it as his Christian duty to revive learning in the kingdom. Probably inspired by the example of Charlemagne, he invited scholars to his court, and established schools. He had those books that he considered 'most necessary for all men to know' translated from Latin into the native tongue. He himself learned Latin and translated the *Cura Pastoralis* (*Pastoral Rule*) of Pope Gregory the Great. He sponsored the creation of the *Anglo-Saxon Chronicle*, a history running back to Roman times, so that his people could know their history. He tried to establish justice, introducing a code of law, attempting to limit the prosecution of blood quarrels and introducing strict penalties for breaking an oath.

ALFRED AND KNIGHTHOOD

In Alfred's time during the late 9th century early forms of knighthood were beginning to take shape in mainland Europe with the emergence of a military elite of mounted warriors rewarded for fighting with the possession of land. In Anglo-Saxon England, the army consisted largely of thegns – warriors bound to their aristocratic lords who took responsibility for maintaining them. Alfred's reign saw the beginning of the theory that warriors were a self-contained group whose existence was essential for good government and a stable society. From the time of the Church Fathers in the 1st–5th centuries AD, it was normal for scholars to debate the right ordering of society and to propose a threefold division – such as clergy,

monks and laity; or nobility, freemen and slaves. As part of his campaign to improve education in his kingdom, King Alfred learned Latin and translated *On Consolation* by the 6th-century Roman philosopher Boethius. To the translation Alfred added the statement that good government required a land that has a good number of people containing (in Anglo-Saxon) '*geberdmen, fyrdmen and weorcmen*' (men who pray, men who fight and men who work). This theory would play an important part in the Church's later view of knights and in the code of chivalry.

ALFRED AS A CHIVALRIC WARRIOR

After the Battle of Edington in 878 Alfred showed considerable forbearance to the defeated Danish force. The Saxon victory came after a period of desperate guerrilla warfare and a great victorious charge across country – it might have been understandable for Alfred and his army to slaughter their enemies. Instead they behaved with restraint.

However, like Charlemagne's defeated Germanic enemies, the Vikings discovered that the price of their defeat was conversion to Christianity. Danish leader Guthrum was baptized with Alfred standing as his godfather and personally raising him from the baptismal waters. Afterwards Alfred recognized Guthrum as an adoptive son. This ability to exhibit generosity in victory, and to recognize the noble qualities of his defeated opponent,

was subsequently made the hallmark of a chivalric warrior fighting according to the code of chivalry.

In his lifetime, as well as after his death, Alfred's contemporaries celebrated him as a Christian warrior. His leading soldiers fought with swords that were decorated with the cross and his troops said prayers on the field of battle; as a contrast, monks recording his exploits always made a point of describing the Danes as pagans. The Welsh monk Asser, who wrote Alfred's biography in 893, called him 'ruler of all Christians in the island of Britain'.

▶ *This heroic statue of King Alfred stands in Winchester, southern England, the place of the king's burial after his death on 26 October 899. The facts of his life were quickly embroidered with legend.*

THE RISE OF THE NORMANS
THE EXPORTERS OF KNIGHTHOOD

The Normans who invaded England in 1066 were descendants of the Viking warrior chieftain Rollo, or Robert, who was granted land in western France in 911 by King Charles III the Simple of West Francia. Between 911 and 1066, Rollo's descendants established a feudal society in Normandy. In warfare they used heavy cavalry and built castles. Following the conquest they imposed feudalism in England, and their descendants later exported it to the Holy Land on the First Crusade from 1095 to 1099.

ARRIVAL OF THE NORTHMEN

Scholars disagree as to whether Duke Rollo was originally Norwegian or Danish. He took part in an unsuccessful Viking siege of Paris in 886 and afterwards established a settlement at the mouth of the river Seine. Charles the Simple established this area as a buffer state against further Viking attacks by granting the lands to Rollo. As well as agreeing to fend off further Viking incursions, Rollo paid feudal homage to King Charles III and accepted baptism as a Christian under the name Robert. The deal was sealed in the Treaty of St Claire-sur-Epte in 911 and Robert married Charles's daughter.

Robert and the settlers were originally known as Northmen or Norsemen, and subsequently as Normans. They quickly

▼ *Viking raiders arrive off the coast of France in the late 9th century. Their war band mentality fed into Norman and later chivalric culture.*

expanded their territory, moving west, and Robert gained middle Normandy (Bassin, Bayeux, L'Huernin and Le Mans) from the king in 924 and Robert's son and successor, William Longsword (Duke William I of Normandy), was granted the seaboard of the Avranchin (the area near Mont St Michel) and the Contentin (the north part of the peninsula) in 933.

DUKE RICHARD I OF NORMANDY

William Longsword was murdered in 942 and a power struggle ensued, but William's illegitimate son finally regained control of Normandy as Duke Richard I. Richard I was known as Richard Sans Peur ('the Fearless'), and in his long reign (942–96) the feudal system was begun in his lands. Normandy was a wealthy realm, with the city of Rouen established as a successful trading centre. Coins bearing the name of Duke Richard I have been found as far afield as Russia and Scotland.

EXPANDING MILITARY POWER

Richard I was succeeded by his illegitimate son Duke Richard II, known as 'the Good'. In his reign Normandy became a great military power: many of his feudal vassals were powerful counts, with large bodies of mounted warriors in their service. Normandy also became a player on the international stage. Duke Richard II established political links with English royalty through the marriage of his sister, Emma of Normandy, to King Aethelred in 1002. However, in the same period he also allowed Danish Vikings to use ports in Normandy as their bases for repeated raids on England.

In 1013 the Danes invaded England, and Emma's sons by King Aethelred, Edward (later Edward the Confessor) and Alfred Atheling, went to Normandy as exiles. Emma remained in England and after Aethelred's death in 1016 went on to marry England's Danish king, Canute.

KING WILLIAM'S FATHER

Richard II was succeeded by his son as Duke Richard III, but Richard III died after just a year in power, and his brother Robert became Duke Robert II of Normandy. Some sources suggest he murdered Richard and he is sometimes known as Robert le Diable ('the Devil') for this reason; he may be connected to the legendary Norman knight of that name, who in the 12th–14th-century tales was the devil's own son and lived a life of the greatest depravity before seeking forgiveness from the pope and saving Rome three times from Islamic attack.

After providing military support for King Henry I of France, Duke Robert II was rewarded with the territory of the Vexin, near Rouen. (Around this time historians generally begin to identify the lands of Francia Occidentalis or West Francia as France and those of Francia Orientalis or East Francia as Germany.) However, despite his nickname of 'the devil', Robert II was clearly also a religious man. He was a sponsor of reform for monasteries in Normandy along the lines

of the new practices promoted by the Abbey of Cluny, and made a pilgrimage to Jerusalem. It was on his return from this voyage that he died in Nicaea (modern Iznik, Turkey) in 1035.

DUKE WILLIAM OF NORMANDY

Robert II fathered an illegitimate son, William, by Herleva, daughter of a tanner or embalmer from Falaise. On his father's death William le Bâtard ('the Bastard') succeeded to the dukedom of Normandy at the age of just eight. He was raised in the household of his late father's steward, Osbern Herfasston, and appears to have had an education alongside several other martial youths in the Norman ways of war, including sword-fighting, the skills of mounted horsemanship and even castle-building – like that of later generations of knights-to-be, as first page and then as squire.

Duke William's biographer, William of Poitiers, described William in his youth as being masterful in the saddle, cutting the air with his sword, grasping his shining shield, and striking fear into his opponent with his fearsome use of the lance. He was knighted by King Henry I of France at the age of 15, in c.1042–43. Before he invaded

▲ *The ability of Duke William's mounted warriors to launch a swift counter-attack made the difference between defeat and victory at the Battle of Hastings in 1066. This image of Norman cavalry preparing to charge is from the Bayeux Tapestry.*

England in 1066, William had proved himself a forceful warrior and leader of men, with victories in Brittany, Maine and Ponthieu.

FEUDAL INVASION

The Norman invasion of England in 1066 could be termed a 'feudal war'. William's noble vassals were fighting for the promise of titles and land if the invasion was a success. At the crucial Battle of Hastings King Harold's army fought entirely on foot behind a wall of shields, while William's cavalry played an important part in the victory – hitting the Anglo-Saxons with a mounted charge after some had lost their discipline and broken out to pursue a feigned Norman retreat. From the very start of the occupation of England, the Normans raised castles to hold conquered territory and frighten the populace, and imposed their own feudal society in place of England's existing nobility.

▼ *Duke William of Normandy, enthroned as King William I of England, makes a grant of lands to Alain de Brittany in return for the promise of feudal military service.*

THE FIRST KNIGHTS

AN EXCLUSIVE FRATERNITY

In the decades after the Norman conquest, in the feudal societies of France, Germany and Norman England, we see the emergence of the first true knights – men who were made knights in a formal ceremony that admitted them to an elite group of warriors. Modern historians argue that soldiers fighting on horseback in the 9th and 10th centuries should be viewed as mounted warriors, rather than true knights. These mounted warriors were, as we have seen, bound to their lords in the developing feudal system, in which they provided military service in return for the right to land. However, an essential element of knighthood was absent: the idea of the making of a knight through the formal admission to a chivalric brotherhood.

Within this view, figures such as Charlemagne and Alfred the Great can be seen as remarkable warrior-kings, as precursors of chivalry, but not as knights; and likewise while mounted soldiers

▼ Feudal service was rewarded with grants of land, so more prominent knights were able to establish themselves on large estates.

riding in the heavy cavalry of Duke Richard II of Normandy, for example, had many qualities of knights, their comradeship as bonded vassals of their lord lacked this quality of a brotherhood following a chivalric code.

SOCIAL STATUS OF KNIGHTS

As both feudalism and knighthood developed, knights became established as one level in an enormously stratified social grouping that also included the barons on their great estates, and poorer mounted warriors who were not admitted to knighthood and provided military service as squires. The relative social status of those formally called 'knights' was constantly shifting as it was challenged from above and below.

EQUALITY AND EXCLUSIVENESS

In theory, according to the code of chivalry, the brotherhood of knights was an elite, but all within it were equal. This equality probably derived from that of the knights' predecessors among the freemen who fought side by side for the Frankish kings. In this tradition knighthood was a reward

▲ The Christian Church sanctioned violence when it was performed in Christ's service. This 12th-century illustration is entitled 'The faithful knight leaving to battle Satan'.

for the brave, and all brave knights were equal. Only a knight could make a knight – but knighthood could be conferred upon anyone who had proved himself worthy of the accolade.

Yet knights were also often a social elite. This was in large part because their feudal rewards for military service set them up as wealthy landowners, who were able to use their position to acquire more land and pass great territories down the generations. On a practical level, it was also because the cost of a knight's equipment excluded poorer warriors.

It became a matter of official policy to maintain the exclusiveness of the knightly fraternity and to exert control over who might confer knighthood. From the early 12th century, royal pronouncements excluded various groups from being knighted. Some of the earlier exclusions were designed to keep the peace by preventing any rowdy elements from becoming knights, and in particular to prevent nobles quickly raising a rebel force through a mass knighting ceremony. For example, a German decree of 1152 excluded peasants from being knights, and in 1140 Roger II, Norman king of Sicily,

▶ *In this manuscript illustration, also from the 12th century, the devils represent vices and heresies. Drawing his sword, the knight prepares to impose Christian law.*

forbade the knighting of men who were liable to disturb the peace. In 1186 Holy Roman Emperor Frederick I banned both the sons of peasants and the sons of priests from being knighted – the latter on the grounds that since priests officially could not marry, their sons were illegitimate.

INHERITED QUALITIES
Gradually the idea developed that the qualities needed to be a knight could only be transmitted through inheritance: only the descendants of knights could be knights. In 1235 the Cortes of Catalonia declared: 'We establish that no man can be knighted unless he is the son of a knight.' Sometimes the ability or right to raise to knighthood those not descended from knights was restricted to kings. For example, Holy Roman Emperor Frederick II declared in 1231: 'No man who is not of knightly descent shall be made a knight

except by our licence or permission.' The royal prerogative could be valuable (see box). These kinds of exclusions were not in force in England. Moreover, even in Germany and France knights were still sometimes 'made' by other knights on the field of battle as a reward for valour.

A LEISURED CLASS
The feudal system delivered knights a leisured life. When not on campaign, they lived in grand style in their castles and fortified manor houses, subsidised by the hard labour of the peasants who worked the land on the grand estates. Knights were free to hunt and hawk, to practise their military skills in tournaments and to develop their taste for literature and music – songs of knightly bravery. In these circumstances the literature and ethos of chivalry developed.

A COMPLEX BOND
In its mature form, from the late 11th century – when European knights rode out against the warriors of Islam in the First Crusade (1095–99) – knighthood was a complex bond, a combination of a badge of warrior honour, a social distinction, an ethical challenge and a religious calling. To be a knight was often a sign of

valorous achievement, while it could also be a title inherited by birth, giving right to certain lands. A knight also voluntarily adopted a code of honour, a duty of service, and was blessed by the Church as a defender of the Christian faith, or *miles Christi* ('soldier of Christ').

▼ *According to chivalric theory, the knight offered his military service to God. Knights and their swords were blessed in church.*

KNIGHTHOODS FOR SALE
Once it was accepted that generally men could not rise to knighthood from lower social ranks, except by royal licence, kings faced the temptation of raising money by putting knighthoods up for sale. This very unchivalric practice was particularly common in France, where for example the king, Philip IV (r. 1285–1314), announced his willingness to grant knighthoods for sums of money. In France in this era, a wealthy merchant might purchase a knighthood as a financial investment since being a knight brought exemptions from tax. Knighthoods were also sold by the Imperial crown in 14th-century Germany, by Charles IV, Holy Roman Emperor in 1355–78, and his subsequent successors.

CHAPTER TWO

HOLY WAR

Knights such as Godfrey of Bouillon and Robert of Flanders won enduring fame on the First Crusade of 1096–99, their exploits quickly embroidered in legends. Yet for every knight such as Godfrey or Robert there were many other crusaders who died uncelebrated and in wretched circumstances – of starvation, of disease, in battle or ambush – many having brought financial ruin on themselves after borrowing very heavily to make the trip. It can be difficult at a distance of several centuries to see why so many men (and women) were moved to risk so much on such a venture. A key explanation is that they were inspired to view the enterprise as a holy war – they saw themselves as the latterday counterparts of the Israelites, whose struggles against enemies of their faith were an inspirational prototype of the crusades. The biblical warrior Judas Maccabeus is said, according to the Second Book of Maccabees, to have gone into battle with a golden sword given to him in a vision by the prophet Jeremiah with words that could happily have given service as a blessing for medieval knights: 'Take this holy sword, a gift from God, wherewith thou shalt overthrow the adversaries of my people Israel'. Judas's soldiers followed him into battle in a manner that was equally suited as inspiration for the crusaders' assault on Jerusalem: 'Thus being exhorted with the words of Judas, which were very good, and proper to stir up the courage, and strengthen the hearts of the young men, they resolved to fight, and set upon them manfully; that valour might decide the matter, because the Holy City and the temple were in danger.'

▲ *The pope had the spiritual authority to judge even royal sinners.*

◀ *The army of Bohemond of Taranto comes under attack while trying to cross the River Vardar en route to fight in the First Crusade. The journey was long and arduous.*

FIGHTING A HOLY WAR

THEORIES OF JUST AND SACRED WARS

The Benedictine historian Guibert, Abbot of Nogent-sous-Coucy, author in the early 12th century of a chronicle of the First Crusade, declared that 'God has instituted in these days sacred wars, so that the body of knights ... can find a means of winning their salvation'. Guibert may have suggested that holy wars were created in his era by a watchful God, but in truth the idea of fighting a just and divinely sanctioned war had its origins centuries earlier, and had roots as far back as the biblical era.

THE EXAMPLE OF THE OLD TESTAMENT

There are many examples in the Old Testament of the Bible of warfare waged on God's instructions or in his name. The God celebrated in the Old Testament appeared to use warfare to achieve his ends; he himself dealt in death. According to the Book of Exodus (Chapter 15), after

▼ *The anger of Israel's warlike God brought ruin on the Egyptians when the Red Sea closed over them, allowing the Israelites to travel on towards the Promised Land.*

escaping from captivity in Egypt the Israelites sang a hymn of praise in which they joyously celebrated their miraculous escape, the parting of the Red Sea and the death of their enemies in its waters: 'The Lord is a man of war: the Lord is his name ... Pharaoh's chariots and his host hath he cast into the sea ... the depths have covered them: they sank into the bottom as a stone. Thy right hand, O Lord, is become glorious in power: thy right hand, O Lord, hath dashed in pieces the enemy.'

The Old Testament God did call on his people to kill on his behalf – for example, when he instructed King Saul (David's predecessor as the king of Israel): 'Thus saith the Lord of hosts, I remember that which Amalek did to Israel, how he laid wait for him in the way, when he came up from Egypt. Now go and smite Amalek, utterly destroy all that they have, and spare them not; but slay both man and woman, infant and suckling, ox, sheep, camel and ass' (1 Samuel 15: verses 2–3).

A gallery of Israelite warriors, including David, Gideon and Joshua, were venerated as proponents of righteous warfare, even as exemplars of the knightly

▲ *'And I beheld when He had opened the sixth seal, and, lo, there was a great earthquake ...' Martial language, such as this quote from the Book of Revelation, encouraged Christians to believe that God sanctioned the use of violence.*

code of chivalry; chief among them and celebrated alongside David and Joshua among the 'Nine Worthies' of the biblical, classical and chivalric worlds was Judas Maccabeus, guerrilla fighter against Seleucid overlords of Jerusalem in the 2nd century BC.

Judas Maccabeus was said to have led his warriors into battle 'fighting with their hands, but praying to the Lord with their hearts' and in battle 'they slew no less than five and thirty thousand'; in the midst of this carnage they were 'greatly cheered with the presence of God'. This quotation is from Chapter 15 of the Second Book of Maccabees, part of the Old Testament for Roman Catholics and Eastern Orthodox Christians but in modern times usually considered by Protestant Christians to be in the Apocrypha, a selection of texts that is associated with the Bible but not seen as part of it.

the 1st-century BC Roman statesman Cicero, who argued that a just war had to be fought using just means or in the right way – for example, with bravery. As developed by St Augustine, the Christian theory of a just or holy war required that it be fought in self-defence or to recover a seized territory or possession, on proper authority, and with the right intentions and means by all involved. Augustine added that wars fought on God's authority did not breach the commandment forbidding killing.

These ideas of sanctioned violence, of just and sacred war, applied to public bodies, such as State or Church. Individuals were required to be obedient to these public bodies, and to fight if commanded to do so. But in their individual lives violence was not sanctioned, and here Christ's troubling commands to love thy neighbour and to show forgiveness applied. Here was the distinction between sanctioned violence carried out in defence of the Church under vows to maintain the peace of God, and private wars, the secular clashes between knights that were condemned by the Church.

▲ St Augustine, kneeling, was inspired by the preaching of St Ambrose, right, the Bishop of Milan. Both men were great intellectuals and rhetoricians who developed theories of a just use of violence.

incentive for travelling to Jerusalem was that the events of the Last Judgement were expected to be played out in the city where Christ died and was buried.

▼ Augustine urged Christians to focus on a mystical heavenly Jerusalem in his work The City of God, *written shortly after 410.*

VIOLENCE OF THE LAST DAYS

In the New Testament, Christian knights and their clerical supporters drew on the warlike imagery of descriptions of the Day of Judgement in the Book of Revelation, in which celestial armies gave expression to the righteous anger of God, which was likened to a winepress. Many of the knights, clerics and ordinary people who travelled to the Holy Land on the First Crusade had a strong sense that they were living in the last days before the Second Coming of Christ, which gave a great sense of urgency to the need to achieve remission of sins. Moreover, a key

JUSTIFICATION OF HOLY WAR

Theoretical justifications of holy war drew on 4th- and 5th-century AD Christian writers, such as St Ambrose, Bishop of Milan, and his pupil St Augustine, Bishop of Hippo. These theologians drew on classical philosophy: in particular those of the 4th-century BC ancient Greek philosopher Aristotle, who developed the notion of a 'just war' waged for the purpose of maintaining peace; ancient Roman ideas that wars could justly be fought to defend oneself, to recover seized territory or property, or to inflict punishment on a wrongdoer as long as the war was fought with proper authority (of the state); and the theory of

DEFENDERS OF THE FAITH

CHRISTIAN WARRIORS IN A HOLY WAR

The great Norman crusader lord Tancred of Hauteville was filled with energy, according to his biographer Radulph of Caen, by Pope Urban II's call to the First Crusade. Before departing on crusade, Radulph writes, Tancred was disturbed by the disjunction between on the one hand the demands of life as a feudal knight, which required him to wage war, and on the other the teaching of Christ to turn the other cheek and act with generosity to the needy. The new idea of crusading, in which waging war against pagans was presented as a form of devotional penance for Christian knights, was tailor-made to address such a difficulty, and Tancred responded with enthusiasm: in Radulph's words, 'as if he had previously been asleep, he came awake, his energy was aroused, his strength increased, his seeing grew sharper and his bravery was born'.

In the context of energizing knights to fight for the Church in distant lands, Pope Urban's conflation of waging war and doing penance was a stroke of genius, and a new departure. But the idea of fighting a holy war – and of being a holy warrior – was not a new one: Radulph may well have been overstating Tancred's sense of discomfort at the disjunction between his life as a knight and his life as a devout Christian. For the knights who travelled

on the First Crusade were descendants of Germanic tribes whose warrior-band philosophy, incorporating celebration of the military lord and of feats of martial vigour, had had a profound effect on thinking and writing about the Christian faith in the centuries since they had been converted in the 5th and 6th centuries AD.

▲ *In the 5th century, King Clovis of the Salian Franks began his people's long association with the Catholic Church when he converted to Christianity in order to marry Princess Clotilde. The faith became increasingly militarized.*

Figures such as Clovis I, the first Frankish king to convert to Christianity, and his successor, Charlemagne, were viewed as warrior heroes as much as they were Christian kings. Christian language and thought became infused with Germanic warrior imagery. For example, in the masterful 8th-century Anglo-Saxon poem *The Dream of the Rood*, the poet uses very military language in describing his dream of seeing Christ on the cross, calling Christ the 'young hero', 'the warrior', 'the Prince' and 'the Lord of Victories', and envisages Christ's actions on the cross as those of a fearless warrior.

HOLY WAR AND DIPLOMACY

One key divide between the westerners, or 'Latins', who travelled on crusade and the easterners, or 'Greeks', they went to help, derived from a distinctly different outlook on life, particularly when it came to diplomacy and war.

The Latins had a developed theory of the just, or holy, war and of the righteousness of combat, but the Greeks viewed conflict only as a last resort and preferred to settle disagreements through diplomacy and compromise. Many of the Latins were only a few generations separated from forebears among the Viking raiders, and the Greeks saw them as uncultured barbarians; for their part, the Latins viewed the Greeks as untrustworthy – particularly in their willingness to negotiate and sign treaties with Muslim powers.

FIGHTING TO PROMOTE CHRISTIANITY

Battle imagery invaded Christian thought, and Christian practices found a place on the battlefield. King Alfred of Wessex prayed with his commanders before battle and his warriors had Christian images on their weapons; in chronicles his wars were always presented as being for Christianity against pagans. Likewise, Charlemagne's battles against pagan enemies such as the Saxons were presented as holy wars. For the 'pagans', the price of defeat by Alfred or by Charlemagne was forcible conversion to Christianity. Such a war was self-evidently a holy one, fought in order to spread the faith. The empire that Charlemagne built was an explicitly Christian one.

FIGHTING TO DEFEND CHRISTIANITY AND THE CHURCH

From c.850 onwards when Charlemagne's empire began to fall apart, the chief foes were marauding pagans – Vikings, 'Saracens' (Muslim Arabs and Berbers) and Magyars. Fighting against these raiders

▲ *Christian Emperor Charlemagne leads his army at the walls of Pamplona, Spain, 778, from a 14th-century manuscript.*

was a defence of Christianity and the idea of 'Christendom' began to inform debate. The community of European peoples who had once been united under the Frankish empire were now bound by their common Christian faith and their opposition to non-Christian, pagan enemies.

In the 9th and 10th centuries, moreover, in increasingly lawless times, church authorities began to promote the theory that armed warriors had a responsibility to protect the weak, and particularly the Church. The churchmen promoted the Peace of God, under which warriors would swear to protect those who were not equipped to protect themselves – principally clergy and monks. In this context, fighting was a form of piety.

This initiative did more than condemn attacks on church property, going as far as to encourage violence in the interests of preventing lawless attacks. As with Urban's call to arms at Clermont, in the Peace of God initiative the Church was not simply giving its blessing to violence, it was rather bringing violence into being.

Throughout the period there were also those churchmen who resisted the glorification of violence, who continued to promote the monastic or clerical life as the ideal Christian one. Killing remained officially a sin. The Norman soldiers who fought at Hastings under William the Conqueror were required to do penance for the blood they had spilled, despite the fact that they were fighting under a papal banner (with the pope's backing) and the explicit approval of their clergy.

▼ *At Hastings in 1066 Christian Normans fought Christian Anglo-Saxons. Duke William's men were supported by the pope.*

MUSLIM EMPIRES
THE SPREAD OF ISLAM

In the late 11th century, prior to the First Crusade, control of the eastern Mediterranean was divided between the Christian Byzantine Empire based in Constantinople, the Sunni Muslim Seljuk Turks nominally ruled from Baghdad, rival Seljuk groups in Anatolia with a capital at Nicaea, and Shi'ite Muslim Fatimids from northern Africa. In eastern Anatolia the Muslim Turkish Danishmends were also a force to be reckoned with.

THE ISLAMIC EXPANSION

The great expansion of Islam began from the Arabian Peninsula in the 7th century AD. In the hundred years following the death of the Prophet Muhammad – founder of the faith – in 632, Muslim warriors created a vast empire stretching from Spain in the west to parts of China and India in the east, and encompassing Palestine, Syria and Mesopotamia.

▼ *Islamic warriors spread north, taking on the Persian and Byzantine empires, then eastwards across Africa to Spain by 711.*

THE PROPHET AND HIS TEACHING

The Prophet Muhammad was born in *c.*570 in the caravan city of Mecca, Arabia, a member of the Quaraish tribe. He began to preach in around 613 and established the new faith of Islam in exile from Mecca at Yathrib (later known as Medina, the City of the Prophet) in 620–30, before returning to Mecca from 630 until his death two years later.

Muhammad taught that there was one God, named Allah, Creator of all that existed, who demanded honour and submission from humans – the word *Islam* means 'surrender' (that is, to the will of Allah), while *Muslims* are so called from the Arabic for 'those who submit'. *Allah* was another name for the 'God of the Christians and the Jews'. Muhammad's teachings were gathered in the Koran, which his followers said completed and superseded the Christian and Jewish books; Muhammad was the final prophet in a sequence that also included Noah, Abraham and Jesus.

▲ *Angels Gabriel, Michael, Israfil and Azrail attend on the Prophet as he travels to Mecca. One of a set of 16th-century Ottoman illustrations on Muhammad's life.*

THE FIRST ISLAMIC LEADERS

Following the death of Muhammad in Mecca in 632, one of his followers, named Abu Bakr, a merchant and member of a minor clan in the Prophet's Quaraish tribe,

Expansion of Islam
- Islamic conquests at Muhammad's death
- Islamic conquests 632–661
- Islamic conquests 661–750
- → Direction of conquest

500 km
500 miles

was elected as *khalifat rasul Allah* (Successor to God's Prophet) or 'caliph': the spiritual and political leader of the faithful. He died in 634, but before his death appointed a successor, another merchant and a member of the Quaraish, named Omar bin Khattab.

Under Caliph Omar's rule (634–44), Muslim Bedouin tribesmen won astonishing victories against the Byzantine and Persian empires, defeating the Byzantines in Syria and the Persians in Mesopotamia. They took Damascus in 635. In 637 they captured the Persian capital Ctesiphon. In 638 they took Jerusalem. In the 640s they established themselves in Egypt, capturing Alexandria in 646. By this time Omar was dead. Disputes over the succession gave rise to schism and centuries-long enmity between Sunni and Shi'ite Islam.

SUNNI AND SHI'ITE SPLIT

Omar was succeeded by Othman ibn Affan, another merchant and also one of Muhammad's original converts and once again a member of Quaraish tribe of Mecca. There was opposition to his appointment, gathered around the Prophet's cousin and son-in-law Ali, husband of Muhammad's daughter Fatima. When Othman was murdered in 656, two rival caliphs vied to replace him: on the

▼ *This image of a Moorish army is from a manuscript made for King Alfonso X of Castile and Leon (r.1252–84).*

one hand Ali, and on the other, Mu'awiyah, a member of Umayyad clan, who had earlier been appointed Governor of Syria by Othman. In 661 both Ali and Mu'awiyah were stabbed as they prayed in mosques in separate cities – Ali later died, but Mu'awiyah survived. Ali's supporters appointed his son Hassan caliph, but in a confrontation with Mu'awiyah he backed down; then when Mu'awiyah died in 680, Ali's second son Hussein claimed the caliphate. In an encounter with Mu'awiyah's son Yazid on 10 October 680, Hussein and all his followers were killed.

The split between Shi'ite and Sunni Muslims derived from this power struggle. Sunnis backed the descendants of Mu'awiyah – the Umayyad caliphs – as the rightful leaders of Islam, but Shi'ites declared them usurpers and argued that Ali had inherited the spirit of Muhammad and that leadership of Islam should be from his descendants. The Shi'ites' name came from that of the followers of Ali in the 7th century – the *shi'at Ali* (the party of Ali), whereas the Sunni were so called because they said they were following the *sunna* (example) of Muhammad.

AN ISLAMIC EMPIRE IN SPAIN

Muslim Arabs spread westwards from Egypt through northern Africa. Their advance was temporarily held up by the Berbers of the Atlas Mountains but after constructing the fortified city of Kairouan (in modern Tunisia) they subdued the Maghreb region of north and north-western Africa, then under the great Arab general Tariw ibn-Ziyad, crossed the Straits of Gibraltar and in just five years took virtually the whole Iberian Peninsula from its previous rulers, the Visigoths.

Arabs began to raid beyond the Pyrenees Mountains into southern and western France. In 732 at the Battle of Tours the marauding Arabs finally met their match in a redoubtable army commanded by Charles Martel ('the Hammer'), King of the Franks. Thereafter the Arabs withdrew into Spain and consolidated their possessions there.

▲ *St James makes a miraculous appearance in the legendary Battle of Clavijo in 844.*

UMAYYADS, ABBASIDS AND FATIMIDS

In the east the Umayyad descendants of Caliph Mu'awiyah ruled the Islamic empire from Damascus until they were ousted in 750 by their cousins and rivals the Abbasids, who established the capital of the empire at Baghdad in Iraq. The Abbasids came to power with Shi'ite support but ruled as Sunni Muslims. In 909 militant Shi'ite Muslims established a rival Fatimid dynasty (claiming direct descent from the Prophet's daughter Fatima) in Tunis and built their capital at Cairo.

By the second half of the 10th century the balance of power in the western Mediterranean was between a resurgent Byzantine empire, which had re-established itself in Syria; the increasingly weak Abbasid caliphate in Baghdad, which had nominal control over Iran, Iraq and the remainder of Syria; and the Fatimids of Cairo, who had extended their territory up through Palestine.

THE RISE OF THE SELJUKS

Then the Seljuk Turks erupted onto the scene. Originally from central Asia, these Turkmen tribes converted to Sunni Islam, conquered Afghanistan and eastern Iran, and in 1055 took control of Baghdad. In the 1070s the Seljuks delivered a crushing blow to the Byzantine army at the Battle of Manzikert, capturing Syria and most of Palestine from the Fatimids.

CHRISTIANS IN THE EAST
THE 'EMPIRE OF THE GREEKS'

The Latin Christians led by the pope in Rome, the faithful who were summoned by Urban II to the First Crusade, did not have a close or easy relationship with their counterparts in the Eastern Church and the Byzantine Empire.

CHRISTIAN ORIGINS IN THE EAST

Christian presence in the eastern Mediterranean dates back to the 1st century AD, when saints Peter, Paul and Barnabus established the first Christian community in Antioch – its members were the first people in history to be called 'Christians'. The origins of the Christian Byzantine Empire lie in the 4th century, when Constantine, the first Roman emperor to support Christianity, established the city of Constantinople as a new capital for the Roman Empire.

Constantine built the city as Nova Roma (New Rome) on the site of the trading city of Byzantium, according to legend created in 667BC by Greek colonists led by

▼ According to tradition, St Peter was the first Bishop of Antioch, then Bishop of Rome – and, as such, was the first pope.

King Byzantas (or Byzas); New Rome was renamed Constantinople (the city of Constantine) after Constantine's death in AD337. In contrast to previous Roman emperors, who had persecuted Christians, Constantine announced that Christianity would be tolerated in the empire in 313 – traditionally he had won power after a vision had inspired him to fight under the sign of the Christian cross. He then laid the groundwork for the establishment of a Christian culture in the empire, although he was not himself baptized until shortly before his death. He called the Church's first ecumenical meeting, the Council of Nicaea, in 325. This council drew up the first statement of uniform Christian doctrine, the Nicene Creed.

Situated on the Bosphorus between the Black Sea and the Sea of Marmara, at the intersection of the mercantile routes of Asia and eastern Europe, Constantinople grew fabulously wealthy on the profits of trade. After the death of Emperor Theodosius I in 395, the Roman Empire was permanently split into eastern and western halves, ruled from Rome and Constantinople, respectively. Following the sacking of Rome by the Visigoths in 410 and the collapse of the eastern empire in Europe culminating in the deposition

▲ Constantine the Great (left) founded Constantinople, while his mother St Helena (right) played an important part in Jerusalem's rise as a centre of pilgrimage.

of the last emperor in Rome, Romulus Augustus, in 476 by the Germanic king Odoacer, the city of Constantine was the capital of the Byzantine Empire.

EXPANSION AND DECLINE

In the 7th and 8th centuries the Byzantine Empire came under repeated attack by the swiftly expanding Muslim empire. Several times, from 674, the Arabs attempted to take Constantinople itself, but without success; they were finally driven back from the city when the siege of 717 was decisively defeated by the Byzantine emperor Leo III. In the period 863–1025 the Byzantine Empire expanded greatly and at one point in 976 the Arabs were driven back as far as the very gates of Jerusalem. But after the death of Emperor Basil II in 1025, the empire's fortunes declined once more, and in the mid-11th century the Seljuk Turks erupted into the region, culminating in the severe defeat of the Byzantine army by the Seljuks at Manzikert in Armenia in 1071. This defeat lost the empire all its lands in Anatolia.

Matters of doctrine also caused controversy: the Eastern Church allowed married priests but the Latin Church insisted officially on celibacy of the priesthood; the Latin Church allowed the use of unleavened bread in the Mass but the Eastern Church was against this. Another major disagreement arose over whether in the Christian Trinity of Father, Son and Holy Spirit, the Spirit derived from the Father or from both the Father and the Son. The Nicene Creed had declared 'I believe in the Holy Spirit, the Lord the giver of Life, who proceedeth from the Father', but western churches had added the words 'and the Son'. This *filioque* clause (so called from the Latin word meaning 'from the Son') had first been used in Spain in the 7th century, then had been backed by Charlemagne, and had finally been accepted by the papacy in 1014; but it was vehemently rejected by the Eastern Church as heresy. In 1089 Urban II sent an embassy to Constantinople asking for full relations to recommence between Western and Eastern Churches but the division – later known to historians as the 'Great Schism' – endured.

▲ *St Mark, author of the Gospel of Mark, is revered by Christians in north Africa, and was Bishop of Alexandria.*

CONFLICT WITHIN

The name 'Byzantine Empire', it should be noted, dates from the 16th century, when it was first used by a German historian. The rulers and citizens of the empire called it 'Roman', whereas those in western Europe called it the 'Empire of the Greeks'. From the 9th century onwards the great powers of Europe were increasingly in competition with the Byzantine Empire to determine who was the successor of ancient Rome – as well as being in dispute over territories in Italy. In 800 Charlemagne was crowned *Imperator Augustus* (August Emperor) by Pope Leo III in Rome, in an attempt to revive the Roman Empire in the west; he also bore the title *Patricius Romanorum* (Protector of the Romans). In the 10th century Otto II of the Germans married a Byzantine

princess – Theopanu, niece of the Byzantine emperor John I Tzimisces – but was in conflict with the eastern empire and declared himself 'Roman emperor'.

TENSION BETWEEN WESTERN AND EASTERN CHURCHES

There was also conflict between the Church hierarchies of west and east. In 1054, the leaders of the Churches – Pope Leo IX in Rome and Patriarch Michael Cerularius in Constantinople – excommunicated one another. The tension went right back to the 5th century, when, following the fall of Rome, the pope assumed the mantle of protector of Christians in the west. Rome was the burial place of the Apostle Peter and the popes claimed direct succession from him and ultimate authority over the entire Church; but the patriarchs of Constantinople claimed they were the highest authority, since Constantinople was the seat of the eastern Roman Empire.

▼ *The Byzantine Empire held territory in Italy. At Ravenna, the basilica of San Vitale contains this beautiful mosaic of Christ.*

THE POWER OF THE PAPACY

POPES STRUGGLE FOR INDEPENDENCE

The second half of the 11th century saw concerted attempts by the papacy to establish the Church in a strong position independent of secular power. The idea of fighting as a form of Christian devotion was taken a stage further when popes presented struggles in support of the papacy as holy wars.

Pope Leo IX (ruled 1049–54) personally led troops to war against Norman adventurers in southern Italy in 1053. He set the precedent of promising his soldiers absolution of their sins and remission of penance as their reward. In this campaign the papal army was defeated at the Battle of Civitate by a Norman force led by Humphrey of Hauteville and containing Robert Guiscard. Ten years later the Normans were papal allies: after Pope Nicholas II (ruled 1059–61) invested

▲ *Cluny Abbey in France was at the forefront of Church reform in the 10th to 12th centuries and its abbot was second in power only to the pope. Otho of Lagery, later known as Pope Urban II, was a prior there. As pope, he visited the abbey in 1095.*

Robert Guiscard as duke of Apulia, Calabria and Sicily, the Norman army fought under a papal banner in invading Muslim Sicily. Another branch of the Norman family also had a papal banner for William of Normandy's invasion of England in 1066.

GREGORY VII AND ST PETER'S SOLDIERS

Pope Gregory VII (ruled 1073–85) became embroiled in a long-running dispute with the German emperor Henry IV (reigned 1056–1105). The main issue of contention in what is known to historians as 'the Investiture Controversy' was whether Henry or Gregory should control

the church: it was focused on who should have control over bishops' investiture (appointment and presentation of symbols of office) in the German church; it followed a period in which the papacy had been very weak, and Henry IV's predecessor, Henry III, had appointed three German popes. Gregory set out to mobilize his own papal force, the *Militia Sancti*

▼ *Pope Gregory VII grants absolution to German emperor Henry IV in 1077. This was an important but temporary victory for the papacy in the long struggle to establish its independence from secular rulers.*

▶ *Pope Leo X and Patriarch Michael Cerularius of Constantinople excommunicated one another in 1054. The quarrel had begun centuries before in a dispute over which church had primacy.*

Petri (the 'army of St Peter'). He told the knights in his service that they were 'vassals of Saint Peter' and as reward would receive Peter's blessing 'in this life and the life to come'.

Gregory and Henry IV clashed dramatically. In 1076 Gregory excommunicated Henry and declared him *anathema*, which meant he was excluded from the community of Christian believers and that none of his subjects had to keep oaths made to him. German nobles forced Henry to back down and in January 1077 he travelled to the pope's castle at Canossa in northern Italy, where Gregory made him wait outside, barefoot and clad in a hair shirt in the snow, before finally allowing him in to receive forgiveness. This decisively changed the balance of power between pope and emperor, but only in the short term: Henry and Gregory clashed again and Gregory excommunicated Henry again in 1080; Henry attacked Rome three times between 1081 and 1084 and on the third occasion Gregory had to be rescued from his castle of Castel Sant'Angelo in the city by his ally and vassal, the Norman adventurer Robert Guiscard.

REFORM AND PAPAL POWER

Gregory is remembered as a 'reforming pope', because he attacked such abuses in the church as simony (the sale of Church offices) and tried to impose celibacy on the priesthood. Both these campaigns were tied up with his efforts to establish the absolute supremacy of the papacy – simony was beneficial to secular leaders who used it to bring about the appointment of their own supporters in key positions, and he made use of the campaign for celibacy to counter the power of rebel bishops who allowed married priests. He was passionately committed to the spiritual renewal of the Church.

GREGORY VII'S 'CRUSADE'

Gregory is also notable for his attempt to launch a forerunner of the crusades – a military expedition to help Constantinople and the Christians in the East in 1074.

THE ISSUING OF INDULGENCES

Popes used the promise of forgiveness, the remission of penances and the granting of indulgences as a lure to mobilize armies in their support. The issuing of indulgences derived from the idea that a punishment remained due for a sinner even when he or she had won forgiveness for a sin through repentance and confession; a sinner might win God's eternal forgiveness through genuine repentance but still be liable for a temporal punishment.

In the early Christian Church 'canonical penances' were calculated to wipe a sinner's slate clean, to do away with the temporal punishment; then in the early medieval Church, parts of the canonical penance were commuted – a repentant sinner was told he or she would achieve the same benefit by donating a specified amount of money to the Church, by giving alms to the poor or by spending an allotted period of time in fasting or prayer. Indulgences were usually partial – they commuted part of the punishment. The first recorded instance of an absolute or plenary indulgence that promised the complete avoidance of temporal punishment was the speech by Urban II at Clermont in 1095, when he issued his call to arms in the First Crusade. He declared: 'Whoever, acting out of devotion and not for the sake of winning honour or riches, travels to Jerusalem to free the Church of God may substitute this sacred journey for all penance.'

▼ *Pope Urban II at Clermont, where he issued his call to take up arms.*

Gregory made the attempt in response to a call in 1073 from Byzantine emperor Michael VII for help against the Seljuk Turks. In a manner that would have many echoes in Urban II's declaration at Clermont in 1095, Gregory promoted the enterprise in 1074 as an act of charity on behalf of those he hoped to involve, and claimed that they would be following the example of Christ, acting under the mandate of God himself; he also offered the promise of 'eternal reward'. Gregory did manage to raise an army but the enterprise foundered and the expedition did not set out.

The First Crusade was a direct descendant of the holy wars that were fought in the name of the papacy, since it was launched by the pope and fought with the aim of establishing his supremacy over the Eastern Church and his rule over a united Christendom. From the outset it was conceived by those involved in it as an expression of papal power.

THE HOLY CITY OF JERUSALEM
PLACE OF CHRIST'S PASSION, SACRED TO THREE FAITHS

Several medieval maps survive to the present day in which Jerusalem is represented as the centre of the Earth, which was at that time believed to be flat. To Christians of this era, the city was the holiest spot in the world, the place where God, through his son Jesus Christ, had redeemed the fallen creation.

Jerusalem was and is sacred to Jews and Muslims, as well as to the followers of Christ. Jews revere Jerusalem as the city of David, founder of the united kingdom of Israel and Judah, and the place where his successor, Solomon, built a great temple. To Muslims Jerusalem is traditionally the third most sacred city in the world after Mecca, the Prophet's birthplace, and Yathrib, or Medina, the city in which he established the Islamic faith in AD620–30. Jerusalem is said to be the place from which the Prophet made an ascent into heaven – according to Muslim tradition,

▼ The Church of the Holy Sepulchre, believed to be built on the spot where Christ was crucified, was the crusaders' goal.

Muhammad was taken up from Mecca by the Angel Gabriel one night in 620 and transported to Jerusalem, from where he ascended a golden ladder to heaven.

REPEATED VIOLENCE
By the time of the First Crusade in the 11th century, the city already had a long and bloody history. Following the era of David and Solomon the city was sacked by the Egyptian pharaoh Sheshonk I in 922BC, and then both city and Temple were destroyed by Nebuchadnezzar of Babylon in 587BC. This cataclysmic event, which resulted in the exile of the Jews in Babylon, was followed eventually by their return under Cyrus the Great of Persia and the building of a second Temple in 515BC.

Under the rule of the Seleucids (the rulers of a kingdom that grew out of the empire of Alexander the Great) in the 2nd century BC, Judas Maccabeus led his celebrated revolt to reclaim the city and cleanse the Temple. In the era of chivalry he became an unlikely role model for the crusader knights as a religious warrior.

ROMAN CITY
At the time of Christ, Jerusalem was part of the province of Judea in the Roman Empire. A Jewish revolt in AD66 resulted in a devastating attack led by the future emperor Titus, in which the city was almost completely destroyed and the Temple once again reduced to ruins. A new city named Aelia Capitolina was built by Emperor Hadrian, provoking another revolt in 132–35, put down again by Roman might; at this time Hadrian renamed the Roman province of Judea 'Syria Palaestina' after the Philistines named in the Bible. Jerusalem remained under Roman rule until the 7th century, although from the 4th century onwards this was under Christian emperors. The city became a well-established site of pilgrimage for Christians.

▲ Jerusalem was depicted as being at the centre of the world in this map from an English psalter c.1262. Christ and two angels preside. The east is at the top, Europe and Africa at the bottom.

CHURCH OF THE HOLY SEPULCHRE
Built by Emperor Constantine in c.325, the Church of the Holy Sepulchre was said to mark the site of Golgotha, or the Hill of Calvary, where Christ was crucified and then buried.

The church consisted of three parts: a basilica named the *Martyrium* built over the place of crucifixion, a colonnade called the *Triportico* built around the Hill of Calvary, and a rotunda called the *Anastasis* (Resurrection) containing the actual cave in which Christ was said to have been buried. The tomb itself was enclosed in a special structure beneath the rotunda called the 'edicule' (from Latin *aediculum*, meaning 'small structure'), and visiting the edicule understandably became a major focus for Christian pilgrims and subsequently crusaders.

AN ARAB CITY

Jerusalem was captured by Bedouin Arabs under Omar bin Khattab, the second caliph, or leader, of Islam, in 638. His successors, the Umayyad caliphs of Damascus and their successors, the Abbasid caliphs of Baghdad, ruled over Jerusalem for more than 600 years, until 969. These regimes were both supporters of mainstream Sunni Islam, but in 969 the rival Fatimid caliphs of Cairo in Egypt, who were Shi'ite Muslims, took control of the city.

THE DOME OF THE ROCK

The city's principal Muslim holy site, the Dome of the Rock, was constructed in 685–91 by the Umayyad caliph Abd al-Malik. It was a mosque built as a *masshad* (pilgrimage shrine) for Muslims, on the reputed site from which Muhammad ascended to heaven on his Night Journey. The site was also sacred on three counts for Jews: as the place where the patriarch

▼ *The army of Nebuchadnezzar, king of Babylon c.605–562BC, brings death and destruction to the city of Jerusalem. The illustration is from the* Commentary on the Apocalypse *(c.776) by Spanish monk Beatus of Liébana.*

Abraham had readied himself to sacrifice his son Isaac to please God; as the rock on which Jacob had dreamt of a ladder ascending to heaven; and as the site of King Solomon's Temple. The al-Aqsa Mosque was built nearby at around the same time. In the crusader era, contemporary reports suggest that many Christian pilgrims, ignorant of their history, believed the Dome of the Rock to be the biblical Temple of Solomon.

▲ *Christ's empty tomb is visible within the Church of the Holy Sepulchre in this 14th-century view of pilgrims visiting Jerusalem.*

The Umayyad, Abbasid and Fatimid caliphs were mostly liberal towards Christian pilgrims. There was a major outbreak of persecution in the early 11th century, when the Fatimid caliph al-Hakim ordered the destruction of Christian shrines, including the Church of the Holy Sepulchre in 1010. This aggression proved to be short-lived, however, and in the 1040s the church was reconstructed by Byzantine builders with the permission of Fatimid caliph Ma'ad al-Mustansir Billah.

In 1071, however, the Fatimids were ousted from Jerusalem by the Seljuk Turks, who were far less tolerant of Christianity, and were unwilling to allow pilgrims to come and go unmolested. The reported attacks by Seljuk Turks on Christian pilgrims to Jerusalem was one of the provocations and justifications of the First Crusade.

Immediately prior to the First Crusade, Jerusalem was in the hands of the Seljuk Turks, but during the crusade (in 1098) it was recaptured by the Fatimid Muslims, so it was from the Fatimids that the crusaders took it in July 1099.

THE PENITENTIAL JOURNEY
A LONG HISTORY OF PILGRIMAGE

The religious tradition of the pilgrimage, or penitential journey, has roots that travel down deep into history. Christians in the 10th and 11th centuries enthusiastically embraced the crusade as a form of pilgrimage, as a means of expiating their sins.

The tradition of making religious journeys to visit shrines dates back to at least the world of ancient Greece, when people would travel to visit the Temple of Diana at Ephesus in Asia Minor (now western Turkey) and other sacred sites. Christ's birthplace, Bethlehem, and the scene of his Passion, Jerusalem, were places of pilgrimage for Christians from as early as the 2nd century AD.

FIRST CHRISTIAN PILGRIMS TO JERUSALEM

Eusebius, an early 4th-century Bishop of Caesarea, made references in his *Historia Ecclesiastica* (History of the Christian Church) to travelling Christians making

▼ *Devout pilgrims patiently wait to receive a papal blessing before embarking on their voyage to the holy places in the East.*

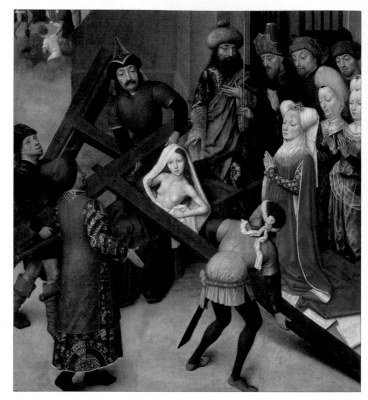

religious visits to Jerusalem. In truth, there was little for Christians to see in the city before Constantine the Great began a programme of identifying sacred sites and building churches.

Before Constantine's time the Jerusalem of Christ's era was almost entirely covered with the new city of Aelia Capitolina built by Hadrian following the near-total destruction of the earlier city by the future emperor Titus in AD70. The only known site associated with Christ's Passion was the cenacle, or supper room, reputedly the place in which Christ shared his last earthly meal with his disciples and gave them the basis of the Christian Mass, or Communion service. The cenacle was in the house said to have belonged to Mary,

▲ *The 'True Cross' is identified when it miraculously heals a sick woman during St Helena's pilgrimage to Jerusalem.*

mother of Saint Mark, author of the biblical Gospel of Mark; she was a prominent early Christian and the house was a meeting place for the disciples and followers after Christ's resurrection.

Constantine identified the site of Christ's burial in an area that, according to Bishop Eusebius, had been built up with earth and used as the site for a temple of the Roman goddess Venus, probably during Hadrian's rebuilding of the city. Constantine excavated the mound and found a cave that was then identified as the place where Joseph of Arimathaea placed Christ's body after it was taken down from the cross. There, Constantine constructed the Church of the Holy Sepulchre in c.AD325.

THE 'TRUE CROSS'

According to a tradition first recorded by the late 4th-century Christian writer Socrates Scholasticus, Constantine's mother Helena – who also converted to Christianity – made a pilgrimage to Jerusalem in c.312–30 and, under the guidance of a local Jew, found Christ's cross together with those of the two robbers who were crucified alongside him. A miracle revealed which one of the three was the cross used to crucify Christ: each of the crosses was laid on a very sick woman and one of them, imbued with divine power because Christ's blood had been spilt on it, brought about a cure. Helena also supposedly found the inscription hung above Christ's head on the cross, which identified him as 'King of the Jews', and the nails used to fix Jesus to the cross: the relics were sent to Constantinople, where the nails were beaten to form the emperor's bridle and helmet.

According to some accounts Helena also took the cross itself back with her to Constantinople, but other versions indicate that parts of the cross were kept in the Church of the Holy Sepulchre: pilgrims were venerating relics of the cross there by about c.380. Shortly afterwards, accounts of pilgrimages indicate that religious travellers were also being told that they could see the Holy Lance that pierced Christ's side, the crown of thorns He wore and the pillar at which He was whipped.

A fragment of the cross was taken from Jerusalem by Persian Sassanid emperor Khosrau II when he took the city in 614, then recaptured by Byzantine emperor Heraclius when he defeated Khosrau in battle. After keeping the relic briefly in Constantinople, Heraclius returned it to Jerusalem, where it remained. It was hidden by Christians early in the 11th century, and reputedly found in August 1099 by Arnulf of Choques, the city's first Latin Patriarch. The fragment became the principal sacred relic of the Kingdom of Jerusalem, kept in the Church of the Holy Sepulchre, and carried into battle by the crusader armies. This was the relic whose loss to Saladin's army during the Battle of Hattin in 1187 caused such lasting concern and consternation.

PILGRIMAGE AS PENANCE

The pilgrimage was a form of penitential discipline. Making a pilgrimage was a form of penance, that is an act performed to win forgiveness of sins. A priest, or in more serious cases a bishop, would specify the particular pilgrimage that a penitent must undertake in order to earn forgiveness. While travelling, the pilgrim might be required to wear a heavy chain or a hair shirt to add to the penance.

THE POWER OF RELICS

The institution of the pilgrimage was supported by the belief – already powerful as we have seen by the 5th century, and strong right through the Middle Ages – in the spiritual force of physical relics of Christ and his saints. In addition to fragments of objects such as the Cross or the Crown of Thorns, pilgrims travelled to venerate miraculously preserved body parts of sacred figures, such as fingers or hair clippings. These relics were believed to be imbued with divine power and regularly, like Helena's piece of the cross, effected extraordinary cures. Pilgrimages did not have to be to Jerusalem or the Holy Land: penitents could make journeys to a wide range of sites closer to home that were associated with the lives of saints or sanctified by the possession of a holy relic.

THE GOLDEN LEGEND OF THE TRUE CROSS

The pilgrims who venerated pieces of the True Cross in various locations were eager to tell and hear stories of its origin. A story developed linking the wood from which the cross was made to the Tree of Life that grew in the Garden of Eden; the form in which this tale has survived is the *Golden Legend* written by Jacopo of Voragine, Bishop of Genoa, in

1260. According to this story, the cross was made of wood grown from a seed of the Tree of Life: as he lay dying, Adam persuaded his son Seth to get the seed from the archangel Michael; when he returned with it, Seth placed it in Adam's mouth. Adam was buried after he died and a great tree grew from the seed and lived for many hundreds of years. Finally it was cut down: the wood was used to build a bridge. It happened that the biblical Queen of Sheba crossed the bridge on her way to visit King Solomon: she saw the wood's true nature and worshipped it, then told Solomon that a piece of the wood would be instrumental in the establishment of a new covenant between God and the Jews. Solomon was afraid and had the wood buried, but 14 generations later it was unearthed and made into the Holy Cross on which Christ died.

◄ *The Queen of Sheba kisses the wood of the Cross in a fresco of the story by Piero della Francesca in the Church of San Francesco, Arezzo, Italy.*

CRUSADER PILGRIMS
A SACRED ENTERPRISE

Access to Jerusalem was the ultimate prize for the crusader armies, for their journey was a pilgrimage as well as a military campaign. Each crusader who took the cross vowed to enter the Church of the Holy Sepulchre and pray there.

PILGRIMS BEARING ARMS

At low points during the First Crusade, such as the long siege of Antioch and the delay following its capture, the rank and file of the army were inspired to endure by their desire to fulfil their pilgrimage vows. Following the taking of Jerusalem, and their visit to the Church of the Holy Sepulchre, many felt that their enterprise was complete and took off for home, despite the fact that the crusaders' hold on Jerusalem was tenuous and that a formi-

▼ *Amid brutal violence, the soldiers who recaptured Jerusalem at the climax of the First Crusade celebrated ecstatically. Their pilgrimage had reached its goal.*

dable Egyptian relief army under the command of Fatimid vizier al-Afdal Shahanshah was marching on the city.

Before the crusades, there was already, as we have seen, a well-established Christian tradition of the pilgrimage as a form of penitential discipline. There was also a precedent for armed pilgrimage: in 1064, 7,000 armed German pilgrims under the command of two archbishops and two bishops marched to Jerusalem – some apparently wearing crosses. In 1095 Pope Urban II conflated the idea of a holy war fought in the name of God and the papacy with the benefits of a penitential journey. Part of the explanation for the response to his call to take the cross and travel on armed expedition to Jerusalem was that it met a keenly felt need – it allowed people to make their piety public and to seek expiation for their sins.

For many, the highest expression of Christian faith in action remained the monastic or clerical life. For example,

▲ *Preaching the Second Crusade in 1146, Bernard of Clairvaux urges Christians to take up the cross of Christ, and demonstrate their willingness to share in His suffering.*

Aelfric Grammaticus (the Grammarian), 10th-century abbot of Eynsham in southern England, declared that monks were the proper soldiers of Christ, those who fought with the words of prayers rather than with the metal of swords. But not all

THE GERMAN PILGRIMAGE OF 1064–65

Various chronicle accounts survive of the German pilgrimage of 1064. It was led by Siegfried, Archbishop of Mainz, and William, Archbishop of Trier, supported by Otto, Bishop of Regensburg and Gunther, Bishop of Bamberg. According to one report, Bishop Gunther cut such a splendid figure on this voyage that when the pilgrims came to Constantinople the people suspected that he must be the Holy Roman Emperor himself, travelling in disguise.

As they moved on towards Jerusalem, the pilgrims met returning travellers who told horror stories about the treatment of Christians by Arabs. On Good Friday 1065 the German pilgrims themselves were attacked by Arab bandits and then besieged at an isolated farmhouse over the entire Easter weekend. But, inspired by their archbishops and

bishops, the pilgrims trusted in God and in their weapons and drove back the besiegers on Easter Sunday, despite having gone three days without food or water. They captured some leading Arabs who had broken into the enclosure and used these men as hostages.

Another much-reported and horrific episode on the pilgrimage involved the rape of an abbess in full view of the travelling pilgrims by a gang of Arabs. The abbess was so badly injured that she died. One account of the pilgrimage, contained in the *Life of Bishop Altmann of Passau*, commented: 'Brought down by events like this and other humiliations in Christ's name, the travelling faithful won high praise in all quarters, from men and from angels above, because they elected to enter God's kingdom, suffering many tribulations.'

could follow this path. As Guibert, the Benedictine abbot of Nogent-sous-Coucy in France, wrote after praising the holy wars of the crusades as giving knights a chance to win their salvation: 'In this way they are not forced to give up secular affairs entirely by entering the monastic life of the clerical professions, as was once the normal practice, but can reach in some degree God's grace while following their own careers, with the freedom and in the dress to which they are used.'

THE CROSS OF SUFFERING

The men (and women) who took the cross did not call themselves crusaders. They were known by contemporaries as *cruces-ignati* – people marked with the cross. Nor did they call the enterprise a crusade. It was variously called a business, a journey or way and a pilgrimage. Urban principally promoted it as a military expedition.

When Bernard of Clairvaux came to preach the Second Crusade in 1146 – with such dramatic effectiveness that his sermons were viewed as a 'divine augury' and

a 'miracle' – he emphasized the expedition to Jerusalem he was urging as an opportunity for Christians to win salvation and, on an individual level, to demonstrate their repentance. In his vision, the cross worn by the crusaders was a sign that they

were willing to share in the suffering of Christ; what pain and difficulty they had to endure en route to victory would only improve the effectiveness of the enterprise in winning salvation for them.

In a sermonizing letter, which he despatched to the people of France and Bavaria in 1146, Bernard called the crusade 'Christ's business, in which is found our salvation' and called for urgency – 'now is the right time, now is the day of total salvation'. He summoned the vision of pagans defiling the Holy City, the place where so many Christian pilgrims had 'confessed their wrongdoings with tears and won forgiveness'; he said that the all-powerful God could of course cleanse the city with a battalion of angels, but that he preferred to test the mettle of his faithful Christian soldiers.

Bernard concluded with the following exhortation 'since your land is bursting with courageous men and is celebrated for the strength of its young warriors, gird yourselves like men and take up arms joyfully in the name of Christ.'

▼ *Bernard of Clairvaux and other crusade preachers painted a picture of terrible outrages perpetrated by Muslim 'Saracens' against the Christians in the East.*

CHAPTER THREE

BECOMING A KNIGHT

The knight was a specialist in mounted fighting. He was well equipped, and often superbly well trained. Many knights underwent a long and difficult apprenticeship in the arts of war, and the thoroughness of this training set them apart from their contemporaries. Although some great martial figures were able to break into knighthood through acts of great chivalry, knights were generally a social elite of princes, magnates or the sons of knights.

In the 13th century the chivalric handbooks that provided instructions on proper knightly behaviour set guidelines on the kind of people who might properly aspire to knighthood. The most celebrated, the *Libre del Orde de Cavalleria* (*Book of the Order of Chivalry*), was written in c.1265 by the remarkable Majorcan troubadour, philosopher, novelist, mystic and missionary Ramon Llull. The book also teaches that it is essential for knights to come from a noble family because such families have an established tradition of chivalric virtue going back generations.

Another handbook, the *Livre de Chevalerie*, or *Book of Chivalry*, was written in c.1350 by French knight Geoffroi de Charny. He stresses the role of chivalric warriors in keeping the peace, and presents them as an arm of the Church alongside the priesthood. Chivalry (the class of knights and men at arms) supports the divinely sanctioned social structure, by making it possible for God's representatives on earth, the king and the Church authorities, to exercise authority and ensure that justice is done.

▲ *The late medieval Bodiam Castle, in East Sussex, England.*

◀ *By tradition, a squire was expected to keep vigil on the last night before he was elevated to the brotherhood of knights.*

ACQUIRING COURTESY
LIFE AS A PAGE

In theory the son of a knight was educated for knighthood from birth. Until the age of seven he was in the care of his mother and her women of the household, then he began the first stage of his knightly training as a page, either at home or in another noble house. Life as a page lasted for seven years before, at around the age of 14, a page moved on to complete his apprenticeship by serving a true knight day by day as his squire. In the later period of his life as a page he was sometimes known as a *damoiseau,* or valet.

▼ *The education of children was divided strictly by gender. While girls learned to spin, sew and manage the household, boys were instructed in martial arts, as shown in this 15th-century illustration.*

FIGHTING AND HUNTING

Squires of the household instructed the pages in horse-riding, tilting at the quintain (riding at and striking a target with a couched lance), tilting at the ring (striking a smaller round target), wrestling, boxing and running. The quintain was a human-shaped dummy holding a shield, and suspended on a stick: the page had to hit the shield right in the centre. The dummy would swing round and round and the page had to be careful to get swiftly out of the way.

The pages also learned how to handle a sword, practising their strokes against a 'pell', or wooden stake. They were trained in hunting techniques, such as caring for the hawks and falcons, and how to use a bow and arrow in competition

les 2 enfans de douicz

> ### GEOFFREY CHAUCER
> English poet Geoffrey Chaucer, whose portraits of a knight and a squire in *The Canterbury Tales* are celebrated for their authenticity, was a page at the court of Elizabeth de Burgh, countess of Ulster. The countess was married to Prince Lionel, duke of Clarence and second son of King Edward III of England, and Chaucer served as a squire in Lionel's company during the Hundred Years War in France. Captured while fighting at the siege of Rheims in 1360, Chaucer was ransomed for a handsome sum – the king himself contributed £16 to the fee. After these early military adventures, Chaucer spent most of his life as a courtier – like many young men who passed through the chivalric education system, he did not progress beyond being a squire and was never knighted. Chaucer was clearly an extraordinarily gifted and talented man, and it is apparent from his later work, which shows that he could read Latin and French, that the quality of education available to all pages and squires in the royal and noble households of this period was of a very high standard – in book learning as well as in chivalric accomplishments.

with their peers. They learned how to handle animal carcasses and prepare them for the kitchen – for example how to cut up a deer.

By watching and helping the squire, the pages also learned to perform the duties that would be required of them when they were older, whether serving knights in hall, working in the kennels and hawkpens, tending horses in the stable or cleaning and storing helmets, armour and weapons in the armoury. They learned

▶ *Pages were trained to serve alongside squires and kitchen staff during banquets. The guest of honour at this feast is Edward the Confessor.*

how to wait at table and carve meat and how to clean armour, weapons and chain mail by rubbing it in a barrel of sand.

In addition the squires were responsible for the pages' training in the courtly arts of singing, dancing, playing the pipes and the harp, and learning Latin and French. These skills were important accomplishments for a mature knight, so it was vital that this area of a page's education was not neglected. The actual teaching of writing and singing was entrusted to minor clergy and to travelling troubadours. The visiting priest would also give the pages religious education.

CORRECTION

If pages were unwilling to learn any part of their studies, squires were permitted to 'correct' them with physical force. No doubt squires were able to get away with a good deal under cover of 'corrections' and probably made themselves feel better

▼ *As well as teaching the pages to read and write, priests made sure that the young men had a proper grounding in Christianity.*

about their own mistreatment when they were pages by handing out orders and harsh punishments.

The pages had a gentler time with the ladies of the household, who also took an interest in the young men's education in chivalric arts, helping with writing and teaching dancing, courtly manners and gallant behaviour. They taught the pages necessary skills of hygiene and personal grooming. The ladies also played chess and other games with them.

BOARDING SCHOOL FOR PAGES

It was normal practice for a son to be sent to the house of his father's *suzerain* (his superior within the feudal system) to undergo his chivalric education in the company of the children of other knights. A lord's son was generally sent to the castle of another great lord or bishop – for example, Stephen of Blois (the future King Stephen of England, and the son of Stephen of Blois who was one of the leaders of the First Crusade) was sent to the court of his uncle, King Henry I of England, at about the age of ten, in 1106. Prominent churchmen took princes and the sons of noble houses into their establishments, to instruct them in the ways of chivalry. Thomas Becket received Henry II's son Henry (later 'the Young King')

alongside princes and nobles of neighbouring kingdoms. He oversaw their education until they attained knighthood.

Above all, pages learned 'courtesy', meaning the kind of behaviour that could only be picked up at a lordly or princely court. The Latin word *curialitas* can be translated as 'courtesy' or 'courtliness', the behaviour practised at the *curia*, or court.

▼ *Pages were expected to learn how to feed, groom and soothe horses belonging to the squires and the knight they served.*

AT A KNIGHT'S RIGHT HAND
LIFE AS A SQUIRE

The second stage of a chivalric education, after seven years living as a page,
was often seven or more years' senior service to a knight as a squire. Typically, this
began at around the age of 14. In these
cases, squires cared for their lords, the
knights whom they served, in all things.
They attended to the knights' needs in the
castle or manor house, at chivalric tournaments and on the field of battle.

It is important to note, however, that
not all squires were trainee knights. There
were many mounted warriors who,
having progressed from being a page to
becoming a squire, remained squires into
mature adulthood, and even for their
whole lives, because they were never
formally dubbed into knighthood. Many
had all the skill, bravery and chivalric

*▼ As well as serving wine and food at
mealtimes, one of a squire's duties in the
banqueting hall was to bring water for
guests to wash their hands.*

accomplishments of their knightly counterparts. At the same time, many more
junior squires served in the knightly
household and oversaw the education of
pages as described on the previous section
and below.

*▲ Life as a knight or a squire required a fit,
strong body. Practice was needed to develop
the skills with sword and lance.*

AT HOME
When a squire was young, and still learning the arts of chivalry in the service of his
lord, he generally lived in the castle alongside his fellows, usually sharing sleeping
quarters. The young men took turns to
serve the lord and other knights. In the
hall the squires carved meat, and served
food and wine at banquets. They also
worked in the knight's bedchamber,
making the bed, helping the knight dress
and bringing a *vin de coucher* (draught of
wine before sleep). It was also one of the
squire's duties to sleep in the knight's
chamber or at his door if requested. Squires
worked with the animals in the kennels
and stables and looked after the armoury.
They also taught the pages in the house.

Squires also served the ladies of the
castle. They were permitted to mingle with
them quite freely, playing chess, walking
in the garden, going hunting and hawking
in their company. It was quite common for
scandals to arise when these interactions
became too intimate.

▲ *Three knights are dressed and armed by their squires, prior to a knighting ceremony.*

AT TOURNAMENTS AND ON CAMPAIGN

If the knight travelled to a tournament, the squire accompanied him. The squire fought in the mêlée, the mock battle that was held at the start of some tournaments. For jousting he had to prepare the knight's horses and be on hand to provide fresh lances and equipment. The squires gathered behind the barriers at the edge of the lists or tournament competition area, ready to rush to the knight's assistance if needed.

When the knight went on military campaign, two squires served him together. They fought alongside him, and were responsible for ensuring he had a good supply of weapons and fresh horses.

Another key part of the squire's training was learning and practising the arts of fighting, jousting and horse-riding. Squires began by fighting without chain mail or other armour in order to accustom themselves to handling the great lances and heavy swords that were used at tournaments and in battle. For example, they would practise hitting targets with their lances while running. Then they would move on to practising with the weapons while wearing armour. The young men needed to be fit and strong to cope with chain mail, for example, because it could weigh as much as 22.5kg (50lb) and the suit's entire weight was felt on the shoulders. Finally they would be ready to practise fighting and jousting while on horseback.

The squires were also educated in other aspects of courtly life and chivalry such as hunting, hawking, dancing and the appreciation of poetry and music. Some learned to read. They were introduced to historical chronicles, books on hunting and battlefield chivalry and treatises on how to be a knight such as Ramon Llull's *Book of the Order of Chivalry*, as well as chivalric romances and songs of courtly love. Squires also learned the basics of blazonry – the language of heraldry, the science of recognizing and interpreting coats of arms. Squires were also responsible for overseeing the education of pages in all these aspects of chivalric life.

LIFELONG SERVICE AS A SQUIRE

As mentioned earlier, not all squires progressed to become knights. Some seem to have fought in campaign after campaign alongside knights and remained squires. Some came from families that could not afford the expense of the ceremony and the equipment needed to be a knight. There were certainly plenty of opportunities for men of this class, well educated in the ways of chivalry, to serve at royal and noble courts throughout Europe whether as warrior squires, heralds or – if they had literary talent – as poets or chroniclers. Examples of notable men of letters who did not progress beyond being squires are Geoffrey Chaucer, author of *The Canterbury Tales*, and Ramon Llull, author of the *Book of the Order of Chivalry*.

KNIGHTING

The ceremony of knighting marked the end of the chivalric apprenticeship as page and then squire. Squires who were princes or sons of great lords could look forward to being knighted in a great courtly ceremony. A prince would often be knighted with a host of his fellow squires to make the ceremony more magnificent. In 1306, for example, Edward of Caernarfon (the future King Edward II of England) was knighted in a ceremony involving 276 squires. He followed the prescribed rituals for preparing to be knighted, including keeping vigil overnight, then was knighted by his father before he himself knighted all the other participants. The main ceremony was held in the grounds of the London Temple, and tents were raised there to accommodate the great crowd of squires. Even so, the space was so full that two knights died in the crush, several others collapsed in a faint, and there was even a fight. There were many other similar examples – such as that of Ulrich von Lichtenstein, knight and poet, who was one of 250 squires raised to knighthood when Duke Leopold of Austria celebrated the wedding of his daughter in 1222.

Some squires of a modest background but with great martial ability were able to win knighthood on the basis of their deeds – for it was possible to be knighted on the field of battle after achieving a great feat or prior to the beginning of fighting.

▼ *Squires attended to a knight's needs in the heat of battle and on campaign, helping him with his weapons and armour.*

'ARISE, SIR KNIGHT'
THE ORIGINS AND DEVELOPMENT OF THE KNIGHTING CEREMONY

The central event in a knight's life was the occasion on which he was knighted. In this proud moment, he was admitted to an elite international group, a brotherhood of equals bound by the demanding code of chivalry. He dedicated himself to serving God, the Church, his king and his lord.

The ceremonies of knighting developed from ceremonial rites of passage practised in ancient Rome and among Germanic tribes in the Roman Empire. In Rome, when a boy was of age to become a man he was given the *toga virilis*, a white toga worn by citizens of the empire. Among Germanic tribes of the 1st and 2nd centuries AD, according to the Roman historian Tacitus, when a young man was ready to assume adult status he was given a sword and shield in a public ceremony by his father, a relative or the tribal chief. Afterwards he was counted among the tribe's warriors.

▼ *According to some accounts, it was in the Norman tradition that only knights could make others knights, and the Anglo-Saxon tradition was to be knighted by a priest.*

INVESTED WITH A SWORD

In the 8th and 9th centuries, a similar coming-of-age ceremony was used among the Germanic tribes for their princes and young lords: the young man was presented with a sword or a sword-belt. Charlemagne's son Louis the Pious, for example, was ceremonially invested with his sword in 791 at Regensburg, in preparation for going on a military campaign with his great father against the Avars. By the late 10th and early 11th centuries, in France and Norman England, the ceremony was being used to describe the elevation of a footsoldier into a mounted warrior; in the ceremony the footsoldier was given the equipment he would need to serve as a knight.

This was originally a secular event, but it became imbued with religious significance as the Christian Church developed doctrines that sanctified violence if performed in the defence of the Church and of God, and knights began to be seen as 'soldiers of Christ'. In Mainz, as early as the mid-10th century, the blessing of a sword and creation of a knight was incorporated into the Christian Mass: the sword was laid on the altar before the reading of the Holy Gospel and this prayer was read: 'Hearken, we pray, O Lord, to our intercessions, and bless with the right hand of thy greatness this sword, with which thy Servant wishes to be girded, that it may be used to defend churches, widows and orphaned children, and all thy people against the attacks of pagans, and that it may strike terror into doers of evil and may be used in justice both to attack and to defend.' Attendants then girded the sword on the aspirant knight.

DUBBING A KNIGHT

Elaborate protocol grew up around the knighting ceremony. The experience of being knighted could be very different depending on the circumstances or the

▲ *After a squire was knighted it was a matter of honour for him to seek an opportunity to prove himself worthy of his knighthood.*

custom prevailing at various times in the chivalric period. For some princely or lordly warriors, knighting took place in the courtly and religious ceremony of investiture, in the presence of a bishop and often at the hand of a king, among many noble peers. For others it was a simpler, though still religiously charged event involving confession and attendance at Mass, while for some squires, knighting was performed on the battlefield – in the simple act of dubbing – either before fighting began or else during or after the battle as a reward for an act of valour.

Dubbing consisted of striking the aspirant knight a blow either with the hand or a sword. In French the blow was known as the *collée* or *paumée* – later it was known in English as an 'accolade'. The striking of the blow may have derived from the ancient Roman practice of slapping a slave to set him or her free, or else from a Germanic tradition of hitting the witnesses to a legal agreement (presumably this was to ensure that they did not forget what they had seen).

THE MEANING OF DUBBING

From at least the 11th century in England and France, dubbing was an important part of knighting ceremonies, both at court and on campaign – the earliest known use of the verb 'to dub' comes in the *Anglo-Saxon Chronicle* for 1086, which records that at Whitsuntide that year King William I 'dubbed his son Henry in making him a knight'. Until the mid-14th century dubbing was found only in England and France, but subsequently it became accepted as one of the essential parts of any knighting ceremony, whether simple or grand.

There is considerable debate among historians about the meaning of the dubbing ceremony. In addition to admitting warriors to the chivalric elite and providing them with the status and equipment that would enable them to function as a knight, the ceremony often also marked the delegation from a lord to the new knight of legal authority to perform

▶ *One of the parallels of the chivalric knighting ceremony was the practice in the 10th century of 'making a knight' by presenting him with military equipment needed to fight in battles and tournaments.*

▲ *Armed soldiers look on as Charlemagne invests a young man as a member of his warrior band. Earlier rituals like this lay behind the development of the formal knighting ceremonies of the Middle Ages.*

feudal duties in his name. In the 11th century the class of knights was increasingly presented as a body created by God to keep order, as a secular arm of His Church. From around this time, bishops were present at formal knighting ceremonies. However, the involvement of

▲ *By the late 15th century, the investiture of knights had developed from the days of Charlemagne into a much more complex ritual, with specific stages that all had distinct religious overtones.*

ordained clergy, and the development of a religious rationale for knightly warfare, did not alter one key element of knighting: only a knight could make a knight. Entrance to the chivalric brotherhood could only be conferred by one who was already a member.

'BE THOU A KNIGHT!'
ACHIEVING KNIGHTHOOD

Accounts in chronicles and romances make it clear that the simplest form of knighting, performed on the battlefield in the immediate aftermath of some great military feat, with the blood still wet on the weapons, was the most highly prized of all. It was probably a very simple ceremony – perhaps no more than a *collée* or blow accompanied by the words 'Be thou a knight'.

If it were possible to achieve this, undergoing such a battlefield ceremony before the fighting began was a very good option for a squire of modest means. Not only did it avoid the need for a costly courtly ceremony, but it also greatly improved the squire's prospects in battle:

a knight could earn more per day than a squire, and was also far less likely to be killed if he were captured in the fighting – for his status as a knight would ensure that he was treated with great respect and ransomed.

KNIGHTED AFTER AN ACT OF GREAT BRAVERY

The great Breton warrior Bertrand du Guesclin, who was a French commander during the Hundred Years War between France and England, was a member of the select band of warriors to be knighted on the battlefield.

Serving Marshal Arnoul d'Audrehem, the French king's lieutenant in Normandy,

du Guesclin was honoured at Easter in 1354 after he defeated a raid led by the English knight Sir Hugh Calverley. Du Guesclin and the Marshal were on reconnaissance in Brittany and staying in the castle of Montmauron, 6 miles (10km) from the key English stronghold of Bécherel, which was commanded by Sir Hugh. Guessing that Sir Hugh might launch an assault on the castle in a bid to capture Marshal d'Audrehem, du Guesclin

▼ *According to chronicler Jean Froissart, at the Battle of Aljubarrota in 1385 between Portugal and Castile, 140 Castilians and 60 Portuguese were knighted. The Portuguese knights, fighting in the front rank, prevailed.*

hid a group of archers beside the route from Bécherel to Montmauron. When the attack came, du Guesclin heard his archers fighting the English and rode out with Marshal d'Audrehem to take part in the battle. In the course of the conflict, Sir Hugh Calverley was flung to the ground and taken prisoner, and afterwards du Guesclin was knighted on the field of battle by Eslatre des Mares, Captain of Caen Castle.

KNIGHTED BEFORE BATTLE

Many squires were knighted at the start of a campaign or before battle commenced. This was partly done for practical reasons – tradition demanded that a squire be knighted before he could command troops in battle.

Sometimes squires were knighted in a great hurry as a battle was about to start. According to historian Jean Froissart (c.1337–1410) in his *Chronicles*, several knights were made in this way in the English army at Vironfosse in 1338. The French and English forces were arrayed in the field, and the morning passed without battle being joined, but at around noon a hare broke from cover in the front part of the French army and ran hither and thither, causing the soldiers there to shout and laugh; this noise was interpreted in the rear part of the English army as the sound of the first fighting of the day, and

▲ This 15th-century illustration of the Battle of Crécy from an edition of Froissart's Chronicles *gives the foreground to English longbowmen. The battle was a famous victory for the English and for Edward, the Black Prince.*

several squires were knighted there and then in order to take part in the battle as knights. The Earl of Hainault made 14 knights in this way; afterwards when it was revealed what had happened these men became known as the 'Knights of the Hare'.

Sir James Douglas, the Scottish knight named the 'Black Douglas' by the English for his fierce border raiding, was another great warrior dubbed on the battlefield – in his case, prior to battle, on 24 June 1314 at Bannockburn.

THE BLACK PRINCE AT CRÉCY

Another knight who swiftly proved his worth as a chivalric warrior was Edward Prince of Wales (later known as 'the Black Prince'), the 16-year-old son of King Edward III of England. The king knighted the prince along with several of the young man's peers at the start of the French campaign of 1346; then on 26 August, at the Battle of Crécy, he placed his young son in charge of the right wing of his army, with Sir Godfrey Harcourt to assist him, and he himself stood back watching the engagement from a windmill nearby.

According to the account in Froissart's *Chronicles*, the fighting was very hard on the Black Prince's wing of the army, and Sir Godfrey Harcourt called for reinforcements, but Edward III refused, saying 'let the boy win his spurs'. By this Edward (or more likely Froissart, who put the words in his mouth) meant that the prince should prove himself worthy of the gilded spurs that were a mark of knighthood.

He did so. The prince fought on and the English prevailed in the battle. When fighting at Crécy finished, after dark, the French had lost no fewer than 1,542 knights. The battle was remembered as significant in two ways – a humiliating disaster for France and a great triumph for the English army – and proof beyond doubt that Prince Edward had a great future ahead of him as a knight.

▼ Breton knight Bertrand du Guesclin kneels before King Charles V. He was raised from humble origins by his bravery and skill.

THE MEANING OF KNIGHTING
THE RELIGIOUS SYMBOLISM OF THE KNIGHTING CEREMONY

In his *Book of Chivalry* (*c*.1350) Geoffroi de Charny gives an idealized account of the knighting ceremony. His version is based on that given a little over a century earlier in an anonymous French poem called *L'Ordre de Chevalerie* (*c*.1225), and presents an account of what should, or ideally might, happen rather than what did routinely occur. The kind of ceremony he describes is rich in religious symbolism. De Charny also provides detailed explanations of the significance of the various parts of the ritual.

RETREAT AND PREPARATION

According to de Charny, a squire was expected to prepare himself to join the blessed company of knights by confessing his sins and receiving communion. On the day before the ceremony, the squire was to take a bath, then rest in a bed newly made with perfectly white sheets. At the given hour, knights were to come to the squire's bedroom to dress him in new white linen, scarlet robes and black stockings, with a white girdle and a scarlet cloak. They would lead him in the evening to church, where he would spend the night in lonely vigil.

In the morning the knights would accompany him to Mass, at which he should pray for divine grace to make him fit to serve as a knight. After Mass, the knights would lead the squire into the presence of the knight who was to confer the order of knighthood upon him. This knight would attach a gilded spur to the squire's foot, gird the squire with a sword and kiss him to confirm the conferral of knighthood. Finally the knight would dub the squire, delivering the accolade or *collée* on his shoulder.

The *Book of Chivalry* explains the knighting ceremony as follows. When the squire takes a bath on the day before he is to be knighted, he washes away the accumulated sins of a lifetime and emerges

with a clean conscience. Then when he rests in a bed newly made with white sheets, this symbolizes the deep sense of peace that arises when his conscience is clean, and he has won God's forgiveness for past wrongdoing. When he is dressed in new white clothes these symbolize his new virtue, while the scarlet robes signify the blood he must be willing to spill in defending Christianity and the Church. The black stockings stand for the earth from which the squire came and to which he will return, and the fact that since he cannot know the hour of his own death he should turn away resolutely from pride and vainglory. His white girdle signifies chastity, and his scarlet cloak is a traditional sign of humility.

Then he keeps a vigil through the night, and this symbolizes that he must be

▼ *King Edward III of England, enthroned, looks on as Edward the Black Prince is invested as a knight of the Most Noble Order of the Garter in 1348. Members wore the garter on their armour in battle or in tournaments as a badge of honour.*

always watchful and renounce evil. When he is given a golden spur in the moment of knighting, this signifies that he must never be covetous, for gold is the most precious and widely coveted of metals but the knight wears it on his foot rather than on his head or close to his heart. When he is girded with a sword, this signifies that he must support justice and reason, defending both the Christian faith and the Church, and when the knight kisses him it is a sign of peace, loyalty and love. The accolade or blow on the shoulder signifies that he should not forget that he is now a knight and must behave henceforth in accordance with the laws of chivalry.

CHIVALRIC SYMBOLISM IN *THE ORDER OF CHIVALRY*

The anonymous French poem, *L'Ordre de Chevalerie*, that provided de Charny with the basis of his inspirational account, describes a fictional encounter between a Christian knight and the great Kurdish Muslim warrior and general Saladin, who captured Jerusalem in 1187 and fought against King Richard I of England during the Third Crusade (1189–1192). The Christian knight, Hue de Tabarie, is captured by Saladin, who was renowned for his chivalric behaviour but, as a non-Christian, could not be expected to know the ceremonies of knighthood. Saladin offers to set Hue free if he will instruct him in the meanings of knighthood and then make him a knight. Hue is not keen to agree this bargain, for he knows that Saladin cannot truly become a knight because he does not accept the Christian faith, but as a prisoner he has little choice.

Hue de Tabarie cuts Saladin's hair and beard, then leads the way to a bath that signifies – as it did for the knight in the *Book of Chivalry* – the washing away of sins, here specifically identified with the Christian rite of baptism. Afterwards Hue takes Saladin to a magnificent bed, which

▶ *Saladin, the crusaders' greatest Muslim foe, exhibited such magnanimity and chivalry in victory that he was hailed as a 'Saracen knight'. He is said to have been knighted in 1167 by Humphrey III of Toron, Constable of the Kingdom of Jerusalem.*

is said to symbolize the place in Paradise that each true knight will attain, then dresses him in white and a scarlet robe, again signifying the willingness to shed blood in chivalric encounters. He then girds on the sword but stops short of giving Saladin the accolade on the grounds that he cannot administer this because he is Saladin's prisoner.

THE SYMBOLISM OF KNIGHTLY FIGHTING EQUIPMENT

Knighting rituals developed from simpler ceremonies in which young men were given the equipment they needed to be warriors or mounted knights. In the literature of chivalry, symbolism was attached not only to the elements of the knighting ceremony but also to the fighting equipment a knight used. In the French prose romance *Lancelot* (c.1225), also known as the *Prose Lancelot*, the Arthurian knight Sir Lancelot is instructed in the symbolism of his armour by the Lady of the Lake. She tells him that his armour signifies various aspects of the duty that he and every Christian knight owes to the Church. His hauberk, or mail tunic, protects his body just as he should defend the Church; his helmet covers his head and symbolizes the way in which he should guard the Church; as his great lance, expertly wielded, strikes fear into wicked men, so it stands for his power to keep the enemies of the Church at bay. His mighty sword has two edges, which stand for the fact that he serves both God and the people, and a sharp point, which signifies that the people must be obedient and follow his leadership. The horse on which he rides stands for the people of the Christian world who support him and follow his guidance, just as a horse follows the directions of its rider.

▼ *King Francis I of France considered it a great honour when he was dubbed a knight by French chivalric hero Pierre du Terrail, the Chevalier de Bayard. This romanticized depiction suggests that the event was blessed by a shaft of light falling from heaven.*

'HOTSPUR'

SIR HENRY PERCY

Sir Henry Percy was probably the greatest knight of the late 14th century, whose effectiveness in patrolling England's border with Scotland – and especially his speed of movement and willingness to attack – won him the nickname 'Hotspur' from his Scottish foes. He was a valued servant and trusted military leader for the English kings Richard II and Henry IV, although he eventually rebelled against both. He was renowned for his knightly prowess, both in the lists and on the field of battle. The chronicler Jean Froissart declared that Hotspur 'desired feats of arms above all other things, and was always first into action at the barriers'.

A PRODIGIOUS YOUTH

Hotspur was raised to arms. He was born at Alnwick Castle, Northumberland, in 1364, the son of another Henry Percy, 1st Earl of Northumberland, and the earl's

▼ Hotspur was England's hero at the Battle of Otterburn in 1388. This two-panelled illustration is to a line from the poet Robert Burns's celebration of the battle, 'But Persie wi his gude braid sword'.

> **SIR HENRY PERCY**
> **Born**: 20 May 1364
> **Died**: 21 July 1403
> **Knighted**: 1377
> **Famous for**: raiding victories against Scots on England's northern border
> **Greatest achievement**: victory in Battle of Homildon Hill, 1402

wife Margaret, who was of the proud Neville family of Raby. Contrary to normal practice, Hotspur was knighted at the age of just 13 in 1377 by King Edward III. The following year, aged 14, he fought alongside his father in retaking Berwick Castle from Scottish raiders.

In 1379 Hotspur married Elizabeth Mortimer, daughter of Edmund Mortimer, 3rd Earl of March, and in 1380 he campaigned with his father-in-law in Ireland. In 1383 Hotspur went on crusade in Prussia against pagan Lithuanians – at this time, the military order of the Teutonic Knights organized crusading trips in Prussia and the Baltic region for the nobility of Europe.

SCOURGE OF THE SCOTS

In 1385 King Richard II of England appointed Hotspur the Warden of the East March (border region) of Scotland, charged with controlling Scottish raiders in the region. In the same year Hotspur accompanied the king's army into Scotland. In 1386 Richard sent him to the aid of the English garrison in Calais, France, because an attack was expected from the French; while there, Hotspur led a number of raids in Picardy.

In 1388 Hotspur was nominated as a Knight of the Garter and returned to the Scottish border. That year he rode into Scotland and fought James Douglas, 2nd Earl of Douglas, at the Battle of Otterburn, which was partly fought in moonlight, and was celebrated by Froissart for being 'as hard a meeting, as well-fought a struggle as ever was'. In this heroic clash, Douglas was killed but Hotspur was captured and ransomed by the Scots. The greater part of his substantial ransom – 7,000 marks – was paid from royal funds and by a subscription from Parliament.

Hotspur's reputation as a knight continued to grow. He took on his fellows in chivalric tournaments, and won admiration for his performance in the lists, notably in the Jousts of St Inglevert that were held near Calais in 1390, and at Smithfield, London, during the celebration of Richard II's 1396 marriage to Isabella of France. He was entrusted by the king with diplomatic missions to Cyprus, to the duchy of Aquitaine and to Calais in 1394–96, and in 1396 was once again appointed Warden of the East March, this time for a period of ten years.

REBEL KNIGHT

Yet despite so much evidence of royal favour, Hotspur turned against Richard II and sided with his opponent Henry Bolingbroke. Hotspur and his father may

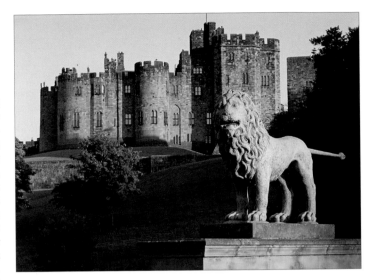

▶ Alnwick Castle, Hotspur's birthplace, was built in the late 11th century to guard England's northern border against the Scots. The Percy family bought it in 1309 and it remains in the family's hands to this day.

have felt that Richard was undermining their authority in the border region, for he took the town of Berwick out of their control; they may have believed that the king was acting in tyrannical fashion in his campaign against the Duke of Gloucester, his nephew Henry Bolingbroke and the earls of Arundel and Warwick. When in 1399 Bolingbroke returned from the exile into which Richard had cast him in an attempt to seize the throne, Hotspur threw his lot in with Henry, meeting him at Doncaster and riding south in his support.

Once established as King Henry IV, Bolingbroke rewarded Hotspur handsomely. He made him Sheriff of Northumberland, Lord of Bamburgh and Justiciar of North Wales and Chester, as well as giving him a further appointment

▼ Hotspur had undoubted greatness as a military commander and as a knight in the saddle. But he displayed little loyalty, twice rebelling against his king – Richard II in 1399 and Henry IV in 1403. This is his effigy, at Wells Cathedral, Somerset.

as Warden of the East March. The appointment in Wales brought him control of the great castles of Beaumaris, Caernarfon, Chester, Conway and Flint. In 1401 Hotspur again proved his prowess by capturing Conway Castle, which had fallen to Welsh rebels, and in the next year trounced the Scots at the Battle of Homildon Hill, capturing several lords including Archibald, Earl of Douglas.

KILLED AT SHREWSBURY

In the wake of this success he rebelled against Henry IV, accusing him of tyrannical government and the breaking of oaths. Hotspur was angry at various royal decisions that he perceived as slights, including Henry's establishment of a military command in Wales under Henry, Prince of Wales. Open conflict ensued. Hotspur led an army south to fight forces under the command of the Prince of Wales at Shrewsbury, but on arriving was surprised to discover a larger royal army led by King Henry IV himself. In the battle that followed, Hotspur was killed – reputedly when he raised the visor of his helmet to gulp some air and was shot in the mouth by an arrow. On seeing the death of their proud leader, the Percy forces abandoned the fight.

Despite the rebellion, King Henry wept when he saw the corpse of his former friend. He ordered Hotspur's burial at Whitchurch in Shropshire, but then had him disinterred. Henry wanted to display the body to counter rumours that Hotspur was still alive and also to make an example of him as a rebel against royal authority. He put Hotspur's corpse on display in Shrewsbury marketplace supported by a pair of millstones, and afterwards had his body cut into four and sent to the four corners of the kingdom. The former knight's head was displayed on a pole at the gates of York.

SHAKESPEARE'S HOTSPUR

Hotspur's fame among later generations rests in part on his appearance as a character in William Shakespeare's historical play *King Henry IV Part I*. Shakespeare rewrites history by making the knight the same age as Prince Henry ('Hal') whereas in reality Hotspur was a good deal older than the future king. The play contrasts Prince Hal's seeming indolence as a young man with Hotspur's great energy, force and bravery.

HOW TO BE A KNIGHT
MANUALS OF CHIVALRY

In the 14th and 15th centuries chivalric manuals such as Ramon Llull's *Book of the Order of Chivalry* were read at courts across Europe. Written in Majorca in the Catalan language in *c.*1265, Llull's book was widely translated and editions have survived that were published in France, Scotland and London – the last a translation by English printer William Caxton, printed in 1484, the year after he published the second edition of Geoffrey Chaucer's *The Canterbury Tales* and the year before he published Sir Thomas Malory's *Le Morte d'Arthur*.

The *Book of the Order of Chivalry* describes an encounter between a hermit and a squire at the former's forest hermitage. The hermit was once a great and wise knight, who had enjoyed a long and glorious chivalric career, in the course of which he had won many renowned victories in battle and excelled at tournaments held for the pleasure of kings and

▲ *Like the hermit knight in the* Book of the Order of Chivalry, *Arthurian knight Sir Lancelot spent a large part of his life in rural retreat. Lancelot was cared for and educated by the Lady of the Lake.*

RAMON LLULL

Ramon Llull, author of the *Book of the Order of Chivalry*, was a remarkable man with many very powerful talents. He is celebrated as a philosopher and religious mystic, as a poet and the author in 1284 of the allegorical novel *Blanquerna*, the first major work of literature in the Catalan language. But perhaps above all he is remembered as the developer of a means of marshalling information by combining attributes from lists: he developed the method, which he published in the *Ars inveniendi veritatis* ('Art of Finding Truth') and the *Ars Magna* ('Great Art'), as a way to reduce doctrine to first principles for use in attempts to convert Muslims to Christianity. His method – claimed by some as an antecedent of modern information science – is commonly

known by the name *ars combinatoria*, applied to it by the 17th-century German philosopher Gottfried Liebniz.

Born in Ciutat de Majorca (probably Palma) in Majorca in *c.*1232, Llull had a chivalric education as page and squire at the royal court of Majorca. He married, then at the age of about 30 (just before he wrote his chivalric manual) he had five visions of Christ crucified, that inspired him to become a lay Franciscan and later a missionary to Muslims in northern Africa and Asia Minor. He visited North Africa three times on mission, on one occasion carrying out reconnaissance for a possible crusade, and according to legend was stoned by angry Muslims at Bejaïa (Bougie) – or perhaps at Tunis – and died in 1315 a Christian martyr on the voyage home.

princes and their ladies. He had often risked his life for the glory of knighthood and in all his dealings had shown wisdom and nobility of character as well as courage and physical strength. Nearing the end of his career, he was aware that his physical strength was failing and rather than attempt to perform acts of chivalry at a level below his customary excellence, he had chosen to retire to a hermitage. A young squire, meanwhile, was riding through the forest on his way to the king's winter court nearby, but he failed to keep his wits about him and fell asleep in the saddle; his horse wandered off the path into the depths of the forest and came to the hermitage.

DEFENDERS OF HONOUR

When the two met, and explained their positions, the hermit offered to teach the young squire all he could need to know about chivalry. He gave the squire a copy of a book on the subject, which contained all his wisdom.

The book explains that long ago, knights were picked from the general population, one from every thousand men, as defenders of justice; and the horse was placed at the service of the knight because of its beauty, speed and strength. It says that knights were an order set apart, coming in the natural social hierarchy above the people, and below the prince, whom the knights must serve alongside God. The knight's principal duties were to defend the honour of the prince and of the Church, and to uphold justice. It is right, the book says, for knights to strike fear into the hearts of the ordinary people, because this prevents the populace doing wrong. In the same way, as knights are placed in an elevated position of trust, it is therefore far worse when a knight does evil than when an ordinary peasant or farmer is wicked.

▼ *Chivalric manuals described how a knight should behave towards the poor, who might need charity as well as protection.*

▲ *Knights were expected to be skilled in the arts of hawking and hunting. Here a hunting party sets out from a castle.*

KNIGHTLY SKILLS

Knights must be taught and must practise essential chivalric skills such as horse-riding, jousting, sword fighting, and the hunting of lions, bears, stags and rabbits. These activities are important for a knight because they keep him fit for fulfilling his duties of chivalric service. A knight who despises the practice of knightly skills is one who despises the very institution of knighthood.

LARGESSE AND COURTESY

Other notable guides to chivalric behaviour include Geoffroi de Charny's *Book of Chivalry*, and an anonymous early 13th-century poem *Roman des Eles*. The *Roman des Eles* argues that chivalric courtesy derives from God and is possessed by knights. The poem has two key aspects: largesse and courtesy. All knights should be able to demonstrate largesse, it states; they should give freely, with boldness and even carelessness. Knights should demonstrate their courtesy by never displaying boastful behaviour, envy, slanderous talk and greed. Rather, they should take pleasure in music and songs, and always honour the Church.

De Charny addresses much of his teaching to men-at-arms, a group of chivalric warriors distinct from knights, from which he himself had emerged. He went on to become one of France's most prominent knights in the service of King John II. He was a member of the Order of the Star and was granted the honour of bearing the Oriflamme, the French standard, into battle. In his *Book of Chivalry* he argues that chivalric warriors should spend their lives striving; even the greatest of them should be seeking to achieve remarkable deeds that would bring them more honour still. He also argues that they can be driven to greater deeds by the fire of courtly love: they should love their lady for love's sake and achieve greatness in the quest for her love.

CHAPTER FOUR

THE KNIGHT
AT HOME

When a knight was not at war, he lived in his castle. If he were a substantial lord he kept his own castle, and if he were less well established he served with honour in the castle of his feudal superior. During peacetime he enjoyed strenuous pastimes such as hunting and tourneying (fighting in tournaments), which helped keep him ready for battle. The knightly class to which he belonged was supported by the labour of the peasants who farmed the lands of the fief, or feudal landholding, and whose agricultural produce supplemented the meat the knights caught in hunting. The knight therefore had plenty of leisure time in which to feast and enjoy the chivalric songs of travelling poets. He also had peacetime responsibilities and duties to carry out.

The knight's role in peacetime changed as feudalism developed. In the early years, he was a mounted soldier and little more, and in periods of peace his main job was to ride out in service of his feudal lord if the need arose, to protect the lord's interests or impose his authority. The knight had a duty to administer and govern his feudal domain or manor, but this work was usually done by his steward or bailiff. In later years, the senior knights, keepers of castles, had more developed duties in the administration of the law and the keeping of the peace, sitting as local judges and, particularly in England and Germany, often having a duty to keep the peace beyond the confines of their feudal domain.

▲ *Courtly banquets were designed to impress, with lavish displays of food and drink.*

◄ *Home and feudal stronghold – the castle of a great lord dominated the country for miles around. Pontefract Castle in west Yorkshire, shown here, was founded in c.1070. It was greatly developed by John of Gaunt and was the scene of King Richard II's murder.*

A LORD IN HIS MANOR

A KNIGHT'S RIGHTS AND DUTIES AT HOME

Knighthood did not necessarily bring a large estate with it. Some knights were in possession of fiefs too small to support them adequately and exploited their military training and skill to make a living through tournaments and on the field of battle by ransoming defeated enemies. But ideally a great knight was master of a substantial landholding.

THE NOBILITY OF LORDSHIP

A great knight was lord to a large number of retainers and lived in great style. This was seen as proper in the chivalric world. Ramon Llull wrote in his *Book of the Order of Chivalry* that knights rightly should be 'made lord of many men, for in seignory is much nobleness'. A lord would take pride in seeing his retainers wearing his arms on their clothing. The larger the household, the greater the glory.

Medieval philosophers held that feudal society was divided into three estates or conditions: the Church was the first estate; the nobility, the knights and lords who held feudal properties were members of

▼ *The main hall of a medieval castle was its central public space, where a lord would eat, dispense justice and entertain.*

▲ *Peasants build a fence on their lord's land while in the background one of their fellows ploughs a field on the farm.*

the second; and the peasantry was the third. It was proper, ordained by God, that the members of the third estate should labour to support the members of the other two. Another image, developed by lawyers in the late medieval period, was that society rightly ordered was like a great pyramid, with the peasants at the bottom, the clergy above them and the knights beneath the king at the top. Above the king was only God himself, and this social structure – in which each man knew his place – was believed to have been blessed and to be sustained by God.

GOVERNOR OF THE MANOR

Under the system introduced in England by the Normans, and current in much of western and central Europe, the knight's landholding as a feudal lord was called a manor, or in France a *seigneurie*. The feudal lord (*seigneur*) had legal and economic power within his manor.

Typically, a manor contained a village and arable and pasture land farmed in strips by the lord's tenants. Some of the land was the lord's and some was farmed on their own behalf by the peasants. The peasants had to farm the lord's lands and in addition had to pay 'taxes', usually 'in kind' in the form of a proportion of the agricultural produce grown on their own strips of land. The lord had duties and responsibilities to govern his tenants. He presided at a manor court. His manor was a self-sufficient community.

The fief-holder supported by his land tenants could be a secular knight or a prominent clergyman such as a bishop or abbot. Many bishops and abbots were knights, and fought in feudal armies. The feudal households described in this chapter could be secular or ecclesiastical.

A NOBLE HOUSEHOLD
From the 12th century, a leading knight's household would contain a range of administrative positions. The *seneschal*, or steward, was in overall charge of food and drink for his lord, while the butler managed its storage. The chamberlain was guardian and manager of the lord's private chambers and their contents, with the help of subordinate valets and janitors. The priest was likely to be one of the few literate people in the castle: he ran the chapel, said religious services and kept the lord's written records in order. The constable and marshal oversaw the security of the castle, and managed the garrison and other troops as well as overseeing the running of the mews and stables.

Among those who provided service to a king or great lord were powerful knights. Chivalry honoured service; there was nothing demeaning about it. In Arthurian literature, King Arthur's seneschal was Sir Kay, who was one of the knights of the Round Table. This arrangement was typical of the period. Knights might provide service in the hall, the stables, the tilt-yard, the armoury and the hunting park. Such was the size of these feudal households that lords with grand positions such as Marshal or Master of the Horse had many more menial staff beneath them. Some of the lower positions were filled by squires.

Those knights and noblemen who occupied elite positions in the inner household were free to offer advice to the lord they served, both as individuals, and gathered together in council. The lord might disregard their opinions, just as the king could go against the will of his

barons, as happened frequently – notably in 13th-century England, under King John and King Henry III.

SPECIALIZATION OF ROLES
During the 13th–15th centuries, the roles of officials in the larger noble households became more specialized and titles were changed. In the 13th century the treasurer took charge of finances, while the role of steward was divided in two, with one managing the lord's estates and tenants and a second in charge of food and provisions. In the 14th century this position was often called the chamberlain, while a clerk managed the butler's store of food.

In a large household of the 15th century, the seneschal was often the lord's deputy, in charge of key roles such as the dispensing of justice when the lord was absent – as he frequently was, either at another of his manors or on campaign.

▲ A feudal estate was a self-sufficient unit, in which each person had a role and a strictly defined social position.

The seneschal was assisted by a chancellor, responsible for keeping administrative documents, writing letters, charters and legal papers. By this time the chamberlain often focused mainly on financial affairs, while the steward managed the estate. The highest authority in the lord's absence was the constable, who was the 'keeper' of the castle and responsible for its defence.

KEEPING A GRAND HOUSE
It was honourable for a feudal lord to entertain men of rank. Even a prince could enhance his status by offering hospitality to a knight. Llull declared that: 'Any baron or lord who honours a knight in his court, in his meetings of council and at his meals does honour to himself'.

KEEPER OF THE PEACE

A KNIGHT'S ROLE IN GOVERNMENT

As feudalism developed, many knights across Europe accepted it as their duty to maintain order in peacetime and to administer the king's law. The knights and their castle strongholds became symbols of a stern authority that demanded respect and kept lawlessness at bay.

JURY SERVICE

By the mid-13th century many leading English knights were no longer simply a warrior caste in the king's service, but were part of the royal administration. They had a major role in delivering justice, both local and national. As we have seen, they presided over manorial courts; they also had to provide jury members for grand assize – the travelling royal court held periodically in English counties. This jury work involved, in addition to attending the hearings, demanding administrative work and in criminal cases law enforcement duties. Such duties were not taken

on by all knights, and those members of the chivalric class who did shoulder these responsibilities shared them with other nobles who were not knights.

▲ *The king's law had to be administered as well as enforced around the country and knights contributed to the work of travelling courts that brought justice to the shires.*

SYMBOL OF ORDER

In chivalric literature the castle is frequently a symbol of order. Within its walls, and on the feudal estate, all is well – the lord and his retainers live in comfort, each knowing his place and providing service. Outside the island of order are all the terrors of an unruly world – symbolized in chivalric literature by the forest, with its monsters and

rogue knights. The medieval world had a fear of disorder – raids by Vikings, Magyars and Saracens were still fresh in folk memory. The castle's structures and discipline would keep the darkness of the forest at bay, while the structures of feudal society guaranteed social order.

▼ *Leeds Castle, Kent, begun in 1119.*

Some knights had a similar role in France and Germany. In France some made a good living as administrators for the king, for these tasks were well paid there. In Germany *ministeriales* were 'serf-knights' who worked mainly as stewards, judges and administrators. Originally the *ministeriales* were not free men, since they were tied to the land on which they served and were without legal rights beyond that domain. But they gradually acquired the right to own property and generate wealth, and in time became members of the knightly class, with the right to hold fief-doms in the gift of other lords in addition to their original suzerain.

KNIGHTS OF THE SHIRE

In the 13th century English knights attended the royal council that was the precursor to Parliament. Two knights from each shire were summoned to the governmental council called by English

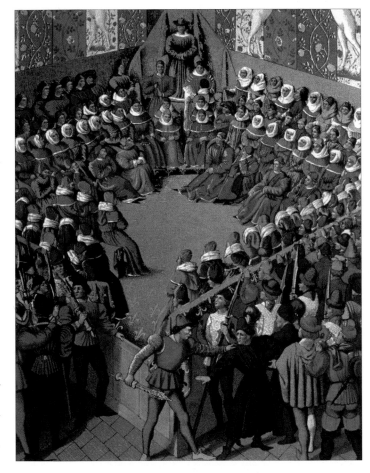

▶ *A convocation of lords enforces the power of the French monarchy, hearing the trial of John II, duke of Alençon, for treason against Charles VII. Alençon was sentenced to death in 1458 but the sentence was not carried out; he died in prison in 1476.*

nobleman Simon de Montfort when he was briefly in power in 1263–65, having deposed King Henry III. De Montfort was then defeated and killed by Henry III's son, the future Edward I, at the Battle of Evesham and his experiment ended, but it had set a precedent. In 1295 Edward I called a representative council later termed the 'Model Parliament' by historians, because it was the first representative English parliament.

The Model Parliament included, in addition to magnates and churchmen, representatives of lesser clergy, two knights from each county, two burgesses from each borough and two citizens from every city. The council began to be called Parliament (from the old French *parlement*, 'a talk') at around this time, and in the reign of King Edward III (1327–77) split into its current format: the House of Commons and the House of Lords. At that point, the knights of the shire, the lesser clergy and the burgesses formed the House of Commons, while the nobles and high clergy formed the House of Lords.

PROTECTORS OF THE WEAK

All knights also had a general duty to provide protection for the Church, widows, children and others unable to protect themselves. In the writings of philosophers and churchmen, knights' elevated position within the feudal system was justified by this role as protectors.

Knights had a particular duty to protect pilgrims. Pilgrimage played a central role in religious life in the Middle Ages. As an act of penance or an expression of Christian devotion, men and women uprooted themselves and travelled along the well-worn routes to shrines such as Canterbury, Santiago de Compostela in Spain, Rome and Jerusalem. They travelled in large numbers: as early as 1064 a party of 7,000 travelled to Jerusalem, which at this stage was in Muslim hands. After the First Crusade in 1096–99 resulted in the recapture of Jerusalem, the number of pilgrims to the Holy Land increased further. All pilgrimages could be dangerous, but the voyage to Jerusalem was particularly long and difficult. The knightly brotherhood of the Knights Templar was established in *c.*1119 to protect pilgrims to the Holy Land.

THE EXPRESSION OF LORDSHIP

The castle was an expression in stone of the knight's mastery and authority. Many castles were built around a great central tower or keep, known as the *donjon*, a French word derived from the Latin *dominium*, meaning lordship. (The English equivalent is 'dungeon'; this word did not come to have its modern meaning, of a dank underground jail room, until later.)

Even when the knight was not in residence – as was often the case, when he was away on campaign, or perhaps visiting another of his residences – the forbidding walls of his castle proclaimed both the greatness of the knight and the solidity of the rule of law that he enforced. The castle was a standing warning to law breakers of the military might that could be brought against them if they rebelled against the lord's authority.

CASTLES AND MANOR HOUSES

LIFE ON A FEUDAL ESTATE

Castles were military instruments, used as bases for expansion and afterwards for dominating conquered territory, but they were also domestic environments. They were a show of power, and a statement of authority, but were also knightly residences, set at the heart of great feudal estates or manors.

EVERYTHING A LORD NEEDED

The great estates were virtually self-sufficient. The castle or fortified house was surrounded by pasture and crop fields, with hundreds of peasants working the land to produce corn and hay, raising animals for the lord's table and chopping the wood needed for fires. On some estates even the cloth worn by the lord and his household was woven on site, but if not, wool produced by sheep on the estate was taken to a nearby centre to be exchanged or woven.

Anything that could not be produced on the estate – salt, say, or iron goods – could be purchased from itinerant merchants or at fairs held in the larger market towns. Larger fairs attracted merchants from as far away as Italy, France and Germany, some selling goods all the way from the far eastern countries of the Muslim world. At the larger markets, a lord's household staff could buy spices, gold, silks, dyes, French or Spanish wine, furs, Flemish cloth and so on.

AN EMPTY HOME

Kings in this period had to keep mobile in order to keep themselves abreast of developments and to maintain their authority. They carried their court with them as they travelled from household to household. Likewise, princes and the greater lords had more than one castle and moved from one to another. Much of their wealth consisted

of land, and its produce, paid to them as rents-in-kind. As the court, and lesser lords, moved from one property to another, their rents – in the form of harvested food and hunted animals – kept them and their courtiers well fed.

When they were away at another house, or indeed on campaign or crusade, the castle was guarded and administered by a castellan, or governor, with a defensive garrison of knights and crossbowmen alongside a team of artisans such as carpenters, smiths and masons to maintain the buildings. The peasants working the estate would of course stay where they were, but the majority of the lord's household would travel with him – necessarily, for they would be needed to provide service in the next location.

DEFENSIVE DESIGNS

Castles took many forms, designed primarily for defence. The Normans who pioneered castle-building often built to a 'motte and bailey' design: the motte was an artificial or natural mound within or adjacent to a wider area called the bailey, set inside a defensive wall and ditch or moat. On the motte stood a tower – made of wood in early castles, later of stone – which usually housed the lord's living quarters and that was a stronghold to which the lord and his garrison could retreat if the castle came under attack and the outer defences were breached.

Later castle-builders – in England and Wales, most notably King Edward I and his builder Master James of St Georges – improved upon this basic pattern. The

◀ *The hall at Penshurst Place, a fortified manor house in Kent, southern England, was completed in 1341. A medieval hall was a space that the lord shared with his retainers, guests and animals. It would be noisy, crowded and full of smoke from the central fire.*

▲ *The kitchens were generally just off the main hall. Often a carved wooden screen disguised the passageway that led from the hall to the larders, kitchens and offices.*

▲ *Banquets were seen by noble households as an opportunity to display wealth and influence, and they would be as lavish and impressive as possible.*

perfection of medieval fortress design was the concentric castle that had two sets of walls: a taller inner set, surrounding the 'inner bailey', and a lower outer set, surrounding the 'outer bailey'. To capture a concentric castle, attackers would have first to defeat the defenders of the outer walls, then cross the outer bailey under fire and begin their assault on the inner, more heavily fortified walls. Fine examples of the concentric castle include the Krak des Chevaliers (near Homs in Syria) which was built and garrisoned by

▼ *This view of Salzburg in 1493 shows how the medieval castle and the fortified cathedral – symbols of the dual powers of State and Church – dominate the city.*

the Knights Hospitaller during the Crusades, and Beaumaris Castle in North Wales built by Edward I and Master James of St Georges.

DOMESTIC BUILDINGS

The large empty baileys or yards that we see in many castles today were once filled with domestic buildings. These were usually constructed of wattle and daub or timber and were either destroyed in conflict or have decayed naturally. They would have included stables, an armoury, a smithy, a servants' hall, the kitchens and the buttery (a storeroom for wines, so called because casks of wine were called butts). In some castles, certain of these halls and rooms were built into the walls surrounding the bailey and so their remains can still be viewed.

The lord of a great castle would have lavish accommodation. His rooms were always in the safest part of the fortress –

initially in the keep or donjon, then, as castle design developed, in the strongly fortified inner bailey. Also in the inner bailey, close to the lord's rooms, would be the chapel and the great hall, the centre of castle life. Even the greatest lord would eat with his retainers in the hall. Robert Grosseteste, scholar and Bishop of Lincoln under King Henry III of England, wrote that it was not proper for a lord to eat alone.

The lord, his family, companions and notable visitors would eat at the high table on finer foods than were served to the mass of soldiers and other vassals in the main part of the room. At the far end of the hall, opposite the high table, was often a raised minstrels' gallery from where musicians entertained diners. In between meals the hall was also a place of business used for judicial hearings and estate management, and by night many of the castle's large population slept there.

Some castles contained more than one chapel. In the lord's private chapel, he and his family would attend a service each morning. A larger chapel in the outer bailey would serve the needs of the members of the garrison. Many castles had a heavily fortified gatehouse guarding the entrance. This usually contained rooms for the castellan, and perhaps a smaller version of the great hall used for receiving visitors and emissaries.

KNIGHTS AT LEISURE

FAVOURED PASTIMES OF THE CHIVALRIC CLASS

Knights had duties both in peace and in war, but they also had plenty of time for leisure. They spent much of this time in pursuits that improved their military skill or their understanding of their knightly calling, although they were also fond of lavish feasts.

THE HUNT

Hunting provided a key opportunity for developing fitness and strength and practising horsemanship as well as the skilled use of weapons such as the bow and arrow, the spear and the sword. The *Anglo-Saxon Chronicle* reports that King William I of England enclosed vast tracts of forest and 'loved the tall stags as if he were father unto them'. The 13th-century English chronicler William Rishanger, a Benedictine monk from St Albans also known as Chronigraphus, described how as a young man Prince Edward (the future warrior-king Edward I) loved to hunt stags on horseback, and when he had chased one down he would kill it at close quarters with his sword rather than from a safe distance with a spear. This was presented as a sign of his bravery and martial spirit.

Manuals on hunting were circulated to complement the handbooks on chivalry. The French nobleman Count Gaston III of Foix-Béarn wrote a treatise on hunting, *Le Livre de Chasse* ('The Book of the Hunt') c.1387. Gaston was a great chivalric figure, who wrote that the three main delights of his life were 'arms, love, and hunting', and whose court in southern France was described in all its knightly splendour by French chronicler Jean Froissart. *Le Livre de Chasse* covered all aspects of hunting in the 14th century, listing the open and close seasons for animals, the best kinds of bait and traps to use, the different kinds of pursuit, including a discussion of which hounds to use for which animal, and even ideal arrangements for dining in the forest.

▲ *A hunting party gathers outside the castle walls. Ladies often rode on the hunt alongside men. Hunting dogs were used to track, chase and kill prey; greyhounds were particularly prized for their speed.*

HUNTING RESERVES

Kings, noblemen and leading knights kept hunting reserves that were strictly guarded. The *Anglo-Saxon Chronicle* reports that William I imposed blinding as the punishment for anyone who killed deer from his forests. They employed specialists to care for the lands, maintain the wild animals and look after the hounds. Hunting was considered a noble pastime and positions involving the management of horse, hounds or the hunt were quite appropriate ones for a knight to take in the household of his feudal superior. The nobles developed a hierarchy among the animals: the noblest target was the stag, then, in descending order, the boar, the female deer, the wolf and the bear, the fox and the hare.

HAWKING

Another favoured pastime of the royal and knightly class was hawking, the use of trained birds of prey such as eagles, falcons and hawks to pursue game. Some contemporary sources suggest that the crusader knights learned of the sport in the Holy Land and brought it back to

▲ *Minstrels were generally employed at the castle, but the troubadours who sang songs of courtly love were wandering musicians.*

Europe, but there is evidence to suggest that in fact it was practised by both Anglo-Saxon and Norman lords before that time. In the 1240s Holy Roman Emperor Frederick II was the patron for a translation of an Arabic treatise on hunting with birds, and he then wrote a book himself on the subject – incorporating some of the translated Arab text and supplementing it with information gleaned from his own lifelong devotion to the sport.

FEASTING AND POETRY

Days could be long in the castle. A favourite way to pass the time was in feasting and drinking. A vast appetite was not considered inappropriate for a great knight – indeed, it was almost a virtue, a sign of a warrior virility and forcefulness. The verse biography of 12th-century English knight William Marshal reveals that in his youth when he was serving as a squire in the household of his uncle, William de

▶ *Chivalric tournaments provided much excitement and colour. A Dutch illumination of c.1475 represents knights and ladies riding through the streets of London to a tournament.*

Tancarville, Chamberlain of Normandy, Marshal was nicknamed *gaste-viande* ('glutton') for, unless otherwise occupied, he filled every waking hour with eating. But the biography makes clear that this was no indication of slothfulness and laziness, noting that de Tancarville predicted a great future for the young man. Likewise in one romance, English knight Guy de Bourgogne made quite an impact on the Saracens merely with his appetite, which was said to be equivalent to that of four normal men – and he demonstrated the general truth that 'a man who eats heartily will never prove to be a coward'.

As many as ten courses would be served on a great occasion. These included such dishes as boar, swan, peacock, fowl, fish, cheese, fruit and pastries, with plenty of wine, cider, spiced mead and sometimes beer to keep spirits high. A medieval document that lists the 'Fifteen Joys of a Knight' identifies the first and foremost of these joys as 'eating well and going swiftly through the supplies of wine'.

Music was usually played by minstrels during the meal and afterwards knights might play at dice or chess. But their favourite after-dinner event was a recitation by a travelling minstrel of *chansons de geste* or *chansons d'amour*, accounts of great

▲ *Chess was invented in India and spread via the Arab world to Europe by c.1000. It was so popular among the nobility that it became known as the 'royal game'.*

knightly doings in battle or romances of courtly love. The 'Fifteen Joys of a Knight' indicates that a knight would always show hospitality to a wandering poet. In this way the knight was sustained in his daily life by the poems and romances of chivalry, which functioned as a mythology of knighthood.

MARRIAGES AND ALLIANCES
THE INCREASING IMPORTANCE OF SOCIAL STANDING

Knights dreamed of doing the great chivalric deeds described in the many chansons, and some had the excitement of riding out on heroic campaigns and fighting great battles, but they also lived in the day-to-day world of social and financial obligations. In this world a knight's standing and that of his family could be a pressing concern.

In the higher levels of feudal society occupied by knights, marriages were normally based on considerations of social standing and wealth, and marital engagements were arranged in order to acquire property or to make a political alliance with a powerful lord. A good marriage for a knight or his daughters could bring with it great landholdings.

THE ROLL OF ARMS
Knights of this era rode into battle and into tournaments bearing their coat of arms on their shield, surcoat or other tunic and horsecloths. These coats of arms developed from simple symbols worn by early knights to identify themselves in battle, and gradually became more complex. When a knight acquired new lands through marriage a new title and coat of arms would come with them; he would then add the new 'arms' to his own coat of arms. In battles and particularly at tournaments heralds were the experts on these arms. A herald might work for a great lord and have jurisdiction throughout the area of his power: he would keep a 'roll of arms' listing the different coats of arms for all the knights in the area.

WILLIAM MARSHAL'S RISE
The great 12th-century English knight William Marshal was the model for those needing to better themselves. He rose from relatively humble origins to be the equal of the leading knights and nobles by dint of his prowess in tournaments and on the field of battle. From a position where, as a junior knight in the house of William de Tancarville, he had to sell his clothes to buy a new horse, he achieved such status within the world of chivalry that in 1189 he married one of the richest women in England, the 17-year-old Isabel de Clare, heiress to Richard de Clare, 2nd Earl of Pembroke. Marshal was made earl and he went on to become Marshal of England and Protector of the Kingdom in the minority of King Henry III.

DAUGHTERS OF A POOR KNIGHT
A rise such as Marshal's was an inspiring dream, of course, but also an exception to the rule. Many knights lived in relatively straitened circumstances, and found it difficult to maintain a good position for themselves and their families in the world of the noble elite. Impoverished or struggling knights were common figures in the literature of chivalry.

In the 12th-century Spanish epic poem *Cantar del Mio Cid* ('Song of the Cid'), the poem's hero, great Spanish warrior Don

◄ *A roll of arms of Yorkshire lords, recorded in c.1483 by William Ballard, March King of Arms under the English kings Edward IV and Richard III.*

▲ Philip the Bold, Duke of Burgundy, made a highly advantageous alliance when he married Marguerite, Countess of Flanders, in 1369, after which he became Count of Flanders and of Artois.

Rodrigo Diaz de Vivar ('El Cid') goes to war in part to provide for his family. He needs to furnish his daughters with suitable dowries, and to find fitting husbands for them. He achieves his aim by raising tribute from Muslim leaders, capturing Valencia and giving his daughters in marriage to the kings of Navarre and Aragon.

In the Arthurian romance *Érec et Énide* ('Eric and Enid') by the 12th-century French poet Chrétien de Troyes, the Lady Enid's father is a knight fallen on hard times, who is too poor to provide a dowry for her or to dress her in finery. Enid is ashamed of her worn clothes, but her father is not a figure of ridicule in the poem: he is presented as pleasing, generous, forthright, attractive – he possesses the virtues of a good knight, despite being poor. The plight of his family is presented with sympathy.

Chivalric literature describes the interaction of the ideal code of chivalry with the real world. According to the code, knightly virtues matter far more than worldly wealth, but the poems make clear that there may be unpleasant consequences of failing to acquire wealth alongside virtue.

CHIVALRIC WEDDINGS

Within noble society, marriages were celebrated with all the trappings of chivalry. Some of the greatest of medieval tournaments were held as celebrations of the weddings of noble lords or their daughters. In 1359 the wedding of John of Gaunt to Blanche of Lancaster at Reading was marked by a tournament in which King Edward III, his sons and 19 other nobles entered the lists clad as the mayor and aldermen of London, and fought against all comers.

▶ Extravagant gestures and declarations of love were an integral part of the social interaction of a court. Attachments were made to single and married women alike.

LOVE AT COURT

In a world in which marriages were made principally in the light of considerations of political expedience or property holdings, love may have seemed like a luxury. Some matrimonial matches began as diplomatic arrangements but became deeply loving. For example, the marriage of the future Edward I of England and Eleanor of Castile started as a diplomatic alliance when he was 15 years old and she was only nine, but ended as a powerful relationship, honoured by Edward after the queen's death in 1290 with the erection of 12 memorial crosses marking the spots at which her funeral cortége stopped on its route from her place of death at Harby, in Nottinghamshire, and her place of burial, Westminster Abbey in London. (Charing Cross in central London is a replica of one of these memorials.) In mourning, Edward wrote: 'In life I dearly loved her and I will not stop loving her in death'.

These deeply loving matches were, however, exceptions to the general rule. The cult of courtly love gave an outlet to romantic passion within the chivalric world. The lady to whom knights would dedicate their service in the courtly love tradition was usually already married to a great lord. The knight may have felt a deep passion for her on account of the connection, and may have expressed his longing for physical union with his beloved, yet very few of the relationships celebrated in these poems would have come to physical consummation.

LIFE IN A KNIGHTLY BROTHERHOOD
DAY-TO-DAY LIFE FOR A KNIGHT TEMPLAR OR A HOSPITALLER

Like other knights, the members of the great chivalric brotherhoods such as the Knights Hospitaller and the Knights Templar also spent periods 'at home', away from the excitement and difficulties of life on the battlefield. For much of the time, they lived a life not unlike that of the monks in Cistercian or Benedictine houses.

Those joining up to military orders took the monastic vows of poverty, chastity and obedience. (One brotherhood, the Spanish Order of Santiago, allowed married men to join.) Mostly the brothers lived a communal existence, in quarters designed like those in a conventional monastery, eating in a refectory and sleeping in a dormitory. They followed the monastic hours and were required to attend services.

The monks were largely lay brethren, many of them illiterate. In addition, there were literate clerical brothers who would serve as chaplains and recite the services or daily offices while the others listened. A typical rule required the lay brothers to repeat the *pater noster* (the Lord's Prayer),a number of times at each of the set offices.

▼ *Krak des Chevaliers, a fortress originally built in 1031 for the Emir of Aleppo, was given to the Knights Hospitaller in 1144, who rebuilt it as the largest crusader castle in the Levant.*

▲ *The Templars wore Christ's cross into battle on clothing, shields and horse coverings. Their full name was 'Poor Fellow-Soldiers of Christ and of the Temple of Solomon'.*

A NOBLE CALLING

It was not an easy life for the knights of these brotherhoods. The address or statement read out before an applicant to the Hospitaller order made it clear that he would have to be willing to sacrifice his own desires and needs and devote himself to the service of the order. It said that to enter the order was a great and noble calling, but that he should not expect to have a magnificent steed or to be kept in comfort. It said that he would find that when he wanted to sleep, the order might require him to be on watch, and when he wanted to eat he might have to fast. The knight would have to be able and willing to travel far away, 'to places that will not be pleasing', and that he would often find it necessary 'to abandon [his] desires in order to fulfil those of another'.

MILITARY RANKS

In the principal knightly orders, the lay brothers were divided into two ranks: sergeants and knights. There were two kinds of sergeant: non-fighting sergeants and sergeants-at-arms. In the monastery the sergeants performed necessary farming and household work, but the knights were of higher rank and were spared this labour. The brothers undertook military exercises to keep themselves prepared for war. Knights had better armour and three or four horses, while sergeants-at-arms made do with basic protection and only a single horse. The sergeants would sometimes fight as infantry alongside their brother-knights. The brothers in the different orders built or repaired and garrisoned many castles.

RULES OF LIVING

The warrior-monks followed a less strict diet than that of their contemporaries in the non-military orders. They were allowed to eat meat, normally on three days a week, in order to keep up their strength for military activities.

Other rules were very strict. Most orders required silence at mealtimes. The favourite leisure activities of secular knights, such as hunting, hawking and fighting in tournaments, were all outlawed – although, as we shall see in Chapter Five, brothers in the Knights Templar were

allowed to take part in *bohorts*, the form of tournament in which there was no physical conflict, presumably as a way of maintaining their fitness and good horsemanship. Another exception to the general rule was made in the case of the brothers of the Spanish military order of Calatrava, who lived in a barren landscape, and were allowed to hunt in order to secure food.

There were strict rules on clothing, which should normally be plain and of

▲ In 1347–48, the Knights Hospitallers, by then based on Rhodes and known as the Knights of Rhodes, came to the aid of King Constantine III of Armenian Cilicia in his conflict with the Mamluk Sultan of Egypt.

wool. It appears that these kinds of rules may have been honoured more in the breach than in the observance – in the 13th century the statutes of the Knights Hospitallers often found it necessary to denounce the use of embroidery on any clothing and even of silver and gold adornment on military equipment. The Templars allowed the brothers in Syria to wear linen, rather than wool, in the hot summer months.

In many of the orders, there was no probationary period or novitiate of the kind followed in the non-military orders. This must have made it difficult to establish whether applicants were really suited to the communal life of the brotherhood. The strict rules were enforced with fierce penalties, which ranged from being expelled to receiving a beating or merely being asked to perform a few days of penitential activities.

YOUNGER SONS

In feudal society property was inherited by the oldest son, which generally made it difficult for younger sons to make their way in the world. At one time, historians argued that many of these relatively poor younger sons went on crusade seeking their fortune, but modern scholars have stressed the enormous expense and financial risk of travelling on crusade and argued that normally only the wealthy could have made the decision to take the cross and become a crusader. The brotherhoods of the warrior-monks, however, offered a way in which younger sons and even those from non-noble families could make a career as a knight; up to the mid-13th century applicants from outside the nobility were able to enter the brotherhoods. There they received very good military training. Their financial position probably meant that they would not have been able to marry outside the order, so that they were not giving up the chance of a wedded life when they took the order's vow of chastity.

CHAPTER FIVE

A KNIGHT
AT ARMS

Mounted knights riding with couched lances in cavalry charges, and wielding mace and sword in close combat, dominate popular visions of battles in the age of chivalry. In reality the exploits of individual knights were usually far less important than we may think in determining the outcome of battles. Accounts in poems, romances and even chronicles were written to praise and memorialize feats of arms by knights, and they exaggerated the number who fought and their importance in battle.

These accounts also overplayed the importance of battles themselves. Pitched battles were rare in the Middle Ages and wars were often conducted through a series of sieges with attacking armies trying to draw out their opponents. However, knights were occasionally the difference between victory and defeat on the battlefield. A celebrated example of such a conflict is the Battle of Bouvines, northern France, on 27 July 1214, in which Philip IV of France was victorious over a German–Flemish army led by Holy Roman Emperor Otto IV. The battle was fought on a front over a mile long, with three areas of fighting: on the two wings and in the centre, where initially the Flemish infantry got the upper hand, but the French recovered and Philip led the cavalry charge. The battle was decided in this central area between the two groups of mounted knights, with daggers and swords. Otto was unhorsed and his imperial standard was captured, but he was saved from capture by the bravery of a group of Saxon knights.

▲ *The reality of medieval warfare involved plunder and looting.*

◄ *After the brutal clash of armies in battle, courtesy was restored in ransom and peace talks. This chivalric encounter is the aftermath of Philip IV's victory at Bouvines in 1214.*

THE MOUNTED WARRIOR

A KNIGHT IN BATTLE

The mounted warriors who fought alongside Duke William of Normandy at the Battle of Hastings in 1066 wore chain mail coats that extended to the knees and the elbows, and were split at the sides and front to make it easier to move. On their heads the warriors wore a conical metal helmet with a single downward protrusion to protect the nose. They carried a long shield shaped like a kite, which when used on horseback offered them protection from head to toe.

▼ *The Norman knights of the 10th and 11th centuries would be dressed in chain mail, which made mounting and dismounting possible in the thick of battle.*

CHAIN MAIL

The basic chain mail tunic (hauberk) or long robe (byrnie), made of circular interlocking links of iron, had changed little since the time of Charlemagne, and continued as the basic defensive armour until the end of the 13th century. Additions were made to it to increase protection. These included a chain mail hood (camail or coif); a chain mail mouth flap (ventail) to protect the lower face; chain mail mittens; and quilted cuisses with metal sewn in to protect the upper legs.

CHARGING WITH A LANCE

Anna Comnena, daughter of Byzantine emperor Alexius Comnenus, was powerfully impressed by the impact of charging crusader knights, which she witnessed at Byzantium in 1096–97. She wrote that the 'first shock' was 'irresistible' and conjectured that they could 'make a hole in the walls of Babylon'. Chronicle accounts may exaggerate the importance of knights in determining the outcome of battles, but there is no denying the force of mounted, armoured knights at full charge.

The knights described by Anna Comnena were charging in a coordinated unit with couched lance. This manoeuvre was developed in the second half of the 11th century in northern France – probably by the Normans. It is a key technique of the age of chivalry, seen both in the lists at tournaments and on the field of battle.

▲ *Norman knights charge at the Battle of Hastings. They use their lances as spears rather than 'couched' under the right arm.*

Mounted soldiers, dressed in chain mail in earlier armies, had used the lance as a spear for overarm throwing when mounted, and for jabbing when fighting on the ground. Knights, however, learned to hold the lance firmly beneath their arm and use it as a weapon of impact. The full force of the knight's charge was delivered at the point of impact, and the knight retained his lance, so that after a charge he could wheel away with the weapon and charge again. Another advantage of the new technique was that the knights could use a heavier lance, because they did not have to lift the weapon up to throw it or jab with it. Lances kept the enemy at a distance, making a knight less vulnerable.

A MIGHTY CHALLENGE

Handling both horse and weapons on the battlefield was extremely difficult. A knight needed to have the ability to control the horse when riding at speed, and when changing direction, through a crowded field if necessary. The knight would be quickly despatched if he were not physically fit and highly skilled in the use of his mount and equipment. For this reason, chivalric literature stressed repeatedly the need for knights to train in the arts of war: tournaments provided an

SADDLE AND STIRRUP

Warriors rode horses in battle for centuries before the solid saddle and the stirrups made them secure on their mounts. The Assyrian cavalry developed the first saddle in about 800–700BC. It was no more than a simple cloth tied around the horse, giving the rider a better grip. The Scythians used an improved, padded saddle. The Nubian mercenaries in the Roman army used a solid saddle built high at the front (pommel) and back (cantle). Of partic-

ular relevance for the massed charge was the use of a high pommel, invaluable for helping the knight to stay mounted at the shuddering moment of impact.

Stirrups made the rider much more secure and allowed him to fight energetically. It is not known for sure when and where the stirrup was invented. Around 500BC, soldiers in India were using a simple leather loop, and the Sarmatians – nomadic contemporaries of the Scythians – used one stirrup-like loop as a help in mounting. The oldest evidence for the use of twin stirrups, one on each side, was in an ancient Chinese tomb of AD322.

From their use by the nomadic groups from Asia, notably the Avars who rode into what is now Hungary, stirrups were gradually adopted in Europe, and more generally by the 8th century.

◄ *An early pair of Avarian stirrups from the 8th century.*

by knocking his knee or ankle. At the end of the hilt was the pommel, a heavy rounded extension, which could also be used as a weapon.

In the late 13th century knights fought with a lance around 2.4m (8ft) in length, and 14th-century lances became longer still – typically 3m (10ft). The spearhead was strong enough to pierce armour.

DAGGER AND MACE

In close combat knights also used daggers and one-handed battle-axes. One type of dagger had a straight blade with a single cutting edge, and was called a misericorde from the Latin *misericordia* ('mercy') because it was used to finish off a badly wounded knight – perhaps by stabbing through the helmet visor or under the gorget. Another dagger was the anelace, a broad double-edged tapering dagger with a blade of up to 45cm (18in).

A knight could also attack a nearby opponent by hitting him with a mace – a wooden club with a metal or stone head. A blow from a mace was often enough to stun an opponent and was the favoured weapon of clerics in battle, for while they were expected to fight, they were not supposed to shed blood. Some spiked maces, such as the flanged mace and morning star mace, could penetrate armour.

The battle-axe was an effective weapon when used with force: at the Battle of Bannockburn, Robert the Bruce reputedly killed the knight Sir Henry de Bohun with a single blow to his head.

▼ *From top: battle-axe, 'morning star' mace, anelace dagger and broadsword.*

essential opportunity to practise, in addition to being an opportunity for self-display and courtly manoeuvring.

A knight could not have fought like this without specialized weapons and equipment. Probably most important of all to the effectiveness of mounted warfare were the saddle and stirrups. Also relevant is that horseshoes were developed in the late 11th century. Horses with horseshoes could travel farther and cross rougher country than those without them.

SWORD AND LANCE

A mounted warrior in the early Middle Ages carried a light sword, weighing less than 1.5kg (3lb), which he used mainly for cutting and slashing. From the 11th and 12th centuries, the sword was usually a little longer with a sharper point so he could thrust with it as well. In the late 13th century a typical knight's sword had a blade of 80cm (2ft 6in) with a handle of

around 20cm (8in). In the following century they used a two-handed broadsword that was almost twice as long, measuring 1.8m (6ft) in total.

All sword handles (hilts) featured a cross-guard, a pair of extensions (quillions) at the blade end of the handle that prevented the hand sliding off the handle. Sometimes knights would reverse the sword when fighting – holding the sword by the covered blade they used the quillions to undermine an opponent's balance

THE ARMOURED KNIGHT

PROTECTION IN BATTLE

The main advantages of chain mail were that it was not too heavy and allowed considerable freedom of movement. However, it could not stop the point of a lance or the edge of a sword. In the 12th century, knights began to wear a padded jerkin beneath the mail, which

▼ *In the 13th century knights began to wear pieces of metal plate armour in conjunction with chain mail. The leg piece is jointed just below the knee for ease of movement.*

helped to absorb the shock of blows, but was still easily penetrated. In addition, a heavy blow, even if it did not break the mail, could force pieces of chain into the wound, making injury and bleeding worse. Chain mail was also difficult to clean and keep rust-free.

THE 'COAT OF ARMS'

The custom of wearing a surcoat, a cloth garment worn over the chain mail, was probably brought back by the crusaders from the Holy Land, where they learned its use from Muslim armies. Soldiers and knights – both in battle and at tournaments – wore coats of arms on their surcoats as a means of identification.

SUITS OF ARMOUR

The first steps towards suits of solid plate armour were taken in the 13th century. Initially chest and back plates of hardened leather were tried, and small pieces of solid metal were attached to the chain mail suit at the elbows, armpits and knees. The next stage was to attach jointed plates of metal to a leather base, making a jacket for the entire upper body.

The first suits of armour in *c.*1330 consisted of many pieces, often connected by complex lacing, which together provided layered protection for the body. It took a long time to put a suit like this on, and there are several accounts of knights being unprepared if an army was surprised.

These suits were gradually improved to counter the devastating effects of the longbow and the crossbow. The breastplate was introduced in the late 1300s, and the gorget to protect the throat, neck and shoulders came in at the start of the 15th century. It was not until the mid-15th century that princes and great lords – the elite among knights – were riding to battle wearing complete suits of plate armour of the kind we may associate with medieval knights

▲ *From top left: the coif, made of chain mail covering the shoulders as well as the head, the chain mail tunic, and the Aketon, a quilted jacket worn beneath armour.*

through depictions in Victorian paintings. The best plate armour was made in Italy and Germany, especially at the Missaglia workshop in Milan. It was made from heat-treated steel, and at vulnerable spots between the main plates were protective roundels – or sometimes pieces of mail were worn beneath the suit.

Armour suits were highly prized, and it was accepted practice for a captured knight to give up his armour as part of his ransom. Froissart reports in his *Chronicles* that at Tournai in 1339, Pope Clement's nephew Raymond was killed after he had surrendered, slain for no better reason than that his captors coveted his beautiful armour – and this unchivalrous act 'drove many good men to anger'. The very best plate armour was superbly well made. Its chief purpose was as protection, but almost as important was its function as a status symbol – a badge of knightly pre-eminence. Plate armour was also remarkably light – hardly any heavier than chain mail. Some of the finest suits weighed as little as 25kg (55lb).

HELMETS AND SHIELDS

The simple conical helmet worn by the Normans at Hastings was gradually developed to protect the head more and more.

▼ *By the 14th century the many pieces of plate provided good protection, although the lack of a breastplate and gorget (neck piece) left knights vulnerable to the bowmen.*

▲ *Horse protection in the 1200s was made of cloth, but horse armour, first of boiled leather and then of plate metal, was developed in the course of the 15th century.*

At first soldiers wore a chain mail coif, or hood, with a padded cap beneath, then in the early 13th century they added a cylindrical helmet with a flat upper surface, a slit at eye level and tiny holes in front of nose and mouth to allow for breathing. Curved helmets were in use by *c*.1270 as experience had shown that a curved upper surface deflected blows better than a flat one. The first helmets with moveable visors were introduced at around the same time. In the 14th century pointed Italian helmets called bascinets became popular – they had a projecting 'snout' covering the mouth and were popularly known as 'hounskulls' (hounds' skulls) or 'pig-faces'.

The long kite-shaped shields carried by Normans were also used by the crusader knights. These shields generally had a

▶ *Open-face helmets were superseded first by flat-topped helmets with eye-slits, then by curved-topped ones, then by helmets with hinged visors.*

rounded top, and were made of wood covered in leather boiled until it was very hard. During the 12th century shields were made with a flatter top. As armour improved the shield was made smaller, and by the 14th century knights carried a compact arm-shield in the shape of a flat-iron known as a 'heater-shield'. By the 15th century, knights in full plate armour no longer needed to carry a shield at all, but shields were still used in tournaments.

A KNIGHT'S ROLE IN BATTLE

HOW KNIGHTS WERE DEPLOYED

The basic pattern of all battles during the age of chivalry was the same: the cavalry attacked in waves, while the infantry was primarily arrayed as a defensive block. If an attack went well, infantry poured forward to support the cavalry.

Knights were usually organized in groups of 30 to 40 fighting beneath a banner. These groups were called *conrois* and several together formed a 'battle', and two or three 'battles' might enter the conflict at once. If a feigned retreat was planned, a further battle would be held in reserve to attack unexpectedly once the enemy had broken out of his defensive position in pursuit of the retreating force.

THE NEED FOR DISCIPLINE

If the cavalry charged too soon, this could spell disaster. Leading knights were sometimes deluded by over-confidence or driven by an intense desire to achieve individual feats of glory: they led attacks

▼ *Christian forces crushed the Almohad army at the Battle of Las Navas de Tolosa in 1212. The battle was fought as part of a crusade called by Pope Innocent III.*

against impossible odds, disregarding the better judgement of more cautious fellow knights. In 1187 at the Battle of Cresson near Nazareth – shortly before the Christians' devastating defeat by Saladin at the Horns of Hattin – Templar knight Gerard of Ridefort led a mere 100 knights in a charge against a large Muslim force. Only three of the knights survived, one of whom was the architect of the disaster, Gerard himself.

Even if a cavalry charge were not against impossible odds it could still spell disaster if it were badly timed. In battlefield conditions it could be very difficult for a group of knights to reform and charge a second time. In the confused mêlée of fighting, an individual knight would have to look for the banner under which he was fighting, and might have to fight his way back to it. Effectively, the charge needed to succeed the first time.

VICTORY – OR DISASTER

Battles could be won quickly with a well-timed charge, but a position of strength could also be thrown away by impulsive knights. If the defending army weathered

the charge, it could launch its own counter-attack, often to devastating effect. It could be difficult for military commanders to maintain discipline within an army containing many proud lords and separate groups in order to prevent this kind of thing happening. For example, on crusades the knightly brotherhoods often competed for the greatest glory.

BATTLEFIELD STANDOFF

Where discipline was maintained, armies sometimes showed great reluctance to make the first move. In Spain in 1212 at the Battle of Las Navas de Tolosa the combined armies of the Christian kings of Castile, Aragon, Navarre and Portugal were arrayed for two full days in opposition to the vast force of the Muslim Almohads before fighting began. These battles often started with preliminary skirmishes between individuals or small groups who rode forward between the two armies, taunting the enemy and trying to tempt a charge. In this case Almohad warriors did just that, trying to goad the Christians into an angry response. But the Christians held firm. The attack when it came was crushingly effective, resulting in a Christian victory that killed or took prisoner 100,000 opponents.

THE EFFECT OF ARMOUR

The development of armour – from mail hauberks and byrnies to full plate armour in the 14th–15th centuries – necessarily had an effect on how knights fought. Different kinds of armour allowed for greater or lesser freedom of movement. It is a common misconception that after the development of plate armour, knights were virtually immobilized by heavy suits of armour and had to be lifted into their saddles using a small crane. In fact the armour was light and they could run and jump on to their horse wearing this equipment. Yet it is true that plate armour in both this final and its various earlier developments did tend to limit the effectiveness of a dismounted knight on the field of battle – he could not move about as easily as his predecessors had in a byrnie, simply because the plate armour was designed to be worn by a mounted warrior and not one fighting on the ground.

KNIGHTS ON FOOT

If a knight in armour were knocked from his horse, he often struggled to regain his mount, and was forced to fight on foot, when he was at a disadvantage. In the Battle of Bouvines, both Philip IV and Otto IV were unhorsed in the close fighting: Otto was saved by the bravery of his Saxon guard, but Philip – who was young and fit – managed to regain his mount and fight on. At the Battle of Poitiers in 1356, many French knights had their horses killed beneath them by English archers and were forced to try to cope on foot – with little success.

A footsoldier could quite easily bring a knight down by stabbing with his dagger through any gaps in the armour or

▼ At the Battle of Bouvines in 1214, French cavalry power won the day in direct and bruising confrontations with the German-Flemish knights of Otto IV's army.

at the joints between armour pieces. In the mid-14th century, at the time of the Battle of Poitiers, plate armour was gradually being developed and many knights wore both chain mail and plate armour in this period. This double armour weighed heavily upon them, and thus they were very severely handicapped once they had been unhorsed.

▲ In many battles of the Hundred Years War, knights chose to dismount and fight alongside infantrymen. It was crucial for these footsoldiers to hold the line and turn back a cavalry charge. Knights also fought on foot after being knocked from the saddle.

THE INFANTRY'S EFFECTIVENESS

In most battles the infantry held the key. The knights in a cavalry charge hoped to scatter the footsoldiers they rode towards, or at least to kill enough of them to break the infantry's unity as a defensive formation. If the infantry were broken up into twos and threes, then the knights could pick them off, but if the footsoldiers were able to maintain their discipline, there was little the attacking cavalry could do to best them – once knight and horse were fighting at close quarters with a solid formation of footsoldiers they were quite vulnerable. At the Battle of Hastings in 1066, the initial Norman cavalry charges had little effect and the Anglo-Saxon footsoldiers, fighting behind a wall of shields, might have carried the day had they held firm rather than breaking out to follow the feigned Norman retreat.

COEUR DE LION
KING RICHARD I OF ENGLAND

King Richard I of England is one of the most celebrated figures in the history of knighthood, hailed as Richard Coeur de Lion ('the Lionheart') for his exploits on the Third Crusade of 1190–92 when he defeated and then wisely negotiated with the great Muslim military leader Saladin. Richard was a superb general who repeatedly took the correct strategic decisions rather than clouding his judgement by a thirst for glory. Yet, like many leading figures of the era, he often did not live according to the code of chivalric honour or the doctrines of Christianity. His actions were often self-seeking and disreputable – he took part in looting, was accused of rape and suspected of murder, and rebelled twice against his own father.

▼ *This statue of Richard I outside England's Houses of Parliament perfectly depicts his heroic status in the English psyche.*

RICHARD I
Born: 8 September 1157
Died: 6 April 1199
Knighted: 1173
Famous for: his charisma, bravery in battle and his ability as a general
Greatest achievement: Defeat of Saladin, Arsuf, 7 September 1191

A TASTE FOR CHIVALRY

Born in Beaumont Palace, Oxford, in 1157, the son of King Henry II and his queen, Eleanor of Aquitaine, Richard evidently had a good education. His mother's influence was strong. She had travelled on the Second Crusade (1147–49) with her first husband, King Louis VII of France, and was a keen patroness of chivalric literature. Richard followed his mother on this path: as well as taking the Cross as a crusader, he was a major patron of poets; he himself wrote poetry in French and Occitan (a French dialect used in romances); and, according to Muslim sources, he had an interest in Arabic culture. By repute, he was a handsome man: tall, with reddish-blond hair and pale skin. He was universally praised for his bravery.

FIRST TASTE OF WAR

Richard's loyalty and sense of responsibility were certainly poorly developed. In 1173, encouraged by his mother, he joined his brothers Henry the Young King and Geoffrey, Count of Brittany, in a revolt against his father, King Henry II. The three sons gathered at the court of Eleanor's first husband, Louis VII of France. At this time, Richard was knighted by Louis, at the age of 15, and then in July 1173 rode out on his first military campaign, an invasion of eastern Normandy. The revolt failed: Henry II succeeded in imposing his authority and in 1174 Richard begged pardon and swore an oath of subservience.

▲ *Richard was a very effective leader. When he landed at Acre on the Third Crusade in April 1191, the town had been besieged for 20 months. He captured it in five weeks.*

A BRILLIANT STRATEGIST

In this period of his life Richard was duke of Aquitaine and count of Poitou, both in France. He quickly proved himself to be an outstanding warrior and general in putting down revolts by the barons in Aquitaine. The troubadour Bertran de Born wrote of the young count, 'he lays sieges and pursues his enemies, seizing their castles, smashing and burning in all directions'.

A particular example of Richard's ruthless and effective military strategy came when he took the castle of Taillebourg, near the river Charente, which was considered impregnable because it had cliff-faces around it on three sides and a town laid out on the other. He ravaged the town, farms and landscape all about, terrifying the garrison into risking all by coming out to confront him. In open battle he defeated them, and entered the castle, which he destroyed. He was merciless in wiping out the challenge of

► *In the Holy Land, Richard came face to face with the other great chivalric figure of his age – the Muslim general Saladin. In 1191 Richard won a great victory at Arsuf. They agreed peace terms at Jaffa in 1192.*

the barons, according to some accounts even taking their wives and forcing them to serve as prostitutes for his leading knights and then afterwards for the army.

CRUSADER KING

In 1187 Richard allied himself with Philip II of France, and then the following year again revolted against Henry II. Richard and Philip defeated Henry's forces, and Henry named his son his heir before dying. Richard was crowned King of England in Westminster Abbey on 3 September 1189 and at once set about raising money for a crusade. In 1190 he departed on crusade with Philip II.

Richard's first act on crusade was to help capture the port of Acre in June 1191. He was very ill with scurvy and laid out on a stretcher, but is said to have been strong enough to shoot down the guards on the city walls one by one using a crossbow, while his retainers carried the stretcher here and there. The garrison surrendered. Meanwhile, Philip II abandoned the crusade he had started with Richard.

After Acre Richard marched his army south towards Jaffa. Saladin launched a major attack at Arsuf, but Richard inflicted a famous defeat on the great Muslim general. Later he might have marched on Jerusalem, but seeing that he would not be able to hold the city even if he were to succeed in taking it, instead opened peace negotiations. This decision is typical of Richard's practical realism as a military commander. He agreed a treaty with

Saladin under which Jerusalem remained in Muslim hands but pilgrims could have access to it, and embarked for Europe in September 1192.

His homecoming was humiliating. He was shipwrecked, captured, imprisoned by Holy Roman Emperor Henry VI and ransomed for 150,000 marks.

DEATH AT CHALUS

After a brief visit to England in April 1194, when he was crowned king for a second time, he spent the final five years of his life fighting over his French possessions. He died after he was shot in the neck with a crossbow bolt at the castle of Chalus and the wound became gangrenous.

REPUTATION AND CHARACTER

Contemporary accounts suggest that as well as being an intelligent strategist, Richard was a charismatic commander,

beloved of his men. He repeatedly showed his bravery in combat and once rode into great danger to rescue a foraging party, with the words: 'I despatched those men there. If they die without me, then I should never again be called king.' According to the 12th-century chronicler Richard of Devizes, King Richard's men were willing to 'wade in blood to the Pillars of Hercules' at his command.

In the 20th century the idea developed that Richard was homosexual: he spent very little time with his wife, and had no children by her – although he had an illegitimate son. Some historians suggest he had a love affair with Philip II, and that this explains the ferocity of their quarrels, and it has been proposed that his wife's brother (later Sancho VII of Navarre) was another of Richard's lovers. Modern historians cast doubt on these arguments – which they say were based on a misreading of texts – and suggest that there is insufficient evidence to make conclusions about his sexuality one way or another.

◄ *Richard was buried beside his father Henry II and mother Eleanor of Aquitaine at Fontrevault Abbey near Chinon. His brain was interred separately, at Rouen.*

THE SPECTACLE OF WAR
PAGEANTRY ON THE BATTLEFIELD

Armies arrayed on a battlefield in the age of chivalry made a stirring sight. Infantry probably impressed mostly by their solid mass, and sometimes their large numbers gathered beneath fluttering banners, but the knights were an imposing sight, in helmet and armour and surcoat, mounted on powerful horses, with a colourful shield bearing a coat of arms or other armorial badge, and sword and lance and other weapons glinting in the light. In chivalric literature and in chronicles – from which we glean so much of our knowledge about how knights saw themselves and understood their calling – a knight's physical appearance was an integral part of the impact he made.

CHIVALRIC DISPLAY

Display was all-important for a knight. His armour's chief purpose was of course protection, but almost as important was its function as a status symbol – the uniform of an elite. In battle, knights were also parading their wealth and seeking to win a glorious reputation – just as they did in the mêlée conflict or individual jousts at a tournament.

▼ Royal or noble members of the chivalric class used fine equipment as a symbol of status. Some even wore golden armour.

▲ Italian adventurer Roger de Flor parades into Constantinople with a splendidly attired army of Almogavar Spanish mercenaries – the 'Catalan Company' – to fight for Byzantine Emperor Andronicus II Palaeologus against the Ottoman Turks.

In the pages of medieval epics, romances and chronicles, battles were presented as being scarcely distinguishable from tournaments – as opportunities for display and knightly encounters. The accounts are full of the glorious spectacle of knighthood in action.

ARMOUR BURNING LIKE FIRE

In the 87th *laisse* or verse-paragraph of the epic *Song of Roland*, for instance, the poet describes the army of Charlemagne as it rides through the Pass of Roncesvalles in the Pyrenees mountains. He reports that the evening sun was reflecting from their armour, so that their helmets and hauberks seemed to be made of fire, while their bright shields, painted with flowers, and their bannerets and pennons, fluttering in the breeze, made a gorgeous vision. Likewise, the Muslim army of King Marsiliun, which sweeps down to engulf Charlemagne's rearguard and kill Roland, is said to present a wondrous sight – the warriors wore golden helmets set with jewels and mail coats varnished with gilt, and carried gleaming shields. Similarly, Froissart in his *Chronicles*, describing

knights and their squires progressing forward, spear in hand, at Noya in Spain in 1387, declares: 'To tell the truth, this was a beautiful sight'.

In battle, chivalric display – wearing the finest armour, using magnificent weapons, and demonstrating great skill in using them – was a way to intimidate the enemy. According to some chronicle accounts of the Battle of Hastings, before the fighting began one of Duke William's knights rode out between the two armies to display his prowess – as a taunting expression of Norman superiority. The knight, a minstrel named Ivo Taillefer, sang a version of the *Song of Roland* while throwing his lance and sword in the air and catching them. An Anglo-Saxon warrior came forth to fight, but Taillefer killed and decapitated him – and paraded the head as proof that God was on the side of the Normans.

THE KNIGHT'S SWORD

The finest weapons were also a sign of chivalric grandeur. The sword, indeed, was the symbol of the knight's calling. In romance literature great knights had magnificent swords, that possessed within them an element of the hero's bravery and nobility: Charlemagne had Joyeuse, his knight Roland had Durendal, King Arthur had Excalibur.

The sword was a precious item, often inlaid with silver in the blade and jewels in the hilt. It was also sacred. The most common design had a sizeable

▶ *The sword a knight carried into battle and stained with blood was a reminder of his calling as Christ's warrior, especially when used as a crucifix during prayer.*

crossbar between blade and hilt so that it took the shape of the Christian cross when held point downwards; squires would pray over the sword before they were knighted and then, when they were knights, before conflict. The sword itself was often blessed during the knighting ceremony.

MASSED RANKS

Aside from the wealth on display among the fighting noblemen, another aspect stressed repeatedly in chivalric literature and chronicles is the sheer size of the spectacle. King Marsiliun's army in the *Song of Roland* is a 'vast host' divided into no fewer than 20 battle formations – this is a force that attacks in a narrow mountain pass. Similarly, various chronicle accounts of the Battle of Bouvines claim that Philip IV's army included around 60,000 French – with no fewer than 9,000 knights – while Otto IV's imperial force totalled 250,000. In reality, even though the battle was fought on a much larger scale than most clashes of the 12th and 13th centuries, Philip's army probably contained no more than 1,200 knights and about 5,000 infantry, while Otto's forces had around 1,500 knights and 6,000 footsoldiers.

USE OF BANNERS

Among the colourful elements on the battlefield were the banners raised above the fighting men. They served a very necessary purpose as a rallying point for knights dispersed after a cavalry charge or by close fighting. These knights often had to fight their way back to their own banner, and it must have been very difficult for a group to reform once they were dispersed. Although military brotherhoods were in competition for glory on the field of battle, the rule of the Knights Templar laid down that if a Templar were cut off from his own banner he should seek out that of the Knights Hospitaller, or failing that any other Christian banner.

▼ *Banners flutter above the mêlée of knights and infantrymen as the English and French armies clash at the Battle of Poitiers on 9 September 1356. Edward the Black Prince led the English to a great victory.*

THE AGE OF SIEGE WARFARE

THE TECHNIQUES USED TO CAPTURE A CASTLE

In early medieval warfare the possession of castles usually provided the key to victory. Military campaigns often entailed a series of sieges. These could last for months at a time, and the fighting when it broke out was often dirty and desperate.

LOCAL STRONGHOLDS

The Normans built castles when invading, initially as a base from which to operate in subduing the territory. Once the land was conquered they used the castle as a consolidating position: its presence dominated the surrounding countryside, intimidating local people. Moreover, if an enemy approached, the castle garrison would not only stoutly defend the fortification but could venture forth from safety to harass the enemy with raids.

For this reason an army could not safely bypass a castle and move on to a more distant target because that would leave its rear and its supply lines wide open to raids from the castle garrison. An invading army had to capture castles, either eliminating or forcing the surrender of the garrison before moving on.

ATTACK OR SIEGE

Castles were designed to withstand attack. An attacking army had two main options: to launch an assault quickly or to mount a siege, cut off supplies and reduce the garrison to desperation.

There were several difficulties with mounting a siege. In a prolonged siege, it could be difficult to hold the besieging army together – feudal levies might come to an end of their period of service and depart for home. It is noticeable that King Henry II of England, who mounted many successful sieges, used mercenary troops who were happy to remain and be paid, however long the siege went on. There was also the risk of sickness setting in amongst the besiegers, as happened to the crusaders at Acre in 1189–91.

Moreover, a well-sited castle could be well-nigh impossible to isolate totally – for example, King Edward I of England established his formidable Welsh castles so that they could be supplied by sea. It was due to this that in the Welsh rebellion led by Madoc ap Llywelyn in 1294 none of the rebels' sieges of the castles was successful.

In 1401, by contrast, Owain Glyndwr, self-styled 'Prince of Wales', succeeded in taking Harlech Castle after a siege because he was able to mount a total blockade – by his own troops on land and by a fleet supplied by his French allies at sea.

SIEGE EQUIPMENT

Attackers often used specialist siege equipment to try to make a hole in the castle defences – machines such as the mangonel and trebuchet, which hurled stones at the walls of the castle. They sometimes used battering rams to try to knock the walls down; at others they tried to scale the walls using ladders – a technique known as escalade. This was highly dangerous since as they mounted, the attackers were liable to be wounded or killed by arrows, missiles or liquids sent their way by members of the garrison on the castle walls.

▼ *The concentric fortifications of Harlech Castle in Wales stand atop a 60m (200ft) rock. The English garrison survived a major siege by the forces of Madoc ap Llywelyn during the Welsh revolt of 1294–95.*

A better technique was to use a belfry, a tall tower that was set up against the besieged castle's walls. The belfry was usually built taller than the defensive walls so that the attackers could climb to the top, then fire down on the garrison before clambering over the walls along a bridge lowered from the belfry top. The belfry was usually made of wood, but covered in water-drenched animal skins to make it harder for the defenders to set fire to it as a way of repelling the assault.

The tactics used to break the spirit of a defending garrison were often highly unchivalrous. For example, King Henry V of England captured Rouen, France, in 1418–19 because he had cut off its water supplies and thrown dead animals into the accessible wells. Eventually a plague broke out in the city and the garrison was forced to surrender.

THE ROLE OF KNIGHTS

Knights did not frequently play much of a role in the initial stages of a siege. Specialist soldiers usually operated the siege equipment such as the mangonel, trebuchet or battering ram. Knights would then lead an assault, clambering up the belfry or pouring through a breach in the

▲ *English troops fire from a siege tower and pour over a ladder into a French town in the Hundred Years War. On the walls the defenders put up a desperate resistance.*

▼ *Three crusader armies – those of the kingdom of Jerusalem (upper left), of France (lower left) and of Germany (right) combine at the Siege of Damascus during the Second Crusade. The abject failure of their attack brought the crusade to an end.*

walls once one was made. On the other side knights were often members of the besieged castle garrison, so once battle was joined over or through the walls chivalric encounters did occur between the two groups of knights.

FIGHTING IN A MINE

Another means of attack was to try to make the walls collapse by digging beneath them. The attackers would dig a mine; within, the defenders would dig a counter-mine in order to repel them. The defenders would place a bowl of water on the ground at various points within the outer walls and if they saw ripples on the water this indicated that digging was going on underground and that a mine was nearby. Where two mines met, it was – rather strangely – the custom for knights on opposing sides to meet in individual combat in the mines. In the autumn of 1420, during his siege of the town of Melun in France, King Henry V of England took part in mounted combat in a mine dug beneath the town walls that was lit by torches along the walls of the mine. These encounters were a good opportunity for acts of high chivalry, and it was the custom for the knights who fought in them to become lifelong chivalric associates – 'brothers in arms'.

PILLAGING AND BURNING
THE REALITY OF MEDIEVAL WARFARE

Many medieval campaigns featured the ravaging of countryside and cities, particularly in the mid-14th century during the Hundred Years War between England and France. These pillaging raids were known as *chevauchée* (from the French term for a 'charge of horses', presumably because the small raiding army moved at great speed across the countryside). The raids were planned as a form of economic warfare to undermine the enemy's capacity to continue the fight by attacking their supplies and resources. Moreover, in an age when the leading generals were often reluctant to risk their infantry and knights in a pitched fight on the field of battle, chevauchée raiding was designed to force a defending army to leave the relative safety of a besieged castle or a fortified town, and to come out to fight in the field.

▼ *When an invading army swept across the countryside, setting homes and farms ablaze, frightened locals were powerless to stand in its way.*

THE PILLAGING OF NORMANDY
In July 1346 King Edward III of England and his son Edward Prince of Wales (later known as 'the Black Prince') landed in Normandy and marched their army along the Contentin Peninsula and westwards to Caen, raiding and pillaging as they went.

▲ *The sack of Aalst and Grammont by the inhabitants of Ghent in 1380, in an illustration from a manuscript of 'Chroniques', by Jean de Froissart.*

With support from an English fleet out at sea, Edward mounted a swift and brutal attack on Caen. His soldiers poured through the streets, taking their pleasure and plundering the city's wealth. If the chronicle reports that Edward had banned maltreatment of women, children and religious houses are to be believed, then the ban was disregarded during the brutal sacking of the city.

Caen was a scene of devastation and rapine. Chronicler Jean Froissart, as always emphasizing chivalric deeds by great knights, reported in his *Chronicles* that Sir Thomas Holland rode through the town, and managed to save the lives of many women, children, nuns and monks from the maddened English mob. The booty was loaded on to the ships of the fleet to be taken back across the Channel – Froissart notes that the ships were 'weighed down with fine clothes, precious jewels, and silver or gold objects'.

SCORCHED EARTH

Chevauchée warfare resulted not only in looting but in wanton destruction and the burning of great swathes of countryside. In 1339 during an early campaign using the chevauchée tactic led by Edward III, a chronicler climbed at night to the top of a church tower in the vicinity of Cambrai, northern France, and saw the countryside ablaze in all directions for many miles around – a vision of hell risen to the earth's surface.

The raids deliberately undermined the capacity of the enemy to fight back by depriving him of resources and support. In 1355–57 Edward the Black Prince led a chevauchée campaign in France specifically designed to hit towns that were strong financial supporters of the French monarchy. Sir John Wingfield, the Black Prince's steward and councillor, wrote that the lands and towns destroyed in the raids 'found for the king of France each year more to maintain his war than did half his kingdom'.

POLITICAL CHALLENGE

If an English army raided with apparent impunity in France it was a demonstration of the power of the English crown, and a calculated insult to the king of France. In the summer of 1370 Sir Robert Knowles (or Knollys) marched unchallenged from Calais to the Île de France (Paris), laying waste the countryside en route, and then taunting the French king in his capital city.

The raids were designed to undermine the French monarch's support among his citizens in the ravaged area. When the local people saw that royal protection counted for nothing, they would lose faith in their king. Often, indeed, the raids forced the enemy to launch reprisals.

Both of the chevauchée campaigns that were conducted by Edward, the Black Prince, in 1346 and 1355–57, drew a military response from the French in the field – they resulted in the celebrated English victories at the Battle of Crécy (1346) and Poitiers (1356). Indeed, this was a principal part of their purpose, for the

English – with their widely feared archers – were confident of victory in the pitched battles that occurred during the Hundred Years War.

ECONOMICAL WARFARE

Chevauchée was extremely profitable because it resulted in the capture of mounds of booty and hundreds of ransomed prisoners. Moreover, it was an economical way to wage war because the raids could be carried out by small armies of a few thousand men and did not call for the expense of long campaigns involving major battles or prolonged sieges. The raids delivered effective blows to the enemy's finances and morale but did not result in conquests that had to be defended with permanent and expensive garrisons.

THE BRUTALITY OF WILLIAM I

Chevauchée is particularly associated by historians with the mid-14th century campaigns in the Hundred Years' War, but

▲ *Women and children, as well as defenders, faced a dreadful fate when a fortified town fell to its besiegers. Army commanders would often turn a blind eye to the activities of their looting soldiers.*

punitive raiding was certainly used elsewhere as an aspect of military policy. For example, William I used similar tactics in his infamous 'Harrying of the North' in 1069–70, when his army burned villages, destroyed the crops and livestock, and devastated the populations across much of northern England. He is reckoned to have killed 150,000 people, with more succumbing to starvation and plague in the course of the long winter that followed in a ravaged landscape. The crusaders also made use of the tactic in the Holy Land. It was also adopted during the raiding in the mid-14th century across the English–Scottish border, when both English and Scots used merciless violence in ravaging the countryside.

'THE BLACK DOUGLAS'

SIR JAMES DOUGLAS, LORD OF DOUGLAS

Sir James Douglas, a great knight in the Scottish wars of independence in the early 14th century, was a brilliant exponent of guerrilla warfare, a man whose violent raids on English castles and towns in the Scottish borders won him the affection of his countrymen and the hatred of his English enemies – the Scots knew him as 'Good Sir James', while the English called him 'the Black Douglas'. He was a close battle companion of Robert the Bruce (King Robert I of Scots). He died fighting against the Saracens in Spain en route to the Holy Land, where he had promised to bury Robert the Bruce's embalmed heart.

SQUIRE IN PARIS

Sir James's father was Sir William Douglas the Hardy (also 'the Bold'), who was Governor of Berwick Castle when it was brutally sacked by the army of King Edward I of England on Good Friday 1296. Sir William was subsequently freed, and supported the Scots freedom fighter Sir William Wallace, but was recaptured and died in captivity in 1298 in the Tower of London. In this period the youthful James Douglas was in Paris, where he had been sent by his family to be safe, and where he entered the service of William Lamberton, Bishop of St Andrews, as a squire. When he returned to Scotland in 1306 with Bishop William, Douglas found that his family estates had been taken and given to one of Edward I's loyal soldiers, Robert de Clifford.

Bishop William introduced Douglas at the English court, but when Edward refused to contemplate restoring the family estates to the young man, Douglas allied himself with Robert the Bruce, who had claimed the Scottish crown after killing his principal rival John Comyn. It was during these years that Douglas learned the guerrilla warfare that he would put to such devastating use.

▲ *At Bannockburn in 1314, Sir James – on the very day of his knighting – commanded one of the four divisions of the 6,500-strong Scottish army of Robert the Bruce.*

THE 'DOUGLAS LARDER'

On Palm Sunday, 19 March 1307, Douglas led a brutal assault on the English garrison in Douglas Castle, the stronghold that should rightfully have been his own possession. He and his troops surprised the garrison celebrating the holy day, breaking into the church with the battle-cry 'Douglas! Douglas!' and slaying many

there and then. Afterwards he beheaded the surviving garrison members, and cast their corpses atop a great fire that he had built from wine casks taken from the castle cellar. He poisoned the wells by throwing dead horses and salt into them. The attack was known as 'the Douglas larder'.

He struck again to capture the English-held Roxburgh Castle in 1314. He ordered his men to approach the castle in the dark on the night of Shrove Tuesday, crawling beneath their cloaks – when the guards looked out from the battlements in the darkness they thought the dark shapes were nothing more threatening than wandering cattle. Suddenly the Scots soldiers threw hooked scaling ladders up the walls, and poured into the castle, surprising the garrison – who were distracted by their pre-Lenten celebrations. He then slighted the castle (damaged its defences so that it was indefensible by the garrison).

A KNIGHT AT BANNOCKBURN

Later that year Douglas fought alongside the Bruce in the Scots' famous victory at Bannockburn over a much larger English army. On the morning of the battle, 24 June, Douglas was knighted – surprisingly late in life, given his many great military exploits, but an interesting example of how many men fought on as squires for several years.

It was in the years after Bannockburn that Douglas won his reputation as 'the Black Douglas' through his relentless raiding of northern England. On these raids he and his men rode on ponies called 'hobbins' and dismounted to fight on foot – soldier and horse together were called 'hobelars'. Douglas defeated many notable

> ▼ An English archer leads an assault on Berwick Castle, whose position in the English and Scottish borders meant it changed hands many times. Sir James endured a siege there by the army of King Edward II in 1318–19.

JAMES DOUGLAS

Born: 1286
Died: 25 August 1330
Knighted: 24 June 1314
Famous for: his lightning raids on northern England
Greatest achievement: defeat of Sir Robert Neville of Middleham, 1318

---

opponents in these conflicts including Sir Robert Neville of Middleham, known as 'the Peacock of the North'.

'DOUGLAS! DOUGLAS!'

In April 1318 Douglas took part in the capture of Berwick Castle, then England's last notable possession in Scotland. Edward II of England rode north with an army to take it back, bringing his queen, Isabella, with him as far as York. In 1319, with the English army encamped outside Berwick, Douglas led a raid into Yorkshire, forcing Isabella to flee southwards, and defeated an English army raised by the Archbishop of York that mainly consisted of clergy, in the Battle of Myton.

Douglas continued to be a thorn in the side of the English. In 1327 when the teenage King Edward III led an army northwards, Douglas launched a night raid on their camp at Stanhope in northern England, his men roaring through the camp with the terrifying shout of 'Douglas! Douglas!', killing 300 Englishmen and almost taking the king himself prisoner.

DEATH IN SPAIN

King Robert the Bruce died in 1329, but before he died he asked Sir James, by now his oldest companion in arms, to take his heart to the Holy Sepulchre in Jerusalem. Sir James set out in 1330, with the dead king's embalmed heart enclosed in a silver casket hung around his neck.

On the way he and his companions heard that King Alfonso XI of Castile and León had declared a crusade against the Saracens in Spain and – as good knights, being ever hungry for glory in the service

of Christ – diverted there. In a battle at Teba, Douglas went to the aid of a fellow knight surrounded by Saracens. They were badly outnumbered, but Douglas plunged into the thick of the conflict, throwing the silver casket with Bruce's heart ahead of him, and shouted 'You go ahead, as was our custom, and I will follow you – even into death!' Douglas was indeed killed and afterwards his body, and the Bruce's heart, were taken back to Scotland. Douglas was buried in St Bride's Kirk, Douglas, and the Bruce's heart was buried at Melrose Abbey.

CHIVALRY IN PRACTICE

Sir James was a celebrated knight of his day, but it cannot be said that he fought according to the laws of chivalry. His favoured method of guerrilla warfare was both necessary, given limited Scottish resources, and very effective, but it relied on subterfuge, deception and ruthlessness. His stirring life story is by no means unique in the medieval period in providing many examples of how the code of chivalry was an ideal that many knights had often to abandon in order to thrive.

> ▼ This tower is all that remains today of Douglas Castle, scene of Sir James's Easter attack on the English garrison in 1307. At that time the castle was just 19 years old, having been built in 1288.

THE BUSINESS OF WAR

HOW KNIGHTS MADE MONEY ON CAMPAIGN AND IN TOURNAMENTS

In raiding and through the raising of ransoms, knights could acquire great wealth. While chivalry emphasized purer motives for fighting, such as seeking glory or exhibiting loyalty to a noble lord, in practice knights accepted the rewards that came their way.

RANSOMS

A knight captured in battle was ransomed, often for very large sums of money. There was a generally accepted understanding that the ransom should not be set at so high a level that the knight would be ruined, and thereafter be unable to keep maintaining himself as a knight.

A king's ransom could be vast. King Richard I of England, captured in 1192 on his way home from the Third Crusade, and imprisoned by Duke Leopold of Austria and Holy Roman Emperor Henry VI, was ransomed for 150,000 marks –

▼ *Many knights, including Bertrand du Guesclin, seen here being made High Constable of France by King Charles IV , made great fortunes through accumulating the legitimate spoils of war.*

RANSOMS AND THE KNIGHTLY CODE

Honoré Bonet, the late-14th-century Provençal prior and writer on chivalry, considered in his *Arbre des Batailles* ('Tree of Battles', 1382–87) whether the setting of ransoms was consistent with chivalric conduct and concluded that it was, declaring: 'All that a soldier can win from his opponent in lawful war he has the right to retain', adding that the act of taking ransom from a prisoner had been 'approved' by 'custom and usage'. He went on, however, to complain that many knights acted without pity or mercy in demanding excessive ransoms, and suggested that they should limit themselves to a 'reasonable and knightly' amount.

---

equivalent to 35 tonnes of gold, and about three times the English crown's annual income. This vast sum was raised from his English subjects by Chief Justiciar Hubert Walter through the seizing of valuable church plate and the imposition of swingeing taxes (a quarter of the value of property) on both clergy and lay people.

After King John II 'the Good' of France was captured at the Battle of Poitiers in 1356, a ransom of 3,000,000 marks was demanded. This was never paid as John was released, with his son Louis held in Calais as a hostage, in order to raise the sum, and then when Louis escaped, John voluntarily gave himself up into captivity once more.

RANSOMS AND HONOUR

A high ransom was in one sense a sign of honour. When the 'Eagle of Brittany', the great Breton knight Bertrand du Guesclin, was captured by Edward the Black Prince at the Battle of Najera (Navarette) in Spain

▲ *Son of a Florentine merchant, Pippo Spano was a knight in the service of Sigismund, King of Hungary and Holy Roman Emperor from 1433 to 1437. Sigismund rewarded Pippo with the control of all the gold mines in Hungary.*

in April 1367, he taunted his captor saying he would not dare grant him his freedom. The Black Prince responded by telling du Guesclin to name his own ransom and he set it at the vastly inflated level of 100,000 francs – boasting that in France he was so highly regarded that even the peasant women would contribute to his ransom. In the event even this enormous payment was given by the French king.

At the other end of the scale, a poor knight might be required to raise a few crowns for his ransom. Sometimes a knight merely forfeited his armour and his horse and weapons and was allowed to go free – even this penalty was considerable, for the cost of horse and equipment was high.

NECESSARY FINANCES

Seeking land and wealth has been a motive in going to war from time immemorial. The mounted warriors of Duke William of Normandy's army at Hastings were not required to be there by feudal loyalty, for their vows of service did not extend beyond the lord's territory: they were drawn, as countless warriors before them, by the promise of the riches they could acquire through conquest. Similarly, one among the many motives for knights going on crusade was seeking riches in the Holy Land.

Throughout the age of chivalry, many lesser knights – those whose fiefs were too small to support them adequately – knew that the wealth acquired with sword and lance was necessary for their very survival. There were knights who rose from a humble beginning to positions of extraordinary power, such as the impoverished Italian knight, Pippo Spano, who became the confidant, trusted strategist and general of the King of Hungary, and as such was granted large portions of land, noble titles, and national assets such as control of Hungary's gold mines, that guaranteed him a substantial income.

In chivalric tournaments, as well as on the field of battle, and in feudal politics, knights could make a living from their martial skills – for defeated opponents in the mêlée and joust could be required to pay ransom and to surrender their horse and equipment. Battles between Christian knights in the European theatre of war,

battles in which there was limited risk of dying because the conflict was not pursued to the death, were thus in many ways highly comparable to tournaments – good opportunities for establishing a public reputation for chivalry and a private fortune.

SHARING OUT THE BOOTY

In the 14th century, when a town was formally besieged and its occupants did not take the opportunity to surrender, according to the laws of chivalry its riches were forfeit to the invaders, save that

▲ *King John II is taken captive at the Battle of Poitiers. Lords had little to fear as their ransoms ensured they were treated well.*

clergy and churches were spared. The normal custom was for spoils to be divided three ways, with the first part being divided among the soldiery and knights, the second part being reserved for the commander, and the remainder sent home to the king. Not all these sieges ended in a frenzied sacking as at Caen – often there was an ordered entry and taking of booty. A more formal system was introduced in England in the second half of the 14th century under the indentures of war. In accordance with these, the commander was required to give up to the king the most important castles, towns and prisoners and he would be rewarded for this. The remaining spoil was split, two-thirds to the commander and one-third to the crown.

◄ *A commander would reward his leading knights and soldiers out of his two-third share of a conquered town's spoils.*

CHIVALRY IN WARFARE

THE CODE OF CHIVALRY ON THE BATTLEFIELD

The code of chivalric behaviour laid down the boundaries of good conduct both on the battlefield and during sieges. However, in practice, fighting was often dirtier than chivalry would readily countenance. In addition, success in war depended on qualities such as discipline that were at odds with chivalry's emphasis on the pursuit of individual glory.

DEMANDS OF CHIVALRY

In battles of the age of chivalry, fighting to the death was only normal in wars against 'the infidel' – meaning those who were not Christians, principally the Islamic soldiers in the Holy Land and in Spain, or pagan fighters in the Baltic region. In conflicts such as the Hundred Years War, particularly in clashes between noble knights, it was normal to take prisoners and to ransom them at great profit.

▼ A Breton warrior surrenders to a French knight at the Battle of Saint-Aubin-du-Cormier in 1488. In such moments of chivalry the brute energy of the medieval battlefield was suddenly stilled.

When a town or castle was besieged, chivalry demanded that the siege be declared by a herald. Once this was done, the garrison or the townspeople could surrender at any point up to the scaling of the walls. There are numerous examples of garrisons and populations being treated with great clemency, in accordance with these rules – such as cases of fighting

▲ When a town fell, its inhabitants were at the mercy of the victorious troops. Even within the code of chivalry, at the end of a siege soldiers could lawfully run riot.

being suspended to allow populations who had taken refuge in a castle to exit while the garrison remained behind to carry on the fight. King Edward III of England allowed non-soldiers free exit from Calais in northern France, when he was besieging the town in 1346; he even gave them food and money. If defenders remained defiant, then when the assault finally came the soldiers of the invading army were entitled to help themselves to the riches within the walls – except that church buildings, priests, monks and nuns could not be touched.

THE SACKING OF LIMOGES

Often when a long siege came to an end the victorious besiegers ran out of control, inflicting dreadful suffering on the garrison or townsfolk. The knights of the First Crusade when entering Jerusalem in 1099 set a terrible example, slaughtering men, women and children until the streets reputedly ran with blood. As we have seen, Edward III and the Black Prince oversaw the horrific sacking of Caen in 1346, while – according to Froissart – at Limoges in 1370 the Black Prince himself took part in a savage raid on the city following the conclusion of the siege. Froissart's account of the attack on Limoges suggests that the prince was maddened with anger that his old ally, the Bishop of Limoges, had gone over to the French side – and ordered the sacking of the city in which more than 3,000 men, women and children were slaughtered.

FAILURE OF DISCIPLINE

On many occasions, it appears that knights were unable to control their men. Armies often contained a good proportion of unruly elements – not least because the English armies in France during the Hundred Years War contained criminals who had been offered a free pardon in return for volunteering for service.

Moreover, it may be that knights felt that the misbehaviour of the lower orders in the army did not reflect badly on them – that the code of chivalry principally bound the noblemen who were knights, and that it was understandable that the lower classes would be unable to live up to chivalry's high standards. This is the view put forward by Froissart when describing the devastation at Caen – that the rampaging mob was full of 'wicked fellows and doers of evil, the sort you inevitably find in a royal army'.

Yet there were also occasions on which knights could not control themselves – when they also took part in the sacking of towns and profited greatly from them; and when they did not adhere to the code of chivalry in battle, abandoning its ties in moments of rage or in the physical excitement and turmoil of the battlefield.

QUEST FOR GLORY

In one important sense self-discipline and the chivalric code were at odds. Knights were expected to seek glory; the code of chivalry demanded that they should be eager to prove again and again their

knightly status through acts of martial endeavour. In battle they were ready to seize any opportunity to do this. Yet then as now, armies required discipline, and to be most effective usually needed to function as a unit. There are countless examples of knights acting rashly and against the interests of their commanders in order to seek glory for themselves or for their knightly brotherhood.

The Templar knights were often a law unto themselves in this regard. In the siege of Ascalon (Ashkelon in Israel) mounted by Baldwin III of Jerusalem in 1153, the Templars even fought against their own side in the search for glory: when a breach was made in the walls opposite the Templar quarters in the camp, a group of 40 knights led by Bernard of Tremblay went in to take the city, while others prevented non-Templars from joining. In the event, the 40 Templar knights had taken

on too much, and they were defeated, captured and killed, and their heads were hung from the city walls.

During the Seventh Crusade at Al Mansourah in Egypt in 1250, the Templar Robert I, Count of Artois, led a charge of fellow members of the brotherhood despite specific orders to hold back. He surprised part of the Egyptian army but then his troops swept on into the streets of the town, where they were ambushed and he was killed; the Egyptians were able to launch a counter-offensive against the main army, which robbed the crusaders of the land they had just won.

▼ *Templar knights pour forward, despite a hail of arrows, towards their Saracen foes. The Templars and Hospitallers were an often unpredictable part of the crusade armies, liable to launch independent attacks in search of their own glory.*

PART TWO

THE FIRST AND SECOND CRUSADES

When Pope Urban II finished the great speech at Clermont in 1095 in which he called knights to the First Crusade, those who rushed to obey his summons at once began to adorn their clothing with the sign of the cross – and the cross was soon established as the sign beneath which the crusader knights rode into battle. In its original biblical context the cross was a symbol of Christ's intense physical suffering, and of his refusal to foment violence and take up arms; through centuries it became emblematic of the power of God and of Christianity, and was worn by pilgrims. But in the hands of the crusade preachers and the knights they inspired, the cross turned into a symbol of dedication and military vigour – an icon that inspired faith, a badge of honour to be worn by those who signed up for the perilous journey to the Holy Land and a sign of the salvation they were seeking. It symbolized the faith and obedience embodied in the cry 'God wills it!' that arose following Urban II's speech, the shout that became the battle cry of the crusader knights on campaign.

▲ *Muslim horsemen often pretended to flee. Crusaders lost many a battle by charging recklessly in pursuit of a feigned retreat.*

▶ *The knights who responded to Urban's call to arms were inspired by tales of the religious campaigns of Charlemagne and his knights, seen here beseiging the walls of Pamplona in AD778.*

TIMELINE OF THE FIRST CRUSADES

March 1095 Byzantine Emperor Alexius Comnenus I sends envoys asking Pope Urban II for help against the Seljuk Turks.

27 November 1095 At Clermont, Pope Urban II calls Christian knights to arms, launching the First Crusade.

1095 Pope Urban declares that Christians fighting Moors in Spain would win full crusading privileges.

April 1096 The first two waves of the People's Crusade, one led by Walter Sans Avoir and one by Peter the Hermit, depart for the Holy Land.

May 1096 Crusaders under Count Emicho of Leisingen carry out attacks on Jewish communities in the Rhineland.

1 August 1096 The armies of the People's Crusade arrive in Constantinople.

21 October 1096 The People's Crusade is routed by Seljuk Turks in Anatolia.

November 1096–May 1097 Crusade armies led by Hugh of Vermandois, Godfrey of Bouillon, Bohemond of Taranto, Raymond of Toulouse and Robert of Normandy arrive in Constantinople.

6 May 1097 Crusaders begin siege of Nicaea, capital of the sultanate of Rum.

19 June 1097 Following secret negotiations, Nicaea surrenders – to Byzantine emperor Alexius Comnenus I.

1 July 1097 Crusaders defeat Seljuk Turks at the Battle of Dorylaeum.

21 October 1097 Crusaders begin the siege of Antioch.

December 1097 Bohemond of Taranto and Robert of Flanders defeat a Turkish army under Sultan Duqaq of Damascus.

January 1098 Morale is low among the crusaders, who suffer severe famine; many, including Peter the Hermit, desert.

9 February 1098 Bohemond of Taranto defeats a relief army under Radwan, Seljuk ruler of Aleppo at Harenc, 25 miles (40km) from Antioch.

10 March 1098 Baldwin of Boulogne creates crusader state: the County of Edessa.

April 1098 Embassy from Fatimid Egypt

▲ *Moors besiege a Christian castle in Spain.*

arrives at Antioch, offering crusaders possession of Syria if they agree not to attack Jerusalem. The crusaders decline the offer.

2 June 1098 Stephen of Blois begins march north to Constantinople.

3 June 1098 Crusaders capture Antioch. The citadel remains in Turkish hands.

6 June 1098 Relief army led by Sultan Kerbogha of Mosul arrives at Antioch and begins siege of crusaders within city.

14 June 1098 Peter Bartholomew claims to have discovered the Holy Lance in the city of Antioch.

28 June 1098 Crusaders defeat Sultan Kerbogha in battle outside Antioch. The citadel surrenders.

December 1098 Crusaders from Antioch capture nearby Maarrat an-Numan.

January 1099 Raymond of Toulouse leads the crusade army south from Antioch, bound for Jerusalem.

January 1099 Bohemond of Taranto establishes the second crusader state, the Principality of Antioch.

8 April 1099 Peter Bartholomew undergoes 'Ordeal By Fire' in an attempt to prove that his claimed discovery of the Holy Lance in Antioch was genuine. He is severely injured and dies on 20 April.

May 1099 Crusaders capture Tortosa and march down the coast as far as Arsuf.

5-6 June 1099 Tancred of Hautville and Baldwin of Le Bourg capture Bethlehem, birthplace of Christ.

7 June 1099 Crusaders begin the siege of the city of Jerusalem.

13 June 1099 Crusade army fails in assault on Jerusalem.

7–9 July 1099 Crusaders hold a three-day penitential fast prior to renewing their assault on the city.

15 July 1099 The crusaders capture Jerusalem. For two days, 15–16 July, they run amok, killing and looting.

22 July 1099 Godfrey of Bouillon is elected Defender of the Holy Sepulchre.

1 August 1099 Arnulf of Choques is elected Patriarch of Jerusalem.

5 August 1099 Patriarch Arnulf announces he has found a piece of the True Cross (the cross on which Christ was crucified) in Jerusalem.

12 August 1099 Godfrey of Bouillon consolidates the victory in Jerusalem by defeating a 50,000-strong Fatimid relief army in the Battle of Ascalon.

1100 Pope Paschal II calls a new crusade in response to calls from crusader lords for reinforcements.

18 July 1100 Godfrey of Bouillon dies; his brother Baldwin of Edessa is elected his replacement.

September 1100 Crusader troops are mobilized in response to Pope Paschal's call to arms depart from Italy.

25 December 1100 Baldwin of Edessa is crowned King of Jerusalem.

1100 Patriarch Arnulf is replaced by Dagobert of Pisa, the new papal legate. Arnulf becomes Archdeacon of Jerusalem.

June 1101 The Italian crusaders, fighting alongside Byzantine troops commanded by Raymond of Toulouse and a French–Burgundian–German force under Stephen of Blois, are routed by Seljuks.

1101 The Kingdom of Jerusalem captures Caesarea and Arsuf.

May 1104 The Kingdom is further expanded with the capture of Acre.

1107 King Sigurd I of Norway embarks on crusade.

12 July 1109 After a long siege Tripoli surrenders to crusaders and Bertrand, illegitimate son of crusader lord Raymond of Toulouse, becomes ruler of the fourth crusader state, the County of Tripoli.

May 1110 The Kingdom of Jerusalem captures Beirut.

4 December 1110 King Baldwin I and King Sigurd I of Norway capture Sidon.

1110 Tancred of Hauteville, veteran of the First Crusade and regent of Antioch, captures the castle of Krak des Chevaliers.

15 February 1113 Pope Paschal II recognizes the monastic order of the Hospitallers of St John of Jerusalem.

1113 Paschal II recognizes the Equestrian order of the Holy Sepulchre of Jerusalem.

1114 In Spain Count Berenguer of Barcelona leads a crusade against the Muslim-held Balearic islands.

1118 Pope Gelasius II declares a crusade against the Moors in Spain.

2 April 1118 King Baldwin I of Jerusalem dies and is succeeded by his cousin Baldwin of Le Bourg as Baldwin II.

19 December 1118 Crusaders in Spain capture the city of Saragossa.

28 June 1119 Artuqid Turkish ruler Ilghazi inflicts crushing defeat on Christian army in the Battle of the Field of Blood.

1122 Pope Calixtus II calls crusades to the Holy Land and Spain. A large fleet sails for Jerusalem from Venice.

c.1123 The brotherhood of the Order of St Lazarus of Jerusalem is established.

1124 With the help of Venetian crusaders, the Kingdom of Jerusalem captures Tyre.

January 1128 Knights Templar recognized at the Council of Troyes.

21 August 1131 King Baldwin II of Jerusalem dies and is succeeded by his daughter Melisende and her husband Fulk of Anjou. They rule as Queen Melisende and King Fulk.

1135 Pope Innocent III offers crusade indulgences for those fighting antipope Anacletus II.

13 Nov 1143 King Fulk of Jerusalem dies and is succeeded by his wife Melisende, co-ruling with their son Baldwin III.

24 December 1144 Turkish general Imad ed-Din Zengi captures the capital of the crusader state of Edessa.

1 December 1145 Pope Eugenius III calls the Second Crusade.

1 March 1146 Eugenius III reissues his call to arms, authorizing Bernard of Clairvaux to preach the crusade.

Easter Day 1146 Bernard preaches the crusade at Vezelay in central France. King Louis VII takes the cross.

25 December 1146 Another crusade sermon by Bernard of Clairvaux inspires Conrad II of Germany to take the cross.

1146 While the Second Crusade is being preached, violence breaks out against Jews in the Rhineland.

13 April 1147 Pope Eugenius III guarantees full crusading privileges to those fighting pagan Wends in the Baltic.

May–June 1147 Armies of the Second Crusade set out for the Holy Land.

July–September 1147 German crusaders campaign against pagan Wends.

mid-September 1147 German crusade army arrives at Constantinople.

24 October 1147 Crusaders aid in the capture of Lisbon from the Moors.

25 October 1147 In Anatolia German crusaders are defeated by Seljuk Turks.

8 January 1148 French crusaders are defeated by Seljuk Turks in Turkey.

19 March 1148 King Louis VII of France arrives in Antioch.

24 June 1148 The Council of Acre determines the future direction of the Second Crusade and decides to attack Damascus.

23 July 1148 Crusader armies arrive at Damascus and lay siege to the city.

28 July 1148 After the arrival of a relief army under Nur ed-Din, crusaders abandon the siege of Damascus. This marks the end of the Second Crusade.

29 June 1149 Nur ed-Din defeats and kills Raymond, Prince of Antioch.

1153 Baldwin III takes power in his own right as King of Jerusalem.

1154 Nur ed-Din captures Damascus.

10 February 1162 King Baldwin III of Jerusalem is succeeded by King Amalric I.

26 September 1164 Pope Alexander III recognizes the Spanish military brotherhood of the Order of Calatrava.

1164–69 A power struggle in Egypt ends in March 1169 with Salah ed-Din Yusuf (later called Saladin) as vizier of Egypt.

c.1170 Spanish military brotherhood of Order of Santiago is established.

11 July 1174 King Amalric I of Jerusalem is succeeded by his son Baldwin IV.

October 1174 Saladin takes Damascus.

25 November 1177 Baldwin IV defeats Saladin at the Battle of Montgisard.

1180 Pope Alexander III approves the establishment of the Knights of Our Lady of Mountjoie in Jerusalem.

1185 Baldwin IV dies and is succeeded by his nephew Baldwin V with Raymond of Tripoli as regent.

1186 Baldwin V dies and is succeeded by his mother Sibylla. She rules as Queen with Guy of Lusignan as her consort.

4 July 1187 Saladin wins a decisive victory in the Battle of the Horns of Hattin.

8 July 1187 Acre surrenders to Saladin.

4 September 1187 Saladin takes Ascalon.

20 September 1187 Saladin besieges the city of Jerusalem.

2 October 1187 Saladin succeeds in recapturing Jerusalem.

▼ *Kurdish general Saladin the Great.*

CHAPTER SIX

A CALL TO ARMS

On 27 November 1095, in a stirring speech to a great crowd at Clermont in France, Pope Urban II set in motion preparations for the First Crusade, which was to prove the start of centuries of violence between European Christians and Eastern Muslims in the Holy Land. Of course, he did not know that his speech was the beginning of hundreds of years of religious conflict, and the pious knights and other European warriors who responded to his call to arms were not aware that they were embarking on the first of a series of wars of the cross – indeed, they were encouraged to believe that the war would be final, victory total and glorious. Urban made the claim that Christ offered the ultimate reward to the knights and infantrymen he was seeking to mobilize. According to the version of the speech recorded by eyewitness Fulcher of Chartres, Urban urged those who waged war to take their courage and martial vigour abroad and put it to good use in combating 'barbarians' and cleansing the Holy Land: 'Let those who have been used to fighting without justice in private wars against faithful men and women, now embark against the faithless infidel and bring to an end with a great victory this war which should have been launched long ago ... Let those who have been earning mercenary pay instead earn eternal reward.' This reward, promised by the pope on behalf of God, was the complete remission of sins, the glory of heaven.

▲ *The People's Crusade sets out for the Holy Land, led by Peter the Hermit.*

◄ *The wealthy and deeply devout Count Raymond IV of Toulouse was the first European nobleman to obey Christ's command – as relayed by Pope Urban – to take the cross. Many pilgrims travelled in his party.*

CONSTANTINOPLE UNDER THREAT

EMPEROR ALEXIUS'S CRY FOR HELP

In March 1095 Alexius I Comnenus, ruler of the Byzantine Empire, despatched envoys to the Council of Piacenza in Italy to ask Pope Urban II for help in fighting the Seljuk Turks. This appeal either convinced Urban to promote a holy war to come to the aid of Christians in the East and reclaim the Holy Land, or else gave him ammunition to justify a decision he had already made to ask the chivalry of Europe to fight for the cross in the East.

Alexius's appeal was one of a number he made in the 1090s. He wanted military help in launching a counter-attack against the formidable Seljuk Turks, who had defeated the Byzantine Empire at the Battle of Manzikert in 1071 and had established the Sultanate of Rum in central Anatolia in 1077. Since becoming Byzantine emperor in 1081, Alexius had succeeded

in halting the invasion of Byzantine lands in Greece by the southern Italian Norman lord Robert Guiscard in 1081–82, then in beating back the incursions of the Turkish Pecheneg nomads in the Balkans. He saw an opportunity in the death in 1092 of the Turkish sultan of Baghdad, Malik Shah, and the collapse of his empire in Iraq, Syria and Palestine. The time appeared to

▲ *Alexius made much of the barbarity of the Seljuk Turks. They were fierce warriors, but maintained a highly civilized court.*

be ripe to strike back against the Seljuks and to reassert Byzantine authority across many of its former lands.

To win the support of Western nobles, Alexius and his envoys emphasized the

---

ALEXIUS I COMNENUS

Alexius I Comnenus, who ruled as Byzantine emperor from 1081 to 1118, proved himself one of the leading statesmen of his era. He came to power, by seizing the throne from Nicephorus III, just ten years after the empire's catastrophic defeat at the Battle of Manzikert by the Seljuk Turks, and ruled through the period of the First Crusade and the establishment of the crusader states of Jerusalem, Antioch, Edessa and Tripoli.

He made the crusader lords swear an oath to return to him the lands they gained on campaign and, although this was not honoured, by the crusaders' efforts he regained control of many cities including Nicaea, Sardis and Ephesus, as well as much of Anatolia. In his 37-year reign he restored the Byzantine Empire to a position of relative strength following its series of defeats at the hands of Normans and Turks. He founded the Comnenian dynasty of Byzantine emperors, who ruled until the late 12th century. In the words of an anonymous Greek biographer, he was a man 'great both in the power of his will and in deeds'.

◀ *The likeness of Alexius I Comnenus, Byzantine emperor between 1081 and 1118, adorns one side of this gold Byzantine soldo (penny coin).*

▼ *Pilgrims arrive at Jaffa (top) and pay a toll before entering Tyre (bottom). Both cities attracted pilgrims because of their role in biblical and early Christian history, and became crusader strongholds.*

threat to Christians and their holy places posed by the pagan Turks. But he did not envisage a holy war – he wanted a mercenary army, whose soldiers he could control with financial incentives. He did not foresee the struggle for the Holy Land launched by the pope; fighting to recapture Jerusalem was never part of his plan – the city had, after all, been in Muslim hands since 638.

LETTER TO COUNT ROBERT OF FLANDERS

One of Alexius's appeals survives in the form of a letter dated 1093 written to Count Robert II of Flanders. Count Robert's father – Count Robert I of Flanders – had stayed with Alexius in Constantinople on his return from a pilgrimage and Alexius had reportedly been impressed by the strength of his escort. His letter tried to appeal on several different fronts, seeking to generate not only righteous anger but also a lust for riches.

The letter described how the Patzinaks (or Pechenegs) and Turks carried out forced circumcision of Christian babies and boys above the baptismal font, and forced them to urinate into its waters; it suggested that they not only abducted and raped Christian women (both virgins and

▲ *The crusaders were awestruck by the beauty and ancient treasures of the walled city of Constantinople. This map was made in c.1485 by the Italian cartographer Cristoforo Buondelmonti.*

venerable matrons), but also performed acts of sodomy on Byzantine men – including Christian clergy, monks and even bishops. He compared their acts to those of the 'impious Babylonians', who, according to biblical accounts, had mistreated the Jews in exile – suggesting

thereby that under the threat of the Turks, the Christian Byzantines were effectively in exile in their own lands.

Alexis lamented that the great expanses of the Byzantine Empire had been snatched away and suggested that the invaders were on the verge of capturing Constantinople itself, 'unless the help of God and faithful Latin Christians should come quickly to us'. He pointed out that the cities of the East – and notably Constantinople – were rich in holy relics and that God would punish any brave lord who refused to come to their protection; those who did come, he said, would win reward in heaven.

Later in the letter, however, Alexius also emphasized that these cities were additionally full of treasures and gold, and of beautiful women – 'Greek women possess a beauty beyond compare that would be a good enough reason to lure the brave armies of the Franks to Thrace'. The Latin Christian lords should not allow these beauties – neither treasures nor flesh and blood – to fall into pagan hands.

▼ *Byzantine forces besiege Messina in Sicily. In Italy, the Byzantines had for centuries been at odds with the Normans and other Europeans, whose help they now requested.*

RIGHTEOUS WARFARE

POPE URBAN II PREACHES THE FIRST CRUSADE

On Tuesday 27 November 1095 at the close of the Council of Clermont in central France, Pope Urban II issued a rousing call to arms, urging the Christian knights of Europe to travel to the aid of their brothers in the East and liberate the holy places of Jerusalem from unbelievers. The speech was the high point of a months-long tour of France promoting the crusade between August 1095 and September 1096.

The Council of Clermont, an assembly for church reform, had been running since 18 November and had been attended by around 300 prominent clerics. They had deliberated on clerical marriage, the elimination of simony (the practice of selling Church positions) and the excommunication of King Philip of France for committing adultery.

Word must have been circulated that the pope was planning to make a great announcement, for the crowd that gathered to hear him was too large to fit into the Cathedral at Clermont and the papal

▼ *Urban is escorted to Clermont, where he asked bishops and abbots to bring the leading lords in their areas to the council.*

▲ *In Fulcher of Chartres's account of the speech, Urban declared 'Let men who have grown used to waging private war against fellow Christians go now against the infidel and win a great victory in this war that should have been started long ago.'*

throne was therefore moved to a field just outside the city. There, Urban delivered the passionate address that launched the First Crusade.

URBAN'S SPEECH

We know that Urban was a highly intelligent man and a great orator and can tell from the response that the speech had an electrifying effect. But it is impossible to know for sure what he said. Five separate substantial accounts of Urban's speech survive, but all were written in the early 12th century in the light of later assumptions about the enterprise and after the First Crusade had ended in triumph at Jerusalem in 1099.

The earliest account was in the anonymous chronicle *Gesta Francorum* (Deeds of the Franks), probably written by a follower of Bohemond of Taranto in *c*.1100. This was used as a source by the other reports. Shortly afterwards, perhaps in 1101, Fulcher of Chartres, an ecclesiastic who travelled on crusade in the party of

Stephen of Blois and Robert of Normandy, wrote a history of the First Crusade that also included a major report of the speech; it is probable that Fulcher was actually present at the Council of Clermont. Another very important description of the speech was given by Robert the Monk, who reworked the *Gesta Francorum* in *c*.1106; he was almost certainly not present at Clermont.

A fourth account was written by the Benedictine historian Guibert, Abbot of Nogent-sous-Coucy, in his *Dei gesta per Francos* (Deeds of God carried out by the Franks) of *c*.1108. He used the *Gesta Francorum* as a principal source but also used material gleaned from discussions with crusaders he knew; he, too, was present at the Council of Clermont, so must have included his memories as an eyewitness in the report. A fifth version of Urban's speech was given by Balderic, Archbishop of Dol-en-Bretagne from 1107–30, who based his account – written 10–20 years after the speech – on the *Gesta Francorum*.

According to the account in the *Gesta Francorum*, Urban primarily focused on the instruction of Christ to his followers that they should take up the cross and follow him, and described how men should seek to save their soul and find reward in heaven by finding the way to the Holy Sepulchre in Jerusalem.

In Fulcher of Chartres's report, Urban presented the expedition as an opportunity for secular warriors to become soldiers in Christ's service. He condemned lawlessness and the actions of robbers and urged that the Truce of God, the general peace agreed on Church authority, should be honoured. Then he called on all present to hurry to the aid of Christians in the East against 'Turks and Arabs', and to 'drive that vile race from the territories of our friends'. He said: 'All who die on the journey, overland or across seas, or in fighting against pagans, shall be rewarded with immediate remission of sins.'

In Robert the Monk's account, meanwhile, Urban emphasized the need to fight for the conquest of the Holy Land more than hurry to the aid of the Christians in the East. He repeated many of the descriptions of pagan infamy listed in the supposed letter of Alexis I to Count Robert II of Flanders – such as forced circumcision of Christian boys, spilling of human blood in the font and brutal rape of Christian women.

▼ *According to Balderic, Urban called on knights to defend the Church of the Holy Sepulchre and other Eastern churches as they would defend their mother.*

▲ *Robert the Monk described Urban calling on Christians to go to the aid of their brethren because, in the words that became the battle cry of the crusaders, 'God wills it!'*

In Robert's account, the pope also emphasized the great history of the Franks and their pedigree as a fighting race – they were above all other nations in arms, and should be inspired by the deeds of their ancestors, great warriors such as Charlemagne: 'O bravest of soldiers, the sons of invincible forebears, do not forget the valour of your ancestors.' He added that France was crowded with men, nd that inevitable competition bred conflict, but that the Holy Land to which he called them was – as noted in the Bible – one that 'floweth with milk and honey'; it was 'a paradise of many delights' and, moreover, a place consecrated by the suffering of Christ. He personified the city of Jerusalem, which he said lay at the centre of the world: 'from you,' he said, 'she asks for help!' He added: 'Take on this journey for the remission of sins, in confidence of the undying glory of God's kingdom.'

Balderic of Dol's version emphasized particularly the desecration of holy places in Jerusalem by pagans and called powerfully on Christian knights to stop fighting one another and, instead, to combat Turks and others in the Holy Land. In this

account, Urban declared 'may you find it is a beautiful thing to give your life for Christ in the city in which he gave his life for us all'; fighting Saracens, he said, was 'righteous warfare', and would deliver 'everlasting glory'. He also pointed out, however, that worldly wealth would be an auxiliary prize – for the enemy was in possession of great riches.

The account of Guibert of Nogent emphasized the notion, current in the 10th and 11th centuries, that the 'Last Days' were at hand prior to the Second Coming of Christ as described in the biblical Book of Revelation and suggested that Christian knights should go to Jerusalem to oppose pagans as part of this final conflict. In this version, Urban described the many sufferings of Christian pilgrims to the Holy Land at the hands of pagans. He promised that knights fighting in the holy war would have Christ as 'standard bearer and inseparable leader'.

GOD WILLS IT! GOD WILLS IT!

THE RUSH TO TAKE THE CROSS

At the end of Urban's speech, a great shout went up among those in the crowd: 'God wills it! God wills it! God wills it!' Adhemar, Bishop of Le Puy, stepped forward and fell to his knees before Urban, and asked to be allowed to take part in an expedition to the East. Urban appointed him to serve on the pope's behalf as leader of the crusade. Some men trembled and wept in the crowd, and others discussed Urban's words earnestly: almost at once, many came forward in imitation of Adhemar to pledge themselves to undertake the task to which Urban called them.

TAKING THE CROSS

According to some accounts volunteers at once began to mark themselves out by attaching a cross to their clothes, in homage to the cross of Christ; clerics and monks surrendered their cloaks to provide

▼ *A monk bestows the cross on a crusader. The symbol of Christ gave weight and meaning to each knight's journey eastwards.*

material from which people cut the crosses. Fulcher of Chartres reported that as soon as people took the oath to go on the expedition, they made 'shining crosses' from cloth of gold or silk and attached them to their shoulders.

It seems obvious from contemporary accounts that the events at Clermont were carefully stage-managed: doubtless Urban had instructed a cleric to set up the chant of 'God wills it! God wills it!' and arranged in advance that Adhemar would step forward and be the first to take a vow. According to Robert the Monk, Urban whipped up the crowd further by claiming that the fact that they all chanted the one phrase was evidence that God was at work among them, in line with Christ's promise that 'Where two or three are gathered together in my name there am I in the midst of them': though the words were issuing from many mouths, they had their origin in one place, in God. And he proceeded to specify that these words should become the battle cry of the crusading armies when they went to war in the East.

▲ *Crusader knights of the Minutolo family kneel in prayer, in a fresco from San Gennaro Cathedral, Naples. Over centuries families became associated with crusading as fathers and sons, uncles and nephews took the cross on different campaigns.*

The visual drama of 'taking the cross' by attaching it to clothing was also seemingly prearranged, with clerics briefed beforehand to provide the necessary material for the eager men in the crowd.

The taking of the cross was a symbolic visual act that gave added physical weight to the verbal vow taken by the participants. The *Gesta Francorum* reported that the Franks who undertook to make the expedition sewed the cross of Christ on their right shoulders. According to Robert the Monk, Urban instructed all those taking the vow to mark themselves with the sign of Christ's cross either on their forehead or on their chest, and said that when they had accomplished what he asked them to do, they should wear the cross on their back between their shoulders. Guibert of Nogent also reported that it was

JERUSALEM ENSLAVED

In December 1095 Urban wrote an open letter to crusaders waiting in Flanders, describing his sermons and in particular his call at Clermont to holy war. In it, he described again how the churches of the East and Jerusalem, the 'Holy City of Christ, made glorious by his Passion and Resurrection', were in 'intolerable slavery' and needed to be freed. He reiterated that the crusade would be in remission of sins, and that Adhemar, Bishop of Le Puy, would be leader of the undertaking in the Pope's place.

▼ *Urban was archdeacon of Rheims and prior at Cluny Abbey before he became pope.*

▲ *Jerusalem, the Holy City, and navel of God's creation, was said to be calling out in her distress to the knights of Europe, begging to be freed.*

Pope Urban's order that people sew the cross, made of any material, on their shirt, cloak or chain mail tunic. In this version, Urban added that any person who took the vow and then did not travel would be an outlaw for all time.

THE REMISSION OF SINS

Although the accounts of the speech at Clermont vary, we can be certain that Urban's appeal did promise the remission of sins for those who took part – the journey itself would bring the same benefits as a pilgrimage to Jerusalem.

The issues of sin and forgiveness were very important for people of all classes at this time, not least because it was commonly held that the expected Second Coming of Christ was imminent, and that the 'Last Days' of the world as described in the Bible were at hand. This meant that the feared Day of Judgement was also imminent, and that it was a matter of even greater than normal urgency to find officially sanctioned ways of seeking forgiveness for wrongdoing.

FIGHTING WITH GOD'S BLESSING

Urban II, who came from the minor nobility of the Champagne region of France, knew how to address the knightly class, and his appeal at Clermont and throughout the preaching tour of which it was a part struck a note that rang true with the warriors in his audience. The Church's initial response to the emergence of knights

had been to try to stifle their enthusiasm for fighting – in the Peace of God and Truce of God movements, to limit knightly conflict to prescribed periods. But on the expedition Urban proposed should take place to the East, knights would be encouraged to fight, and would do so with the full blessing of the Church and of God. Moreover, in doing so they would gain spiritual blessings as well as impunity – as Christ's soldiers they would win forgiveness of their sins and ultimately their salvation after death.

THE QUEST FOR GLORY

MOTIVES OF THE KNIGHTS WHO UNDERTOOK THE FIRST CRUSADE

The primary motivation of the knights who departed on the First Crusade was religious. Taking the cross was an act of piety, a statement of faith.

Taking the cross as a knight was likened to becoming a monk, which in this period was put forward as the spiritual ideal for a Christian life. Those who took the cross were treated like the clergy, and acquired certain associated privileges – while on crusade they did not, for example, have to pay taxes or settle debts or carry out feudal military service. It was understandably a matter of concern for those considering going on crusade that they were leaving their family and property behind, but the Church promised protection on their behalf. In the account of Urban's speech at Clermont given by Guibert of Nogent, the pope announced that anyone who molested the property or family of a soldier of Christ while he was on pilgrimage to the Holy Land would be subject to 'a fearful anathema' – that is, excommunication.

▼ *Before embarking upon crusade a knight receives Holy Communion. Crusading was comparable to the quests in search of honour taken by knights in chivalric poems.*

GLAMOUR AND HONOUR

But there were also secular attractions for the crusaders in addition to these primary religious motives. The knights were seeking honour and glory as well. Glamour was attached to the crusade proposed by Urban: it was an adventure and, as we have seen, it allowed the knights of Europe to indulge their taste for conflict.

The code of chivalry, which in the late 11th century was in the early stages of its development, taught that knights must seek opportunities to practise their martial skills and to prove themselves worthy of the honour of being a knight. In Europe they could be frustrated in doing this by the Peace of God and by secular or ecclesiastical authority, but on crusade they were encouraged to do so. The knights were – and saw themselves as – an international elite: the landowners of northern France and of England and of southern Italy had more in common with each other than they had with their countrymen; the crusade gave them an enemy and a target, and the opportunity to ride out among their peers seeking glory.

THE LURE OF WEALTH?

For many decades historians argued that the crusaders also rode eastward in search of a fortune. The accounts we have of the appeal that was made to the knights of Europe certainly included the promise of wealth. Alexius Comnenus's letter to Count Robert II of Flanders pretended that in Constantinople there was more gold than anywhere else in the world – and that the city's churches were overflowing with silver and precious stones and fine silks as well as gold; moreover, he claimed that the riches of all the emperors of the ancient Roman Empire were hidden in the palaces of the city. In Balderic of Dol's account of Pope Urban's speech at Clermont, the pope promised the crusaders the spoils of the enemy: 'the

▲ *A knight offers his service to God. This celebrated crusading image is from the English Westminster Psalter of c.1250.*

possessions of the enemy will be yours, too,' he said, 'since you will make their treasures your spoils'.

The knights, of course, were happy to take what spoils of war came their way in line with conventional practice in the medieval period. But they did not set out principally to seek their fortune.

At one time, historians argued that crusade armies contained many younger sons, men who seized on Urban's call to reclaim the Holy Land as a chance to make a place for themselves in the world and win a fortune. This traditional account pointed out that within the feudal system in northern France and England, younger sons in noble families could not inherit their father's wealth and had limited opportunities for self-advancement. And even in southern Europe, where inheritances were shared out among all sons, many found their prospects were poor because the property was split so many times among

▲ *Committing to crusade required bravery, a willingness to risk all fighting far from home. Most knights were sustained by their faith that they were carrying out God's will.*

descendants that it became insignificant. However, modern historians dismiss this argument, pointing out the great expense of equipping oneself to go on crusade. To travel on crusade cost a knight many times his annual income.

From surviving charters and other documents we can see that the great majority of crusaders intended to return, if they did not die on the adventure overseas, and were not deliberately setting out to make a new life in a strange land. Moreover, it is simply not true that younger sons rather

▶ *Knights had to equip themselves at great expense with a horse, weapons and finery. Crusading was a chance to demonstrate social standing and chivalric qualities.*

than their older siblings went on crusade – great lords and eldest sons travelled as well as their younger brothers. It is true that following the success of the First Crusade and the establishment of the crusader kingdoms of Jerusalem, Edessa, Antioch and Tripoli, a number of Europeans settled in the Middle East. But

historians now question whether these settlers were primarily crusaders, as was once assumed, or whether they were emigrants after the crusade taking advantage of the new opportunities.

There were certainly individual cases of young men who made their name and fortune on crusade, but they were not a general type among the crusaders. Many knights, in fact, made significant financial sacrifices to go on crusade – some had to mortgage their property to pay for the expedition – and pay high rates of interest on the loan; others sold their land – and often accepted a poor price because in France, for example, the 1090s were a time of agricultural depression. The fact that so many knights made substantial sacrifices to take the cross is testament to the power of Pope Urban's stirring appeal and runs quite counter to the proposal that knights travelled to the Holy Land out of financial self-interest.

WALKING TO THE HOLY LAND

THE PEOPLE'S CRUSADE

The sermon at Clermont may have been meticulously planned and the accompanying pageantry carefully staged, but the response to Urban's plea took him by surprise. In addition to a well-equipped military force of great princes, lords and knights of the kind Urban had hoped to mobilize, a vast army of peasants and poor townspeople also left their homes, determined to put their trust in God and make their way to the Holy Land.

PETER THE HERMIT

A monk and popular preacher from Amiens named Peter the Hermit toured northern France and Flanders on a donkey, calling for crusade volunteers. He was a small man, known as 'Little Peter' by his contemporaries, with a long thin face, like

▼ *Peter shows knights their duty. Byzantine princess Anna Comnena wrote that Peter had tried before to make a pilgrimage to Jerusalem, but had been tortured by Turks.*

that of his donkey, and eccentric habits – he dressed only in a cloak, was often unwashed and lived on nothing but wine and fish. Yet Peter had the orator's gift, the ability to transfix a large crowd; according to Guibert of Nogent, who met him, Peter's charisma was such that his acts and deeds seemed 'half divine'. Peter claimed that Christ himself had appointed him to preach the crusade – and even pretended that he had a letter from God to prove it. The crowds flocked after him.

This first wave of crusaders contained many hangers-on with little or no military equipment or experience of fighting, although the core of the group was adequately fitted out with horses and weapons. But remarkably there were only eight knights. The most notable of these was the experienced Walter of Sans Avoir in the Seine Valley. (He was not, as is commonly written, a penniless knight. This traditional reputation derives from a misunderstanding of his name – for

generations historians interpreted Walter Sans Avoir to mean he had nothing, that he was penniless; in fact, it refers to his feudal base, a place of that name in the Seine Valley.)

DEPARTURE FOR THE HOLY LAND

Pope Urban had declared the Feast of the Assumption of the Blessed Virgin Mary (15 August 1096) to be the starting point for the expedition, but the people who gathered to travel on what historians call the People's Crusade were impatient to depart. Peter the Hermit assembled his followers at Cologne, Germany on 12 April. His plan was to gather more followers by preaching among the Germans.

A French contingent of a few thousand under the leadership of Walter Sans Avoir could not brook even this minor delay and departed at once. They followed an overland route, and were in Hungary by 8 May. They then proceeded without incident as far as Belgrade, on the border of Byzantine lands. However, the governor of Belgrade refused them entry and the French crusaders looted the countryside – in the market town of Semlin, 16 of them were captured and stripped of their armour, which was hung from the walls of the castle there. Eventually the main group reached Nish (now in Serbia) and waited for a troop escort from the Byzantine emperor in Constantinople.

A second wave of around 20,000 left Cologne under Peter the Hermit's leadership on 20 April and followed the same route as the French pilgrims who had gone before. The first part of their journey was uneventful, but when they reached Semlin and saw the armour of the earlier crusaders hanging from the castle walls, they rioted and attacked the city, killing 4,000 locals. Afterwards, they crossed the River Save before attacking and looting Belgrade. At Nish, where they arrived on 3 July, the garrison commander was the crusaders – especially in the Rhineland, where there were dreadful massacres in Worms, Mainz, Cologne and Trier. Count Emicho's troops massacred 800 Jews at Worms on 18 May and at least 1,100 at Mainz on 27 May.

Anti-Semitism had been current for centuries, but these were the first organized attacks against the Jews in European history. Some of the crusaders, including Count Emicho himself, felt that the Jews – culpable for the crucifixion of Christ – were just as much enemies of the cross as the Muslims, and believed that the crusading spirit could be given expression close to home. Feeling was also running high against the Jews among crusaders who had to borrow money to finance the crusade since, because money-lending was forbidden among Christians, they usually had entered into debts with Jewish lenders. Many of these crusaders now grew rich by stealing the Jews' money. Some historians refer to these attacks as the 'First Holocaust', linking them to the official attempt to exterminate the Jews by the Nazi government of Germany during the 1930s and World War II.

initially peaceable and promised an escort to Constantinople if the crusaders would move quickly on, but then a skirmish broke out between locals and some German crusaders and the commander unleashed the full force of his garrison, routing the motley crusader force and killing about 5,000 crusaders. Peter the Hermit and the chastened survivors carried on, and on 12 July arrived at Sofia (now in Bulgaria), where they awaited a military escort from Constantinople.

▲ Faith drove them on. The unlikely looking forces of the People's Crusade march across Europe in an image from the 15th-century Les Passages faits Outremer.

CRUSADES AGAINST THE JEWS

Some sections of the great population mobilized for a crusade did not travel to the Holy Land, but carried out attacks against Jewish communities in France and Germany. The most serious slaughter was carried out by a 10,000-strong army commanded by Count Emicho of Leisingen, who claimed that Christ had appeared to him and promised to make him emperor if he would convert the Jews of Europe. The Church authorities largely tried to protect the Jews, but Jews were forcibly converted or killed in their thousands by

WHY DID SO MANY PEOPLE JOIN THE PEOPLE'S CRUSADE?

In the late 11th century there was a resurgence of belief that the Second Coming of Christ was imminent. This fired a popular desire to make a mass pilgrimage to Jerusalem and to return the Holy City to Christian control. At the same time, a series of celestial events – including a comet, a lunar eclipse and a meteor shower – seemed to reinforce the sense that the enterprise preached by Pope Urban and Peter the Hermit had God's blessing. In addition, there had been an outbreak of ergotism, or 'St Anthony's fire', food poisoning (caused by long-term consumption of cereals

containing fungi). This poisoning results in convulsions and gangrene, and it was interpreted as evidence of God's displeasure and made people desire to expiate their sins by making a pilgrimage. Some historians argue that in the years prior to 1096, the peasants of northern Europe had been suffering very severely as a result of the plague, drought and famine and were seeking escape from these terrible conditions.

▶ For most people in Europe, life was harsh. Some may have seen the crusade as a chance for a new beginning.

CHAPTER SEVEN

THE JOURNEY TO PALESTINE

The vast contingent of pilgrims and soldiers led by the monk Peter the Hermit and the knight Walter of Sans Avoir was followed to Constantinople by no fewer than five armies commanded by minor royals and some of the leading noblemen of Europe – including Duke Robert of Normandy, eldest son of King William I of England, and Hugh of Vermandois, younger brother of King Philip I of France, as well as counts and noblemen such as Raymond of Toulouse, Godfrey of Bouillon and Bohemond of Taranto. The second wave of armies, some of whom travelled overland and some by sea, is known to historians as the Princes' Crusade to distinguish it from the earlier People's Crusade, which was so called because it contained many unarmed pilgrims and peasants. As had the People's Crusaders before them, the Princes' armies endured their share of mishaps and disasters before they ever arrived at the glittering capital of the Byzantine Empire; and, arriving there confident in the knowledge that they were riding to the help of beleaguered Christians, their leaders faced an uncertain welcome from an emperor suspicious of their motives, who in particular feared that they aimed to establish themselves as rulers in his territory. In the event, the two crusades merged – after a catastrophic defeat at the hands of the Seljuk Turks in Anatolia, the chastened remnant of the People's Crusade returned to Constantinople, joined up with the still fresh and confident armies of the Princes' Crusade and set off for Jerusalem.

▲ *A messenger is sent for help at the siege of Antioch.*

◄ *The main strength of a crusader army was in its mounted cavalry bearing lances, but the soldiers were also a very effective force when battle broke down into hand-to-hand combat.*

MORE THAN THE STARS OF HEAVEN
THE PEOPLE'S CRUSADE ARRIVES IN CONSTANTINOPLE

The two main branches of the People's Crusade, one under the leadership of impoverished knight Walter Sans Avoir and the other following charismatic monk Peter the Hermit, had both arrived at Constantinople by 1 August 1096.

Anna Comnena, daughter of the Byzantine emperor Alexius I, described how the armed contingent was accompanied by a vast crowd of crusader-pilgrims 'outnumbering the grains of sand on the sea shore or the stars sparkling in the sky, carrying palms and crosses on their shoulders'. This group included many women, children and old people. She wrote that 'to look upon them was like watching powerful rivers flooding from all sides to a confluence'.

▼ *Peter the Hermit's charismatic preaching convinced many to abandon home and loved ones to honour the cross. Arriving in the East, they began to realize the immense difficulty of the task they had taken on.*

ACROSS THE BOSPHORUS

Alexius had expected a disciplined and cohesive army to be sent from Europe; instead he was confronted with a motley band of largely ill-equipped travellers who expected to be fed and given assistance. He refused them entry into the city, and made them camp outside the city walls. Within five days he had ferried them all across the Bosphorus into Anatolia.

It may be that the emperor simply wanted to be rid of them, and sent them on without much help to face almost certain death; on the other hand, it is possible that the crusaders insisted on marching on towards Jerusalem despite his best efforts to dissuade them. Anna Comnena – whose account in the *Alexiad* (*c*.1148), a biography of her father, understandably cast Alexius in a sympathetic light – claimed that the emperor tried to persuade Peter to await the arrival of reinforcements before moving on, but that Peter insisted on crossing into Anatolia and pressing on

towards Jerusalem. Alexius also warned the hermit not to be drawn into battle, because he saw that the crusaders were evidently no match for the Turkish army.

The crusaders were joined by several contingents of Italians, newly arrived from home. The group marched on, pillaging the towns they came to until they reached Nicomedia (now Izmit in Turkey), where they quarrelled. The Italians and Germans, under the command of an Italian by the name of Rainald, separated themselves from the French under Geoffrey Burel. Peter the Hermit and Walter Sans Avoir were no longer in control of events.

RAIDS IN ANATOLIA

The crusaders established a camp at Civetot, on the Sea of Marmara (the inland body of water that connects the Black and Aegean seas). Groups set out from the main crusader camp, competing with one another in attempts to progress the crusade. A French contingent marched as far as Nicaea, wealthy capital of the Turkish sultanate of Rum, and looted the edge of the city – according to Anna Comnena's colourful version of events, they committed atrocities there, torturing venerable old men, killing children and even cooking babies over spits and eating them.

Meanwhile, a 6,000-strong German troupe took the city of Xerigordon. In response the Turks sent an army to lay seige to Xerigordon, which captured the only source of water, located outside the city walls. The Germans lasted eight days, and surrendered only after they were reduced to drinking their own urine and the blood of their donkeys to survive. In defeat, they were slaughtered, or forced to convert to Islam and sold into slavery.

CRUSADERS MASSACRED

The Turks then set a trap for the remainder of the crusaders. In the main camp at Civetot, Turkish spies spread a rumour

▲ *The dreams of glory summoned by Peter the Hermit fell apart in the unfamiliar territory of Anatolia, where the crusaders were ravaged by the Seljuk Turks.*

that the Germans had not only triumphed at Xerigordon, but had also taken Nicaea. The rumour spread like wildfire, and generated a clamour to travel swiftly on to Nicaea and share in the looting. Peter the Hermit was absent, having travelled back to Constantinople to negotiate for supplies; Geoffrey Burel convinced the entire remainder of the force, some 20,000 strong, that they should move out at once.

On 21 October at dawn they marched out of the camp towards Nicaea. Anna Comnena commented at this juncture that the 'Latins' (Italians and Europeans) were known for their love of money, and that when they went on a military campaign

their lust for wealth grew even stronger, becoming so overpowering that it robbed them of their judgement and made them rush headlong, as here, into trouble. In her account, they simply ran out of the camp towards Nicaea, without arming themselves, clamouring for money, with no semblance of discipline: they were entirely unprepared for what followed.

The Turks had laid an ambush in a narrow valley just 3 miles (5km) from the crusader camp. There they set on the army led by Geoffrey Burel, provoking a wave of blind panic among them. The slaughter was most terrible. Anna Comnena reported that when after the battle men went to clear the battlefield they gathered together the corpses of the fallen crusaders and made not merely a mound or a hill but a grisly flyblown mountain. Only 3,000 crusaders survived, and they took refuge in an abandoned castle. The Turks pursued them there and laid siege, but in time a Byzantine force sailed across from Constantinople, chased the Turks off and freed the crusaders.

A RABBLE OR AN ARMY?

The conventional view of the People's Crusade has been that the people who made this long and fruitless pilgrimage were little more than a rabble roused by an unscrupulous charismatic preacher, and that their 'armies' contained no more than a handful of properly equipped and trained soldiers. However, it is worth considering that this first wave of crusaders maintained their discipline sufficiently to march all the way across Europe as far as

▲ *Peter distributes crosses to eager volunteers. He convinced many of his poorer followers that a host of angels would defend them if they came under attack.*

Constantinople and that in Anatolia they did win military victories before their ultimate defeat. Even granted this, however, the ill-conceived People's Crusade cannot ultimately be adjudged anything more than a disaster. Scores of thousands of people lost their lives – the 3,000 crusaders who survived defeat in Anatolia were the only survivors of the crusade.

After they were freed by the Byzantine relief force from the castle in which they had taken refuge, the survivors made their way slowly back to Constantinople, where they eventually joined up with the better equipped armies that had followed them from Europe.

▼ *The crusaders arrive in Constantinople. A significant proportion of the peasants on the People's Crusade died of starvation or were sold into slavery.*

PRINCES ON CRUSADE
THE LEADERS OF THE FIRST CRUSADE

The European princes and nobles who responded to Pope Urban's call to crusade travelled in five main armies to Constantinople by different routes. They began to leave in mid-summer 1096 and arrived at Constantinople at various times between November 1096 and May 1097.

The first army to arrive was that of Hugh of Vermandois, who as younger brother of King Philip I of France was a prince of a royal house and one of the highest-ranking of the crusaders. He was reputedly convinced to embark on the crusade by an eclipse of the moon in February 1096, which he interpreted as divine guidance. The chronicler William of Tyre called him 'Hugh Magnus' (Hugh the Great), but despite high birth Hugh did very little of note, being an ineffective soldier and leader. He certainly had a high opinion of himself, however: according to Anna Comnena, he sent a breathtakingly arrogant letter to Alexius, in which he declared: 'Be advised, O Emperor, that I am the King of kings, highest-ranking of

▼ Godfrey of Bouillon. The crusade made him into a figure of legend, celebrated in literature as one of the 'Nine Worthies'.

all beneath the sky. My will is that you should attend me upon my arrival and give me the magnificent welcome that is fitting for a visitor of the noblest birth.'

Hugh's army travelled by way of Italy, where they were joined by a number of soldiers previously under the command of Count Emicho, leader of the German Crusade against the Jews – soldiers who had been dispersed by a Hungarian army. The army set sail from Bari across the Adriatic Sea, but were shipwrecked off the Byzantine port of Dyrrhachium (now Durres in Albania) and had to be rescued by the Byzantine governor of that locality before being escorted to Constantinople, arriving in November 1096.

GODFREY OF BOUILLON
The second army was from northern France and Belgium, led by Godfrey, Lord of Bouillon and duke of Lower Lorraine, with his younger brother Baldwin and his older brother Eustace III, Count of Boulogne. The army, perhaps 40,000 strong, set out from Lorraine in August

▲ Bohemond of Taranto's crusading feats won him the hand of Constance, daughter of King Philip I of France, in 1104.

1096 bound for Constantinople: they followed largely the same route as the People's Crusade, through Hungary and the Balkans (part of the Byzantine Empire), where they crossed the River Danube at Belgrade and proceeded via Sofia and Adrianople (modern Edirne in Turkey) and arrived at the Sea of Marmara in mid-December. On 23 December they pitched their camp beneath the walls of Constantinople. In some accounts, this army was referred to as 'the Lorrainers'.

BOHEMOND OF TARANTO
The third army was made up of Normans from southern Italy and led by Bohemond of Taranto. Bohemond was the son of Norman adventurer Robert Guiscard and was an old enemy of Emperor Alexius, having fought against him during his father's failed invasion of the Byzantine Empire in the early 1080s. In his company

was his nephew Tancred, the son of Bohemond's sister, Emma of Apulia.

Bohemond did not hear Pope Urban's call to arms. He joined the crusade only in October 1097 after he encountered knights making their way towards the Holy Land by way of southern Italy, where he and his army – including Tancred – were besieging the town of Amalfi, which had rebelled against his authority. Among these knights was Tancred's brother William: learning of the purpose of their journey, the Normans under Bohemond elected to join the crusade. The army set sail in October 1096, crossing the Adriatic from Brindisi to Avlona (a seaport now in Albania) and marched overland to Constantinople, where it arrived on 9 April 1097.

RAYMOND OF TOULOUSE

The fourth army belonged to Raymond, Count of Toulouse, Duke of Narbonne and Margrave of Provence. He was the first noble knight to take the cross after Pope Urban's speech at Clermont, and was profoundly religious: according to one account in an Armenian chronicle, he had made a pilgrimage to Jerusalem before the First Crusade, and during the course of this journey lost an eye; he had also fought in Spain against Muslim armies. He was 55, the oldest and also the wealthiest of the crusading lords, and he might have expected to be named leader of the expedition, but Pope Urban gave no special position to any of the secular lords, vesting his authority in the papal legate Adhemar, Bishop of Le Puy, who travelled in Raymond's party.

Raymond, in the company of his third wife Elvira (the illegitimate daughter of King Alfonso VI of Castile) and Bishop Adhemar, departed from Toulouse with a large army and a significant contingent of unarmed pilgrims in October 1096. They took an overland route by way of Genoa and Venice and along the coast as far as Dyrrhachium, before heading inland. They arrived at the gates of Constantinople on 27 April 1097.

DUKE ROBERT OF NORMANDY

The fifth main army was jointly led by Duke Robert of Normandy, his brother-in-law Stephen, Count of Blois, and Count Robert II of Flanders.

Duke Robert of Normandy was the eldest son of King William I of England, who, on his deathbed, had bequeathed the duchy of Normandy to Robert and the English throne to his second son, William Rufus. The two brothers had been at war on and off since William Rufus had become King of England on the Conqueror's death in 1087: in September 1096, Robert pawned the duchy of Normandy to William Rufus in return for 10,000 silver marks, which he used to fund his part in the crusade.

Stephen, Count of Blois, was married to Robert's sister, the formidable Adela of Normandy, and according to contemporary accounts went on the crusade only because he was ordered to do so by his wife. (He was to be father of a king of England, for his son Stephen – born at

▲ Robert II, Count of Flanders, was one of the co-leaders of Robert of Normandy's section of the crusading army.

Blois in 1096 before the crusade – was King Stephen of England from 1135–54.) Count Robert of Flanders was an experienced campaigner and skilled knight, who had proved his worth by governing Flanders while his father had been away on a pilgrimage to Jerusalem from 1085–91. Also in this army was Bishop Odo of Bayeux.

This fifth army left northern France in October 1096, but was waylaid in southern Italy where Duke Robert and Count Stephen settled for the winter, enjoying the hospitality of local lords. But Count Robert of Flanders pressed on with his force, sailing from Brindisi and marching overland to Constantinople. The remainder of the army followed in the spring, leaving Brindisi in April and arriving in Constantinople in May 1097, just a month behind Raymond's army.

THE CRUSADERS IN CONSTANTINOPLE
NEGOTIATIONS WITH EMPEROR ALEXIUS

Alexius quite naturally viewed the princely crusaders with suspicion. The princes and lords had mobilized great armies and brought them on to imperial Byzantine territory officially to supply help to Christians in the East, but it was difficult to be sure of their true motives.

The emperor could not be certain that the Latin lords were not plotting to capture pieces of his empire for themselves. In any case, the crusaders were also talking of capturing Jerusalem, which Alexius still viewed as a possession of the Byzantine Empire, even if one that was temporarily in Muslim hands. Moreover, among the leaders was a major former adversary, Bohemond of Taranto.

Alexius determined to make each of the crusader lords swear an oath of allegiance to him, under which they would pledge to be his vassals and would promise to return any Byzantine lands that they won in the course of the crusade. In return, he would supply the crusade with provisions, money, horses, guides and a supporting

▲ *Constantinople had formidable defences. Its magnificent double walls, with 142 fortified towers and 11 gates, were built in 412–22 during the reign of Theodosius II.*

military force. In demanding personal oaths of loyalty, Alexius adopted the established practices of Europe: in his own domain he could expect the total obedience of his subjects, but in the feudal lands from which these lords had come, he knew, great men generally held they were bound only by oaths they swore in person to an emperor, a king or a suzerain (feudal superior).

HUGH OF VERMANDOIS
The first of the princely crusaders to arrive, Hugh of Vermandois, expected a grand welcome; Alexius was happy to provide gifts and to spout honeyed words, but he kept Hugh under close supervision – virtually as a prisoner – in a monastery. For all his self-aggrandizement, Hugh did not object when asked to swear an oath of loyalty as vassal to the emperor.

GODFREY OF BOUILLON
When the second main army arrived under Godfrey of Bouillon and his brothers, Alexius made them camp outside the

THE IMPACT OF CONSTANTINOPLE

The city of Constantinople amazed the crusaders. Emperor Alexius had decided to make the armies camp outside Constantinople's great city walls, but he allowed small groups of five or six at a time to enter the city in order to pray in the churches and see the sights. They were astonished by what they found – by the

city's size and wealth, by its baths and sanitation and by the beauty of the churches and the rich collections of treasures and of sacred relics. Fulcher of Chartres wrote: 'Oh what a splendid and noble city! What fine monasteries, what elegant palaces we saw, what superb workmanship! How many superb works … It would take too long to describe the richness of all kinds of goods, of silver and gold, fine clothes and sacred relics.' The Frankish lords were also suspicious of, and perhaps a little intimidated by, the courtly ritual of the Byzantine Empire.

◄ *Constantinople retained its great beauty through centuries of conflict.*

▲ *Godfrey of Bouillon and his army praise God as they make the passage across the Bosphorus into Anatolia, moving closer to their ultimate destination, Jerusalem.*

city walls. Godfrey was unwilling to swear the proposed oath of loyalty, maintaining that he could not became a vassal of Alexius since his feudal lord was the German emperor Henry IV. He attempted to play for time, since he wanted to wait for the other European lords to arrive. Alexius, on the other hand, was concerned about what might happen if Godfrey, Bohemond of Taranto and other lords marshalled their armies at Constantinople at the same time: he was absolutely determined to move on Godfrey's troops before Bohemond arrived, but he could not do so until Godfrey agreed to swear the oath. Alexius cut off the food supplies to the crusader camp, but when this provoked an outburst of looting and then scavenging he began to provide food once more.

The waiting game continued until, growing desperate, Alexius cut off the food to the camp again. This time Godfrey and his army launched a military attack on Constantinople, which provoked panic among the citizens. Alexius decided to move the army on without requiring Godfrey to swear the oath but the men he sent with this message were attacked by the crusaders before they could deliver the information. Finally, Alexius lost his patience and unleashed the imperial military on the crusader camp. This was enough to bring Godfrey and his brothers to heel and on Easter Sunday, 5 April 1097 they swore the required oaths, recognizing Alexius as their overlord and promising to return to him any conquests they made in former Byzantine territories. The next day, Godfrey and his troops were transported across the Bosphorus.

THE NORMAN CONTINGENT

Three days later, on 9 April, Bohemond of Taranto arrived. According to contemporary sources, Bohemond declared 'I come by my own free will to be a friend to your Majesty'; Alexius housed him in magnificent quarters and gave him splendid gifts. Contemporary accounts report that Bohemond asked to be named as deputy or chief commander to Alexius in Asia, but Alexius was noncommittal. Bohemond was happy to swear the oath that Alexius

suggested, although he set little store by it and had no intention of keeping it. They moved on: on 26 April the Norman army was transported across the Bosphorus and joined the troops of Godfrey of Bouillon in Anatolia. Bohemond's nephew Tancred, however, had refused to swear the oath and slipped out of Constantinople by night to escape having to do so.

RAYMOND OF TOULOUSE AND ROBERT OF NORMANDY

That very same day saw the arrival at Constantinople of the army of Raymond of Toulouse. It had not had an easy march, and had even come under attack from imperial forces. Raymond refused to swear an oath to Alexius as his overlord, but promised to return conquered lands.

The final groups of arrivals, Duke Robert of Normandy, his brother-in-law Stephen, Count of Blois, and Count Robert II of Flanders agreed to swear the oath. According to chronicler Fulcher of Chartres, who travelled in their company, swearing the oath was 'essential to make good our friendship with the emperor, for without his advice and help we would not be able to make the journey we planned'.

THE SIEGE OF NICAEA

THE CRUSADERS MAKE THEIR MARK

The princely and noble leaders of the First Crusade were now gathered in Anatolia at the head of an army of perhaps 60,000 men. They agreed that they should move first against Nicaea, the capital of the Turkish sultanate of Rum, for it was clear that the crusade could not safely advance beyond Nicaea towards Jerusalem if the city remained in Turkish hands.

The crusaders were not a united force, for there were many rivalries between lords, and regional, cultural and linguistic differences among the knights and

▼ Under heavy attack by the forces of the Seljuk sultan, Kilij Arslan, the crusaders' rally was later attributed to heavenly aid.

soldiers. In addition to the main army there were many non-combatants – women and children, some of them families of crusaders, as well as aged pilgrims and clergy – and the battered remnants of the People's Crusade. There was also a Byzantine force, around 2,000 strong, supplied by Alexius and under the command of an experienced general named Taticius; Alexius's order was that the crusaders would give the command of cities and territories they captured to Taticius.

CRUSADERS ENCAMP AT NICAEA

The crusader army arrived at Nicaea in instalments – the first groups, under Godfrey of Bouillon, Robert of Flanders,

▲ During the siege of Nicaea, the crusaders lobbed the heads of corpses into the city.

Tancred and Taticius arrived on 6 May and were reinforced a few days later by Bohemond of Taranto. On 14 May a large force under Raymond of Toulouse swelled their numbers, and the final contingent, under Robert of Normandy and Stephen of Blois, joined the camp on 3 June.

The city of Nicaea, on the eastern side of Lake Iznik, was an ancient Christian town, where, in AD325, the Church's first General Council had agreed the statement of Catholic Christian beliefs still known as the Nicene Creed. Situated just 50 miles (80km) from Constantinople, it was for centuries part of the Byzantine Empire, but had been captured by the Seljuk Turks in 1077. The crusaders surrounded it on three sides and settled in for a siege; they were unable, however, to blockade the lake approaches so the city could still bring in supplies. Emperor Alexius provided the crusader army with supplies and siege equipment.

ABSENT RULER RETURNS

Kilij Arslan, the Sultan of Rum, was not present to defend his capital. Not expecting any greater threat from the new wave of crusaders than he had experienced from the ineffective armies of the People's Crusade, he had departed to fight rival ruler Ghazi ibn Danishmend in Sivas (also

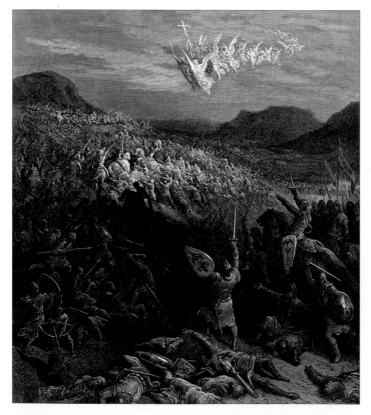

known as Sebastea), several hundred miles away at the eastern edge of his territory. (The Danishmends were named after dynastic founder Ghazi ibn Danishmend; he had captured the Roman city of Sebastea and renamed it Sivas, making it his capital in c.1080.) When Kilij Arslan received messages to the effect that a large and apparently well-equipped army was besieging Nicaea, he made a hurried peace with Danishmend and rushed back.

By mid-May Kilij Arslan was in the vicinity of Nicaea, viewing the crusader forces with dismay. On 16 May he launched a surprise attack on the recently arrived army of Raymond of Toulouse, which was still setting up camp to the south of the town. It was a fierce clash, in which Raymond showed great skill to hold his force together until reinforcements sent by Godfrey of Bouillon arrived and decided the conflict in the crusaders' favour. A notable casualty, according to the account in a letter written by Stephen of Blois, was Baldwin, Count of Ghent. Kilij Arslan withdrew and gathered his forces in the hills to fight another day.

The siege of Nicaea lasted six weeks. The crusaders had only lightweight siege equipment and were unable to do significant damage to the town walls; they were

▼ *Nicaea's walls, about 32ft (10m) tall, ran for a total of 3 miles (5km). The west wall gave directly on to the lake.*

limited to hurling small rocks, flaming missiles, beehives, the heads of corpses and other foul objects at the defenders. They could not smash their way into the town and since the town garrison could bring in supplies across the water of the lake, there was no hope of starving them out. There seemed to be no end in sight.

OUTMANOEUVRED BY ALEXIUS

Emperor Alexius was keeping a close watch on events from a camp at Pelecanum nearby. He wanted to regain control of Nicaea in good condition for the Byzantine Empire, and so wanted to prevent the crusaders destroying its defences, overrunning the city and looting its wealth. With typical cunning, he went behind the backs of the crusaders, opening secret negotiations with the Turks in Nicaea. He promised them good treatment if they would surrender to him; if they did, he would protect them with his own troops against the crusaders.

On the morning of 19 June the crusaders prepared to launch a major attack on the town and saw to their initial puzzlement and then dismay that the Byzantine standard was flying above the walls. The Byzantine troops were in control of the city. They acted as guards, only

▲ *Nicaea was an important city for Christians, where a groundbreaking council had taken place in AD325 to formulate what became known as the Nicene Creed.*

allowing the crusaders inside the walls in small groups. Alexius laid on food and wine for the crusading army and made gifts of jewels and gold to the leaders, but the crusaders remained deeply unhappy at having been outmanoeuvred and denied the riches they had expected to gain from looting.

In the aftermath, Alexius had a stand-off with Tancred: he refused to give Tancred his share of the gold unless the prince swore an oath of fealty. Tancred insisted that his loyalty was to Bohemond, not to Alexius; and he demanded as much gold as all the other lords put together, plus the amount it would take to fill Alexius's campaign tent. The tense situation was only resolved when Bohemond persuaded Tancred to give way.

Despite the crusaders' disappointment at the outcome in Nicaea, the future looked bright. Stephen of Blois wrote to his wife Countess Adela declaring they would be in Jerusalem in just five weeks. In fact, the crusaders' journey to the Holy City was to take more than two years.

MEN OF IRON
THE BATTLE OF DORYLAEUM

Near Dorylaeum (modern Eskiehir) on the Anatolian plateau, the crusaders were attacked by a Seljuk Turkish army led by Kilij Arslan, Sultan of Rum. The battle, on 1 July 1097, was fierce and long – from the third hour to the ninth, according to the Frankish chronicle the *Gesta Francorum*. After weathering a Turkish assault, the crusaders were reinforced when the rear of their army caught up and turned the tables to win a great victory.

BUILD-UP TO THE BATTLE
Following the capture of Nicaea, the crusaders set out eastwards across the Anatolian plateau towards their ultimate goal, Jerusalem. In the vanguard of the army were around 20,000 Normans under Bohemond of Taranto, his nephew Tancred and other noblemen; in the rear, around a day behind, were some 30,000 Franks led by Raymond of Toulouse, Godfrey of Bouillon and other lords. Kilij Arslan, who was smarting at the loss of his

capital city Nicaea, had retreated to the mountains and, in alliance with Ghazi ibn Danishmend, prepared an ambush for the Christian invaders. The Turkish army was probably about 20,000–30,000 strong – although the contemporary crusader accounts claim it was much bigger, with Raymond of Aguilers suggesting 150,000 and Fulcher of Chartres reporting 360,000 men under Kilij Arslan's command.

Bohemond noticed that Turkish scouts were watching the crusaders' vanguard, and on the evening of 30 June, three days' march out of Nicaea, set up a defensive camp near the town of Dorylaeum. At once, he sent a messenger riding at breakneck speed back to the army's rearguard, with an urgent summons for the Franks to come to the rescue of their comrades.

DAWN ONSLAUGHT
The Turks attacked at dawn the next day, 1 July. Bohemond ordered his knights to form a defensive line, while the foot

soldiers and women took refuge in the camp. He ordered that no one was to try to charge the attackers – they were to put all their efforts into holding them at bay. The plan was to defend the camp until the rest of the army caught up.

Rather than engaging the crusaders in a pitched battle of foot soldiers and cavalry of the kind fought in Europe, the Turks surrounded the camp and attacked from all sides. The Turkish army was all cavalry: its horsemen swept in from every direction, then swerved away at the last moment, sending a storm of spears and arrows into the camp. The attack was strange and terrifying for the crusaders – as Fulcher of Chartres wrote, 'this form of warfare was not known to us'. The *Gesta*

▼ *Heavily armoured crusaders clash head on with the Turks. At Dorylaeum the Franks were amazed at the size of the Turkish army, while the Turks marvelled at the ferocity of the crusaders' charge.*

▲ *When properly deployed, a fully armoured cavalry backed up by foot soldiers and archers was a formidable force.*

Francorum reported, 'the Turks were attacking us from all sides … we were not able to resist or weather the force of so many'. The defence was brave, but seemed ultimately hopeless.

Many of the pilgrims who accompanied the soldiers were killed, and those huddled in the camp feared that they would be slain. According to contemporary accounts, while some women ran tirelessly back and forward bringing water to the cavalry, others seem to have been quickly convinced that defeat was inevitable and set about making themselves as attractive as possible as a way of averting death by winning admirers among the Turks.

REINFORCEMENTS TO THE RESCUE

For six hours the army of Kilij Arslan and his allies kept up the assault. They were breaking through the crusaders' defences and an end to the battle was in sight. But at this moment, the rear of the crusaders' army rode in to the rescue.

On their arrival, a group of knights under Raymond of Toulouse attacked the Turks from the flank. Then the crusader cavalry drew up swiftly in battle formation, with Godfrey of Bouillon and Hugh

of Vermandois aligning themselves to the right of Bohemond, and Stephen of Blois and Robert of Normandy to the left. They attacked, a great wall of cavalry, bristling with lances, thundering across the field.

THE LURE OF RICHES

The battle continued. The crusaders were no longer in desperate straits, but they were unable to drive the Turks off. According to the *Gesta Francorum*, the crusaders marvelled at the size of the Turkish army and knowing that these essentially nomadic men carried their riches with them, they looked forward to seizing some of the wealth they had missed out on when they had been denied the chance to sack Nicaea. They declared: 'Let us all be one in faith in Christ and in the victory of the Holy Cross because this day, God willing it, we shall become rich!'

Then knights under the papal legate Bishop Adhemar of

Le Puy launched a surprise attack on the Turks from the rear, having ridden round under cover of some low hills. The army of Kilij Arslan, now tiring, and fearing being surrounded, broke and fled. The crusaders rode in triumph through the enemy camp, setting it afire and looting the riches in its tents.

VICTORY FOR THE 'MEN OF IRON'

The Turks' casualties were very heavy. Probably around 4,000 crusaders died; among them was Tancred's brother, William. Disaster had been very close at Dorylaeum: defeat would have brought the crusade to a premature end, but victory reinforced the crusaders' belief in their holy mission.

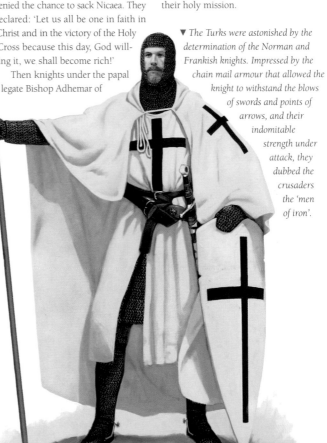

▼ *The Turks were astonished by the determination of the Norman and Frankish knights. Impressed by the chain mail armour that allowed the knight to withstand the blows of swords and points of arrows, and their indomitable strength under attack, they dubbed the crusaders the 'men of iron'.*

DEFENDER OF JERUSALEM
GODFREY OF BOUILLON

French knight Godfrey of Bouillon did not play a leading role in the First Crusade until its final stages, when he was one of the first Christians into Jerusalem on 15 July 1099 and after its capture became the first ruler of the Latin Kingdom of Jerusalem. He died only a year later, but he succeeded in consolidating the kingdom, and within a century of his death had become a hero of medieval legend, celebrated in chansons about the crusade that were told by *trouvères* (troubadours) at the noble courts of Europe as early as the 12th century.

Born in 1060 in northern France or Belgium, perhaps in Boulogne-sur-Mer, Godfrey was lord of Bouillon, a castle and village in the Ardennes forest of France, and from 1087 duke of Lower Lorraine. Most of Godfrey's life before he left in his

▼ *When Jerusalem was taken by the Christians on 15 July 1099, Godfrey is said to have been one of the first knights to scale the battlements of the city.*

mid-30s on crusade was spent asserting his right to the lordship of Lower Lorraine against attempts by Henry IV, King of Germany and ultimately Holy Roman Emperor, to take these territories away.

FINANCING THE CRUSADE
In 1095, inspired by Pope Urban's call to crusade, Godfrey either sold or agreed loans against his substantial landholdings and thereby raised a large force of knights. He also accepted money from Jewish communities in the Rhineland who were desperately attempting to buy safety in the face of repeated atrocities by crusaders. With his brothers Baldwin and Eustace, Godfrey embarked with an army of perhaps 40,000 from Lorraine in August 1096. They reached Constantinople in November, the second of the princely armies to arrive, following that of Hugh of Vermandois, brother of Philip I of France.

When the following year the crusaders set out for Jerusalem, Godfrey and his knights played only a supporting role in

the conflicts en route, such as the capture of Nicaea and Antioch, while in between those two events, he and his contingent were part of the force that rode to the rescue of the beleaguered vanguard of the crusader army at the Battle of Dorylaeum. After Antioch, he took part in the march on Jerusalem and the siege of the city and was one of the first knights to climb the walls when it was taken on 15 July 1099.

DEFENDER OF THE HOLY SEPULCHRE
A week later, in a meeting of the crusade leaders in the Church of the Holy Sepulchre in Jerusalem on 22 July, Godfrey was elected ruler of the newly established Latin Kingdom of Jerusalem. He did not accept the title of king in a city where the crusaders believed that Christ himself was the only true ruler, and was known either as *Princeps* (Prince) or as *Advocatus Sancti Sepulchri* (Defender of the Holy Sepulchre).

According to the *Gesta Francorum*, Godfrey's task as ruler was to 'subdue the pagans and defend the Christians'. He set about ensuring the survival of the new kingdom, which was by no means certain, for the great majority of the crusaders departed, leaving him with a force of only 300 knights and 2,000 infantry and without a fleet with which to mount naval blockades of Muslim cities along the coast. He agreed truces with the cities of Acre, Ascalon and Caesarea and, most important of all in the short term, succeeded in defeating the Egyptian army in the Battle of Ascalon.

DEATH AND LEGACY
On 18 July, less than a year after his election, Godfrey died in Jerusalem. He was around 40 years old. Accounts of how he died differ: the Muslim chronicler Ibn al-Qalansi reported that Godfrey was shot by an arrow while besieging Acre, but

Christian chroniclers wrote that he fell ill in Caesarea in June and succumbed to the illness on 18 July in Jerusalem – some versions allege he was poisoned by the emir of Caesarea.

Godfrey was succeeded by his younger brother Baldwin – according to the chronicler Radulph of Caen, before he died he called the Patriarch of Jerusalem and leading secular lords and warned them, saying they needed to consider formally who should succeed him, but they asked him to nominate his successor and when he named Baldwin they were pleased and pledged to be loyal subjects to him.

THE LEGEND OF GODFREY OF BOUILLON

It was Godfrey's position as the first ruler of Jerusalem and his achievement in securing the future of the Latin kingdom there that established his towering reputation in medieval legend. In the stories that

▼ The enduring fame and memory of Godfrey of Bouillon is honoured by a fine equestrian statue in Place Royale, Brussels.

▲ The clergy, knights and citizens of the young Kingdom of Jerusalem mourn Godfrey at his funeral on 23 July 1100.

quickly began to circulate, he was presented as an exemplar of fearless chivalry and a man of immense strength – in one story he wrestled a bear into submission, in another he beheaded a camel with one skilful stroke of his sword. William of Tyre, whose chronicle of the Kingdom of Jerusalem was written in the late 12th century when the myth of Godfrey was already established, described him as taller than average, with solid limbs, a brawny chest and 'strong beyond any comparison'; William reported that the hero was good-looking, with blond hair and beard. Godfrey was certainly an intelligent man and a forceful character, but there is little evidence that he was truly devout, and he was certainly not the paragon of Christian virtue that he became in his legend.

THE MARCH ACROSS ANATOLIA
AND THE ESTABLISHMENT OF THE COUNTY OF EDESSA

Following their victory in the Battle of Dorylaeum, the crusaders rested for two days and then marched onwards to the south. They headed across the Anatolian plateau bound for Antioch in Pisidia and thence on to Iconium.

A HELLISH SUMMER
It was summer and the gruelling heat took a heavy toll on the army. According to chronicler Albert of Aix, the suffering was terrible: children, women, animals and soldiers died at the roadside from thirst and heat exhaustion; some women gave birth in the dust and were too weak to do anything but stagger on, abandoning their babies in the roadway; when a river was reached, many more people and their ani-

mals died from drinking too much. Albert claims that 500 people died in a single day from the effects of the heat. It seemed to the crusaders that far from arriving in the paradise of a land flowing in milk and honey, as promised by Urban II, they had arrived in hell.

Near Heraclea, the crusaders had to muster the strength to fight a Turkish army under two emirs from Cappadocia; the battle was soon over, for the Turkish army – perhaps made nervous by reports of the crusaders' exploits at Dorylaeum – dispersed and fled when Bohemond gathered his finest knights and charged at speed with couched lance.

In September the crusaders arrived at the Cilician Gates, the daunting pass

▲ *The people of Edessa pay homage to Baldwin I, King of Jerusalem.*

through the snow-covered Taurus Mountains that lay between the Anatolian plateau and the Mediterranean coast. By this stage almost all the travellers' pack animals had died and many knights were without horses, having to ride on oxen and force dogs to pull carts.

The weather was still hot and dry and the crusaders decided that if they took the pass, they would be vulnerable to guerrilla attacks from the Turks. The main body of the army now marched north-east, away from the Cilician Gates, into easier wooded country towards Armenian lands. In these territories, the crusaders could expect a welcome: the Armenians were Christians who had been evicted from their lands in the southern Caucasus by Byzantine forces and so had little affection for the emperor of Constantinople. They were also enemies of the Turks.

FIGHTING OVER TARSUS
A smaller force of around 100 knights and 200 foot soldiers under Tancred elected to split off from the main army, risk the passage through the Cilician Gates and attempt an assault on the Turkish-garrisoned town of Tarsus on the plain beyond. At Tarsus, Tancred succeeded in driving out the Turks and raising his own banner, with the help of reinforcements of 500 knights and 2,000 foot soldiers led by

---

FIRST-HAND ACCOUNTS OF THE FIRST CRUSADE

Such was the impact made by the crusaders' success in librating Jerusalem that several histories were written soon afterwards. *Gesta Francorum* (Deeds of the Franks) was written almost immediately after the capture of Jerusalem in *c.*1100 by an anonymous follower of Bohemond of Taranto. Fulcher of Chartres, a churchman who travelled in the party of Stephen of Blois, also wrote a history of the crusade perhaps as early as 1101–06. The history of Raymond of Aguilers, chaplain to Raymond, Count of Toulouse, is rich in accounts of visions and miracles – including the discovery of the Holy Lance at Antioch. Radulph of Caen was chaplain to Bohemond of Taranto and he wrote a biography of Bohemond's nephew, Tancred, in *c.*1112. Albert of Aix (also known as Albert of Aachen) wrote a 12-volume history of the First Crusade and the early history of the Latin Kingdom of Jerusalem in *c.*1125–50; Albert's is the most detailed chronicle of the First

Crusade. Among other first-hand accounts of events of the time are Anna Comnena's biography of her father, Emperor Alexius, and the writings of Armenian Christian Matthew of Edessa. There are also later accounts of events of the First Crusade written by Muslim chroniclers, including Ibn al-Athir and Sibt Ibn al-Jawsi.

▼ *In the aftermath of the crusade, churchmen recorded God's triumphs.*

Baldwin of Boulogne, brother of Godfrey of Bouillon. The two knights then disputed the spoils: Baldwin had led his men through the Cilician Gates not to help Tancred but in order to prevent him (and thereby his uncle Bohemond) from taking control of the coast.

Rival lords were coming into open and bitter conflict as they disputed control of captured territories. In this instance, Baldwin had many more knights and soldiers than Tancred, so Tancred gave way. When more of Bohemond's knights arrived at Tarsus, Baldwin refused to open the city gates and they were put to the sword in an attack by Turkish troops. Tancred moved on and took control first of Adana and then of Mamistra. Baldwin followed. The two armies fought, but finally agreed to withdraw from the coast.

ON TO ANTIOCH

The main army had a terrible time crossing the Anti-Taurus Mountains that stood inland, behind the Taurus range. By this time it was October and heavy rains had begun – in wet conditions, the steep tracks were almost impassable. The army limped across the mountains and moved on

▼ *During the lengthy siege of Antioch, various plots to take the city by stealth were attempted, and rumours of secret truces and intercepted messengers were rife.*

towards the city of Antioch. Tancred, meanwhile, had captured Alexandretta, crossed into Syria and was reunited with the main army as they prepared to besiege Antioch in October 1097.

BALDWIN ESTABLISHES THE COUNTY OF EDESSA

For his part, Baldwin headed north-east to the town of Edessa, an important and wealthy Armenian town to the east of the River Euphrates, while the main army settled in for the siege of Antioch. Edessa was governed by an Armenian Christian

▲ *Baldwin of Boulogne, seen here in a particularly viciously fought battle against the Seljuk Turks, became the King of Jerusalem in 1100.*

named Thoros, who had only two years earlier captured it from the Turks. Thoros's position was far from secure: he was surrounded on all sides by Seljuk emirs who were all too keen to depose him. He was happy to welcome a fellow Christian in Baldwin, and to accept the support of his fighting men. Baldwin, clearly sensing possibility, demanded that Thoros adopt him as his son and heir, which he did in a public ceremony.

Shortly afterwards, Thoros was killed during a revolt by the townspeople, who were said to hate him because he was a Greek Orthodox rather than an Armenian Orthodox Christian. Baldwin became ruler, calling himself Count of Edessa. Thoros's death was highly convenient for Baldwin, but we do not know for sure that he masterminded it – indeed, his contemporary supporters vehemently denied that he had any involvement.

Baldwin thereby established the County of Edessa, the first of the crusader territories that would be created in the course of the First Crusade.

BOUND FOR JERUSALEM

The extraordinary events of June 1098 at Antioch were the turning point of the First Crusade. In that month the crusaders twice went from despair to wild elation. At the start of June they were bogged down in a siege of the city that they had been enforcing since October 1097 with little progress, and were expecting the arrival within days of a vast Seljuk Turkish army led by Sultan Kerbogha of Mosul, who had every intention of lifting the siege. One of their leaders, Stephen of Blois, abandoned the enterprise and departed for home. They were starving, and frightened, and desperate. Then they took the city through cunning and subterfuge on the night of 2 June, and rejoiced wildly and raucously. But within three days they were plunged into despair again, when Kerbogha arrived and besieged them. Within the city they wondered if the entire crusade would come to nothing, but after visions of St Andrew and the discovery of what was purportedly the Holy Lance – the spear with which Christ's side was pierced on the cross – morale soared. On 28 June the crusaders threw open the gates of Antioch and rode out behind Bishop Adhemar bearing the Holy Lance to take on the huge army of Sultan Kerbogha. Despite being vastly outnumbered, they won, and claimed it as a miracle. Antioch was safe, and as soldiers of Christ riding in a divinely ordained mission to liberate Jerusalem; the crusaders must triumph.

▲ *The town of Latakia was one of the key ports in Syria. The crusader armies were dependent on it for the delivery of supplies.*

◄ *The crusaders at last reach Jerusalem, and give thanks and praise to God for a hard-won achievement that has taken so much longer than expected.*

THE SIEGE OF ANTIOCH
A LONG STRUGGLE TO WEAR DOWN THE CITY'S DEFENCES

The crusader army drew up before Antioch in October 1097. The city lay in a vital position on the route from Anatolia into Syria, and the crusader lords knew that they had to capture it before moving southwards through Syria and on down the Mediterranean coast towards the city of Jerusalem.

FORBIDDING DEFENCES

At once the crusader lords saw that capturing Antioch was a daunting task, for it had 400 towers set in 25 miles (40km) of defensive walls running across very hostile terrain. A siege would be difficult – the city stood on the bank of the River Orontes, so was very well supplied with water, and there were even areas of pasture set safely within the forbidding walls. Military attack was impossible from the north, because of the river, and from the south because of the forbidding bulk of Mount Silphius, site of Antioch's citadel. Writing home, Stephen of Blois called the city 'unassailable' and by general consensus the city was deemed to be impossible to take by force: the Arabs had captured it in AD637, and since that time it had only been taken twice – by the Byzantine Empire from Arabs in 969 and by Seljuk Turks from the Byzantines in the 1080s – both times by treachery.

In October 1097 when the crusaders set up camp before the city, Antioch was in the hands of a Turkish governor, Yaghi-Siyan, ruling on behalf of the Seljuk sultan in Baghdad, Barkiyaroq. The citizens were mostly Christians, a combination of Orthodox Greeks, Armenians and Syrians, most of whom disliked their governor heartily. Taking a precaution against possible treachery, Yaghi-Siyan made himself more unpopular by expelling the leading Christian citizens and jailing the Patriarch of Antioch, a very senior ecclesiastic on a par with the patriarchs of Constantinople and of Jerusalem.

TO ATTACK OR TO BESIEGE?

The crusader lords discussed how to proceed: Raymond of Toulouse argued for a military assault, but Bohemond urged a siege and an attempt to foster treachery within the city. Caution prevailed, and the army settled in for a siege. As autumn passed into winter, they had to deal with dwindling food supplies, regular sallies by the garrison and the taunting behaviour of Yaghi-Siyan, who put the Patriarch of Antioch in a cage, and hung it from the walls to enrage the Christians without. Stephen of Blois wrote to his wife, reporting that: 'We have lived through great

▲ Like the cities of Nicaea and Jerusalem, Antioch was surrounded by massive walls that demanded the construction of siege towers for any attack to be successful.

suffering and evils beyond counting. Many people have exhausted their finances, and others were saved from starvation only by the kindness of God. The cold is excessive and there are terrible deluges of rain.' In these months, having come so far, thousands of the poorer crusaders died of starvation; some people ate their horses, while there were even reports of cannibalism among the most desperate.

TWO RELIEF ARMIES ROUTED

The need for food grew so severe that in late December Bohemond and Robert of Flanders risked riding out on a foraging expedition up the fertile valley of the River Orontes. There they encountered a large Turkish army under Sultan Duqaq that was marching from Damascus to raise the siege of Antioch. In a tense battle, the crusaders recovered from a disastrous start, in which Robert of Flanders and his men were almost defeated, to launch a powerful counter-attack that drove the Turks off. Bohemond and Robert returned safely to Antioch, but without the supplies they had been seeking.

The New Year brought little comfort. Godfrey of Bouillon and Raymond of Toulouse fell ill. Robert of Normandy left the siege, withdrawing to Laodicea in Anatolia (near modern Eskihisar in Turkey). In February the Byzantine general Taticius took his troops north, either in search of supplies or else because he judged it more important to consolidate Byzantine gains in Anatolia than continue

▲ *Wearing his mitre in battle, papal legate Adhemar of Le Puy takes the battle to the Seljuks at Antioch. He carries the Holy Lance discovered within the city.*

▼ *During the long months of the siege at Antioch, the crusaders spent a great deal of time building siege equipment to drive home their assault, but they made little progress.*

a hopeless siege. Many began to despair, losing their faith in what they were doing; some deserted, including Peter the Hermit who was caught and forcibly brought back to Antioch by Tancred.

Then a fresh threat emerged: news arrived that a large relief army under Radwan, Seljuk ruler of Aleppo, had approached and had set up camp at Harenc, only 25 miles (40km) from Antioch, in preparation for launching an attack on the besieging army. The crusaders struck first: Bohemond led a company of knights out by night and surprised Radwan's army, winning a stunning victory despite being vastly outnumbered.

SIEGE EQUIPMENT

In March an English fleet under Edgar the Atheling, a claimant to the throne of England, arrived at St Symeon, the port of Antioch, with supplies, siege equipment and building materials. The crusaders tightened their grip on the city by building tall siege towers and a fort called the 'Castle of Raymond' opposite the city's Bridge Gate; Tancred established a position in a monastery opposite St George's Gate. Spring turned to summer and although the city was almost entirely encircled, the crusaders were no closer to taking it by force. It was clear that they would need to find someone in the city who was willing to betray his masters.

THE FALL OF ANTIOCH
THE CRUSADERS CAPTURE THE CITY

In May 1098 the crusading army encamped around Antioch received news that a mighty relief army was approaching under the command of the powerful Sultan Kerbogha of Mosul. It was clear that they needed to take the city before Kerbogha arrived, otherwise his force would either destroy the crusader army or drive it away – and all their efforts and suffering during the eight-month siege would have been wasted.

THE CRUSADERS ABANDONED
At this crucial moment Stephen of Blois, who had been elected commander-in-chief of the besieging army, abandoned the crusade. Deciding that the enterprise was doomed to failure and taking a sizeable contingent of French soldiers with him, he marched back towards Constantinople to take a ship for Europe.

▲ Betrayed to its besiegers, Antioch is overrun. The city has a European look in this 15th-century French illustration.

His timing could not have been worse, for Bohemond had found the ally he had been seeking within Antioch. This man was an Armenian, a Christian convert to Islam named Firuz, who commanded key defence towers overlooking the Gate of St George. Firuz had been fined for hoarding foods and according to some versions had discovered that his wife had been seduced by his superior officer. He was happy to have his revenge and profit by it.

BOHEMOND TAKES THE CITY
On the night of 2 June 1098 the crusading army feigned a retreat from the city walls. To Antioch's Turkish governor, Yaghi-Siyan, it looked as if the news of

Sultan Kerbogha's imminent arrival had forced the invading Christians to take fright and abandon the enterprise, or else to lift the siege in order to fight Kerbogha's army in open countryside.

But in the middle of the night, the treacherous watchman Firuz let down a rope beside the Gate of St George and allowed Bohemond to climb into the city. At the top, in the darkness, Bohemond felt his hand seized by another and heard a voice whisper: 'Long life to this hand.' He was followed in by a group of 60 knights. They succeeded in surprising the watchmen and guards and at dawn opened the Gates of St George and of the Bridge.

LOOTING AND DESTRUCTION
Meanwhile the main army had returned under cover of darkness and now they swept into the city. Terrible scenes followed, as the starving crusaders gave vent to their fear and greed, raping and killing, looting and burning. Many of the Christian citizens burst out from their houses into the streets to seek revenge against the Turkish overlords, but were killed in the confusion and lawlessness by the blood-crazed crusaders.

A few Turks survived by taking refuge in the citadel under the command of a son of Yaghi-Siyan. As for Yaghi-Siyan himself, he escaped on horseback, but fell and was knocked unconscious during his flight to the mountains; his companions left him for dead, but some Armenians found him and, recognizing his face, cut off his head. They brought the corpse and its head to Bohemond in Antioch and were given a substantial reward.

The crusaders, when their heads cleared, praised God. Another victory had been achieved that had seemed impossible. They had taken the impregnable city of Antioch. It was beginning to seem as if their success in the crusade truly was to be guaranteed by God.

THE TAFURS

The most intense members of the crusader army were the Tafurs, poor soldiers originally part of the People's Crusade who were fired with wild religious fanaticism. According to Guibert of Nogent they marched barefoot and without weapons, living on the roots of plants, as a kind of holy army, and led by their own king of the Tafurs. They were notorious among the enemy – their name comes from the Arabic *tafuria*, meaning 'poverty-stricken'. They were always associated with the most extreme behaviour of the army, for instance performing acts of cannibalism during the siege of Antioch or later at Maarrat an-Numan, and were said to have urged on soldiers to acts of cruelty against the enemy at Antioch and in Jerusalem. The Tafurs were later celebrated as the deserving poor in the crusade chanson, the *Chanson d'Antioch*, which suggested that God had led the crusaders to victory because of the Tafurs' religious devotion.

▶ *The 'king' of the Tafurs was reputedly a wealthy Norman knight, who took pity on their plight and gave up his position and comforts to become their leader.*

TRAPPED INSIDE THE CITY

But in the days following their victory, the Christians' delight turned to fear once more. Sultan Kerbogha arrived on 6 June and set his army before the city. The besiegers became the besieged.

There was little food within Antioch. Kerbogha's troops took possession of the citadel and the crusaders had to fight determinedly to prevent them flooding over its walls into the city.

The crusaders pinned their hopes increasingly desperately on relief from Emperor Alexius, who had set out with an army from Constantinople in the spring. But these hopes were empty: Alexius had met the fleeing Stephen of Blois, who had described the critical situation at Antioch. Alexius, convinced that the crusaders' cause was lost, had turned back.

The crusaders' numbers were cut further by desertions – those who fled were derided as 'rope-danglers', presumably because they used ropes to climb from the city walls. By this stage, the Christian army probably numbered no more than 30,000. The crusaders' position was desperate.

▶ *Flooding into the city after months of frustration, the crusaders ran amok. Terrified citizens jumped to their deaths to avoid being torn limb from limb.*

MIRACLES AT ANTIOCH

FIRED WITH BELIEF, THE CRUSADERS DEFEAT SULTAN KERBOGHA

In early June, as we have seen, the crusaders were at the lowest of ebbs. Once the euphoria of breaking into Antioch had died down, they found themselves besieged and starving in the city.

Then, on 11 June, a priest named Stephen of Valence reported to the papal legate Bishop Adhemar that he had had a vision of the Blessed Virgin Mary and of Christ himself and that Christ had promised to come to the army's aid. Around the same time, a Provençal peasant named Peter Bartholomew reported that he had had a whole series of visions of St Andrew, who had revealed that the Holy Lance – the spear with which Christ's side was pierced on the cross – was within Antioch, buried beneath the Church of St Peter. There were other portents, including a meteor that seemed to fall directly on to Sultan Kerbogha's besieging army.

▼ *Soldiers fall to their knees in awe as Peter Bartholomew presents the Holy Lance (the spear that pierced Christ's side on the cross). The illustration is from an edition of William of Tyre's crusade history made for King Edward IV of England.*

THE DISCOVERY OF THE HOLY LANCE

On 14 June an excavation was carried out in the Church of St Peter: at first the digging soldiers found nothing, but then Peter leapt into the hole, dressed only in a shirt, and triumphantly brandished a length of metal that he declared to be the lance. A few sceptics doubted, but most were swept up in a wave of delirious rejoicing. Here was proof that God was on their side. They need fear no more.

THE DEFEAT OF KERBOGHA

The leaders prepared for battle and on 20 June elected Bohemond commander-in-chief. Bishop Adhemar ordered a three-day fast (not much of a challenge, since most were already without food) in repentance of their sins and preparation for battle. At first light on 28 June the soldiers attended Mass then flung open the city gates and marched out to take on the army of Sultan Kerbogha.

They marched behind Bishop Adhemar holding the Holy Lance and priests dressed in white and carrying crosses

▲ *Reported visions of the Blessed Virgin Mary and of Christ himself in Antioch, together with the discovery of the Holy Lance, raised feelings among the crusaders to such a fever pitch that they came to believe themselves invincible.*

while they prayed aloud. Their chances of success seemed to be nil. The encircling army was vast. The crusaders were weak from hunger. In previous encounters on crusade, their strength had been the mounted charge of knights with couched lances, but now they had only around 200 horses left alive. Many of the knights had to fight on foot.

According to the *Gesta Francorum*, as the crusaders emerged from the city they saw a great host on white horses and bearing pure white banners charging to their aid. This was – they afterwards reported in awe – nothing less than a heavenly army commanded by saints George, Demetrius and Mercury riding in to ensure that God's will was done. This was in line with the prophecies of the Last Days in the biblical Book of Revelation,

▶ *At Antioch the crusaders built this façade in front of a cave believed to have been used as the very first Christian place of worship by St Peter and followers in* c.AD40–50.

which declared that the heavenly armies following the Word of God 'were upon white horses, clothed in fine linen, white and clean'.

The crusaders, calling on God's name, charged the Turkish army. Amazingly, the Turks broke up and fled. A letter written by the leaders of the crusade to Pope Urban II, describing the victory, declared 'from the very first clash on the battlefield we drove the enemy back'.

Kerbogha had split his force between an advance group near Antioch's Bridge Gate and a main camp no less than 3 miles (5km) away. Charged by the crusaders, the advance group fled just as Kerbogha arrived with the main army from the camp. The main force then also abandoned the battle – perhaps partly because they were surprised by the discipline and ferocity of the crusaders' assault but principally, according to Islamic sources, because the sultan's rivals in the army wanted to prevent Kerbogha capturing Antioch and so called off their men at the very last moment.

Finally Kerbogha set fire to the sun-dried battlefield in a last desperate attempt to change the course of the conflict, but to no avail. The crusaders were afire with belief, and fought like men possessed; they had no desire to flee since behind them was only the empty city where they had been starving to death. In the citadel above the city, the Turkish garrison watched Sultan Kerbogha's army flee and knew that their chance had gone. They sent a message of surrender to Raymond of Toulouse. The crusaders had complete control of the city. The letter to Pope Urban II continued: 'the right hand of God fought on our side … our Lord Jesus Christ brought the entire city of Antioch to the Roman religion and faith.'

THE HOLY LANCE AND ITS EFFECT ON THE CRUSADERS

In the medieval era Christians had a deep and powerful belief in the miraculous powers of relics of the life of Christ and other biblical figures. The astonishing effect of the Holy Lance on the crusaders can partly be explained as an effect of this belief. In addition, the majority of the crusaders were under extreme mental and physical stress – starving and desperate for hope – which would increase the likelihood of mass hysteria. The relic supposedly discovered by Peter Bartholomew was presented as the lance used by a Roman soldier to pierce the side of Christ while he was hanging on the cross, an event described only in the Gospel of St John and said to be the fulfilment of a prophecy in the Book of Psalms concerning the Messiah. Many crusaders in Antioch must have known and chosen to forget that a spear said to be the Holy Lance had been found in Jerusalem, where it was seen by many Christian pilgrims in and around the 5th–6th centuries AD; by the time of the First Crusade, this other spear was being kept in Constantinople.

▶ *In John's Gospel, the soldier was said to have pierced Christ's side with the lance rather than break his legs, which was normal practice with the crucified.*

THE PRINCE OF ANTIOCH

BOHEMOND OF TARANTO

Bohemond of Taranto, the Calabrian-born Norman knight who established himself as Prince of Antioch, was an inspirational leader of men and by far the most effective general among the knights of the First Crusade. He was also powerfully ambitious and primarily self-interested; the realization of his dream of establishing a personal principality meant far more to him than the official aims of the First Crusade. He did not even take part in the triumphant conclusion of the crusade, the capture of Jerusalem, having remained in Antioch to consolidate his position there.

BOHEMOND'S APPEARANCE AND CHARACTER

Anna Comnena, daughter of the Emperor Alexius, met Bohemond in Constantinople at the start of the First Crusade and left a vivid portrait of the man. She reported that Bohemond was astonishingly tall – she claimed he was 18 inches (45cm) taller than the tallest men; he had a narrow waist but broad chest and shoulders and very strong arms; he had a sturdy frame, she said, but a slightly stooping stance. His skin, she reported, was noticeably white, but his cheeks were red; his hair was light brown and worn shorter than was normal among the crusaders, cut just above the ears. He had grey eyes, which suggested (according to Anna) that he was a man of indomitable courage and great dignity. People were astonished at the sight of him.

Anna noted that Bohemond's size and strength made him frightening – even his laugh, she remembered, caused people to be nervous; in fact the mere mention of his name made people jittery. But he certainly also had charm. It was clear that courage and love ran deep in him, and he found expression for both these qualities in warfare. His intelligence was sharp – he always made ambiguous, non-committal replies to questions, and his mind 'ran

▲ *Bohemond climbs into Antioch on the night of 2 June 1098 after the watchman let down a rope ladder. He then threw the gates open to admit his fellow crusaders.*

over all possible outcomes' and 'dared all things'; his actions were often unpredictable, for he rushed into undertakings. Overall, he was 'like no other man ever found in the Byzantine Empire, whether a foreigner or a Greek'. It is a measure of the impression that Bohemond made that Anna's account, with its vivid details, was written around 40 years after she met him and that he was the only one of the crusader lords she described so closely.

THE YOUTHFUL GENERAL

Bohemond's father was the powerful Norman adventurer Robert Guiscard. As a baby, the future prince of Antioch was christened 'Mark' but as he grew was given the name 'Bohemond' by Guiscard in tribute to a legendary giant of that name. In 1080–85, in his early 20s, Bohemond proved himself a great general during Guiscard's daring invasion of the Byzantine Empire, and in 1082–84 while commanding the Norman army when

Guiscard was recalled to Italy, he won two major victories over Emperor Alexius. Bohemond was forced to abandon the campaign in 1084 through illness, and returned to Italy. Guiscard's death in 1085 was followed by a succession conflict in which Bohemond fought his half-brother Roger; this was ended by a settlement, favourable to Bohemond, imposed by Pope Urban II.

In 1096 Bohemond joined the First Crusade: in some accounts, he was besieging the rebel town of Amalfi (near Naples) when he encountered knights riding to the crusade and, impressed by their zeal, opted to join them. In other versions, such as that of the 11th-century Benedictine chronicler Geoffrey Malaterra, Bohemond saw the crusade from the start as a chance to continue his father's attack upon the Byzantine Empire and to carve out a principality there for himself.

A LEADER OF MEN

Throughout the early part of the First Crusade, Bohemond was the effective commander of the enterprise, an inspirational general and leader for the crusaders. At Dorylaeum through his quick thinking and tactical nous he averted disaster and held off the Turkish attacks until the main force of the crusader army could arrive. During the difficult months of the siege of Antioch Bohemond again proved his excellence as a general – not only defeating a large force under Sultan Duqaq that he encountered during a foraging mission, but also routing and driving back a substantial relief army under Radwan, Seljuk ruler of Aleppo.

Bohemond then almost single-handedly brought about the capture of Antioch through clandestine negotiations with the rebel Firuz within the city and a daring night-time raid. Afterwards, when the crusaders were besieged within the city by Sultan Kerbogha, when despair was

▲ *The crusader army had feigned a retreat but turned around and flooded into Antioch after Bohemond had opened the gates.*

mounting and desertions were commonplace, he remained inspirationally upbeat, touring the defensive positions, making sure that they were manned and lifting the spirits of the defenders with the example of his courage and self-belief.

After the discovery of the Holy Lance, Bohemond was privately sceptical that a miracle had occurred, but he knew well enough how to marshal the outpouring of emotion among the rank and file: he was elected commander-in-chief of the army by the lords, and in this capacity planned the army's tactics and oversaw the astonishing victory over the besiegers on 28 June 1098.

SEEKING CONTROL IN ANTIOCH

Throughout this period, however, Bohemond was also plotting to outmanoeuvre the other crusader lords and establish a private holding in his name at Antioch. He was even apparently willing to put this objective above the success of the crusade itself: during the siege his men spread discontent within the crusader camp, suggesting that a military assault would never succeed and that their cause was hopeless, so that when he established contact with an ally within the city and with the news that Sultan Kerbogha was approaching fast, he could negotiate hard, knowing that he held all the cards. From the other leaders he wrung the concession that he could keep Antioch if they won it. He proceeded with the capture of the city only when he knew that it would be his.

Bohemond remained in Antioch when the main crusading force marched on towards Jerusalem in January 1099. He watched the conquest from afar, and then visited Jerusalem at Christmas 1099 to fulfil his vows. On this occasion, wily as ever, he engineered the election of Dagobert of Pisa as Patriarch of Jerusalem to counteract the strength of the Lorrainer faction under Godfrey of Bouillon, who was by that time the effective king of Jerusalem.

AFTER THE CRUSADE

In 1100 Bohemond launched an attack on Danishmend, the warlike emir of Sivas (Sebastea), but was captured and thrown in jail. He stayed there for three whole years until being ransomed in 1103 by Baldwin of Le Bourg, at that time Count of Edessa and later King Baldwin II of Jerusalem. In the following year, Bohemond was heavily defeated by a Seljuk army after he attacked and besieged the city of Harran. After this setback Bohemond returned to Europe, where in 1105–06 he was hailed as a conquering hero for his part in the crusade.

Now Bohemond felt that he was poised for enduring greatness and after raising a large army he launched an attack on the Byzantine Empire. The enterprise failed, and Bohemond was forced to accept a peace treaty in 1108 by which he became the emperor's vassal. He died, humiliated and with his dream of creating a powerful independent principality broken.

However, he was able to pass Antioch on to his heirs, and was assured of everlasting fame for his reputation as a charismatic diplomat and general. Without his leadership, the crusade would have foundered at Dorylaeum or Antioch before it ever reached Jerusalem.

▼ *On his death in 1111, Bohemond was buried in this mausoleum at the Cathedral of San Sabino in Canosa di Puglia, Italy.*

THE WAY TO THE HOLY CITY
DELAY IN ANTIOCH PRECEDES THE MARCH SOUTH

The capture of Antioch appeared to open the way to Jerusalem. The army's morale was sky high, bolstered by the conviction that with the Holy Lance in their possession they were invincible because they fought with God's blessing. But this impetus and energy was wasted, allowed to drain away, while the princely and noble leaders of the crusade were locked in dispute over what should be done with Antioch.

Raymond of Toulouse insisted that Antioch be returned to Alexius in order to honour the vow that he and other lords, including Bohemond, had made while in Constantinople, to return captured lands to the Byzantine Empire. Bohemond claimed the city for himself and, as we have seen, before beginning the assault he had negotiated an agreement with the other lords that he should keep it; he argued that because Alexius had not come to the crusaders' aid when they were besieged in Antioch, and left them to God's mercy, that the vow no longer held. Nevertheless, Raymond sent a message to Alexius with Hugh of Vermandois to the effect that they would return Antioch to the empire if the emperor now agreed to bring an army to help them in the conquest of Jerusalem.

THE UNTIMELY DEATH OF BISHOP ADHEMAR

Just over a month after the capture of Antioch, the crusaders lost their spiritual leader when Bishop Adhemar, the papal legate, died of a plague that swept through the city. Adhemar's death was a great setback, for he had been a guiding presence, presiding over councils of leading lords, reminding all involved of the original purpose of the undertaking and attempting to restrain the leading lords from personal conflicts that might derail the crusade.

He had also been a visible leader of the army and played a major part in determining battle tactics. For example, prior to the siege of Antioch a crusader force under Robert of Normandy captured the Iron Bridge across the River Orontes 15 miles (24km) from Antioch, defeating a garrison sent from the city to do so; in this battle, on Bishop Adhemar's advice, they used a tortoise formation – the crusaders held their shields above their heads to form a protective barrier to hold off arrows fired by the defenders, and were able to advance largely unscathed and overpower the garrison. The formation was inspired by the *testudo* formation of the ancient Roman army, which the bishop probably read about in a Roman military treatise.

▲ *The crusader army finally began its march southwards from Antioch towards Jerusalem. Rank and file soldiers were convinced Heaven was lighting their way.*

THE ATTACK ON MAARRAT AN-NUMAN

The months dragged on, with little happening. Groups of crusaders raided the countryside around Antioch; some went north to join Count Baldwin in Edessa. In December an expedition was mounted to take the strategically significant town of Maarrat an-Numan to the south of Antioch. The army captured the town and slaughtered its 20,000 population and then, finding little or no food, they were allegedly reduced to cooking and eating some of the freshly slain inhabitants.

JERUSALEM BECKONS

The Holy City to which the crusaders were ultimately headed was no longer in the hands of the Seljuks. In 1098, while the crusaders were occupied at Antioch, an army of the Fatimid Vizier of Egypt, Al-Afdal Shahanshah, had retaken Jerusalem and Palestine as far north as Beirut – lands which they had only lost to the Seljuks in the early 1070s. The Fatimids had

---

CANNIBALISM AMONG THE CRUSADERS

According to accounts by Tancred's biographer Radulph of Caen, and in a letter to Pope Urban II, the troops at Maarrat an-Numan were driven by desperation and maddening hunger to commit acts of cannibalism. Guibert of Nogent, who discussed incidents of cannibalism in his *Historia Hierosolymitana*, reported that perhaps because of incidents such as this or perhaps because of wild rumour and speculation, the Turks and other 'Saracens' became convinced that it was common practice among the crusaders, whom they regarded as savages, to eat the flesh of their dead enemies. He then described an act of provocation by the Tafurs, who openly spit-roasted a slain Turkish prisoner in view of the Turks in order to madden and anger them – they had no intention of eating the man's flesh. It is probable that accounts of crusaders eating flesh were propaganda on behalf of Christian writers seeking to make the crusaders seem fierce.

---

declared that the city was open to Christian pilgrims, who could come and go safely – the city's holy places did not need rescuing.

Although the crusaders did not know this, the Byzantine emperor Alexius had effectively disowned them, declaring to the Vizier that he could not control and did not support them, and renewing an alliance with Fatimid Egypt. Yet the bulk of the crusaders were desperate to march on Jerusalem, determined to fulfil their vows to reach the city and worship in the Church of the Holy Sepulchre, and driven by the conviction that they were engaged in a divinely inspired war fighting for Christ and his saints.

While the leading crusaders continued to hesitate, the lesser lords and knights – together with members of the army's rank and file – urged the continuation of the crusade. They offered to recognize Raymond of Toulouse as leader of the crusade if he would command them on the way to Jerusalem. Raymond accepted, giving way in the stand-off and allowing Bohemond to keep Antioch.

Finally, in mid-January 1099, walking barefoot as a pilgrim, Raymond finally left Antioch and began the journey southwards towards Jerusalem, leading a force of 5,000 crusaders. Tancred and Robert of Normandy followed with their troops almost immediately, while Robert of Normandy and Godfrey of Bouillon caught up around a month later.

PROGRESS SOUTHWARDS

The crusaders encountered little opposition as they marched south, partly because local lords – following the defeat of Kerbogha and the advance of the Fatimids – thought that dealing with the Christians was a way of exploiting the changing balance of power to their own advantage, and partly because the rulers simply wanted

▼ *As the crusader army advanced through the Holy Land, its reputation for ferocity and acts of barbarity preceded it.*

▲ *Local lords were willing to make deals with the crusaders so they would pass by and become someone else's problem.*

to keep the crusaders moving on, avoiding the devastation that would follow from conflict, and making the bedraggled army another ruler's problem.

The crusaders captured the port of Tortosa, strategically important for maintaining their supply line, and then passed Tripoli on the coast of Lebanon on 16 May without attacking, after its emir agreed to pay them protection money and supplied them with horses and provisions. They proceeded down the coast past Beirut and into Fatimid-held territory, past Acre and Caesarea to Arsuf, about 50 miles (80km) north-west of Jerusalem, from where they headed inland towards the Holy City.

They stopped for four days at the town of Ramla, which they found deserted of its Muslim garrison but well supplied with food. Here, according to Fulcher of Chartres, they installed a bishop in the Church of St George and left a Christian garrison holding the fortress before setting out once more for Jerusalem on 6 June.

ROBERT OF JERUSALEM
CRUSADER KNIGHT COUNT ROBERT II OF FLANDERS

French knight Robert of Flanders fought bravely in the major sieges and battles of the First Crusade, including the capture of Jerusalem in 1099, and when he returned to Europe after fulfilling his vows he won acclaim and adulation for his part in events that were quickly becoming the stuff of legend. Hailed as Robertus Hierosolimitanus (Robert of Jerusalem) and as 'Robert the Crusader', in the ensuing decades his fame was almost equal to that of Godfrey of Bouillon.

THE 'ARDENT WARRIOR'

The eldest son of Robert I, Count of Flanders (the nobleman known also as Robert the Frisian), Robert the younger had ruled the county as regent while his father had undertaken a pilgrimage to Jerusalem in 1085–91. After his father's death in 1093 he took power as Count Robert II, but within two years had committed to the First Crusade. He was already an experienced knight, and on the crusade he proved himself a great general and soldier, often in close association with Bohemond of Taranto. *Gesta Francorum* described Robert as an 'ardent warrior'.

EXPLOITS ON CRUSADE

Robert travelled on crusade in the company of Godfrey of Bouillon, leaving northern France in October 1096. In Constantinople he was easily persuaded to swear the oath of loyalty to Emperor Alexius in the company of Bohemond and Godfrey. After taking part in the siege of Nicaea, Robert marched on in the vanguard of the crusader army with Bohemond of Taranto – the part of the

---

THE CULT OF ST GEORGE

Robert played a significant part in the establishment of the cult of St George in Europe, for on his return he brought with him a precious relic, supposedly the arm of St George, which had been given to him as a gift by Emperor Alexius. Robert gave the relic to the Church of Anchin in Flanders, which established the church as a pilgrimage centre. He also founded the Monastery of St Andrew at Betferkerke near Bruges.

▼ *An artist's impression of Count Robert and Godfrey of Bouillon depositing trophies, supposedly won in the Battle of Ascalon, in the city of Jerusalem.*

army that came under attack in the Battle of Dorylaeum. He and his men fought bravely to keep the Seljuk Turks under Kilij Arslan at bay until the arrival of the main part of the crusader force, then fought on in the centre section of the crusader army alongside Raymond of Toulouse, when it launched the counter-attack that managed to decisively break the Turkish advance.

In the long siege of Antioch, Robert took part in key manoeuvres at the side of Bohemond of Taranto. In December they rode out to forage for food in the fertile valley of the River Orontes and, on 30 December, they together encountered and defeated a relief army sent by Duqaq, the Seljuk ruler of Damascus. As at Dorylaeum earlier, the charge of the Frankish and Norman knights riding with lances couched was too much for the Turkish horsemen to endure. When Antioch was subsequently taken, Robert was among the first of the crusaders to enter the city with Bohemond.

Then on 28 June 1098, when the Christian army broke out of the city to attack Sultan Kerbogha's besieging force – behind the Holy Lance, to the sound of prayers chanted by priests and in the face of a blinding vision of heavenly warriors under St George riding to their rescue – Robert together with Hugh of Vermandois commanded the first regiment to emerge, which deployed along the riverbank in a line. Contemporary accounts of the battle suggest that leadership was exemplary, for the crusader deployment and tactics were highly disciplined. After this battle, Robert took part with Bohemond in the capture of the citadel of Antioch, which had held out against the crusaders when the rest of the city had fallen.

LOYAL TO BOHEMOND OF TARANTO

Subsequently, Robert backed Bohemond in the dispute with Raymond of Toulouse over whether the crusaders could keep the city or must return it to Alexius. In December that year he rode out with

Raymond of Toulouse to attack the strategically important town of Maarrat an-Numan to the south of Antioch: Robert took part in the siege and capture of the town and presumably also in the massacre of its 20,000 inhabitants. He probably did not become involved in the alleged instances of cannibalism in which, according to Radulph of Caen, the starving crusaders cooked and ate the freshly slaughtered locals, both adults and children – this was most likely limited to the rank and file, while the nobles and commanders would have had the resources to buy scarce and overpriced food.

The crusaders recommenced their movement towards Jerusalem in January 1099, led by Raymond of Toulouse. Robert of Normandy and Tancred swore oaths to become Raymond's vassals and marched in his army, but Robert of Flanders and Godfrey of Bouillon refused to swear and initially remained in Antioch with Bohemond, subsequently joining the army at the siege of Arqa in March.

Robert largely remained with the army all the way down the coast to Jerusalem, except that at one point he and Tancred made a diversion into Samaria to find wood for building siege engines to use in the expected siege of Jerusalem. Robert then took part in the siege and capture of Jerusalem and in the subsequent Battle

▲ The ancient port of Latakia in Syria, taken by Count Robert and Raymond of Toulouse in 1099, became an important holding of the Principality of Antioch.

of Ascalon, in which the crusaders drove off a Fatimid army commanded by al-Afdal Shahanshah, Vizier of Egypt. Having been warned of the approach of the Fatimid army, the crusaders rode out to meet them and caught them by surprise in their camp near Ascalon. In this battle, he fought in the centre of the crusader force with Tancred, Robert of Normandy, Eustace of Boulogne and Gaston of Bearn, while Godfrey of Bouillon commanded the left wing and Raymond of Toulouse led the right flank. The crusaders triumphed despite being outnumbered by as many as five to one.

HOMEWARD BOUND

Robert of Flanders left Jerusalem in the company of Robert of Normandy and Raymond of Toulouse at the close of August 1099. On route to Constantinople, they conquered the Syrian port of Latakia, which became part of the crusader Principality of Antioch. In Constantinople, both Roberts declined an offer from Emperor Alexius to remain there in his service and took ship for Europe and a wildly enthusiastic homecoming.

JERUSALEM! JERUSALEM!
ARRIVAL AT AND BESIEGING OF THE HOLY CITY

As spring turned to summer in 1099 the crusaders neared their goal day by day. They were encountering little opposition, and even receiving a welcome of sorts, but they got an inkling of the locals' true attitude when a carrier pigeon was killed by a hawk above their camp and was found to have been carrying a message from the governor of Acre calling on faithful Muslims to take up arms and repel the Christian invasion.

A WELCOME IN BETHLEHEM

Christian inhabitants of Bethlehem sent out envoys begging the crusaders to liberate them from Egyptian occupation. Tancred and Baldwin of Le Bourg accepted the call and were welcomed as a liberating army by citizens and priests. The sight of their banner flying above Christ's birthplace was an enormous boost to the

crusaders. They were further cheered by an eclipse of the Moon that occurred at that very time – they interpreted it as portending the imminent eclipse of the crescent, the symbol of Islam.

'MOUNT JOY'

On 7 June 1099, the very day after the taking of Bethlehem, the crusader force crossed the hill known as Mountjoie ('Mount Joy') to generations of pilgrims and saw the walls of Jerusalem before them. 'Jerusalem!' went up the cry, and echoed down the lines. According to William of Tyre, the crusader-pilgrims fell to their knees and sobbed tears of joy, offering prayers of gratitude that God had led them to their destination; they cast off their shoes and bowed low to the ground in order to kiss the earth of the Holy Land. It had taken them three years to get there,

▲ At last the crusaders see the cherished city of Jerusalem. They offer prayers to God for having delivered them to their goal.

a long period of suffering and desperate exertions in which the pull of the Holy City and of their pilgrims' vows had inspired them to carry on. Now Jerusalem's walls were spread out before them. But their task remained a daunting one, for this city was one of the world's most strongly fortified, in a commanding position with deep valleys on two sides, to the east and west.

Assault was really only feasible from the north, for in the south on Mount Zion conditions could not support anything other than a small encampment. Expecting a siege, its governor, Iftikhar al-Daula, had prepared well, bringing in provisions and poisoning wells around the city, and sending urgent communication to Cairo calling for a Muslim relief army. He also expelled the city's Christian inhabitants to prevent any of them betraying Jerusalem to the crusaders.

AN ATTACK IN FAITH

The crusader army was not large enough to surround the city fully. On the northern wall, Godfrey of Bouillon arrayed his troops, alongside those of Robert of Flanders and Robert of Normandy, while to the south was the army of Raymond of Toulouse. In the gruelling heat of the summer and with very little water available, the crusaders decided to act quickly. They launched an attack on 13 June, although they had insufficient siege equipment. They had been spurred on by a hermit who reported that he had been told in a vision that if they proved their faith by attacking at once even without the necessary equipment God would grant them instant success. The attack failed, and brought home to the besiegers their urgent need for wood and other equipment with which to build proper siege towers.

Then, as if in answer to their prayers, Tancred found a hidden collection of

timber in a cave, and six English and Genoese ships put in at Jaffa bearing wood, nails, bolts, ropes and other supplies. Hidden from sight of the Jerusalem garrison, the crusaders set to work building two siege towers. They even took apart two ships to get more wood.

THE EXAMPLE OF JOSHUA

As at Antioch, they were working against time, for they received a warning that Governor Iftikhar al-Daula's cry for help had been answered, and a large relief army

▲ *Exaltation strengthened the crusaders' resolve to take the city into Christian hands.*

was on its way from Egypt. But they found time to mount a penitential procession around the city. A crusader priest named Peter Desiderius had been visited by the late Bishop Adhemar in a vision, and been instructed that if the army marched barefoot around the city walls Jerusalem would fall within nine days. This was inspired by the example of Joshua, Israelite leader in *c.*1200BC, who, according to biblical accounts, led his army seven times around the city of Jericho – and, as promised by God, the walls of the city fell down and the Israelites captured it. The entire crusader army held a three-day fast and on the second day, Friday 8 July, marched barefoot around the city, singing hymns. Members of the garrison gathered on the walls to jeer at the soldiers, who proceeded to the Mount of Olives to hear sermons by Peter the Hermit and others.

Five days later, the siege towers were ready. The plan was to mount the main assault on the north wall, using the two towers, one commanded by Godfrey of Bouillon and the other by Robert of Normandy, while a second assault was led by Raymond's force from the south side.

▼ *Godfrey rallies foot soldiers and knights at Jerusalem. Victory now seemed as certain as that of Joshua at Jericho.*

THE HOLY CITY CAPTURED
THE CRUSADERS' TRIUMPH – AND SHAME

After dark on the night of 13 July, the crusaders began to move their siege towers up to the walls of Jerusalem. They worked beneath a murderous storm of arrows, missiles, pitch and Greek fire. All night and all the next day, while behind them the mangonel hurled great rocks at the walls of Jerusalem, sweating and toiling beneath a searingly hot sun and through great clouds of dust, they laboured at hauling the machines forward.

At last, on the morning of 15 July, Godfrey of Bouillon's tower was close enough to the wall to make a bridge across on to the city ramparts near Herod's Gate. Godfrey and his brother Baldwin fought bravely on the tower. At around noon, despite the defenders' desperate attempts to repel them using fire and boiling water, the first crusaders made it on to the ramparts from Godfrey's tower. Among the first across were two brothers from Flanders, Lethold and Gilbert of Tournai. Just afterwards, the second tower under Robert of Normandy established a bridgehead to the wall.

THE CITY TAKEN
The defenders on the north wall retreated in order to take refuge in the al Aqsa mosque. Crusaders clambered over the walls and opened gates from within, and their comrades flooded into Jerusalem, unleashing a frenzy of bloodletting.

During the long struggle to get the towers up to the walls, according to the author of the *Gesta Francorum*, the crusaders had been surprised by how difficult it was, 'numbed with astonishment and extremely frightened'. Now, in the moment of triumph they had dreamt of for years, they unleashed their pent-up emotions in a bloodbath. According to the same author, 'the defenders of the city fled … and our men, following Lethold, ran after them, slaughtering them and dismembering them all the way to the Temple of Solomon. And in that place there was so much killing that the blood

▼ *The besiegers endured a heavy assault from the battlements as they moved their siege towers, little by little, up to the walls.*

came up to our ankles.' According to the Provençal chronicler Raymond of Aguilers, 'in the streets and squares of the city, piles of heads, hands and feet could be seen. People were making their way over the corpses of men and horses. But this is only to describe the minor horrors …'

The defenders of the north wall were pursued by Tancred and his men, and surrendered to him, promising to pay a large ransom. They took refuge in the al Aqsa mosque praying for their lives. Tancred claimed the Temple quarter in his name, and set his banner flying above the building. The Jews of the city also fled for their lives, taking refuge in their main synagogue, by the Western Wall.

The *Gesta Francorum* account goes on to describe how the pilgrims followed the soldiers into the city and also slew 'Saracens' indiscriminately to left and right. At the Temple of Solomon, it reports, attackers and defenders 'fought a furious battle all day so that their blood flooded all over the Temple. At last the pagans were defeated and our men took a good number of men and women prisoner in the Temple. They killed whichever prisoners they wished and chose to allow others to live.'

THE HONOUR OF RAYMOND OF TOULOUSE
On the south wall, meanwhile, the defenders kept Raymond of Toulouse's attack at bay until they saw that behind them the city had been lost. Then they made a swift retreat to the citadel, the Tower of David, and finally surrendered there to Raymond. He gave his word that they would have safe passage out of the city – and, remarkably, amid such chaos was able to honour it, escorting them from Jerusalem as far as the Muslim garrison in the port of Ascalon. This honourable enactment of the safe escort was a brief interlude of restraint.

THE CITY IS STRIPPED

The account given by Fulcher of Chartres describes how crusaders ran into deserted houses and seized whatever they found. Whoever was first into a building was able to claim it – 'in this way, many poor folk became rich'. For it was a frenzy of greed, as well as of bloodletting. According to the *Gesta Francorum*, 'the crusaders seized silver and gold, mules and horses, and buildings full of all manner of riches'.

A VIOLENT CLEANSING

It was normal practice in 11th-century warfare for an army to loot a city it had conquered after a long siege. The attack on the inhabitants of Jerusalem had an extra intensity, fuelled as it was by papal and priestly rhetoric about the need to sweep the city clean of 'Saracens'. After the killing, the soldiers and pilgrims piously gave thanks to God in the Church of the Holy Sepulchre. Fulcher of Chartres presented this dreadful slaughter as a purgative cleansing: 'O day so fiercely longed for! ... O deed above all other deeds! ... [the crusaders] desired that this place, for so long made unclean by the pagan practices of its inhabitants, should be cleaned of its filth.' Raymond of Aguilers declared that: 'after the city had

▼ *In the 15th century, when this illustration was drawn, the battle for Jerusalem was reimagined as a civilized encounter.*

been taken, it was a rich reward to see the devotion of the pilgrims at the Holy Sepulchre; the manner in which they clapped in their exulting, singing a new song to the Lord.'

The slaughter continued for almost two days. Tancred was not able to protect the Muslims in the al Aqsa mosque. On 16 July the crusaders forced their way into the building and killed every man, woman and child. The synagogue, filled with refugees, was burned to the ground. A letter from the crusade leaders to the pope declared proudly that in the portico of Solomon and in his Temple, 'our men rode in the blood of the Saracens even up to the knees of their horses'. A reference, perhaps, to the Book of Revelation, whose apocalyptic accounts of the Last Judgement were familiar to the crusaders: 'And the winepress was trodden without the city, and blood came out of the winepress, even unto the horses' bridles.'

▲ *The crusaders dedicated their attack to Christ and proclaimed a desire to win Jerusalem for God.*

▼ *In the heat of the moment, bloodlust took over from pious righteousness, and one act of barbarity was followed by another.*

AFTER THE VICTORY
THE CITY SECURED WITH TRIUMPH AT ASCALON

In the immediate aftermath of the slaughter of 15–16 July, the crusaders had had to deal with cleaning the city, since the piles of corpses made such a terrible stench. The *Gesta Francorum* reports that the bodies of the Saracens were dragged out of the city and burned in huge pyramids. The smoke hung over the city in a dreadful pall.

DEFENDER OF THE HOLY SEPULCHRE

On 22 July, the eighth day after the taking of Jerusalem, the crusaders elected Godfrey of Bouillon to rule the city as Defender of the Holy Sepulchre. The first choice had been Count Raymond of Toulouse as king, but he declined the offer saying no mortal man should wear a crown in the city that belonged to Christ. Godfrey agreed with this statement, but came up with a compromise title that allowed him to take power.

▼ *With the city of Jerusalem secured, normal rules of pillage did not apply, and the victors became rich overnight.*

In many ways, Godfrey was an understandable choice. He had proved himself pious, steadfast and brave. Among the other lords, Bohemond had established himself in Antioch and Baldwin in Edessa, while Robert of Normandy had truly joined the crusade in order to liberate Jerusalem and was now set on returning to France. Raymond's refusal of power in Jerusalem is less easy to understand, given that he had shown himself elsewhere to be ambitious and not averse to putting political ambition above Christian piety. It is possible that his refusal was a ploy to prevent any of the lords claiming the kingship or that he considered Jerusalem too difficult a prize to defend and was planning to establish a principality in Tripoli.

JERUSALEM'S FIRST LATIN PATRIARCH

Then on 1 August Arnulf of Choques, the chaplain in Robert of Normandy's army, was elected Patriarch of Jerusalem. Arnulf had been one of the most prominent sceptics voicing doubts about the validity of Peter Bartholomew's claims that he had

▲ *When the Church of the Holy Sepulchre gave up a piece of the True Cross it was seen as a further validation of the attack.*

discovered a piece of the Holy Lance in Antioch, and his opposition had played a major part in forcing Peter to undergo a trial by fire in April during the march south, after which the visionary had died. During the siege of Jerusalem, Arnulf had made a statue of Christ to stand on one of the siege engines. Then, on 5 August, he announced that he had discovered a piece of the True Cross (the cross on which Christ had been crucified) in the Church of the Holy Sepulchre. This became one of the most treasured possessions of the Kingdom of Jerusalem.

Arnulf's election was supported by Godfrey, and in return Arnulf backed Godfrey's decision to make the Kingdom of Jerusalem a secular state rather than one under Church – and ultimately papal – rule. He imposed the Latin form of Christianity, barring the priests of other denominations, such as the Orthodox Greeks and the Coptic, Armenian or Georgian Christians, from the Church of the Holy Sepulchre. He also reportedly authorized the torture of other Christians to force them to reveal where they had hidden other parts of the True Cross. The events of these first weeks of the Kingdom of Jerusalem created a fierce hatred in the Eastern churches for the Latin Christians that would endure for centuries.

BATTLE OF ASCALON

Godfrey's first job as ruler was to repel the Fatimid relief army summoned from Egypt by Jerusalem's governor, Iftikhar al-Daula, before the fall of the city. The Fatimids had raised a force of perhaps 50,000 men under the command of Vizier al-Afdal Shahanshah, who intended to mount a siege of Jerusalem. On 10 August, Godfrey received reports from scouts that the Muslim army was massing in the vicinity of Ascalon, a port about 35 miles (55km) east of Jerusalem. Godfrey led his army out of Jerusalem to confront the Fatimid force, with Robert of Flanders and Arnulf; they were followed the next day by Raymond of Toulouse and Robert of Normandy. On the way, at Ramla, they met up with Tancred and Eustace of Boulogne, Godfey's brother.

In total, the crusader force numbers totalled around 10,000, with probably as few as 1,200 knights and the rest infantry. They were severely outnumbered by the Fatimids, although not as badly as is suggested in the *Gesta Francorum*, which claims the Egyptian army was 200,000-strong. The crusaders had their relics to comfort them: they marched behind Arnulf carrying the piece of the True Cross he had found and Raymond of Aguilers carrying the relic of the Holy Lance.

On 11 August the crusaders discovered a large number of goats, cattle, sheep and even camels grazing near Ascalon: they presumed the creatures were intended as a source for food for the large Fatimid army, although a few captives taken in a small encounter by Tancred indicated that the animals were intended as a decoy in the hope that the crusader army would lose its discipline and begin pillaging.

When the crusader scouts discovered the precise location of the Fatimid force, the Christian army marched on with the animals in tow, making their army seem larger than it otherwise would have done.

The two forces met in open conflict outside Ascalon. Most contemporary accounts suggest that the crusaders caught the Fatimids unprepared and that the battle was quickly over. It began with an exchange of arrows, and then the two main contingents fought at close quarters with lances, the kind of battle in which the crusaders were at their best. The Fatimids broke and fled, some into the city, some into the sea. They abandoned their camp, and all its treasures, which were claimed by Tancred and Robert of Normandy.

QUARREL OVER ASCALON

The crusaders rejoiced, but prepared for a second battle. However, after spending the night in the abandoned Fatimid camp, they discovered the next day that the Fatimid survivors had begun a retreat to Egypt. The city lay at their mercy, but its garrison declared that it would only surrender to Raymond of Toulouse – doubtless because he had behaved honourably in providing safe escort for Iftikhar al-Daula and his troops during

▲ The crusaders rejoice as the symbol of Christ's Passion is raised at the end of their long and desperate campaign.

the capture of Jerusalem. Raymond and Godfrey quarrelled over the spoils: Godfrey refused to accept the surrender on these terms, declaring that the city should come to him as ruler of Jerusalem, Raymond, furious at being thwarted again by Godfrey; marched back to Jerusalem, with Robert of Normandy. Godfrey alone was not strong enough to capture Ascalon, and so it remained in Muslim hands. Allowing this to happen was a grave mistake, for taking Ascalon would have been an important step towards consolidating the fledgling Kingdom of Jerusalem.

CRUSADE COMPLETED

For the great majority of the crusaders, the enterprise was now at an end and most went home. At the end of 1099 Godfrey remained in Jerusalem with only around 2,000 foot soldiers plus perhaps just 300 knights – in the estimation of William of Tyre. Robert of Normandy and Robert of Flanders were among those who departed for Europe and with them Godfrey sent word that the Kingdom of Jerusalem needed reinforcements.

CHAPTER NINE

THE LAND OVERSEAS

The many settlers who stayed after the First Crusade in 1099 created an outpost of Latin Christendom in the East. The land in which they made their homes became known as *Outremer* – from the French word meaning 'overseas'. Outremer encompassed the four crusader states established during or as a result of the First Crusade: the County of Edessa; the Principality of Antioch; the Kingdom of Jerusalem; and the County of Tripoli.

The settlers organized life along familiar lines, introducing the feudal system and imposing the rites of the Latin Church on other Christians. But in many respects, also, they went native. Fulcher of Chartres, who became chaplain to King Baldwin I of Jerusalem, wrote: 'We were once Westerners, but now we are men of the East. You may once have identified yourself as a Roman or a Frenchman, but here, in the present, you are a man of Galilee or of Palestine.... For we do not remember the lands of our birth; to the majority of us they are unfamiliar, foreign lands.' He went on to describe how the lords of the new estates came to appreciate local customs and food and married local women, whether Armenians, Syrians or even 'Saracens' – of course, he added, 'only to those who have been baptized'. It is clear that for the settlers life in Outremer represented the start of something permanent. When the soldiers of the Second Crusade arrived in 1148, they were shocked to find that the leading men of Outremer in their eyes were more like 'Saracens' than Christian princes.

▲ *The coastal crusader citadel of Sidon, in Lebanon.*

◄ *The impressive remains of Krak des Chevaliers at Qal'at al-Hisn in Syria are an enduring symbol of the might of the military orders and the kingdoms of Outremer.*

THE KINGDOMS OF PALESTINE

To understand the movements of the great crusading armies, and appreciate the drama of their adventures, it is helpful to know the routes they took and the boundaries they crossed.

Tracing the long and dangerous journey made on the First Crusade underlines the enterprise's vast ambition and daring (shown on the map below). From central and northern Europe, some from as far north as England, or from southern France, by a variety of routes – across the Holy Roman Empire and Hungary, or through Italy and by sea across the southern Adriatic – the great armies marched under the banner of the cross to Constantinople, capital of the Byzantine empire, then on across Anatolia and down the Mediterranean coast towards their glittering goal, the Holy City of Jerusalem.

Across these thousands of miles trailed many, many thousand men (and some women), first the somewhat ragged forces of the People's Crusade – according to Byzantine princess Anna Comnena, to see them was 'like looking at rivers flooding together from all directions' – then no fewer than five princely armies. The routes of the four main princely armies are detailed on the map. Faith and the inspirational words of Urban II and the crusade preachers drove them on and helped them keep their nerve: this was a great adventure but also a daunting and frequently terrifying challenge. In taking the cross many had cried 'God wills it!' and the belief that they were destined to achieve their goal bore the core of the crusaders onward in the face of hardship, defeats and the deaths of comrades. More than

three years elapsed between the departure of the first elements of the People's Crusade in April 1096 and the bloody capture of Jerusalem in July 1099.

JERUSALEM

With the Holy City in Christian hands for the first time since AD638, the crusaders began building. They erected a palace beside the al-Aqsa Mosque, in the place

▼ *The first of the main princely armies to depart was that of Godfrey of Bouillon, who left Lorraine in August 1096. Bohemond of Taranto set sail from Bari in October 1096. At the same time Raymond of Toulouse left southern France and Robert of Flanders set out from the north. Their combined forces took Nicaea in June 1097 and marched across the Sultunate of Rum.*

The City of Jerusalem during the First and Second Crusades

- St. Stephen's Gate
- Church of St. Mary Magdalen
- Church of St. Anne
- Jehoshaphat's Gate
- Jehoshaphat Street
- Via Dolorosa
- Pool of Bethesda
- PATRIARCH'S QUARTER
- Tancred's Tower
- Church of the Holy Sepulchre
- Golden Gate
- TEMPLE AREA
- Hospital of St. John
- Church of St. John the Baptist
- Pool of the Patriarchs
- David's Gate
- David Street
- Temple Street
- Royal Palace
- St Mary's Hospital
- The Tower of David
- Church of St. Martin
- Hospital of the Knights Templar
- Tanner's Gate
- Church of St. James the Great
- Church of St. Peter in Chains
- Zion Gate

▲ *Pilgrims entered the city by David's Gate in the west and went directly to the Church of the Holy Sepulchre. Christ reputedly entered the city on Palm Sunday through the Golden Gate, beside the Temple Area.*

believed to be the site of the ancient Temple. Later this became the headquarters of the Knights Templar, and a new palace was built in the west of the city at the Tower of David, by David's Gate. In this place King David had reputedly written the Book of Psalms in the 11th-10th century BC. Under the Muslims, bells had been banned from churches, but now they were restored and rang out over the capital of a Christian kingdom in the Holy Land, a city perceived as the centre of the world.

In the course of 50 years to c.1150 the crusaders built the great Romanesque Church of the Holy Sepulchre, containing the rock of Calvary on which Christ was

crucified, and the site of his tomb. Pilgrims visiting Jerusalem could follow the 'Way of the Cross' from the site of Pontius Pilate's palace on Jehoshaphat Street to the site of Christ's crucifixion and burial.

THE CONQUESTS OF SALADIN

Less then a century later, beginning in July 1187, Muslim leader Saladin won a series of victories that brought the Christian Kingdom of Jerusalem close to extinction (shown in the map right). Crossing the River Jordan from the east with an army of around 30,000 on 30 June 1187, Saladin defeated Guy of Lusignan, King of Jerusalem, and a 20,000-strong army in the Battle of the Horns of Hattin on 4 July. Jerusalem was an easy target after this victory, in which the crusaders famously lost their treasured relic of the 'True Cross' on which Christ died, for the Kingdom's military force was all but wiped out.

Saladin and his troops captured Acre and other strongholds along the Mediterranean coast: from Acre he headed north and took Sidon and Beirut, then marched south and took Jaffa and Ascalon before moving inland to capture Jerusalem on 2 October 1187. He campaigned again in 1188, in the north, and won several further victories, including the capture of the fortress of Saone. But he did not take Tyre, and this would be an invaluable foothold for a Christian revival in the Holy Land.

▼ *Saladin campaigned at great speed, determined not to allow the Christians to regroup. He took Acre just four days after the victory at the Horns of Hattin, then captured Ascalon, during a solar eclipse, exactly two months after Hattin. By 20 September he had marched inland to begin the siege of Jerusalem.*

The Conquests of Saladin

- Saladin's territory 1190
- Christian outpost 1190
- Christian castle
- Battle

CILICIAN ARMENIA
- Alexandretta
- Antioch
- Aleppo
- St Simeon

PRINCIPALITY OF ANTIOCH
- Maraclea

Mediterranean Sea

COUNTY OF TRIPOLI
- Tripoli
- Beirut
- Sidon
- Belfort
- Damascus
- Tyre
- Chastel Neuf
- Battle of the Horns of Hattin
- Jacob's Ford
- Acre
- Haifa
- Lake Tiberias
- Nazareth
- Tiberias
- Belvoir
- Caesarea
- KINGDOM OF JERUSALEM
- Nablus
- Arsuf
- Jaffa
- Ascalon
- Jerusalem
- Gaza
- Dead Sea

DOMINION OF SALADIN

50 km
50 miles

THE FOUNDATION OF OUTREMER
EDESSA, ANTIOCH, JERUSALEM AND TRIPOLI

The first crusader states had been established in 1098 en route to Jerusalem, when Baldwin of Boulogne created the County of Edessa based on the ancient city of that name (now Urfa, Turkey), and Bohemond of Taranto established the Principality of Antioch in Syria.

THE KINGDOM OF JERUSALEM
The third state, the Kingdom of Jerusalem, did not technically come into existence until 17 months after the Christian conquest of Jerusalem on 15 July 1099. As we have seen, Godfrey of Bouillon, refused to be called king in the city where Christ wore a crown of thorns and took the title 'Defender of the Holy Sepulchre'. But following Godfrey's death in July 1100 his brother Baldwin, no longer 'of Boulogne' but 'of Edessa', had no such qualms, and was crowned king on 25 December 1100 by Daimbert, Patriarch of Jerusalem.

Daimbert had arrived in Jerusalem from Rome in 1099. The Archbishop of Pisa, he had been sent from Italy as the new papal legate, the replacement for Bishop

▼ *Baldwin of Boulogne became Baldwin of Edessa and then, on the death of his brother Godfrey, King Baldwin I of Jerusalem.*

Adhemar of Le Puy, who had died of the plague in Antioch. Daimbert engineered the removal from office of the recently elected Patriarch of Jerusalem, Arnulf of Choques, on the grounds that Arnulf's election had been illegal, and took his place. He allowed Arnulf to occupy the lesser position of Archdeacon.

Then Daimbert set to work to bring about the creation of the papal state in the Holy Land that had been Pope Urban II's dream. He recognized the rule of Bohemond as Prince of Antioch and Tancred as Prince of Galilee, thus guaranteeing their independence from Jerusalem. From Godfrey he won the assurance that on his death the church would inherit control of Jerusalem – according to William of Tyre, Godfrey's plan was to cede rule to the Church in the Kingdom of Jerusalem and to carry on crusader conquest as far as Egypt, where he would establish his own secular kingdom.

But when Godfrey died unexpectedly, fate and conspiracy among the secular lords combined to prevent Daimbert achieving his and the papacy's wish of establishing a theocracy (a state ruled by God through churchmen). At the time of Godfrey's death, Daimbert was away on a campaign with Tancred against Haifa, and Baldwin was secretly summoned to come to Jerusalem and take power. When

▲ *The crusaders called this fortress on Mount Hermon 'L'Asibebe'. In English it is called Nimrod Fortress after the biblical hunter – and 'Citadel of the Mosquitoes'.*

Daimbert heard that Godfrey had died and that Baldwin was marching on Jerusalem, he wrote to Bohemond offering him rule of Palestine under Daimbert's authority – and asking him to prevent Baldwin reaching Jerusalem. The letter was intercepted, however, and Bohemond was captured while attempting an attack on Danishmend, emir of Sivas (Sebastea).

Baldwin marched into Jerusalem and secured his power base. Daimbert was forced to crown him king. Baldwin gave his previous holding, the County of Edessa, to his cousin Baldwin of Le Bourg. Early in 1101 Tancred abandoned his rule as Prince of Galilee, moving to take up power in Antioch – he reigned as regent for Bohemond, who was in Danishmend's jail (where he remained until 1103).

THE FOURTH CRUSADER STATE
The crusader state of the County of Tripoli was created in the course of the war waged by Raymond of Toulouse, from 1102 onwards, against Fakhr al-Mulk, emir of the coastal city of Tripoli (now in Lebanon), in power there as a vassal of the Fatimid caliphs in Cairo. Raymond died

in 1105, before the city fell, naming his cousin William-Jordan as regent and his infant son Alfonso-Jordan as heir; but subsequently, one of his illegitimate sons, Bertrand, who had been serving as regent of Toulouse in his father's absence, arrived in the Holy Land. Bertrand and William-Jordan agreed, as a result of King Baldwin I's intervention, that they would each keep the conquests they individually made. Bertrand was the main beneficiary, for he captured Tripoli and became sole ruler when William-Jordan died a little while afterwards; Alfonso-Jordan meanwhile returned to France with his mother.

Bertrand ruled the County of Tripoli as a vassal of the king of Jerusalem. Within his realm, the castle of Krak des Chevaliers was given to the military order of the Knights Hospitaller in 1142.

THE GEOGRAPHY OF OUTREMER

The County of Edessa was the farthest north of the crusader states and set in a remote, landlocked position, with half of its territory lying far away from the Mediterranean, on the east bank of the River Euphrates; the other three states were all coastal domains. The Edessa territory west of the Euphrates was governed from the castle of Turbessel, strongly fortified against attacks from the Seljuk Turks of the Sultanate of Rum, which lay to the north. To the west lay Armenian Cilicia, parts of the Byzantine Empire where the crusaders had made conquests, including the city of Tarsus.

▲ *The majority of Outremer territories were coastal, and the Christian lords grew rich on trade passing through their ports.*

▼ *Krak des Chevaliers, the 'Castle of the Knights', in the County of Tripoli, was the foremost crusader fortress of Outremer.*

The Principality of Antioch bordered the County of Edessa to the south-west, and ran down to the Mediterranean coast. When Tancred was regent in 1100–03 he expanded the Principality north-west to take the cities of Tarsus and Latakia from the Byzantines. To the south was the County of Tripoli, leading south again to the Kingdom of Jerusalem. By the mid-1100s, when the Kingdom was at its largest, it extended north to south from Beirut (now capital of Lebanon) to Rafia (modern Rafah in the Gaza Strip). In the north it was separated by the district of Lebanon from the Emirate of Damascus; in the south-east it ran all the way to the Arabian desert and even encompassed the Red Sea port of Aïla (modern Elat). After the First Crusade, some parts of Cilicia remained in European hands, but they never formed into a state or principality.

GOVERNMENT OF THE CRUSADER STATES

THE FEUDAL HIERARCHY IS EXPORTED TO OUTREMER

The crusader states were governed on the lines of the feudal system. The crusaders imported this social system from Europe because in their eyes it had God's blessing as the perfect way to create stability within a hierarchy of duties and responsibilities. Each man had his place, by divine plan, beneath the king. Detailed accounts of the government of the Kingdom of Jerusalem survive, and we know that the other crusader states had a parallel system.

THE KING OF JERUSALEM

Within the Kingdom of Jerusalem, the king was paramount. Great lords held land as his tenants in chief – men such as Tancred, Prince of Galilee, or Eustace Grenier, Lord of Caesarea. These lords in turn packaged land out to their tenants or rear-vassals. Only Catholic Christians were permitted to hold fiefs – Jews, Muslims and all other Christians were excluded from the system.

As in Europe, the lords and their vassals were required to provide military service – for example, Caesarea was required to provide 100 knights, as was Galilee; even the inhospitable lordship of

▼ *The port of Caesarea, a major crusader possession on the Mediterranean coast, dates back to around the time of Christ. It was built by Herod the Great in c.25BC.*

Oultrejourdain (the land east of the Jordan river containing the Negev Desert) had to raise 60 knights.

In 1166 the second tier of tenants, the rear vassals, took vows of liege homage to the king – at that time, Amalric. The chief city of Jerusalem was naturally reserved for the king himself, part of a royal domain that he governed directly.

THE KING'S POWER STRUCTURE

The king's most senior officers were: a seneschal, with control of royal castles and the treasury; a butler, in control of the royal household; and a constable, in charge of the military establishment. The collection of revenue from the countryside largely used pre-crusade methods, and then the moneys were passed via scribes and bailiffs, through local treasuries to the Grant Secrete, or principal treasury.

The king's power was limited by the great lords as tenants-in-chief and the rear-vassals, in their capacity as members of the High Court. The king took an oath in its presence, and was forbidden to seize any lord's fief-holding unless the decision was approved by the Court. The High Court, and not the king, made the kingdom's laws or assizes – the Assizes of Jerusalem. (These are sometimes wrongly said to have been drawn up by Godfrey of Bouillon.) Under these assizes, if the king broke his oaths, his feudal dependants had the legal

right to resist. In addition, if two members of the royal family came into dispute over succession to the throne, the Court had the power to determine the new king. However, the Court met only when summoned by the king so, if necessary, he was able to sideline its powers.

The High Court also functioned as the kingdom's highest legal tribunal, and there was no appeal against its judgements. Beneath it was a network of burgess courts to judge cases involving Western settlers; these courts had the power to impose the death penalty or to send offenders into exile. In addition, within the larger fiefs there were courts of knights and burgesses. These courts were limited to Latin Christians. Other Christians used a separate group of port and market courts. For Muslims and Jews, cases were divided into spiritual or secular: spiritual cases were judged by the existing religious authorities of qadis or rabbis, while secular ones went to newly established native courts called the Courts of the Syrians.

Assemblies of leading citizens – including senior churchmen, top members of the military orders and prominent townsmen as well as the king and nobles – were occasionally held to debate matters of consequence such as the necessity of levying taxes to pay for wars or policy problems such as where help could most profitably be requested among western lords. These meetings were called *parlements*.

THE INDEPENDENCE OF MAJOR LANDOWNERS

As in feudal Europe, the king often struggled to impose his will on the most powerful lords, who possessed strongly fortified castles and their own military forces – for example, Reynald of Châtillon, lord of the important fief of Montreal from 1174, was largely a law unto himself and waged a private war against Muslims, ignoring the royal policy of his king,

Baldwin VI. The lordship of Montreal was a wealthy one, for its main castle, Al-Shaubak (also known as Montreal) controlled lucrative caravan routes from Damascus to the Red Sea and Egypt.

THE RICHES OF THE KING

This difficulty was balanced by the fact that the king's domain made him richer than any of his lords: it contained the ports of Tyre and Acre as well as the city of Jerusalem. The king imposed customs duties at ports along the Mediterranean coast, and taxed overland trade caravans; he also had a monopoly on some local industries and was the only lord permitted to coin money in the realm; he had the right to claim shipwrecks; he could also, with the approval of his *parlement* or the High Court, levy one-off taxes – as when, in 1182, Baldwin IV imposed a tax of 2 per cent on all incomes, including those of the Latin Church, in order to raise money to fight Saladin. These large and varied incomes made the kingship of Jerusalem very profitable indeed: the king of this small eastern kingdom was probably richer than most European princes in the 12th century. And he was able to use his wealth to hire mercenaries.

THE POWER OF THE CHURCH

After the king, the Patriarch of Jerusalem was the most important person in the kingdom. The Latin Church in Palestine quickly became powerful, establishing a number of monasteries on land donated by wealthy crusaders and ruthlessly

▲ *The prosperity of Outremer depended on trade. The king of Jerusalem amassed great wealth from taxes on desert caravans.*

sidelining other Christians, such as the Coptic, Syrian, Greek Orthodox and others. The Patriarch was elected by the clergy, then acclaimed by the people: his position was subject to the approval of the pope, who would confirm the Patriarch's powers after the election.

▼ *The city of Tyre, an important port on the Mediterranean coast, had a Christian community from the 2nd century onwards. Its Muslim rulers surrendered in 1124.*

THE MILITARY ORDERS

One of the principal difficulties for the crusader authorities was the low number of settlers. They made repeated attempts to attract immigration from Europe, but they remained vastly outnumbered – a ruling minority with a very large subject population of Syrians, Greeks and Muslim Arabs who could not be relied on if the kingdom came under attack. By the 1180s, only an estimated 35 per cent of the population was European in origin.

The establishment of the military orders such as the Knights Hospitaller, the Knights Templar and the Teutonic Knights helped to boost the Kingdom's strength. The increasingly wealthy orders, funded by lavish donations in Europe, were able to buy castles and land from impoverished noblemen among the settlers and were an important means of maintaining order.

However, the ultimate loyalty of the military orders was to the papacy; they were not bound by feudal ties to the king, and technically did not owe military service in the defence of the kingdom, although in practice they fought in all the major campaigns. They also had the right to negotiate directly with Muslims.

LIFE IN THE CRUSADER STATES

THE RICH ENJOY LOCAL LUXURIES

▲ *In this image of Bertrand of Saint-Gilles receiving submission from Seljuk qadi Fakhr al-Mulk it can be seen how the Westerners adapted their lifestyle to the climate and landscape of Outremer.*

In Jerusalem and other cities of the crusader states, the great lords and many of their retainers lived in fine style. They had their pick of the cargoes of Chinese silk, rare stones and spices that were brought to the Mediterranean coast overland from central Asia by camel caravan; in addition, they chose from the finest locally produced cotton and glassware.

In their city dwellings and their castles, they surrounded themselves with the finest luxuries, including silk wall hangings, woven carpets and beautifully carved Arabian furniture; the richest even used gold and silver plates. They adapted to the local diet, learning to enjoy dates, olives, watermelons, lemons, oranges and sugar cane, and to spice up their foods with pepper, ginger and cinnamon; they dressed in flowing robes, and began to wear open-toed sandals; some even adopted the turban. They married beauties among the local womenfolk – often in addition to European wives. Many lords kept elaborate Arabian-style gardens as havens from the dust and heat.

LIFE IN THE COUNTRYSIDE

The majority of the Europeans lived in the cities and castles but there was some settlement in the countryside. Some occupied existing villages and towns. In the Mediterranean port of Caesarea, for example, the crusaders who captured the town in 1101 simply drove out the Muslim population and made their homes in the existing city. Initially they just adapted mosques to use them as churches. In the longer term, they dismantled the Great Mosque and built in its place the Catholic Cathedral of St Peter.

There were also new settlements, in which land was given to European peasants in return for a 10 per cent tithe paid to the local secular or religious landowner. For example, the village of Magna Mahumeria (modern day al-Bira) north of

Jerusalem was established on these lines in 1120 by canons of the Church of the Holy Sepulchre on land bequeathed to them by Godfrey of Bouillon.

For poor Eastern Christians and Jews in the parched countryside, however, life probably seemed to have changed very little as a result of the crusade: their Muslim landlords had been replaced by Christian lords, but little else was different. The Muslims, of course, had to come to terms with being cast among the poor.

One way in which the feudal system in the East was different to that in Europe was that the Christian lords were largely absentees, for they chose to live in Jerusalem or other cities rather than on their estates. Although technically they were the property of the Latin Christian master who owned their land, the Muslims, Jews and Eastern Christians had a significant amount of freedom. There was freedom of religion in that in the countryside, Jews, Muslims and Eastern

▲ *The crusaders drove the local inhabitants out of Caesarea in 1101 and simply took what they found for their own use.*

Christians could follow their own faith and in religious matters at least were subject to their own authorities.

The farmers grew cereals and summer crops such as maize and millet. They kept vineyards, orchards and olive groves, and a few grew sugar and cotton. They paid a tax of up to one-third of their arable crops and one-half of the produce from olive groves and vineyards.

RELIGIOUS FREEDOM

In the cities, Muslims, Jews and Eastern Christians had their freedom – except that Jews and Muslims were allowed only to visit Jerusalem and were officially not permitted to live there. The Armenians, Jacobites and Maronite Christians were allowed to worship according to their own rites, but as we have seen were excluded from the Church of the Holy Sepulchre.

The degree of tolerance that developed between the Catholic Christians and other groups was a matter of necessity. For example, trade connections had to be made with Muslims and Jews. The Catholics' treatment of Jews was considerably better in the crusader states than in 11th–12th-century Europe, and there were no pogroms against the Jews in the crusader states.

MERCHANT ENCLAVES

Within the cities – particularly the coastal ports, such as Tyre and Acre – were colonies of merchants from the cities of Genoa, Venice, Pisa, Marseille, Narbonne and so on, who lived in independent, self-contained districts under the control of their own consul; they were not subject to the feudal system and did not have to perform military service. These merchant colonies had landholdings on the edges of cities, where they grew sugar cane and cotton. They were allowed a monopoly on trade between the Kingdom and Europe and sent home ships heavily laden with highly profitable cargoes. Ships from European ports brought goods necessary to the settlers' way of life, although most adapted quickly to local conditions.

The ports grew very rich. Traders from the Byzantine Empire, Syria, Iraq and north Africa worked alongside those from the European mercantile cities of Europe. Taxes imposed by the authorities could be as high as 25 per cent. The most valuable trade of all was in spices leaving the Mediterranean ports bound first for Constantinople and then on to the towns and cities of western Europe. Among the richest and most profitable of the ports was Acre. The Muslim geographer Ibn Jubayr, born in Valencia, described Acre in 1185 as 'a trading stop for all ships. It is a major attraction for vessels and caravans, the meeting place for Christian and Muslim traders from all around the area. Its streets are hard to walk, so crowded are they by men from all countries.'

▼ *Acre was a key crusader city, which was taken, lost and recaptured many times.*

PRINCE OF GALILEE

TANCRED OF HAUTEVILLE

A Norman lord from southern Italy, Tancred of Hauteville rode on the First Crusade with his uncle Bohemond of Taranto and afterwards established himself first as Prince of Galilee and then as regent of the Principality of Antioch and the County of Edessa. Through his feats of bravery leading up to, during and after the capture of Jerusalem in 1099, and his staunch defence of the independence of the crusader state of Antioch against the Byzantine Empire, Tancred won enduring fame as a knight that made his name resonate down the centuries.

Grandson of the great Norman–Italian adventurer Robert Guiscard, Tancred shared his name with the founding father of the Hauteville clan, the relatively minor 11th-century nobleman from near Coutances in Normandy, whose sons – including William Iron-Arm, Guiscard himself and Roger, Count of Sicily – travelled south to achieve greatness. Tancred

▼ Tancred (right) meets King Philip I of France prior to marrying the king's daughter, Cecile.

the Crusader certainly lived up to the expectations that such ancestry aroused. His life was recorded in the *Gesta Tancredi in Expeditione Hierosolymitana* (The Deeds of Tancred on Crusade to Jerusalem), written in Latin by Norman churchman Radulph of Caen in the years after 1112, based on eyewitness accounts.

IN CONSTANTINOPLE AND CILICIA

Tancred took part in the early episodes of the crusade. Notably in Constantinople, when other crusader princes swore oaths to Alexius in which they promised to return any conquered lands to the Byzantine Empire, doubtless with the full intention of breaking them, Tancred avoided taking the oath at all by slipping out of the city at night.

He took part in the siege of Nicaea and the Battle of Dorylaeum, but Tancred first made his name on the crusade when taking Tarsus during an excursion in Cilicia in 1097; in this part of the crusade he came into open conflict with Baldwin of Boulogne (later King Baldwin I of

Jerusalem). Tancred went on to capture Adana, Mamistra and Alexandretta, before taking part in the siege of Antioch.

In the course of the siege at Antioch, when spirits in the camp were very low and members of the crusader armies were sorely tempted to abandon the adventure, Tancred encountered no less a figure than Peter the Hermit attempting to flee and make his way back to Constantinople. Peter was the itinerant French monk who had preached the crusade so enthusiastically in Europe and become one of the leaders of the 'People's Crusade'. Tancred forced him to return to the crusaders' camp before Antioch.

A BROKEN PROMISE TO PROTECT MUSLIM PRISONERS

During the capture of Jerusalem in 1099 Tancred took hundreds of Muslim prisoners and famously pledged to protect them from the rampaging soldiers who had taken over the city, in return for the offer of a large ransom. He flew his banner over the al Aqsa mosque where the prisoners were gathered, but on the second day of looting he allowed the Muslims to be slain – man, woman and child.

AFTER THE FIRST CRUSADE

In the aftermath of victory, Godfrey of Bouillon, newly elected as Defender of the Holy Sepulchre, gave Tancred the title Prince of Galilee. Then, in the following year, when his uncle Bohemond was taken prisoner during an ill-fated military expedition against Danishmend, the emir of Sivas (Sebastea) in eastern Anatolia, Tancred became regent of the Principality of Antioch. He extended its territories by seizing land from the Byzantine Empire, and resisted attempts by Emperor Alexius to bring him to heel.

In 1104 Tancred also became regent of the County of Edessa, when its ruler Baldwin of Le Bourg was taken prisoner

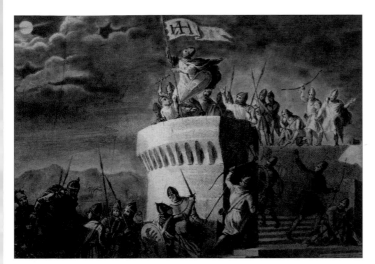

▲ *Tancred raises his banner above Bethlehem. He and Baldwin of Le Bourg established a crusader presence in Christ's birthplace before the attack on Jerusalem.*

by the Seljuk Turks at the Battle of Harran. In 1105–06 when Bohemond, having been released, returned to Europe to raise reinforcements, Tancred remained as regent in Antioch. He attempted to hold on to the regency of Edessa when Baldwin was released in 1107, but later agreed to relinquish his claim.

HUSBAND OF A PRINCESS
Around this time, Tancred married Cecile, daughter of King Philip I of France; she had travelled to the Holy Land to become the wife of Bohemond of Taranto, but that marriage had not taken place. He remained very powerful in Antioch and staunchly defended the Principality's independence from the Byzantine Empire – despite the fact that Bohemond, having been defeated in battle by Emperor Alexius, had signed the humiliating Treaty of Devol in 1108, in which he agreed that Antioch should be a vassal state of the empire. In 1100, moreover, Tancred gained a foothold in the crusader state of Tripoli when he gained possession of the powerful castle of Krak des Chevaliers.

DEATH AND REPUTATION
Just two years later, however, Tancred died of typhoid while still in power in Antioch. He had no children, but his memory was kept alive in Radulph of Caen's *Gesta Tancredi*. In addition to his status as a warrior in the key engagements of the crusade, Tancred demonstrated considerable strength of purpose and political nous, as he carved out a position for himself as the pre-eminent Catholic Christian magnate in northern Syria.

AFTERLIFE OF A CRUSADER
In the 16th century, Tancred was a hero of the epic poem *La Gerusalemme Liberata* (Jerusalem Delivered) by Italian poet Torquato Tasso. The poem used historical events from the First Crusade as a frame on which to hang a chivalric romance, and borrowed many narrative elements from the *Orlando Furioso* of Tasso's fellow-Italian, Ludovico Ariosto. In Tasso's work, the character of Tancredi falls in love with a Muslim warrior maiden, Clorinda, a character based on Bradamante in the *Orlando*; Tancredi himself is loved by Princess Erminia of Antioch, who betrays her city to the crusaders because of her love for him.

Italian composer Claudio Monteverdi used parts of Tasso's poem in his operatic dialogue *Il Combattimento die Tancredi e Clorinda* (The Fight Between Tancred and Clorinda), composed in 1624. In 1759 French writer Voltaire wrote a tragedy about the hero called simply *Tancrède*, and this, together with Tasso's poem, formed the basis of the opera *Tancredi in Siracusa* by Gioacchino Rossini in 1813.

▼ *In* La Gerusalemme Liberata *the distraught Erminia finds Tancredi heartbroken by the death of Clorinda.*

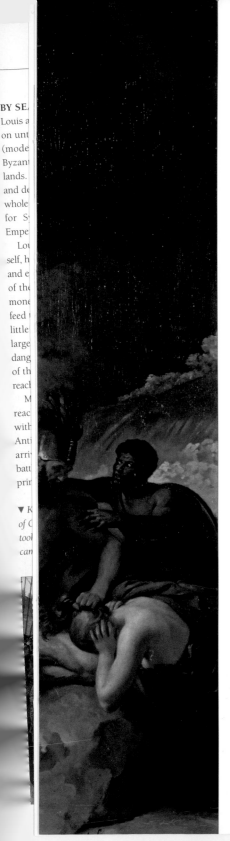

BY SE
Louis a
on unt
(mode
Byzant
lands.
and de
whole
for S
Empe
Lo
self, h
and e
of the
mone
feed
little
large
dang
of th
reach
M
reac
with
Anti
arri
batt
prin

▼ K
of C
too
can

CHAPTER TEN

MUSLIM RESURGENCE AND THE SECOND CRUSADE

The Europeans who fought in the First Crusade and subsequently established the crusader states of Jerusalem, Antioch, Edessa and Tripoli benefited from division among their opponents. Fierce rivalries between Muslim lords meant that in many cases, they preferred to ally themselves with the crusaders than with their countrymen. But in the 12th century great Muslim generals such as Ilghazi, Zengi, Nur ed-Din and Saladin began to develop unity and inflict great defeats on the Christians. These men mobilized their armies and people with the call to jihad, or holy war. The capture of Edessa at Christmas 1144 provoked European Christians to mount the Second Crusade of 1147–49; the abject failure of that enterprise only boosted Muslim morale and inspired Nur ed-Din to further great exploits of jihad. Then, in 1187, Saladin annihilated the strength of the crusader states at the Battle of the Horns of Hattin, and later that year recaptured Jerusalem. According to his biographer Imad ed-din al-Isfahani, Saladin envisaged an even more sweeping holy war. After Hattin he declared: 'When Allah grants me possession of the rest of Palestine I shall divide my lands, make a will laying down my wishes, and then embark by sea to the Franks' faraway lands, and pursue them there, so as to clean the earth of all those who do not believe in Allah.'

▲ Qalaat ar-Rahba in Syria was built by the great Muslim general Shirkuh.

◄ The culmination of the Islamic fight back in the Holy Land was the recapture of Jerusalem by Saladin's army on 2 October 1187, seen here through the eyes of a 19th-century artist.

THE COUNCIL OF ACRE
AND THE HUMILIATING SIEGE OF DAMASCUS

When King Louis VII and Eleanor arrived in Acre, a great council was convened there on St John's Day (24 June) 1148 to discuss the future direction of the crusade. At this council the assembled lords agreed to attack Damascus, and the abject failure of this expedition was to bring the Second Crusade to an end.

CRUSADERS IN JERUSALEM

By the time Louis reached Acre, the remnants of the German pilgrim contingent under Bishop Otto had reached Jerusalem. Also in the Holy City was their king, Conrad III, who had recovered in Constantinople from his sickness and sailed directly as far as Tyre before travelling on to Jerusalem.

Other crusader groups had also made it to the Holy Land. Those who remained of the first wave of crusaders who had fought in the siege of Lisbon had arrived by sea, and the Provençal army that had

▼ *On three thrones, Louis VII of France, Conrad III of Germany and Baldwin III of Jerusalem hold court at the Council of Acre.*

▲ *This illustration from William of Tyre's History of Outremer (c.1280) shows the three kings at Acre and, below, the siege of Damascus that they decided to attempt.*

departed under Alfonso Jordan, Count of Toulouse, had landed. Alfonso almost immediately met his end, reputedly poisoned while at Caesarea by Raymond II, Count of Tripoli, who was fearful that Alfonso had come to claim the lands in Tripoli he had held in his infancy as the legitimate son of Raymond of Toulouse. (Count Raymond II was, in fact, Raymond of Toulouse's great-grandson, descended through an illegitimate brother of Alfonso Jordan named Bertrand of Toulouse. This made him Alfonso Jordan's great-nephew.)

The council in Acre was officially a meeting of the High Court of the Kingdom of Jerusalem. In attendance were: Queen Melisende and her son King Baldwin III of Jerusalem; Manasses of Hierges, the constable of Jerusalem; Patriarch Fulk of Jerusalem; Louis VII; Conrad III; Bishop Otto of Freising; Duke Frederick of Swabia; and Henry II, Margrave of Austria. In addition, the masters of the military orders were there – Robert of Craon, master of the Knights Templar, and Raymond du Puy of Provence, master of the Knights Hospitaller. Other leading nobles of Outremer at the council included Walter Grenier, lord of Caesarea, Philip of Milly, lord of Nablus and Humphrey II, lord of Toron; but none of the lords of Antioch, Tripoli or Edessa were in attendance.

King Baldwin and the Knights Templar urged an attack on Damascus. Several local lords argued against this line of action, particularly on the grounds that

Mu'in ad-Din Unur, emir of Damascus, was an ally of the Christians against the Zengid lords of Syria – including the increasingly formidable Nur ed-Din of Aleppo. King Louis and King Conrad, however, were persuaded to back the attack on Damascus; the European lords, unversed in local politics and diplomacy, could not readily accept arguments in favour of making alliances with Muslim rulers and wanted principally to pursue a holy war against 'the infidel'. Moreover, while Aleppo meant nothing to them, Damascus was a city they knew from the Bible. An army was raised and in July assembled at Tiberias.

THE ORCHARDS OF DAMASCUS

The crusader lords decided to attack Damascus from the west, where a thick band of orchards would provide them with a steady food supply. They arrived there on 23 July, with the troops of the Kingdom of Jerusalem leading the way, followed by Louis and the French and then Conrad and the remainder of the German contingent in the rear. Emir Unur was warned of their approach, and had poisoned water sources, taken steps to strengthen his fortifications and sent out appeals for help to rival Muslim lords.

Taking the orchards was the crusaders' first task, but it was not an easy one: according to William of Tyre, they stretched for more than five miles 'like a dense, gloomy forest', the trees growing close together and accessible only by way of narrow footpaths between mud walls; in addition, there were defensive towers set at regular intervals. The crusaders poured into this difficult terrain, losing many men to arrow shots from the towers or to sudden attacks with spears from the darkness between the trees. They also had to face the city defenders who poured out of Damascus across the Barada river.

Both sides fought fiercely – according to a contemporary account, Conrad III made himself the talk of the entire army by dealing an overwhelming blow to a Turkish warrior that sliced through his

entire body, cutting off his head, neck and left shoulder. By the end of July 24 the crusaders had prevailed, taking control of the orchards and driving the Damascene defenders back behind their city walls.

Within the city, the people began to build barricades in the streets, fearing that they would be overrun. But at this point the crusaders paid the price for not encircling the city, for a relief army began to arrive from Aleppo in response to Emir Unur's cry for help – and this force, approaching from the north, was able to march right up to the city and enter through its North Gate. They began to launch counter-attacks on the Christian position in the orchards.

EASTERN APPROACHES

On 27 July the crusader lords took the fateful decision to move the army around the city to its open east side. Here they thought they might better be able to defend their camp. But – as they discovered the moment they arrived – there was

▲ *The crusader armies fought bravely at Damascus, but were undone by their leaders' bad tactical and strategic decisions.*

little or no food or water available there, and the eastern section of the city wall was very heavily fortified.

The crusaders and their leaders must have looked about in dismay. They could not return to the orchards, for by this stage Nur ed-Din himself had arrived and encamped his army there. In the burning heat of July, with insufficient water and the city strongly reinforced, their chances of taking Damascus had melted away; their position became untenable.

At dawn on 28 July, the Christian army began to abandon the siege, retreating in despair and disarray, harried all the way by the Turks. They lost many more men and horses during this humiliating retreat, and according to local chroniclers the human and animal corpses that lined the road sent up a stench powerful enough to make birds fall from the sky.

THE BATTLE FOR EGYPT
SYRIA LOOKS TO EXTEND MUSLIM POWER

In 1162, with Syria secure against intervention from the crusader lords, Nur ed-Din went on pilgrimage to Mecca. He had achieved his ambition of uniting Syria. His eyes – and those of his nominal masters, the Abbasid caliphs of Baghdad – began to turn to Egypt, and to view the possibility of overthrowing the Shi'ite Fatimid caliphate there and establishing a united Sunni Muslim state of Syria and Egypt. The same year, a new king mounted the throne in Jerusalem – Amalric I, brother of Baldwin III.

POWER STRUGGLE IN CAIRO

In Egypt, although rule was nominally by the religious leader or caliph, real power lay in the hands of the chief administrator, or vizier. In 1163, at a time when the caliph was the inexperienced 14-year-old al-Adid, the vizier Shawar was ousted and replaced by Dirgham. King Amalric of Jerusalem, seeing an opportunity,

mounted an expedition into Egypt claiming that the Fatimids were not paying tribute that had been pledged during the reign of Baldwin III. This campaign failed and he was forced to withdraw to Jerusalem. Meanwhile, Shawar visited the court of Nur ed-Din begging for military help to restore himself to power, and offering lavish rewards.

In 1164 Nur ed-Din sent an army under his leading general Asad ed-Din Shirkuh bin Shadhi to Egypt. Shirkuh had risen from relatively humble origins by dint of his energy, leadership qualities and military excellence. His name, of Kurdish-Iranian origin, meant 'Mountain Lion'. William of Tyre described him as a short and 'very stout' man, and already in the early 1160s 'advanced in years', with a cataract in one eye; he presented him as a formidable leader, experienced in military affairs, possessed of 'great endurance in the face of hardships' and beloved of his

men because of his profound generosity. With him to Egypt rode his nephew, Salah ed-Din Yusuf (later known as Saladin).

Shirkuh did his job: Dirgham was killed and Shawar reinstated. But at once Shawar reneged on his promises and entered an alliance with Amalric against the Syrians. Amalric invaded Egypt once more and with Shawar's troops besieged Shirkuh in the fortress of Bilbeis.

CRUSADERS HUMILIATED IN ANTIOCH

In response, Nur ed-Din launched an attack on the Principality of Antioch, where he besieged the castle of Harim and won a crushing victory against the crusader armies of Tripoli and Antioch. He

▼ *Qalaat ar-Rahba in Syria was one of the strongholds of the 'Mountain Lion' Asad ed-Din Shirkuh, general in the service of Nur ed-Din and uncle of the great Saladin.*

▲ *View of Cairo and the valley of the River Nile from the citadel constructed in the city by Saladin after he became vizier of Egypt.*

captured a roll-call of crusader lords: Bohemond III, Prince of Antioch; Raymond III, Count of Tripoli; Joscelin III, Count of Edessa; and French nobleman Hugh VIII of Lusignan, who had recently arrived on pilgrimage. Nur ed-Din had them all led in chains into Aleppo and cast into jail there. As many as 10,000 were killed in the crusader army, according to the Arab historian Ibn al-Athir.

But Nur ed-Din did not capture Antioch itself; it remained officially a Byzantine possession and he did not want to provoke Emperor Manuel Comnenus, with whom he had lately agreed a treaty. He did, however, capture Banias, and then kept up a constant harrying of the crusader states for the following two years. Meanwhile in Egypt, Amalric and Shirkuh made terms, agreeing to lift the siege and return home.

EGYPTIAN BATTLES

But in 1167 Shirkuh and Saladin invaded Egypt again. They were followed by Amalric's army in 1167. Initially there was a stand-off between the Christians and Shirkuh's army at Cairo. Shirkuh offered Shawar the chance to make a deal and unite against the crusaders, but he turned it down and instead renewed his alliance with Amalric. Shirkuh then led his men south, followed by the crusader army. The

two sides fought without clear result: Shirkuh occupied Alexandria, where he was welcomed by the largely Sunni Muslim population, but was then besieged by the crusader army.

Shirkuh broke out of the city in the hope that the crusader troops would follow him and engage in battle. But they sat tight, and Saladin was left in control of a starving population within the besieged city. Finally the standoff was broken not by a battle, but a truce; Saladin played no small part in brokering a deal under which both leaders took their armies home.

THE TAKING OF CAIRO

In 1168 Amalric entered an alliance with the Byzantine Empire and invaded Egypt once more. He captured Bilbeis, massacred the inhabitants and then besieged Cairo. Shawar changed sides once more, turning to Nur ed-Din and the great Shirkuh for help. Shirkuh and Saladin responded with all speed to the summons, marching south with an army containing 8,000 cavalry. The crusader army, badly outnumbered, withdrew once more and Shirkuh entered Cairo in triumph on 9 January 1169.

THE KURDS

Originally a pastoral people living in the mountains to the north and north east of what is now Iraq, the Kurds were subjects of the Abbasid Empire who established independent warrior principalities when the power of Baghdad waned in the 11th century. These states were overwhelmed by the invasion of the Seljuk Turks, but in the 12th century the Kurds rose to prominence again as soldiers of fortune in the pay of the Syrian rulers Imad ed-Din Zengi and Nur ed-Din. The brothers Najm ed-Din Ayub and Asad ed-Din Shirkuh made their names under Nur ed-Din: Ayub was governor of Damascus while Shirkuh was Nur ed-Din's leading general. Saladin was Ayub's son.

▼ *Kurdish mounted warriors battle against Arab counterparts.*

At first Shirkuh dealt amicably with Shawar, but then, ten days later, Shawar was killed after Saladin and his associates dragged him from his horse and had him beheaded – notionally on the orders of the caliph. Shirkuh then became vizier of Egypt. But within thee months Shirkuh had died, reportedly from overeating, and Saladin was in power in his place.

CRUSADERS DESTROYED

SALADIN'S VICTORY AT THE HORNS OF HATTIN

In July 1187 Saladin moved again against the Kingdom of Jerusalem. On 4 July he annihilated the crusader army at the Battle of the Horns of Hattin, on one day destroying the Kingdom's united military capability and making inevitable his triumphant capture of Jerusalem later in the same year.

THE PROVOCATION OF REYNALD OF CHÂTILLON

Following Saladin's defeat at the Battle of Montgisard in 1177 and his revenge at Jacob's Ford in 1179, conflict between Saladin and the crusaders continued throughout the 1180s. A constant provocation was Reynald of Châtillon, a highly controversial figure in his own lifetime and beyond, the former Prince of Antioch (1153–60) who had spent 16 years in jail in Aleppo after being captured by Nur

▼ *Guy of Lusignan was crowned King of Jerusalem in 1180. He came to the throne as consort of Sibylla, daughter of Amalric I and sister of the leper-king Baldwin IV.*

ed-Din in 1160. Following the death of his wife, Reynald had made a powerful second marriage in 1183 when he wed Stephanie of Milly, heiress of the lordship of Oultrejordain, which included the powerful fortress of Montreal. From here, Reynald repeatedly attacked Muslim trade and pilgrim caravans, provoking Saladin to besiege the castle without success in 1183 and 1184. Reynald briefly practised restraint, but he was soon back to his old ways, attacking a caravan of pilgrims making the *hajj* (pilgrimage) to Mecca in 1185. (According to the 13th-century Old French *Continuation of the Chronicle of William of Tyre*, in this attack Reynald captured no less a figure than the sister of Saladin, but this is probably an invention since it is not confirmed in any of the contemporary accounts.) In May 1187 he attacked again, sweeping down from Montreal to attack a Muslim trade caravan from Cairo headed for Damascus. Saladin decided to act. He reputedly swore then that if he were ever to capture Reynald, he would kill him with his own hand.

THE SUCCESSION DISPUTE IN JERUSALEM

Saladin was also encouraged to attack by the weakness of the regime in Jerusalem, which had been undermined by a succession dispute. The dispute had begun in the reign of Amalric I's son, Baldwin IV, who, although a great military commander, was also a leper and was often too ill to govern and was unable to leave an heir. Two factions fought over the succession: on one side was Baldwin's eldest sister Sibylla and her ambitious husband Guy of Lusignan, supported by (among others) Reynald of Châtillon; on the other side was Raymond of Tripoli and the powerful Ibelin family, who backed the cause of Baldwin and Sibylla's half-sister Isabella, whose mother, Maria Comnena (widow of Amalric I), had married Balian of Ibelin.

▲ *Guy of Lusignan was banished from France by the future King Richard I of England. Guy arrived in the Holy Land some time after 1174, and can be seen here at his coronation as King of Jerusalem.*

Baldwin IV had Sibylla's young son Baldwin V crowned as co-ruler and heir in 1183 and when Baldwin IV died in spring 1185 the boy became king at the age of 8, with Raymond of Tripoli as regent. Baldwin V lasted less than 18 months: he died in summer 1186, and in the aftermath, Sibylla and Guy won the power struggle and Sibylla was crowned Queen with Guy as her consort.

A RECKLESS ADVANCE

Saladin gathered his army in May–June 1187 and on July 2 attacked Tiberias. The Christians gathered their forces at Sephoria under the leadership of Guy of Jerusalem (as Guy of Lusignan was known following the coronation of his wife Sibylla as Queen of Jerusalem). The army numbered around 1,200 knights and perhaps 20,000 infantry, representing the entire military strength of the Kingdom of Jerusalem. In attendance was the Bishop of Acre carrying a piece of the True Cross, the Kingdom's most sacred relic.

The position at Sephoria was a strong one, but Saladin was hoping that by his attack on Tiberias he could lure the crusaders out into open country. He got his way. Guy ignored advice from Raymond of Tripoli who counselled him not to risk a pitched battle against Saladin, and – urged on by the hot-headed Reynald of Châtillon – advanced towards Tiberias on 3 July. This was desert country, and the crusaders marched for hours without food or water, being harassed by Saladin's advance troops, until in the evening they encamped just to the south of the twin-peaked hill known as the Horns of Hattin.

SURROUNDED IN THE DESERT

In the morning they found that they were surrounded. Ahead of them, within sight, was a green valley and a lake, but Saladin's army barred the way. Saladin's men set fire to the dry grass around the crusaders, increasing the searing heat. Thirst maddened the crusaders, smoke billowed around them and arrows rained down on them from the sky. Saladin's secretary and chronicler Imad ed-din al-Isfahani later

▲ *The crusaders were overrun and all but wiped out by Saladin's army at the Battle of the Horns of Hattin. Fires set by Saladin's men swept smoke across the battlefield.*

▼ *Knights of the Kingdom of Jerusalem lie dead on the battlefield following the defeat at Hattin. By tradition, a heavenly light shone over them for three nights.*

recalled that: 'the people of the Trinity were eaten up by a worldly fire of three kinds, each irresistible and overwhelming: the fire of racing flames, the fire of raging thirst and the fire of whistling arrows.'

The crusaders tried to drive back the advancing army of Saladin, but without success. Only one sortie succeeded: Raymond of Tripoli, Reynald of Sidon and Balian of Ibelin broke out but were then unable to rejoin the battle; they rode away, knowing that Guy's rashness had brought the Kingdom to the brink of extinction.

Back in the heat of battle, the crusader army was driven up the hill towards the tent of King Guy, visible on the summit. To the despair of all, while fighting, the Bishop of Acre was robbed of the relic of the True Cross. Templars and Hospitallers fought bravely but they could not prevent the inevitable and eventually King Guy's tent fell and the battle was over.

HONOUR AND REVENGE

Guy and Reynald of Châtillon were still alive and were brought to Saladin's tent. Saladin gave the thirst-maddened Guy a drink of iced rosewater and the king

handed it to Reynald. Saladin grew angry, and made it clear that he had not offered the drink to his enemy Reynald – for by the Muslim warriors' code of war if a prisoner were offered food or drink by his captor his life had to be spared. Saladin did spare Guy, but slew Reynald by his own hand. 'Kings do not kill kings,' he said to Guy, but looking at Reynald added, 'that man's insolence went beyond what can be tolerated.'

On the following day Saladin ordered the execution of the surviving warriors among the Knights Templar and the Knights Hospitaller. Muslim holy men and Sufi mystics, who had joined the army in answer to the call to take part in jihad, begged to be allowed to perform the deed. Saladin seated himself on a mounted platform and watched, with his assembled soldiers, as the Christian warriors were put to death agonizingly slowly by these inexperienced swordsmen.

JERUSALEM RECAPTURED
SALADIN TAKES THE HOLY CITY

On 2 October 1187 Saladin and his army recaptured Jerusalem, ending almost 90 years of Christian rule.

CONTROL OF THE KINGDOM
Defeat at the Horns of Hattin had wiped out the crusader states' military strength and Saladin proceeded through the Kingdom virtually unopposed. Acre surrendered within days of the battle, and shortly afterwards Saladin's brother Al-Adil captured Jaffa. Nazareth, Caesarea and Haifa were taken and on 4 September Saladin captured Ascalon. Darkness fell by day because there was an eclipse of the sun; Christians who had heard of the eclipse of the moon witnessed before the capture of Jerusalem in 1099 may have seen this as an omen – and shuddered.

On 20 September 1187 Saladin began a siege of Jerusalem. The city's defence was

▼ In triumph the Muslim army was highly disciplined. Saladin had his enemies at his mercy but treated them respectfully. There was no repeat of the lawlessness of 1099.

the responsibility of Balian of Ibelin, one of the knights who had broken out of the Muslim encirclement at the Horns of Hattin; he had returned to the city in order to rescue his wife Maria Comnena (the city's former queen and widow of Amalric I). He did not have sufficient manpower to mount an effective defence of the city walls – according to one contemporary account, there were only two other knights and a limited number of men-at-arms. Nevertheless, he inspired the defenders to hold out for nine days.

TERMS OF SURRENDER
On 30 September, after the Muslim siege equipment had made a breach in the wall near the Gate of the Column, Balian rode out to Saladin's camp to discuss terms under which the city might be given up. At first Saladin did not want to negotiate. He reminded Balian of the terrible behaviour of the Christian knights in taking Jerusalem in 1099. He wanted nothing less then unconditional surrender.

Balian responded by threatening that if they could not agree a truce and ransom, he would order the Christians within the city to slaughter the 5,000-odd Muslim slaves and prisoners, then to kill their own wives and children, destroy their valuable

▲ Within Jerusalem, Balian of Ibelin led a few knights in desperate resistance to the siege, but they were vastly outnumbered. The Holy City passed into Saladin's hands.

possessions, attack the Muslim holy places and then fight to the death on the city walls. The city would be a bloodbath, loot would be destroyed, sacred places desecrated, and many of Saladin's soldiers would be killed unnecessarily in taking the city by force.

Saladin wanted to capture the city intact and did not want to cause the deaths of his fellow Muslims, so he agreed a ransom deal with Balian: ten dinars for each man, five for each woman and one for each child, with a lump sum of 30,000 dinars payable for 7,000 of the population who were too poor to pay their own ransom, the remainder of the unransomable poor were to be sold into slavery.

THE REOCCUPATION OF JERUSALEM
On 2 October 1187 Saladin and his disciplined army took the city peacefully. He was true to his word and the Franks were allowed to leave unmolested. Saladin sent groups of armed soldiers into the city to ensure that there was no looting or

SALADIN'S CHARACTER

Saladin was celebrated for his lively mind and sense of honour. Crusaders praised him for his generosity in victory and his wit in negotiation. His Muslim biographer Baha ed-Din ibn Shaddad wrote of him that he was a mine of fascinating information in conversation, a caring leader who would always ask after friends, and attempt to raise people's spirits. He would not allow fellow Muslims to be criticized in his presence, wanting to hear of people's good qualities instead. When he encountered orphans he always made sure that they were helped. Baha ed-Din ibn Shaddad recounted the story of how a distraught crusader woman demanded to see Saladin after her daughter had been stolen by Muslim soldiers: Saladin not only saw her and listened to her, but also sent men to scour the markets to see if they could find the girl; they did and he reunited her with her mother.

▼ *A monument to Saladin in Damascus.*

▲ *An illustration of c.1400 looks back to the fight for Jerusalem in 1187. The besieging Islamic army has been reimagined as a conventional European force.*

rampage. He then set about cleaning up the city, restoring the al Aqsa mosque and the Dome of the Rock to sacred use for Muslims. Although he was urged by his compatriots to destroy the Church of the Holy Sepulchre, he merely ordered it to be closed for three days, then reopened to pilgrims. The manner in which they reoccupied Jerusalem was a great and lasting credit to Saladin and his men, and should have shamed the Christian knights of 1099 had they been alive to see it.

Saladin's reputation for magnanimity and piety were enhanced by his treatment of the ransomed prisoners. Forty days were allowed for the Christians to raise the necessary ransoms. Throughout, Saladin behaved with the utmost generosity: when his brother, growing distressed at the vast numbers of captives, asked for some to be spared, Saladin freed 1,000; he gave another 700 their freedom in response to a request by the Patriarch of Jerusalem; and set another 500 free as a tribute to Balian. He then went even further, freeing the elderly and the infirm and all the husbands of women already freed.

MUSLIM JOY

According to Imad ed-din al-Isfahani, Saladin held a joyful court in the days after his retaking of Jerusalem, and was visited by many leading Muslims who 'covered his carpet with kisses'. He maintained a sober and dignified bearing, but his face was 'bright with joy' and 'his expression shone'; the great triumph he had achieved, Imad ed-din wrote, appeared to give him a halo of moonlight.

CHRISTIAN DESPAIR

The Kingdom of Jerusalem appeared to be close to extinction. In the two years following the Battle of the Horns of Hattin, Saladin captured more than 50 crusader strongholds. He did not move against Tripoli or Antioch and Tyre remained in Christian hands, but the taking of Jerusalem was a great propaganda victory that suggested there was no future for the Christians in Palestine.

News of the defeat at the Horns of Hattin and the loss of Jerusalem reached Europe in the autumn of 1187 and Pope Urban III is reported to have died of grief. Writers and preachers lamented the terrible turn of events. One declared: '... on that day, October 2, 1187, the queen among all the cities in the world was cast into slavery.' It was an end, but also a beginning – within weeks, Urban's successor Pope Gregory VIII issued a call for a fresh military expedition to the Holy Land and a new crusade began.

PART THREE

THE LATER AND EUROPEAN CRUSADES

The kings, princes and knights who conducted the Third Crusade of 1189–92 – and those of the ensuing centuries – were inspired by tales of the heroic deeds of Christian warriors on the First and Second Crusades (1096–99 and 1147–49). In particular, they were driven by a desire to repeat the extraordinary achievement of the knights of the First Crusade, who succeeded against all odds in capturing Jerusalem for Christ and for the Western Church. They had little political or economic motive in fighting in the East – they were inspired principally by religious motives. The later crusades in the Holy Land were paralleled by wars of the cross fought against pagans of middle and northern Europe, against the Muslim 'Moors' of the Iberian Peninsula, against enemies of the Catholic Church in Italy, and against the French dualist Cathars and other Christians denounced as 'heretics' – a collection of campaigns characterized by historians as Baltic or European Crusades to distinguish them from those in the East. These crusades were different in character: while the Eastern Crusades remained essentially wars of religion, the European Crusades were mostly political or economic struggles, in which the powerful religious rhetoric was merged with political agendas and causes.

▲ *Holding key ports was essential in the crusading era so that vital supplies could be shipped in to maintain the long sieges.*

▶ *In 1249, on the Seventh Crusade, an army led by Louis IX of France landed in Egypt, aiming to destroy Muslim power in north Africa before attacking Syria.*

TIMELINE OF THE LATER CRUSADES

29 October 1187 Pope Gregory VIII calls the Third Crusade.

January 1188 Kings Philip II of France and Henry II of England take the cross.

March 1188 Frederick I of Germany takes the cross.

11 May 1189 German crusaders under Frederick I depart.

6 July 1189 Henry II of England dies; his successor Richard I sets about raising money to go on crusade.

27 August 1189 King Guy of Jerusalem begins siege of Acre.

17 May 1190 German crusaders defeat Seljuks and capture Iconium.

10 June 1190 Frederick I drowns in River Saleph (modern Göksu).

25 July 1190 Queen Sibylla of Jerusalem dies, sparking succession dispute.

20 April 1191 Philip II arrives at Acre.

8 June 1191 Richard I arrives at Acre.

12 July 1191 Acre surrenders.

7 September 1191 Richard I defeats Saladin in the Battle of Arsuf.

April 1192 Sibylla's sister Isabella and her husband Count Henry II of Champagne take power in Jerusalem.

5 August 1192 King Richard I defeats Saladin at Jaffa.

2 September 1192 Richard I and Saladin agree a peace treaty that brings an end to the Third Crusade.

4 March 1193 Saladin dies.

25 July 1195 Pope Celestine III calls a new crusade; German emperor Henry VI takes the cross and a crusade sails in 1197 but melts away following Henry's death in Sicily in September 1197.

August 1198 Pope Innocent III calls the Fourth Crusade.

October 1202 The armies of the Fourth Crusade set off.

24 November 1202 Crusaders sack the Christian city of Zara in Hungary (modern Zadar in Croatia).

1202 The military order of the Livonian Brothers of the Sword is established.

12–15 April 1204 Forces of the Fourth Crusade sack Constantinople.

16 May 1204 Count Baldwin of Flanders is crowned emperor of the new Latin Empire of Constantinople in the Church of Haghia Sophia, Constantinople.

1208 Pope Innocent III declares a crusade against the Cathars, a heretical Christian sect of southern France.

July 1209 A crusade army takes Béziers from the Cathars, killing 20,000.

15 August 1209 The crusaders capture Carcassonne and evict the Cathars from the city.

1212 Pope Innocent III proclaims a crusade in Spain against the Almohad caliphs.

16 July 1212 A Christian army led by Alfonso VIII of Castile and Sancho VII of Navarre defeats the Almohads under their caliph Muhammad al-Nasir in the Battle of Las Navas de Tolosa.

April 1213 Pope Innocent III proclaims the Fifth Crusade.

November 1219 The Fifth Crusade army captures and sacks Damietta, Egypt.

July 1221 The Fifth Crusade army is defeated by Ayyubid sultan al-Kamil after

▼ *Soldiers at the gates of Jerusalem, from 13th-century manuscript Velislavovy.*

its attempt to march on Cairo is stopped by the flooding of the River Nile.

***c*.1228** The Prussian Cavaliers of Christ Jesus are established to maintain a permanent military presence in Prussia.

1228 Despite having been excommunicated, Holy Roman Emperor Frederick II embarks on the Sixth Crusade.

17 March 1229 At the climax of the Sixth Crusade Frederick II takes possession of Jerusalem for Christendom. He triumphs through diplomacy rather than military force.

1233 Pope Gregory IX establishes an Inquisition to counter the continuing activity of the Cathars in southern France.

1233–34 Pope Gregory IX calls a crusade against pagan Prussians, led by the Teutonic Knights. The knights build fortresses at Marienwerder and Rehden.

1236 King Ferdinand III of Castile and León captures the city of Córdoba from the Moors as the Christian Reconquista in Spain continues.

March 1244 The Cathar stronghold of Montségur castle is taken by French royalist forces.

August 1244 Khwarismian Turks take Jerusalem. Only 300 Christians escape.

17–18 October 1244 In the two-day Battle of La Forbie, a Turkish–Egyptian army commanded by Baybars (the future Mamluk sultan of Egypt) crushes a Christian–Syrian army.

1245 Pope Innocent IV grants the Teutonic Knights the right to issue crusading indulgences to those fighting on their behalf.

1248 King Ferdinand III of Castile and León captures Seville.

25 August 1248 King Louis IX of France embarks on the Seventh Crusade.

6 June 1249 The armies of the Seventh Crusade capture Damietta, Egypt.

6 April 1250 After a failed advance, the crusade army surrenders and Louis IX is captured by Ayyubid sultan Turan Shah.

May 1251 Louis IX is released from captivity in Egypt after payment of a large ransom. He sails to Acre.

April 1254 After three years in the Holy Land, Louis returns to France.

1255 The Cathars abandon their last stronghold at Quéribus in southern France, and flee.

3 September 1260 Mamluk general Baybars defeats a Mongol army in the Battle of Ain Jalut in Galilee. Later the same year, he seizes power as sultan.

1265 Baybars invades Outremer, taking Caesarea and Arsuf.

24 March 1267 Responding to Baybars' attacks, Louis IX of France takes the cross once more.

May 1268 Baybars captures Antioch.

July 1270 Louis IX and the army of the Eighth Crusade besiege the city of Tunis, in north Africa.

25 August 1270 Louis IX dies during the siege of Tunis.

30 October 1270 The army of the Eighth Crusade lifts the siege of Tunis.

May 1271 Prince Edward (the future King Edward I of England) lands in Acre leading the Ninth Crusade, causing Baybars to abandon the siege of Tripoli.

May 1272 King Hugh of Jerusalem agrees a truce with Baybars.

16 June 1272 An assassin sent by Sultan Baybars fails in an attempt to kill Prince Edward in Acre.

24 September 1272 Edward quits Palestine and departs for England.

1289 Tripoli is captured by Mamluk sultan Qalawun.

11 April 1291 Mamluk sultan Khalil begins the siege of Acre.

18 May 1291 The Christians are driven out of the Holy Land as Acre is captured by Khalil.

22 November 1307 King Philip IV of France orders the arrest of Jacques of Molay, Grand Master of the Knights Templar, and other French Templars.

1309 Having left the Holy Land following the fall of Acre in 1291, the Teutonic Knights build a new headquarters at Marienberg, Prussia.

▲ *Copies of Albigensian books are burned by monks of the Dominican order, under orders from the Inquisition.*

1312 With support from King Philip IV of France, Pope Clement V dissolves the Order of the Knights Templar.

1330 King Alfonso IX of Castile defeats Sultan Muhammad IV of Granada in the battle of Teba in Andalusia; Sir James Douglas, boon companion of the late Robert the Bruce, dies in this battle.

1332 King Alfonso founds the chivalric Order of the Sash.

30 October 1340 King Alfonso defeats a Marinid army in the Battle of Rio Salado.

1344 King Alfonso captures Algeciras from the Moors.

27 June 1365 King Peter I of Cyprus leads a crusade against Mamluk Egypt.

9 October 1365 King Peter's army captures and sacks Alexandria. Shortly afterwards, the army melts away as many of its leading members return home, and Peter has to abandon the city.

1390 Count Louis of Bourbon leads a crusade against Mahdia, Tunisia, a base for Muslim pirates attacking Genoan ships. It ends in a profitable settlement.

25 September 1396 Ottoman Sultan Bayezid I trounces a European crusading army at the Battle of Nicopolis.

1420 The First anti-Hussite Crusade is mounted against the followers of executed preacher Jan Hus, in Bohemia.

6 January 1422 Jan Zizka leads a Hussite army to defeat the Second anti-Hussite Crusade at the Battle of Nemecky Brod.

1422–31 The Third, Fourth and Fifth anti-Hussite Crusades are mounted but come to nothing.

10 November 1444 At the Battle of Varna Sultan Murad II's Ottoman army defeats a European Christian army.

29 May 1453 Ottoman sultan Mehmed II captures Constantinople. This marks the end of the Byzantine Empire.

21–22 July 1456 In the 'miracle of Belgrade', a vast army commanded by Sultan Mehmed II fails to capture the city. Belgrade's Christian defenders are led by Janos Hunyadi of Hungary and Italian monk Giovanni da Capistrano.

26 September 1459 Pope Pius II calls a new crusade, but it comes to nothing.

28 July 1480 Mehmed II abandons his attempt to capture Rhodes having been repulsed by the Knights Hospitaller.

1485 As part of a final push to drive the Moors from Spain, the army of King Ferdinand II of Aragon and Queen Isabella I of Castile takes Ronda.

1487 Ferdinand and Isabella capture the island of Malaga.

1491 Ferdinand and Isabella besiege the Muslim stronghold of Granada.

2 January 1492 King Ferdinand II of Aragon and Queen Isabella I of Castile take possession of Granada, marking the end of the centuries-long Reconquista.

22 December 1522 The Knights Hospitaller surrender Rhodes to Ottoman sultan Suleyman I 'the Magnificent' after a six-month siege.

Sept 1565 The Ottomans fail to take Malta from the Knights Hospitaller.

7 October 1571 The Christian Holy League defeats the Ottoman fleet in the naval Battle of Lepanto in the Ionian Sea.

1588 Spanish forces fight for English Roman Catholic insurgents against the ruling Protestant establishment, with the support of crusading privileges.

CHAPTER ELEVEN

RICHARD THE LIONHEART AND THE THIRD CRUSADE

On 7 September 1191, during the Third Crusade, King Richard I of England won a stunning victory over the great Saracen general Saladin at the Battle of Arsuf. Richard's battle tactics, which demanded total discipline from his knights in holding back from attacking under enormous provocation, were almost spoiled by a hasty charge led by the Knights Hospitaller, but ultimately were triumphantly vindicated as the Christians swept the Saracens off the battlefield in three unstoppable mounted advances.

The Third Crusade is forever associated with Richard I and his encounters with Saladin. The Battle of Arsuf was one of three victories Richard won over Saladin – and they had other memorable diplomatic encounters. In the chivalric literature of chansons and of chronicles, the clash of these great generals shines as an example of chivalry at its finest. The origins of the Third Crusade were notably different from those of the first two crusades, since it was called by the will of secular rulers as much as by that of the pope. Richard's participation – along with King Philip II of France and Emperor Frederick I of Germany – made the 'Kings' Crusade' one of the greatest and most glamorous of the wars of the cross – but, equally, the involvement of these monarchs was its undoing, for they were unable to put aside their fierce rivalries.

▲ *Frederick Barbarossa, King of Germany, invades Italy by sea in 1157.*

◄ *According to* jongleur *Ambroise, an eyewitness of the Battle of Arsuf, Richard was like a crossbow bolt fired against the enemy, who cut down his foes like a farmer harvesting wheat.*

THE CATHOLIC EXPANSION

The sense of glorious achievement felt by the Christian world after the success of the First Crusade was never to be repeated. Later crusades in the Holy Land and Europe were more complex and often severely compromised by mixed or deliberately duplicitous motives. The Fourth Crusade spiralled out of control amid political machinations and ended in the sacking and looting of Constantinople. In Europe, the crusading model was applied both to the fight against Muslim power in the Iberian peninsula and to campaigns waged against enemies both religious and political. The religious exaltation felt in 1100 did not accompany these events.

THE FOURTH CRUSADE

The Fourth Crusade was called by Pope Innocent III in August 1198. Its forces, which took some time to gather, departed from Venice in October 1202, bound initially for the former Venetian colony of Zara, which had become part of Hungary in 1186. (Today the city, on the Adriatic coast of Croatia, is called Zadar.) The crusade was vastly in debt to the city of Venice after negotiating an extravagant deal to supply a crusade fleet, and paid off part of the money owed by attacking and capturing Zara; from this point on they lost papal backing, for Zara was under the protection of a Roman Catholic monarch, King Emeric of Hungary, and Pope Innocent III had outlawed attacks on Christian cities. Some crusaders wanted no more to do with the enterprise and sailed directly from Zara to the Holy Land, but the bulk of this now badly flawed expedition became embroiled in the attempt by exiled Byzantine prince Alexius Angelus to oust Emperor Alexius III and claim the throne for himself.

Promised great wealth – nominally to help fund the recapture of Jerusalem – the crusaders left Zara on Easter Monday 1203 and arrived at Constantinople on 24 June that year. They landed on the far side of the Bosphorus but on 5 July crossed in transports and began a siege of the city. They took the Byzantine capital on 17 July, but then were forced to wait in their encampment for several months while the former Prince Alexius (now Emperor Alexius IV) raised the money he had promised them. Before he could do so, Alexius was deposed and a courtier named Alexius Doukas took power as Alexius V. A new siege began. The crusaders captured the city on 13 April 1204 and looted it wildly over three days. They established the Latin Empire of Constantinople; Count Baldwin of Flanders was elected Emperor Baldwin I. The crusade did not move on to the Holy Land.

RECONQUISTA

The *Reconquista* (Reconquest) of the Iberian Peninsula from its Muslim rulers was regularly promoted as a crusade from the 1090s onwards. The war against Islam in what became Spain and Portugal had

▼ *The papacy lost control of the Fourth Crusade, an enterprise in which religious crusading rhetoric was used to mask nakedly political motives. After the capture of the Byzantine imperial city, and the establishment of the Latin Empire of Constantinople, a large part of southern Greece was captured in winter 1204–05.*

The Reconquista in Spain
— Christian-Muslim border 1050
— Christian-Muslim border 1100
— Christian-Muslim border 1157
— Christian-Muslim border 1224
— Christian-Muslim border 1275
■ Christian territory in 1275
■ Muslim territory in 1275
▮ Castle
✕ Battle

▲ *The final war waged by Ferdinand and Isabella was explicitly a Christian crusade, and their army – as well as being equipped with the latest artillery – was reinforced by Christian troops from around Europe.*

actually begun almost 400 years earlier, not long after Arabs and north African Berbers seized most of the Christian kingdom of the Visigoths in AD711–716. Catalonia was recaptured in the late 8th century and became known as the 'Spanish March'. By the late 9th century Christian territory extended right across the north of the Iberian Peninsula; the remainder of what is now Spain and Portugal was ruled by a Muslim caliph from Córdoba.

After the Caliphate of Córdoba collapsed in 1002, the 30 or so independent Muslim kingdoms that succeeded it proved vulnerable to Christian advance: King Alfonso VI of Léon took Toledo in 1085 and looked set to recapture the entire peninsula but was defeated by the Almoravids of north-west Africa in the Battle of Sagrajas in 1086. They made southern Spain and Portugal part of the

Almoravid Empire, but this too collapsed after 1140 and was succeeded by the Almohad Caliphate, which held roughly the southern third of the country. The Muslims were pushed farther and farther south by the expansion of Christian Castile, Aragon and Portugal – until by the last quarter of the 13th century the Muslims held only the small Kingdom of Granada in the far south. This territory survived for 200 years until it was finally

conquered by King Ferdinand and Queen Isabella of a united Castile and Aragon in 1482–92. With the capture of the city of Granada on 2 January 1492 the monarchs of the fledgling Spain ended 750 years of reconquest.

CATHAR CRUSADES

The first major battle of the decades-long Albigensian Crusade against the Cathar heretics of southern France was at Béziers on 21 July 1209: around 20,000 were killed. Carcasonne surrendered the next month. A Cathar fightback, supported by Peter II of Aragon, was defeated at Muret near Toulouse in September 1213. After 1216 the Cathars under Raymond VI of Toulouse and his son, Raymond VII, did win back a good deal of territory.

The war ended in 1229 but the fight against heresy continued through the often brutal activities of the Dominican Inquisition. The final Cathar strongholds in the hills and mountains east of Perpignan were captured in 1240–55.

▼ *The Cathars were especially numerous in what is now western Mediterranean France, then part of the Kingdom of Aragon. Although Cathar ideas did not originate in Languedoc, one of the most urbanized and populated areas of Europe at the time, it was there that their theology found its most spectacular success.*

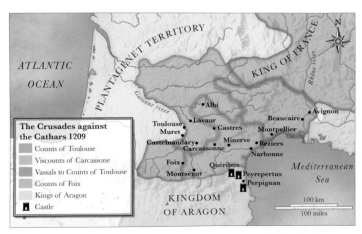

The Crusades against the Cathars 1209
■ Counts of Toulouse
■ Viscounts of Carcassone
■ Vassals to Counts of Toulouse
■ Counts of Foix
■ Kings of Aragon
▮ Castle

ONCE MORE TO JERUSALEM
A THIRD CRUSADE IS CALLED

On 29 October 1187, in Ferrara, Pope Gregory VIII issued a crusading bull known to historians from its first words in Latin, *Audita tremendi* (the first part of a Latin phrase that translates as 'On hearing of the dreadful and profound judgement inflicted on the land of Jerusalem by the divine hand'). The papal bull was issued in response to the defeat at the Battle of the Horns of Hattin in July, before news of the fall of Jerusalem had reached Europe.

The bull called the defeat at Hattin and the loss of the relic of the True Cross in the battle 'a terrible judgement inflicted by the Lord on the land of Jerusalem' and declared that the news – which had reputedly ended Pope Urban III's life, by bringing on a heart attack – had thrown his successor as pope and other church leaders into confusion and left them battered by 'such a deep horror and resounding grief that it was not apparent what we should do'. But it called for all to maintain their faith and to believe that God 'once softened by our repentance' would bring 'gladness after grief'; Christian warriors should see this as 'a chance to repent and do a good deed', offering themselves and their wealth for recovery of 'the land where Truth itself was born from the earth in order to bring about our salvation'.

Those who made the journey with 'humble and contrite heart' or who died 'in repentance of their wrongdoing and in the right faith' would earn a plenary indulgence and eternal life 'by the mercy of God Himself, on the authority of the apostles Peter and Paul' and that of the papacy. As in previous crusades, the property of those who took the cross would be protected by the Church and those who incurred debts making the journey should be free of the requirement to pay interest. The bull also urged those travelling to avoid ostentation and aim for simplicity – not to take dogs,

▲ *When elected to the papacy Alberto di Morra took the name Gregory in honour of Pope Gregory VII (r.1073-85), pictured here, a key establisher of papal primacy.*

hawks and expensive clothes but to have plain robes and equipment, to make clear that they are travelling in penitence rather than indulging idle vanity.

CRUSADE SERMONS
A Church campaign to preach the new crusade was put in train. In the British Isles, the Archbishop of Canterbury, Baldwin of Exeter, made a tour of Wales in 1188 to preach the cross. Baldwin's journey was described by the colourful Norman–Welsh churchman and chronicler Giraldus Cambrensis, or 'Gerald of Wales', in his *Itinerarium Cambriae*, written in 1191.

According to Giraldus Cambrensis Baldwin convinced 3,000 men-at-arms to take the cross. The sermons were delivered in Latin and French, sometimes with a Welsh interpreter, but even when the crowd could not have understood the words, knights and men-at-arms still rushed forward to take the cross. According to Gerald, a miracle occurred that showed God's blessing on the enterprise and the holiness of Archbishop Baldwin – in the area near Haverfordwest,

an old lady who had been blind for many years was cured when she rubbed her face with earth upon which the archbishop had stood when giving the sermon.

SALADIN TRIUMPHANT
In Outremer in July 1187, in the immediate aftermath of Saladin's victory at the Battle of the Horns of Hattin, the Muslim general's armies marched virtually unchallenged and imposed his will where they went. City after city passed out of crusader control. But the important port of Tyre was saved at the last moment following quick thinking by the charismatic European lord Conrad of Montferrat.

Conrad had sailed from Italy for Jerusalem in 1185 in order to join his father, William V of Montferrat, but he had been waylaid in Constantinople, where he had married Princess Theodora, sister of Byzantine emperor Isaac II Angelus. In July 1187 Conrad set out for the Kingdom of Jerusalem, probably fearing reprisals after he killed a rebel general named Alexios Branas when putting down a rebellion on behalf of Isaac. He set sail on board a Genoese merchant ship.

When Conrad arrived by sea at Acre on 14 July he found the place eerily quiet and cautiously dropped anchor offshore; then he and his companions saw Saladin's standards above the walls – the town had just fallen to the Muslim general. When messengers from the port approached by ship, Conrad pretended to be a merchant ally of Saladin; he promised to bring his goods ashore the next morning. But in the night he lifted anchor and inched away, setting sail for Tyre.

TYRE SAVED FROM SALADIN
There are differing versions of precisely what happened next. According to the 13th-century Old French *Continuation of the Chronicle of William of Tyre*, Conrad arrived in Tyre just as the port, which was

▲ At Tyre, Saladin and his apparently invincible army were defeated for the first time since the Battle of the Horns of Hattin.

▼ The victory at Tyre, snatched as it was from seemingly inevitable defeat, was the kind of triumph against all odds that had occurred on the First Crusade and inspired later generations to try to emulate it.

in the hands of crusader lord Reginald of Sidon, was preparing to mark its surrender to Saladin by raising his banners. But Conrad – resolute, determined and charismatic – threw the banners into the city ditch and convinced the people to transfer their allegiance to him; when they did so he led them to a last-gasp defence.

The truth may have been more prosaic. Other accounts suggest that Conrad arrived in advance of Saladin's army while Reginald was absent seeking to fortify his castle of Belfort; Conrad strengthened the town's defences and inspired its merchant community and other residents to put up a stout defence. Whatever truly happened, Saladin's attempt to take the city of Tyre was repulsed and he moved on to take Caesarea, Arsuf and Jaffa.

In November Conrad repulsed another, larger-scale attack on Tyre by Saladin, who had blockaded the city by land with his troops and by sea using an Egyptian fleet. Saladin paraded Conrad's aged father, William, who had been captured at the Battle of the Horns of Hattin, before the walls of Tyre and threatened to kill him if Conrad did not surrender; but Conrad was unmoved, declaring that his father had already lived a long life, and even – it is said – aimed a crossbow at the old man. His bluff worked, Saladin backed down and later released William. Again Conrad drove him off, leading an assault on the Egyptian fleet, and then a brave charge out of the city gates that surprised the besiegers and forced them to retreat.

The saving of Tyre was a turning point for the crusaders. This strategically placed port was to be a vital point of access for Western ships bringing supplies and troops in order to make the Third Crusade possible. Saladin's decision not to press home his advantage by taking Tyre was one of the very few strategic mistakes he made in a long and glorious career.

KINGS OF EUROPE TAKE THE CROSS

HENRY II, PHILIP II AND FREDERICK I JOIN THE CRUSADE

At Gisors, north-west of Paris, in January 1188 a crusading sermon by Archbishop Joscius of Tyre convinced two kings, Philip II of France and Henry II of England, to take the cross. According to the account given by the English chronicler Roger of Howden in his *Chronica* (*c*.1191), the sermon was accompanied by a miracle, when the Cross of Christ appeared in the sky above the kings.

Joscius had been sent to the west by Conrad of Montferrat after Conrad had repulsed Saladin's initial assault on Tyre. Joscius sailed in a ship with black sails to spread the news of Saladin's victories and call for urgent help and, according to Arabic accounts, carried with him pictures designed to outrage the Christians in Europe – for example, one of Saladin's army horses urinating in stables he had supposedly set up within the Church of the Holy Sepulchre, and another of a 'Saracen' hitting Christ in the face.

Roger added that the kings, who had been at war, were inspired by Joscius to put aside their enmity and agreed to

▼ *Frederick Barbarossa and his crusaders are called on to liberate the Holy Land, and begin their journey in 1157.*

pursue a common goal in the Holy Land – as Roger commented: 'those who were once enemies were persuaded to become friends on that day, through his preaching and the help of God'. At their meeting the kings also agreed on distinctive crosses to be worn by their armies to help tell them apart on campaign: the English army would wear a white cross, while the French would wear a red one. The troops of Philip, Count of Flanders, who also took the cross on this day, would wear a green cross.

DECISIONS AT LE MANS

In a meeting at Le Mans in February, Henry and Philip discussed ways to finance the crusade and decided on a tax of 10 per cent on income and property for an entire year to be applied to both Church and laity. This tax became known as the 'Saladin tithe' because it was imposed to raise money for a campaign against the Muslim general. It was administered by the Church rather than by lay authorities; clerics and knights who took the cross were exempt from the tax, but those who refused either to go on crusade or to pay the tax were excommunicated. The tax was extremely unpopular, and sparked fears that it was not a one-off but the beginning of a permanent taxation of the people; Philip II was faced with such opposition that he had to issue a proclamation in summer 1189 to the effect that the tax was an extraordinary measure and would not be perpetuated.

The kings also agreed on a sober code of conduct for the crusading armies. In order to generate a penitent and suitably sombre mood, furs and other fine clothes, games of dice and swearing were all outlawed; in addition, no knight or yeoman was permitted to bring a woman with him – 'save possibly a washerwoman on foot, to be beyond suspicion'. Anyone who died on crusade would be required to give up

▲ *Clockwise from top left: King Henry II, 1133–89, Richard I, 1157–99, John, 1167–1216, Henry III, 1207–72, from Matthew Paris'*, Historia Anglorum, *1250.*

the money he carried with him: it would be divided to meet immediate needs, such as maintaining his bondmen, helping the land of Jerusalem or feeding the poor.

FREDERICK TAKES THE CROSS

At Pentecost – the church festival celebrating the descent of the Holy Spirit on early Christians – in 1188, Emperor Frederick I of Germany took the cross at a special 'Court of Jesus Christ' convened in Mainz. By now in his mid-sixties, Frederick was a veteran of the Second Crusade on which he had travelled, as Duke of Swabia, in the company of his uncle, Emperor Conrad III. He had called the court the previous December, when, according to contemporary reports, he was visibly moved by a sermon at Strasbourg (modern Strasbourg, now in France) that

▲ *A stained-glass window in St Stephen's Cathedral, Vienna, represents Holy Roman Emperor Frederick I taking the cross.*

cast Christ in the role of a feudal lord wronged by his enemies and left unsupported by his liegemen.

On that day of Pentecost, around 13,000 princes, bishops, dukes, margraves, counts, nobles as well as many lesser knights took the cross alongside Frederick and his son Frederick, Duke of Swabia. According to the author of the anonymous *Historia de Expeditione Frederici* (Narrative of Frederick's Expedition), many men were in tears as they listened to a reading of Pope Gregory's encyclical, and a sermon from Bishop Godfrey of Würzburg. Frederick put himself forward as leader and standard-bearer for the crusade. No warlike man in Germany ignored the call, said the chronicler, and those who took the cross: 'burned with a great passion for fighting. For them, life was in Christ and death was a prize to be gained.' They set the departure for St George's Day (23 April) 1189.

WAR OF WORDS

Frederick traced his descent from Charlemagne himself and in 1165 had brought about the elevation to sainthood of that great leader, the creator of a Christian empire. Frederick had also, since 1157, used the term *Sacrum Imperium* (Holy Empire) to describe his own territories; and he believed it was the necessary and rightful task of a leader of a Christian empire to come to the aid of the faithful in the East against their 'infidel' opponents. He had even in 1165 considered launching a crusade on his own initiative.

Now, according to the crusade history called the *Itinerarium Regis Ricardi* (The Voyage of King Richard), he sent a proud missive to Saladin, demanding his retreat from the Holy Land and threatening a 'trial by battle' on 1 November 1189, 'by the merit of the life-giving Cross of Christ'. He claimed that Saladin would be shocked by the ferocity and strength of the warriors of the German empire: the untamed warriors of the Rhine, young soldiers from the Danube who would never flee, the towering Bavarians and canny Swabians, Saxons expert with the sword, circumspect Franconians, Bohemians unafraid of death, men from Bologna wilder even than their own beasts. And he said that he himself could still enforce his imperial will with a sword, for his arm was not wearied by age.

The *Itinerarium* also gave details of Saladin's equally proud response, in which he boasted that only three cities – those of Tyre, Tripoli and Antioch – remained in Christian hands in all the lands of Outremer and that 'these will inevitably be captured'. He also said that he was quite happy to undergo a trial by battle but that peace was a possible outcome if the three cities were handed over; in which case, he would allow Christian pilgrims to come and go freely.

▼ *Passions run high at Mainz on Pentecost 1188 when Frederick I accepted the call to take up the cross once more, together with many great men of the empire.*

BARBAROSSA'S CRUSADE
THE CAMPAIGN LED BY FREDERICK I OF GERMANY

The German army under Frederick I was the first crusading force to depart, leaving on 11 May 1189. Contemporary reports claim that his army was 100,000 or even 150,000 in number – easily the largest ever to set off on crusade – and took three days to march past an observer.

DISCIPLINE AND BELIEF
Frederick, now 67, must have had a good amount of grey in the red beard that gave him his nickname 'Barbarossa', but he still cut an imposing figure at the head of his vast force. He attempted to maintain strict discipline, reportedly turning away a group of 500 small-time criminals at Vienna and accepting into the army only those who could prove their capacity to support themselves. He had absolute confidence in his ability to regain Jerusalem and the Holy Land for Christianity: in common with the soldiers of the First Crusade, he believed that the Last Days

▲ *Frederick and his vast army survived a long overland journey, with many difficulties, and then boarded ships in Constantinople to sail across the Hellespont to Anatolia.*

as described in the Bible were upon humankind, and that when the emperor laid his sceptre down in Jerusalem the final act would begin with a reign by the Anti-Christ prior to the triumphant Second Coming of Jesus.

BY LAND ACROSS EUROPE
The German army departed from Ratisbon (modern Regensburg, in Bavaria, Germany) and followed the overland route to Constantinople taken by the soldiers of the First Crusade almost a hundred years earlier. Frederick led the way through Hungary and Serbia into Byzantine territory. Frederick had planned ahead, and conducted prolonged negotiations with Byzantine emperor Isaac II Angelus to ensure the crusader army's safe passage across Byzantine territory, but they did not receive the warm welcome they expected. Isaac was in negotiations with Saladin, who wanted Constantinople's troops to

▼ *An idealized portrait from the 19th century of Frederick I Barbarossa, Holy Roman Emperor.*

impede the progress of the crusader army in return for support against the Seljuk Turks in Anatolia and his help in ensuring that the church in Palestine would be under Orthodox Christian control. The Byzantine emperor was also suspicious of Frederick's motives – and reports reached him that parts of the army wanted to conquer his empire for Latin Christianity.

CONFLICT WITH BYZANTIUM
In October there were several open clashes between German and Byzantine troops in the Balkans. Frederick reported in a letter to his son Henry (the future Emperor Henry VI) that the crusader army had endured 'plundering' and 'massacre', and

▲ After setting out from Germany in a spirit of religious devotion, Frederick had a rude awakening when he encountered what seemed to be attempts by the Byzantine emperor to undermine the crusade.

At this point the crusade seemed well-starred. The army had survived a difficult passage from Europe, had won a great victory and appeared to be on the threshold of great deeds in the Holy Land. But in a twist of fate on 10 June, Frederick died when he fell from his horse while crossing the River Saleph (now called the Göksu) and drowned in its icy though shallow waters. In that moment, all the energy and conviction went out of the German wave of the crusade.

Saladin and the other Muslim leaders declared that Frederick's death was the work of Allah, who had acted to deliver them from a great impending threat; to the Christians it appeared that God was not supporting their march on Jerusalem. Many Germans gave up and returned to Europe; some were reportedly so shocked that they renounced Christianity entirely.

Barbarossa's son Frederick of Swabia took control of the army and marched on to join the crusader siege of Acre, where they arrived in October 1190.

▼ Frederick drowns in the icy River Saleph – like many crusaders before and after, he died in humiliating circumstances far from home, without having achieved the crusading mission he saw as his destiny.

that attacks had been 'obviously instigated by none other than the emperor'. They were, he wrote, attacked by bandits, had their way blocked with great rocks and felled trees and even found castles fortified against them. Nevertheless, they progressed and spent the winter of 1189–90 in Philippopolis (modern Plovdiv, Bulgaria).

In the letter Frederick indicated that Isaac 'with little concern for his reputation' had also imprisoned German ambassadors in Constantinople and seized 'upwards of two thousand marks' of their money – and that relations had deteriorated to the extent that Frederick was planning to attack Constantinople. He asked Henry

to gather a fresh force of knights to embark by sea to help in the battle. He instructed him to send more money to Tyre, where he would collect it – and he also asked to be remembered in Henry's prayers and those of the people at home.

In the event, full-scale war between Germans and Byzantines was averted, the German army bypassed Constantinople, and crossed the Hellespont into Anatolia – on board transport ships provided by Isaac – on 28 March 1190. They marched across Anatolia and won a great victory over the Seljuks, capturing the capital of the Sultanate of Rum at Iconium (modern Konya in Turkey) on 17 May. They stayed in the city for almost a week, restocking the army with horses and supplies, before moving on towards Armenian-held Cilicia. They also captured the town of Laranda (modern Karaman) around 60 miles (100km) farther south and just to the north of the Taurus Mountains.

IN SICILY AND CYPRUS
RICHARD I AND PHILIP II STOP EN ROUTE TO THE HOLY LAND

The kings of France and England did not follow the German army to the Holy Land until July 1190. Although in their meeting at Gisors in January 1188 Henry II and Philip II had agreed to put disagreements to one side in the interests of Jerusalem, feuding had resurfaced.

In particular Henry II's eldest surviving son, Richard of Poitou, had allied with Philip II and invaded Henry's territory in Anjou. Henry was defeated, and was broken by this, the latest of a series of rebellions involving his sons, and he died at Chinon on 6 July 1189. He was succeeded by the Count of Poitou, who became King Richard I of England. Richard set about raising money for the crusade: he cancelled the Treaty of Falaise

▼ *On 24 June 1190, Philip II receives the royal standard in the abbey church of St Denis prior to embarking on the crusade.*

of 1174, thus freeing the Scots from their acknowledgment of English overlordship, and in return received a payment of 10,000 marks from King William of Scots.

FROM FRANCE TO SICILY

Richard and Philip II embarked together from southern France, bound initially for Sicily, where, following the death of William II of Sicily, his successor Tancred, Count of Lecce, had imprisoned William's widow, Joan of England (Richard's sister), seized her dowry and stolen a legacy intended for Richard himself.

Arriving in Sicily in September 1190, the crusader armies came into conflict with the locals; but they were given an outlet for their energies when on 4 October Richard captured and sacked the capital city of Messina. The *Itinerarium Regis Ricardi* reported that the attack was so swift and easy that it took less time than

▲ *Leaving on crusade, Richard appointed William of Mandeville, Earl of Essex, and Bishop Hugh of Durham as his regents. But William died and his position was taken by the chancellor, William Longchamp.*

a priest needs to sing the Mass; Richard spared the citizens, but his army seized vast quantities of loot. Tancred backed down, freed Joan and returned the moneys he had taken.

But Philip and Richard quarrelled fiercely about who should take most credit for the victory, with Philip enraged that Richard flew his standard above the walls rather then Philip's banner. In the end, on 8 October they made up and swore an oath to defend one another and each other's armies on the campaign ahead. Nevertheless, the differences between the two kings would dog the entire crusade.

The armies of France and England then spent the winter on the island, while their leaders continued to squabble – principally now over a marriage, for Richard had pledged to wed Philip's sister Alys, but then proposed to renege on that promise in order to marry Princess Berengaria, the daughter of the king of Navarre. According to the *Chronica* of Roger of Howden, Richard took time in Sicily to listen to the prophecies of Joachim, Abbot of the Cistercian monastery at Corazzo, who had visions of St John the Evangelist, and declared to Richard: 'the Lord is to grant you a great victory over his enemies, and will raise your name above that of any other prince on the Earth'.

THE KINGS PART COMPANY

Finally the two kings went their separate ways. Philip left Sicily on 30 March 1191, and landed at Tyre in the middle of May. He moved on towards Acre, and joined the crusader siege of that city on 20 April. Richard made another diversion, for several of his ships – including the one carrying his intended wife Berengaria and his sister – had been caught in a storm and put in to Cyprus. There, the Cypriot ruler, Isaac Dukas Comnenus, had seized a large load of treasure that Richard was carrying and had imprisoned many of Richard's men.

Isaac Comnenus had come to power by treachery and trickery and ruled as a tyrant, so when Richard landed and

▼ *Philip and Richard swore a vow like that of chivalric brothers in arms after their quarrel in Sicily. They promised to protect one another throughout the crusade. But they would soon be at loggerheads again.*

ANTI-SEMITIC RIOTS IN ENGLAND

The Third Crusade was no different to its two predecessors in that the preaching of the cross sparked widespread anti-Jewish rioting. The violence afflicted England particularly, where Richard's coronation was marred by a major anti-Semitic riot in London, sparked when onlookers saw wealthy Jews apparently gaining access to the celebration. The following year violence against the Jews swept the country. The

▲ *Members of the London mob run riot in a Jew's house during Richard I's reign. Crusading rhetoric drove violence at home as well as in the disputed territories of Outremer.*

worst outbreak was in York, where on 16 March around 150 Jews committed suicide by setting fire to the tower in which they had taken refuge rather than face the mob in the streets below.

attacked Limassol the people welcomed him as a bringer of freedom. Isaac agreed to return the treasure and pledged to add 500 troops to the crusading army.

Once he had ensconced himself within his castle of Famagusta, however, Isaac attempted to take a hard line, ordering Richard's departure from the island. At this point, a ship arrived from the crusader camp at Acre, seeking news of Richard; on board were leading members of the Knights Templar, to whom Isaac owed a large amount of money. With their backing and encouragement, Richard led the conquest of the island, which was thereafter to be an important ally of the

crusader states in Palestine. The campaign took 15 days and, according to the *Itinerarium Regis Ricardi*, Richard found extraordinary stores of wealth that had been hoarded by the miserly Isaac – treasure was piled high in the castles of the island: the king and his knights found golden cups, silver jars, gilded saddles, precious spurs, silken cloth and fine scarlet robes, and they took them all, thinking it a gift of God to help finance the crusade.

Also during his stay on Cyprus, on 12 May, Richard married Berengaria at the port of Limassol and made her his queen. Richard finally left Cyprus and arrived at Acre on 8 June 1191.

THE CAPTURE OF ACRE
RICHARD I'S ARRIVAL BRINGS LONG SIEGE TO AN END

◀ The turning point in the seemingly endless siege at Acre came with the arrival of the charismatic Richard Coeur de Lion. Sure of success, the crusaders celebrated.

Philip II arrived at Acre on 20 April 1191 with a Genoese fleet. He was followed on June 8, by Richard I with an English fleet carrying a force of 8,000 men. Within five weeks of Richard's arrival, the city of Acre, which had steadfastly withstood a siege since August 1189, fell to the crusader army.

Richard's reputation had preceded him to Palestine. Saladin knew from his military intelligence that although Philip II was the highest-ranking of the European kings on the crusade, Richard was the leader in terms of battle prowess and charisma, a far more powerful warrior than his rival, driven by a burning desire for warfare. For several weeks before Richard arrived, Saladin and his officers heard boasts from crusader lords in the besieging camp to the effect that when this king of England arrived, the siege of Acre would be swiftly brought to its conclusion. The day of his arrival turned into a festival. According to the *Itinerarium Regis Ricardi*, trumpets, pipes and drums sounded out 'until the earth shook with the happiness of the Christians'; as darkness fell, people celebrated with carousing and dancing and lit bonfires that burned so brightly that the garrison of Acre thought the land around them was on fire.

SIEGE TIGHTENED

After his arrival in April, Philip II had put in train the construction of several powerful new siege engines, and Richard now personally supervised the erection and use of many more as the crusader army stepped up its attacks on the city. One of his military catapults had sufficient range to hurl great stones far over the walls and into the heart of the city; it reputedly killed 12 men with one shot. Richard fought in the front line: he had his men build a moveable protective shed beneath which the army's foremost crossbowmen could shelter as they fired; he himself worked a crossbow and killed many of the defenders manning the walls.

The garrison fought back forcefully, using Greek fire to consume the laboriously constructed siege towers and engines, manning the battlements and clearing the ditches, but they were outnumbered and increasingly desperate. On 3 July the crusaders made a substantial breach in the walls. There was intense fighting at close quarters as the crusader army, containing many hastily armed lords, including the Earl of Leicester and the Bishop of Salisbury, tried to enter the city – but the Turks rallied strongly and held them at bay. On 4 July the city's defenders offered their surrender, but Richard was unhappy with the terms: the crusaders were asking for the Kingdom of Jerusalem to be restored to its boundaries prior to the Battle of the Horns of Hattin.

ACRE SURRENDERS

On 7 July the garrison sent a message to Saladin indicating that if he did not come to their aid they would be forced to surrender. Saladin attacked the crusaders once more on 11 July but without driving them off and on 12 July the garrison formally surrendered.

They did so without the agreement of Saladin, who reportedly wept tears of frustration and grief when he heard the news, for he had just received yet more reinforcements and was confident that a final assault might drive the crusaders off and save Acre. The garrison, moreover, had agreed punitive terms on Saladin's behalf, as negotiated by Conrad of Montferrat (or of Tyre, as he was often now known): a vast ransom of 200,000 gold dinars for the lives of the garrison, 3,000 of whom would be held as prisoners; the cherished relic of the True Cross, in Saladin's possession since it had been captured at the Battle of the Horns of Hattin, would be returned, and around 2,000 Christians held prisoner by the Muslim army would be released; the city, all its possessions and the ships in its harbour would be handed over to the crusaders. Despite his anger, Saladin felt honour-bound to accept the terms agreed in his name.

The English army took possession of the city. King Philip II installed himself in the Acre mansion of the Templars, while Richard made himself at home in what had been the royal palace. Almost at once Richard quarrelled openly and fiercely with Duke Leopold of Austria – in a disagreement almost identical to the one that

▼ *Their long months of suffering at an end, the crusaders establish themselves in Acre after the garrison's formal surrender.*

had followed his capture of Messina. Duke Leopold saw himself as the commander of the German contingent on the crusade, for Frederick Barbarossa had died in Cilicia and his son Frederick, Duke of Swabia, had died during the siege; Leopold, therefore, demanded equal ranking with Philip II and Richard I. He issued an order that his standard should fly alongside that of

▲ *Saladin was impressed by the valour of Hubert Walter, Bishop of Salisbury, at Acre and later asked to meet him. On returning from crusade to England, Walter was named Archbishop of Canterbury.*

Richard on the city walls; but shortly afterwards the standard was found in the ditch, having been torn down and thrown over the wall. The result was that Leopold and the force at his command abandoned the crusade and set off for home.

KING PHILIP'S DEPARTURE

Philip II also left shortly afterwards. He had been severely ill with dysentery and also needed to settle the succession in Vermandois and Flanders, for the lord of that region, Philip of Alsace, had died in the camp at Acre and left no heirs. Philip left behind in Acre a French army of 10,000 under the command of Duke Hugh III of Burgundy and set sail for Genoa, bound for France. His departure greatly displeased Richard, who declared: 'It is a pity and a shame on my lord to leave this place without having brought to an end the enterprise that brought him here. But if he finds himself in bad health, and in fear perhaps lest he should die here, his will must be done.' His displeasure was no doubt principally caused by the knowledge that his territorial possessions in northern France would be open to interference from Philip while he himself was engaged in pursuing the crusade.

ATROCITY AT ACRE?

RICHARD I AND THE MASSACRE OF MUSLIM PRISONERS

On 20 August Richard had 2,700 Muslim prisoners from Acre beheaded on the plain in front of the city, in full view of Saladin's camp. He said that he did it because Saladin was refusing to honour the agreed terms of the surrender.

The prisoners killed included soldiers from the garrison, but also women and children. Many historians have expressed horror at the deed, contrasting it with Saladin's frequent magnanimity in victory. The Muslim army launched an attack in an attempt to stop the killing, but were driven back.

▼ *Kings Philip II and Richard I oversee the surrender of Acre and the taking of the city's garrison and people into captivity.*

It may be that Richard's decision was a justified act of war. It is certainly true that Saladin was dragging out the settlement of the ransom payment. Saladin had made an initial payment of the ransom fee on 11 August but according to the 12–13th-century Muslim historian Baha ad-Din ibn Shaddad, the general had then refused to hand over the next instalment until all the garrison prisoners had been released, and had wanted to provide a new batch of prisoners from his own camp to stand in place of the members of the Acre garrison. His motive was probably to make the settlement of the agreement drag out so long that the campaigning season would end before Richard could succeed in launching an attack on Jerusalem.

A LION IN A HURRY

Richard, on the other hand, was in a hurry. He had seen Philip II set sail for home, and had had time to consider the possible ramifications of the king of France being at large in Europe unchecked by the presence there of the king of England – Richard himself. He wanted to hasten the crusade towards its conclusion, so that he could return to manage his European affairs. He wrote to his justiciar in England from Acre on 6 August describing his victories on campaign, but indicating that he would soon be returning home – 'as soon as we have brought Syria back to its previous position'. He promised to be back in English waters by the following Lent.

▲ Barbarous act or necessary military decision? On Richard's orders, one by one, 2,700 Muslim prisoners are put to death.

He was in any case a decisive man who liked to act swiftly: already on the crusade he had conducted two whirlwind campaigns, one in southern Italy, where he had captured several Byzantine possessions, and one in Cyprus, where he had captured the island in just a fortnight.

He wanted to move on from Acre, and he did not have sufficient manpower to leave an army behind to guard the prisoners. Among the garrison were many crack Turkish soldiers who had fought bravely and with great skill to prolong the siege – he could not allow these men to escape or be released and then rejoin Saladin's army. Some writers have argued that the killing of the prisoners was an act of barbarity, but it can be viewed as a sensible and necessary strategic decision.

ALL THINGS FAIR IN WAR?

Moreover, it would appear from Saladin's ... er friendly relations with Richard that ... Muslim general did not view the killing at Acre as an act of brutality – he did not conceive a contemptuous hatred for Richard as he had done for Reynald of Châtillon. While Saladin was certainly often notable for his clemency in victory, he, too, was capable of acts of great ferocity, such as when he ordered the beheading of the captured Knights Templar and Hospitaller after their defeat at the Battle of the Horns of Hattin. On that occasion, the killing of the knights was made into an amusing spectacle, as the Muslim army jeered and laughed while untrained and unskilled army followers hacked at the knights.

Richard's actions did, however, have consequences that cannot have been good for army morale. The killing of the prisoners naturally brought an end to negotiations. As a result, the 2,000-odd Christian prisoners in the Muslim camp were not released and the sacred relic of the True Cross, captured at the Horns of Hattin and held in Saladin's camp, was not returned to the crusaders. However, the failed attack by the Muslim army left the crusaders in even stronger control of Acre than previously.

FIERCE AND RUTHLESS

Throughout his career, Richard demonstrated ruthlessness and decisiveness and a knack for making correct strategic decisions. In most ways the man known as *Coeur de Lion* was the very type of the chivalric knight – a great leader of men, charismatic, brave, strong, skilful, good-looking, hearty, and not lacking courtly accomplishments as a well-educated lover of poetry and song. But he was not the kind of knight who placed a greater importance on chivalry than on victory.

The massacre at Acre should probably be viewed in this light, seen alongside his treachery towards his father, Henry II of England, or his ruthlessness on European campaigns as another example among many of a clear-eyed desire for victory – a willingness to do whatever is necessary to win. The killing of the prisoners freed the crusader army to move on swiftly from Acre and impressed his ferocity and strength of purpose on his opponents. (Later, Saladin was unable to garrison Ascalon against Richard, for his men were too frightened by reports of Richard's behaviour at Acre to volunteer.) *Coeur de Lion's* heart was not only brave and strong, but also ferocious – and dangerous.

▼ Ruthless in victory, Richard does away with the prisoners. He saw them as a threat that had to be eliminated.

RICHARD'S MARCH TO JAFFA
AND A GREAT VICTORY AT THE BATTLE OF ARSUF

Richard set out from Acre on 22 August with the intention of moving swiftly on to Jerusalem. He led his army southwards along the coast to Jaffa (modern Tel Aviv-Jafo), accompanied at sea by a fleet carrying supplies and water. But Saladin's troops shadowed them all the way and launched wave after wave of skirmishing attacks. In a pitched battle at Arsuf on September 7, the crusaders drove off their persecutors, winning a resounding victory over the Muslim force.

THE MARCH
Richard imposed absolute discipline on his army. He knew that over-enthusiasm and a lack of respect for the harshness of climate and terrain had led to disaster at the Horns of Hattin: for this reason, he decreed that the army would march no more than 4–5 miles (6–8km) per day, moving only in the cooler hours of the morning and making camp each afternoon by a source of water.

On the march Richard insisted that his men kept in a tight formation, with the infantry on the landward side to fend off attacks by the Muslim army and protect the mounted knights riding in the centre of the column. The infantrymen carried large crusader shields and wore heavy armour over thick felt jerkins. According to Muslim historian Baha ed-Din, the arrows of the Turkish archers could make little impression on them: 'I saw,' he wrote, 'warriors with no fewer than ten arrows stuck in their back armour, marching on unperturbed without breaking rank.' Periodically, the infantrymen on the landward side were replaced by fresher men who had been marching on the seaward side, where there were no attacks.

In the centre of the main column was the royal standard, mounted in a wagon and guarded by an elite reserve. In front of this rode the Knights Templar and behind it the Knights Hospitaller. The rear of the army had to cope with repeated attacks, and take care not to fall behind. The Muslim force harried the column, hoping to force the crusaders to break rank, but they failed. King Richard was constantly vigilant, barking out orders, tirelessly riding out to meet attacks with his great sword shining in the harsh sun.

▼ *Richard's troops make their way in searing heat and through bare desert from Acre to Jaffa, his men under strict orders not to respond to attacks by Saladin's army.*

▲ *The crusaders fought fiercely, but it was Richard's ability to make instant tactical decisions that triumphed at Arsuf. When the Hospitallers broke rank it was a potential disaster, but with a swift general charge Richard won the day.*

There was no great crowd of campfollowers as there had been on previous crusades – only this strictly disciplined column. Baha ed-Din described the Muslims' frustration at being unable to break the self-control of the Christians: 'You could not help but admire the patience of these soldiers, who put up with the most extreme difficulties.' Richard would not allow women to accompany the army, save for a corps of washerwomen who were responsible for cleaning the soldiers' linen, washing their hair and delousing them.

THE ATTACK AT CAESAREA
The crusader army reached Caesarea on 30 August. A major Muslim attack succeeded briefly in isolating the rear of the crusader column under Hugh III, Duke of Burgundy, but with the help of Richard himself they managed to drive off the attack and reunite the column. As the fought the crusaders called out 'Help u Holy Sepulchre!'

THE BATTLE OF ARSUF

On 7 September Saladin unleashed a full-scale onslaught on the crusader army at Arsuf. His plan was to draw the Christian knights out into a series of charges, and then attack and overpower them once they were split up into small groups.

The first attack came at nine in the morning, accompanied by a fearful noise of gongs, cymbals and trumpets and by the Muslim soldiers screaming. A second attack concentrated on the Hospitallers in the rear of the army column. Each attack came in waves: first Nubian and Bedouin soldiers unleashed a storm of arrows and javelins, and then moved aside to allow a follow-up onslaught from the Turkish mounted archers who rode swiftly forward before wheeling away in the hope of drawing out a charge. Here and there along the columns were pockets of fierce hand-to-hand fighting.

All this time the crusaders continued to march forwards towards Arsuf. Richard's plan was to hold the line and keep his

▼ Richard was everywhere at Arsuf, leading his men by personal example and trying to ensure that they kept their discipline.

knights back for one overwhelming charge. This demanded extraordinary discipline, for the Christians were under extreme pressure and the natural response of many of the knights in the army was to break out and charge.

In mid-afternoon, the vanguard of the Christian army marched into Arsuf just as the Hospitallers in the rear came under very severe attack. The Hospitaller general, Garnier of Nablus, begged Richard for the order to charge but the king commanded him to hold the line. But at this point discipline snapped: the Hospitallers charged, with a great shout of 'St George!' They were followed by the French knights who were just ahead of them in the line.

Richard acted decisively, making the best of what had happened by ordering a Templar-led charge right along the line. Saladin's army was driven back, but regrouped; Richard managed to gather his knights for a second charge and the Muslim force scattered. According to the *Itinerarium Regis Ricardi*, Richard led by example: the author likened Richard's sword to a sickle, harvesting a crop of warriors: he claimed that Richard covered the battlefield with Muslim corpses.

▲ Saladin's attack was carefully planned at Arsuf. He thought he had Richard trapped, but the crusaders turned the tables on him.

The crusaders still had to weather one more storm, for Saladin's nephew Taqi al-Din led an attack on the left flank, but Richard managed to regroup his knights for a third charge. This time Saladin's army fled in disarray into the hills. Richard's knights mounted his standard on the hill where Saladin's had flown and looted the abandoned Muslim camp. Since darkness was now falling Richard ordered his men to abandon the chase.

A GREAT BUT NOT DECISIVE VICTORY

The Battle of Arsuf was a major victory. It blew a hole in Saladin's reputation for invincibility and demonstrated Richard's superb generalship and personal bravery. But it was not a victory on the scale of the Horns of Hattin, for it wasn't a decisive blow against Saladin's military strength. The Muslim general prepared to block the route to Jerusalem: Richard's triumph at Arsuf did not leave the way open to the Holy City as Saladin's victory at the Horns of Hattin had done. In the short term, instead of marching on Jerusalem Richard occupied and refortified Jaffa.

AN UNCERTAIN FUTURE

RICHARD'S NEGOTIATIONS WITH SALADIN, AND THE JERUSALEM SUCCESSION

After the immense demands of the siege of Acre, the difficult march down the coast and heroic victory in the bruising Battle of Arsuf, Richard and his army recuperated in Jaffa. Saladin went to Ascalon and broke down the fortification to prevent Richard taking it and using it as a stronghold. In October Richard opened negotiations with Saladin in search of a diplomatic solution to bring the war to an end.

With the year drawing to a close, Richard saw the difficulty of mounting a swift campaign to capture Jerusalem, given Saladin's surviving military strength and the fact that elements of Richard's own army had drifted back to Acre. He also saw that lack of manpower would make it virtually impossible to defend the Holy City even if he succeeded in capturing it, especially because many in his army were crusader-pilgrims and could be expected to return to Europe having entered Jerusalem and worshipped in the Church of the Holy Sepulchre. On 1 October 1191 Richard wrote to the abbot of Clairvaux, describing his successes at Arsuf and reoccupation of Jaffa, and look-

▼ Richard and Saladin were exemplars of chivalry throughout the medieval period. These tiles representing the adversaries date from the 13th century.

ing hopefully forward to future conquests. Richard indicated that he and his men were exhausted and that the land of Palestine needed reinforcement, for if they captured more territory they would need men to hold it: he asked the abbot to inspire more European lords and yeomen to travel to the Holy Land.

NEGOTIATIONS AT JAFFA

Meanwhile, Saladin sent his brother al-Adil to Jaffa to carry out the negotiations. Richard was negotiating from a position of relative strength, and initially made a remarkably bold demand: the handover of Jerusalem together with all the territory between the coast and the River Jordan, and the return of the sacred relic of the True Cross, which was still in Saladin's possession following the breakdown of negotiations after the slaughter of prisoners at Acre. Saladin returned a cautious response, noting that Jerusalem was as much a Muslim as a Christian city, that the wider territory in Palestine had been in the possession of the crusaders for only a century or so and that he was willing to hand over the True Cross if he received something of equal value in return.

Then Richard made a shockingly original suggestion to al-Adil. He proposed that al-Adil marry Richard's sister, Joan of England, who, since the death of William

II of Sicily, had been the Dowager Queen of Sicily. Richard would give them possession of Acre and Jaffa and Saladin, should he agree, would give them the remainder of Palestine: then together they would rule the entire country from Jerusalem. Richard would return to England; the war would be over. The only problem he could see, Richard said, was that the pope would not agree: in which case, Richard suggested, one of his nieces could take the place of Joan.

Saladin, remarkably enough, agreed to this proposal – although according to Baha ed-Din, only because he knew it was a practical joke. But Joan of England refused to marry a Muslim; and Richard's suggestion to al-Adil that he convert to Christianity was also rejected. The negotiations ended amicably but without lasting results.

MARCH ON JERUSALEM

Richard then marched to Ascalon and began to rebuild the fortifications that Saladin had dismantled. In the winter, when Saladin had largely disbanded his army, Richard marched the crusader force towards Jerusalem. He got within 12 miles (20km) of the Holy City in January 1192, but in terrible weather that made rivers of the roads he decided not to risk an assault; the waterlogged, mountainous terrain did not play to the strengths of the crusader cavalry and instead favoured the mobile Turkish horsemen and archers. He returned to Ascalon.

Negotiations continued. Richard felt an increasingly urgent need to return to Europe to safeguard his possessions, for he was receiving reports that his brother John was seeking to seize power in England while Philip II was eyeing Normandy. At the end of March a workable compromise seemed to have been reached: the crusaders would retain Acre, Jaffa and Ascalon and would have the relic

◄ Richard's decision to pull back from an assault on Jerusalem in 1191–92 may be a sign of his willingness to compromise.

Isabella's consort from 1192 to 1197, although for unknown reasons he was never crowned.

Rumours soon began to circulate as to who had been behind Conrad's murder, with some claiming that Richard had hired the Assassins to do the deed. But it seems unlikely, given that he did not try to force Guy of Lusignan on the kingdom but accepted the elevation of the kingship to Henry of Champagne. More likely the cause lay in conflict between Genoese merchants who had Conrad's backing and their rivals from Pisa who would have been excluded by a Genoese monopoly had Conrad succeeded, but under Henry won important concessions in Acre.

of the True Cross returned; in addition, they would have the right to visit Jerusalem as pilgrims and maintain priests there. On Palm Sunday, 29 March, Richard knighted al-Adil in a splendid ceremony.

THE JERUSALEM SUCCESSION

In April the long-running succession dispute between Guy of Lusignan (also known as Guy of Jerusalem), the husband of the deceased Queen Sibylla, and Conrad of Tyre (also known as Conrad of Montferrat), husband of Sibylla's younger sister Isabella, was decided in Conrad's favour at a meeting of a council of Jerusalem's leading knights and barons. Richard had backed Guy but Guy received no votes at all in council. Richard subsequently arranged for him to buy the Kingdom of Cyprus. But then, on April 28, before he could be crowned, Conrad was killed in the streets of Tyre by two Assassins (see box).

Within a week of Conrad's death Henry II, Count of Champagne, nephew to both Richard I of England and Philip II of France, had married Conrad's wife Isabella and been acclaimed King of Jerusalem. He ruled as king on account of being Queen

THE ASSASSINS

The Assassins who killed Conrad were members of a militant Shi'ite Muslim sect, founded in 1094 in opposition to the new Shi'ite Fatimid caliph in Cairo and in support of his deposed brother Nisar. They believed in terrorist murder as a sacred duty, and were known as *hashshashin* in Arabic, from their reported practice of smoking hashish before embarking on suicide murder missions. The English word 'assassin' comes from *hashshashin*.

The Assassins carried out deadly missions against Sunni and certain Shi'ite Muslims whom they considered religious enemies as well as against crusaders. Their first leader, Hasan-e Sabbah, oversaw the establishment of a string of castle strongholds in Iran and Iraq from which terrorist killers emerged on missions. In the 12th century they captured several fortresses in Syria,

including the celebrated castle of Masyaf, from which their Syrian chief Rashid ad-Din as-Sinan and his successors sent men out on a series of murder missions. Sinan and his successors were called *shaykh al-jabal* (mountain chieftain in Arabic), which the crusaders rendered into English as the 'Old Man of the Mountain'.

► The fortress that became the Assassins' castle at Masyaf in Syria was originally built by the Byzantines.

THE TREATY OF JAFFA
LAST BATTLES AND FINAL TREATY OF THE THIRD CRUSADE

In May–June 1192, when Richard and his troops came within striking distance of Jerusalem for the second time in just six months, Richard elected not to launch an assault. Subsequently, back on the coast, he won two astonishing victories over Saladin before agreeing the terms of the Treaty of Jaffa, which brought the crusade to an end.

SECOND APPROACH TO JERUSALEM

In May 1992 Richard marched southwards down the coast from Ascalon and captured the fortress of Darum. Then he marched inland towards Jerusalem and encamped in the hills about 12 miles

▼ *In war and diplomacy Richard and Saladin treated each other with respect, each aware of the other's prowess. Chivalric authors and storytellers ever since have imagined encounters between the two men.*

(20km) from the city. Two events occurred in the hills before Richard ordered a surprising retreat to the coast.

The first was that he attacked a trade caravan heading from Egypt to Jerusalem and seized rich booty, including several hundred camels and horses – according to Saladin's secretary, Imad ed-din al-Isfahani, Richard disguised himself as an Arab in order to reconnoitre the landscape as the caravan approached. On another occasion, while pursuing some Turks in the hills he looked up and saw the Holy City in the distance. This was to be the only time he saw Jerusalem – and because he had made a vow that he would look on the city only as its conqueror, he raised his shield in front of his eyes to block off the view and rode away.

After the attack on the caravan, Saladin expected an assault on Jerusalem and prepared for a siege by poisoning water sources around the city and calling his

military advisers to a council of war. But on 5 July he received reports from his scouts that the crusaders had broken their camp in the hills nearby and were marching away from Jerusalem, back to the coast. Saladin rode out to watch the retreat. Many in the crusader army were puzzled and angered by Richard's decision. It would appear that he again decided that it would be pointless to launch a major assault against a target that he could not hope to hold even if he won it.

THE BATTLES OF JAFFA

Richard retired to Acre, expecting the stand-off to continue, but Saladin launched a heavy attack on Jaffa. Here, for once, the great Muslim general lost control of his men, who ran amok looting and plundering in defiance of Saladin's orders to allow the Christians to leave the city peacefully with their possessions. Some contemporary reports suggest that Saladin urgently communicated with the Christian garrison, encouraging them to take refuge in the citadel while he struggled to impose order on his troops.

Richard meanwhile gathered a small force and sailed along the coast from Acre to Jaffa. Arriving on 31 July he anchored off the city: a priest from the garrison, seeing the royal standard, swam bravely out to the ships to let Richard know that, although the city was in Saracen hands, the garrison was holding out in the citadel and negotiating terms of surrender.

What followed was truly the stuff of chivalric legend. Richard leapt immediately from the boat and swam ashore, loyally followed by his knights. This force of just the king and 54 others succeeded against all odds in driving the Saracen forces back. Richard and his knights camped outside the city, for inside it was in ruins following its earlier sacking and the stench of corpses in the streets made it uninhabitable. At dawn on 5 August

Saladin launched an attack with 7,000 cavalry; Richard and his knights had just 15 horses between them but – supported by around 2,000 Italian crossbowmen – they went resolutely forward to defend the edge of their camp, which was marked by a line of sharpened tent pegs. That day the crusaders won another extraordinary victory, holding the camp and the city against the Saracen attack. Saladin abandoned the campaign and retreated to Jerusalem.

Richard and Saladin were both exhausted, and both fell ill in the days after the extraordinary battles of Jaffa.

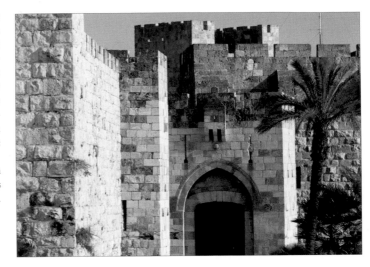

▼ *Richard's heroic assault on Jaffa with just 54 knights really was an occasion when history matched the brave feats of legend.*

▲ *These stones, in the gateway to the Old City at Jaffa, witnessed the clash of armies and the great deeds of kings and knights.*

With typical chivalry, Saladin sent fruit and mountain snow to Richard to speed his recovery.

PEACE AT LAST
Negotiations for a peace settlement were reopened and the two leaders reached agreement and signed the Treaty of Jaffa on 2 September. Under its terms, there would be a three-year truce between the two sides. The Christians agreed to demolish Ascalon and not rebuild it in those three years; they were to keep the coastal lands from Acre down to Jaffa, as well as the Principality of Antioch and the County of Tripoli; they would be allowed access as pilgrims to the churches and shrines of Jerusalem; and Roman priests would be able to celebrate services in the city.

In the weeks following the agreement, hundreds of crusaders made their way to Jerusalem to fulfil their vows. But Richard refused, declaring that he could not enter the city since God had denied him the chance to do so as conqueror. He was in any case very keen to return to Europe to look after his possessions there. He set sail on 9 October.

AFTER THE THIRD CRUSADE
THE AFTERMATH AND LEGACY OF THE 1189–92 CAMPAIGN

The Third Crusade ended in 1192 without the capture of Jerusalem. The crusade did not have a dramatic conclusion, and although it succeeded in preventing the complete destruction of the Latin Kingdom of Jerusalem, there remained in many quarters a sense of unfinished business. Just three years later, in 1195, another crusade was being organized by Pope Celestine III (ruled 1191–98) and German emperor Henry VI.

▼ *Coeur de Lion's martial prowess counts for nothing as he is fatally injured by a crossbow bolt from Chalus-Chabrol castle.*

RICHARD LEAVES PALESTINE
Richard I's homeward journey from the Holy Land was a disaster. Shipwrecked in the Adriatic, he attempted to cross the lands of the Holy Roman Empire in disguise, well aware that he could not expect a hospitable welcome from either Duke Leopold of Austria (with whom he had quarrelled violently at Acre) or German emperor Henry VI (angry that Richard had recognized Tancred as King of Sicily). By rights, these lords should have offered Richard immunity from attack because he was returning from the crusades, but both were keen to punish and to profit by him.

Richard was betrayed to Leopold who passed him on to Henry. Richard languished in prison for months before being ransomed for 150,000 silver marks.

His great opponent, Saladin, died after morning prayers on 4 March 1193 in Damascus, just five months after Richard's departure from Acre. Baha ed-Din ibn Shaddad declared that the Islamic world was filled with a grief so profound that only Allah himself could plumb its depths. Famed for his generosity, Saladin died bankrupt – at his death his treasury contained a gold coin and 47 pieces of silver – not enough to pay for his funeral.

Saladin's death presented an opportunity for the crusaders at an extremely inopportune moment. The great general's army was dispersed, and his power evaporated in family squabbles as one of his sons, al-Afdal Nureddin, marched on Damascus, while a second son, al-Aziz Uthman, was besieged in Cairo by Saladin's brother, al-Adil. Had Richard I waited in the Holy Land just six months longer, he would almost certainly have been able to capitalize on Saladin's death by capturing Jerusalem and re-establishing it as a Christian city. In the event, it took al-Adil ten years to reunite Saladin's territorial possessions.

Richard was never to return to the Holy Land. He spent most of the remainder of his life fighting over his French possessions with Philip II and died in April 1199 aged 41 after being shot in the neck by an archer during a siege of the unimportant castle of Chalus-Chabrol in the Limousin.

THE 'CRUSADE' OF 1195
On 25 July 1195 Pope Celestine III issued a call to arms for a fresh crusade. His letter, as reported by English chronicler Ralph of Diceto, declared that although the most recent crusade had not entirely succeeded in its aims, Christian folk should be strong in faith that God would

'exalt in his miracles' and 'instruct their hands in battle and their fingers in fighting'. As his predecessors had done before him, Celestine promised a plenary indulgence for the crusaders' sins 'and afterwards eternal life'.

German Emperor Henry VI, the son of Frederick I Barbarossa, responded to the call. Between October 1195 and March 1196 a great throng of Germans took the cross; they departed from southern Italy for the Holy Land in spring 1197. The army, sent by Henry, Duke of Brabant, landed at Acre in September 1197 and occupied Beirut and Sidon. But Henry died of malaria in September 1197 in Messina while campaigning in Sicily; and the German crusaders, as their predecessors had in 1189, simply melted away when they heard the news of the emperor's untimely death. The crusade of 1195 ended in a hurried truce.

LEGACY OF THE THIRD CRUSADE

The Third Crusade did not succeed in achieving one of its principal targets, capturing Jerusalem, but in many ways it was a success. At the outset in 1187 Saladin appeared to be invincible and it seemed

only a matter of time before the greatest of Muslim generals drove the Latin settlers out of Palestine altogether. Yet Richard I managed to inflict stunning defeats on this towering figure at Acre, Arsuf and Jaffa and in the process re-established the Kingdom of Jerusalem on a relatively secure footing. Moreover, the island of Cyprus, which Richard captured in 1191, proved to be a very valuable conquest,

▼ *Saladin died in Damascus, where he was buried close to the Umayyad Mosque.*

▲ *German crusaders capture Beirut in 1197, but the victory was to be short lived.*

since it provided a vital long-term partner for the Latin states in the Holy Land.

The Third Crusade set the pattern for future crusades to the Holy Land. After the campaign of 1189–92, crusaders no longer made their way to Palestine by way of Constantinople and Anatolia, but by sea directly to the ports of Acre or Tyre. In the first two crusades the European soldiers had chosen violence over diplomacy in every impasse, but after the use by Richard of truces and negotiated settlements with Saladin, relations between the crusaders and the Muslims were transformed. Moreover, just as the crusade had failed to capture Jerusalem, but still achieved certain valuable goals in consolidating the Latin presence in Palestine, so in future crusades the focus shifted away from the earlier narrow focus on liberating Jerusalem to a more general focus on aiding the Christian settlers in the Holy Land.

In 1198 a young, power-hungry pope, Innocent III, began to organize another crusade. The fruit of his labours would be the Fourth Crusade of 1202–04.

CHAPTER TWELVE

CRUSADES OF THE EARLY 13TH CENTURY

In the first three decades of the 13th century, popes Innocent III (ruled 1198–1216), Honorius III (ruled 1216–27) and Gregory IX (ruled 1227–41) oversaw three major crusades to the East – the Fourth of 1202–04, the Fifth of 1217–21 and the Sixth of 1228. In his 18-year reign Innocent III also proclaimed a whole series of European crusades, including two against fellow Christians (the German lord Markward of Anweiler and the Albigensian heretics of southern France), one against Baltic pagans in northern Europe and one against the Muslim Almohad caliphs in Spain. In all of these encounters, Innocent and his successors worked with their utmost force to maintain papal control, for they saw crusading as a means to extend the power of Rome.

But the popes often failed to keep control of the powerful lords and complex alliances engaged in the crusades to the East. Of the three major Eastern crusades in these years, only the Fifth can be said to have remained under papal control through the office of papal legate Pelagius. It ended in abject failure, with the agreement of a humiliating peace treaty. Of the others, the Fourth slipped entirely from the papal control and ended up as little more than a pillaging expedition, while the Sixth ended as a seeming success, with Jerusalem in Christian hands and the position of Outremer bolstered. However, these successes had been achieved by the fiercely independent Frederick II of Germany working quite unilaterally to the papacy.

▲ *Venetian and French lords take stock after the sacking of Constantinople in 1204.*

◄ *The armies of the Fourth Crusade ignored an excommunication threat from Innocent III when they sacked the city of Zara in 1202.*

FIGHTING FOR VENICE

CRUSADERS DIVERT TO ATTACK ZARA

The newly elected Pope Innocent III called for another crusade to reclaim the Holy Land in August 1198. French barons responded to the call in 1201 and, choosing to travel by sea, negotiated with the doge of Venice, Enrico Dandolo, to transport them to the Holy Land. Failures of organization and recruitment resulted in them being in such severe debt to Venice that they had to agree to divert the crusaders to fight on the doge's behalf against the city of Zara, in Dalmatia (Croatia).

INNOCENT'S CALL TO ARMS

Pope Innocent's call to arms was largely directed at knights and noblemen rather than royalty. Like many others, Innocent believed that the Third Crusade had failed to liberate Jerusalem because it had been led by kings, and principally because of the inability of Richard I and Philip II to overcome their rivalries. This time the pope set out to establish the crusade as one strictly under papal control and nominated two legates, Soffredo of Pisa and Peter of Capuano, to be leaders 'humbly and religiously' of the crusade. Innocent

▼ Venice rose to prominence as a centre for trade between western Europe and the rest of the known world – both the Byzantine Empire and Islamic territories beyond.

later authorized the preaching of the crusade by a French priest named Fulk of Neuilly, a gifted orator.

The response to Innocent's call to arms was initially underwhelming, but then in November 1199 at a grand chivalric tournament at Ecry-sur-Aisne in Champagne, the 22-year-old host, Count Theobald of Champagne, and one of the leading competitors, the 27-year-old Count Louis of Blois, both took the cross after hearing a crusade sermon by Fulk of Neuilly. (Theobald was the younger brother of Henry of Champagne, then reigning as king of Jerusalem since he was the husband of Queen Isabella of Jerusalem, having married Isabella right after the assassination of her previous husband, Conrad of Montferrat.)

Theobald and Louis were followed by other noblemen, including Count Baldwin of Flanders and Simon of Montfort, 5th Earl of Leicester. (Simon was later captain general of French forces in the Albigensian Crusade and father of the Simon of Montfort who led baronial opposition to King Henry III of England and briefly ruled the country in the 1260s.) Also among the French noblemen who took the cross was Geoffrey of Villehardouin, who wrote an account of the crusade. Count Theobald was elected leader.

▲ Earlier in his career, wily Venetian leader Enrico Dandolo had served his city as an ambassador to the Byzantine Empire. He knew the wealth of Constantinople.

NEGOTIATIONS WITH VENICE

Theobald, Louis and Baldwin appointed six envoys to negotiate the necessary practical arrangements. The envoys approached Venice, the world's leading maritime power at the close of the 12th century, and commissioned a fleet to transport the crusader army to the Holy Land. They asked for sufficient ships to transport an army of 33,500 men – a wildly ambitious number, no less than seven times larger than the force taken by Philip II in 1190. The proposed army was to consist of 4,500 knights (with their horses), 9,000 squires and 20,000 infantry.

To supply a fleet to carry this army, plus nine months' supply of food and fodder, the Venetians demanded 85,000 marks; in addition they offered to provide 50 additional armed galleys 'for the love of God', on the condition that the city be granted one-half of any plunder that was seized by, either by land or sea. The deal was agreed, and consecrated in a lavish service in St Mark's, Venice.

The envoys' overambitious planning was to have severe consequences. The envoys also secretly agreed among themselves that the initial target for the crusade should be Egypt rather than Palestine. It had been proposed before, not least by Richard I during the Third Crusade, that the key to undermining Muslim strength in the Holy Land would be found in attacking Egypt. However, the revised target was kept secret because the majority of the knights and others who had taken the cross had done so with Jerusalem as their inspiration and goal.

A NEW LEADER

In May 1201, crusade leader Count Theobald died of a mysterious malady. He was replaced by the Italian count Boniface of Montferrat. In June 1202 crusaders began gathering in Venice. Only around 11,000 men had arrived by October, partly because some had sailed directly from ports in southern France; the original target of 33,500 had been far too ambitious. The fleet of ships was ready – but the crusaders could not pay for it in full. After a prolonged stalemate, the Venetian doge offered to postpone full

▼ *Pope Innocent III felt the Christian church had to strengthen its position against heretics within it.*

▲ *Baldwin of Flanders played a leading role in the Fourth Crusade from start to shameful finish. He was made emperor of the Latin Empire of Constantinople.*

payment of the shortfall until the crusaders were able to raise the money through looting, but only if the crusaders came to the aid of Venice by reconquering its former colony of Zara in Hungary (modern Zadar in Croatia). This was a Christian city, under the protection of the Roman Catholic king, Emeric of Hungary, who had himself taken the cross.

The crusaders effectively had no choice. The doge, Enrico Dandolo, elected to take the cross and sail with them – despite being in his 80s and virtually blind. He was an extremely capable and intelligent man, and remarkable healthy for his age.

THE ATTACK ON ZARA

The crusade fleet sailed in November 1202, bound for Zara. The papal legate Peter Capuano approved the deal as the only way to prevent the crusade foundering altogether, but Pope Innocent III wrote a letter threatening the crusade leaders with excommunication if they attacked fellow Christians. The citizens of Zara hung banners emblazoned with the cross from their windows and on the city walls in the hope of forestalling the assault. But the attack went ahead.

After a siege of five days, Zara surrendered to the crusade leaders, and accepted Venice's claim of suzerainty. The victorious army entered the city and systematically looted it. They then decided to spend the winter there before proceeding with the crusade.

CHAPTER THIRTEEN

CRUSADES OF THE MID-13TH TO 15TH CENTURIES

For the most part, the news of the fall of Jerusalem to the Khwarismian Turks and the devastating defeat of the armies of Outremer and Damascus at the Battle of La Forbie had little effect in Europe, but it did provoke one very powerful man to plan a military response. In December 1244. Louis IX of France was revered by contemporaries as the embodiment of Christian chivalry, the perfect Christian ruler. He was fiercely devout, a great leader, respected by knights and men-at-arms – but even he could not bring success to the crusading cause. In fact, he led two crusades, the Seventh of 1248–54, and the Eighth of 1270. The Seventh Crusade, to Egypt, ended with a humiliating surrender. The Eighth Crusade, in Tunisia, ended in his death and the abandonment of the enterprise with only a trade treaty with the city of Tunis to show for it. The year after Louis's death saw the expedition traditionally regarded as the Ninth and last Crusade, led by Prince Edward (the future King Edward I of England). This enterprise brought about a ten-year peace treaty between Christians and Muslims in the Holy Land, but it was followed through the 14th and even 15th centuries by further crusading expeditions despatched from Europe to counter the power of the Mamluk sultanate of Egypt and then later of the Ottoman Turks.

▲ *Rukn al-Zahir Baybars destroys a Christian-Syrian army at the devastating Battle of La Forbie near Gaza in 1244.*

◄ *After four years' preparation, Louis IX of France embarked on the Seventh Crusade in 1248, heading to Cyprus and then to Egypt.*

CRUSADE IN EGYPT

KING LOUIS IX CALLS THE SEVENTH CRUSADE

King Louis IX declared his intention to lead a crusade to the East in 1245. But he certainly did not rush to war, for he spent no less than four years recruiting and preparing, raising money and even building a special port at the sleepy village of Aigues-Mortes in southern France, before he finally embarked in 1248.

Louis imposed a swingeing tax on the French Church, demanding one-tenth of ecclesiastical revenues for five years, raising 950,000 livres tournois. (The livre tournois, or 'pound of Tours', was one of a number of currencies used in France in Louis's time.) He demanded municipal grants from the towns of his royal domain, raising another 275,000 livres tournois. In all, he raised around 1.5 million livres tournois – a sum so vast that he campaigned in the East for four years before he needed to borrow more money.

FRENCH LORDS

Louis's recruitment campaign resulted in many of France's great lords taking the cross, including: Peter of Vendôme; Hugh X of Lusignan (Count of La Marche); John of Montfort; and Louis's brothers Alphonse of Poitou, Robert of Artois and Charles of Anjou. Many of these great lords' feudal dependants and blood relatives also joined the crusade. Another notable participant who joined the crusade in France was John, lord of Joinville in Champagne, who later wrote a life of King Louis that is a major source for our knowledge of the Seventh Crusade.

The army that finally embarked from southern France in 1248 numbered around 15,000 and included some 2,500 knights as well as 5,000-odd crossbowmen. As many as half of those who travelled received loans or agreed contracts

▲ *The holy warrior-king, as seen by his enemies. This image of Louis IX on horseback is from a 13th-century Egyptian or Syrian brass medallion inlaid with silver.*

from Louis, meaning that they were effectively subsidized by the king. Practical arrangements included the advance purchase of supplies and equipment, and the contracting of 36 ships from Marseilles and Genoa to carry the army.

DEPARTURE

The French crusade army left from Marseilles and from the specially built port and arsenal at the Aigues-Mortes on 25 August 1248 and sailed initially to Cyprus. They landed at Limassol on 17 September, and there united by prior arrangement with various other crusade participants, including Scottish and Italian forces, around 200 English knights led by William, Earl of Salisbury, and barons from Outremer led by Guillaume of Sonnac, Grand Master of the Knights Templar. The crusade leaders agreed that their first target should be Muslim Egypt: the plan was to defeat the sultan's army there before moving against Syria.

◀ *Louis IX of France embarks at Aigues-Mortes on the 7th Crusade. This depiction is from a mid-16th century stained-glass window in Champigny-sur-Veude, France.*

▲ *Encamped before Damietta in June 1249, Louis and his barons pray for the triumphant ending they envisaged for their painstakingly planned enterprise.*

DAMIETTA

Having overwintered on Cyprus, they embarked for Egypt on 14 May 1249. The fleet, which by now numbered as many as a hundred ships, was scattered by a storm, but the royal ships held together and arrived off the beaches near the target of Damietta (modern Damyut) in early June. They saw an Egyptian Muslim army drawn up on land. Disregarding the advice of senior campaigners to wait for reinforcements, Louis led an immediate assault that drove back the Muslim force in the course of a fierce battle on 5 June.

The Muslims retreated along a pontoon bridge of boats to Damietta and that night, in a panic, the Damietta garrison of Bedouin troops and the town's Muslim population fled. The following day, having been alerted to this development by Christians in Damietta, the French army marched in triumph, unopposed across the bridge of boats, into the port.

▶ *This 17th-century Ottoman map shows Muslim power bases around the Mediterranean as well as the movements and origins of crusaders, marking Jerusalem with an image of Christ.*

JOHN, LORD OF JOINVILLE, AND FRIEND OF LOUIS IX

John came from a family of lesser nobles from the Champagne region of France who, nevertheless, had a proud history of crusading – and is a good example of the way taking the cross became a tradition in certain families. John's grandfather, Geoffrey of Joinville, had travelled on the Third Crusade and was killed during the siege of Acre in 1189; John's father, Simon, had crusaded against the Cathars in southern France and fought on the Fifth Crusade, taking part in the capture of Damietta; he also had two uncles who had gone on crusade. John himself took the cross in 1244. In the catastrophic defeat that ended the Seventh Crusade he was later captured with King Louis and travelled with him to Acre, where he became friends with the king before returning in the royal party to France in 1254. He served as seneschal of Champagne, and lived both at the royal court and in Joinville. In 1270 he refused to take part in the ill-fated Eighth Crusade (on which Louis died): before Louis departed, John told him the enterprise was folly. He began writing his life of

▲ *This statue of Louis IX is believed to be true to life. The king was canonized in 1297, just 27 years after his death. He is revered as the perfect Christian king.*

King Louis in the 1270s, but did not complete it until 1309, when it was presented to Louis X. By this time, Louis IX had been canonized and the work was called the *Histoire de Saint-Louis* (The Story of St Louis).

THE FALL OF TRIPOLI AND ACRE

THE END OF OUTREMER

The ten-year truces signed by Tripoli and Acre with Muslim Egypt were essentially worthless, for neither Sultan Baybars nor his successors in Cairo were the type of men to be bound by such a nicety as a peace treaty. Following the death of Baybars in 1277, sultans Qalawun and Khalil led the Mamluk Egyptian army to the conquest of Tripoli in 1289 and of Acre in 1291.

CRUSADING INITIATIVES

In the immediate aftermath of the Ninth Crusade there were further attempts in Europe to mount expeditions to come to the aid of Outremer. Pope Gregory X entered negotiations with the Mongols to mount a combined campaign in the Holy Land and preached a crusade in 1274, but the plans came to nothing following

▼ In Tripoli the forbidding Castle of Raymond of St Gilles, named for the leader of the First Crusade, was expanded by the Mamluks after they captured it in 1289.

Gregory's death in January 1276. In 1282 Louis IX's brother, Charles of Anjou, King of Sicily and in name King of Jerusalem (after he had bought the succession rights from Mary of Antioch) attempted to mount a campaign to retake Constantinople for Latin Christianity. (Constantinople had been recaptured by the Byzantine Greeks under Emperor Michael VIII Palaeologus in 1261 – see box.) But Charles had to abandon the campaign to deal with an uprising against his rule in the War of the Sicilian Vespers.

THE MAMLUK SUCCESSION

In the year of his death, in 1277, Sultan Baybars achieved two final triumphs: the defeat of a combined Mongol–Seljuk Turk army and the capture of Caesarea. When he died in June of that year, Baybars was initially succeeded by his son Baraka, who was forced to abdicate by a revolt in Egypt. He was replaced by Salamish, his seven-year-old brother – then Qalawun, established himself as regent from 1279.

▲ Acre was held by the crusaders from 1104 until 1187, when it was taken by Saladin, and from 1191 to 1291. For its last century in Christian hands, Acre was the capital of the Kingdom of Jerusalem.

EVENTS IN OUTREMER

Charles of Anjou died in 1285, and King Henry III of Cyprus was crowned King of Jerusalem at Acre on 15 August 1286. After two weeks of celebrations including an 'Arthurian Round Table' chivalric tournament, Henry returned to Cyprus leaving his uncle, Philip of Ibelin, to rule in Acre as his bailiff. Then, in 1287, Bohemond VIII, Count of Tripoli, died. The citizens of Tripoli chose to become a republic rather than accept the accession of Bohemond's sister Lucia and asked the republic of Genoa to send its fleet.

This was the impetus for Sultan Qalawun to march on Tripoli with a vast army and settle in for a siege. He had earlier moved against the remaining crusader possessions, capturing the Hospitaller fortress of Margat in 1285 and taking the main Syrian port, Latakia, in 1287. The siege of Tripoli lasted less than a month. Qalawun's troops slaughtered the population and destroyed the city and its port so that a new wave of crusaders would have nothing to inherit.

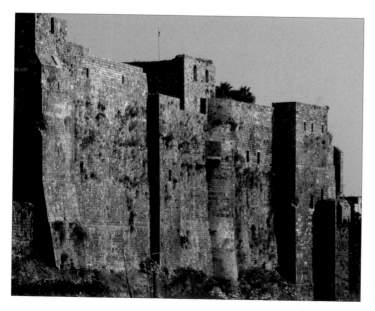

THE FALL OF ACRE

Determined to achieve the destruction of the crusader states, Qalawun next moved against Acre. But he died in November 1290 before he could effect its capture. His son and successor, Khalil, began the siege, bringing an army perhaps 75,000 strong and a huge siege train containing more than 90 mangonels and trebuchets. The siege began on 11 April 1291.

The garrison numbered 800 knights and 14,000 infantry. From Europe came a contingent of English knights sent by Edward I of England under the command of Odo of Savoy, and a contingent of French knights under Jean of Grailly. The defenders manned Acre's double line of walls, with the Templars on the northern section, the Hospitallers alongside them, the French on the southern walls and Venetians, Genoans and Pisans defending the port area. Further reinforcements under King Henry II of Cyprus and Jerusalem arrived on 4 May.

The besiegers set up their great engines: one directed at the quarter defended by the Templars, another aimed at the Hospitallers' area of walls and a third wheeled machine trained on the Accursed Tower, on the eastern wall and defended by knights of Cyprus and Syria.

Early in the siege Frankish envoys rode into the Egyptian camp and spoke to the Sultan, asking him to have mercy on the poor and vulnerable of the city. He made them an offer: abandon the city and he would let them leave freely. They refused to negotiate, perhaps remembering the many promises broken by Sultan Baybars.

The knights of the military orders made two night-time sorties – the first (by the Templars) was essentially successful, although it did not result in the hoped-for destruction of siege equipment, but the second (by the Hospitallers) was met with fierce resistance.

The continual assault by the siege engines and the digging of sappers beneath the walls inevitably had its effect. On 15 May, following the collapse of the towers of Blois, of St Nicholas and of Henry II, the defenders were forced to abandon the outer walls and retreat to the inner defences. On 18 May Sultan Khalil ordered a general assault, which was launched before dawn to the beating of a kettledrum and accompanied by a hail of Greek fire and a storm of arrows. The Accursed Tower was the first to be taken by the attackers, and in the bitter struggle the Grand Master of the Knights Templar, William of Beaujeu, was killed in the fighting. The attackers poured through and overran the city. Acre fell to Sultan Khalil on 18 May 1291. Only a small group of Knights Templar, in the Templars' palace, carried on the resistance – but they were forced to surrender after a week. The population of the city was put to the sword, and its buildings, including the warehouse and port, were utterly destroyed.

END OF OUTREMER

In the days following the fall of Acre, the crusader towns of Beirut, Tyre, Haifa and Tortosa were all abandoned by their defenders. A few thousand refugees managed to escape in ships bound for Cyprus, which remained in crusader hands; other survivors were sold into slavery. A little less than two centuries after the First Crusade, the Latin Christians had been expelled from the Holy Land. Outremer was a thing of the past.

▼ *William of Clermont at the forefront of the last stand in defence of the Kingdom of Jerusalem on the walls of Acre.*

PETER I OF CYPRUS

THE CRUSADER KING

Peter of Cyprus is known to history as the crusading king, who briefly in the mid-14th century made Cyprus a major participant in international affairs. He reigned for just 11 years, 1358–69, but established himself as a well-known figure of chivalry, the founder of a chivalric order and leader of holy war against Egypt of 1365. This enterprise was known by contemporaries as 'King Peter's Crusade'.

THE ORDER OF THE SWORD

Peter, sometimes also called Pierre I of Lusignan, was the second son of King Hugh IV of Cyprus and had the title of King of Jerusalem from 1358–69. Born in 1328 in Nicosia, Peter was just 19 when, in 1347, he had a religious vision that inspired him to found the chivalric Order of the Sword. According to the account given by French poet and musician William of Machaut (see box), Peter had a vision of a cross floating in mid-air, venerated by many as the cross on which the Good Thief hung. (The Gospels report that Christ was crucified between two thieves, one of whom railed against Christ, but the second of whom rebuked his fellow thief and addressed Christ as Lord; in later Christian tradition he was known as

the 'Good Thief' or St Dismas.) Peter heard a voice addressing him as 'Son' and urging him to wage holy war to regain the lands promised by God to the holy patriarchs; as a result, he founded the Order of the Sword for knights professing a determination to regain the promised land and for men-at-arms with the desire to save their souls. The emblem of the order was a silver sword, set with the point downward to resemble a crucifix, against a blue background and the words 'With this maintain loyalty' inscribed in gold.

Two years later Peter left secretly for Europe with one of his brothers, perhaps with the intention of trying to raise or join a crusade. But his father, King Hugh, tracked the pair down and had them brought back to Cyprus, where he jailed them for having left without permission.

SEA RAIDS

Following his father's abdication in 1358, Peter assumed power and was crowned King of Cyprus and titular King of Jerusalem in Famagusta in 1360. He achieved a number of successes against Muslim Turkish emirs along the eastern seaboard of the Mediterranean. In 1360 he was invited by the citizens of Corycos,

▲ *King Peter's Crusade in 1365 ended is disarray but Peter himself, seen here issuing orders to his men, had a great reputation a military strategist and leader.*

in Armenian Cilicia, to take control of their harbour settlement and protect them against Turkish attacks. Peter accepted and sent a Cypriot force commanded by Robert of Lusignan to defend the port. The city was then besieged by Turkish forces, but the garrison held firm and Corycos was made part of the Kingdom of Cyprus.

Peter was now seen as a threat by the Turkish emirs on the mainland, and these men united to plan a maritime attack on Cyprus. Peter, however, received news of the plan and launched a pre-emptive strike with the help of the Knights Hospitaller on Rhodes, and some European and papal forces. With a fleet of 120 ships, he attacked and besieged Adalia (now Antalya in south-western Turkey) and forced the Turks to sue for peace. He made them pay a yearly tribute to Cyprus.

TOUR OF EUROPE

The following year Peter embarked on a trip to Europe, intending to generate enthusiasm for a general crusade for the

▲ *Pope Urban V told Peter to bring the 1365 crusade to an end after it broke down, and in the wake of violent reprisals against Christian merchants in Egypt and in Syria.*

recapture of the Holy Land. He took part in a succession of chivalric tournaments and was hospitably received by monarchs and princes, but was unable to win the widespread support he had hoped for.

Nevertheless, by 1365 Peter had managed to raise an army of sorts, and he embarked on his crusade against Egypt in October of that year. As we have seen, the enterprise began well, with the taking of the city of Alexandria, but this quickly degenerated into ill-disciplined looting before the crusaders departed for home, refusing to obey Peter's command to march on Cairo. In contemporary accounts of the events, Peter's own participation was highly praised – he was represented not only as an inspirational leader, but also as a brave warrior and a

▶ *Peter was represented (back row, second from right) with Emperor Charles IV and Pope Urban V (third and fourth from right) in Andrea Bonaiuti's fresco of 'The Church Militant' at St Maria Novella in Florence.*

skilled and capable general who achieved what could have been a significant gain for Christendom if he had not been let down by greedy and self-interested troops.

Peter returned to Cyprus, where he continued to mount raids on Turkish holdings along the coasts of what is now Turkey and Syria. He raided Tripoli and was preparing an attack inland, on Damascus, but abandoned that venture after Venetian merchants – afraid of damage to trade – bribed him handsomely not to carry it through. In 1367 he made another trip to Europe, again to try to raise a crusade force, but without success. Increasingly he ruled with an iron hand: when he discovered that his wife Eleanor had conducted an adulterous affair with John of Morphou, Count of Edessa, he embarked on a bitter campaign against her favourite members of the nobility. Some began to question his sanity.

ASSASSINATION AND LEGACY

On 17 January 1369 Peter was assassinated. Two of his knights allowed conspirators – including Philip of Ibelin, lord of Arsuf, and Henry of Jubail – access to the king's bedchamber early in the morning. There, half-dressed, he was repeatedly stabbed, then beheaded and even had his genitals mutilated by an angry knight, James of Nores.

> ### WILLIAM OF MACHAUT
> Born in c.1300 in Champagne, the poet William of Machaut was in his mid-70s when he wrote his account of the crusade to Alexandria. He was a celebrated figure, who had served one of the great chivalric monarchs of the age, King John of Bohemia. John insisted on fighting on the French side at the Battle of Poitiers in 1356 despite being almost blind and was killed and then honoured by Edward the Black Prince, who took his emblem of an ostrich feather and motto *Ich Dien* (I serve) as his own. William wrote several poems in praise of royal knighthood and also composed many lays and ballads.

Peter's reign was brief and he died a humiliating death. His crusading endeavours achieved little – the only real effect of the attack on Alexandria was to provoke the Sultan of Egypt and damage trade. Nevertheless, because of his devotion to crusading ideals, the fact that he founded a chivalric brotherhood and cut a impressive figure in the courts of Europe (as well as when fighting during the crusade to Alexandria), he was remembered as a paragon of 14th-century chivalry.

CRUSADE TO MAHDIA
ATTACK ON TUNISIA UNITES WARRING CHRISTIANS, 1390

In 1378 the Catholic Church split, in an event known as the Great Schism: there was one pope in Rome and one in Avignon, and the schism continued until 1417 when rule by a single pope was reintroduced. The rival popes combined in 1390, however, to call a crusade against the town of Mahdia, in Tunisia, home to a corsair fleet.

CHRISTIANS DIVIDED

In 1305, at a time when Italy was riven by the papacy's conflict with the Holy Roman Empire, Pope Clement V moved the Roman curia (papal court) from Rome to Poitiers in France, and then in 1309 moved on to Avignon. In 1378 Pope Gregory XI moved back to Rome, but died the same year; there was a dispute over the succession and while Bartolomeo Prignano took power as Pope Urban VI in Rome, in France cardinals elected Robert of Geneva

▲ *John of Gaunt is received by the citizens of Bayonne. John campaigned in Europe in the 1360s–70s, fought with Edward, the Black Prince, in the Battle of Najera (1367) and led a 'crusade' to Portugal in 1386, which ended in a financial settlement.*

as a rival pope to rule from Avignon. Robert took the papal name of, Clement VII, and swiftly excommunicated Urban, declaring him to be the Antichrist.

CRUSADES OF THE GREAT SCHISM

In the years following the Great Schism, supporters of the rival popes fought crusades against one another. In general terms, the Avignon pope enjoyed the support of France and her allies Scotland and Castile, while the pope in Rome had the backing of most of the rest of Europe. In 1383 Sir Henry Despenser, Bishop of Norwich in England, a supporter of Rome and a veteran of papal wars in Italy, led a crusade against Louis of Mâle, Count of Flanders and a supporter of Avignon. In a bloody campaign, beginning in May 1383, Sir Henry took Gravelines, Bourbourg, Dunkirk, Diksmuide and other coastal towns, as well as many castles and a fortified church at Veume. He then drove off

an army raised by the Count of Flanders at Dunkirk and laid siege to Ypres. However, the crusade army became bogged down in the siege and after eight weeks, hearing that the French army under Charles VI was approaching, retreated to Dunkirk. In the end, Sir Henry left for England after a negotiated settlement and the crusade came to nothing – although the settlement with Charles VI reportedly made the bishop and his leading knights considerably richer.

A second crusade took place in 1386 when John of Gaunt, 1st Duke of Lancaster, led a campaign in alliance with Portugal on behalf of Rome against Castile. The enterprise doubled as an attempt to

▼ *John of Gaunt was the fourth son of King Edward III of England and was father of King Henry IV. Lady Margaret Beaufort, mother of the first Tudor king (Henry VII) was Gaunt's great-granddaughter.*

enforce Gaunt's claim to the Castilian throne (through his marriage to Constanza, daughter of the late King Pedro I of Castile), and before he left he was formally recognized as King of Castile by King Richard II of England. However, like its forerunner of 1383, this crusade was settled by a financial agreement under which Gaunt abandoned his claim to the Castile in return for a substantial payment.

CRUSADE OF 1390

The warring halves of Christendom were united by proposals for a crusade against Tunisia in 1390. The idea of the crusade came from Genoese traders whose Mediterranean ships had been raided repeatedly by corsairs from the town of Mahdia, Tunisia. The Genoese, supporters of Pope Boniface IX (Urban VI's successor in Rome), won the backing for the project of King Charles VI of France, who supported Clement VII in Avignon. The proposal was then enthusiastically taken up in France and won the backing of both Boniface IX and Clement VII. Contingents joined from the Low Countries, England and Spain to bolster the mainly French and Genoese army. The leader was named as Count Louis of Bourbon.

▼ *Boniface IX, second Roman pope of the Great Schism of 1378–1417, is crowned. The 1390 crusade, which had his backing, showed the benefits of Christian unity.*

The crusaders set sail from Marseilles and went by way of Genoa to northern Africa. They expected to have a fierce fight on their hands when they landed before Mahdia, but they disembarked unopposed and began a siege, with Count Louis's army surrounding three sides of the city by land and the Genoan fleet blockading the seaward wide. The inhabitants of the town waited three days before launching any attack: when it came, it was easily beaten back by Count Louis's troops, who drove the Mahdians back and reached as far as the gates of the city, fighting fiercely, but unable to force their way into the city.

After that the crusade went on for nine weeks, until finally the Genoans negotiated a peace treaty with Ahmad, emir of Tunis, under which the Tunisians would pay handsome taxes to Genoa for 15 years as well as furnishing them with 12,000 gold sovereigns to cover the cost of this campaign. The crusade turned out well for Genoa, but achieved none of its wider goals – although it certainly had benefits for Christian morale at a time of schism. Its success probably lay in the fact that it gave considerable weight to the argument that the disputes of the Great Schism would be best solved not by wars between rival camps but by creating a united front against the Turks. A further crusade would be proclaimed by Avignon and Rome in 1394 – this time against the rising power of the Ottoman Turks.

▲ *In 1417 the Great Schism was over and the Church was reunified with the deposition of two popes, the abdication of a third and the election of Pope Martin V, seen here at the Council of Constance, 1418.*

THE ENDURING SCHISM

The division within Christianity continued, however. Indeed, the two-way split became a three-way one in 1409, when patriarchs, cardinals and bishops at the Council of Pisa declared the Holy See to be vacant and elected Peter Phillarges as Pope Alexander V. Finally in 1417, at the Council of Constance, Pope John XXIII (successor to Alexander V) was deposed, the Avignon Pope Benedict XIII was deposed, Pope Gregory XII abdicated and Pope Martin V was elected as sole pope.

DEFEAT AT NICOPOLIS
THE RISE OF THE OTTOMANS

As the 14th century progressed the Christian powers of Europe were increasingly aware of the rising threat posed by the Muslim Ottoman state as it expanded from its original base in Anatolia into the Balkans and towards the lands of the mighty Holy Roman Empire. In the 1390s the Ottomans, under their great general Bayezid I, took Salonika (modern Thessaloniki) in Greece, blockaded Constantinople and invaded Hungary. The Christian response was a major Venetian–Hungarian crusade, with the backing of both the Avignon and Roman popes, in 1396. It ended in yet another crusading humiliation, a crushing victory for Bayezid and his Ottoman army at the Battle of Nicopolis.

OTTOMAN ORIGINS AND EXPANSION

The Ottomans were descended from Turkmen tribes driven from their homes in Turkestan in the early years of the 13th century by the raids of the Mongols. They took their name from Osman I, who reigned from 1299–1326, and was known

as Uthman or 'Ottoman' in Arabic. He was the son of Ertogrul, chief of a principality in Anatolia based at Sögüt (now in Turkey); Osman greatly expanded the principality, taking a series of towns including Eskisehir, Yenisehir and Bursa from the Byzantine Empire. Osman's son Orhan (r.1324–60) continued the expansion, capturing Nicaea (modern Iznik) in 1331 and Nicomedia (Izmit) in 1334.

In 1341–47 Orhan intervened in a Byzantine succession crisis, providing the military support that enabled John VI Cantacuzenus to overcome his rival John V Palaeologus. As a reward for this, John Cantacuzenus gave Orhan the hand of his daughter, princess Theodora, and allowed him to raid Byzantine lands in Thrace and Macedonia. Under Orhan, and as a result of the policy of John Cantacuzenus, the Ottomans won their first permanent holding in Europe, taking Gallipoli in 1354.

In 1361 Orhan's son, Murad I, captured Adrianople and Philippopolis in Thrace

◄ *The Ottomans became a major naval power, mostly acquiring their ships by theft. They stole an entire fleet from the Byzantines in the course of a daring night raid in 1356 led by Sultan Murad's brother Süleyman.*

▲ *King Sigismund of Hungary was forced to retreat at Nicopolis and took refuge in Venetian shipping. He was frustrated that the crusaders, refusing to listen to the advice of those familiar with Ottoman battle tactics, brought defeat upon themselves.*

and forced the Byzantine emperor (by now John V Palaeologus once more) to become a vassal. Making Adrianople his capital, renaming it Edirne, Murad then expanded deep into Serbia and Bulgaria, making local princes accept him as their overlord.

CRUSADE OF 1366

In 1366 Murad faced a crusade from Venice under the command of Italian nobleman Amadeus of Savoy. This small enterprise, which set sail with just 15 ships and 1,700 troops, was intended to restore Byzantine power in the face of Ottoman expansion and to help John Palaeologus, who was Amadeus's second cousin. Amadeus allied with Francesco I of the Aegean island of Lesbos and together they drove the Turks from Gallipoli; afterwards Amadeus, discovering that John Palaeologus had been taken captive by the Bulgarians, captured the ports of Mesembria and Sozopolis on the

Black Sea and besieged Varna, demanding his release. Finally the emperor was freed and the crusade saw no further action.

THE THUNDERBOLT STRIKES

Murad's son was Bayezid I, nicknamed *Yildirim* (the Thunderbolt) for the speed of his military campaigns. He came to power following the death of Murad in battle against Bosnian, Serbian and Bulgarian princes at Kosovo in 1389, and just two years later began a siege of Constantinople, the principal buffer between the Ottoman power base in Anatolia and Europe. He also began to extend Ottoman power towards and into Europe, capturing most of the Balkans and expelling Bulgarian tsar Ivan Shishman from his capital, Nicopolis.

A crusade was proclaimed by both Pope Boniface IX in Rome and his rival, the Avignon pope Clement VII. Kings Richard II of England, Charles VI of France and Sigismund of Hungary (who was later to be Holy Roman Emperor, 1433–37) backed the enterprise: initially the plan was for Charles and Richard to fight on the crusade, but in the event an army of 10,000 French, 1,000 English and around 6,000 from the German states gathered under Sigismund in Buda (now part of the Hungarian capital Budapest) in

▼ *The Battle of Nicopolis became a rout. Admiral of France, Jean of Vienne, fought off attackers trying to capture the French standard six times. In the end he was killed.*

TAMERLAINE AND BAYEZID

The seemingly invincible Bayezid met his match in the Turkish–Mongolian warlord Timur, or Tamerlaine. In 1402 Bayezid again abandoned his siege of Constantinople to deal with a troublesome enemy, but this time was heavily defeated by Tamerlaine at the Battle of Ankara. Bayezid was taken prisoner and kept in captivity by Tamerlaine.

Colourful contemporary reports suggested that the Ottoman sultan was kept chained in a cage but this is thought to be false. Bayezid certainly died in captivity, however, one year later; his sons, who had escaped to Serbia after the Battle of Ankara, were later able to re-establish Ottoman rule. In the 16th century English playwright Christopher

▲ *Bayezid died after a year in captivity.*

Marlowe wrote a celebrated play, *Tamburlaine the Great*, about the warlord's exploits. He was also the hero of an opera of 1724, *Tamerlano*, by Handel.

July 1396. The plan was to force the Turks from the Balkans, relieve the siege of Constantinople, and then march across Anatolia and Syria to take Jerusalem for Christ. Mircea, Prince of Wallachia, joined the crusade with a substantial army despite being an Orthodox Christian rather than a Roman Catholic; a contingent from Transylvania also joined up. Venetian and Genoese fleets and a contingent of Hospitaller knights from Rhodes also arrived to lend their support.

The army marched southwards, pillaging towns and massacring locals, before settling in to a siege of Nicopolis, the

Bulgarian capital recently taken by the Turks. Bayezid then showed why he was called 'the Thunderbolt', acting with astonishing decisiveness and speed in lifting his siege of Constantinople and marching against the crusade army. He met them in battle near Nicopolis on 25 September.

Wallachian prince Mircea, who was familiar with Ottoman tactics and had won previous victories against Bayezid, proposed that he should lead an initial assault with his skilled Wallachian light cavalry prior to a main charge by the Western army. But the crusade leaders were suspicious of his motives and instead chose to make a full-scale frontal assault. The battle was a disaster for the crusaders: although the French knights won initial successes against the Ottoman vanguard, they were overwhelmed by the main bulk of Bayezid's men; the Wallachians and Transylvanians deserted and Sigismund escaped. It was a triumph for Bayezid serving to consolidate the Ottomans in the Balkans, and leaving Constantinople even more vulnerable. Bayezid built the magnificent Ulu Mosque in Bursa to commemorate his victory in what became known as the Crusade of Nicopolis.

THE END OF BYZANTIUM
CRUSADERS FAIL TO SAVE CONSTANTINOPLE

The Ottomans repeatedly threatened Constantinople, and Western powers sent intermittent expeditions to the aid of the city. The most significant, in 1444, ended in another heavy defeat for the crusaders at Varna. Then, on 29 May 1453, the Ottomans under Sultan Mehmed II 'the Conqueror' captured Constantinople, marking the end of the Byzantine Empire.

CRUSADES OF BOUCICAUT
French knight Jean Le Meingre, Marshal of France and known as 'Boucicaut', had taken part in the Christians' defeat by Ottoman sultan Bayezid at the Battle of Nicopolis in 1396. Boucicaut was captured in the battle and later ransomed. Then, in 1399, the same year in which he established his chivalric order, the *Emprise de l'Escu Vert à la Dame Blanche* (Enterprise of the Green Shield of the White Lady), he sailed once more to the East. With 21 galleys, three transports and six ships and around 1,200 men, he succeeded in lifting the Ottoman blockade of Constantinople and rescuing the embattled Byzantine emperor, Manuel II

Palaeologus. Manuel then returned with Boucicaut to Europe to try to drum up interest for a further crusade.

In 1401 Boucicaut was made French Governor of Genoa and in 1403 he sailed to Rhodes with a fleet of 16 Genoese ships and from there led a series of raids against ports in Anatolia and Syria held by the Ottomans and the Mamluk Sultanate of Egypt. He attacked Ottoman Alanya in Anatolia, then (with the help of the Knights Hospitaller from Rhodes) raided Mamluk-held Batroun, Tripoli and Beirut.

A NEW CRUSADE
In 1443 Pope Eugenius IV (ruled 1431–47) issued a rallying call to Christians in the West to go to the aid of their brethren in the East against the Ottomans. Murad II, grandson of Bayezid 'the Thunderbolt', had re-established Ottoman supremacy after a period of decline and in-fighting following Bayezid's defeat by the Turkish-Mongolian general Tamerlaine in 1402 and his subsequent death in captivity. Murad II defeated two rivals, forced the Byzantine Empire to pay

▲ Pope Eugenius IV did much to restore the power of the papacy after the Great Schism. The crusade he called in 1443 almost ended in success at Varna in 1444.

tribute, and in 1430 recaptured Salonika (Thessaloniki) from the Venetians. Then he annexed Serbia in 1439.

However, the Hungarian army, commanded by King Ladislas of Hungary and his illegitimate son Janos Hunyadi, known as the 'White Knight', won victories against the Ottomans at Nis, Sofia and Snaim in 1443, on the celebrated 'long campaign', and again at Jalowaz in 1444, encouraging Christendom to dream once more of a lasting victory over Islam. A motley collection of crusaders gathered in the Balkans in 1444: the force included Hungarians, Poles, Germans, Ukrainians, Lithuanians, Croatians, Bulgarians and Bosnians. The plan was for a fleet of Genoese, Venetian and papal ships to blockade the Dardanelles to prevent Murad crossing from Anatolia into Europe to fight the crusaders; the fleet and the crusader army would rendezvous at Varna in Bulgaria, then march and sail down the coast of the Black Sea to Constantinople and relieve the siege there, pushing the Ottomans out of Europe in the process. However, the blockade of the Dardanelles failed, and Murad marched to meet the crusaders at Varna.

BATTLE OF VARNA

In the Battle of Varna on 10 November 1444 Murad's Ottoman army of around 60,000 men faced a much smaller crusade army of no more than 20,000 troops commanded by Ladislas and Janos Hunyadi. Not only were the Christians outnumbered, but they also had an unbalanced army, with very few foot soldiers and a great preponderance of heavy cavalry.

The Christians pinned their hopes on the arrival of reinforcements by sea from Constantinople. The papal legate on the crusade, Cardinal Julian Cesarini, called on the army to retreat, but they were in a difficult position, trapped by the enemy between the Black Sea, Lake Varna and the hills. The cardinal then proposed that they attempt to defend their position until they were relieved by Christian reinforcements, but Ladislas and Janos Hunyadi argued for attack – famously declaring: 'Escape is not possible, surrender inconceivable, so let us fight bravely and do honour to the arms we bear!'

The plan almost worked. The crusaders came close to victory: a group of around 500 Polish knights smashed the centre of the Ottoman deployment, breaking through the elite Janissary infantry; Sultan Murad began to flee on horseback but a soldier seized his reins to prevent him, and Murad regained his composure; Janos Hunyadi and his cavalry devastated a company of Sipahis (Ottoman cavalry) and drove them from the battlefield; King Ladislas went in pursuit of Murad, but was cut down by the Ottoman imperial

▶ *'The White Knight' Janos Hunyadi was a formidable opponent of the Ottomans for 20 years from the 1430s to his death in 1456. He was regent of Hungary in 1446–53.*

bodyguard, also of Janissaries. Ladislas was beheaded on the battlefield and, seeing the king cut down, the Polish cavalry lost heart and retreated. Janos Hunyadi escaped. King Ladislas's head was subsequently carried off to the Ottoman court.

SECOND BATTLE OF KOSOVO

In 1448 Janos Hunyadi raised another mainly Hungarian Christian army and fought Murad II again, in the Second Battle of Kosovo, which ran over two days in October. (The clash is known as the Second Battle of Kosovo to distinguish it from the earlier battle at the site between a Serbian army led by Prince Lazar and an Ottoman force under Murad I in 1389 – the battle in which Murad I died.)

Once again, as at Varna, Hunyadi was badly outnumbered by Murad II's Ottoman army, and once again he almost won the battle despite this numerical disadvantage; and, as at Varna, it was the

resilience and bravery of the sultan's elite Janissary corps that won the day. The battle began with an attack by Hunyadi's flanks that was driven back, but this was followed by a strong assault by the main part of his army. This defeated the Janissaries and reached as far as the Ottoman camp before falling back; during this latter part of the battle, with Hunyadi's forces retreating, the Janissaries recovered from their earlier setback and delivered a powerful attack that killed many of the finest Hungarian knights and forced Hunyadi himself to flee. Fighting went on with missiles and artillery fire through the night; on the next day the Ottomans launched a final and decisive attack.

The Christians' defeat in this battle left the Ottomans in the ascendant in the Balkans, with the Byzantine Empire at their mercy. Within five years, Murad II's son and successor, Mehmed II 'the Conqueror', had captured Constantinople.

CHAPTER FOURTEEN

THE WARRIOR MONKS

On 1 May 1187 a small Christian force of foot soldiers and 140 knights under Gerard of Ridefort, Master of the Knights Templar, encountered a Muslim Ayyubid army of 7,000 in the Battle of Cresson near Nazareth. When the Ayyubid horsemen feigned a retreat Gerard rashly ordered a charge, his knights were isolated from the foot soldiers and the two parts of the army cut down. The account in the crusade chronicle *Itinerarium Regis Ricardi* (The Voyage of King Richard) describes the extraordinary heroism and death of Templar knight Jakelin of Mailly, who reportedly fought to the last, surrounded by Muslim soldiers and entirely alone, until he sank to the ground and his soul rose at once to heaven, wearing a martyr's crown and covered in glory.

The Knights Templar and other monastic military brotherhoods – such as the Knights Hospitaller, the Teutonic Knights, the Knights of St Lazarus or the Knights of St Thomas Acon – were famed for their ferocity in battle and the powerful commitment to the crusading cause celebrated in the account of Jakelin of Mailly's death. In battle, they provided a highly disciplined, well-trained fighting force, although their leaders often were drawn by overconfidence or the desire for glory into rash and even disastrous acts. The monastic military brotherhood – consisting of men who like Jakelin of Mailly sought salvation through their exploits in religious warfare – was an institution unique to European chivalry of the Middle Ages, without counterpart in other cultures or eras.

▲ *At Cresson in 1187, Templar Jakelin of Mailly fought to the end.*

◄ *The defence of Rhodes by Fulkes of Villaret and the Knights Hospitaller, against Sultan Osman I in 1307. The Knights held the island until 1522.*

HOSPITALLERS SAVE RHODES

KNIGHTS OF ST JOHN DEFEAT MEHMET THE CONQUEROR

After the loss of Jerusalem in 1187 the Knights of St John removed to Acre and, following the fall of Acre in 1291, took up residence on the island of Cyprus, so maintaining a presence in the East. The Hospitallers did not stay long in Cyprus. Within 20 years they had transferred to the island of Rhodes, where they would remain for more than 200 years, in that time twice defeating seaborne armies – one in 1444 from Muslim Egypt and a second in 1480 from the Ottoman sultan Mehmet II 'the Conqueror'.

ESTABLISHMENT ON RHODES

On being driven from the Holy Land following the fall of Acre in 1291, the leading figures in the hierarchy of the Hospitallers saw that the sea would inevitably play an important part in the order's future. The admiral of the Hospitaller fleet, Fulkes of Villaret, joined the inner council of the order in 1299. In 1307 the knights captured Rhodes, in part to curb the operations of Muslim corsairs who used the island as a base of operations for raiding Christian shipping in the East, but also perhaps with an eye to establishing their own landholding.

The knights found it difficult to maintain their independence from court politics on Cyprus and elected to move permanently to Rhodes in 1310. By now Fulkes of Villaret was Grand Master. The order also took control of a number of small neighbouring islands, including Bodrum and Kastellorizo. Using these bases, the Hospitaller knights waged a determined sea war against Muslim corsairs from northern Africa who preyed on Christian shipping in the western Mediterranean. (These ruthless Muslim operators were also known as 'Barbary pirates' because the north African coast from which they emanated was called the Barbary coast.)

The Hospitallers also took part in the various minor crusades of the 14th cen-

▲ *The Ottoman fleet, commanded by Palaeologos Pasha, approaches Rhodes, at the top right of this picture. The island appears secure behind stout walls.*

tury, notably those of 1345 in which Smyrna was captured; 'King Peter's Crusade' of 1365, which degenerated into the sacking of Alexandria; and the Nicopolis Crusade of 1396.

A NEW ORGANIZATION

In this period, the order also became immeasurably richer: after the Knights Templar were disbanded in 1312, all their property was assigned to the Hospitallers by Pope Clement V (ruled 1305–14). The Hospitallers organized their new territory

well, dividing their landholdings into eight *langues*, or 'tongues' (Provence, Italy, Germany, France, England, Castile, Auvergne and Aragon), each with its own prior and with key positions of authority in the order distributed among the langues. In this way, the Knights Hospitaller avoided difficulties caused by national feelings at a time when such feelings were increasingly powerful in Europe.

On Rhodes the brothers of different langues lived in their own *auberges*, or hostels, within an enclosed area of the city known as the *collachium*. They fortified both the city and the island's main harbour and established a commercial area, as well as inviting Latin and Greek farmers from the mainland to settle.

ATTACK ON RHODES

In 1426 Cyprus was conquered by Muslim Egypt and Rhodes was more than ever isolated and vulnerable. In 1435 the warlike Egyptian sultan Baybars planned an invasion of Rhodes, and the Knights brought reinforcements in from Europe at full speed, but the threat came to nothing. In 1444 the Egyptians tried again, mounting an invasion of the island and a month-long siege of the town of Rhodes.

In 1480 Ottoman sultan Mehmet II 'the Conqueror' launched a major attack on Rhodes – ostensibly because Muslims on the islands had reported being persecuted, but really as part of military expansion towards southern Italy. A vast Ottoman fleet, reputedly carrying 70,000–100,000 men, appeared off Rhodes in May. It was commanded by Palaeologos Pasha.

On the island, the garrison, under the command of Grand Master Pierre d'Aubusson, had just received reinforcements of around 2,000 foot soldiers and 500 knights from France. D'Aubusson had been vigilant and had prepared well against possible attack, laying in substantial supplies and military equipment.

The Ottomans settled in to a siege. Coming under attack from the citadel, where the garrison was ensconced, the Ottomans launched an assault: they succeeded in building a bridge from the boats in the harbour to the citadel walls but as their men began to pour across it to attack, this makeshift structure collapsed and thousands were drowned in the ensuing panic. A second attack was more successful and some of the Ottoman troops succeeded in raising the sultan's standard on the walls.

HEAVENLY ARMY

Accounts differ as to what happened next. According to the version given by Flemish writer Guillaume Caoursin, the Ottomans were terrified by a vision of the Virgin Mary and a saintly army in the sky above the citadel. Caoursin reports that the Knights had raised banners showing Christ, the Virgin Mary and St John the Baptist on the walls of the citadel, but that when the Ottoman attack was at its height a golden cross appeared in the clear sky above these banners, together with a miraculous image of the Virgin Mary carrying a spear and a shield and next to her a man in simple clothing standing before a great host of warriors of light. The Ottomans were paralyzed with fear and the Hospitallers were able to cut them down and drive them back.

The Ottoman account, however, suggests that their soldiers were poised for victory when their commander issued the order that there was to be no looting since the wealth of the citadel, and the merchants in the town, belonged to the sultan. This apparently caused the Ottoman warriors to stop fighting and many were slain in their moment of wavering.

OTRANTO PUNISHED

In the wake of this defeat, the Ottoman fleet lifted the siege of Rhodes and sailed away on 28 July 1480. On the island, the merchants, farmers and knights of the Hospitaller garrison rejoiced at their delivery by a seeming miracle from a force of such size. The Ottomans, for their part, sailed on and wreaked a terrible vengeance for the frustration at Rhodes on the people of Otranto in Italy. Having overrun the port, they killed Archbishop Stefano Agricoli in the cathedral and slaughtered 800 citizens of the town who refused to convert to Islam.

▼ *The Ottoman forces preparing for battle outside the walls of Rhodes in 1480. Their attack failed, reputedly after an appearance by the Virgin Mary.*

SULEYMAN TAKES RHODES
BUT THE HOSPITALLERS HOLD MALTA

In 1522, the Hospitaller garrison on Rhodes was forced to surrender after a six-month siege by Ottoman sultan Suleyman I 'the Magnificent' and his army. The Hospitallers departed Rhodes to take up residence on Malta.

PREPARATIONS FOR THE SIEGE

Philippe of L'Isle-Adam was elected Grand Master of the order in 1521 and began at once to prepare for the defence of Rhodes. He sent out an appeal throughout Europe for reinforcements to defend this outpost of Christendom, but received no response save a small contingent from Venice and Crete. He laid in a year of provisions and organized the defence of the town's reconstructed walls and bastions with most particular care, assigning the protection of different areas to groups of knights.

▼ *The Hospitallers had a powerful fleet and were a force to be reckoned with at sea.*

The Ottoman fleet arrived on 26 June under the command of Mustafa Pasha; Sultan Suleyman sailed in around a month afterwards to take command. The Turks launched a concerted assault on a section of the town walls defended by knights of Aragon and England, using both artillery and the digging of mines. This went on for as much as a month, with little progress, but on 4 September the Ottoman attack opened a breach almost 40ft (12m) across beside the bastion of England. The Ottomans gained control of this area, but then a fearless Hospitaller assault led by English knight Nicholas Hussey managed to force the Turks back.

GENERAL ATTACK

On 24 September the Turks mounted a general assault on the town, with particular concentration of fire against the bastions of England, Italy, Provence and Spain. Twice in one day the bastion of

Spain was captured by the Ottomans and then retaken by the Hospitallers. After hours of fierce fighting, with the garrison's powerful cannon killing vast numbers of Ottoman warriors, the attack was at last called off. Suleyman was enraged and ordered the execution of Mustafa Pasha because he had failed to take the city despite his vast numerical advantage; the sultan was persuaded to spare Mustafa, but he replaced him with Ahmed Pasha.

The Ottomans launched another powerful attack in late November, but it was driven back once more. However, the Knights and the townspeople of Rhodes were close to exhaustion and by mid-December were ready to negotiate terms of peace. A truce was called on 11–13 December, but when the townspeople asked for further reassurances regarding their safety, Suleyman ordered the artillery attacks to begin again. His troops took the bastion of Spain on 17 December – and from this point on there seemed no doubt the city would eventually be taken.

PEACE AT LAST

On 20 December Grand Master of L'Isle-Adam requested another truce and on 22 December a peace treaty was agreed under which the Knights who wished to depart would be allowed 12 days to leave the island in peace, with their weapons and religious relics, while the islanders would be permitted to leave for up to three years. Suleyman was very impressed with the fight put up by the Knights and the bearing of Grand Master of L'Isle-Adam. After the peace negotiations, the sultan is reported to have said of of L'Isle-Adam 'it gives me no pleasure to force this fearless old man from his home' and when he entered Rhodes he dismissed his imperial bodyguard, declaring that he had his safety guaranteed on the honour of the Grand Master of the Hospitallers, and that this was 'worth more than all the world's armies'. A further tribute to the heroism and faith of the Hospitallers came from Holy Roman Emperor Charles V, who declared: 'Nothing in the world was ever so well lost as Rhodes.'

IN MALTA

After leaving Rhodes, the Knights Hospitaller took up residence in Sicily, but in 1530 moved on to Malta, which was given them as a fief, along with the nearby island of Gozo and the port of Tripoli in north Africa, by Holy Roman Emperor Charles V (r.1519–56). In return, they were required to send one falcon a year to the Viceroy of Sicily and to celebrate Mass for Charles on All Saints Day.

From their new base they launched regular attacks on Muslim shipping, and fought a running war against the Muslim corsairs who operated from north Africa across the Mediterranean. In 1551 the corsair Turgut Reis and the Ottoman admiral Sinan combined in an attack on Malta: they did not take the main island, but captured Gozo and, also during the same campaign, drove the Hospitaller garrison from Tripoli. In response the Knights greatly expanded and strengthened fortifications on Malta. In 1559, the Knights took part in an expedition organized by

▼ *Jean Parisot of Valette masterminded the defence of Malta. He was a veteran of the Hospitallers' campaigns in Rhodes.*

▲ *In the defence of Malta the Hospitallers fought with heroic courage.*

Philip II of Spain to drive Turgut Reis from Tripoli. It was a significant enterprise – involving more than 50 galleys and 14,000 men – but ended in a heavy defeat in the Battle of Djerba in May 1560.

THE ASSAULT ON MALTA

Nevertheless, the Hospitallers kept up their attacks on Muslim shipping, and in 1565 Suleyman determined to stop them once and for all. A vast Ottoman war-fleet landed a force of around 40,000–50,000 men on Malta in mid-May. Grand Master Jean Parisot of Valette had sent out a summons to members of the order around the world, but even so its defending garrison numbered no more than around 6,000. He further strengthened the fortifications on the three main forts of Malta – St Elmo, Fort St Michael and Fort St Angelo.

The Ottomans could not use the mining that had worked so well on Rhodes because the fortresses on Malta were built on solid rock. Instead they relied on their mighty artillery, training their guns on the fortress of St Elmo at the entrance to the Grand Harbour. The Ottomans launched three major attacks on St Elmo, on 3, 10 and 16 June, and each time were driven back by the determined defenders; the attackers suffered very heavy losses, and many of the elite Janissary troops were killed. But finally on 23 June, in another major attack, the entire defending garrison of that fort was killed – even the

wounded men who had fought heroically to the last, sitting on chairs on the ramparts. The fort was taken.

Next the Turks attacked the Senglea Peninsula to the south of Fort St Angelo. There was fierce fighting over several days in early August, but the Ottomans were driven back. Another attack on Fort St Michael and the town of Birgu on 7 August seemed to have brought the Turks close to victory when they made a breach in the walls, but they had to retreat to defend their camp against a daring attack by Hospitaller cavalry from Mdina.

THE OTTOMANS DEPART

Further attacks on Fort St Michael and on Mdina also failed and in early September the Ottomans abandoned the attack when a relief force arrived from Sicily. The holding of Malta against seemingly impossible odds was an extraordinary and famous victory that ranked alongside any of the Hospitallers' other feats.

The Knights Hospitaller continued to fight for Christendom at sea and in land wars in eastern Europe and on Crete. They were to remain on Malta until 1798, when they were finally driven out by French general Napoleon en route to Egypt, on the expedition that was to discover the Rosetta Stone.

KNIGHTS OF THE TEMPLE OF SOLOMON
FOUNDATION OF THE KNIGHTS TEMPLAR

The military brotherhood of the Knights Templar was founded in the aftermath of the First Crusade, initially for the care of Christian pilgrims travelling to Jerusalem. The order received the official blessing of the Church at the Council of Troyes in 1129 and this was confirmed and many privileges granted to the order by Pope Innocent II in 1139.

French knights Hugues of Payens and Godfrey of Saint-Omer, both veterans of the First Crusade, took on the responsibility of protecting pilgrims on the road between the port of Jaffa and the Holy City, and in c.1120 proposed the formation of a religious brotherhood to perform this task. King Baldwin II of Jerusalem gave them his backing and provided space for a headquarters in the former al-Aqsa mosque on Temple Mount. At the time, this building was believed to stand on the ruins of the biblical Temple of Solomon and the brotherhood took the name of the 'Poor Knights of Christ and the Temple of Solomon'. Initially there were nine knights in the brotherhood and they had very few resources; their emblem, which shows two

▼ With the backing of Bernard of Clairvaux, the Templars received the ceremonial blessing of the Roman Catholic Church at the Council of Troyes in 1129.

▲ In crusader Jerusalem the al-Aqsa mosque was used as a palace. The Knights Templar were given space in one wing.

knights mounted on a single horse, reflects their poverty-stricken beginnings. They took vows of poverty, chastity and obedience and agreed to share all their property.

BERNARD OF CLAIRVAUX
In 1126 Hugues of Payens, by now known as *Magister militum Templi* (Master of the Temple Soldiery) travelled to Europe to raise finances and seek Church support. He had a powerful ally in the Cistercian monk Bernard of Clairvaux, founder and first abbot of the Cistercian Abbey of Clairvaux in north-eastern France, who was also nephew to Andre of Montbard, one of the initial members of the brotherhood. Bernard wrote a pamphlet called *De Laude Novae Militiae* (In Praise of the New Soldiery), in which he set up the Templar knights as ideal exemplars of chivalry and contrasted their Christian poverty and religious devotion with the lack of these qualities in the secular knights of the day, men who expended their God-given energy in private quarrels driven by greed.

The pamphlet took up the imagery used by St Paul in his *Epistle to the Ephesians*, which urged readers to put on 'the whole armour of God' and 'the breastplate of righteousness', to use 'the shield of faith' and 'the helmet of salvation' and fight with 'the sword of the spirit'. Bernard

FOUNDER MEMBERS
Hugues of Payens was initially a vassal of (and cousin to) Count Hugues of Champagne in France and fought alongside his suzerain on the First Crusade, probably in the army of Godfrey of Bouillon. In addition to Godfrey of Saint-Omer, there were seven other founding members of the order: Payen of Montdidier; Archambaud of St Agnan; Andre of Montbard (Bernard of Clairvaux's uncle); Geoffrey Bisot; two knights known as Gondamer and Rossal; and an unknown knight – who may perhaps have been Count Hugues of Champagne himself. Legend tells that the image on the Templar seal of two knights on a single horse (seen below) in fact represents the actual practice of Hugues of Payens and Godfrey of Saint-Omer, who shared a horse because in the early days of the order they could not afford one each.

wrote of the new 'fearless knight, secure in every direction, who dons the breastplate of faith to protect his soul just as he dons an iron breastplate on his body'; he added that with this 'double armour' knights need fear nothing, and urged them to go forward in safety, with undaunted spirits, to fight back those who oppose the Cross of Christ.

Hugues of Payens, almost certainly with Bernard's help, drew up a rule for the new order, which was to be committed to protecting pilgrims and the holy places in Jerusalem, and this was approved at the Council of Troyes in January 1129. Five Templars, led by Hugues of Payens, attended the council and received the rule from Bernard. The rule was based on that of the Cistercians.

On his trip of 1128–29, Hugues of Payens also visited England and Scotland, where he established the first Templar house in London and also one close to Edinburgh on land granted to the order by King David I at Balantrodoch (now known as Temple, in Midlothian).

ROBERT OF CRAON

Hugues of Payens died in 1136 and was succeeded as Grand Master by Robert of Craon. Robert won papal approval for the order in 1139. In his bull *Omne Datum Optimum*, Pope Innocent II confirmed the order's rule and granted the Templars exemption from local laws and taxation and also from all secular and religious authority save that of the papacy. He wrote: 'since your religious order and your

▼ The Templars meet, with great ceremony, in Paris in April 1147, shortly after they were granted privileges by the Church.

ancient institution is praised throughout the whole world … you should be regarded especially as part of God's knighthood.' By this date, the order was well established, having already received several substantial gifts of land and finance from the nobility of Europe, many as a result of Bernard of Clairvaux's tract in praise of the order.

The Templars gained further significant privileges in the papal bulls *Milites Templi* of 1144 (issued by Pope Celestine II, who ruled 1143–44) and *Militia Dei* of 1145 (issued by Pope Eugenius III, who ruled 1145–53), which permitted them to build

▲ Burgundian nobleman Jacques of Molay is inagurated into the Knights Templar. He became Grand Master in 1292, and was also the last Grand Master, for the order was accused of heresy and dissolved in 1312 under his leadership.

their own places of worship, to bury their dead in the grounds of these establishments and to gather taxes on Templar property once each year. In 1147 Eugenius III granted the knights to right to wear a red splayed cross (one with spreading ends) on their white surplice. The sacred design was sewn above the heart.

ORGANIZATION

The head of the order was the Grand Master. Major decisions were taken by the Grand Chapter, a council of leading officers. Only the Grand Chapter could agree treaties or declare war. Its officers included the Marshal, in charge of military affairs, and the Seneschal, in control of administration, plus eight provincial masters in Aragon, Apulia, England, France, Poitiers, Hungary, Portugal and Scotland.

TEUTONIC KNIGHTS

GERMANIC BROTHERHOOD

The German order of the Teutonic Knights was established in Acre in the late 12th century and granted approval by Pope Celestine III (ruled 1191–98) in 1192. In the 13th century the order established itself in Prussia, initially as part of a crusade against pagans in the region and subsequently against the non-Christian people of central and northern Europe. The order suffered a crushing defeat at the hands of a Polish–Lithuanian force at the Battle of Tannenberg in 1410 and became gradually secularized.

ORIGINS AND FOUNDATION

The earliest origins of the order of the Teutonic Knights lie in a hospital for German pilgrims run in Jerusalem from c.1140 by German knights under the overall control of the Knights Hospitaller. It was known as the *Domus Teutonicorum* (House of the Germans). In 1189–90 during the siege of Acre on the Third Crusade, German merchants from Lübeck and Bremen set up a sister German hospital in the crusader camp. After the

▼ *The Teutonic Knights' Montfort Castle was originally so called from the French for 'strong mountain'. The Knights' name for it, Starkenberg, means the same in German.*

▲ *Holy Roman Emperor and sometime King of Jerusalem, Frederick II, seen here receiving a delegation of Arabs in 1230, was a major patron of the Teutonic Knights. His chancellor, Petrus of Vinea, pictured on the left, was a Master of the Order.*

capture of Acre in 1191 the hospital was established as a permanent institution in Acre, known as the Hospital of St Mary of the German House in Jerusalem. Initially a simple monastic brotherhood, as recognized by Pope Celestine III in 1192, it became a military order with the approval of King Amalric II of Jerusalem in 1198.

The Teutonic Order received substantial grants of land from popes Celestine III and Innocent III in the Latin Kingdom of Jerusalem and in Germany, Italy and elsewhere. It was Innocent III who, in 1205, granted the knights the use of their white habits, or surplices, decorated with a black cross. The order based its organization on that of the Knights Templar and its head was known as the Grand Master.

MONTFORT

The order's original base was in Acre, but in 1220 the brotherhood bought the Castle of Montfort, or Starkenberg, to the north-east of the city and on the route between the Mediterranean coast and Jerusalem. From 1229 this was the principal seat of the Teutonic Grand Masters, as well as the home of the order's treasury and archive. In 1266 the Knights repelled an attack by Mamluk sultan Baybars, but when he returned in 1271 the garrison surrendered at the end of a seven-day siege. Baybars for once honoured his promise made during negotiations to allow the knights to leave Montfort with their belongings. They returned to Acre.

IN TRANSYLVANIA

Hermann von Salza, Grand Master of the Teutonic Order in 1210–39, was a close friend of Holy Roman Emperor Frederick II. Under von Salza's leadership, the brotherhood began to transfer its operation from the Holy Land to central Europe.

▲ *The Teutonic Knights' days of glory ended when, under Grand Master Ulrich von Jungingen, they were roundly defeated at the First Battle of Tannenberg in July 1410.*

In 1211 the Teutonic Knights entered the service of King Andrew II of Hungary (r.1205–35) and settled on land he gave them in Burzenland, Transylvania; his aim was to establish a buffer against the border incursions of the nomadic Turkish Cuman people. However, when the Teutonic Knights attempted to establish an independent principality on the territory by appealing to Pope Honorius III (ruled 1216–27) to be placed under his authority rather than that of the Hungarian crown, King Andrew expelled them from the country.

IN PRUSSIA

In 1226 the Teutonic Knights answered a call from Duke Konrad I of Masovia in Poland to fight on his borders against the pagan Prussians who had been provoked to violent uprising by the first Prussian Crusade of 1221. Over 50 years between 1233 and 1283 the knights fought with great ferocity for the conversion of the Prussians. From 1245 the order even had the power to grant crusade indulgences in this struggle without prior papal approval.

The Teutonic Knights governed Prussia as a sovereign 'monastic state' under charters from the Holy Roman Emperor and the papacy. They founded several fortress settlements including Konigsberg (now in the Russian enclave of Kaliningrad Oblast, situated between Poland and Lithuania), Elbing (modern Elblag in northern Poland), Allenstein (modern Olsztyn in north-east Poland) and Memel (modern Klaipeda in Lithuania). But they faced sustained and brutal opposition from pagan Prussians, who (according to the order's chronicles) would 'roast' captured knights in their armour over fires 'like chestnuts'. The order also tried to expand eastwards to convert Russia to Roman Catholicism, but suffered a devastating defeat at the hands of Alexander Nevsky in the Battle of Lake Peipus, 1242.

MARIENBURG

The knights maintained their presence in the Holy Land at Acre but following the fall of that port in 1291 and the final collapse of Outremer, they briefly made their main base in Venice, Italy, from where they planned ways to retake the Holy Land. In 1309, however, they built a vast castle in Prussia named Marienburg (Mary's Castle)

▼ *Teutonic Knights encounter pagan east German farmers during their attempts to impose Christianity in the region.*

in honour of the Virgin Mary. This place (now Malbork in Poland) was thereafter their main base. In the 14th century they waged a long war against pagans in the Baltic, in the area known as Livonia (now Lithuania, Latvia and Estonia).

The knights were also engaged in wars against Poland, because their expansion cut the country off from its access to the Baltic Sea, and with Lithuania even after that country's conversion to Christianity in 1387. In 1410 Poland and Lithuania joined forces and defeated the Teutonic Knights at the Battle of Tannenberg. The brotherhood ceded territory to Poland, and further landholdings in 1466 following defeat by the Poles and the knights' own Prussian vassals in the Thirteen Years War (1454–66). The order survived in East Prussia, but the Grand Master held the land as a vassal of the Polish king.

DECLINE AND REBIRTH

In 1525 Grand Master Albert of Brandenberg dissolved the order and founded a secular duchy in Prussia under his own rule. Gradually over the ensuing 400 years, the order's territories were ceded to secular authorities. In 1809 the French emperor Napoleon dissolved the order entirely and seized its remaining holdings. However, the Teutonic Knights enjoyed a rebirth in Vienna in 1834 as an ecclesiastical body engaged in charitable work.

KNIGHTS OF ST THOMAS
THE HOSPITALLERS OF ST THOMAS OF CANTERBURY AT ACRE

The English military brotherhood of the Knights of St Thomas of Canterbury at Acre was established after the capture of the city by crusader armies led by King Richard I of England (r.1189–99) and King Philip II of France (r.1180–1223) in 1191. Some sources suggest its founder was a certain William, chaplain to the Dean of St Paul's Cathedral, London, although there is also evidence that the knights celebrated no less a figure than Richard Coeur de Lion himself as their founder. Their brotherhood was named in honour of Saint Thomas Becket, the Archbishop of Canterbury who had been slain in his own cathedral by English knights in 1170 and canonized in 1173 (*see* box). The order survived for around 340 years, until it was wound up by King Henry VIII of England (r.1509–47) as part of the Dissolution of the Monasteries in 1538.

▼ *The Fifth Crusade was mainly against Ayyubid Egypt, but its initial stages took place in the Holy Land, and at this time Peter Roches established the Knights of St Thomas as a military order.*

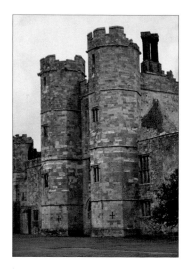

CARING FOR THE SICK
In its first years the brotherhood was a religious rather than a military order, dedicated to caring for the wounded and sick, burying the knights who had died in the wars of the cross and seeking to raise funds in order to ransom Christian warriors who had been taken prisoner by Saladin and his Muslim generals. The

◄ *Peter Roches, Bishop of Winchester and the man who transformed the St Thomas brotherhood from monks to knights, founded Titchfield Abbey in Hampshire in c.1222.*

brothers took vows of poverty, chastity and obedience like their counterparts in other monastic orders. In Acre they built a church and a hospital, both dedicated to St Thomas of Canterbury.

The brotherhood was made into a military order by Peter Roches, Bishop of Winchester, when he was in the Holy Land for the Fifth Crusade of 1217–21. He established the brotherhood under the rule of the Teutonic Knights with the backing of the Latin Patriarch of Jerusalem and leading magnates of Outremer. The brotherhood was recognized by Pope Gregory IX (ruled 1227–41) in 1236. The order became more generally known as the Knights of St Thomas Acon (the last word being an anglicized form of Acre). In the first 80 years or so of its existence, the brotherhood had a prior as its senior figure, but from *c.*1279 – reflecting increasing militarization – the pre-eminent individual was the master.

Historians are not certain why members of religious brotherhoods initially dedicated to providing medical and other care for pilgrims and soldiers became themselves soldiers. It is likely that the constant shortage of warriors in Outremer was an important incentive for the brothers to take up arms and further the Christian cause themselves. Bishop Peter Roches would surely have been encouraged in his militarization of the Order of St Thomas of Acre when he sought the counsel of Outremer's leading barons, for these men faced a constant struggle to find enough soldiers to fight their wars and maintain hard-won territories.

The brothers fought in defence of Christian holdings in the Holy Land and, in particular, to protect Acre. They did not become wealthy. In 1279 they were forced to appeal to King Edward I of England (r.1272–1307) for funds. But they did succeed in establishing a house in London and various provincial quarters in both England and Ireland.

▼ Mercers Hall in Ironmonger Lane, London, stood on the site of the former Hospital of St Thomas Acon, which was destroyed in the Great Fire of London (1666). The hall as shown here was itself destroyed by German bombs in May 1941.

THE CULT OF ST THOMAS BECKET

King Henry II of England (r.1154–89) elevated Thomas Becket to greatness, making him Chancellor in 1155 and Archbishop of Canterbury in 1162 but the pair quarrelled over Henry's attempts to impose his authority on the Church and, despite an apparent reconciliation, four knights claiming to be acting on Henry's wishes killed Becket in Canterbury Cathedral on 29 December 1170. The whole of Christendom was outraged and in 1173 Pope Alexander III (ruled 1159–81) canonized the archbishop. Becket's cult was immediately very strong and his tomb at Canterbury became a major draw for pilgrims. For his part, Henry II strongly denied having ordered the murder of his archbishop, but was forced to make a public demonstration of penance at the saint's tomb in July 1174.

▲ Two murderous knights violate the sanctuary at Canterbury Cathedral and slay Thomas Becket at his prayers.

IN CYPRUS

After the fall of Acre in 1291 the brothers removed, with the Knights Templar, to Cyprus. There they built the fine Church of St Nicholas in Nicosia. But very difficult times followed. In the early 14th century the London house of the Knights of St Thomas was reported to be in ruins and the brothers had to fight off two proposed takeovers, firstly by the Knights Templar and secondly by the convent of Bonhommes at Ashridge, Hertfordshire.

In c.1320 the master of the order in Cyprus, Henry of Bedford, removed to London and established himself in power there. He sent a deputy to rule in Cyprus, but the brothers rejected this man and there was a spilt in the order. Overall power briefly returned to Cyprus after Henry's death, but in c.1360 it was finally confirmed in London; there are no records of a master in Nicosia after this date.

From this period onwards, the brothers appear to have abandoned their military role and exchanged the rule of the Teutonic Knights for that of the monastic

rule of the Augustinians. They concentrated on charitable and educational work in London, where they established St Thomas of Acres grammar school in the city in c.1450. The order was dissolved by Henry VIII in 1538 in the Dissolution.

MERCERS

Henry put the brothers' London hospital and chapel up for sale and the buildings were bought by the Worshipful Company of Mercers. Incorporated under royal charter in 1394, the Worshipful Company of Mercers was established as a trade association for merchants in the cloth trade, especially importers of velvet and silk and exporters of wool. The Mercers had already established links with the Knights of St Thomas and had been worshipping in the brotherhood's London chapel for some years. This was destroyed in the Great Fire of London in 1666, but a statue of Christ was salvaged and reused both in the second Mercer's Hall and Chapel (destroyed in World War I) and in its modern replacement.

THE ORDER OF ST LAZARUS
AND OTHER MINOR CHIVALRIC ORDERS

A number of smaller chivalric orders complemented the major brotherhoods of the Knights Templar, the Knights Hospitaller and the Teutonic Knights. Among these, as we have seen, was the brotherhood of the Knights of St Thomas at Acre. Others included the Order of St Lazarus of Jerusalem, established *c*.1123, and the Order of the Sword, founded by King Peter of Cyprus in 1347.

THE ORDER OF ST LAZARUS
Another group of knights in the Holy Land who were dedicated to relieving the suffering of pilgrims and soldiers in the wars of the cross belonged to the Order of St Lazarus of Jerusalem, which specialized in the care of lepers. Like the Order of St John (Hospitallers), St Lazarus grew into a military order from a brotherhood offering hospitality and medical care. Under the Templar rule, any Templar knights who contracted leprosy were required to transfer to the Order of St Lazarus, and

▼ The Knights of St Lazarus are named after the man raised from the dead by Christ, as told in the Gospel of St John.

▲ Henry II of England was an important patron of the Order of St Lazarus. His effigy is at Fontevrault Abbey, France.

these Templars trained the St Lazarus brothers in military ways. The Order of St Lazarus of Jerusalem was established as a military brotherhood in *c*.1123.

The order became very wealthy, and was left endowments by European kings including Louis VII of France (r.1137–80), Henry II of England (r.1154–89) and Holy Roman Emperor Frederick II (r.1220–50). The order followed the Augustinian rule. Knights of the Order fought at the Battle of La Forbie in 1244 against the alliance of Khwarismian Turks and Sultan as-Salih Ayyub of Egypt (r.1240–49), in the army of the Seventh Crusade led by King Louis IX of France (r.1226–70) and at the fall of Acre in 1291.

The order received papal recognition under Augustinian rule in 1255 in the reign of Pope Alexander IV (ruled 1254–61), and was granted the same privileges and exemptions as the principal monastic orders in 1262 under Pope Urban IV (ruled 1261–64). Its numbers were swelled after 1265 when Pope Clement IV (ruled 1265–68) issued an order that Catholic clergy send all lepers to the houses of St Lazarus.

After the loss of Jerusalem in 1187, the Knights of St Lazarus (like the Hospitaller counterparts) removed to Acre. Then, following the fall of Acre in 1291, the Order

of St Lazarus disappeared from the East altogether while the Hospitallers as we have seen took up residence on Cyprus. The Knights of St Lazarus continued to maintain leper hospitals in Europe.

THE ORDER OF THE SWORD
The future Peter I of Cyprus, the titular King of Jerusalem in 1358–69 and the monarch known as the 'Crusading king', led a military expedition in 1365 against Muslim Egypt. He founded the chivalric brotherhood of the Order of the Sword

▼ Those afflicted with leprosy, who entered the Order of St Lazarus, were required to pass their worldly goods to the brothers.

▲ *Mary the mother of Christ, was honoured in the brotherhood of Our Lady Of Bethlehem, established to counter the power of the Ottomans in the mid-15th century.*

in 1347. In a powerful mystical experience, Peter had a vision of a floating cross and heard a voice urging him to liberate the Holy Land: the order he formed was for knights and men-at-arms prepared to dedicate themselves to freeing Jerusalem and other parts of Outremer from Muslim control. Its emblem was a silver sword, point down, against a blue backing inscribed with the words 'With this maintain loyalty'.

THE ORDER OF OUR LADY OF BETHLEHEM

After the Ottoman Turks under Sultan Mehmed II 'the Conqueror' (r.1444–46, 1451–81) captured Constantinople in 1453, Pope Pius II (ruled 1458–64) established the Order of Our Lady of Bethlehem on the island of Lemnos in the Aegean Sea. Its knights were charged with defending the island against the Ottomans and countering the Turks' activity in the Aegean and Hellespont. The knights of the order wore a white surplice with a red cross and followed a rule similar to that of the Knights Hospitaller.

Pope Pius suppressed a number of orders, including that of St Lazarus, in order to provide the knights of Our Lady of Bethlehem with property and revenues.

But the enterprise came to nothing when the Ottomans succeed in capturing Lemnos. The orders Pius had suppressed were re-established.

OTHER GERMANIC ORDERS

A number of minor Germanic military-monastic orders of knighthood were established in the 13th century. The Order of Dobrzyn, also known as the *Fratres Milites Christi de Prussia*, (the Prussian Cavaliers of Christ Jesus), was created in the 1220s by Christian of Oliva, the first Bishop of Prussia, in order to fight against raids on Masovia by pagan Prussians who had risen in defiance of Duke Konrad I of Masovia's efforts to force them to convert

to Christianity. The establishment of the order was approved by Pope Gregory IX (ruled 1227–41) in 1228. The order was granted possession of the town of Dobrzyn and surrounding regions (Dobrzyn Land). The order initially had 15 German knights in membership under the command of Master Brunon. In 1235 the majority of the knights joined the Teutonic Order.

The monastic order of the Livonian Brothers of the Sword was established by Albert of Buxhoeveden, third Bishop of Riga in Livonia, in 1202 and was granted official sanction by Pope Innocent III in 1204. Bishop Albert wanted the German warrior monks to help in the forcible conversion to Christianity of pagan Curonians, Livonians and others in the region. The knights, who were also known as 'Christ Knights', 'Sword Brethren' and 'The Militia of Christ of Livonia', made their headquarters at Fellin (modern Viljandi in Estonia) and the remains of their Grand Master's castle can still be seen there. They suffered a heavy defeat by Lithuanians at the Battle of Schaulen in 1236 and in 1237 most of the members joined the Teutonic Order.

▼ *Two minor Germanic orders – those of Dobrzyn and of the Livonian Brothers of the Sword – were established by bishops.*

CHAPTER FIFTEEN

THE EUROPEAN CRUSADES

Christian wars were waged against Muslims in Spain from as early as the 8th century, and against the pagan peoples of northern Europe from the time of the Second Crusade (1147–49) up until the 14th century. In southern France the Albigensian Crusade of the 13th century brutally attacked the Cathars, who were denounced as heretics by the papacy; in Bohemia the Hussites (followers of Czech nationalist preacher Jan Hus) were likewise declared heretics and attacked by crusaders in 1420–32; and in Italy during the 12th–14th centuries, several holy wars were called against enemies of the Catholic Church.

Many of these wars were thinly disguised secular struggles – those in Italy, for example, were fought to promote the territorial interests of the papacy. They were different in kind to the crusades in the Holy Land, and would probably have been fought even if the ideology of crusading was not deployed. One of them, the war to reconquer Spain, predated the crusading era, for it began in the immediate aftermath of the Muslim conquest of the Iberian Peninsula in the early 8th century. Yet, once available, crusading rhetoric and the apparatus of crusade indulgences and taxes were enthusiastically applied to this Spanish struggle from the time of the First Crusade in the 1090s. The call to fight for the cross also gave an added force and charge to all the struggles termed as the Northern Crusades against Muslims, heretics or pagans.

▲ *King Alfonso XI of Castile waged war against Muslims in Spain with such determination he was called 'the Implacable'.*

◀ *After the conquest in 1492 of Granada, the last remaining Muslim territory in Spain, Ferdinand and Isabella receive Arab tributes.*

THE RECONQUISTA

THE STRUGGLE IN SPAIN

◄ *At the Battle of Guadalete (711) in the far south of the Iberian Peninsula, invading Muslim cavalry routed the Visigoths.*

Umayyads were the successors of the fourth caliph, Mu'awiyah, a member of the Umayyad clan of caravan merchants.

In 750 the Umayyad caliph Marwan II was defeated by a rival leader, Abu al-Abbas, who established the Abbasid caliphate. Abu al-Abbas was known as *as-Saffah* ('the Bloodshedder') on account of the ruthlessness with which he eliminated his rivals, but one prominent Umayyad, Abd ar-Rahman, escaped to Spain and established himself in Córdoba. His successors were in theory subordinate to the Abbasid caliphs, who were now based in Baghdad, in Iraq, but were in practice independent and ruled as emirs of Córdoba. When Abbasid power declined sharply and their realm fell into anarchy in the early 10th century, the then emir, Abd ar-Rahman III, declared himself the

▼ *The Arabs capture Córdoba. Under their rule it became one of the world's largest cities, home to as many as 500,000 people.*

The *Reconquista* – from the word in Spanish and Portuguese for 'reconquest' – was the struggle by the Christians of Europe to retake the Iberian Peninsula from its Moorish rulers. The Reconquista lasted a full 750 years, from the early 8th century, when Muslim Arabs and Berbers captured the peninsula from the Visigoths, to 1492, when the combined armies of Aragon and Castile conquered the city of Granada, the last Muslim territory in the peninsula. These Iberian wars were promoted as holy wars by popes who offered crusading privileges to those taking part in the struggle.

VISIGOTHS AND MUSLIMS

In the 5th century AD the Visigoths, an East Germanic tribe, took power in the Roman province of Hispania (incorporating the whole of the Iberian Peninsula and part of southern France) under the auspices of Rome. After the fall of the Roman Empire in the west, the Visigoth territory became an independent territory.

A Muslim army of Arabs and north African Berber tribesmen invaded the southern part of the peninsula in 711 and in five years captured most of the large

Visigoth kingdom. The Muslims then attempted to push on northwards but were defeated by Odo, Duke of Aquitaine, at the Battle of Toulouse in 721 and by Frankish leader Charles Martel in the Battle of Tours in 732. Thereafter they largely abandoned attempts at northward expansion and settled in what is now Spain and Portugal.

Only in the north of the Iberian Peninsula did the Visigoths maintain a foothold. The Visigoth nobleman Pelayo established the Kingdom of Asturias, which was subsequently to be an important base for the reconquest of Spain. His defeat of a Muslim army in the Battle of Covadonga (722) is often identified as the first conflict of the Reconquista.

AL-ANDALUS AND THE MOORS

The Muslim state in the Iberian Peninsula was known by the Arabic name al-Andalus – and its people were known by the Christians as 'Moors'.

Al-Andalus was at first nominally subject to the Umayyad caliph in Damascus, Syria. 'Caliph' was the title for the leader of Islam as a successor to the founder of the faith, the Prophet Mohammad; the independent caliph of Córdoba in 929. Historians call al-Andalus the Umayyad caliphate province from 711 to 750, the Emirate of Córdoba fom 750 to 929, and the Caliphate of Córdoba from 929 to 1031. After 1031, the caliphate broke up into small Muslim kingdoms.

ST JAMES THE GREAT

Descendants of King Pelayo of Asturias seized territory in Galicia (the north-west part of the peninsula). In the reign of King Alfonso II of Asturias (r.791–842), the bones of St James were reputedly discovered at Compostela, which became established as one of Europe's foremost pilgrimage sites. St James the Great was one of Christ's 12 Apostles and traditionally brought the Christian Gospel to the Iberian Peninsula. According to legend, his bodily remains were brought to what is now Spain by sea after his death. In 844 the saint then supposedly made a miraculous appearance to lead the Christian army of King Ramiro I of Asturias (r.842–50) against the Moors of Córdoba in the Battle of Clavijo.

PROGRESS IN THE RECONQUISTA

Gerona and Barcelona were taken from the Muslims in 785 and 801 by Carolingian armies from France, and the region of Catalonia became part of the Carolingian realm known as 'the Spanish March'. After 850 the Christian buffer between southern France and the Iberian Peninsula established by the Kings of Asturias was expanded to the valley of the River Duero. In 913 the rulers of Asturias moved their seat of power from Oviedo to León and the kingdom became known as León. Christian kingdoms were also established in Pamplona and Aragon.

In 1002 the caliphate of Córdoba collapsed and divided into around 30 small *taifa* (successor) kingdoms that were to prove vulnerable to the continuing Christian recovery. In 1029 the independent kingdom of Castile was founded in what had been a county within the kingdom of León.

ALFONSO VI AND EL CID

King Alfonso VI of León temporarily reunited his kingdom with Castile, reigning as king of Castile and León from 1072, until his death in 1109. When he captured Toledo in May 1085, he appeared to be on the brink of a major onslaught against the taifa kingdoms: in 1077 he had declared himself Emperor of Spain. But the beleaguered rulers of the taifas appealed to the Muslim Almoravids of north-west Africa, and Almoravid armies defeated Alfonso at Sagrajas in 1086 and Ucles in 1108.

In this period, Don Rodrigo Diaz of Vivar, the Spanish knight celebrated as 'El Cid', performed his great feats of chivalry. He was cast into exile by King Alfonso in 1081, entered the service of al-Mu'tamin, Moorish king of Saragossa, and then fought for al-Mu'tamin and his successor al-Musta'in II for almost ten years, before returning to Alfonso's service and capturing the Muslim kingdom of Valencia in 1090–94; he ruled Valencia until his death in 1099, when it was captured by the Almoravids. (León and Castile remained reunited until 1157.)

▼ *In the legendary Battle of Clavijo, a Christian army was vastly outnumbered by the Moors but triumphed nonetheless after a miraculous appearance by St James.*

CRUSADING PRIVILEGES

War against Muslims in Spain was promoted as crusading, with privileges identical to those offered for military service in the Holy Land, from the 1090s onwards. In 1095 Pope Urban II (ruled 1088–99) urged the Spanish to respond to his call to crusade by fighting the Muslims in their own land rather than by travelling to Palestine. In 1123 Pope Callixtus II (ruled 1119–24) declared a crusade in Spain at the same time as he called a fresh military expedition to the Holy Land.

At the time of the Second Crusade during 1145, Pope Eugenius III (ruled 1145–53) also called a crusade in Spain, guaranteeing King Alfonso VII of León and Castile (r. 1126–57) the same indulgence he had given to the French crusader knights. In 1147 crusader armies from England, Scotland, Normandy and Germany stopped in Spain and Portugal en route to the Holy Land and helped to recapture the city of Lisbon; around the same time, as part of the crusading campaign, Alfonso VII of Castile and Count Ramon Berenguer IV of Barcelona conquered Almeria in south-eastern Spain from the Moors. The next major crusading activity in the Iberian Peninsula was to come in 1212.

THE SPANISH CRUSADE OF 1212

AND OTHER 13TH-CENTURY CRUSADES IN SPAIN AND PORTUGAL

In 1212 Pope Innocent III (ruled 1198–1216) proclaimed a crusade in Spain against the Almohad caliphs. The Almohads had ousted their Almoravid predecessors and defeated the kingdom of Castile in the Battle of Alarcos on 19 July 1195. With the support of troops from the Spanish kingdoms of Aragon and Navarre and with crusaders from France, King Alfonso VIII of Castile (r.1158–1214) won a resounding victory over the Almohads at the Battle of Las Navas de Tolosa, one of the greatest and most important Christian victories in the entire period of the Reconquista.

RISE OF THE ALMOHADS

The Almohads were originally followers of a Berber religious teacher named Ibn Tumart from the Atlas Mountains of

▼ *King Alfonso VIII led the army of Castile and a vast force of crusaders and Knights Templar to victory over the Almohads at the Battle of Las Navas de Tolosa in July 1212.*

Morocco. Ibn Tumart established the Almohads as a religious order dedicated to bringing purity back into the faith of Islam, and after declaring himself the *mahdi* (a promised Islamic redeemer) in 1121, he led armed resistance against the Almoravid caliphs ruling in northern Africa. His successor, Abd al-Mu'min, defeated the Almoravids by 1147 and made himself Emir of Marrakech in 1149; another Almohad leader, Abu Ya'qub Yusuf (r.1163–84), conquered the Almoravid empire in Spain and established a capital in Seville.

Meanwhile King Alfonso VIII of Castile led resistance to the Almohads in Spain. In 1190, following a defeat, Alfonso was forced to agree an armistice, but when this expired in 1194 he attacked the Almohad province of Seville. Almohad caliph Abu Yusuf gathered an army and inflicted a heavy defeat on Alfonso near the fortress of Alarcos, making the Castilian king retreat to Toledo.

In the aftermath of this defeat, the Almohads took a great deal of territory – capturing Trujillo, Talavera, Cuenca, Ucles and the fortress of Calatrava, stronghold of the Spanish monastic military brotherhood the Order of Calatrava. These Muslim successes forced the border between Muslim and Christian Spain many miles northwards, until it lay in the hills just south of Toledo.

Alfonso's ally Rodrigo Jiménez of Rada, Archbishop of Toledo, sought Church backing for a crusading response. Pope Innocent III issued a call to arms, and in 1212 crusaders – including Frankish knights under Archbishop Arnold of Narbonne and members of the military-monastic brotherhood of the Knights Templar – arrived at Toledo. They marched southwards, accompanied by the armies of Aragon, León and Castile. They captured Calatrava, Alarcos and Benevente before they met the Almohad army.

LAS NAVAS DE TOLOSA

The Almohad caliph, Muhammad al-Nasir, gathered his army on the plains of Las Navas de Tolosa. The Christians, trying to reach them though the mountain pass of La Llosa, found it heavily guarded, but then with the help of a local shepherd found a different route through the Despenaperros Pass.

After a prolonged stand-off, the two armies clashed. King Alfonso led the Christian forces into battle, and they won a famous victory – killing, wounding or capturing no fewer than 100,000 of the Almohads at the cost of 2,000 of their own men dead or wounded. Tradition has it that King Sancho VII of Navarre (r.1194–1234) humiliated the Almohad emir in his tent following an act of great

▲ *King Ferdinand III of Castile and León receives homage from a Moor after taking Seville in 1248. The city had been in Moorish hands since its conquest in 712.*

bravery (*see* box). The Almohad caliph, al-Nasir, fled to Marrakech in Morocco, where he died shortly afterwards. Alfonso went on to capture the southern towns of Baeza and Ubeda.

CHRISTIAN TRIUMPHS

In the following years, the victory at Las Navas de Tolosa proved to have been a truly significant one, for the Almohad empire fell apart in dynastic struggles after 1224 and without strong leadership was unable to hold back the armies of the Christian reconquest. King Alfonso IX of León (r.1188–1230) captured Caceres (1227) and Merida and Badajoz (1230), opening the way to the recapturing of Seville. Ferdinand III, who reigned as King of Castile 1217–52 and of León 1230–52, captured Córdoba in 1236), Jaen in 1246 and Seville in 1248. (Ferdinand is celebrated as San Fernando after he was canonized on 4 February 1671.)

King Alfonso X of Castile and León (r.1252–84) defeated the Muslim emirates in Niebla and Murcia. (Alfonso was the father of Eleanor of Castile, beloved wife of King Edward I of England, and it was at his court that the law code known as the *Siete Partidas*, or Seven-Part Code, was composed; he was a great patron of learning and is remembered as Alfonso 'the Wise' or 'the Learned'.)

King James I of Aragon (r.1213–76) captured the Balearic Islands (1229–35) and the kingdom of Valencia (1233–38). Both these campaigns were crusades. James was renowned as *El Conquistador* (the Conqueror). In Portugal, King Sancho II (r.1223–47) reconquered from the Moors a number of cities in Alentejo (south-central Portugal) and the Algarve (the southernmost part of the country). By the close of the 13th century, the kingdom of Granada was the only part of the entire peninsula to remain under Muslim rule.

▼ *Knights embark by sea for the Holy Land on crusade. The illustration is from a book made for Alfonso X of Castile and León, a great patron of court learning who also played his part in the Reconquista.*

THE ALBIGENSIAN CRUSADE

WAR ON HERESY

In 1208 a papal legate named Pierre of Castelnau was murdered in the Languedoc region of southern France and Pope Innocent III (ruled 1198–1216) declared a crusade against the Cathars of that region, who were viewed as heretics by the Catholic Church. The Cathars were subsequently called the Albigensians (from the town of Albi that was inaccurately identified as their headquarters).

The Albigensian crusade lasted 20 years, from 1209 to 1229, and although it began as a religious war aimed at curbing what the Church hierarchy saw as a popular and dangerous heresy, it became little more than an exercise in territorial expansion by northern French barons. The

▲ *The seal of Raymond VI of Toulouse. It was his vassal who murdered Pierre of Castelnau and provoked Pope Innocent to declare his crusade against the Cathars.*

▼ *St Dominic worked for years to convince the Cathars that their beliefs were heretical. After the celebrated trial by fire, in which Cathar books burned while orthodox Catholic volumes were spared, he gave one of the orthodox books to the Cathars.*

religious victory over the Cathars when it came was achieved not in battle but through the efforts of the Dominican Inquisition (a tribunal to investigate heresy), established in 1233. Military action against the Cathars continued inter-

mittently until 1255. The Cathars were driven from France into Italy, where they died out and were heard of no more after the end of the 14th century.

CATHAR BELIEFS AND BACKGROUND

The Cathars took their name from the Greek word *katharos*, meaning 'pure'. They were dualists, believing in two gods – an ultimate embodiment of goodness, and a lesser and evil creator god who had made the material world. They believed the material world therefore to be evil: the human soul was naturally good and trapped in this evil creation; people should seek salvation through extreme asceticism. Cathars avoided meat and animal products, were sexually chaste, lived in poverty and were pacifists.

Cathars divided themselves into two groups: 'the perfect' and 'the believers'. The perfect passed through an initiation ceremony called the *consolamentum* and lived lives of extreme asceticism, devoting their energy to contemplation. The believers were not required to attain the very high standards of asceticism and religious devotion attained by the perfect.

ROOTS IN GNOSTICISM

Cathar beliefs may have derived from ancient Gnosticism, a dualist faith system popular in the Mediterranean and Middle East from the last centuries BC onward, but suppressed in the Christian Roman Empire from the 4th century AD. Like Cathars, Gnostics believed in dual divinities. The highest god was good and the lesser one evil; the evil one had created the material world. Humans were divine souls trapped in the material world, from which they could only escape through *gnosis* or knowledge held by the elite. The Cathars did not place strong emphasis on spiritual knowledge, but they did have an initiation ceremony, and an initiated elite.

BOGOMILS AND PAULICIANS

The Cathars certainly had links with the Gnostic-influenced Christian groups of the Bogomils and the Paulicians. The Bogomils had emerged in the 10th century in Bulgaria and spread from there into the Byzantine Empire, as well as into Italy and France: they were dualists, who rejected the doctrine of Christ's divine birth and the veneration of the Virgin Mary and declared that reverence for the cross and for saintly relics was no more than idolatry.

The Paulicians had their origins earlier, in the 7th–9th centuries, in Armenia: they rejected the Old Testament, veneration of the Virgin Mary, worship of the Cross and the sacraments of Baptism and Communion. The Cathars for their part denied the divinity of Christ and declared him to have been an angel come to earth; they said that his apparent sufferings and death as a human being was an illusion. Cathar teaching also rejected the doctrines of purgatory and hell and that of the resurrection of the body, arguing in favour of reincarnation.

▲ *Pope Innocent III sent out wandering preachers to bring heretics back to the true faith. He gave St Dominic and St Francis (shown here) his blessing to do this work.*

The Cathars were first established in Flanders, northern Italy and western Germany in 1000–50. They expanded in 1140–70, particularly under the influence of a resurgent Bogomil Church that sent missionaries throughout Europe; historians also believe that soldiers and pilgrims on the First Crusade picked up dualist ideas and brought them back to Europe in the early 12th century. In the 1140s the Cathars established themselves as a church: their first bishop in c.1149 was in northern France, but soon afterward he was joined by counterparts in Lombardy and in Albi. By 1200 they had five bishops in France and six in Italy.

SERIOUS THREAT

Remarkably, in the Languedoc Catharism became a popular religion – unlike many sects, attracting a wide following among the nobility, educated townspeople and the peasantry. Cathars attacked the wealth and corruption of the Church, while rejecting the authority of Catholic priests and of the pope; they posed a threat to the very structure of society, for they rejected the taking of oaths that was one of the central features of the feudal system. Moreover, the fact that they had many followers among both nobility and peasantry served to undo the natural, God-given social hierarchy that orthodox believers saw in the feudal system.

Pope Innocent III initially tried to bring the Cathars back to orthodoxy by peaceful means, sending preachers – including Dominic Guzman (later St Dominic), founder of the Dominican Order – to attempt to convert the heretics. The preachers had little success. Innocent then found that local nobles and even bishops were protecting the Cathars. In 1204 he suspended the bishops and replaced them with papal legates, and he demanded that Philip II of France (r.1180–1223) force the nobles to return to Catholicism. Philip refused to take action. Innocent demanded that the powerful local count, Raymond VI of Toulouse, take action but he, too, refused and was excommunicated.

In January 1208 Raymond held a meeting with the papal legate, Pierre of Castelnau, which ended angrily. The following day Pierre of Castelnau was murdered by one of Raymond's vassals. Pope Innocent III declared war, issuing a call to a crusade against the Cathars.

Innocent offered a full crusade indulgence to all who responded to his call to take up arms against the Cathars. He also declared that they would have the right to seize the land of the heretics, which attracted a number of northern French barons to the cause. It should be noted that the indulgence offered to the anti-Cathar crusaders was remarkably generous – the annulment of sins was being offered for a mere 40 days campaigning (the normal period of feudal military service) and for a war fought in nearby southern France rather than for a potentially very hazardous journey over land and sea to the Holy Land.

MASSACRE OF THE CATHARS

TWENTY YEARS OF BRUTAL WAR, 1209–1229

The crusade armies raised against the Cathars by Pope Innocent III won a series of brutal victories in 1209–15, in which local people – both Cathars and Catholics – were slaughtered in their thousands. During the next ten years, many of these bloody victories were overturned by rebels, but in 1226 King Louis VIII of France (r.1223–26) entered the fray on the side of the Church and following his death in November that year, his son Louis IX (r.1226–70) took up the fight. The Languedoc region was conquered by 1229 and peace was finally agreed in the Treaty of Paris that year.

COUNT RAYMOND RECANTS

In 1209 a crusade army of around 10,000 massed in Lyon and marched south under the leadership of papal legate Arnaul Amalric, Abbot of Cîteaux. Suddenly persuaded of the error of his ways, Raymond VI of Toulouse agreed at last to move against the Cathars and was reconciled to the Church in a ceremony before carvings of the Passion of Christ on the west front

▼ At the Battle of Muret on 12 September 1213, Simon of Montfort's small crusader force roundly defeated the much larger army of Peter II of Aragon and Raymond of Toulouse. Peter was killed in action.

of the Benedictine abbey church of Saint-Gilles. The crusaders then marched towards Montpellier; Raymond-Roger Trencavel, viscount of Béziers and Albi and a vassal of Raymond VI of Toulouse, attempted to make peace with them but was refused an audience. He fled back to Carcassonne to arrange its defence.

THE SLAUGHTER AT BÉZIERS

The crusade army marched to Béziers, where it arrived on 21 July 1209. The soldiers demanded the surrender of the Cathars and the submission of any local Catholics; both groups refused. But the crusaders gained access to the town when an attempted sortie by the defenders went wrong and they burned Béziers to the ground and savagely killed every man, woman and child.

According to one account, soldiers asked the Abbot of Cîteaux how they would tell Cathars from Catholics and the abbot replied: 'Kill them all. God will recognize his own.' Afterwards the Abbot wrote gleefully to the Pope: 'Our soldiers spared neither rank, nor sex, nor elderly. About 20,000 people lost their lives … the entire city was put to the sword. Thus did God's vengeance vent its wondrous rage.'

CATHARS EVICTED FROM CARCASSONNE

Many settlements were terrified into submission and surrendered to the army. The crusaders marched on Carcassonne and took it after a two-week siege on 15 August 1209. The Cathars were forcibly evicted, having been stripped naked to humiliate them. At this point, French nobleman Simon of Montfort took charge of the crusade army and was granted territory that included the Cathar strongholds of Carcassonne, Albi and Béziers. (Simon of Montfort, a veteran of the Fourth Crusade, was the father of Simon of Montfort, 6th Earl of Leicester and main

▲ Fighting during the siege of Carcassonne. In the rear the Cathars emerge from the city to take on the besieging crusaders.

leader of baronial opposition to King Henry III of England; the 6th Earl was the effective ruler of England in 1263–64 and is remembered as a pioneer of parliamentary democracy.)

Town after town surrendered or was conquered by the crusader army over the following months. In June–July 1210 the city of Minerve put up a brave resistance but finally surrendered on 22 July; many Cathars accepted Catholicism, but fully 140 remained defiant and were burned at the stake. In 1211 Raymond of Toulouse was again excommunicated after he fell out with Simon of Montfort. In May hundreds of Cathars were burned at the stake and Aimery of Montréal was hanged after his castle fell to Montfort.

The crusaders besieged Raymond in Toulouse, but the siege failed and the army withdrew. Raymond then led a successful rebellion, capturing Castelnaudary from Simon of Montfort and 'freeing' more than 30 towns for the Cathar cause.

THE BATTLE OF MURET

In 1212, however, much of Toulouse was captured. In 1213 King Peter II of Aragon (r.1196–1213), famous victor over the Moors at the battle of Las Navas de Tolosa, led an army in support of Raymond, who was his brother-in-law. With Raymond, he besieged Montfort in Muret, but was defeated and killed in the ensuing battle. The Aragonese army broke and fled on seeing their king slain.

In 1214, Raymond was forced to flee to England and his lands were given by the pope to Philip II, who became involved in the war. In 1214–16 Montfort captured the remaining Cathar strongholds and also ceded his lands to Philip II.

CATHAR RESURGENCE

In 1216 the tide began to turn. In that year, Pope Innocent III died and was replaced by Honorius III (r.1216–27), who was not so strongly committed to waging war on the Cathars. Raymond returned from exile and captured first Beaucaire and then, in 1217, Toulouse. Montfort besieged him there and was killed in fighting outside the city on 25 June 1218, his head crushed by a stone hurled from a mangonel. The Cathar side made a number of gains, including

▼ *The Cathar stronghold of Carcassonne had grown from a Roman fortification, and parts of its northern walls date from when France was under Roman rule.*

Castelnaudary, Montreal and Fanjeaux and, in 1224, Carcassonne. Raymond VI of Toulouse had died in 1222 , and been succeeded by his son, another Raymond; and Philip II had died, in 1223, and been succeeded by King Louis VIII. Amaury of Montfort, son of Simon, offered his claim to territory in the Languedoc to the new French king, who took up the challenge.

▲ *Naked and frightened, the Cathars were expelled from Carcassonne after the city fell to the crusader army in August 1209.*

Louis led a new crusade army into the region in June 1226. Many castles and towns surrendered without a fight but it took a three-month siege to capture Avignon. That same autumn, Louis VIII died and was succeeded by his son, Louis IX, at the age of just 12. Louis VIII's widow, Blanche of Castile, acted as regent and ordered the continuation of the crusade under the command of Humbert of Beaujeu. The crusaders crushed Cathar resistance, taking Labécède in 1227 and Toulouse in 1228.

A peace treaty was finally agreed in 1229 under which Count Raymond was recognized as ruler of Toulouse, but was forced to agree to hand his castles over into royal control, to dismantle the defences of Toulouse and to attempt to suppress the Cathars.

THE BALTIC CRUSADES
HOLY WAR AGAINST NORTHERN PAGANS

The Baltic Crusades were military campaigns against the pagan peoples on the southern and eastern shores of the Baltic Sea. They were cast as wars of religion but were often fought to gain territory for local bishops and feudal lords. The Baltic Crusades are often said to have started in the 1190s when popes Celestine III and Innocent III called what became a standing crusade. Its purpose was to support the Catholic Church in the region of Livonia (now Estonia, Lithuania and Latvia), but as early as 1147 crusading privileges had been officially granted to Saxon, Danish and Polish Christians fighting against the pagan Wends of the Baltic.

THE WENDISH CRUSADE

In 1147 when Bernard of Clairvaux was preaching the Second Crusade to the Holy Land on behalf of Pope Eugenius III, he was told by the north German Saxons that they were not willing to travel to the Holy Land but wanted to conduct a holy war against the pagan Wends in the Baltic. Eugenius sent out the *Divina dispensatione*

bull, on 13 April 1147, guaranteeing those fighting on this Baltic crusade the same benefits as those who took the cross to fight in the Holy Land. Bernard himself wrote of the crusaders' attack on the Wends: 'We expressly forbid that for any cause they should agree peace with these people until either their false religion or their nation has been destroyed.'

Papal legate Anselm of Havelberg was put in command of an army that included Danes and Poles as well as Saxons. Some of these crusaders were genuinely fighting in order to convert the pagans, but many bishops and lords were primarily seeking to increase their landholding in the region.

◄ *The Wends of the Baltic region were descendants of Slavic tribes who settled in eastern Germany in the 5th century AD. King Wandalus was a mythical ancestor, and was supposedly originally a Trojan.*

▲ *The Baltic Crusades had begun as much as 50 years before Pope Celestine III called a crusade in Livonia following the failure of a Church mission to the region.*

The campaign followed the annexation by Count Adolph of Holstein of Wendish lands, which he had parcelled out among Christian immigrants from western Germany. Wendish leader Niklot led an invasion of Wagria (now eastern Holstein in northern Germany) and Adolph fought back with part of the crusader army. This part of the campaign was swiftly over, and ended in a peace treaty, but other crusaders attacked Dobin and Demmin. At Dobin, the members of the Wendish garrison were baptized following a siege. The crusade army marching on Demmin sacked a castle and pagan temple at Malchow, but their siege of Demmin was unsuccessful and so they marched on into

Pomerania on the Baltic coast where, reaching the Christian city of Stettin (now in Poland), they were greeted by Bishop Albert of Pomerania and Prince Ratorbor I of Pomerania and then disbanded.

The crusade achieved a few conversions, but many of these Christianized Wends reverted to their own religion after the crusaders left. It had the effect of strengthening Christian landholdings in the region and of weakening the resistance of the local people to future campaigns.

THE CRUSADE IN LIVONIA

Before Celestine and Innocent unleashed the power of the crusading machine on Livonia in the 1190s, the Church had made peaceful efforts to convert the local populace. In the 11th century Adalbert, Archbishop of Bremen in 1045–72, had sent missionaries into the region, but with little effect. In 1180 an Augustinian monk called Meinhard led missionary work at Uxhull (modern Ikskile) on the River Dvina (now called the Daugava) and established himself as bishop.

▼ *Prince Niklot, who fought against the crusade army in 1147, had renounced Christianity and reverted to paganism. He is an ancestor of the dukes of Mecklenburg, and is honoured with this statue in their castle at Schwerin, north-eastern Germany.*

▲ *The Livonian Brothers of the Sword fought in Finland in 1232 on the orders of Pope Gregory IX. After they merged with the Teutonic Knights in 1236, they still had their own Master. He was subject to the Grand Master of the Teutonic Knights.*

After Meinhard's successor, Berthold, reported that the mission to Livonia was close to failure, Pope Celestine III called a crusade in the area. A Saxon crusading army led by Berthold won a battle against the Livonians in 1198, but Berthold was killed. Subsequently the crusaders went home and the missionary monks had to abandon their work after the Livonians issued death threats against them.

In 1199 the Archbishop Hartwig of Bremen appointed his nephew Albert of Buxhoeveden as Bishop of Livonia, with instructions to conquer the region and impose Christianity on its people. Albert embarked on a tour to preach a crusade in Livonia, and Pope Innocent III issued a papal bull guaranteeing those who fought in Livonia the same crusading privileges as knights and men-at-arms fighting in the Holy Land. At the bishop's request, Innocent also dedicated the Baltic region to the Virgin Mary, in order to encourage recruits to the cause, and the area is still sometimes known as 'Mary's Land'.

In 1200 Albert landed at the mouth of the River Dvina with a crusade army of around 1,500 men aboard a fleet of 23 vessels. In the next year he abandoned his mission station at Uxhull and founded the trading settlement of Riga at the mouth of the river. Previous efforts at conquest had foundered when temporary crusading armies disbanded, so in 1202 he founded the military order of the Livonian Brothers of the Sword to ensure a continuous military presence. (Albert founded the Cathedral of Riga in 1215; he was later named a Prince of the Holy Roman Empire, with Livonia as his fief, and was known as a 'Prince-Bishop'.) The Livonian Brothers of the Sword suffered a heavy defeat at the hands of a Livonian army in 1236 and the order's few survivors joined the Teutonic Knights.

For more than 25 years, until his death in 1229, Albert was engaged in the conquest of Livonia. He converted some of the locals – for example the Livs accepted Christianity when Bishop Albert guaranteed them military protection against incursion by rival Lithuanians and Estonian tribes; he also achieved the conversion of some Latvians. Otherwise he achieved his goals by military means. By c.1230 the conquest and conversion of Livonia was complete.

▼ *The seal of the Livonian Brothers of the Sword. They were called* Fratres militiae Christi Livoniae *in Latin.*

CRUSADES IN ITALY
WARS IN THE PAPAL INTEREST

In the 12th–14th centuries a series of crusades were called against Christian princes and noblemen who had been declared enemies of the Catholic Church in Italy. Many of these enterprises were in fact thinly disguised attempts to enforce the interests of the papacy.

TERRITORIAL CONFLICTS
In the 12th century the popes established themselves as secular rulers of a strip of territory across the middle of what is now Italy – bound to the north by a collection of independent city-states in Tuscany and Lombardy, and to the south by the Kingdom of Sicily, which at this time included the southern part of the mainland as well as the island of Sicily. As early as the 1120s, crusading indulgences were offered to those fighting the opponents of the papacy, King Roger II of Sicily, for example, who had a crusade declared against him by Pope Honorius II.

▼ *Farinata degli Uberti, a 13th-century Ghibelline leader from Florence, fights the pro-papal Guelphs at the Battle of Serchio.*

In the 12th and 13th centuries, Italy was divided between the Guelphs (those who supported the papacy) and the Ghibellines (who supported the rule in Italy of the Holy Roman Emperors). The conflict between Holy Roman Empire and papacy in Italy went back to the investiture conflict between Holy Roman Emperor Henry IV (r.1084–1106) and Pope Gregory VII (ruled 1073–85) over control of church appointments. The names of the Guelphs and Ghibellines probably derived from rallying cries used at the Battle of Weinsberg (1140) between the house of Hohenstaufen, who called the name of a castle, 'Waiblingen!' (later Ghibelline) and the rival house of Welf, who shouted 'Welf!' (later Guelph), which had the support of the papacy.

MARKWARD OF ANWEILER
At the close of the 12th century Pope Innocent III (ruled 1198–1216) called a crusade against Markward of Anweiler, a former follower of Hohenstaufen emperors Frederick I 'Barbarossa' and Henry VI. Markward was appointed Margrave of

▲ *This coin was issued by the Ghibelline government of Genoa, northern Italy.*

Ancona and Count of Abruzzo by Henry; his service to the emperor in Italy brought him into territorial conflict with the papacy and he was excommunicated by both Celestine III and Innocent III.

Following Henry's death he entered the service of the emperor's brother, Philip of Swabia, by whom he was granted the lordship of Palermo in Sicily. In 1198 Henry VI's widow, Constance of Sicily, died, placing her son, the future Emperor Frederick II (r.1212–50), in the care of Pope Innocent III. Markward challenged the pope, however, and established himself as guardian of the heir and Regent of Sicily.

In 1199 Innocent declared a crusade against Markward, likening him to the greatest of defenders of Islam by calling him 'another Saladin' and claiming that Markward was working in alliance with Muslims resident in Sicily and attempting to undermine preparations for the Fourth Crusade, which had just been proclaimed. Knights who joined up to fight Markward were to receive the same indulgences as those who travelled to the Holy Land on crusade; Innocent declared that because Markward was attempting to hinder the crusade, fighting him was as crucial as actually going to Jerusalem.

▲ *Prominent Ghibelline Ezzelino III da Romano was* podestà *(magistrate and representative of the Holy Roman Emperor) in first Verona, then Vicenza, then Padua.*

When he had earlier excommunicated Markward, Innocent had placed him under anathema, cursed him and damned him to hell. For all that, however, and although he suggested that Markward was in league with Muslims, in calling the crusade Innocent did not accuse Markward of being a heretic, and so the cause of the war remained transparently political rather than religious; many historians identify it as the first purely political crusade. The crusade itself did not really come to anything, although an army under Walter of Palear, Chancellor of Sicily, fought against Markward in 1202 as a result of Innocent's call to arms.

CRUSADE OF CHARLES OF ANJOU

For the next 70-odd years, the papacy preached a series of crusades in Italy, most aimed at countering the power of Emperor Fredrick II and his Hohenstaufen descendants in Sicily. Most notable was the holy war waged in Sicily in 1265 by Charles of Anjou, brother of King Louis IX of France.

Following Frederick II's death in 1250 and the death of his heir Conrad in 1254, Frederick's illegitimate son Manfred

(Conrad's brother) had seized power in Sicily and declared himself regent, then entered an alliance with the Saracens to defeat a papal army at Foggia. Pope Alexander IV (ruled 1254–61) excommunicated Manfred, and his successor, Urban IV (ruled 1261–64), offered the crown of Sicily to Charles of Anjou.

Urban's successor, Clement IV (ruled 1265–68), had Charles declared King of Sicily in Rome in May 1265. Charles led his army on campaign and defeated and killed Manfred at the Battle of Benevento on 26 February 1266 to become King of Sicily in fact as well as in name.

WARS OF THE SICILIAN VESPERS

Charles was driven out of Sicily in 1282 and the people allied themselves with the royal house of Aragon. Almost 20 years of fighting followed, known as the Wars of the Sicilian Vespers (1283–1302), and in this period the papacy called a series of crusades in an attempt to restore the rule of Charles and his Angevin descendants. (Charles's descendants were known as the Second Angevin Dynasty, since the first was that otherwise known as the House of Plantagenet, established in England by King Henry II in 1154.) None of these crusades succeeded and, in 1302, the

Treaty of Caltabellotta divided the old Kingdom of Sicily into a mainland portion, to be ruled by the Angevins (and subsequently known to historians as the Kingdom of Naples), and the island of Sicily itself, to be ruled by Aragon.

CRUSADES OF AN EXILED PAPACY

In 1305, the papacy established itself in France, first at Poitiers and then from 1309 at Avignon. Through the period of the papacy's French exile (until 1378), various popes in exile declared crusades against the Ghibellines in Italy. Crusades were launched against the Ghibelline Visconti lords of Florence, for example, in the 1320s and 1360s. But none of these crusading initiatives succeeded in defeating the Ghibellines.

During the ensuing Great Papal Schism of 1378–1417, when there were rival popes in Rome and Avignon, the two sides used crusades against one another with no success. After this date, the holy war as an instrument of papal policy was little seen, found only occasionally in the 16th century under popes such as Julius II.

▼ *War of the Sicilian Vespers. The people of Sicily rise up against Charles I and his French followers on the island in 1282.*

PART FOUR

THE GLORY OF CHIVALRY

The Christian Church and the brotherhood of knights were the two main institutions of the Middle Ages. Christianity and the code of chivalry together moulded the motives and inspired the actions of the dominant figures of the era. Knights drew inspiration from portrayals of knighthood in the literature of chivalry – in heroic *chansons de geste*, poems of courtly love and prose and verse romances that told of knights' great deeds in war and love. The knights judged themselves and their own behaviour in terms of the ideals portrayed in poems and romances. At the same time, romance leaked into reality – chronicles of the age, biographies of knights and practical handbooks on chivalric behaviour were strongly influenced by fictional portrayals. Together the books of chivalric literature embodied a vision of how knights should and could behave. They amounted to nothing less than a mythology of knighthood.

▲ *The death of Roland, legendary knight of Charlemagne.*

▶ *King Arthur and the Knights of the Round Table, ideals of romantic notions of chivalry, depicted in the 15th-century French manuscript of* Le roman du roi Arthur et les Compagnons de la Table Ronde (Book of King Arthur and the Knights of the Round Table) *by Chrétien de Troyes.*

TIMELINE OF CHIVALRY

938 King Henry I of Germany reputedly holds glamorous tournaments in Magdeburg. However, this is according to a possibly unreliable account in the 16th-century *Book of Tournaments* (c.1530).

c.975 Mock battles fought by Frankish cavalrymen across open countryside in northern France are a forerunner of the chivalric tournament.

1062 Norman knights are said to take part in a tournament fight during a siege in Sicily, according to chronicler Geoffrey of Malaterra.

1066 Another later chronicle claims that Frankish nobleman Geoffrey de Preilly invented the tournament in this year.

1095 According to a 12th-century church history, Count Henry III of Brabant is killed in a tournament between his warriors and those of Tournai in 1095.

1095–99 On the First Crusade, Frankish knights train between battles by 'tilting at the quintain' (riding towards a target with a couched lance).

1095–1291 In the period of the Crusades, the crusading knight embodies the ideal of religious chivalry. He is seen as a warrior in Christ's service.

1114 A law issued by Count Baldwin III of Hainaut contains the first known use of the word 'tournament' to mean martial competition.

c.1125 In early tournaments jousting was less common than the mêlée, a pitched battle fought between two teams of knights in an enclosure.

1127 Jousts are held during a siege of Würzburg in Germany.

1130 In banning tournaments, Pope Innocent III issues a declaration that says 'We firmly prohibit those detestable markets or fairs at which knights … show off their strength and boldness.'

January–February 1141 Knights engage in jousting during the siege of Lincoln Castle by King Stephen's forces.

1167–68 William Marshall and another

▲ *Sir Perceval, one of the legendary knights of King Arthur's round table, came to represent the embodiment of chivalry.*

unnamed knight show that tourneying can be profitable: in a ten-month partnership they capture 103 knights, together with their costly horses and equipment.

1170–91 In his Arthurian romances (entitled *Narratives of the Knights of the Round Table of Legendary British King Arthur*) French poet Chrétien de Troyes promotes holy innocence – as embodied by one of the knights, Sir Perceval – as a key chivalric quality.

1180–1207 In *The Epic Letter* Raimbaut de Vaqueiras, court poet at the court of Montferrat, praises Boniface of Montferrat (leader of the Fourth Crusade in 1202–04) for embodying key chivalric virtues including compassion and generosity as well as military prowess.

1186 Geoffrey Duke of Brittany, King Henry II of England's fourth son, is trampled to death at a tournament near Paris.

1194 King Richard I of England licenses tournaments in England in defiance of Pope Innocent's ban of 1130. Richard sees

tournaments as a training ground for knights, and wants to improve the martial skills of English knights.

1197 During a truce to halt fighting at Tours, the army of King Richard I holds a tournament.

c.1200 Another form of tournament is a pitched battle or contest of horsemanship known as a bohort.

1207 Peter II of Aragon hosts a tournament at Montpellier to honour his mistress. This is the first recorded instance of a tournament in honour of a lady, which later becomes common.

1219 Prior to his death in 1219 and in fulfilment of a vow he made while on crusade in 1183–86, English knight William Marshall – described as 'the greatest knight who ever lived' – is invested in the Knights Templar.

1240 German knight Ulrich von Lichtenstein takes part in a tournament at Neustadt: six knights from his Round Table fight against 17 attackers.

1241 Eighty knights die from suffocation fighting in heavy suits of armour at a tournament in very hot and dusty conditions at Neuss, Germany.

c.1250 The Bishop of Acre denounces tournaments, declaring that knights who take part in them commit all seven deadly sins – pride, envy, anger, greed, lust, sloth and avarice.

c.1250–1284 King Alfonso X of Castile and Leon compiles *Cantigas de Santa Maria* ('Songs to the Virgin Mary'), a collection of 427 songs celebrating courtly and sacred love. Alfonso writes many of the songs himself. Other poets include Airas Nunez.

1258 Edward I fights in his first tournament, at Blyth. He wears padded armour.

1285 A lavish tournament at Chauvency, France, is described by the trouvère Jacques Bretel.

September 1293 King Edward I holds a tournament at Bristol to celebrate the wedding of his daughter, Eleanor, to Count Henri III of Bar.

c.1300 Jousting is commonly the main event in tournaments by this period. Some tournaments feature only jousting.

c.1300–c.1500 The knightly class share a more secular conception of chivalry, contrasting with the religious chivalry celebrated in the era of the crusades. Knights fight more in the service of kings and worldly leaders than in the cause of Christ and the Church.

February 1308 King Edward II of England holds a tournament as part of his coronation at Westminster.

1316 One hundred and eighty–six years after it was imposed by Pope Innocent III in 1130, the papal ban on tournaments is raised by Pope John XXII.

1332 The statutes of the Order of the Sash brotherhood of knights, created by King Alfonso XI of Castile and Leon in this year, declare truthfulness and loyalty to be the qualities essential to knightly behaviour.

1334 King Alfonso XI of Castile and Leon fights incognito in a tournament at Valladolid among the knights of his brotherhood of knights, the Order of the Sash, against a team of challengers.

1336 King Edward III of England successfully rescues Katherine, Countess of Atholl, from a besieged Highlands castle during a Scottish campaign; the very stuff of chivalry.

January 1344 King Edward III announces his intention to form the Most Noble Order of the Garter during a tournament and feast at Windsor. The order is established in 1348.

1344 Henry 3rd Earl of Lancaster founds a 'tournament society', whose knights commit to gather for jousting at Lincoln each Whit Monday.

1346 According to chronicler Jean Froissart, Edward III sees his teenage son Edward the Black Prince come under great pressure at the Battle of Crécy, and declares 'let the boy win his spurs'.

1347 Chronicle accounts describe how King Edward III chivalrously spares the lives of six leading citizens of the besieged town of Calais at the request of his lady, Queen Philippa.

1350 French royal official, poet and legal expert Philippe de Beaumanoir affirms a knight's right to use violence in a good cause, saying: 'A knight can wage war in line with tradition.'

c.1350 Under the rule of Holy Roman Emperor Charles IV a knight is entitled to wage war in pursuit of his own ends, provided he gives his enemy three days' notice of attack.

1353 According to chronicle accounts, half the knights of the French Order of the Star are killed in a single battle in Brittany; they had sworn never to retreat in battle.

1357 At Rennes the Breton knight Bertrand Du Guesclin fights a series of jousts against an English opponent during the siege of the town by an English army commanded by Henry of Grosmont, Duke of Lancaster.

1370 English knight Sir John Chandos, a great figure in English chivalry and a

▼ *Edward III established the Order of the Garter in 1344, here he confers the Black Prince at Windsor on 23 April 1349.*

lifelong follower of Edward the 'Black Prince', dies. According to Jean Froissart, Chandos was 'the most courteous and gentle knight alive'. Chandos was celebrated also for his moderation and self-control.

1370 John of Gaunt, duke of Lancaster, jousts against French knight Jean de Villemur in tunnels dug beneath the city walls during the siege of Limoges.

c.1375 Lavish themed tournaments known as *pas d'armes* ('passages of arms') are held in this period by leading royals and nobles.

1390 Scottish knight Sir David Lindsay of Glenesk defeats Lord de Welles, England's ambassador to Scotland, in a trial of strength on London Bridge. He spares his defeated opponent and visits him daily through a long convalescence. Sir David's conduct is praised as exemplary.

1391 Sir William Neville and Sir John Clanvowe, both Knights of the Garter, die and are buried alongside each another in 1391 near Constantinople. They epitomize the 'brotherhood of arms' between a pair of knights.

1398 Seven French knights issue an open 'challenge to arms' to any seven English knights, open for three years, for a fight with lance, sword, axe then dagger.

1421 Two squires in King Henry V's army, Nicolas Molyneux and John Winter, swear to become brothers in arms in the Church of St Martin at Harfleur: each is liable to find the first £1,000 if the other needs to be ransomed.

1430 Duke Philip the Good of Burgundy holds a banquet and six-day tournament in Bruges to mark his marriage to Isabella, daughter of King John I of Portugal.

1466 Sir John Tiptoft's *Ordinances* provides details of rules for scoring at a tournament. The highest score is given for knocking your opponent's horse down with him.

1468 Duke Charles the Bold of Burgundy hosts a lavish 14-day tournament at Bruges to mark his third marriage, to Princess Margaret of York. Its theme is 'Florimont: the Knight of the Golden Tree'.

CHAPTER SIXTEEN

THE GOLDEN AGE OF THE CHIVALRIC KNIGHT

In the 14th century, Jean Froissart wrote in the preamble to his *Chronicles* that he intended to record 'the honourable adventures, noble enterprises and feats of arms' achieved in the long wars of his era between England and France. He wanted to do this, he wrote, in order that the deeds should be 'held in perpetual remembrance' and act as an example and encouragement to fearless men. These wars were hard-fought, often in a quite unchivalric manner, with brutal raiding campaigns that used 'scorched earth' tactics, and frequent incidences of murder, theft and rape during the sacking of towns. Yet Froissart saw 'noble enterprises' because he viewed them through the lens of chivalry.

By the time Froissart was writing, the code of chivalry had been established for 300 years as a guide to the behaviour of knights, inspiring them to exhibit qualities of loyalty, bravery, courtesy, generosity and humility in both war and peace. The code emerged in the late 11th century and endured as a powerful ideal and ethic for many centuries. That this code was often at odds with the way knights behaved does not diminish its importance: it coloured and influenced all aspects of knights' lives, determining their self-image and aspirations, rather as religious faith affects a person's life even if he or she does not always live up to its codes of behaviour.

▲ *The return of King John II of France to London in 1362.*

◀ *Jean Froissart presents a copy of his* Chronicles *to the duchess of Burgundy. He saw noble knights performing acts of chivalry where a viewer with a different perspective might have seen battle-hardened warriors often driven by necessity to act cruelly.*

A KNIGHT LOYAL AND BRAVE

LOYALTY, COURAGE, PROWESS AND HONOUR

On the field of battle, in tournaments and on the quests described in chivalric literature, a knight welcomed the difficulties that he often encountered as opportunities to prove his courage. He knew that he should always act out of loyalty and be true to his lord, his faith and his lady. Bravery and loyalty were key virtues of the chivalric code.

COURAGE AND LOYALTY

In *The Book of the Order of Chivalry* (*c.*1265) Ramon Llull described courage as the knight's primary virtue, and promoted loyalty as one of the ways in which he could prove his bravery. The 13th-century German knight Wolfram von Eschenbach, author of the poem *Parzifal*, a masterpiece among medieval romances, put the main emphasis on loyalty among chivalric virtues. In *Parzifal* Sir Perceval, one of the knights of King Arthur's Round Table, learned through many adventures

and on the quest for the Holy Grail the key importance of loyal faithfulness – in love, to God and Christianity and to his fellow knights. In the vision of *Parzifal*, the essential chivalric virtue of loyalty guided the knight in love, in religion and in the secular world of service as a knight.

The statutes of the Castilian chivalric brotherhood, the Order of the Sash – which was established in 1332 in Vittoria, Castile, by King Alfonso XI of Castile and León (r. 1312–50) – had a similar interpretation of chivalry. The order declared that 'of all in the world the qualities most appertaining to a knight are truthfulness and loyalty'.

PROWESS

A knight needed prowess to exhibit his bravery to its fullest extent: prowess meant skill in arms, and to an extent this depended upon natural ability of the kind possessed in abundance by great knights

such as William Marshal, Jacques de Lalaing or the Black Prince. To a lesser extent, however, prowess could be developed through practice, and knights were expected to work at their horsemanship and weapon-handling.

THE EXPRESSION OF CHIVALRY

In the medieval period, there were three principal arenas in which knights could exhibit the qualities of this ideal. In the different arenas the knight might express key chivalric qualities in different ways.

The first was the knight's life as a feudal warrior – his loyalty was to his lord, and he would exhibit courage in his lord's service in battle. The second arena was the knight's life as a religious warrior – his

▼ *It was natural that kings such as King Alfonso XI of Castile and León (1311–50), founder of the Order of the Sash, should emphasize loyalty among chivalric virtues.*

loyalty was to Christ, and he would be expected to show bravery in fighting against Saracens and other infidels, and in protecting the Church, pilgrims, women and children. The third arena was the knight's life as a noble lover, within the context of the conventions of courtly love – his loyalty was to his lady, and he would demonstrate his bravery in showing obedience to her and striving to win her favour on quests and in tournaments.

THE MEANINGS OF CHIVALRY
The word chivalry appeared in a wide variety of documents from the 11th to the 15th centuries, with various meanings. At times the word was used as a collective noun to refer to a group of medieval knights armed for battle, and as an alternative term for 'knighthood' – a label for the position of being a knight. In a romance, or chanson, chivalry might mean knightly action performed in battle. Beginning in the late 11th century, the idea of a code of chivalry developed as a guide to knightly behaviour. Chivalry began occasionally to be used to refer to the actions and life of an ideal knight. Finally, it came to have its modern meaning, as an aspect of this type of behaviour – a kind of gallantry and honourable conduct.

▼ *One of the knights most revered as the epitome of chivalric virtues was Sir Galahad of King Arthur's court.*

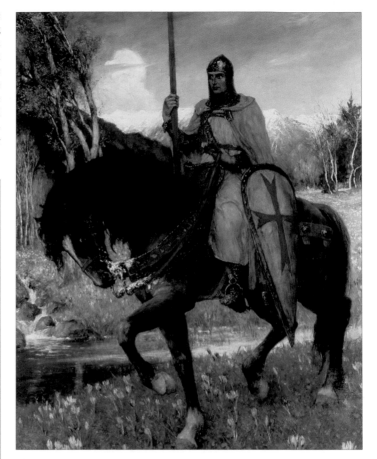

There were distinct periods within the history of chivalry. The ideal of religious chivalry was at its height from the late 11th to the 13th century – the period of the Crusades. The crusader was in theory the perfect incarnation of chivalry, who used his weapons not in political struggles between princes or barons, nor in search of glory at tournaments, but in the service of Christ and his Church. This period of religious chivalry was followed by one of secular chivalry, the time of the struggles of the Hundred Years War in the 14th and 15th centuries, when the ideal of the crusading knight was in decline and knights fought principally for king and country. Before the end of the first period, courtly love began to rival religious ardour as the

▲ *Before Wolfram von Eschenbach's Parzival, an earlier poem about Sir Perceval (written by Chrétien de Troyes in c.1181–91) emphasized his holy innocence. The story has similarities with a Welsh tale in which an innocent, raised like Perceval in the forest, rides out to learn about chivalry.*

inspiring ideal for many knights. A further development was that of courtly chivalry: secular chivalric brotherhoods such as the Order of the Garter and the Order of the Star were founded in the 14th and 15th centuries, when knights were courtiers who took vows of service not to God or the brotherhood of knights but to their monarch, and distinctions of rank began to appear among them.

CRUSADER KING
KING EDWARD I OF ENGLAND

A great knight from his youth, Edward took part in the Ninth Crusade (1271–72) while still a prince and was hailed by contemporary chroniclers as the new Richard Coeur de Lion. After he became King Edward I of England, he directed his military attentions particularly against his country's neighbours in Wales and Scotland, and following his death in 1307 his marble tomb in Westminster Abbey was marked with the tribute *Edwardus Primus, Scottorum Malleus* ('Edward I, Hammer of the Scots'). This inscription was probably added in the 16th century, by which time the king's status as a great exemplar of English chivalry was well established – he was the subject of a play *The Famous Chronicle of King Edward the First* by 16th-century dramatist George Peele.

KNIGHTING AND FIRST EXPLOITS
Edward was knighted at the age of 15 by King Alfonso X of Castile, prior to his marriage to Alfonso's 13-year-old daughter Eleanor on 1 November 1254. He first proved himself in battle aged 20 fighting in his father's campaigns against Welsh

▼ *King Edward's crusading partner, King Louis IX of France, died in 1270.*

KING EDWARD I OF ENGLAND
Born: 17 June 1239
Died: 7 July 1307
Knighted: 1254
Famous for: conqueror of Wales and persistent enemy to the Scots
Greatest achievement: the subjugation of Wales

---

prince Llywelyn ap Gruffydd in 1259, and in 1265 exhibited sound strategic sense in isolating the small army of the rebel knight Simon de Montfort in order to defeat him at the Battle of Evesham in Worcestershire.

CRUSADER KNIGHT
In 1268 he travelled with around 130 knights to take part in the Eighth Crusade alongside King Louis IX of France. The crusade was called to relieve the Christian-held port of Acre, the capital of what remained of the Kingdom of Jerusalem, but was diverted to Tunis in Africa; Louis died of disease before Edward even arrived and the crusade came to nothing.

However, Edward pressed on to Acre in a campaign that became known as the Ninth Crusade. He succeeded in lifting the siege of Tripoli and survived an assassination attempt during negotiations for a truce. He was preparing to abandon negotiations and launch an attack on Jerusalem when the news arrived that his father Henry III had died; the treaty was swiftly signed so that he could depart for England to be crowned King Edward I.

WARS IN WALES AND SCOTLAND
Edward proved himself a great general and strategist in wars against the Welsh. In 1276–77 he crushed Welsh resistance raised by Llywelyn ap Gruffydd and again in 1282–83 defeated Llywelyn's brother Dafydd. He raised ten castles to enforce English control of Wales, including those

at Beaumaris, Caernarfon and Harlech. In 1284 Wales became part of England under the Statute of Rhuddlan.

In relations with Scotland he was equally forceful, storming Berwick in 1296 in an attack that killed almost the entire population, and then defeating a Scottish army at Dunbar before taking the Scottish coronation stone, the Stone of Scone, to London. He forced the abdication of King John Balliol, and stripped him of his finery and crown in a humiliating ceremony.

He was determined to conquer Scotland and bring it into England but Scottish resistance could not be broken as the Welsh had been, and Edward had to fight several other campaigns on and beyond his northern borders, including in 1298 when he defeated Scottish freedom fighter Sir William Wallace at the Battle of Falkirk; indeed, when Edward died from the effects of dysentery in 1307 he was near Carlisle on his way north to combat the Scots once more. It would appear that he was sorely troubled by the unfinished business of the conquest of Scotland, for according to the chroniclers, he wanted to have his bones carried on campaign in

▼ *Edward was crowned on 19 August 1274 in Westminster Abbey.*

▲ *Kings of Edward's era were expected to demonstrate piety. Edward complied.*

▲ *Edward was married in a Castilian convent to Eleanor of Castile in 1254.*

Scotland, and was buried in a lead casket, asking to be moved to the gold casket of the kind reserved for kings only when Scotland was finally conquered.

EDWARD AND CHIVALRY

Physically Edward was extremely imposing: he stood 6ft 2in (1.9m) tall, which was a remarkable height in the 13th century, and had thick curly hair, which was blond in youth. He was nicknamed 'Longshanks'. He may have been lacking in some aspects of military chivalry. He was merciless in his treatment of defeated enemies: Simon de Montfort in 1265, Prince Dafydd of Gwynedd in 1283 and Sir William Wallace in 1305 were horribly mutilated in death. But in other ways his life was a model of chivalry.

He was certainly possessed of knightly prowess and was fond of chivalric pastimes, notably hunting and hawking. According to tradition, he had three favourite horses: a war horse named Lyard; a hunting horse named Ferrault; and his favourite, named Bayard after the great horse of Renaud de Montauban.

He was a very keen tourneyer from his teenage years on, and was deeply interested in Arthurian tradition. He was responsible for the reburying of what were believed to be the bodies of Arthur and Guinevere, found at Glastonbury and

reinterred in the abbey there in 1278; he held an Arthurian 'Round Table' at Nefyn in Wales in 1284, to celebrate the conquest of Wales, and resided over several others at Kenilworth in 1279, Warwick in 1281 and Falkirk in 1302.

He also exhibited religious devotion, most notably in founding Vale Royal Abbey in 1277 in Cheshire, allegedly in honour of a vow he made to build an abbey for the Cistercian monks after he was saved from shipwreck during a Channel crossing in 1263–64. He supposedly brought back from the Ninth Crusade a piece of the cross on which Christ was crucified, and gave it to the monks. He was as devoted to his lady as

any knight could be, particularly to his first wife Eleanor of Castile, who travelled with him whenever she could, even on crusade. On her death in 1290 he built a magnificent series of 12 memorial crosses to mark the places at which her funeral cortège stopped on its route from her place of death in Nottinghamshire to her burial place in Westminster Abbey.

▼ *The construction of Beaumaris Castle was begun in 1295. It is the greatest of the castles built by Edward to consolidate his conquest of Wales.*

THE GENTLE QUALITIES OF A KNIGHT
COURTESY, GENEROSITY AND HUMILITY

In addition to courage, loyalty and prowess, other qualities were deemed to be proper in a knight. These included *largesse* or 'generosity', *mesure* or 'moderation', and *franchise* or 'noble bearing'.

There was never a definitive statement of the qualities of behaviour associated with the code of chivalry. Various authorities – some active knights, others religious commentators or philosophers, others, poets whose works praised acts of chivalry – put emphasis on different qualities according to the focus they brought to bear. Philosopher of chivalry Ramon Llull took care in *The Book of the Order of Chivalry* to stress the variety of ways in which a knight could give expression to his bravery. Llull warned against the showiness of display that was often an aspect of knightly behaviour. He wrote that a knight should not devote himself to fine speech, for this could be misleading;

▼ *Sir Lancelot – otherwise the embodiment of perfection in chivalry – stained his name when he embarked upon adulterous relations with Queen Guinevere. In this 15th-century illustration other knights see Lancelot creep out of the queen's bedroom.*

he should not believe that fine armour and splendid horse trappings were necessarily signs of true courage, for they could conceal cowardice. Courage, he wrote, was not guaranteed by fine equipment, but must be genuine and find expression in qualities such as 'faithfulness, hope, charitable love, a commitment to justice, physical strength, moderation and loyalty'.

THE QUALITIES OF LANCELOT

In Sir Thomas Malory's 15th-century masterpiece of chivalric literature, *Le Morte d'Arthur*, Sir Ector gave a moving lament for Sir Lancelot that provides an insight into the range of gentle virtues to which a medieval knight was expected to aspire. Sir Ector called Sir Lancelot the 'head of all Christian knights' and declared that he was 'the most courteous knight who ever carried a shield', 'the truest friend who ever rode a horse', the 'most honest lover that ever honoured a woman', the 'kindest warrior who ever fought with a sword', 'the goodliest person among the whole body of knights', the 'meekest man and the most gentle among knights gathered to dine in the company of ladies'.

▲ *On his adventures Lancelot encountered many hermits and treated them with courtesy. From one he learned that the perfect knight Sir Galahad was his son.*

In addition to all these gentle qualities, Sir Ector said, Sir Lancelot was also fierce in battle – 'the sternest knight who ever took up lance' when faced with his enemy. In Malory, Sir Lancelot was presented as the knight without equal, the epitome of chivalry, despite other parts of Arthurian literature undermining his greatness by his adulterous love for Guinevere.

LARGESSE

It was an important element of the code of chivalry that knights should give freely. Generosity, or *largesse,* was interpreted as demanding lavish, even sometimes reckless spending. This principally took the form of large payments to reward military followers and retainers for loyal service and deeds of arms – as we have seen, the Black Prince rewarded Sir John Chandos and Sir James Audley very generously after the Poitiers campaign of 1356. But a great lord could also demonstrate his nobility of character and social standing by spending extravagantly on hospitality and entertainment. King John's son Richard, 1st Earl of Cornwall, reputedly had 30,000 separate dishes of meat at his wedding ceremony when he married Princess Sanchia, daughter of Ramon Berenguer IV, Count of Provence, in 1240. The great French knight, the Chevalier de Bayard (1473–1524) maintained his generosity, according to his biography, even when he did not have ten crowns himself.

MESURE AND FRANCHISE

The code also emphasized the counter-balancing virtue of *mesure* ('moderation'). English knight Sir John Chandos, negotiator of several truces in the Hundred Years War between England and France, was as well known for his diplomacy as he was for his abilities as a war captain. A key aspect of his sense of chivalry was *mesure*: he had the other key chivalric virtues such as bravery, loyalty and courtesy, but, according to Jean Froissart, moderation, self-control and a disciplined spirit were qualities that marked him out from other knights. Froissart noted approvingly that his strong sense of duty prevented him from indulging in 'acts of high romance'.

Knights were also expected to exhibit *franchise*, meaning 'noble bearing'. The word's roots were associated with freedom from servitude but the concept became associated with nobility. It began to be seen as part of the noble character of a knight and one of the reasons why young men had to be descended from chivalric families to be considered fit for the honour of being knighted.

VIRTUES OF A COURTLY KNIGHT

Boniface of Montferrat, leader of the Fourth Crusade and a great chivalric patron, was praised for his embodiment of the courtly virtues of generosity, elegance, honesty and compassion, as well as the martial ones of force, bravery and prowess. The *Epic Letter*, a poem by Boniface's friend and court poet, the Provençal troubadour Rambaut de Vaqueiras (1180–1207), gave a stirring account of the virtues, courtly as well as martial, that were thought to embody the highest expression of chivalry at Montferrat, which was one of the most celebrated knightly courts of the late 12th and early 13th centuries.

The *Epic Letter* praised Boniface's understanding of all aspects of courtly life, the elegance of the clothing, the beauty of the armour, the sophistication of games, the quality of the music and poetry and the richness of the table at the court of Montferrat. It also underlined Boniface's good judgement as a lord: it said that he never listened to slander from a dishonest man's lips, but always knew how to distinguish between good and evil, raising up the deserving and exiling the wicked.

▼ *Troubadours praised deeds of knights in love and war but often knew little of military life. This illustration of poet-singers is from the fine 13th-century Portuguese collection* Songs to the Virgin Mary, *which combines poems of sacred and courtly love.*

THE GENEROSITY OF A PATRON

Of great importance among Boniface's many chivalric virtues, the *Epic Letter* said, was generosity. Rambaut said his lord had always been generous at his table, and beyond that had shown compassion to those who were in need, helping widows and orphans. On a personal level, Boniface had raised the troubadour up from a 'nobody' to a 'highly valued knight, always welcome at court and worthy of the praises of ladies'.

For the poets who played a key part in formulating the code of chivalric conduct, generosity was of course an essential virtue in a patron. At Montferrat both Boniface and his sister Azalais, the Marchioness of Saluzzo, were noted patrons of courtly poetry and literature. In addition to the court poet Rambaut de Vaqueiras, they supported the poets Peire Vidal (a favourite of Raimon V of Toulouse), Gaucelm Faidit (author of a celebrated lament on the death of King Richard I of England), and Arnaut de Mareuil (who was another troubadour particularly associated with the court at Toulouse).

'THE MOST COURTEOUS KNIGHT ALIVE'

SIR JOHN CHANDOS

In the mid-14th century, English knight Sir John Chandos was revered for his sense of chivalry. Jean Froissart reported that at the height of Sir John's fame, in *c*.1350–70, he was the most courteous and gentle knight alive.

NORMAN DESCENT

Like many of his peers among the great knights of medieval Europe, Chandos had a long chivalric heritage: he was descended from the Norman knight Robert de Chandos, one of the close companions of King William I. Born in Derbyshire, John made his name at the very start of the Hundred Years War when he fought in single combat against a French squire at the siege of Cambrai in 1339, and attracted great renown. In the same year he was knighted, and given an annual annuity of 20 marks to support himself 'in the estate of knight'.

JOUSTER AND DIPLOMAT

In the 1340s Sir John established himself as a lively leading chivalric figure at the court of King Edward III. He won a great reputation fighting in the king's tournaments from 1344 onwards, and was a close associate of Edward Prince of Wales (later 'the Black Prince'). He was kept lavishly, receiving royal gifts of horses and jewellery and wearing the prince's livery. In August 1346 he fought alongside the prince in the English vanguard at the

▲ *In the Battle of Poitiers in 1356, Chandos was one of Edward the Black Prince's key advisors and fought alongside the prince.*

Battle of Crécy. In 1350 at the naval battle off Winchelsea he sang a ballad, on the king's orders, before fighting began – and the minstrels played a new German dance that Sir John had introduced at court. In 1348 he was a founder member of the Order of the Garter, although curiously he was one of the 12 companions on King Edward's side rather than the 12 on the Black Prince's side.

In 1356 during the campaign that culminated in English victory at the Battle of Poitiers, he and Sir John Audley had charge of scouting in the Black Prince's army. On this campaign Chandos first demonstrated the great diplomatic skills for which he was later renowned, negotiating a truce before the battle proper during which peace talks took place. He then fought bravely at Poitiers and was richly rewarded by his royal master with the grant of two English manors, together with an annual sum of £40, in addition to a one-off payment of 600 crowns.

Sir John again led negotiations with the French in 1357 and 1359. In 1360 he won the admiration of the great French

knight Bertrand du Guesclin when he negotiated the release of du Guesclin's brother Olivier, who had been captured by the English during a period of truce.

DEFEAT OF DU GUESCLIN

Sir John oversaw the establishment of English rule in the duchy of Aquitaine in 1361–63. In 1364 he supported John de Montfort, Duke of Brittany and a supporter of English rule, in the Breton War of Succession against Charles, Duke of Blois. At the Battle of Auray in September that year, Chandos helped defeat the French and captured Bertrand du Guesclin. The bulk of the very large ransom of 40,000 gold francs set for the French knight came to Sir John, establishing him as a wealthy man once and for all. He served King Edward III as lieutenant in France and constable of Aquitaine, and was made viscount of Saint-Sauveur-le-Vicomte in Normandy.

SIR JOHN CHANDOS

Born: unknown

Died: 1 January 1370

Knighted: 1339

Famous for: his diplomacy and chivalric *mesure* (moderation)

Greatest achievement: capture of French knight Bertrand du Guesclin at the Battle of Auray, 1364

CHANDOS'S HERALD

Sir John Chandos's herald wrote a life of Edward, the Black Prince, which is greatly valued by historians as a source for the events of the period. It describes the Hundred Years War and the civil war in Castile, during which Chandos and the prince helped to reinstate King Pedro. After Sir John's death his herald became king-of-arms in the service of King Richard II.

▶ *King Richard II, seen here with his father, Edward, the Black Prince, both dressed in heraldic robes.*

▲ *John Chandos's career was closely linked with the reign of King Edward III.*

THE PASS OF RONCESVALLES

In 1366 Sir John served alongside the Black Prince in his campaign in Spain to reinstate King Pedro on the throne of Castile, after the king had been driven out by his illegitimate brother Henry of Trastamera. En route Sir John (as constable of the army) followed in the footsteps of Charlemagne in leading the vanguard of the force through the Pass of Roncesvalles in the Pyrenees, the scene of the events so beautifully described in the *Song of Roland*. At the Battle of Najera in April 1367, Chandos and the Black Prince defeated Henry and once again took Bertrand du Guesclin captive. This was the occasion, described in Chapter Four, when the Black Prince allowed du Guesclin to name his own vastly inflated ransom – and received no less than 100,000 francs as a result.

DEATH IN THE WINTER ICE

Back in France, Sir John apparently quarrelled with the Black Prince and retired to his estate at Saint-Sauveur-le-Vicomte. He was fatally injured in a skirmish on New Year's Eve 1369 at Lussac-les-Châteaux near Poitiers. Froissart's account gives colourful details: Sir John gallantly led an attack against the French, but slipped on his surcoat and fell on the frozen ground; before he could recover he was stabbed in the face by a French squire – he could not see the blow coming because he was blind in one eye from an old wound. He died the next day, 1 January 1370.

According to Froissart, French knights mourned Sir John's passing because they believed he might have been capable of establishing peace between France and England; Sir Thomas Walsingham reported that King Charles V of France commented that Chandos's death meant there was 'no knight left capable of bringing peace between France and England'.

▼ *In 1369 Sir John Chandos and Sir Robert Knowles successfully besieged Domme, a bastide (fortified town) founded by King Philip III 'the Bold' of France in the Dordogne in 1283.*

A CHRISTIAN WARRIOR
FAITH, HUMILITY AND HONOUR

True knights were inspired by a strong Christian faith, exhibited through great deeds in fighting for the Church. They were expected also to cultivate Christian virtues such as humility and truthfulness.

FAITH
The ideal knight channelled his martial skills into the service of Christ, and the crusader fighting for the cross was regarded as the embodiment of this ideal. In this context religious faith could be manifested in bloodthirsty violence, if it were directed against the Saracen enemy, as in the case of Charlemagne's knights in the *Song of Roland*, or Richard Coeur de Lion, who was celebrated in the romance of his life for the relish with which he killed Saracens, even eating their flesh as a sign of his enthusiasm.

PURITY AND PRACTICALITY
The chivalric code also celebrated purity of life and mind, most notably in the figures of Sir Perceval and Sir Galahad in the Arthurian tales, who were presented in some versions as sexual innocents and

travellers on a mystical path of self-denial. But these qualities had to be balanced by martial energy and strength in conflict.

The practicalities of life as a knight, even in a religious brotherhood, were emphasized in a sermon by 13th-century French theologian Jacques de Vitry to the Knights Templars. He spoke of a brother knight who paid a great deal of attention to self-denial and private devotions, but whose performance in battle suffered as a result: characterized as 'Lord Bread and Water', this knight was so weak after his self-denial in the refectory that he was defeated by the first blow of the lance he received from his Saracen enemy, and had to be rescued by a fellow Templar; put back in the saddle, he rode back into battle and was knocked down again at

◄ *The cross, once a symbol of Christ's love, became the sign under which Christian wars were waged. 'Taking the cross' came to mean swearing an oath to go on crusade.*

▲ *According to the Arthurian romances, the pure Sir Galahad was the first knight to carry the white shield with a red cross, later used by the Knights Templar.*

the first Saracen blow. The same knight rescued him a second time, and told him to eat more heartily in future, for he was not about to rescue him a third time. The sermon commented: 'You ought not to put God to the test, but do what you are capable of, following behind as Heaven leads the way, and then you can safely go to your death for Christ's sake.'

HONOUR
The ideal quality of honour was central to chivalry as a focus for a knight's actions. Maintaining honour was a knight's main goal: to do so he had to win renown and behave always in line with the rules of good conduct. If a knight swore on his word of honour to do a deed there was no going back – it was his most solemn and

▲ *The Battle of Pavia in 1525 was a crushing defeat for French King Francis I, when his knights were shot down by Spanish gunmen and his 28,000-strong army was annihilated. Yet he felt that because he had not disgraced himself, his honour survived.*

HOW REAL WAS CHIVALRY?

There were so many occasions on which knights did not live up to the code of chivalry that we are justified in asking to what extent they believed in it. Many institutions presented as noble expressions of chivalry had a very mundane side: for example, in one light, the 'brotherhood of arms' was little more than a very practical risk-sharing and profit-sharing arrangement, in which knights agreed to pay one another's ransoms and also to split any money they made. While the chronicles wrote up deeds of high chivalry, knights were indulging in pillage and looting, and often making great fortunes as a result. It could be argued that knights used chivalry as a smokescreen behind which they were happy to fight dirty wars.

Yet knights did often act in accordance with chivalry when dealing with one another – for example they went to great lengths and into personal danger to keep their honour. They saw knighthood as an international elite body, and it appears that they believed in the code of chivalry only as it applied to other members of the elite.

kept his honour safe, all other things could be lost. King Francis I of France famously declared after his humiliating defeat in the Battle of Pavia, northern Italy, in 1525, 'All is lost save honour'.

pressing vow. It depended upon honesty. In theory, honour reigned in both history and literature, as countless deeds were done because a knight had given his word of honour. For example, Sir Walter Manny led a contingent of just 50 knights in a highly dangerous attack on the French in 1339 because he had made a vow to be the first into combat in the war that had recently been declared (which became the epic Hundred Years War).

In reality, many a blind eye must have been turned to knights' actual behaviour. For instance, Sir John Talbot – one of the great English commanders in the Hundred Years War – was mourned at his death in 1453 as one of a dying breed of great knights, exemplars of chivalry, yet in his lifetime he was also known as a disturber of the peace and a ruthless operator.

Honour was all, the supreme concept of the chivalric code. Thus, if a knight

---

AFTER THE FALL

Medieval philosophers traced the origin of warfare and violence to the biblical Fall. According to the account in the Book of Genesis, our first ancestors Adam and Eve were expelled from the paradise of the Garden of Eden after they had defied God's commandment not to eat from the Tree of Knowledge in the garden. The Fall referred to this lapse from the original state of grace, living alongside God in the Garden, to the familiar conditions of life in the world. The medieval writers argued that war was the result of the Fall, and that God oversaw the rise of knights and the development of chivalry in order to regulate violence and defend those who

▶ *Warfare followed the Fall and knights had to keep order and protect virtue.*

were defenceless in the fallen world. Some authorities saw the origin of the knight in the Roman era, when they believed armed forces of 1,000 expert warriors were created.

TALES OF WAR AND LOVE

HOW EPIC CHANSONS, ROMANCES AND COURTLY POEMS SHAPED CHIVALRY

By the *chansons de geste* and prose or poetry romances of chivalric literature, knights were educated in chivalry. As they listened to tales of great deeds, of battles won, tournaments fought, quests pursued or dread marvels encountered and overcome, they participated in the growing development of a vision of knighthood that would have a major influence on their own behaviour as knights.

THE MYTHS SURROUNDING KNIGHTHOOD

This vision embodied how knights should behave and how they should conduct themselves in an ideal world. These ideals often filtered through stories about how knights used to behave in a legendary or quasi-historical golden age of the past. Tales of Charlemagne and his paladins, of King Arthur and his knights, of biblical or classical warriors such as the Jewish freedom fighter Judas Maccabeus or the Macedonian conqueror Alexander the Great, were expositions of knightly virtue.

HEROIC DEEDS FROM A GOLDEN PAST

The first flowering of chivalric literature came in the 12th century, with the appearance of *chansons de geste* ('songs of heroic deeds'). These were epic poems in Old French that celebrated the exploits of Christian knights fighting for Charlemagne and other Frankish kings against warriors of Islam from Spain, usually called 'Saracens' (a word traditionally said to be derived from the Arabic *sharqiyin*, which meant 'easterners').

Some of the great deeds celebrated were based on historical fact – like those recounted in the first and greatest *chanson de geste*: the *Chanson de Roland* (*Song of Roland*) of c.1130–70, which as we have

▲ Minnesänger, *the German musician poets, were counterparts of the Provençal troubadours. Their songs included some written by kings and other leading nobles.*

seen was inspired by an ill-fated expedition to Spain led by Charlemagne in 778. The poems usually looked back to a lost golden age when knights behaved better, and so had an elegiac quality that is a strong part of their appeal.

The chansons were recited and sung by *jongleurs*, or minstrels, who would usually accompany themselves on a *vielle* – the medieval version of the violin. Chansons were probably composed and performed for around 200 years before the mid-12th century, the date of the oldest surviving manuscript. Around 100 chansons survive in manuscripts dating from the 12th to the 15th century.

◄ The warlike feats and noble deeds of Charlemagne, seen here on the right, and his retainers, were the subject of many chansons de geste, *most famously in the* Song of Roland, *illustrated here.*

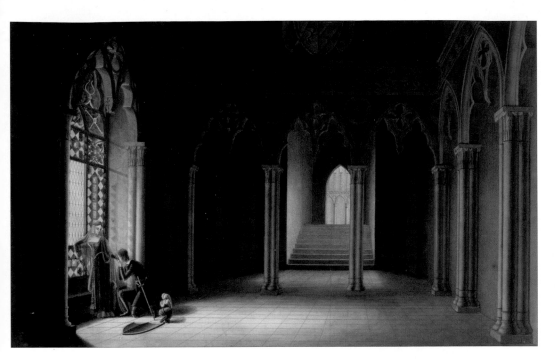

RISE OF ROMANCE

Alongside the *chansons de geste*, and ultimately superseding them, arose chivalric romances – narratives of heroic deeds written in prose or poetry. The romances flourished from the mid-12th century onwards throughout the age of chivalry – right up to the 16th and 17th centuries – but were at their most popular in *c*.1150–1300. According to the 12th-century Old-French poet Jean Bodel, there were three principal subjects for romances: 'the Matter of Rome', narratives about heroes of the classical world such as Julius Caesar; 'the Matter of France', principally stories about Charlemagne, his great knight Roland and other paladins; and 'the Matter of Britain', recounting the doings of King Arthur and the Knights of the Round Table. There was some common ground between chansons and the early romances. Both were written not in Latin, the language then used for scholarly and ecclesiastical writing, but in vernacular languages; the Old French word *romanz* means 'the language of the people'. A great

▲ In the tradition of courtly love, knights were inspired to deeds of chivalry by their burning desire to prove themselves worthy of their lady's love.

literary figure such as Chrétien de Troyes was the author of both romances and chansons, and they could have very similar subject matter. But one key difference was that chansons were performance poems that were sung to an audience by a professional troubadour, while romances were written down in a book and then read aloud.

COURTLY LOVE

In the late 11th century, in what is now southern France, poets developed a new emphasis in songs about knights. Working at the largely peaceful and prosperous courts of princes and dukes in Aquitaine, Burgundy, Champagne and Provence, the poets sang about knights' intense devotion to noble ladies. The knights conceived a fierce love for the ladies at court, who were often already married; the poets said

that the knights were bound to the ladies by the bonds of feudal service, as a knight conventionally was to his feudal lord.

This culture or literary convention has been known as one of 'courtly love' since the Frenchman Gaston Paris first used the term in the 19th century. It referred to the fact that the conventions flourished at royal and noble courts, and also to the supposed 'courts of love' at which, according to some of the poems, ladies sat in judgement on the exploits of their devoted admirers. Modern historians point out that the term 'courtly love' appeared only once in chivalric literature – in the form *cortez amor* in the 12th-century poem written by Pierre d'Alvernhe – and some writers prefer the name *fin'amors* ('fine love'), which was used frequently in poems of the period. It was an elevated form of love, characterized by the knight's feelings of devotion, almost to the point of religious worship, for the lady, and by humility and courtesy; it did have a sexual element, but actual physical consummation was not its principal goal.

NOBLE WARFARE
FIGHTING TO KEEP GOD'S PEACE

Knights believed that armed conflict was a quite proper way to settle disputes. It was honest and noble to confront an enemy in a trial of strength and martial skill. The chivalric attitude was that war is man's natural condition.

The 14th-century Provençal writer on chivalry, Honoré Bonet, declared in his *Arbre des Batailles* ('Tree of Battles') from 1382–87: 'Fighting is not a bad thing, but excellent and full of virtue, for it cannot be denied that war only seeks to put wrongs right, and turn disagreement to concord, in line with the teachings of Scripture'. Bonet's book, which is based on the *Tractatus de Bello* ('Theories of War') by the 14th-century Italian canon lawyer Giovanni da Legnano, argued not that all fighting was good, but that in the right context and for the right purpose, warfare was a noble and just cause. Churchmen and those who wrote on chivalric issues

generally agreed with this position, and argued that knights were ordained by God to keep order and peace while protecting and fighting in the Church's interests.

ATTEMPTS TO CONTROL PRIVATE WAR

There were often incidental victims when knights worked out their disagreements in 'private wars'. Peasants or churchmen might have livestock killed or lands ravaged in the fighting; they were not equipped to defend themselves against a lord and his well-armed warriors. From the 10th century onwards, the Church aimed to control rather than prevent the knights' outbursts of martial energy. Through the 'Peace of God' and the 'Truce of God' movements, churchmen tried to guarantee exemption from violence for certain groups such as peasants and clergy and attempted to outlaw fighting between knights on certain days – initially, Sundays and holy days and later the period of Lent.

Repeatedly kings, too, attempted to end the fighting of private wars, but with very limited success. The waging of private war remained a jealously guarded chivalric right – less in England, where knights did

▲ A French manuscript illumination from c.1310–25 depicts the belief in those times that the crusaders were the knights of Christ in their campaign against Islam.

not fight in this way after the 1200s, than in France and Germany. In France c.1350 the knight's right to wage war was reaffirmed by the French royal official, poet and legal expert Philippe de Beaumanoir, who wrote: 'A knight can wage war in line with tradition.' This entitlement was governed by certain rules: before attacking, a knight had to make a formal complaint against another, giving due cause, and the combatants were not permitted to burn or ravage property. In Germany private war also had a legal basis in the mid-14th century: Holy Roman Emperor Charles IV accepted the knight's entitlement to wage private war provided he gave his enemy three days' notice of attack.

PURSUING A QUARREL

Even when knights did not openly pursue private wars, there were many opportunities for them to settle grievances or seek out old opponents. When knights fought at tournaments, they had a good chance

▼ In his youth Holy Roman Emperor Charles IV was wounded at Crécy; later he was known chiefly for his diplomatic skills and dedication to learning.

▲ Medieval writers generally agreed that knights could justly wage war to keep the peace or protect the Church, but these battles could involve the knights in political maneouvrings – such as the campaigns to promote the interests of the papacy in Italy.

to come up once more against former adversaries. Private war could also be fought under cover of national war – many old quarrels were pursued during the Hundred Years War or the Scottish border raids on northern England.

Knights who fought private wars or who sought out former foes in this way were not merely pursuing a grudge, for often there was a strong chivalric element to the conflict: the knight who tracked down an old foe might not so much be seeking to get even as to pit himself once more against an honoured adversary in a 'joust of war' or a 'feat of arms'.

CHIVALRY IN COMBAT

In one of the most celebrated feats of arms, Scottish knight Sir David Lindsay of Glenesk fought Lord de Welles, England's ambassador to Scotland, on St George's Day 1390 on London Bridge in the presence of a great crowd and of King Richard II of England. Lord de Welles had boasted of English chivalry and so Sir David had challenged him to a test of strength, the rules of which called for a joust.

When the two knights met in the charge their lances both splintered, and onlookers taunted Sir David by calling out that he was tied to the saddle in contravention of the rules of conflict. To prove them wrong, the Scottish knight leapt from his horse then vaulted back into the saddle unaided before riding on.

At the second charge both lances again shattered; at the third joust, Sir David unseated Lord de Welles, who fell heavily but recovered in time to fight on foot, when he was again defeated and this time quite badly injured. The Scots knight had Lord de Welles at his mercy but rather than press home his advantage, he revived his opponent – and after the contest visited him daily for three months during the lord's recuperation.

Sir David was widely praised for his gallantry – and chroniclers noted that he had fought in the true chivalric manner, not from anger but seeking glory. Later Sir David served as Scotland's ambassador to England, and he also commemorated his victory on St George's Day by founding a chantry at Dundee.

Three years afterwards, a second match between the leading lights of Scottish and English chivalry was held at London Bridge. On this occasion the English knights were the victors, in a conflict once again fought in the spirit of chivalry.

▼ How a knight fought was as important as why he did so – he was called upon to conduct himself bravely and to demonstrate that glory was more important to him than mere victory.

A KNIGHT FEARLESS AND BLAMELESS

PIERRE DE TERRAIL, CHEVALIER DE BAYARD

French knight Pierre de Terrail achieved remarkable feats of chivalry while in the service of Kings Charles VIII, Louis XII and Francis I of France in the late 15th and early 16th centuries. In an age when chivalry appeared to be in severe decline, and when many knights were fighting as mercenaries for whoever paid the most, he was revered as a great example of the knightly creed and an unconditionally loyal servant of the French crown.

Pierre de Terrail was hailed as *le chevalier sans peur et sans reproche* ('the fearless and blameless knight'), and was the subject of a romanticizing biography by Jacques de Mailles.

▼ *The Chevalier de Bayard acted with typical gallantry in the siege of Brescia in 1512, when he was wounded, but his fellows in the victorious French army embarked upon a five-day sacking of the city, killing thousands.*

PIERRE DE TERRAIL

Born: 1473

Died: 30 April 1524

Knighted: 1495

Famous for: chivalrous bearing at all times

Greatest achievement: the defence of Mézières with a force of just 1,000 men against an army of 35,000

PAGE, SQUIRE AND KNIGHT

Born at Château Bayard in the Dauphiné, Pierre came from a great chivalric family, and in his youth served as page to Charles the Warrior, Duke of Savoy, before, at the age of 14, becoming a squire in the service of King Charles VIII of France. Even at a young age he was renowned for his handsome looks and his courteous and charming manners, as well as for his bravery and skill at jousting. He was a squire

in Charles's army at the start of the Italian Wars, launched by the French king against the kingdom of Naples, and fought in the Battle of Fornovo in 1495. The French lost the battle against a combined army from Venice, Milan and Mantua, but Terrail won glory when he captured an enemy standard, and afterwards he was knighted on the field of battle for his prowess. Subsequently Terrail was captured when pursuing an enemy, alone, into Milan, but he impressed and charmed his captor Ludovico Sforza, Duke of Milan, so much that the duke released the knight without demanding ransom.

HERO OF THE ITALIAN WARS

Terrail won repeated acclaim for his feats of bravery and chivalric deeds during the Italian Wars, on one occasion being the hero of a contest that took place between 12 French and 12 German knights, on another reputedly holding a bridge over the river Garigliano in central Italy alone against a force of 200 Spanish knights. As in the chronicle accounts of Jean Froissart, the romantic nature of chivalry must have coloured the telling of his life story.

He was praised for his part in the sieges of Genoa in 1508 and of Padua in 1509 and was injured attempting to be the first on to the ramparts at the siege of Brescia in 1512. He was left unable to defend himself, but his soldiers took him to safety in the house of a nobleman; even severely wounded, he managed to do enough to prevent the nobleman's family from being insulted later in the siege. Then, before he was even properly recovered, he rode from Brescia to fight in the Battle of Ravenna under Gaston de Foix, Duke of Nemours.

In addition to bravery in combat, the Chevalier was known for his careful planning and sound knowledge of enemy movements gathered through painstaking reconnaissance and the use of spies.

▼ *A king kneels before a knight at Marignano, in 1515, when the Chevalier de Bayard knights young King Francis I.*

CAPTIVE OF KING HENRY VIII

The following year, in the wake of the French army's heavy defeat by King Henry VIII of England at the Battle of the Spurs, he attempted to rally the French but was isolated on the battlefield and, unwilling to surrender, he rode up to an English captain and demanded that he instead surrender; when the Englishman did so, the Chevalier de Bayard gave himself up. Henry VIII was delighted by the French knight's courtesy and chivalry and once again Terrail was released without ransom. He gave the English king his *parole*, or word of honour, that he would not fight in the war for a period of six weeks.

SAVIOUR OF FRANCE

In 1515 after playing a great part in the French victory in the battle of Marignano against a Swiss army in Italy, Terrail had the honour of knighting his own king, the 21-year-old Francis I. His biographer noted that despite the Chevalier's relative lack of social status, his bravery in battle meant that there was no one knight more worthy to raise the king to knighthood.

The Chevalier de Bayard was appointed Lieutenant-General of the Dauphiné and in 1521 defended the town of Mézières in northern France against the invading army of Holy Roman Emperor Charles V. For six weeks Terrail and his small garrison defied the imperial army, until eventually they lifted the siege. His actions prevented the invasion of central France and won time for Francis I to collect the army that would go on to defeat the imperial forces in 1521. He was hailed as France's saviour and made a knight of the Order of St Michael. He was given his own command of a unit of 100 mounted cavalry – an honour only previously given to scions of the royal family.

A CHIVALRIC DEATH IN ITALY

In Italy once more, in 1524, he took command of the French army after Admiral Guillaume de Bonnivet was wounded at Robecco. Terrail was himself fatally injured on 30 April when he was hit by a ball fired

▲ *Perhaps the Chevalier's finest achievement was inspiring a garrison of just 1,000 men to hold Mézières for six weeks against a 35,000-strong army of the Holy Roman Empire in 1521.*

from an arquebus (an early gun) during a skirmish at the crossing of the River Sesia. Like the English knight Sir John Talbot, he was killed by a gun, a fact that only reinforced the sense that here was one of the last of a dying breed of chivalric knights, representatives of an old and increasingly outmoded way of fighting. In Terrail's case, another important part of his appeal for contemporaries was that in addition to great prowess and spotless honour, he also showed kindness and had a light, carefree and charming manner. His second nickname was *le bon chevalier* ('the good knight').

The Chevalier died in the middle of battle, amidst his enemies, and attended by his old comrade in arms, Charles, Duke of Bourbon. Tradition has it that his dying words were as purely chivalric as his life: 'Do not pity me, for I died an honourable death while doing my duty. Pity rather those who fight against their king, their country or the sworn oath.'

BROTHERHOOD OF ARMS

A PARTNERSHIP BETWEEN KNIGHTS

The chivalric virtue of faithfulness was given powerful expression in the custom of the brotherhood of arms. Two knights pledged loyalty to one another, even to death.

BLOOD BROTHERS

Knights who swore to be brothers in arms took an oath to support one another in war and in peace: they would fight together, in some cases sharing the same coat of arms. Their vows meant that an enemy of one would be an enemy of the other, and likewise they would share friends and allies. The oath was stronger than any other tie that bound them except for the feudal duty to lord or king. It even took precedence over a knight's promises to his lady.

The custom probably had ancient roots that run back to the bonds of blood brotherhood made between Germanic and ancient Greek warriors who mixed their blood and swore to brave injury and death in defending one another. The medieval brotherhood of arms was usually formalized in a written document and to mark this contract the two men would take the Sacrament of Holy Communion as well as mixing their blood. They also exchanged a 'kiss of peace'.

KNIGHTS BOUND IN DEATH

The bond of Sir William Neville and Sir John Clanvowe epitomized the brotherhood of arms – although the written document giving evidence of their union unfortunately did not survive. The two men, both Knights of the Garter, died and were buried alongside one another in 1391 near Constantinople – and their tombstones are now exhibited in Istanbul's archaeological museum.

The stones depict the men's coats of arms combined, so that both bear the same shield showing the Neville and Clanvowe arms side by side – in heraldry

▲ *Chivalric encounters took place in the intervals between bouts of fighting during sieges and on campaign. Remarkably, even the tunnels excavated beneath castle walls to weaken the fortifications were large enough to be used for jousting.*

this is called 'impalement' and was customarily done to the arms of married couples. Sir William and Sir John were prominent knights who were constantly in each other's company from 1378 onwards, and their deaths were recorded in the chronicle of Westminster Abbey; we know from this source that when Sir John died, Sir William pined away – refusing to eat, weakening swiftly and dying himself just two days later. The chronicle refers to Sir William as Sir John's 'companion on the march'.

SHARING THE KISS OF PEACE

Many leading knights and princes were brothers in arms through the age of chivalry. As early as the 10th century, according to the chronicler Henry of Huntingdon, the kiss of peace was shared by Edmund Ironside and King Canute. In the 11th century Godfrey of Bouillon and the Prince of Edessa became brothers in arms. In the 14th century the great French warriors Bertrand du Guesclin and Olivier de Clisson made an agreement of this kind. They swore to guard one another as brothers, and to keep the other apprised of any impending threat. In the 15th century King Louis XI of France became brother in arms to Charles the Bold, Duke of Burgundy.

BROTHERS NO MORE

Although the agreement, like that made by a married couple, was 'till death', there is a notable example of a brotherhood in arms being cancelled. As Earl of Hereford, Henry Bolingbroke swore to be brother in arms with Louis, Duke of Orleans, but when Henry deposed King Richard II of England to become King Henry IV in 1399, Louis cancelled the treaty of brotherhood. The brothers became enemies as Louis challenged King Henry to meet him at any place in France for combat with 100 knights and squires in each company. Although he deposed his king, Henry was a great chivalric figure and was renowned as one of the foremost jousters and fighters at tournaments in his day.

PROFIT-SHARING AGREEMENT

Chivalry cast a glow over the real world. Its ideal forms often had a very practical side. The brotherhood in arms was an expression of faith and martial brotherhood, but among kings, princes and leading nobles it could be a very useful diplomatic tool, used to promote or cement alliances.

The brotherhood sometimes had strong elements of a business arrangement. As part of their brotherhood agreement, described above, the French knights Olivier de Clisson and Bertrand du Guesclin swore to share equally all the lands and ransoms gained in conflict. Similarly, two squires in the army of King Henry V, Nicolas Molyneux and John Winter, agreed detailed financial arrangements when they swore to become brothers in arms in the church of St Martin at Harfleur in 1421: for example, they were each pledged to find the first £1,000 if the other needed to be ransomed, and they agreed that any money they made while on campaigning should be despatched quickly to England to the safety of London banks.

In this context, the brotherhood is comparable to a profit-sharing agreement made by knights in tournaments. As we have seen, William Marshal and Roger de Gaugi, a knight in the household of his royal master Henry the Young King, made a substantial fortune competing in tournaments of 1177–79.

BROTHERS IN THE MINES

During the sieges of castles, when the attackers dug mines in an attempt to undermine the walls, the defenders would excavate countermines, thereby creating tunnels in which fighting took place. The conflict, strangely, usually took the form of formal jousting between knights on the opposing sides – and it was the custom for the knights who fought in this way to afterwards become brothers in arms. At Limoges in 1370 John of Gaunt, Duke of Lancaster, reputedly fought French knight Jean de Villemur in this way, and subsequently it appears that de Villemur was spared when the city was captured.

GODFATHER IN ARMS

The *Siete Partidas* (Seven-Part Code), a law code composed in the reign of King Alfonso X 'the Wise' of Castile (1252–84), described a relationship between knights that was comparable to the brotherhood of arms. The man who ungirded the sword of a new knight would thereafter stand as the knight's 'godfather in arms': the knight was forbidden to fight against his godfather in arms or in any way work to his detriment; he was expected to support his godfather in arms in any conflict unless it were against his feudal lord or one of the members of his own family. As well as formulating statutory codes, the Seven-Part Code also contained writings on philosophy and theology.

▼ *Alfonso, King of Spain – known also as 'the Learned' – set up a school of translators in Toledo, whose work accelerated the transmission of Arabic and ancient Greek learning into Europe.*

KING OF CHIVALRY

KING EDWARD III OF ENGLAND

King Edward III of England was an internationally renowned chivalric figure, celebrated as the foremost Christian warrior of the mid-14th century. He did a great deal to foster chivalry in England. As an inspirational general, he led his army to major military victories in France; he was father to the warrior-prince Edward the Black Prince; he presided over many tournaments and he founded the Order of the Garter, which was openly based upon the Round Table of King Arthur.

PROTECTOR OF THE REALM

In his youth Edward had a solid education in the practical skills of knighthood, and he learned to read and write Latin and to speak French and English. However, as a teenager he became a pawn in the power struggle between his father Edward II and his mother Queen Isabella, supported by

▼ *The surrender of the Burghers at Calais, 1347, to the English army. Six townsmen offered their lives to King Edward III if the besieged populace could be spared.*

> **EDWARD III**
> **Born**: 12 November 1312
> **Died**: 21 June 1377
> **Knighted**: 1 February 1327
> **Famous for**: embodiment of chivalry, a great general, co-founder of the Order of the Garter
> **Greatest achievement**: victory at Crécy (1346)

---

her lover Roger Mortimer. Isabella and Mortimer used him to depose Edward II and he became 'Protector of the Realm' at the age of 14. He was knighted by the Earl of Lancaster prior to his coronation on 1 February 1327.

EARLY HUMILIATION

Edward's first military campaign, against the Scots in 1327, was not a success and almost resulted in his capture by a raiding party led by Sir James Douglas; when the English prepared to retaliate, the Scots fled, reputedly making Edward weep tears

of frustration. England agreed a peace with the Scots that recognized Robert the Bruce as King Robert I, but the humiliation of the campaign and the treaty rankled with Edward for many years.

In 1330 Edward seized power in England, aged 18, when he launched a night raid on Nottingham Castle and surprised his mother and Mortimer in their bedchamber. He sent Mortimer to the Tower of London and exiled his mother at Castle Rising, Norfolk.

TOURNAMENTS

From the start Edward was an enthusiastic tourneyer, and used the tournaments he organized and attended as opportunities to consolidate relations with the leading knights. In 1330 he attended tournaments at Dartford, Stepney and Cheapside.

In 1331 he attended three days of jousts at Stepney: 26 defending knights and 26 challengers, all dressed in costumes bearing a motif of a golden arrow, rode through London to St Paul's and said prayers before jousting in the marketplace. For another three-day joust in the same year, at Cheapside in London, all the defenders were dressed as Tartar knights and were led through the streets by a lady in costume as a 'damsel'. The king's enthusiasm for tournaments and the store he set by them as opportunities to foster unity can be seen in the fact that for both these events, he ordered all able-bodied knights in the country to attend.

IN SCOTLAND

Edward soon built a military reputation for himself. In the war against the Scots in 1333, he won a resounding victory over Sir Archibald Douglas and a Scottish army at the Battle of Halidon Hill by using the new defensive tactics that combined dismounted knights with archers. Edward fought again in Scotland in 1334–35 and 1336, during which he achieved an act of high chivalry by rescuing Katherine, Countess of Atholl, from the besieged castle of Lochindorb in the Highlands, but thereafter his attention was largely taken up with wars against France.

CLAIM TO THE FRENCH THRONE

From the start of his reign Edward had been pressing his claim to the French throne. This followed the death without issue in 1328 of his uncle Charles IV of France. In 1340 Edward declared himself King of France, defeated a French fleet in the naval Battle of Sluys, and invaded France – with little success on land. His first major victory came in 1346 with the campaign in Normandy that saw him win the famous Battle of Crécy, achieved by using the same defensive tactics that he had used at Halidon Hill 13 years earlier.

The triumph of Crécy was followed by the surrender of besieged Calais in 1347, and the defeat of the Scots (in Edward's absence) near Durham, where the Scottish king, David II, was captured. At Calais, according to chroniclers, Edward held six

▲ *Edward laid claim to the French throne prior to the campaign that led to his famous victory in the naval battle of Sluys in 1340.*

▼ *King Edward III released David II (right) from captivity in 1357. The Scots paid a ransom of 100,000 marks for their king.*

leading citizens of Calais as hostages, and was preparing to put the men to death when Queen Philippa begged him to spare them. Ever the chivalrous knight, he acceded to the wishes of the lady and the citizens were spared. (Chroniclers made much of Queen Philippa's involvement, but she was not in fact at Calais.)

CHIVALRIC CELEBRATIONS

These military successes in France and Scotland were celebrated with a great series of chivalric events that were used as an opportunity to parade prisoners of war and to make a statement of the king's international power. In 1348 Edward hosted tournaments in various cities, and it was during a Windsor event that he began the brotherhood of the Order of the Garter. The founding knights were all veterans of Crécy and tourneying companions of the king and the Black Prince, and the two 'sides' of knights (one led by the king and one led by the Black Prince) may have

been based on tournament teams. The year 1356 brought further military triumphs, including victory at Poitiers in which the Black Prince led an 8,000-strong army to victory over 50,000 French, and captured King Jean II. This year may have been the high point of Edward's international standing. He was unable to translate his successes into lasting gains in France: in 1360 Jean was released for a ransom of 3 million gold crowns and Edward renounced the claim to the French throne. Over the next two decades the land in France that Edward held was gradually lost to a resurgent French military.

A CHIVALROUS KING

Edward's standing in Europe was built on his success as a warrior and his status as a chivalric figure. The chronicler Jean le Bel of Liège called him 'noble', and most contemporary accounts stressed his honourable behaviour – especially in his dealings with women. Stories of the Countess of Atholl's rescue and Edward's giving way to Queen Philippa's plea for the lives of the Calais hostages presented him as a model of chivalry.

ORDERS OF CHIVALRY

KNIGHTLY IDEALS AND THE LAY CHIVALRIC BROTHERHOODS

From a distance, the 14th century's lay chivalric brotherhoods, such as the English Order of the Garter and the Castilian Order of the Banda, appear to be a stirring embodiment of knightly romance. However, their creation as national organizations with oaths of loyalty to the king ran counter to the international ideals of religious chivalry that found expression both in the stateless class of knights mobilized to fight the crusades, and in the deeply religious brotherhoods like the Orders of the Templars and the Knights Hospitallers.

▼ *The establishment of the Order of the Garter was a celebration of Edward III's famous victory at the Battle of Crécy, as well as a statement of the power and nobility of English knighthood.*

KNIGHTS OF THE GARTER

The model for the secular brotherhoods was the Round Table of knights described in the romances of King Arthur. King Edward III initially emphasized the romance of his proposed brotherhood. He announced his intention to form it at a feast and tournament held at Windsor Castle in January 1344. He invited knights and their ladies from throughout the realm; and the king, his minstrels and no fewer than 200 squires and knights were decked out in fine tunics for the occasion. After a day of feasting and jousting, on the second morning of the festival Edward and Queen Philippa attended Mass, then the king solemnly swore upon the Bible that he would found a brotherhood of knights of similar type and standing to the one established by King Arthur. He said

▲ *Edward III confers the Order of the Garter on the Black Prince. The order's first meeting was at Windsor on 23 April 1349.*

the brotherhood would have 300 knights, and that they should meet at Whitsun – which was the traditional time for the assembly of knights in the Arthurian romances. He began the building of a hall to be the headquarters of the brotherhood: St George's Hall, Windsor.

However, when the Order of the Garter was finally established in 1348, it was at least as much a ploy in support of Edward's claim to the French throne as it was a tribute to the legendary chivalric feats of King Arthur and the knights of Camelot. The knights were each given a blue and yellow garter – in the colours of France – and their motto *Honi soit qui mal y pense* ('Shame come to him who thinks evil of it') was almost certainly a reference to the king's claim in France, a suggestion that only those who backed Edward in his designs on France could be his brothers in chivalry. The colourful account of the motto being the king's response to an embarrassment for his mistress (see box) was a later embellishment.

The Order had only 26 members instead of the proposed 300. They were King Edward and the Black Prince, with 12 knights each in their company. The knights selected by King Edward and the Black Prince were their brothers in arms, who had fought beside one another at the Battle of Crécy two years earlier and won honour in the lists at the king's many tournaments. The creation of the order was a celebration of the great victory at Crécy and a statement of the power of English knighthood. The statutes of the order established that Edward would call on the Knights of the Garter first when he was planning a war campaign or any other act of chivalry – France should beware.

ENDURING FAME OF THE ORDER OF THE GARTER

Other secular chivalric brotherhoods of the 14th century included, as we have seen in Chapter Five, the Order of St George (created in Hungary in 1325), the Order of the Sash (created in Castile in

▼ French knights of the Order of the Star take their oath before its founder, John II of France, then celebrate at a banquet.

▲ Philip III the Good, Duke of Burgundy, wears the jewel-encrusted collar of his chivalric Order of the Golden Fleece.

1332), the Order of St Catherine (created in the Dauphiné in the 1330s) and the Order of the Star (created in France in 1352). None of these achieved the reputation or enduring glory of the Order of the Garter. The Order of the Star failed principally because it required its knights to swear that they would never retreat in battle, and according to one chronicler half of its member-knights were killed in one battle in Brittany in 1353. Another reason was that its founder, King John II, was very unpopular among the nobility of his country, after clashes with leading nobles earlier in his reign.

CHIVALRY AND DIPLOMACY

The Order of the Golden Fleece, created by Philip the Good, Duke of Burgundy, in 1430, was modelled on the Order of the Garter. Duke Philip's brotherhood initially had 24 members plus the king, but this number was raised to 30 in 1433 and 50 in 1516. Its badge was a piece of sheepskin hanging from a jewel-encrusted collar and its motto was *Pretium laborum non vile*

('The reward of labour is not cheap'). The order's statutes provided that all disputes among members would be settled by the order and that the king was required to take the advice of the knights before embarking on a war.

The original membership of the Order of the Garter included three French knights who had served the English cause in France. It became common practice for other secular brotherhoods, especially the Order of the Golden Fleece, to use offers of membership as a tool in diplomatic negotiations.

THE BLACK PRINCE

EDWARD OF WOODSTOCK, PRINCE OF WALES

Edward the Black Prince was a central figure of English knighthood in the mid-14th century. Eldest son of King Edward III of England, he was famed for his martial prowess: he 'won his spurs' aged 16 in the great victory at Crécy in 1346, was a founder member of the Order of the Garter and was celebrated as a conquering hero for his part in the Battle of Poitiers ten years later, when he captured the French king Jean II.

THE YOUNG KNIGHT

Son of a great devotee of chivalry, Edward was truly born to knighthood. He had his own suit of armour by the age of seven, and was already a friend of knights by the age of ten, in 1340, when he lost money at gambling to Sir John Chandos. At the age of 13 he went with his father on military campaigns abroad, and in 1346 he fought at Crécy, where he acquitted himself superbly in the vanguard of the army and became a hero of the English while little more than a boy.

At one point in the battle, he was knocked to his knees and was captured by the count of Hainault, but almost at once was freed by English knight Sir Richard Fitzsimon. One report suggests that King Edward, seeing his son under pressure, sent knights to his aid, but that when they arrived at the spot they found the prince and his companions leaning nonchalantly on their swords. (The account of the battle

▲ *The Black Prince is celebrated for his crushing victories over the French at Crécy and Poitiers. The French lost more nobles in these two battles than to the Black Death.*

in Froissart's *Chronicles*, which suggests that King Edward watched while the prince's section of the army came under powerful attack and refused to send help with the words 'Let the boy win his spurs', is believed to be a legend.)

After the battle, Edward paid a tribute to King John of Bohemia, a great chivalric figure who had been killed fighting on the French side. Prince Edward adopted King John's emblem, an ostrich feather, and motto *Ich Dien* ('I serve') as his own; at first the prince's badge showed a single feather but later versions had three feathers, and this has remained the emblem of the Prince of Wales to this day.

RETURN FROM POITIERS

At the Battle of Poitiers in 1356, Prince Edward captured the French king Jean II and afterwards, according to the account by Jean Froissart, behaved with great

chivalry – serving the king at table, and praising the sovereign's performance in battle, as having outdone that of all the great French knights. Afterwards Edward took Jean to Bordeaux, where they were delayed by three months of peace negotiations, and then by sea to Plymouth, where the party arrived in May 1357.

▼ *Victory at Poitiers was helped by great leadership from Edward and superb discipline among his troops.*

THE BLACK PRINCE

Born: 15 June 1330

Died: 8 June 1376

Knighted: 12 July 1346

Famous for: bravery in battle, co-founder of the Order of the Garter

Greatest achievement: victory at the Battle of Poitiers, 1356, and capture of the French king, Jean II

Edward made a magnificent triumphal entry into London later that month amid great pageantry: on the road, he was 'attacked' by 500 knights disguised as bandits in a mock ambush, and in London he was welcomed by the city guilds in streets decorated with armour and beside fountains running with wine. His reputation and chivalric prestige could get no higher.

PRINCE EDWARD AND CHIVALRY

In many ways, Edward was an exemplar of chivalry. In addition to his treatment of Jean II, he was a great jouster and was noted for his generosity, his willingness to exhibit the knightly virtue of *largesse*. After Poitiers he rewarded his leading knights Sir James Audley and Sir John Chandos with gifts of 600 crowns, in addition to large annuities. He was also known for his piety – he made pilgrimages before campaigns (to Walsingham and Canterbury in 1345 and again to Walsingham in 1354), and made a number of generous donations to Canterbury Cathedral. He is believed to have been devoted to the Holy Trinity and is represented in a lead badge doing religious homage.

Prince Edward was surely destined to be one of England's greatest kings, but the length of his father's 50-year reign (1327–77) and the prince's own death in

▲ After being captured at Poitiers by Prince Edward, John II of France was escorted in style to captivity in England. He was valued at no less than 3 million crowns by his English ransomers.

his mid-40s from dysentery denied him that honour. In his time he was England's most famous knight. His use of some unchivalric methods, such as chevauchée raiding, was common in his time.

NAMED FOR HIS ARMOUR

In his lifetime the prince was called 'Edward of Woodstock' after his place of birth. The name of 'the Black Prince' was first used in an English chronicle that was

published by the Tudor printer Richard Grafton. Modern historians suggest that the name may have been made up by French chroniclers, and referred to his string of victories over the French or the cruelty of the chevauchée raiding he planned. The traditional view, however, is that the name was used because of an ornate black cuirass, or breastplate, given to the young prince by his father at the Battle of Crécy.

▼ A gilt-copper effigy of the Black Prince surmounts the knight's tomb in Canterbury Cathedral. Above the tomb is a panel of the Holy Trinity, to which Edward dedicated his chivalric achievements.

CHAPTER SEVENTEEN

KNIGHT OF THE TOURNEY

In January 1430 Philip the Good, Duke of Burgundy, hosted a magnificent banquet followed by a six-day tournament to celebrate his marriage to Isabella, daughter of King John I of Portugal. To welcome the new duchess to Bruges he hung vermilion cloth in the streets, laid on fountains of wine and built a magnificent temporary banqueting hall containing a gilded tree hung with his heraldic arms. During the tournament two teams of knights jousted in three sets of lists built in the city's marketplace. Each day a golden chain or sparkling jewel was presented to the best knight and squire of each team. At the end of the tournament Philip announced the creation of a new chivalric order, the Order of the Golden Fleece. The duke's tournament was one of the most lavish of the entire Middle Ages, and the culmination of a long tradition of chivalric competitions. Tournaments were absolutely central to the world of medieval knights. They developed from martial manoeuvres, and throughout their history were always valued by knights as a form of military training. Crucially, also, they provided a setting for knights to display their chivalric virtues such as bravery, courtesy, humility and generosity. They were inspired by, and themselves inspired, the developing culture of chivalry and courtly love, an arena where knights competed for the approval of watching ladies. The tournament was also a place of opportunity, for knights could grow rich on the winnings.

▲ *Medieval jousts were the extravagant entertainment spectacles of the day.*

◀ *Sir Tristan and Sir Palomides fight in the lists as other knights of the Round Table look on. According to Arthurian legend, Palomides was inspired by a glimpse of the lady he adored, Iseult, to become unbeatable in the tournament – despite the fact that she loved Tristan.*

MARTIAL GAMES
THE ORIGIN OF TOURNAMENTS

A spectacle incorporating military training, tournaments have precursors going back to the classical world. In the medieval era the lavish and formal courtly entertainments of the kind held by Philip the Good developed from the rough and tumble of cross-country cavalry manoeuvres.

THE EXAMPLE OF ROME
From the time of ancient Greece and Rome, if not earlier, soldiers and their generals understood the need for martial games and manoeuvres as part of military training. The young men of Sparta and of Rome developed their strength and their soldierly prowess in mock combats. In the medieval period, knights and writers on chivalry saw tournaments as emulating the fighting contests of the classical world. Tournaments, particularly when they took the form of a pair of knights jousting in the lists, also had forerunners in classical and pre-medieval combats, such as the gladiatorial contests so popular in ancient Rome and in the trials by combat used by Germanic tribes to resolve their disputes.

▼ *Most gladiators in ancient Rome were slaves. Like a joust, gladiatorial combat was both a trial of strength and entertainment.*

FRANKISH CAVALRY MANOEUVRES
The Frankish cavalry practised riding at speed, changing direction sharply and controlling a horse among a crowd of many others. One celebrated account of these manoeuvres describes 'war games' held at Strasbourg in 842 to celebrate the alliance of Charlemagne's grandsons, Louis the German and Charles the Bald.

In the games, groups of cavalry rode fast towards each other, then one group wheeled away, protecting themselves with shields, and pretending to flee, drawing their opponents into a charge before suddenly turning and driving back the charge. Finally the kings, Louis and Charles, rode into the battle with their lances aloft, urging on the two sides. Frankish historian Nithard described the event, noting that the encounter was a great sight, partly due to the many nobles taking part and also because they were so well ordered. Some modern historians have claimed this was the first medieval tournament, although it was not a true tourney because it was not a combat – the two sides charged and fled but did not fight.

▲ *The city-state of Sparta rose to power in the 8th–5th centuries BC with an army of super-fit soldiers who fought mock battles to develop their skills – similarly, tournaments honed the prowess a knight needed for war.*

BATTLES IN OPEN COUNTRY
The first proper tournaments were probably mock battles that took place between groups of Frankish cavalry in France in the late 11th century. Two sets of knights, often from different areas, fought across open countryside. They rode across farmland and forests and took full advantage of the opportunities for ambush provided by buildings and natural features. There were often as many as 200 knights on each side, led by the same lords they followed in war. The purpose of the game was to capture and then ransom as many knights as possible from the other team.

The knights fought with real weapons including lances, bows and arrows – and injuries were common. There were no rules, save that fighting must not be to the death, and that knights could take refuge and rest in fenced-off neutral areas.

▲ *When tournaments were held in the streets, onlookers ran the risk of being hurt by the galloping horses and flailing knights.*

TOURNEYING ON CRUSADE

Formal tournaments developed out of these cross-country battles. The Franks probably carried the sport with them when they went on the First Crusade – the chronicler Robert the Monk noted that when not fighting they practised tilting at the quintain (riding towards a target with a couched lance). Tournaments, indeed, emerged at the time that the Franks or Normans began using the couched lance in battle, a very demanding technique that required a lot of practice – and it may well be that tournaments developed initially out of the need to practise it.

FIRST REFERENCES

The first use of the word 'tournament' is in legislation of 1114, issued by Count Baldwin III of Hainaut, which describes keepers of the peace neglecting their jobs and leaving the town of Valenciennes to partake in 'javelin games, tournaments and similar sports'. Around the same time, in c.1115–20, the Benedictine monk and chronicler Geoffrey of Malaterra observed that in campaigns in Sicily by his fellow Normans, the young knights tourneyed during the course of a siege in the year 1062 – this indicates that tournaments were being held in c.1120, when he was

writing, even if his account of 1062 is fictitious. Then in the 1140s, a history of the Church of St Martin of Tournai referred to the death of Count Henry III of Brabant in a tournament between his warriors and those of Tournai in 1095.

CREATIVE ACCOUNTS

Caution is advised when reading accounts of early tournaments since in later years a way of proving knightly heritage was to demonstrate that one's ancestors had fought in tournaments for generations; medieval chroniclers often rewrote the

past, inventing great encounters at tournaments to add lustre to the reputation of their lords. The 16th-century herald Georg Ruexner claimed in his *Book of Tournaments* (c.1530) that King Henry I of Germany held glamorous tournaments in 938 in Magdeburg; but certain details in his description cast doubt on his account. The chronicle of St Martin of Tours refers to the supposed origin of tournaments: it says that a nobleman named Geoffrey de Preilly, who it says was ambushed and killed at Angers in 1066, should be remembered as the inventor of the sport.

WHAT WAS A TOURNAMENT?

Strictly speaking a tournament was a mock battle between two sets of knights – the combat also known as a mêlée. The knights fought as units, just as in battle, with the aim of defeating the other side and so winning their opponents' equipment and horses. In France and England this was often also called a *hastilude* ('spear contest'), and it was the principal form of the tournament in England in the 13th century when Sir William Marshal rose to prominence due to his martial skills. It was a distinct

contest from jousting. However, the word 'tournament' began to be used, especially in Germany, for the courtly events that encompassed both mêlées and jousting, and it certainly has the more general meaning in modern usage.

▶ *Two teams of knights from Arthur's Round Table compete as groups in the form of the tournament known as a hastilude.*

PROWESS ON DISPLAY

TYPES OF TOURNAMENT

The 12th-century English chronicler Roger of Hoveden defined tournaments as 'military exercises performed not in a hostile spirit but only to practise and put prowess on display'. Across the centuries of the chivalric period, the tournament took a number of forms – most, in line with Roger's definition, devoted to the sport of mounted contests, but some much closer to actual warfare.

THE MÊLÉE

The earliest formal tournaments seem to have taken the form of mock battles of the kind fought by the Franks in the fields of northern France, but in an enclosed area rather than in open country. In this type

▼ *Knights take an oath before participating in the tournament. The competitors are split into two 'teams' to fight in the mêlée.*

of encounter, called a mêlée, two teams of knights fought with couched lances.

The two groups represented home and away teams – the 'defenders' (those associated with the town or region in which the tournament was being held) and the 'attackers' (visitors from elsewhere). The two sides first paraded into position and called out their cries of war, then rested briefly while in the land between the two sides young knights charged at one another in individual jousts.

At a signal the main charge began: the two groups headed for one another with couched lances, then turned swiftly to fight individually or in small groups. The word 'tournament' is believed to derive from the French *tournement* ('turning'), a reference to the quick reversal of direction. Squires stood by to offer up to three replacement lances to their lords.

From an account in Wolfram von Eschenbach's great 13th-century poem *Parzifal* we learn that a knight in one of these charges aimed for his opponent to the left and carried his couched lance across the neck of his mount, aiming at his rival's shield. After the charge, the mêlée often spread out beyond the original lists into a designated area of countryside or even into the streets of the town as knights carried on the fight, trying to take as many of their opponents captive as possible.

THE JOUST

The mêlée was quite dangerous and often resulted in serious injury or death. Over time it became less common and tournaments primarily featured jousting between two knights. In a joust the knights rode towards one another with couched lance, each aiming to unhorse his opponent.

From about 1400, in an attempt to limit injuries, the knights rode either side of a central barrier called the tilt. Probably developed in Spain or Portugal, the tilt spread throughout Europe during the 15th century; it was already common in France by 1430. At first it seems to have been no more than a cloth hanging from a rope, but quickly this became a stout wooden barrier with padding.

In the 11th–12th centuries individual jousting was often a sideshow to the main event, which was the mêlée. Jousting might take place on the eve of the tournament or on the morning of the contest, prior to the main combat. The 13th and 14th centuries saw jousting becoming more popular, and some tournaments featured only individual combat with lances.

Although the conditions of the mêlée provided better practice for battle than did a joust, knights tended to prefer jousting because their individual prowess was more obvious in individual combat. Jousting certainly had its dangers but it was generally safer than the mêlée, with less danger of the horses trampling unseated riders.

THE BOHORT

Less formal contests between mounted knights continued to be held alongside tournaments. One of these was the *béhouard*, also known as the *buhurt* (in 12th-century German) or, in English, the bohort. This was more sport than conflict, an encounter between knights relying principally on their horsemanship, and using weapons less than in a tournament. For this reason, while the tournament was often condemned by state and Church authorities, the bohort was viewed more kindly. The rules of the Knights Templar stated that brothers must not compete in tournaments but were allowed to take part in bohorts. Sometimes bohorts were enacted by squires rather than knights.

Bohorts were described often in chivalric literature, where they were the natural conclusion to a wedding or knighting ceremony. In Geoffrey of Monmouth's *History of the Kings of Britain*, King Arthur's knights

are described as riding out to hold an impromptu bohort after feasting at one of the king's courts: and while the ladies cheered from the town walls, the knights sported in the meadows, riding and throwing lances and competing with bows and arrows. Geoffrey emphasizes that the competition was only for sport, and never in earnest, and that it did not provoke the smallest display of bad feeling.

PRACTICE MEETINGS

New knights needed practice before they entered the very demanding mêlée arena and the jousting lists. Practice sessions called vespers were often laid on for the inexperienced on the eve of major tournaments, but sometimes entire contests were held specifically to give the young knights practice. In Germany this type of tournament was called the *tirocinium*.

PAS D'ARMES AND CHALLENGES TO ARMS

In the late 14th and 15th centuries very lavish tournaments called *pas d'armes* ('passage of arms') were held. These were so magnificent in conception and presentation that only kings, princes and leading nobles could afford to mount them. Examples include the tournament held by Philip the Good in 1430.

▲ *Jousts were often fought until a specified number of lances had been broken. In this tournament, fought in the reign of King Charles V of France (1338–80), broken lances litter the ground in the lists.*

Poorer knights, who could not afford to organize a *pas d'armes*, arranged their own chivalric contests by issuing 'challenges to arms'. A good example is the open challenge issued by seven knights of France in 1398 to any seven knights from England. The French knights agreed to wear a diamond on their armour for three years and to be ready to fight on challenge by an English knight, with lance, then sword, then axe, then dagger. Should the English knight win, he could keep the diamond, but should he lose he would be required to supply seven golden rods, one for each of the French victors, for them to pass on to their devoted ladies. We have no record of the result of this challenge.

Four French knights travelled to Parliament in London to issue a challenge for jousts at Calais, and the king granted licences to English knights to respond. Another example is the celebrated Joust of St Inglevert in northern France in 1390, when four knights proclaimed that they would occupy the lists for a period of 30 days and fight all comers.

HERALDS AND CHALLENGES
WHEN AND HOW TOURNAMENTS WERE HELD

Tournaments were often held to add pageantry and colour to great royal or noble state occasions. These entertainments needed careful organization.

COURTLY CELEBRATIONS

At royal and noble courts tournaments were associated, first and foremost, with weddings. The chivalric Edward I held a tournament at Bristol in September 1293 to celebrate the wedding of his daughter, Eleanor, to Count Henri III of Bar. Nobles also laid on tournaments to entertain their wedding guests, as we have seen in the example of Duke Philip the Good of Burgundy in 1430.

The tournament was also considered fitting for a royal coronation. King Edward II of England had a tournament at his

▼ *The tournament survived into the 17th century. This one was held in Turin in 1619 to mark the marriage of Victor, Duke of Savoy and Prince of Piedmont, to Christine, third daughter of King Henry IV of France.*

coronation in Westminster in February 1308. Farther afield, at Acre in 1286, the crusaders fought an Arthurian 'Round Table' tournament in honour of the coronation of King Hugh III of Cyprus as King of Jerusalem. Events were also a frequent addition to diplomatic meetings as late as 1520 – King Francis I of France and King Henry VIII of England met with ceremony, feasting and jousting at the Field of the Cloth of Gold near Calais in France.

Tournaments were also associated with festivals of the Church year – particularly at Shrovetide, the celebrations prior to the self-denial of Lent, as well as at Easter and Christmas. Sometimes tournaments were also held in late autumn, prior to the onset of winter, notably on St Martin's Day, 11 November, the festival of the 4th-century churchman Martin of Tours.

Tournaments could last for a week or more, often beginning on Monday or Tuesday. They were not held on Sundays or Fridays, which were kept sacred, or on holy days of the Church calendar.

SEEKING GLORY

Between the 11th and 13th centuries knights would often travel in search of tournaments. Young noblemen and royals such as King Henry II of England's sons Henry the Young King and Geoffrey, Duke of Brittany, kept a permanent group of knights and squires for competing. In the summer of 1260, the 21-year-old Prince Edward (the future Edward I) travelled to France with a company of 80 companions to seek glory by fighting in tournaments – surprisingly, given his later status as a warrior, with little success. At this time it is probable that events were publicized by word of mouth among the participants, who before leaving at the end of a tourney would arrange to meet again in the future at a particular time and place.

More formal arrangements for planning and publicizing the events came into use in the 14th and 15th centuries. King René I of Naples, known as René d'Anjou and an artist and poet as well as a patron, gave details of tournament organization in his book *Le Livre des Tournois* (*The Book of Tournaments*), written in *c.*1450.

ISSUING A CHALLENGE

Often letters were sent out to particular knights to advise them of a coming tournament. Heralds rode out to proclaim the date, place and duration of the tournament; the rules under which it would be fought; the type of arms and armour to be used; and the arrangement of the tournament area – known as the lists. This would be announced at least a fortnight before the tournament was due to start.

Sometimes an invitation to a particular knight was issued by a challenge: the herald would ride to the court of the king, prince or noble knight to be invited, and present to him a blunt sword (the kind used in some tournaments), and taking the sword would signify acceptance of the challenge by the recipient. It was expected

▶ *In the close and highly dangerous combat of the mêlée, brute strength counted for as much as skill. This manuscript depicts a German tournament of the early 1300s.*

that he swear to fight not out of anger or a desire for violence, but in order to please his challengers and the ladies of the tournament court. The recipient then chose four judges of the tournament from a list of eight carried by the herald.

Invitations were often sent far and wide. For King Edward III of England's 1344 tournament at Windsor, the invitation was proclaimed by heralds as far afield as Brabant (in the Netherlands), Burgundy, Flanders, France, Hainault (in the Low Countries) and Scotland. Knights were promised safe conduct to and from the event. For a 1358 tournament, Edward spent £32 on sending heralds to Scotland, Flanders, Brabant, Germany and France.

GATHERING FOR THE EVENT

The knights who wanted to take part in a tournament gathered at least four days before the event was due to start. The

▼ *Knights usually made sure they could be identified in the lists by their coat of arms on shields and horse coverings. Occasionally knights deliberately avoided being identified – and competed as 'an unknown knight'.*

more important would make a formal processional entry into the city or town where the event was taking place. The appointed judges were required to take up residence in a local monastery or other religious establishment. All the knights planning to fight had to display their escutcheon, or shield, bearing their coat of arms, in the window of the inn and in the courtyard of the judges' residence. They also had to display it on the place they were staying, whether that was a room or a tent.

This gave knights or others the chance to make a complaint against particular contestants: a 'blot on the escutcheon' was a stain on a knight's reputation. On the eve of the contest the shields were inspected by the judges and if a complaint were upheld, then the knight in question would be excluded. There were a number of complaints liable to cause exclusion – for example being a proven murderer or a fugitive, having slandered a woman or broken a knight's duty to be honest, or having been excommunicated.

Tournaments also attracted merchants, who would gather in the days before jousting started. These included horse traders, sellers of fine clothes and moneylenders offering knights help in covering a possible ransom. Entertainers such as jugglers and fortune tellers also attended, giving the events the atmosphere of a fair.

THE LISTS

Lists, usually rectangular or oval, were set out within barriers either in a town – perhaps the marketplace – or in open countryside. Stands were set up for noble spectators. A strong wooden barrier was built around the lists to keep the spectators safe. This soon became a double fence, and in the area between the fences the squires stood, ready to rush to the assistance of the knights whom they served. The ground in lists was covered with dung, straw and sometimes sand.

A SEA OF COLOURS

THE PAGEANTRY OF THE TOURNAMENT

Tournaments were a magnificent sight, drenched in gorgeous colours, full of dramatic movement. They also had the extra spice of the passions of courtly love between knight and lady, and the promise of martial combat, even serious violence.

From specially constructed stands or balconies decorated with pennants and tapestries, lavishly dressed ladies and eager courtiers looked down on the knights and the poorer spectators gathered below, sometimes throwing coins into the crowd as an expression of their benevolence. Pavilions, also decked with flags, often lined the edge of the lists – the area laid out for competition. The knights wore elaborate armour sometimes decked only

with the 'tokens' – the scarves, gloves or veils – of the ladies they represented, sometimes partly covered with colourful surcoats bearing the armorial bearings that adorned their shield as well as the horse-cloths and trappings. Heralds, who were familiar with the coats of arms of the contestants, proclaimed the names of knights as they entered the lists. We draw much of our knowledge of tournaments from accounts in chansons and romances, which presented an idealized version of tourneying. In practice, of course, there was great variety in the type of tournaments held, and many must have been far less splendid than the very grand ones glorified in chivalric literature.

FIGHTING IN COSTUME

Display was central to the event. Knights often fought in disguise, dressed as monks, cardinals, ancient Romans and women – but most often as knights from chivalric literature. When assuming a character, knights must have had a 'costume' simple enough to slip over their armour without affecting their ability to fight – perhaps a simple coat bearing a crest or arms, plus a symbol on horsecloths and trappings.

▼ *The colour and excitement of tournaments are evident in this scene from a 14th-century event. A herald (right) is master of ceremonies; in the grandstands, ladies and courtiers debate the outcome.*

Frequently, in the 13th–15th centuries, tournaments were devised as theatrical celebrations of chivalry, and those taking part either represented great knights of history or played out typical scenes from romance literature. In 1468 Charles the Bold, Duke of Burgundy, celebrated his third marriage, to Princess Margaret of York, with a lavish 14-day tournament at Bruges. It was set within a romance narrative, based on the story of Florimont, the Knight of the Golden Tree, whose service was to the Lady of the Secret Isle. A tree was erected in the market place in Bruges and a champion knight defended it against four challengers every day for eight days. The tree was guarded by a dwarf dressed in white and red satin and by a giant; each challenger had to knock four times on a barrier and identify himself to a herald before taking a lance from those proffered. He would then fight in the lists with the Knight of the Golden Tree, for a defined period of 30 minutes: the knight who broke the largest number of lances was to be the winner. The dwarf sounded a horn to begin the 30-minute challenge. After the eight days of jousting the tournament culminated in a mêlée for two competing teams of 25 knights on the final day.

Ladies and courtiers watching the main action of the tournament also dressed in costume and finery. To preside over her wedding jousts Princess Margaret, for instance, wore a glorious golden coronet set with pearls and precious stones and the white roses of York made from enamel – with her initials and those of Duke Charles picked out alongside lovers' knots.

ARTHURIAN 'ROUND TABLES'

There was a whole series of 'Round Table' tournaments in which knights played the parts of Arthur's leading warriors. In 1223 the crusader knight John of Ibelin, Lord of Beirut, held the first, a 'Round Table' in Cyprus to celebrate the knighting of his son. The German Ulrich von Lichtenstein took part in one at Neustadt in 1240, when six knights from his 'Round Table' fought against 17 attackers; it was planned

▲ *In the evenings, after vigorous exercise in the lists, the knights joined their ladies for courtly entertainments, dancing and feasting. The lower part of this fresco of c.1390 depicts this other part of tourneying.*

as jousting, one to one, but was fought rather more loosely, with knights competing two against one, in an event halfway between a joust and a mêlée. The fighting was fierce – Ulrich records that more than 100 spears ended up broken.

King Edward I of England held two 'Round Table' tournaments – once while a prince (in 1254) and once as king (in 1284). Perhaps the most celebrated of all is the one held at Windsor by Edward III of England in 1244, where he announced the formation of a secular chivalric brotherhood. The Most Noble Order of the Garter was formed four years later, in June 1348: it consisted of 26 knights, Edward and his son, the Black Prince, with 12 companions each.

SCENERY, PROPS AND DANCING

These events used props and scenery as well as costumes. It is probable, for instance, that the celebrated 5.5m (18ft)-diameter Round Table at Winchester was made for Edward III to use at one of his Arthurian tournaments; the design on the table, which features the names of Arthur's knights, was painted in the mid-16th century, probably for another royal devotee of chivalry, King Henry VIII. In 1328 Roger Mortimer, Earl of March, erected a castle

made from canvas as scenery for one of the tournaments he arranged to celebrate his engineering of the accession of the teenage Edward III to replace Edward II (the deposed king was later horribly murdered in Berkeley Castle, Gloucestershire). At the tournament held in 1430 by Philip the Good, described in the introduction to this chapter, there were many 'stage props' and large amounts of scenery, including a vast wooden lion and sculptures of a stag and a unicorn that dispensed drinks.

Such tournaments were important social events in the medieval calendar. They were accompanied by feasting and dancing from as early as the 12th century – we know that there was dancing at the tournaments in which William Marshal (1146–1219) competed. It became a tradition for there to be dancing on the night before the tournament began, and at many events – such as during a celebrated tournament held at Chauvency, France, in 1285 – there was dancing every night.

QUEEN OF THE TOURNAMENT
THE IMPORTANCE OF LADIES TO THE EVENT

Ladies played a central role in the tournament. As well as providing an audience, they were often patronesses of tournaments, which were proclaimed as being held in their honour, and served as inspiration for the competing knights. They were also, nominally at least, judges of the jousting and often awarded prizes to the best-performing knights.

A GLAMOROUS AUDIENCE

The first tournaments were more military manoeuvres than courtly entertainments and did not cater for audiences, but ladies were increasingly present as spectators and as patronesses of tournaments from the 13th century. The first record of an event held to honour a lady is from 1207, when Peter II of Aragon hosted a tournament at Montpellier to bring glory to his mistress.

In England the presence of ladies at tournaments was certainly the norm by

▼ The king and queen look on from the royal box as two knights break their lances in combat. Note the sturdy wooden barrier (the 'tilt') built down the centre of the lists.

c.1330. King Edward III's queen, Philippa of Hainault, was a regular attendee at her husband's tournaments after their marriage in 1328 and she probably helped popularize the attendance of noble ladies at the events. Earlier than this, however, English ladies were involved in themed events; for

▲ Within the code of courtly love, a knight was driven to acts of bravery in tournament and in battle by the fact that his passion for his lady was pure and impossible.

example, King Edward I of England's Round Table at Kenilworth Castle in 1279 was for 100 knights and their ladies.

As we have seen, tournaments were very often associated with grand courtly celebrations with dancing and feasting. King Edward III's great tournament at Windsor in 1344 began with a feast in the castle for the queen and her ladies, while the knights ate equally lavishly in specially erected pavilions. After the banquet came an evening of dancing; the jousting took place over the following three days.

ARTHUR'S QUEEN

In the elaborate tournaments planned on Arthurian and other themes, ladies took a part as queen, princess or damsel within the chivalric make-believe. At Le Hem, Picardy, in 1278 a two-day Arthurian tournament was held in honour of a lady portraying Queen Guinevere; it was described in some detail in the poem 'Le Roman du Hem' written by an Anglo-Norman *trouvère* named Sarrasin. All the knights had to bring a lady with them, as a knight-errant in a romance would bring a damsel, and the tournament was opened by Dame Courtoisie ('Lady Courtesy').

The tournament, held by the lords of Bazentin and Longueval, provided a narrative setting for the jousting. At the start, seven knights of Guinevere humbled themselves before their queen, reporting that they had all been bested by a noble warrior named the Knight with the Lion. Immediately, this knight arrived, bringing a number of damsels in Guinevere's service, whom he had saved from a dreadful fate, and also a live lion. He was intended to represent Yvain, and was played by Robert II, Count of Artois, a devoted tourneyer who took part in the event despite having been excommunicated for attending tournaments while they were officially banned. He would later lead the French army to a heavy defeat by the Flemish at the Battle of Courtrai in 1302.

Subsequently, a noble lady claimed that these knights of Guinevere were the best in the world, but her lord angrily challenged her and ordered her to be beaten in public. Guinevere's knights were then able to prove themselves by defeating this lady's champion one at a time. The event was less a performance before an audience than a shared theatrical experience, for all those present were required to act in the pretence that these events were taking place at the court of King Arthur.

THE LADY AS INSPIRATION

As the courtly love tradition developed, knights often fought to honour a lady. The knight would enter the lists wearing a 'favour' – a token such as a scarf that she had given him. The knight's desire to win the lady's favour inspired him to fight more bravely. She became his protector. In Thomas Malory's *Morte d'Arthur*, Sir Palomides – who, like Sir Tristan, loves Iseult – becomes unbeatable in the lists after a glimpse of Iseult laughing in a window overlooking the contest – 'he struck down with his sword or his spear every knight he encountered'. In this case, Palomides is inspired, despite the fact that Iseult's love is for Tristan – the laugh he saw was prompted by the sight of Sir Tristan riding past in his knightly finery.

▲ *A knight pays homage to the lady who is presiding over the tournament. These brief, formal encounters, bound by convention, were the very stuff of chivalric romance.*

PRIZEGIVERS

The lady or ladies presiding over an event were often asked to give prizes for the best performances in the mêlée and the jousts. Some accounts suggest that they chose the winners, but it is more likely that they just presented the prizes to winners who were chosen by heralds and other nominated judges familiar with the complex rules and scoring for a tournament.

▼ *This illustration of a 15th-century Italian tournament depicts the knights competing fiercely in a mêlée.*

WAR AND PEACE

TOURNEYS ON CAMPAIGN AND PEACETIME REGULATION OF EVENTS

Jousts and mêlées were often fought by knights during wartime as a diversion while they were far from their home on a campaign. In peacetime, because of the not infrequent deaths and attendant violence, tournaments provoked opposition from state and Church authorities.

JOUSTS OF WAR

From the very earliest days of tournaments, knights fought mêlées and jousts during military campaigns – particularly at a time of truce or during the longueurs of a siege. We have seen that, according to chronicler Geoffrey of Malaterra, Norman knights fought a tournament during a siege in Sicily as early as 1062; in the 12th century, jousts were held during sieges at Würzburg (Germany) in 1127, and at Lincoln during the siege of the castle by King Stephen's forces in January–February 1141; and in 1197, the army of Richard I held a tournament at Tours during a truce. Other examples include that of the great Breton knight Bertrand du Guesclin, who

▼ *Although the Church disapproved of them, tournaments were often a recruiting ground for holy war, when knights agreed to undertake a crusade to the Holy Land.*

in 1357 at Rennes fought a series of jousts against an English opponent, while he was also masterminding the defence of the town against a besieging English army commanded by Henry of Grosmont, Duke of Lancaster.

In England's 14th-century border conflicts with Scotland there were often prolonged periods of inactivity between engagements because the Scots used guerrilla tactics and could be difficult to engage. Knights from opposite sides arranged to hold jousts of war during these periods, which were neither really truces nor periods of full war. In 1341 at Berwick, jousts between 20 knights on each side left three dead and many injured, but nevertheless were ended with the giving of prizes to the best knights, as if it were a peacetime tournament.

CHIVALRIC ARENA OR DEN OF SINNERS?

For a knight the tournament was the chivalric arena par excellence in peacetime, a place in which he could display the key chivalric virtues of *prouesse* (prowess) and courage in fighting, and *courtoisie* (courtesy) in his dealings with the ladies; he could show *franchise* and *debonnaireté*

▲ *Pope Innocent II, who banned tourneying in 1130, had to use violence in his struggle to win the papacy from rival claimant Anacletus II. Innocent sent German king Lothair II to Italy to fight on his behalf.*

(good breeding and noble manners), and exhibit *largesse* (generosity) in dealing generously with crowds at the tournament.

For the Church, on the other hand, the tournament was a sinful indulgence in violence and pride. In the mid-13th century the bishop of Acre wrote that knights at a tournament committed all of the seven deadly sins, for they felt pride when they were praised, and envy when others were lauded more highly; they allowed themselves to feel and act on anger in the combat of the lists; they were avaricious because they greedily eyed the horses and shining equipment of other knights; they indulged in lust when they set out to please ungodly women by wearing their favours; they were slothful when they were defeated and slunk back to their quarters; and they were gluttonous at the feasting that followed the fighting.

In the light of this sermonizing, it would appear that at a 1362 tournament in Cheapside, London, seven knights meant mischief when they entered the lists in the guise of the seven deadly sins and fought against challengers.

TOURNAMENTS BANNED

Pope Innocent II banned tournaments in 1130. At the Council of Clermont in that year he declared: 'we firmly prohibit those detestable markets or fairs at which knights … show off their strength and boldness,' adding that aside from the real danger of death or serious injury there were many 'dangers to the soul' in attending a tournament. Those who ignored the prohibition risked excommunication. Knights killed at tournaments were denied a church burial.

Kings added their authority to that of the Church in outlawing tourneying. The bans were of variable effectiveness: in England, strong kings such as Henry I and Henry II were able to enforce their will but a weak ruler such as King Stephen could not, and as a result in the reigns of the two Henrys (1100–35 and 1154–89), English knights routinely travelled to France to tourney, while under King Stephen (1135–54), knights took on themselves the right to fight at tournaments and Stephen could do nothing about it.

REGULATION OF TOURNAMENTS

In 1194 King Richard I of England defied the papal ban and introduced a licensing arrangement under which tournaments could be legally held in England. Richard, though a great knight and a devoted chivalric patron, was not himself a keen tourneyer. While in France, before he was king, he devoted his martial energies to fighting wars in the duchy of Aquitaine rather than competing in tournaments. But he reputedly saw the benefit of tournaments as training for knights, and wanted to establish them in England to improve military skills.

Under Richard's scheme there were to be five licensed tournament areas in England: Wiltshire, Warwickshire, Suffolk, Northamptonshire and Nottinghamshire. A knight who wished to hold a tournament in one of these areas had to buy a charter and a personal licence. Knights from outside England were not permitted. Historians note that Richard I was continually short of funds as king, due partly to his expensive crusading campaigns, and no doubt designed the scheme partly because of the income it would generate through licences and charters – and also through the hefty fines imposed on those who ignored the regulations.

▲ *Depictions of dancing (bottom) and feasting (top) join riding out to war and competing in tournaments among the works of the devil in this illustration from an early 14th-century manuscript.*

In France, where the kings had a closer relationship with the papacy, kings continued to ban tourneying – with little effect. The papal ban on the sport stayed in place until it was eventually lifted in 1316 by Pope John XXII, the second pope of the Avignon Papacy (the period in the 14th century when seven successive popes, all French, made their residence at Avignon in France).

DEATH AND DANGER
THE RISK OF DEFEAT IN A TOURNAMENT

Especially in the early years, tournaments were dangerous and knights were sometimes killed in the full-blooded encounters of the mêlée. Even in later, more stylized events, a knight's defeat in a tournament could bring ruin and humiliation, severe injury or occasionally death.

KILLED IN THE LISTS

Several knights died as a result of the conditions in which early tournaments were fought. Some were killed by frightened or stampeding horses – King Henry II of England's fourth son, Geoffrey, Duke of Brittany, was trampled to death in 1186 at a tournament near Paris. Sometimes, in hot and dry conditions, the heat and dust during a tournament could be overpowering – in 1241 at Neuss, in Germany, as many as 80 knights died from suffocation.

Many knights also lost their lives because of the force of the conflict. In 1344 Sir William Montagu, 1st Earl of

▼ The shuddering impact between two knights hurls one to the ground. This graphic woodcut of c.1516 is thought to be by the great German artist Albrecht Dürer.

Salisbury, died from severe bruising he had received after fighting in a tournament at Windsor. The Montagu family suffered badly in this regard – in 1383 Sir William's grandson, another Sir William Montagu, also died from wounds received in a Windsor tournament – the injuries were delivered by his own father Sir William Montagu, the 2nd Earl, a veteran of the Battle of Poitiers and one of the first Knights of the Garter. Earlier, in 1252, Sir Roger of Leybourne killed Sir Arnulf de

▲ The main danger in the lists was being injured in the head by the other knight's lance. Jousters might also be badly hurt if knocked at high speed from the saddle.

Munteny, a knight in King Henry III of England's household, in a tournament at Walden. Sir Roger, seeking revenge for a slight by Sir Arnulf at an earlier tournament, used a sharpened lance, which struck Sir Arnulf under the helmet. Sir Roger recovered from this early disgrace by taking the cross and going on crusade. He succeeded in winning the king's forgiveness, and had a long and chequered chivalric career, fighting both with Simon de Montfort and for the royalist cause in the 1260s.

TRAGIC ACCIDENT

Late in the history of chivalry, King Henry II of France sustained a fatal injury while jousting in July 1559. The tournament, in the Place des Vosges in Paris, was held to celebrate his daughter's marriage to King Philip II of Spain, as well as the Peace Treaty of Cateau-Cambrésis that ended the Italian War of 1551–59. During a joust the lance carried by Henry's opponent, Gabriel, Count of Montgomery, shattered – and a piece of it went through the king's

▲ *With pride, a great deal of status and personal safety at stake, jousts and subsequent sword fights could become very heated. Judges were on hand to intervene if a contest got out of hand.*

visor and through his brain. The king lived for nine days in agony, and although he was able to absolve Gabriel of blame, the royal physicians were unable to save him and he succumbed to the injury.

JOUSTS OF WAR

Several died in the jousts of war that were fought between knights during breaks in military campaigns. In 1341 Scottish knight Sir William Douglas was killed in a joust between four Scottish and four English knights at Roxburgh. In 1351 in the celebrated Combat of the Thirty, two teams of 30 knights competed near Ploërmel, Brittany: a French force of 30 Bretons against an English group of English, Germans and Bretons. (The two groups were garrisons attached to rival lords disputing possession of the duchy of Brittany.) In this event, at least three of the French knights were killed, while no fewer than nine of the English knights died including the English commander, Sir Robert Bramborough.

RUIN IN DEFEAT

When a knight was unhorsed, his opponent had to dismount to continue the fight: the pair abandoned their lances and fought on with maces and swords. They would fight until one was unable to carry on through injury or exhaustion and cried 'quits' to end the contest. A judge or patron(ess) of a fight could also intervene to stop it. A defeated knight was liable to pay a ransom for his freedom and would also be expected to give up his horse, his armour and his weapons. To be released he would have to pledge to raise the ransom fee – he would give his *parole* (word of honour) to do this, and be released 'on parole'.

A knight who was repeatedly defeated would soon build up a sizeable debt in promised ransoms. The 15th-century French nobleman Robert de Baudricourt reported of a relative who often lost at tournaments and was able to survive only because his wife, remaining behind on the family estate, was so careful with the money that she was able to meet these commitments on his behalf. On the other hand, a knight who regularly won could quickly build a fortune – not through the acquisition of prizes, which were small, but through ransoms and seizing his opponent's arms, armour and horses.

JOUSTS *À OUTRANCE*, JOUSTS *À PLAISANCE*

The jousts of war were the most dangerous form of the sport, fought with sharpened weapons, and clearly in some encounters to the death. They were termed jousts *à outrance* ('to the uttermost'). Alongside them in the 14th and 15th centuries courtly tournaments were often fought *à plaisance* ('for the pleasure of the encounter'), with blunted ('rebated') lances, maces and swords.

▼ *At tournaments, even with blunted weapons, deaths were common.*

'THE GREATEST KNIGHT THAT EVER LIVED'

SIR WILLIAM MARSHAL

Sir William Marshal rose from humble origins to become a great knight and statesman, initially establishing his reputation through his astonishing prowess at tournaments. Some claim that in the many tournaments he fought he remained undefeated. Stephen Langton, Archbishop of Canterbury (1207–28), declared him 'the greatest knight that ever lived'.

After Sir William's death in 1219, his son William Marshal II and his squire and executor John d'Earley commissioned a biography of the great man. The result, *L'Histoire du Guillaume le Maréchal*, was a 19,214-line poem, written in rhyming couplets, giving a full account of the exploits of this remarkable figure.

AN EARLY ESCAPE

In 1152, aged just six, William was given up as hostage by his father John Marshal when John's castle at Newbury was besieged by the army of King Stephen. The king lifted the blockade, expecting surrender negotiations to begin, but John – apparently untroubled about the safety of his son – instead used the opportunity to bring provisions into the castle. Stephen

◀ *King Stephen, who threatened to kill the 6-year-old William in order to force the cooperation of his father, John Marshal.*

tried several times to convince John that he would kill young William if he did not co-operate but John reputedly replied: 'I have a hammer and anvil on which I can forge better sons than he!' In the end, Stephen spared William and kept him at court as a royal ward until 1153.

In c.1159–66 William underwent his chivalric education as a squire at the court of William de Tancarville, Chamberlain of Normandy, who was his mother's cousin. In 1166, aged about 20, he was knighted. His first engagement was in war, that same year, when with de Tancarville and as part of the garrison of the castle at Neufchâtel-en-Bray, he fought in a frontier war between King Henry II and the counts of Boulogne, Flanders and Ponthieu. His bravery almost got the better of him – his master called him back at one stage of the conflict and told him not to be a 'hothead', and he lost his horse to an opponent.

HIS FIRST TOURNAMENT

He was at a low ebb. De Tancarville, clearly displeased, refused to supply him with a new horse and he was of such

▲ *William Marshal was largely responsible for raising the first stone fortifications at Pembroke Castle in Wales. He built on the site of a wooden structure erected in 1093.*

limited means himself that he had to sell his clothes to procure one. But shortly afterwards, his life changed when he fought in his first tournament, at Le Mans. He was an immediate success: in the mêlée he captured a number of prisoners including a notable Scottish courtier, and at the end was richer to the tune of four horses, with a half-share in another.

William spent two years, 1167–68, winning repeatedly (and growing rich) on the tournament circuit of France. He went into partnership with another talented knight in the party of King Henry II's second son, Henry the Young King. In ten months, William and his partner captured no fewer than 103 knights along with their horses and equipment.

In 1168 William entered the service of his uncle, Patrick, Earl of Salisbury, and while fighting on his side in Poitou was injured and captured by soldiers serving Guy de Lusignan (the French knight who later became king of Jerusalem). William was imprisoned, but was ransomed by Henry II's queen, Eleanor of Aquitaine.

ROYAL SERVICE AND CRUSADES

In 1170 William was appointed tutor in arms to the 15-year-old Henry the Young King. Over the next decade they fought together often at tournaments and William became rich enough to maintain his own household knights. However, he was banished from the Young King's court in 1182, accused of having become too intimate with the Young King's wife, Margaret. This was probably a false accusation put about by jealous courtiers, but we cannot be sure.

The following year Henry and Marshal were reconciled and Marshal returned but only in time to see the Young King die of dysentery in June 1183. The Young King had taken the cross, and on his deathbed he gave William Marshal his cloak and made him promise to take it to Jerusalem. William thereafter went on crusade, and in the Holy Land made a solemn vow that his burial would be as a Knight Templar.

FIGHTING THE COEUR DE LION

On his return to Europe he served King Henry II from 1186 until the king's death in July 1189. Marshal fought in the king's household guard on campaigns against Philip II of France and Henry's rebellious

▼ *Temple Church, London, where William Marshal was buried in 1219.*

sons. He reputedly had the chance to kill Prince Richard (the future King Richard I of England) when the latter was suddenly isolated – an encounter between perhaps the two most celebrated chivalric men of the 12th century. Richard is said to have begged for his life and Marshal chose to kill the rebel prince's horse instead.

As king, Richard chose to honour Marshal. In 1189 he arranged Marshal's marriage to the 17-year-old Isabel de Clare, heiress to Richard de Clare, 2nd Earl of Pembroke. Marshal, now a great magnate, undertook substantial building at the de Clares' Pembroke and Chepstow castles.

PROMINENT NOBLE

For the rest of his long life, Marshal was one of the leading men in England. He was on the council of regency while King Richard I was away on the Third Crusade (1189–92), then was named Marshal of the Kingdom. After Richard's death he served King John, supported Magna Carta (he was a signatory) and on John's death was named as Protector of the Kingdom during the minority of King Henry III.

He was by now an old man of 70, but still fought with astonishing vigour in Henry's army against the rebel barons at the Battle of Lincoln of 1217. He died in 1219 and, in fulfilment of his vow while he was on crusade, was invested as a Knight Templar on his deathbed. He is buried in the Temple Church in London, where a fine effigy of this great knight lies with those of his sons.

▲ *The signing of Magna Carta by King John in June 1215. Sir William Marshal was also a signatory.*

WILLIAM MARSHAL

Born: c.1146
Died: 14 May 1219
Knighted: 1166
Famous for: sparing Richard Coeur de Lion's life and rising from obscurity to be Marshal of the Kingdom
Greatest achievement: remained undefeated in European tournaments

▼ *The effigy of William Marshal in Temple Church, London.*

RULES OF THE GAME
TOURNAMENT LAWS AND TECHNIQUES

The rules governing the fighting in a tournament were created as the sport developed. If the first tournaments were effectively war without the killing, the more refined events that took place from the mid-15th century onwards were governed by complex rules. These covered how to score points, and detailed the manoeuvres that were illegal and would lead to disqualification.

WAR GAMES

In tournaments of the 12th century, as in the Franks' very first countryside battles of the mid-11th century, knights could use any techniques to unhorse and then defeat an opponent, but should not fight to the death nor deliberately aim even to injure one another. There were fenced-off areas where engagement was suspended and knights could take a rest for their horses or themselves. In these early tournaments ordinary weapons were used – knights could use lances, swords, battle-axes, maces, and bows and arrows.

Some of the techniques and tactics reported seem scarcely chivalrous. For example, the 12th-century noble Philip of Alsace, Count of Flanders, was renowned for refusing to take part in the mêlée until the other knights involved were near to exhaustion – he would then sweep into the lists to attack a group of opponents from the flank and claim a large number of easy ransoms. (Philip later went twice on crusade, once in 1177, and once in 1190 on the Third Crusade, when he died during the Siege of Acre from sickness.)

RULES OF ENGAGEMENT

There exists only limited evidence of the rules of engagement for tournaments in the 13th and 14th centuries. It would seem that there was a developing set of general rules and also that rules were agreed for individual tournaments. At the 'Round Table' events, so popular in the 13th century and afterwards, knights agreed to rules laid down when they entered the tournament.

Typical rules in these 'Round Table' tournaments specified the use of blunted weapons, and said that knights should not have concealed weapons. They also set the limit on the number of squires who were allowed to enter the lists to assist a knight in the tournament, and usually required that the squires and all other supporting retainers must be unarmed. The rules often declared that once a knight had surrendered he could not be attacked further, or launch another attack himself. The early 13th century saw the first use of blunted weapons, which greatly helped in making the combat in tournaments safer, and the rounded coronal head was used on the lance in place of a point from the mid-13th century.

The rules usually also laid down details about the kind of armour worn and the length of the lance. It was the normal practice for knights to use lances supplied by the defending knight to ensure that they were both fighting with identical equipment and challengers could gain no secret advantage by using their own weapon. It is known from the account in the romance of Fulk Fitzwarin (c.1230) that judges were in charge of settling any disputes in the tournament by the early to mid-13th century.

SCORES AND DISQUALIFICATION

Complex scoring rules were in use at some tournaments by the mid-15th century. They are detailed in Sir John Tiptoft's *Ordinances* of 1466. According to this list, the best score was achieved by the knight who knocked his opponent from his horse and brought the horse down with him. The next best point-scoring move was to make two spears break by the collision of their coronals or rounded tips. The third best score was achieved by hitting an opponent's visor three times, and the fourth best score was gained by breaking the largest number of spears.

▼ By the 15th century tournaments were much better regulated, with rules of entry, engagement and scoring.

▲ *Charles the Bold, Duke of Burgundy (1433–77), dressed in the splendid robes of the Order of the Golden Fleece.*

We have seen that in the 1468 tournament in Bruges held by Charles the Bold, Duke of Burgundy, the knights jousted for a set period of 30 minutes, measured on an hourglass, and the winner was the one who broke the most lances. However, this arrangement was unusual, and completely unknown in tournaments before the mid-15th century, when knights generally competed for a set number of jousts, agreed in advance.

Sir John Tiptoft's *Ordinances* also indicated that a knight could be disqualified if he struck a horse, struck an unarmed knight or one who had turned his back, hit the tilt (the central barrier in the competition area) three times, or took off his helmet twice, unless this was caused by trouble with his mount. When fighting in a general mêlée, knights were required to give up their sword for inspection by the judges before entering the fight, and they could be disqualified if they dropped a sword, tied the sword to their hand, hit an opponent beneath the waist with a pike, or rested on the barrier.

TECHNIQUES IN THE LISTS

Duarte, King of Portugal, wrote a manual on jousting and the management of horses, *The Art of Good Horsemanship*, in 1434. The book contains detailed advice on how to hold and support the lance, the best type of equipment to use, the training methods needed for effective jousting and even, perhaps most interestingly, on the mental strength needed to supplement physical bravery if a knight were to succeed in jousting.

Duarte stresses the importance of balancing the lance and, among a number of options for carrying it, suggests that the best way in a tournament is on the leg, supported by a bag placed on the saddle bow or on the leg itself. He adds that a knight should never use a lance that is too heavy for him to handle comfortably. He writes that it is a useful technique to aim slightly below the point of impact – this method enables a knight to see the exact place he intends to strike as clearly as possible, and prevents the frequent error of pulling the lance too far down at the last moment.

In addition, King Duarte stresses that it is important to banish fear and to maintain steadfast commitment in the lists: many jousters fail, he writes, because they look away or close their eyes or pull the lance imperceptibly off target just prior to impact. But it is important, he adds, not to be too tense because this may also cause the jouster to pull the lance off target. A knight should be confident in his abilities and able to ride into the impact with his eyes open and trained right to the last on the place on his opponent he intends to hit. Furthermore, he adds, a knight should never seek unfair advantage – and if he perceives that he is far better equipped than his opponent, he should lower his shield to even things up a little. He writes: 'I believe that you cannot prove yourself a skilled jouster if you are unwilling to take a risk.'

▼ *The squire's role in a tournament was an important one, and tourney rules reflected this by including various regulations on how many squires could attend, and how they should be armed.*

PROTECTION IN THE LISTS
TOURNAMENT ARMOUR AND EQUIPMENT

In the tournaments of the 11th and 12th centuries and for much of the 13th century, knights used the same armour and equipment in tournaments as they did in battle. Conditions of combat in a mêlée were similar to those on a battlefield, so there was no need to develop specialist tournament equipment. But from the late 13th century, the elite armour makers who

▼ *In early tournaments knights wore chain mail, often with a surcoat for identification over the top. The great helm gave better protection but restricted the wearer's view.*

served kings, princes and leading knights began to make specialist armour and other equipment designed for use in jousting.

EARLY ARMOUR
Knights at the first tournaments wore a chain mail hauberk and camail, or mail hood, with a simple conical helmet with nose piece of the kind shown on Norman knights in the Bayeux Tapestry. Gradually they began to use chain mail sleeves that also protected the wrist and hand – although the palms were necessarily left exposed to make it easier to hold and manipulate the lance and other weapons.

A full helmet design was introduced in the late 12th or early 13th century, and is commonly known as the 'great helmet'. These helmets were generally flat-topped and cylindrical in shape and provided much better protection, but had definite drawbacks – it was very hard to see out through the two small eye-slits, and also difficult to breathe through the holes situated near the mouth.

CRESTS AND COATS OF ARMS
When knights began wearing a full helmet, it became impossible to tell them apart. They started to sport armorial bearings to proclaim their identity. It was important to do so because the display of individual *prouesse* (prowess) was a key motive for fighting in the tournament. One of these identifiers was the crest, worn on top of the helmet. This could be a few feathers or else a heraldic beast or symbolic feature, made probably from cloth and wood. Another was the surcoat, a cloth garment worn over the armour and decorated with coats of arms.

LINEN AND LEATHER ARMOUR
A knight or soldier who received a heavy blow when wearing chain mail could be very badly bruised. In the 13th century, knights at tournament began to

▲ *A knight takes leave of his lady. He does not wear a surcoat but has his coat of arms emblazoned on his horsecloth.*

wear padded linen armour instead: as the use of blunted or rebated weapons spread, knights at tournament needed protection not against cutting and penetration, as they did in battle, but against bruising following heavy impact. Bruising was a very serious problem: Sir William Longespee was very badly bruised while jousting in 1256 and reportedly never fully recovered. Prince Edward (the future King Edward I of England) wore padded linen armour in his first tournament, at Blyth in 1258.

In the late 13th century, armour makers experimented with other materials including plates of metal, horn, whalebone and leather. The last of these became a popular choice – the leather was boiled and soaked in hot wax so it was soft enough to be fashioned into pieces that fitted tightly, but it was also sufficiently hard to repel a blow by a lance or sword, and it was light. Armour made from *cuir bouilli* (boiled leather) was popular until the 15th century; King Edward I of England held a bohort tournament at Windsor in 1258 in which participants were only permitted leather armour. A particularly popular piece of leather armour was the cuirass, a moulded piece that protected the chest, stomach and back, and was worn beneath the surcoat.

PLATE ARMOUR

As we have seen in Chapter Four, the first suits of plate armour, which appeared in c.1330, consisted of several plates of tempered steel, either laced in place or sewn on to a coat of leather or cloth and worn

▼ *Tournaments were flamboyant public displays of a knight's wealth, as well as their military prowess and skill, and helmet plumes became an expression of both.*

beneath the surcoat. They also included gauntlets, sabatons or shoes, and pieces to protect the throat and the upper and lower arms. The first solid breastplates were developed very quickly, probably as early as c.1340.

SPECIALIST TOURNAMENT ARMOUR

At around the same time, amid this rapid development of new types of armour, there appeared the first pieces designed for use in tournaments. These included the *maindefer* and *poitrine pur justes* – we do not know for sure what they were, but they were probably a gauntlet made to hold a lance, and a breastplate with a support on which to rest the lance. In the years of the late 14th to

the mid-15th century, knights could wear full suits of jointed plate armour. At this time, the original great helmet was widely replaced by a smaller design called the 'frog-mouthed helmet' (so called because of its profile), with a rounded top and curved front. As pageantry played an increasingly important role in tournaments, knights needed armour not only for protection but also to give them a splendid and glamorous appearance. Heraldic devices were emblazoned on surcoats and horse trappings, and elaborate, attention-seeking plumes adorned helms.

WEAPONS AND SHIELDS

In early mêlées and later jousts of war, knights fought with the ordinary weapons of contemporary warfare: lances, axes, maces and swords. In jousts of peace they used weapons with blunted blades; in par-

ticular, the sharp end of the lance was replaced with a coronal, shaped like a tiny crown with three short protrusions, from the mid-13th century. In battle, knights of this era carried a triangular shield, but in jousts of peace they used the oval ecranché shield, which had a part missing on the right-hand side to allow aiming of the lance. In the 16th and 17th centuries, as tournaments became displays more than contests, knights began to use mechanical devices that produced memorable effects for spectators. Chief among these was the spring-mounted shield that shattered dramatically into pieces when it was struck by the opponent's lance. During this period elite competitors such as King Henry VIII of England and the Holy Roman Emperor Maximilian I wore magnificent, highly ornamented jousting armour, with delicate chasing and fluting. This type of armour is so closely associated with the emperor that it is called 'Maximilian armour'.

▶ *The two most common kinds of horse used for jousting were chargers and destriers. Chargers were medium-weight horses bred and trained for agility and stamina, while destriers were heavy war horses.*

BROTHERS IN ARMS
CHIVALRIC ORDERS AND TOURNAMENTS

Beginning in the mid-14th century, a number of lay chivalric brotherhoods were formed. They were modelled on the religious brotherhoods such as those of the Knights Templar and Knights Hospitallers, which had come into existence in the era of the First Crusade (1196–99). However, these lay orders required members to swear an oath of loyalty to their secular lord and to fight on his behalf in war. Most of these orders were closely connected to tournaments.

▼ *The cult of St George, a soldier in the Roman army who was martyred in AD303, was popularized by knights returning from the First Crusade. The story of George and the dragon was recast within the conventions of medieval chivalry, with the saint riding a white horse and using a lance.*

THE ORDER OF ST GEORGE
The first of these was probably the Order of St George, founded in Hungary by King Charles in 1325. It was a brotherly union of knights who swore to defend the realm and protect the king, and to follow him in 'pastimes and knightly sports' – doubtless a reference to tournaments they contested. Unlike the later orders, described below, the Order of St George did not have the monarch at its head.

THE ORDER OF THE BANDA
In 1332 in Vittoria, Castile, King Alfonso XI of Castile and León (r. 1312–50) established the first lay brotherhood of knights, the Order of the Banda – or Sash. The members wore a white surcoat with a broad vermilion sash running diagonally from the left shoulder down to the waist.

▲ *Knights at a session of the Order of the Golden Fleece, formed in 1430 by Philip the Good, Duke of Burgundy. Philip based the brotherhood on the Order of the Garter.*

They swore an oath of loyalty to the king, and were to be grouped together in an elite unit within the royal army when at war. They also promised to love their fellow knights as brothers, and to avoid conflict among themselves.

The order was specifically linked to fighting in tournaments: it was a duty for each member knight to attend any tournament within a day's ride of where he was if he were summoned by the king. Moreover, it was laid down as an expectation that every meeting of the order would include a tournament. Chronicle reports reveal that Alfonso was a dedicated tourneyer and believed tournaments to be a valuable means of keeping his knights trained up and ready for war. He made new members by giving a surcoat and sash to any knight who performed great deeds in war against his enemies.

At a tournament held in Valladolid at Easter 1334, Alfonso fought incognito among the Banda knights against a team of challengers. Great deeds of chivalry were performed, and the fighting became so heated that the four appointed judges had to break the contest up for fear that the king would be badly hurt – according to the chronicles, he was receiving bruising blows in the midst of the press. The combat then moved to a second location, at a bridge just outside the town, and again the judges had to break the fighting up because it was so fierce.

The knights of the Banda are also reported to have fought at the pilgrim destination of Santiago de Compostela in 1332 and many years later at a Christmas tournament in Seville held by King Henry II of Castile and León (r. 1369–79) in 1375. But the prime of the order lasted no more than 20 years, and after Alfonso's death in 1350 it was in decline although it continued to exist for around 100 years.

THE ORDER OF ST CATHERINE

Formed in the Dauphiné, south-eastern France, in the 1330s, the Order of St Catherine was another lay brotherhood. Its knights swore to serve the lord of the Dauphiné and were committed to help one another and to be ready to lend one another horses and jousting equipment at tournaments. They carried a shield bearing an image of St Catherine, and were required to attend celebrations on her feast day at Côte-St-André each year – only those who were not able-bodied or who were more than three days' journey distant were excused.

THE ORDER OF THE GARTER

The most celebrated of these lay orders is certainly the Most Noble Order of the Garter, established at Windsor Castle on St George's Day, 23 April, 1348 by King Edward III of England. It consisted of 26 knights – Edward and his son, the Black Prince, with 12 companions each.

Four years earlier, during a tournament held at Windsor, Edward had vowed to form an order of Arthurian knights called the Order of the Round Table. Initially, the plan was for 300 knights to be in the

▲ *These illustrations of the badges of King Edward III, Richard II and Henry IV are from Writhe's Garter Book, a late-15th-century heraldic and genealogical volume.*

order, but Edward had scaled down the plans (perhaps influenced by the Order of the Banda) by the time he created the Order of the Garter. The 1348 foundation established a college of 12 canons and an almshouse for impoverished knights at Windsor. The vows of the order required knights never to fight on opposing sides, never to leave England without the king's permission, and not to be seen in public without the insignia of the order – a dark blue garter. Edward inaugurated the order with a feast and tournament at Windsor. The founding knights were regular contestants at Edward's tournaments in this period – and most had fought alongside Edward and the Black Prince at the Battle of Crécy in 1346.

THE ORDER OF THE STAR

This French order was formed in 1352, with 500 knights. It was dedicated to the Virgin Mary, and its motto was *Monstrat regibus astra viam* ('Kings see their way by the stars'). Its stated aims were to promote chivalry and increase honour.

TOURNAMENT SOCIETIES

In Germany in the mid-14th century groups of knights would gather in tournament societies. Tournaments were organized among these groups, with one society issuing a challenge to another. A similar body was formed in England in 1344 by Henry, 3rd Earl of Lancaster. The knights in Henry's society made a commitment to meet for jousting at Lincoln once a year on Whit Monday, and under a royal licence they were permitted to hold tournaments even during times of war or during a general ban.

▼ *Early shields bore very simple designs.*

PART FIVE

LEGENDARY KNIGHTS

In medieval chronicles, chivalric biographies, poems or romances, writers amplified the feats of arms performed by historical figures such as Godfrey of Bouillon, Sir William Marshal or King Richard I of England. Godfrey was an 11th-century French knight, a leader of the First Crusade of 1095–99 and the first 'Defender of the Holy Sepulchre'. William Marshal, 12th–13th-century Englishman, was a peerless fighter at tournaments who was dubbed the 'greatest knight who ever lived'. King Richard, celebrated as we have seen under the name Coeur de Lion for his endeavours on the Third Crusade of 1189–92, was a mighty warrior on the battlefield. Ancient figures from the biblical and classical worlds also featured in the works of these medieval poets, warriors such as the Jewish freedom fighter Judas Maccabeus, Hector of Troy, or Julius Caesar were reimagined as knights of chivalry and so presented as exemplars for medieval warriors. Other more legendary figures such as Roland, the Germanic warrior Siegfried, the British heroes King Arthur or Guy of Warwick were likewise presented as protagonists in affairs of the heart at court, as heroes in tournaments or on the field of battle, even as 'soldiers of Christ' on crusade. Medieval knights listened – and were inspired.

▲ *The legendary figure of Roland, knight of Charlemagne, blew his horn to request aid but help came too late to save him.*

▶ *The fate of a noble knight was often entangled with a beautiful damsel, and there were many tales of unwary and impressionable young knights being lured into fairy kingdoms, robbed of all energy and purpose or used in some wicked scheme against the maiden's enemies.*

TIMELINE OF LEGENDARY KNIGHTS

c.500 A British war leader who achieves a significant victory over the Saxons at 'Mount Badon' may be the historical basis of the legendary King Arthur.

c.550 Arthur is a hero in Welsh works by poets Aneirin and Taliesin.

778 In the Pass of Roncesvalles in the Pyrenees, Basques or Muslims attack the army of Frankish king Charlemagne.

793 William of Gellone (Charlemagne's cousin and Count of Toulouse 790–811) defeats the Muslim 'Saracens' of Spain at Orange in southern France. This is the basis of the 12th-century chanson *La Prise d'Orange* ('The Taking of Orange'). He is known as 'William of Orange'.

c.817–30 The *Vita Karoli Magni*, a biography of Charlemagne by Einhard, identifies 'Hroudland' or 'Roland' as one of those killed in a skirmish at Roncesvalles in 778.

c.830 Welsh monk Nennius mentions Arthur in his *History of the Britons*. He lists 12 battles in which Arthur fought the Saxons, including a famous victory at Mons Badonicus (Mount Badon).

c.950 The anonymous *Annals of Wales* report that Arthur won victory at Mount Badon in 516 and was killed fighting at Mount Camlann in 539.

973 William I, Count of Provence (another model for William of Orange in later chansons), defeats Saracens at the Battle of Tourtour.

c.1050–1130 The *Chanson de Roland* ('Song of Roland') mourns the loss and celebrates the heroism of a knight in the service of Frankish king Charlemagne, and is one of the first of the *chansons de geste* ('songs of heroic deeds').

c.1050–1150 The legend of Arthur develops in Welsh legend *Culhwch and Olwen*, which describes Arthur as foremost among a band of warriors with a court at Kelliwic ('wooded grove') in Cornwall; this may be Callington (near Launceston).

1096–99 The feats of Norman knight Robert Guiscard are celebrated by Norman

▲ *King Arthur, a knightly legend who features repeatedly, and for centuries, throughout historical and literary works.*

chronicler William of Apulia in *The Deeds of Robert Guiscard*.

1099 Spanish knight Don Dodrigo Diaz de Vivar dies in Valencia. His exploits in the service of the Spanish crown and in that of the Moors (Muslim Saracens) are the subject of the 12th-century poem *Song of My Cid*.

1100–50 Alberic of Besançon writes the oldest surviving romance about Alexander the Great. His work is a key source for the *Alexander Romance*, written before 1200 by Norman poet Alexander of Bernay.

1126–71 Henry de Blois, abbot of Glastonbury, orders a search of Glastonbury Tor for King Arthur's remains. A coffin is reputedly found inscribed with the legend 'Here is found the grave of King Arthur, buried in the Isle of Avalon'.

1130–90 French troubadour Bernart de Ventadorn is active.

c.1150–1300 Chivalric romances – accounts of knightly deeds in prose or poetry – are at the height of their popularity. They will remain a notable art form throughout the age of chivalry, right up to the 16th and 17th centuries.

1155 The *Roman de Brut* by Anglo-Norman chronicler Wace of Jersey is a translation of the *History of the Kings of Britain* (c.1135–39) by Geoffrey of Monmouth and transmits Welsh/British traditions about King Arthur to continental Europe.

c.1155–60 *Tristan* by Anglo-Norman poet known as 'Thomas of Britain', and another roughly contemporary poem of the same name by Norman poet Béroul, are the oldest surviving versions of the story of Tristan and Iseult.

c.1160 The Romance of Aeneas, the Romance of Thebes and the Romance of Troy, all attributed to trouvère Benoit de Sainte-Maure, are early examples of the roman d'antiquité, romances about figures from the classical world.

c.1160–1215 Marie de France writes several songs including the *Lay of Lanval*.

1170 *Erec and Enide*, a 7,000-line poem by French poet Chrétien de Troyes, is the first Arthurian romance. Sir Erec is also known as Sir Geraint in other contexts.

1176–81 Chrétien de Troyes's poem *Lancelot, the Knight of the Cart* develops the story of Sir Lancelot and is the first work in the Arthurian tradition to mention Arthur's court at Camelot.

c.1180 In his chanson *Girart de Vienne*, troubadour Bertrand de Bar-sur-Aube identifies three cycles for chansons: the *Geste du roi*, (mainly about Charlemagne), the *Geste de Garin de Monglane* (mainly about William of Orange) and the *Geste de Doon de Mayence* (about rebellions against royal authority).

1180 *The Four Sons of Aymon*, also known

as *Renaud of Montauban*, is one of the most popular *chansons de geste* in the Geste de Doon de Mayence.

c.1180 The Chanson d'Antioche ('Song of Antioch') by trouvère Bertrand de Bar-sur-Aube features Godfrey of Bouillon and other knights of the First Crusade and is based on a poem reputedly written by Richard the Pilgrim during the crusade.

1181–91 Chrétien de Troyes's poem Perceval, the Story of the Grail introduces the story of Sir Perceval and the search for the Holy Grail. It is dedicated to Count Philip of Flanders.

1190 French churchman and courtier Andreas Capellanus ('Andrew the Chaplain') writes *The Art of Courtly Love*.

1191-1202 French poet Robert de Boron's *Joseph of Arimathea* develops the story of the Holy Grail. Around the same time, his *Merlin* is the first Arthurian tale to describe the sword that could be drawn from the stone only by the rightful king.

c.1194 The romance *Lanzelet* by Swiss cleric Ulrich von Zatzikhoven is the first work in the Arthurian tradition to describe Sir Lancelot's upbringing by the Lady of the Lake. His work is based on an Anglo-Norman original.

c.1200–20 In his poem *Parzival* (another version of the story of Arthurian knight Sir Perceval) German poet Wolfram von Eschenbach promotes loyalty as the foremost chivalric virtue.

1210 Old French poet Jean Bodel (1167–1210) identifies three proper subjects for chivalric romances: 'the Matter of Rome' (on heroes of the classical world), 'the Matter of France' (about Charlemagne and his knights) and 'the Matter of Britain' (about King Arthur and his knights).

c.1220 The attitudes and engagements of courtly love are described in French poet Jean Renart's narrative poem *The Lay of the Shadow*.

c.1225 *The Search for the Holy Grail* presents Galahad as the unique perfection of chivalry, who gradually comes to understand the meaning of the Holy Grail.

1225–26 The Anglo-Norman poem *History of William Marshall* describes the

exploits of the man described as 'the greatest knight who ever lived'.

c.1250 In the Welsh collection *Triads of the Island of Britain*, Arthurian knight Sir Kay is celebrated as a great enchanter – able to grow as tall as an oak tree.

1254 The future King Edward I of England, later a great chivalric figure, is knighted at age 15 by King Alfonso X of Castile prior to marrying Princess Eleanor of Castile. He later fights on the Ninth Crusade (1271–72) and takes great interest in the Arthurian tradition. He holds several Arthurian 'Round Tables' (jousting tournaments) in 1279–1302.

1255 Ulrich von Lichtenstein, a noble from the Duchy of Styria (now southern Austria), writes the courtly love poem *In Service of the Lady*.

1278 The supposed remains of King Arthur and Queen Guinevere are reburied in the presence of King Edward I in front of the High Altar in Glastonbury Abbey.

1279 King Edward I holds a 'Round Table' tournament at Kenilworth Castle for 100 knights and their ladies.

1286 Crusaders compete in an Arthurian

'Round Table' tournament in Acre to mark the coronation of King Hugh III of Cyprus as King of Jerusalem.

c.1300 Middle English poem *Sir Orfeo* transports the ancient Greek myth of Orpheus to the medieval world. It is probably based on a now lost Old French Breton lay or song.

c.1310–14 In *The Divine Comedy* the poet Dante Alighieri celebrates Norman knight Robert Guiscard as one of the greatest of all knights.

1312 Jacques de Longuyon, from Lorraine, is the first to list the 'Nine Worthies', figures from the biblical and classical world celebrated as exemplars of chivalry: three biblical figures (Joshua, David and Judas Maccabeus), three classical warriors (Hector of Troy, Alexander the Great and Julius Caesar) and three Christian leaders (King Arthur, Charlemagne and Godfrey of Bouillon, leading knight of the First Crusade).

c.1320 *The Deeds of the Romans*, probably written by monks, features classical figures including Alexander the Great.

1330–44 Roman general Julius Caesar is portrayed as a medieval knight in the courtly love tradition in the 14th-century French romance *Perceforest*.

1348 King Edward III of England makes St George the patron of his knightly brotherhood the Order of the Garter.

c.1375 In the English poem *Sir Gawain and the Green Knight*, Gawain is the first figure to be called 'knight errant'.

1380 *The Chronicle of Bertrand du Guesclin*, a poem by Cuvelier, celebrates the life of the Breton knight.

1485 In Sir Thomas Malory's Arthurian masterpiece *Le Morte d'Arthur*, Sir Lancelot is celebrated as the foremost Christian knight, embodying key chivalric virtues of courtesy, loyalty, honesty, kindness and humility – as well as ferocity in conflict.

1493 Louis de Hédouville hosts an Arthurian *pas d'armes* at Sandricourt set in locations from romance narratives.

◄ *Sir Lancelot became known as the knight who embodies all aspects of chivalry.*

CHAPTER EIGHTEEN

KNIGHTLY HEROES OF THE BIBLICAL AND CLASSICAL WORLDS

In his *Historia Regum Britanniae* (*History of the Kings of Britain*), written in *c*.1135–39, the chronicler Geoffrey of Monmouth claimed that the people of Britain were descended from Brutus, great-grandson of Aeneas of Troy. Geoffrey wrote that Brutus and his fellow Trojan Corineus were the first settlers of the British Isles: Brutus founded the city of Troia Nova ('New Troy'), which became London, while Corineus gave his name to Cornwall. Britain was thereby linked to the heroic past of legend, and perhaps also to the Roman Empire, which according to some was founded by Aeneas.

In the same way the strand of knightly poems and romances centred on classical heroes and biblical warriors added glory to contemporary knights by creating an ancient pedigree. Romance authors described the classical and biblical warriors as if they were medieval knights. Characters in the stories were intended to inspire knights to perform similar acts of chivalry.

For the purposes of this book, great figures such as the Jewish King David or the Greek warrior Achilles are of interest not in their own right as warriors, although their reputation makes them major figures in military history, but because the way they were presented in chivalric literature gives us important insights into how medieval authors and knights understood chivalry and their own world.

▲ *Medieval-style Trojans setting off for battle in a 15th-century manuscript.*

◄ *In the 15th century Alexander the Great was depicted riding into battle against the Persians in the manner of a late medieval king, with 12th-century armour and weapons.*

GOD'S SOLDIERS

AN INSPIRATION TO CRUSADERS

Knights of the Middle Ages saw the Jewish warriors of the Old Testament as exemplars of chivalry. Chief among these biblical prototypes of the medieval knight were King David, Judas Maccabeus, Joshua and Gideon.

THE CITY OF DAVID

In the 10th century BC David became the second king of Israel (after Saul) and created a united kingdom with a capital at Jerusalem (later called 'the city of David'). David was a great warrior as well as a king. The most famous of the many celebrated biblical stories featuring him was doubtless his slaying of the Philistine giant Goliath in single combat, using a stone from his sling. In the medieval Christian tradition he was likened to Christ himself, and his victory over Goliath was said to be the precursor of Christ's victory over evil in the form of Satan.

David was also a poet and musician – and is traditionally believed to be the author of much of the Book of Psalms in the Bible. He was one of the prototypes for those ideal chivalric figures and historical knights – such as King Richard I – who wrote poetry and songs as well as being great warriors.

THE HAMMER

Judas Maccabeus was a Jewish guerrilla fighter of the 2nd century BC, who led a revolt against the Seleucid empire, the Hellenistic state stretching from Thrace to India that followed Alexander the Great's empire. The Seleucid King Antiochus IV Epiphanes had attempted to prevent the Jews from practising their religion, had defaced the Temple in Jerusalem and rededicated it to the Greek god Zeus. Judas's rebellion against the Seleucids was celebrated for having saved Judaism.

Using mainly guerrilla tactics, Judas defeated four Seleucid armies and restored the Temple in Jerusalem. The name Maccabeus was given to him in his lifetime, and is thought to derive from the Aramaic word *maqqaba* ('hammer') – a reference to his fierceness in battle. In later years both Frankish king Charles Martel (Charles 'the Hammer') and English monarch Edward I (known as *Scottorum Malleus* – 'the Hammer of the Scots' – because of his victories in Scotland) were similarly honoured.

Judas's achievements were described in Books 1 and 2 Maccabees, which were part of the Bible in the medieval period. (The books are still part of the Old Testament in the Roman Catholic and Eastern Orthodox Christian traditions, but not in the Hebrew Bible. Protestant Christians usually consider them to be part of the Apochrypha, a group of texts associated with the Bible but not included in it.) Judas featured also in the history written by the 1st-century AD Jewish priest and historian Josephus.

AN EXAMPLE FOR CRUSADERS

Judas Maccabeus was celebrated for his strength, bravery and piety, and the combination of these qualities made him the ideal model for knights. In defending his faith of Judaism (seen as the forerunner of Christianity) and driving imposters

◄ *An illustration in a 16th-century French manuscript shows the Jewish warrior Judas Maccabeus giving money to pay for services for those killed in battle.*

◄ *The Israelites commanded by Joshua sack the city of Ai (top), and (below) the people of Gibeon, afraid of the receiving the same treatment, make peace with Joshua. Both images are from a 13th-century manuscript of the Old Testament.*

Sadly, in victory the crusaders also followed the example of Joshua's army, when his men slaughtered every living person in Jericho except for a woman, Rahab, and her family who had helped spies sent ahead by Joshua before the attack. Once in Jerusalem, the crusaders likewise went on a violent rampage, until the streets ran with blood. (Joshua's exploits were described in the Bible, chiefly in the books of Exodus, Numbers and Joshua.)

Another great biblical warrior, Gideon, was hailed by medieval writers for his combination of martial power and deep religious faith. As described in the Bible's Book of Judges, he restored the true faith in God after his fellow Jews had turned to the worship of the Canaanite god Baal. Gideon won a great victory over a tribe of desert raiders called the Midianites. His name meant 'Great Warrior'.

out of the holy city of Jerusalem, he was a prototype for the knights of the crusades.

The example of the biblical warrior Joshua was also a model for the crusader knights, particularly those on the First Crusade. After the Israelites had escaped from captivity in Egypt in *c*.1200BC, Joshua succeeded Moses as their leader and led them into the 'Promised Land' of Canaan (the eastern Mediterranean shore, from southern Turkey to Egypt).

On arrival in Canaan, Joshua famously inspired the Israelites to attempt to capture the fortified city of Jericho. This was done by ordering the army to march around the city for seven days – after which the walls miraculously collapsed. In 1099 the priest Peter Desiderius convinced the crusaders to employ the same tactics at Jerusalem – and reputedly they were again successful.

THE NINE WORTHIES

Joshua, David, and Judas Maccabeus were celebrated as the three great exemplars of chivalry of the biblical age in the list of the Nine Worthies accepted by medieval writers. The idea of the Nine Worthies was introduced in a *chanson de geste* called *Les Voeux du Paon* ('A Peacock's Vows'), written in 1312 for the Bishop of Liège; the poem was traditionally said to have been written by Jacques de Longuyon from Lorraine, but this claim has been shown to be false. The list of the Nine Worthies also includes figures from the classical world – Hector of Troy, Alexander the Great and Julius Caesar; and the Christian era – King Arthur, Charlemagne, and crusader knight Godfrey of Bouillon.

▲ *The warrior Judas Maccabeus, portrayed as one of the Nine Worthies.*

HEROES OF ANCIENT GREECE
ANCIENT WARRIORS PRESENTED AS FEUDAL KNIGHTS

The 12th-century trouvère Benoit de Sainte-Maure gave the classical story of the Trojan War a feudal setting in his poem *Le Roman de Troie* (*The Romance of Troy*). In Benoit's 40,000-line poem, written in *c*.1160, all the Greek and Roman heroes of the narrative behaved as feudal warriors. They had abbeys and castles, and they fought according to 12th-century techniques of war.

The story of the Trojan War, which describes historical events that occurred in Anatolia in the 13th century BC, is principally familiar to modern audiences through the *Iliad,* by the ancient Greek poet Homer. However, Benoit de Sainte-Maure did not have access to the works of Homer, since these were not rediscovered until the 15th century in Italy. He had two main sources: a Latin history believed in the Middle Ages to have been written by Dares the Phrygian, a participant in the events described, which in fact probably dated from the 5th century AD; and another Latin account, supposedly written by a second contemporary, Dictys of Crete, but in fact dating from the 4th century AD.

Benoit's version was strikingly different from the accounts familiar to modern readers because it did not include the frequent interventions in the story by Greek gods and goddesses. It made the Trojan warrior Hector, rather than the Greek warrior Achilles, the main hero of

the narrative. This was in line with the prevailing enthusiasm for Troy and its heroes – Hector was celebrated, as we have seen, as one of three principal warriors and chivalric figures of the classical age in the list of Nine Worthies.

THE *ROMANS D'ANTIQUITÉ*

Benoit's poem inspired an entire literary genre, the *romans d'antiquité*, which consisted of poems of the feudal age featuring classical warriors – the 'Matter of Rome' described by Jean Bodel. Of these ancient warriors, the Greek Achilles and the Trojan

▲ Hector leads the mounted warriors of Troy into the kind of battle fought by knights in the 15th century, when this edition of Benoit's Trojan poem was published.

Hector were viewed as the finest exemplars of chivalry. The poems were intended to inspire contemporary warriors in the audience by their examples of great chivalric behaviour. The poets who wrote them invented love affairs for their protagonists so they could treat themes of courtly love, and added episodes of knight-errantry and fighting of tournaments so they could describe acts of gallantry and chivalry. Classical narratives of this kind were, alongside Arthurian stories, the favourite subjects for enactment in tournaments and the courtly pageants that surrounded them.

Benoit was attached to the court of King Henry II of England and dedicated *Le Roman de Troie* to Henry's queen, the

◄ An illustration from an edition of Benoit de Sainte-Maure's Romance of Troy *shows the Trojans building their city.*

▲ *This portrait of Hector of Troy is from a fresco of the Nine Worthies made in c.1430.*

great royal patroness of chivalric literature, Eleanor of Aquitaine. He may also have been the author of a slightly earlier romance called *Le Roman de Thèbes* (*The Romance of Thebes*), a 10,000-line account of the assaults by the city of Argos on the city of Thebes. It was based on an abridgement of the Latin poem the *Thebaid*, written in the 1st century AD by Publius Papinius Statius, and again represented the Greeks using 12th-century methods of warfare and behaving according to the dictates of courtly love.

Another near-contemporary poem is the 2,000-verse *Le Roman d'Eneas* (*The Romance of Aeneas*), again sometimes attributed to Benoit. Written in *c.*1160, it was presented as a translation of the Latin poem the *Aeneid* (written in the 1st century BC by Roman poet Virgil). However, rather than reproducing Virgil's account of the travels of Trojan warrior Aeneas from Troy to Italy and his defeat of the Latin people there, it instead concentrated on a medieval courtly love affair between Aeneas and Lavinia, daughter of Latinus, King of the Latins.

TROILUS AND CRESSIDA

Benoit's *Le Roman de Troie* imported the concerns of 12th-century courtly love into the world of the Greek war against Troy. He invented a love affair between a Trojan prince and Briseida, the daughter of a Trojan priest, and this was the first telling of the story of Troilus and Cressida, which was later retold by three major writers.

In Homer's narrative (which, as we have seen, was not available to Benoit) Troilus was the son of King Priam and Queen Hecuba of Troy, and was killed before the Trojan War began. In other ancient versions Troilus was killed by the Greek hero Achilles. In Benoit's poem, Troilus was presented as a young and innocent warrior, who fell deeply in love with the beautiful Briseida, but was betrayed by her when she took up with the Greek warrior Diomedes. The heroine was renamed Cressida in the three later accounts of the tale: the 14th-century version *Il Filostrato* (*c.*1335) by the Italian poet Giovanni Boccaccio; Englishman Geoffrey Chaucer took Boccaccio's work as the outline for his poem *Troilus and Criseyde*, written *c.*1385–90; and then, in the 17th century, William Shakespeare used Chaucer's poem as the source for his play *Troilus and Cressida* (*c.*1602).

In Boccaccio's poem, Cressida mourned for her father, Calcas, who had powers of prophecy and had seen the future defeat of Troy and so taken up residence in the Greek camp. Troilus noticed her at a festival and fell passionately in love with her. With the help of his friend Pandarus, a cousin of Cressida, he was able to meet her. As part of a truce agreement Cressida was then allowed to join her father in the camp, leaving Troilus in the city. He begged her to elope with him, but she said he should remain to defend Troy. She promised to guard her honour closely and meet him again after ten days.

Subsequently, however, Cressida was seduced by the Greek warrior Diomedes and she did not keep her promise to return to Troilus. He suspected the worst, and although Cressida sent him letters promising continuing love his fears were confirmed when his brother Deiphobus returned from battle with a piece of Diomedes' clothing – it had a favour from Cressida attached to it. Troilus sought revenge in battle, and fought for many hours against Diomedes, and in the style of a hero of chivalric romance killed no fewer than a thousand warriors in his righteous anger, but did not kill his rival. He was finally despatched by Achilles.

▼ *The go-between Pandarus talks to Cressida on behalf of her courtly lover Troilus. This image is from an edition of Giovanni Boccaccio's poem* Il Filostrato, *printed c.1475.*

THE ADVENTURES OF ALEXANDER
MEDIEVAL ROMANCES ABOUT ALEXANDER THE GREAT

A series of medieval romances recounted the larger-than-life exploits of Alexander the Great, the 4th-century BC Macedonian warrior who conquered the Persian Empire and northern India. The Alexander romances – like the *romans d'antiquités* that featured narratives of the heroes of Greece and Troy – used an anachronistic approach, presenting the great general and other ancient heroes as feudal warriors. They were also full of marvels and enchantments, monsters and magic, and tales of the Orient that appealed strongly to a noble audience that had developed a taste for the exoticism of the East, by listening to the eye-witness accounts of grizzled crusaders.

Alexander's extraordinary career combined stirring military achievements with explorations far into the east, beyond the limits of the known world. Even in his lifetime, colourful legends collected around his name and following his death in 323BC, a folklore rich in exotic oriental marvels grew up. A number of these stories, written in Greek, were gathered in

c.AD300 by an author masquerading as one of Alexander's own generals named Callisthenes, and the scholars call the text the pseudo-Callisthenes; many translations of this source in Latin were available to the authors of the romances in the 12th and 13th centuries.

ALBERIC OF BESANÇON
The oldest surviving medieval version of the life of Alexander was written in c.1100–1150 by Alberic of Besançon. Alberic told how Alexander's birth was

▲ According to legend, the great warrior had a remarkable education. A French edition of The Alexander Romance, *c.1400, shows him with his tutor Aristotle.*

marked by marvels: the sky grew dark as the sea raged and the rain fell red as blood, but with the birth of the baby who was destined to be a conqueror all fell quiet. According to the legend recounted by Alberic, Alexander's father King Philip II of Macedon appointed great men of the age of antiquity including Homer, Aristotle and Ptolemy to be tutors to Alexander in his youth; and they saw to it that he had a good chivalric education, of the kind enjoyed by the nobles in the audience for the poem, combining knowledge of letters with training in the arts of knighthood such as swordplay, jousting and hunting – as well as singing and playing music.

THE ALEXANDER ROMANCE
Alberic's work survives only in a fragment of 105 lines, but it was one of the major sources for other medieval stories about the legendary general, notably *Le Roman d'Alexandre* (*The Alexander Romance*), a

◄ The people of Babylon give the keys of their city to Alexander. The world-conquering general died in Babylon, perhaps of food or alcohol poisoning, aged 33 in June 323BC.

poem in lines of 12 syllables written by the Norman poet Alexander of Bernay, also known as Alexander of Paris, before 1200. (The 12-syllable lines he used to such good effect were named 'alexandrines' in his honour.)

EXTRAORDINARY FEATS

One section of *The Alexander Romance* told how as a youth the future general prefigured his wide conquests on land by claiming the heavens as his own. It happened that one day as he rode to hunt he saw two gryphons, creatures of Greek myth that combined a lion's body with an eagle's head and wings. He was seized by a desire to fly the creatures as high as the sun, and called a squire to him, commanding the young man to capture and starve the gryphons for two days, so that on the third day they would be willing to obey his commands if he brought them food. Meanwhile he constructed a chair and added a canopy to guard against the light when he was near the sun.

When the day came, he easily mastered the gryphons, tied the chair to them, and by luring them with juicy meat suspended just out of their reach he drove them into the sky as easily as he was able to make his horse gallop and turn in the hunt. He flew so high that the gryphons' wings were burned and the creatures swooped down away from the great heat; Alexander mastered them once more and brought them safely to land in his father Philip's fields.

Another episode recalls how he went on campaign to the land of the Amazons, the race of terrifying female warriors in Greek mythology, and forced them to pay tribute. Their queen, Thalestris, was so impressed with the general that she came to him with 300 women hoping to breed children in his image – she herself waited on him for 13 days and nights, in hopes that she might conceive a daughter by him.

THE WISDOM OF INDIA

Two other tales recounted incidents that occurred during Alexander's campaigns in India. In the first, Alexander encountered

a group of Indian sages, who informed him that they were not afraid of him because in their village there was nothing to steal except wisdom – and for all his strength, he could not take that from them against their will. In the story, Alexander reacted with grace and intelligence, allowing his army to rest in a camp and sitting with the sages in order to learn from them. They told him that all his campaigning would in the end be for nothing since he, like all men and women, would die, and another man would come and take what he had worked so hard to conquer; but they also taught him that death was not the end, for although darkness covered the soul when a person died, soon the soul would rise to new life just as the sun rose at the end of night.

▲ *After being impressed by war elephants in the Persian army during his victory at the Battle of Gaugamela in 331 BC, Alexander incorporated the animals into his own forces and used them in battle charges.*

In the second story, which was framed as a letter from Alexander to his tutor Aristotle, the great general encountered in India a holy grove containing talking trees that were sacred to the moon and sun gods. The trees delivered the chilling news that Alexander would be killed by his own men and that his death would come in Babylon – a prophecy that proved only half-right, for although Alexander did die in Babylon in 323 BC at just 33 years of age, it was from fever rather than as a result of treachery.

KNIGHT OF ROME

JULIUS CAESAR

Another great general of the classical world revered as an embodiment of chivalry was Julius Caesar, the Roman general and statesman, conqueror of France (then known as Gaul) in 58–50BC and invader of Britain in 55BC and 54BC.

ALL FOR LOVE

As we have seen, Caesar was one of the Nine Worthies who were presented as exemplars of chivalry. In the 14th-century French romance *Perceforest* (*c*.1330–44), he was portrayed as a young knight in the courtly love tradition, who decided to invade Britain because one of his own knights named Luces had fallen passionately in love with the wife of Perceforest, King of England.

The seeds of Caesar's death were sown in the invasion: after Caesar killed a British knight with a lance, the knight's nephew Orsus Bouchesuave vowed revenge, and taking the lance, made 12 iron weapons from its head. These were the weapons used by Brutus and his allies (with Orsus in their number) to kill Caesar on the Ides of March in 44BC.

The romance also found room for Alexander the Great: it claimed that he conquered Britain, but then set out for Babylon and left Perceforest in charge;

▲ A 15th-century French manuscript of the Deeds of the Romans *depicts Caesar's army in full medieval armour preparing to disembark after defeating a Breton army.*

Perceforest then converted Britain to Christianity and ruled over a golden age, with bands of great knights in his service.

GEOFFREY OF MONMOUTH'S 'HISTORY' OF CAESAR

Geoffrey of Monmouth included an account of the Roman general's invasions of Britain in his *History of the Kings of Britain* (*c*.1135–39). To the various existing accounts by early medieval writers such as Bede and Nennius, Geoffrey added a number of legendary elements that reflected the preoccupations of the medieval knights in his audience.

According to Geoffrey's account, Julius Caesar decided to invade Britain after he had conquered Gaul (whereas in reality he undertook the invasions while still engaged in the conquest of Gaul) and dispatched a letter demanding tribute to Cassibelaunus, the King of Britain. (Cassibelaunus was Geoffrey's literary version of the historical British chieftain

◄ The Roman army uses medieval siege engines and ladders to break into a fortress in this illustration from a 14th-century French edition of the Deeds of the Romans.

Cassivellaunus of the Catuvellauni tribe, who led British resistance to the second Caesarian invasion that occurred in 54BC.) Cassibelaunus refused to pay tribute and claimed equality with Caesar, on account of the Romans' and Britons' common descent from the heroes of Troy.

CAESAR'S MAGICAL SWORD

Caesar then invaded via the Thames estuary and during the ensuing battle engaged in a hand-to-hand duel with Nennius, Cassibelaunus's brother. In the course of the struggle, Caesar struck Nennius a brutal blow to the head and then his sword *Crocea Mors* ('Yellow Death') became stuck in Nennius's shield. Nennius kept the weapon and – like the swords carried by great chivalric figures such as Charlemagne or King Arthur – it proved to be a sword of magical power that laid low any person that Nennius encountered during the remainder of the battle. The Britons fought with such heroism that Caesar was forced to take flight and sailed back to France. Nennius, however, survived for only 15 days after the battle and died from the effects of the head wound. He was buried in Trinovantum (London) with the magical sword beside him.

BRITONS BETRAYED

Subsequently, according to Geoffrey, Caesar invaded a second time and was driven back once more. The British used the cunning tactic of driving stakes into the Thames mud so they were hidden beneath the water at high tide and holed the Roman ships. During the victory celebrations after this triumph, however, the seeds of future disaster were sown when Cassibelaunus's nephew Hirelglas was killed by Cuelinus, the nephew of another royal, Androgeus, during a bout of wrestling. In Caesar's third invasion, Androgeus betrayed Cassibelaunus by

▲ *Caesar's assassination on the Ides of March 44BC is reimagined as a moment of 15th-century Italian court life in this panel of c.1450 by Giovanni di Tommaso Angelo.*

launching an attack on the rear of the British, and driving Cassibelaunus into retreat. Finally Cassibelaunus agreed to pay tribute to Caesar and became his friend.

AN ISLAND FOR A HORSE

Caesar and the invasion were also covered in the *Welsh Triads of the Islands of Britain*, a 13th-century collection of history, mythology and folklore. In this version, Cassibelaunus (here called Caswallawn) travelled to Rome to find his lover Fflur and initially allowed Caesar to land in Britain, in return for a horse of great strength and beauty named Meinlas.

ANCIENT VERSUS MEDIEVAL

Also in the 13th century a French work, *Le Faits des Romains* (*Deeds of the Romans*) detailed Caesar's invasion of Britain. In this the invaders overcame the underwater stakes by burning them with Greek fire. The mysterious Greek fire was a sulphur-based weapon developed in c.AD670 and used by the Byzantine Greeks. The use of the stakes was a partial invention of the medieval writers: in the historic invasion, the Britons did use sharpened stakes and did conceal some beneath the waterline, but they intended them as a defence against Roman infantry, not the ships.

ONE OF THE NINE WORTHIES

As with all the Nine Worthies, Julius Caesar (depicted below second left in an early 15th-century fresco) represents all facets of the perfect warrior. All, with the exception of Hector of Troy and arguably King Arthur, are conquering heroes. Most came from royal families.

All brought glory and honour to their nations and were noted for their prowess in arms. As individuals, each displayed some outstanding chivalric quality which, in combination with their historical context, made them exemplars of knighthood.

SIR ORFEO

CHIVALRIC LORD, LOYAL HUSBAND AND COURTLY MUSICIAN

An English poem from the 13th and 14th centuries transposed the Greek myth of Orpheus and Eurydice to the world of medieval England. The hero and heroine, in the Greek myth a minstrel and his beloved wife, a tree-spirit, became Sir Orfeo, ruler of a medieval kingdom, and his queen, Heurodis. The poem *Sir Orfeo* appeared to be derived from an earlier Old French Breton lay or song and it showed the strong influence of Celtic folktales about faery kingdoms existing alongside the day-to-day world.

WHAT MEDIEVAL POETS KNEW OF THE GREEK MYTH

The earliest surviving manuscript of *Sir Orfeo* dates from *c*.1330. There are references to a Breton lay about Orpheus in earlier French narratives, such as the 12th-century romance *Floire et Blanchefleur* (*Floris and Blanchefleur*) and the 13th-century *Prose Lancelot*, but this version of the story has not survived. The ancient Greek myth of Orpheus and Eurydice

▼ *According to the ancient Greek myth, Orpheus was killed by Maenads, female worshippers of the mystery god Dionysius. They were angry that after Eurydice's death he had abandoned the love of women.*

dates back to at least the 6th century BC, and would have been available to the medieval period poets through the Roman poets Virgil and Ovid.

In the Greek myth Orpheus was a musician from Thrace so gifted that animals, and even trees and stones, would come to listen to his playing of the lyre. When his wife Eurydice was killed by a snakebite he followed her into the underworld, and there played so beautifully that the god of the dead, Hades, allowed him to have Eurydice back – on the condition that as he led her out of the land of the dead, back to the world of the living, he did not look back. In older versions of the myth he succeeded, and Eurydice was restored to life, but in the better known, and less happy versions (found in Ovid and Virgil) he looked back – and Eurydice dissolved into mist.

FROM WINCHESTER TO THE OTHERWORLD

The poet of *Sir Orfeo* began by situating the narrative in England, declaring that Thrace (Orfeo's kingdom) was in fact an old title for Winchester, King Alfred the Great's capital. The king lost his beloved wife, Heurodis, when she was stolen by the king of the fairies from under an apple tree haunted by spirits. In this version, she did not die, but was taken at the moment before death to a faery Otherworld.

Sir Orfeo was undone by grief, and renounced his kingdom in order to search for Heurodis. Like a good feudal lord he thought of the well-being of his vassals, and left his steward in charge of the kingdom; he announced that the people should hold an assembly to elect a new ruler if they heard reports of his death. Then he cast off his fine clothes and put on the simple robes of a pilgrim, and retreated into the forest. He took only one thing with him: his harp. In his solitude and grief, deep in the woods, he played

▲ *Orpheus and Eurydice in elaborate medieval courtly dress, from an illustration to a c.1412 edition of the works of Venetian female writer Christine de Pizan.*

songs of unearthly beauty on this instrument, and even the wild animals were charmed to stillness.

Ten years passed, then one day Sir Orfeo saw Heurodis riding by in the fairy king's hunting expedition, and followed her into the Otherworld. There he played songs of exquisite beauty on his harp and the king offered him one 'boon', or favour. Seizing his chance, Sir Orfeo chose Heurodis and led her back to the earth.

With Heurodis safely restored to him, Sir Orfeo returned, rejoicing, to Winchester. He remained disguised as a poor beggar in order to test the loyalty of his steward, and finding the man to be honest and true, he then revealed his identity and resumed his rule as king.

▶ *The myth of Orpheus, with the journey to the underworld realm of the dead and the celebration of the power of music from above, has remained a symbolic tale of loss and redemption through the centuries.*

CHRISTIAN INTERPRETATIONS

The abduction of mortals by fairies, the appearance of the fairy hunt and the idea of an Otherworld that mortal men and women could travel to and return from, were all traditional motifs that appeared in Celtic folklore. At the time of the poem's composition, there were many Christian commentaries written on the original myth. One 14th-century interpretation identified Eurydice as the soul of a Christian, the king of the underworld as Satan, and Orpheus as Christ (who travelled to hell to save lost souls after his death on the Cross).

Another interpretation of the story from the same period saw Orpheus as a Christian and Eurydice as his soul; in the version in which Orpheus lost Eurydice by looking back, this interpretation said that after regaining his soul through leading a religious life and turning away from the things of the world, the Christian was tempted once more by temporal concerns and in looking back lost his soul to Satan.

CHIVALRIC MEANINGS

For the medieval audience of *Sir Orfeo,* the harp that the king played was both a courtly and a sacred instrument, and would recall the lyre played by the biblical psalmist, and paragon of chivalry, King David. Sir Orfeo's withdrawal into the forest was suggestive for the audience of a religious retreat or pilgrimage – indeed, after his temporary abdication, the king wore pilgrim robes; moreover, the fact that Sir Orfeo was granted a glimpse of Heurodis (on the fairy ride) while he was on retreat rather than on a quest would suggest the grace of God in granting spiritual benefit to pilgrims.

In addition to supporting such a religious interpretation, *Sir Orfeo* could be understood in the light of the code of

chivalry and of courtly love. The knight's loyalty to his lady, tested to the utmost limit when he gave up his worldly pre-eminence and lived in the wilderness of the forest for ten years, proved that he was worthy of her love. He demonstrated great bravery in his journey to the unknown

faery Otherworld, and his prowess (in this case with the harp rather than lance or the mace) won him his reward. In addition, he proved himself a worthy ruler, putting his people in the care of a trusty steward, and arranging for them to elect a new king if necessary.

CHAPTER NINETEEN

KING ARTHUR AND THE KNIGHTS OF THE ROUND TABLE

King Arthur and the knights of the Round Table at Camelot were honoured in the Middle Ages as the epitome of chivalry. The knights who took inspiration from the medieval cycles of Arthurian romances sought to emulate the deeds of Sir Lancelot or Sir Galahad, while many kings, princes and lords used the Round Table as the model for the organization of tournament knights or chivalric brotherhoods. As early as 1223 the Crusader knight John of Ibelin, Lord of Beirut, used the deeds of the knights of the Round Table as an inspiration for a 'Round Table' of jousting in Cyprus. Knights looked on Camelot with pride, admiration – and sadness, for the golden age of King Arthur contained within it the seeds of its own decline and failure. The medieval romances told of the great adventures of Arthur's knights, but also of the adulterous love between his queen, Guinevere, and his most trusted knight, Sir Lancelot. Their treachery, combined with the chivalric quest for the Holy Grail – the cup used by Christ at the Last Supper – led to the dissolving of the Round Table fellowship, Arthur's death and the passing of his glorious kingdom. Taken as a whole, the romances – and the wider body of Arthurian legend – were coloured with a deeply affecting elegiac tone, the sense that all great things, such as the age of Camelot, must pass away.

▲ *The Lady of the Lake meeting Guinevere, from 'The Story of Lancelot'.*

◄ *The Round Table – at which no knight could claim precedence – was presented as the ideal organization for a body of brave warriors, but when the knights departed on the Grail quest the brotherhood of fellow knights was fractured.*

LORD OF CAMELOT
KING ARTHUR'S HISTORICAL ROOTS AND THE GROWTH OF HIS LEGEND

In the great body of medieval literature celebrating Arthur and his knights, the king was cast in a number of roles – as squire called to greatness, noble ruler, peerless warrior, perfection of knighthood and the emblem of a perfect past who might one day return to lead his fallen people into a glorious future. The origins of this figure, whose appeal endures to this day, are found in an uncertain blend of Celtic history and legend.

ARTHUR'S GRAVE

Medieval knights in England were in no doubt that King Arthur was part of their history. In the 12th century a search was mounted for his place of burial.

The familiar tales of his life told that he was carried away for burial on the Isle of Avalon. This has been associated with St Michael's Mount, a sea island just off the coast in Cornwall, and L'Ile d'Aval off the coast of Brittany, but a parallel tradition, current from the early 11th century, held that Avalon was Glastonbury Tor, a hill that looked like an island among the water meadows of Somerset before the meadows were drained.

In the time of Henry II of England, Henry de Blois, abbot of Glastonbury in 1126–71, ordered a search of the Tor for Arthur's remains. Reputedly a coffin was found buried in the hillside inscribed with the legend *Hic jacet sepultus inclitus rex*

Arthurus in insula Avalonia ('Here is found the grave of King Arthur, buried in the Isle of Avalon'). In the 13th century the remains were reburied in front of the high altar in Glastonbury Abbey, in the presence of King Edward I. They were visited by pilgrims until well into the Tudor era.

HISTORICAL ROOTS

Most modern historians believe that the legend of King Arthur grew up around the military achievements of a minor British or Welsh prince of the 5th or 6th century, who led a united resistance to the invasions of the Saxons. He may have been the leader of a British army that won a celebrated victory over the Saxons at 'Mount Badon' in *c.*500.

The earliest references to Arthur are Welsh. He was named in poems of the late 6th century by Welsh poets Aneirin and Taliesin, which praised his bravery and referred to him as the 'great holder of feasts'. In the *Historia Brittonum* (*History of the Britons*) of *c.*830, the Welsh monk Nennius catalogued no fewer than 12 battles in which Arthur fought the Saxons, and mentioned the great victory at Mons Badonicus (Mount Badon); in the following century the anonymous chronicler of

▲ *In his youth Arthur thought himself a mere squire, but without knowing it he was, in fact, a prince, destined to wear the crown.*

the *Annales Cambriae* ('Annals of Wales') stated that Arthur won a battle at Mount Badon in 516 but was slain in fighting at Mount Camlann in 539. The Annals also mentioned that a warrior named Medraut (a Latin form of Mordred) met his end in this fateful battle. Arthur's name appeared in 11th- and 12th-century Welsh accounts of the lives of the saints, in which he was portrayed as a great warrior.

Mount Badon is identified by many historians as the hill fort of Little Solsbury Hill near the city of Bath in southern England. Archaeologists have uncovered evidence that the fort was in use by the British at the close of the 4th century. Other theories hold that Camlann, the proposed place of Arthur's death, might

▼ *Glastonbury Tor, proposed as the site of the Isle of Avalon, takes its name from the Celtic word (tor) for a cone-shaped hill.*

be in northern England at Bidoswald in Cumbria, which was called Camboglanna in the Roman era.

ARTHUR THE BEAR GOD

Other historians, however, disagree that there was a single historical figure at the heart of the Arthurian legend. Arthur's name may mean 'bear man' from the Welsh *art* ('bear'), and some experts argue that Arthur was originally a Celtic bear god who was given a historical setting in legends. Others suggest that the name may have been a *nom de guerre* adopted by a succession of war leaders who fought against invaders.

THE LEGEND IS BORN

The legend of Arthur developed in Welsh folklore and early romances. Perhaps the earliest of these was *Culhwch and Olwen* (11th–12th century), which described Arthur as the leader of a band of heroes (forerunners of the knights of the Round Table) and placed his court at Kelliwic ('forest grove') in Cornwall; this has been identified as Callington (near Launceston) or as Castle Killibury, a hill fort near Wadebridge in North Cornwall.

The Arthurian legend was established by Geoffrey of Monmouth in his *Historia Regum Britanniae* (*History of the Kings of Britain*) in c.1135–39. In his fictionalized account, which was highly influential across Europe, many now familiar elements of the Arthurian cycle were present: the magician Merlin gave the British King Uther Pendragon the appearance of Gorloise, Duke of Cornwall, so that Uther could satisfy his desire to sleep with Ygerna, Gorloise's beautiful wife; as a result of this union, Arthur was born; he became king when his country was at the mercy of Saxon invaders, but drove them back decisively; he married the beautiful Guinevere and his rule was a golden age of peace and chivalry. But Camelot could not last forever: when the Roman Emperor Lucius Tiberius demanded that Britain pay tribute, Arthur travelled to France to defeat a Roman army, leaving the country

▲ *A stained glass window depicts King Arthur beside his foremost knight, Lancelot.*

in the care of his nephew Mordred; ungrateful and unchivalrous, Mordred seduced Guinevere and seized the throne. Arthur returned and killed Mordred but was fatally wounded in the last battle, at Camlann, and his body was borne off to the Isle of Avalon (which Geoffrey said meant 'island of apples').

THE ROUND TABLE AND THE GRAIL QUEST

The Anglo-Norman author Wace of Jersey translated Geoffrey of Monmouth's *History* into French as the *Roman de Brut* (1155). This work was the first to describe the round table at King Arthur's court. The French author Chrétien de Troyes, author of five Arthurian romances (c.1165–80), introduced the theme of the quest for the Holy Grail, the cup used in the Last Supper, which Christ had supposedly given to Joseph of Arimathaea who had brought it to Europe.

The legend was further developed in French romances of the 13th century, which added the narratives of Arthur's childhood and how his destiny as king was revealed when he drew the sword Excalibur from the stone; of the liaison between Guinevere and Arthur's most trusted knight, Lancelot; and of Lancelot's son, Sir Galahad, whose purity allowed him to succeed as far as possible in the Grail quest. These legends were made available to English audiences by the 15th-century knight Sir Thomas Malory in his *Le Morte d'Arthur* (c.1470).

In the development of the Arthurian legend, very little changed in the main story between Geoffrey of Monmouth and Sir Thomas Malory. One key change came with the development of the code of chivalry and theories of knighthood: Arthur himself, a warrior in the early legends and in Geoffrey of Monmouth's account, became a more courtly figure, a chivalric patron and lord of the Round Table, rather than a knight finding sport in tournaments and on the battlefield.

A KING BETRAYED

SIR TRISTAN AND LADY ISEULT

Sir Tristan was the hero of a Celtic legend about a warrior's love affair with his lord's wife. This was recast in the 12th century by Anglo-Norman poets within the conventions of courtly love, then assimilated in the first quarter of the 13th century into the cycle of Arthurian romance, so that Sir Tristan became a knight of the Round Table, where he was a rival of Sir Lancelot and participated in the quest for the Holy Grail. The story of Tristan's joyful but doomed adulterous love affair with Iseult, wife of King Mark of Cornwall, came before and probably influenced the narrative of Sir Lancelot's affair with Guinevere, wife of King Arthur.

TRISTAN'S CELTIC LEGEND

The earliest surviving versions of the story of Tristan and Iseult are in the Old French poem *Tristan* (c.1155–60), by Anglo-Norman poet Thomas of Britain, and the 12th-century Norman poem *Tristan* by Norman poet Béroul. An earlier story in Celtic folklore, from which all later versions were derived, is now lost but can be reconstructed with confidence.

▲ *Returning from Ireland with Lady Iseult, Sir Tristan mistakenly drinks the potion that makes him risk all for his lady's love.*

According to this version, Sir Tristan was a knight in the service of his uncle, King Mark of Cornwall, and was himself prince of the kingdom of Lyonesse. He was Mark's champion, and after defeating an Irish knight named Marhaus in a duel, was sent to Ireland to seek the hand of Princess Iseult on Mark's behalf.

In Ireland Sir Tristan killed a dragon that had been terrifying the local population, then set sail for Cornwall with the princess. On their journey they mistakenly drank a love potion that Iseult's mother had prepared for her daughter to share with Mark, and were swept away by a deep love that could not be denied.

Iseult married King Mark, whom both she and Sir Tristan liked and honoured, but secretly she carried on her love affair with Tristan. Mark was suspicious and many times tried to catch the lovers out, but they used trickery to maintain an appearance of innocence.

Finally Mark had proof of his suspicions, and sent Tristan to death at the stake and Iseult to a leper colony. But Tristan made a miraculous escape by leaping from a clifftop chapel and rescued Iseult, and the lovers took refuge in the forest of Morrois, where they lived a life of simple fulfilment.

There Mark discovered them again, sleeping naked together with a drawn sword laid between them. Shortly afterwards, remarkably, the three made peace: Iseult returned to Mark's court as his wife and Tristan departed for Brittany, where he married a second Iseult, 'for her name as well as her beauty' – Lady Iseult of the White Hands, the daughter of Duke Hoel of Brittany.

The story ended in tragedy, however: Tristan fought Morholt, uncle of the original Iseult (of Ireland) and although he performed heroically and killed Morholt, he was stabbed with a poisoned spear in the struggle; only Iseult of Ireland knew the magic to draw this poison and save his life, so he sent for her from his sickbed with the message that if she could come she should sail in a ship with white sails, whereas if she could not come the ship should sail with black sails.

Tristan called out to his wife, Iseult of the White Hands, from his bed to tell him whether the ship was coming, and she, jealous of his undying love for her rival, lied to him, telling him that the ship had

---

PAS DE LA JOYEUSE GARDE

▲ *René d'Anjou, Duke of Anjou was a chivalric legend in his own lifetime. The epitomy of a knight, he excelled in all the necessary skills and accomplishments.*

Typical of the elaborate 15th-century *pas d'armes* devised to dramatize scenes from the Arthurian cycle was the *Pas de la Joyeuse Garde* held in Anjou in 1446. A castle was built from wood near Saumur in imitation of the 'castle of love' in which, according to various versions, both King Arthur and Queen Guinevere and Tristan and Iseult took refuge. The pageant included two 'Turks', two real lions, a company of musicians mounted on horseback, a dwarf and Duke René d'Anjou on a horse led by a maiden. The best jouster won a gold clasp adorned with rubies and diamonds.

loved both Iseult and Tristan as nephew and wife; and Iseult loved Mark as her husband. Typically in the earlier versions, with the strongest influence of the magical elements in Celtic folklore, Tristan and Iseult were viewed as being under the power of the love potion and so not morally responsible for their adultery.

In the prose romance versions of the story, however, Mark became a villain who raped and murdered his niece and killed his brother Baldwin. He also slew Tristan – in this version, Tristan did not die in Brittany, but at King Mark's court: the king crept upon him and stabbed him while the knight played his harp beneath a tree.

RETURN FROM EXILE

In some versions Tristan returned from exile to visit Iseult. Two 12th-century poems, now known as the *Folie Tristan*, told of how the knight came back to King Mark's court disguised as a fool or madman, while another called the *Luite Tristan* recounts how he made his return in the guise of a minstrel. The 12th-century poet Marie de France told in her lay *Chèvrefoil* (*Honeysuckle*) of how Tristan signalled to Iseult by leaving out a hazelnut branch inscribed with the legend *Ni moi sans vous, ni vous sans moi* ('I cannot live without you, nor can you live without me').

hoisted black sails. So Tristan, believing himself abandoned by his one true love, turned to the wall and died.

When Iseult of Ireland arrived, and discovered Tristan was dead, she was inconsolable – and herself died in a final embrace with her lover. Two trees, one honeysuckle and one hazel, were planted on the lovers' grave, and their branches intertwined as a symbol of their undying love: although King Mark tried three times to cut and separate the branches, they grew back and linked once more so he allowed them to grow.

PRINCE OF LOTHIAN?

Tristan's name (which also appears as Drystan or Drustanus) was a common Pictish name, while his kingdom of Lyonesse may be a transcription into French of Lothian (a region in south-east Scotland, once part of Pictish territory). King Mark of Cornwall was a historical figure who ruled in the early 6th century, and it is possible that the legend of Tristan grew up around a historical Pictish prince

▲ *The legend of Tristan and Iseult's doomed love has inspired many reworkings. German composer Richard Wagner's opera* Tristan und Isolde *was first performed in 1865.*

who was sent to the Cornish court. Another theory is that Lyonesse refers to the Isles of Scilly off south-west Cornwall.

The earliest versions of the Tristan legend probably had no connection to the Arthurian legend cycle. However, the names of Tristan and Iseult are found in early Welsh poems in connection with King Arthur's court: Iseult was listed as one of the key figures at the court in the 11th-century *Culhwch and Olwen*, while Tristan was identified as one of Arthur's advisers in the 12th- or 13th-century *Dream of Rhonabwy*.

In the early versions of the story, King Mark was a sympathetic character, wronged by circumstance; Mark, Tristan and Iseult all honoured one another – as in the later narrative of Arthur, Lancelot and Guinevere. Tristan loved and honoured Mark as his king and lord; Mark

▼ *King Mark was present at the funeral of Tristan and Iseult, according to this 15th-century manuscript version of the story.*

KING ARTHUR'S SQUIRE AND SENESCHAL

SIR KAY

S ir Kay was the son of Arthur's foster
father Sir Ector, and so was the future
king's foster brother. Kay's character dif-
fered markedly in different versions of the
Arthurian legends, ranging from being one
of the first and bravest of the knights of
the Round Table to being a boastful fool
and even a treacherous coward. He
appeared often with Sir Bedivere, the
knight who returned Arthur's magical
sword Excalibur to the mysterious Lady
of the Lake.

Sir Kay was best known in the guise
presented by the French Arthurian prose
romances and in Sir Thomas Malory's *Le
Morte d'Arthur*. As an infant, Arthur was
removed by Merlin the magician from his
true parents, King Uther Pendragon and
Ygrayne, and placed in the care of Sir
Ector. Arthur grew up in the company of
Sir Ector's son, Sir Kay, and came to serve
as his squire. At a tournament in London,
Arthur lost Kay's sword and thought he
could replace it by drawing the magical
weapon Excalibur from the stone. In so
doing he revealed that he was destined to
be King of the Britons. Initially Sir Kay
tried to claim that he had drawn the sword
himself, but in the end had to admit that
it was his foster brother, Arthur, who was
the chosen one. The tables were turned:
Sir Kay became Arthur's squire, and then
went on to serve as one of the knights of
the Round Table.

A WELSH LORD, AN 'ENCHANTER KNIGHT'

Welsh folklore celebrated Sir Kay – known
as Cai Hir ('Kay the Tall') – as a leading
warrior with a hot temper. Some writers
identify him as the 5th-century Welsh
Lord of Caer Gai, who had this nickname.

The folk tales collected in the
Mabinogion told of his great feats of bravery and chivalry. In the 11th-century tale
Cuhlwch and Olwen, for example, Cai,
Bedwyr and Gwalchmei (Kay, Bedivere
and Gawain) were chosen among six
champions to ride out with Culhwch from
Arthur's court in Cornwall, on the quests
Culhwch was set by the giant Ysbaddaden
before he could marry Ysbaddaden's
daughter Olwen. In the course of these
adventures, Kay killed a giant named
Wrnach and defeated Dillus the Bearded,
making a dog's lead from his hair. Arthur
made fun of his defeat of Dillus, and the
two knights were briefly estranged.

In the 13th-century Welsh collection
the *Triads of the Island of Britain*, Kay was
celebrated as one of the three great
enchanter knights of Britain. He was said
to have the ability to grow as tall as a great
oak, to hold his breath for nine days and
nights under water and to go without
sleep for the same period. He possessed a
magical sword, capable of delivering
wounds that would never heal, and had
such bodily heat that his companions

▲ *Kay's character varied in different accounts,
but he was loyal to the last. Arthur avenged
Kay's murder before his own death.*

could warm themselves on his skin when
the weather was cold in the wet forest –
indeed when it rained, anything that Kay
held would remain dry because his hand
was so hot.

A CELTIC SAINT

Breton legend gave Sir Kay a further career
as a hermit, churchman and saint.
According to this tradition, he stood down
as a knight of the Round Table in order to
become the Bishop of Glastonbury. Later
he went to Brittany and established a
monastery there at Cléder, where a shrine
was kept for centuries in honour of St Ké.
He only returned to the English court in
its last days when he tried without success
to make peace in Arthur's war with
Mordred. He also persuaded Guinevere to
enter a nunnery.

A BUFFOON AT CAMELOT

In Geoffrey of Monmouth's *History of the
Kings of Britain* (*c*.1135–9), Sir Kay was
identified as the Count of Anjou and was
said to serve as King Arthur's steward.
Together with Sir Bedivere he rode out
with the king to defeat the giant of Mont
St Michel in Normandy. In the works of
Chrétien de Troyes, however, Sir Kay was

presented as a boastful and incompetent
fool, a somewhat humorous figure who
made fun of truly heroic knights such as
Sir Lancelot or Sir Gawain, and who himself proved incapable of great deeds. In
Chrétien's poem *Lancelot, le Chevalier de la
Charrette* (*Lancelot, the Knight of the Cart*),
Sir Kay persuaded Arthur to allow him to
attempt the rescue of Guinevere when she
was taken captive by Sir Meleagant. He
failed, and ended up in prison, setting the
scene for Sir Lancelot's triumph. In the
tournament held at Le Hem, Picardy, in
1278 and described in the poem *Le Roman
du Hem*, the participating noblemen took
the roles of Arthurian knights and one
played Sir Kay as boastful buffoon.

SIR KAY THE MURDERER

From Chrétien de Troyes' time onwards,
Sir Kay was often presented as a fool and
braggart, but he was only once a villain –
in the early 13th-century French romance
Perlesvaus. In this narrative, Kay killed
Arthur's son Sir Loholt in an attempt to
take the credit for Sir Loholt's slaying of a
giant, but was found out when Sir Loholt's
head arrived at court in a box that would
only open to his murderer. Banished from
Camelot, he sided with Arthur's enemies
Sir Meliant and Brian of the Isles.

SIR KAY'S DEATH

The main tradition held that Sir Kay died
as a loyal knight in King Arthur's service.
According to Geoffrey of Monmouth, Sir
Kay was killed while fighting the fictional

Roman emperor Lucius Tiberius in France,
and the French prose romances likewise
suggested that he met his end in Arthur's
war in France against the Romans. Welsh
sources reported that Sir Kay was slain by
one of Arthur's enemies, Gwyddawg, and
that Arthur, enraged at the death of his
foster brother, avenged the murder.

▲ *Kay breaks his sword at a tournament.
He was diminished by being transformed
from the enchanter of the Welsh sources to a
middling knight in the Arthurian romances.*

▼ *According to Chrétien de Troyes, Lancelot
succeeded where Kay had failed in rescuing
Guinevere from Meleagant's castle.*

THE MARRIED KNIGHT ERRANT

SIR EREC'S CONFLICT BETWEEN MARRIED LIFE AND CHIVALRY

Sir Geraint, also known as Erec, was one of the first knights in Arthurian romance to embark as a knight errant on a journey of chivalric encounters. These marvellous adventures included combats against magical foes, visits to spellbound castles and intense jousts with unknown knights, events that inspired jousts of war and stately *pas d'armes* tournaments in the 14th and 15th centuries. By tradition Sir Geraint, variously said to be a Welsh knight or a king of Dumnonia (roughly Devon and Somerset), was famous for his great prowess in tournaments. He even won the hand of his wife, Lady Enid, at a tournament.

EREC AND ENIDE

As Sir Erec, Geraint was the hero of the first romance written by the great French poet Chrétien de Troyes, *Érec et Enide* (*c.*1170). This 7,000-line poem in Old French, called a 'tale of adventures' by its author, predates all other Arthurian romances – save perhaps the Welsh tale *Culhwch and Olwen*, which although it survives only in 14th-century manuscripts has been dated in its original form (now lost) to the 11th century. Chrétien's romance described the conflict experienced by Sir Erec between married love and the call of chivalry.

SHAMED BY SIR YDER

At the start of the story, Sir Erec – who was not wearing armour – attended on Queen Guinevere while the other knights of the Round Table rode through the forest hunting a stag. Guinevere and Sir Erec were approached by a knight named Sir Yder, accompanied by a dwarf, who treated Sir Erec discourteously before riding off. Guinevere, feeling slighted by the insult to her serving man, ordered Sir Erec to follow him and avenge the slight.

On this adventure Sir Erec rode to a far-off town where he met the Lady Enid, whose father was the archetype of a poor knight, a warrior blessed with honour and prowess but who had lost his title and worldly wealth; Sir Erec fought in the knight's old and rusty armour at a great tournament, where he defeated Sir Yder, who was competing in disguise as the 'Sparrow Hawk Knight', and made him beg for Guinevere's forgiveness. Sir Erec married Lady Enid.

MARRIAGE PROBLEMS

Sir Erec and Lady Enid settled into a happy marriage. However, Lady Enid became distressed to hear rumours accusing Sir Erec of losing some of his knightly stature because of his attachment to her and their marriage. His companions felt he was becoming soft, and failing in his duties because he was neglecting the life

◀ *Lady Enid leads the way on Sir Geraint's rather unusual chivalric quest. At the end of their adventure, they settled at Camelot.*

▲ *English poet Alfred, Lord Tennyson made Lady Enid and Sir Geraint the subject of one of his first four Arthurian poems, published as* Idylls of the King *in 1859. He celebrated their faithfulness in marriage.*

of tournaments and chivalric sports in order to spend time with his wife. Erec found Enid weeping over these rumours, and he suspected that she no longer loved him, and even that she had been unfaithful to him, and at once ordered her to prepare for a journey in his company.

They set out on a series of adventures during which he was able to prove again his prowess as a knight and she was able to demonstrate her continuing love for him. He treated her roughly and ordered her to be silent throughout the quest, but she often disobeyed his command in order to save him from dangers. At the end, after he had fought no fewer than three giants, they returned to their original home in King Arthur's court and settled back into a life of great domestic happiness.

▶ *On their travels there is a marital power struggle between Erec (Geraint) and Enid, which is happily resolved at the end of their journey, with each taking their natural place in the partnership.*

CELTIC ORIGINS

The same story was told in the Welsh romance *Geraint mab Erbin* (*Geraint, Son of Erbin*), which survives in a 14th-century manuscript associated with the *Mabinogion*. Some historians argue that Chrétien's poem and the Welsh romance were both based on a common Celtic original, others that the Welsh poem was derived from Chrétien's work. Geraint was a well-known figure in Welsh and Celtic folklore and romance, where he appeared as King of Dumnonia (a Celtic kingdom in south-west England that included Devon and Somerset). In some versions he was said to have died fighting alongside King Arthur against the Saxons at the Battle of Llongborth; his death in this battle (perhaps in *c.*500) was lamented in the poem *Elegy for Geraint*, which celebrated

the speed and strength of Geraint's horses and named Arthur as 'emperor'. Other Welsh sources identified Sir Geraint as one of three great 'seafaring knights' in Britain. In Cornish legend Geraint was buried on Carne Beacon close to the village of Veryan in the Roseland Peninsula, Cornwall, and was celebrated as the patron saint of the village of Gerrans, near Falmouth.

SJOUSTERS AS KNIGHT ERRANT

At Sandricourt in September 1493 Louis de Hédouville organised an Arthurian *pas d'armes* set in a series of locations taken from romance narratives: one part of the entertainment took place at a 'dangerous barrier', another at a 'dark crossing of ways', another in a 'thorny field', another in a 'forest wilderness'. The tournament featured ten defenders taking on all-comers. The defenders were reported to have taken up their positions 'like knights errant in search of adventures'.

▼ *The Arthurian legends were rich in mysterious settings of the kind used for the Sandricourt tournament. On one of his quests, Sir Lancelot rode into a magic wood.*

THE HOLY KNIGHT

SIR PERCEVAL

Sir Perceval was a knight marked by a profound – almost childlike – innocence. Raised away from courtly civilization, in the forest, he left his home to prove himself a knight and, after achieving great feats of chivalry at Camelot, became one of the knights of the Round Table. Set aside from the other knights by his innocence, he embarked on a sacred journey in search of the Holy Grail, the cup or dish used by Christ at the Last Supper before his crucifixion, said to be imbued with miraculous power.

The narrative of Perceval and the Grail quest first appeared in the late 12th century in Chrétien de Troyes' poem *Perceval, ou Le Conte du Graal* (*Perceval, or the Story of the Grail*), written in 1181–91. Chrétien wrote the poem towards the end of his life, and it was unfinished, ending after only 9,000 lines. But such was its popularity that four later authors wrote further sections – known as the 'Four Continuations' – that altogether added an extra 54,000 lines to the poem.

▼ *The Welsh romances that fed into the Perceval story weighed the qualities of courtliness and worldliness a knight might need to acquire during his rise to greatness.*

THE KNIGHT WITHOUT COURTESY

According to Chrétien's version, Perceval was raised in the forests of Wales by his mother, who had fled civilization following the death of her husband. When some knights rode by, Perceval was awestruck by their splendid appearance, and decided to become a knight himself. Ignoring his mother's pleas to remain, he rode to King Arthur's court, where he was knighted.

Sir Perceval was taunted by the foolish Sir Kay, then set out on a series of adventures, determined to make his name. He rescued a princess named Blanchefleur from a besieged castle, and received instructions in the ways of knighthood from Sir Gornemant. He quickly picked up the necessary physical skills, but because of his lack of a courtly education he was wanting in sophistication and the chivalric quality of courtesy; Sir Gornemant ordered him not to ask so many questions.

▲ *In some versions of his legend, Perceval married a maiden he had rescued, and fathered two sons; in others, he was devoted purely to the quest for the Grail.*

FIRST GLIMPSE OF THE GRAIL

This instruction had major consequences later in the adventures, when Sir Perceval reached the castle of two ailing kings set amid a wasteland. There were two kings, father and son, both crippled by being injured from the waist down; the elder was confined to the castle while the younger was able to come and go, well enough to visit the castle grounds.

Sir Perceval saw a mysterious procession in which young women and men passed before the younger king and his guests, carrying first a bleeding lance, then a pair of candelabras and finally a mysterious vessel (the Holy Grail) containing one wafer for the Christian Mass, said to be the only food that sustained the elder

CHRÉTIEN DE TROYES

The French poet Chrétien de Troyes was the author of five Arthurian romances. After *Erec and Enid* in c.1170, he wrote *Cligès*, in c.1176; *Lancelot ou Le Chevalier à la Charrette* (*Lancelot, or the Knight of the Cart*), and *Yvain, ou Le Chevalier au Lion* (*Yvain, or the Knight of the Lion*), both in 1176–81; and *Perceval, ou Le Conte du Graal* (*Perceval, or the Story of the Grail*), in 1181–91. He was one of the great poets of the medieval age, but we know very little about his life.

As his name indicates, he was from or was associated with the town of Troyes in north-eastern France. He served at the court of Marie de Champagne, daughter of Eleanor of Aquitaine, in the years 1160-72, and may have been herald-at-arms there. In his later years he was associated with Count Philip of Flanders, to whom he dedicated the Perceval poem. He also wrote four poems based on the *Metamorphoses* of Roman poet Ovid (1st century AD) but only one, *Philomela*, has survived.

seven years, Perceval returned to the woods, living as a hermit until he died. The poet suggested that on his death he took the Holy Grail with him to Heaven.

There were many other versions of the story. In later material, Sir Perceval was secondary to Sir Galahad in the Grail quest, but still retained a key role: with Sir Bors, he accompanied Sir Galahad in the final stages of the sacred quest, reaching the castle and achieving completion.

PERCEVAL WITHOUT THE GRAIL

The Welsh romance *Peredur ab Efrawg* (*Peredur, son of York*), which survives in two 14th-century manuscripts, told much of the same story about a knight raised in the woods and embarking on a long series of adventures in which he learned how to be a knight, but it left out the matter concerning the Holy Grail. It is possible that the Welsh romance and Chrétien shared a common Celtic or Breton source. There were various possible historical prototypes for Peredur – including a Welsh king of Gwynedd mentioned by Geoffrey of Monmouth and the Welsh Triads as fighting in the Battle of Arfderydd in AD573.

The Welsh romance told the same story as Chrétien up to Perceval's stay at King Arthur's court and his shaming by the boorish Sir Kay (here called Cei). Then, embarking on his adventures, Perceval met two uncles. The first trained him in knighthood, just as Sir Gornemant did in the other account, while the second was the equivalent of the crippled king: he also showed Sir Perceval a mysterious procession of objects, but instead of the Holy Grail he revealed a man's decapitated head on a platter. After an encounter with the Nine Witches of Gloucester, meeting his destined love, Angharad Golden-Hand, and many more adventures, Sir Perceval discovered that the decapitated head was that of his cousin and took vengeance upon his killers. The romance ended with celebrations of Sir Perceval's heroism. A Middle English romance, the 14th-century *Sir Perceval of Galles*, also omitted the Grail material from Percival's adventures.

▼ *Pre-Raphaelite painter Arthur Hacker makes the innocent Sir Perceval completely oblivious to temptations of the flesh – and even gives him a halo.*

▲ *On the ...*
and Sir ...
sister An...
cure a l...

two kni...
other's...
sword...
of his ...
noble...
covere...
then p...
the Gr...
ficient...
questi...
plete...

king. Because of Sir Gornemant's warning, Sir Perceval did not ask what the procession meant, or what the Grail was; and it later emerged that if he had asked, the old king would have been healed. Back at Arthur's court, Perceval pledged to make his way back to the mysterious castle and find the Grail and its meaning.

SIR P... THE STORY CONTINUED

Acco...
versic... Chrétien's poem continued with a section
he res... describing the adventures of Sir Gawain,
Blanc... in this context King Arthur's best knight,
Cond... but it did not complete Sir Perceval's nar-
had... rative. However, in the last of the Four
Lohe... Continuations the story was brought to a
lege... conclusion: Sir Perceval achieved his
Lohe... quest, the Grail King died and Perceval
sent... was crowned king in his stead, then after
a m... a rule of peace and prosperity lasting

THE FLAWED KNIGHT

SIR LANCELOT

Sir Lancelot was King Arthur's greatest and most trusted knight, blessed with unmatched chivalric prowess but undone by his love for Queen Guinevere. By entering into an adulterous relationship with Guinevere, he failed his king and set in motion the events that brought about Arthur's death and the end of the golden age of Camelot.

In his earlier appearances in the Arthurian cycle, Lancelot's love for Guinevere was celebrated within the conventions of courtly love, but as the story was developed in the Prose *Lancelot*, his adultery was presented as his undoing – both as a chivalric figure and as a religious knight. In the Grail romances, Lancelot was unable to achieve success in the quest

▼ *Lancelot fell unconscious at the sight of the Grail. He was unable to complete the quest because his love for Guinevere, and subsequent betrayal of his king, gave his knightly character a fatal flaw.*

because of his illicit love for the queen, but much of his extraordinary potential was realized in his son, Sir Galahad.

THE STORY OF LANCELOT

The story, as developed by the time of the 13th century Prose *Lancelot*, told that after his father King Ban of Benoic lost his kingdom and died of a broken heart as a result, Lancelot was carried off as a boy by a water-spirit, the Lady of the Lake, who brought him up in her own kingdom. In the version told in the 12th-century German poem *Lanzelet*, this was in a magical land, where no other men were permitted, but in the Prose *Lancelot* many other fine knights lived there, including Lancelot's cousins Lionel and Bors.

When Lancelot came of age he left, bound for King Arthur's court, without having been told his name or royal background; in the *Lanzelet* he was at this stage entirely untrained in knightly pursuits, and could not even handle a horse, but in

▲ *The Lady of Shalott, heroine of a work by 19th-century poet Alfred, Lord Tennyson, was based on Elaine of Astolat, who in the Arthurian legends fell hopelessly in love with Sir Lancelot.*

the Prose *Lancelot* he had benefited from a good chivalric training.

In the Prose *Lancelot*, from the moment of his arrival at court Lancelot was in love with Queen Guinevere. He rescued her from the castle of Sir Meleagant (as told in Chrétien de Troyes' poem). He recovered his father's kingdom, taken previously by the wicked Sir Claudas, but chose to live principally at King Arthur's court. At the castle of the Fisher King, he was tricked by the king into sleeping with his daughter Elaine and fathered the perfect knight, Sir Galahad. But Queen Guinevere, discovering the fact, was furious and drove him into madness and exile from Camelot.

He took part in the Grail quest, but – tainted by his sin with Guinevere – was unable to reach the end of the quest: he passed out at a mere glimpse of the Grail and remained unconscious for a length of time said to match the number of days on which he had sinned against Arthur with

► *One of the darker sides of the legend of the quest for the Grail was that it emptied Camelot of its knights, left Arthur's court open to attack and corruption, and caused individual self-doubt and failure.*

Guinevere. Subsequently, recovered and forgiven by Guinevere, he returned to Camelot, but then – after his love affair was betrayed to the king – he and Guinevere were discovered together by Arthur, who condemned the queen to death. Lancelot escaped and returned in time to save Guinevere, but in the battle kinsmen of Gawain were killed, sparking a long and bitter struggle between Gawain's kinsmen and Lancelot.

Finally, when Arthur travelled to France to defeat the Romans, the king was betrayed by Mordred. Lancelot took no part in this revolt, but his earlier treachery had destroyed the unity of the Round Table. Lancelot had to look on as Arthur

was killed in battle, Guinevere also died and the golden age of Camelot came to an end. He ended his life in a hermitage.

THE COURTLY LOVER

Lancelot first appeared in the Arthurian stories in the work of Chrétien de Troyes. Chrétien mentioned him in his poem *Erec et Enide* (c.1170) and made him the principal character of the poem *Lancelot, le Chevalier de la Charrette* (*Lancelot, the Knight of the Cart*), where he rescued Queen Guinevere after she had been taken captive by the wicked knight Sir Meleagant. The poem was the first to mention Lancelot's illicit love for Queen Guinevere; it was also the first to mention Arthur holding court at Camelot – although in this its first appearance, it is a minor court, less important than the king's main court at Caerleon.

Before the end of the 12th century the Swiss cleric Ulrich von Zatzikhoven developed the knight's character in his romance *Lanzelet* (c.1194), the first Arthurian work to describe Lancelot's upbringing by the Lady of the Lake. The poet wrote that his work was a translation of an Anglo-Norman work brought to Germany by the Crusader knight Sir Hugh de Morville, who stood hostage for King Richard I of England when he was captured by Holy Roman Emperor Henry VI. *Lanzelet* made

no mention of the knight's love for and adultery with Guinevere, and described his love for a princess named Iblis. It is possible that the original source legend about Lancelot was similar to that given in *Lanzelet*, and did not include the adulterous love, which would then have been added by Chrétien de Troyes, perhaps influenced by the Celtic legend of Tristan and Iseult. (Chrétien claimed that he had written a poem based on the Tristan story, but if he did it has been lost.)

A COURTLY INVENTION

Lancelot's relations with Guinevere as described by Chrétien in *The Knight of the Cart* were only comparable with those of Tristan and Iseult in the most general terms. As lovers Lancelot and Guinevere followed the conventions of courtly love whereas Tristan and Iseult's affair had far more of the magic associated with Celtic and Breton folklore. Chrétien wrote *The Knight of the Cart* for Marie de Champagne, a great patron of courtly love poems. Lancelot did not appear in earlier Arthurian material, such as Geoffrey of Monmouth's *History of the Kings of Britain*, in which Guinevere did have a lover, but he was the villain Mordred. Lancelot's story appears to have been invented with no antecedent in the Celtic legends that fed into so much of the Arthurian cycle.

SIR HUGH DE MORVILLE

Sir Hugh de Morville, the English knight who supposedly gave Ulrich von Zatzikhoven the Anglo-Norman source for the romance *Lanzelet*, served King Richard I of England in the 1190s before standing hostage for the king. He may well be the same Sir Hugh de Morville who served Richard's father King Henry II and was one of the four knights who assassinated Thomas Becket in 1170 in Canterbury Cathedral after misunderstanding the king's forlorn complaint 'Who will rid me of this meddlesome priest?' as a command. The assassin Sir Hugh de Morville was disinherited by the king of his holdings as Lord of Westmoreland and sent to obtain forgiveness from Pope Alexander III (r. 1159–81). The pope told the four knights to travel to the Holy Land, and so perhaps Sir Hugh was on the Third Crusade with Richard I in 1189–92.

THE PERFECT KNIGHT

SIR GALAHAD

In the later Grail romances Sir Galahad, son of Sir Lancelot, was the perfection of chivalry and the only knight capable of completing the Grail quest. These profoundly religious romances contrasted the religious inspiration of Sir Galahad's chivalry, based on spiritual fervour, with the courtly inspiration of Sir Lancelot's knightly achievements, which were done to impress his lady, Queen Guinevere.

Sir Galahad first appeared in Arthurian narratives in the early 13th-century *Queste del Saint Graal* ('Search for the Holy Grail'), part of the Prose *Lancelot* (also known as the Vulgate Cycle). His story was developed in the later romances of the Post-Vulgate Cycle and in *Le Morte d'Arthur* of Sir Thomas Malory.

▼ *The spear Sir Galahad carried on his sacred quest was said to be the holy lance that pierced Christ's side.*

SIR GALAHAD'S STORY

The Grail story as presented in the *Queste del Saint Graal* revealed the influence of Cistercian monks and of the mystical writings of the Cistercian St Bernard (1090–1153), founder of the great abbey of Clairvaux in France. The Cistercian ideal demanded sexual virginity for the leading heroes of the Grail narrative. As we have seen, Sir Perceval was no longer described as finding married love with Lady Blanchefleur, but was a virgin. Likewise, Sir Galahad possessed absolute purity, and was also a virgin. The stages by which Galahad rose to understanding and full vision of the Grail matched those of a mystic's movement towards realization of God, as described by St Bernard. The *Queste del Saint Graal* appears to have been written by a Cistercian clerk.

Sir Galahad was born after his father, Sir Lancelot, was tricked by magic into believing that Elaine, daughter of the Fisher King, was his beloved, Guinevere. Upon learning the truth Sir Lancelot returned at once to King Arthur's court, and when Galahad was born he was given to his great-aunt, who was an abbess. He had a profoundly religious upbringing in a nunnery. The great Merlin prophesied that Galahad would be braver even than Sir Lancelot and was the knight destined for success in the Holy Grail quest. The story stated, without giving details, that through his mother's side Sir Galahad was a descendant of the biblical King David.

Galahad was later brought to King Arthur's court at Camelot by a hermit and knighted by his father. Not knowing what he was doing, he sat down in the Siege Perilous – a magical empty seat at the Round Table that would kill any knight except the one capable of succeeding in the Grail quest. King Arthur, having knights – guided by Sir Perceval's sister – set sail across the sea, where they came to a second ship and boarded it to find the Holy Grail once more, covered and set upon a silver table.

Bors, Perceval and Galahad then sailed on to the city of Sarras, where, Christ-like, Sir Galahad healed a cripple and made him walk. The three knights were thrown in jail by the local king, but in time the king died and Sir Galahad succeeded him; then at a celebration of the Mass Sir Galahad was taken aside and shown the glorious mysteries of the Grail by a man who revealed himself to be Joseph of Arimathea. Afterwards Sir Galahad bade his companions farewell and died, and Sir Bors and Sir Perceval saw their friend's soul carried up to heaven. The Grail was taken with him.

▼ *Sir Galahad was one of several Arthurian knights raised in obscurity but destined to prove their greatness at court and on quests.*

▲ Sir Galahad, fighting here incognito with Sir Lancelot, had the military prowess of a great knight as well as a religious seeker's determination and drive.

witnessed the proof of Galahad's special status, gave him another test – to draw the sword from the stone. Galahad also passed this test and Arthur proclaimed him the foremost knight of all and welcomed him to the company of the Round Table. They then had a vision of the Holy Grail and Sir Galahad, Sir Bors and Sir Perceval were chosen as the best knights to pursue the quest, for Galahad had such remarkable purity of character and motive that he lived without sin.

The assembled company then retired to a meadow close to Camelot where they fought a great tournament, in which Sir Galahad, even on his first day as a knight, outdid all the other knights of the Round Table except for his father, Sir Lancelot, and Sir Perceval.

SIR GALAHAD'S SHIELD

A pure knight needed the purest weapons, hallowed by sacred history. Sir Galahad embarked on the quest carrying a shield – white as snow, with a red cross at its centre reputedly drawn in blood by Joseph of Arimathea. This shield, a red cross on a white background, was the one carried by the Knights Templar. Sir Galahad later acquired the sword of David.

In one version of the conclusion of the Grail quest, he travelled with Sir Bors and Sir Perceval to the castle of the Fisher King, where they discovered the Holy Grail. Galahad used the spear (which was identified as the spear used to pierce Christ's side as he hung on the cross) to cure the Fisher King.

Some versions ended at this point, with Sir Galahad being granted a vision of the Holy Grail and then being raised to heaven. Others provided further adventures overseas in the city of Sarras in the Middle East. According to this version, the

A KNIGHT STRONG AS THE SUN

SIR GAWAIN

The character of Sir Gawain, King Arthur's nephew, changed with the development of the Arthurian legends. In early literature he was a trusted knight and exemplary warrior, but by the time of Sir Thomas Malory he was a treacherous lord known for his rough treatment of women.

From the beginning Gawain was associated with women: altogether, in the various legends told of him, he had no fewer than 21 lovers. He was also the hero of a story in which he stepped forward to marry an ugly lady for whom Arthur had promised to find a husband, in return for help that saved his life, and she turned out to be a great beauty cast under a spell.

The magic of folklore attended Gawain, and some of his feats may be distantly connected to folktales about the Irish hero Cúchulainn; although possessed of extraordinary strength, he was flawed as a chivalric figure, because he did not live up either to the ideal of courtly knight or to the ideal of the religious-mystical knight.

Sir Gawain's character is a case study in a knight's maturing understanding of the meaning of chivalry: moving from celebration of feats of physical strength and

▼ *In a scene based on the English poem* Sir Gawain and the Green Knight, *Gawain is tempted by the wife of his host Sir Bercilak.*

▲ *Gawain was renowned for his martial ability. In 13th-century romances he was often the only knight able to match a new hero, freshly arrived at court, in combat.*

martial endeavour, to praise for courtesy and the ability to thrive, as Sir Lancelot did, within the convention of courtly love, to reverence for humility and purity as embodied by Sir Galahad.

THE HISTORICAL GAWAIN

Sir Gawain's legend appears to have grown up around the life of a late 5th-century Welsh king, Gawain Gwalltafwyn. In the Arthurian narratives, however, he had Scottish roots, as the son of King Lot of Orkney and Lothian. His connection to Arthur was through his mother Morgause, Arthur's half-sister. Gawain's brothers were Sir Agravain, Sir Gaheris, Sir Gareth and Sir Mordred. In some accounts, but not in the early Welsh Arthurian legends, Sir Mordred was the product of Arthur's incestuous liaison with his half-sister.

A CELTIC SUN GOD?

In Malory and in a number of the romances, Sir Gawain's strength grew greater and less in the course of the day –

often it was said that he was three times stronger at noon than in the evening. For this reason, it has been suggested that he was based on a Celtic sun god. In early Welsh versions of the Arthurian legends, Gawain was known as Gwalchmei. He appeared with Cai and Bedwyr (Sir Kay and Sir Bedivere) in the 11th-century *Culhwch and Olwen*, where he was King Arthur's nephew and one of his foremost knights, who was selected to travel with Culhwch on his quest.

In the following century Geoffrey of Monmouth's *History of the Kings of Britain* presented Sir Gawain as one of the leading warriors of Arthur's court, who served as the ambassador to Rome. William of Malmesbury described Sir Gawain as an enduring foe for the Anglo-Saxons, although he was finally driven from the kingdom by the brother of the semi-legendary Anglo-Saxon king, Hengest. William also recorded that Gawain's grave had been discovered in south-west Wales.

WORLDLY KNIGHT

In the romances of Chrétien de Troyes, Gawain was one of the most prominent of Arthur's knights, but was often compared unfavourably with Sir Lancelot or Sir

Perceval. With the development of the Grail theme, Gawain was increasingly presented as lacking in the necessary spiritual qualities for the mystical quest – brave and forceful he might be, but too reliant also on his own strength and unable to understand the significance of the Grail.

HATRED FOR SIR LANCELOT

In the romances of the Vulgate Cycle (c.1210 onwards) Gawain played an important role in the end of the Round Table fellowship. He refused to take part when his brothers Agravain and Mordred exposed the secret love of Sir Lancelot and Queen Guinevere to King Arthur, but after Arthur had condemned his wife to death and Sir Lancelot returned to rescue Guinevere, a battle broke out in which all the brothers save Mordred were killed. Gawain's respectful friendship with Sir Lancelot became an implacable hatred that was the bitter backdrop for the final days of Camelot. In this version Gawain lost his life fighting against Mordred and before he died wrote to Lancelot asking for his forgiveness.

Sir Gawain's character had been transformed into a villain and even a murderer by the time of the Prose *Tristan* and the Post-Vulgate Cycle romances (both written c.1240). In his *Le Morte d'Arthur* (c.1450–70) Malory reproduced the largely negative image of Sir Gawain presented in the French romances.

ENDURING ENGLISH POPULARITY

Yet more positive images of Sir Gawain survived and endured: the English poem *Sir Gawain and the Green Knight* (c.1375) presented Gawain as a brave and loyal knight. His popularity endured: the story of his encounter with the Green Knight was retold in a rhyming romance of c.1500, and we know from a description by courtier Robert Laneham that a minstrel performed a Gawain romance as part of the festivities laid on at Kenilworth Castle in 1575 for Queen Elizabeth I.

The story of *Sir Gawain and the Green Knight* was based on an old folkloric nar-

rative of a beheading game, which was told of heroes including Cúchulainn. At Camelot when the court was celebrating New Year's Day a knight dressed in green armour arrived unannounced and proposed a game: he would allow anyone to strike him with an axe if the person agreed to the Green Knight returning the blow in one year's time. Sir Gawain took up the challenge and decapitated the knight. But after receiving this blow the knight stood and picked up his own head; before leaving, he instructed Sir Gawain to meet him at the Green Chapel in one year's time.

One year later, searching for the Green Chapel, Sir Gawain came to a fine castle and was welcomed by its lord Sir Bercilak and his ravishing wife. Sir Bercilak embarked on a hunt and proposed a deal with Sir Gawain: he would give Sir Gawain whatever game he caught while Gawain would give the lord whatever he gained during the day. When he was gone, the lady of the castle visited Sir Gawain's chamber to try to seduce him, but he resisted her advances, only allowing her to give him one kiss; in the evening, he gave the kiss to the lord. On the second day, the same thing happened, but the

▲ Sir Gawain and Sir Yvain failed in the Grail quest. In one story Gawain saw the chalice but allowed himself to be distracted by the beauty of the maiden carrying it.

lady gave two kisses; Sir Gawain later passed these on to Sir Bercilak. On the third day the lady gave him three kisses and a green girdle that she said would keep him safe from physical harm; in the evening he gave the three kisses to Sir Bercilak but withheld the girdle.

The following day being New Year's Day, Sir Gawain met with the Green Knight at the Green Chapel, wearing the girdle. The Green Knight swung his great axe three times, only injuring Gawain slightly on the third swing. He revealed himself to be Sir Bercilak, and said that he would not have hurt Sir Gawain at all had he been honest about the girdle; they had, he said, been taking part in a game arranged by the sorceress Morgan le Fay. Sir Gawain returned to Camelot wearing the green girdle as a sign of his shame at having been outwitted, but King Arthur on hearing the tale announced that all the knights of Camelot should henceforth wear a green sash in honour of Gawain.

CHAPTER TWENTY

KNIGHTS IN HISTORY

In November 1095 at the Council of Clermont in France, Pope Urban II issued the call to arms to Christian knights that resulted in the First Crusade. To stir up enthusiasm for a war against Muslims in the Holy Land, he held up the example of the great Frankish king Charlemagne and his knights, whose military encounters in Spain and southern France with Islamic warriors from the Iberian Peninsula and northern Africa were already celebrated, in works such as the epic Anglo-Norman poem the *Chanson de Roland* (*Song of Roland*), as great feats of war against Muslims. Urban's speech, which had such momentous consequences, is an indication of how literary tales of chivalry were intertwined with the historical deeds of knights.

The *Song of Roland* and other *chansons de geste* – songs celebrating the great figures and heroic exploits in the era of Charlemagne – were the first flowering in a long tradition of poetry and romances that wove colourful legends of chivalry around the past adventures of knights. These works, whose accounts of chivalric deeds were strongly influenced by legend, presented exemplary images of knighthood that were held up by Urban and others as an inspiration for the knights of their day. In addition, the accounts in the poems and romances were to some extent determined by the prevailing culture – in particular, they often filled a need for 'crusading propaganda', showing knights fighting heroically for Christ and their Muslim foes acting with dishonesty and cowardice.

▲ *An imagined joust between Richard I and a blue-skinned General Saladin.*

◄ *Charlemagne was said to have 12 paladins or leading knights – just as Christ had 12 disciples. This ceiling fresco of the great king is from the Palace of Justice in Paris, France.*

CHRISTIAN KNIGHTS IN BATTLE

ROLAND, CHARLEMAGNE'S FIRST KNIGHT

The *Song of Roland* is the earliest surviving example of the Anglo-Norman and French *chansons de geste* ('songs of heroic deeds'), epic poems that celebrated feats of arms performed by knights in the service of Charlemagne and other Frankish kings. It is the oldest surviving epic poem in French and because of its quality as well as its antiquity enjoys a preeminent place in medieval literature. Traditionally the poem was seen as a French work, but recent scholars have established that it belongs in the Anglo-Norman tradition.

The poem survives in a number of manuscripts, the oldest of which dates to *c.*1130–70, but it was composed by the time of the First Crusade and perhaps even earlier: according to the 12th-century Anglo-Norman poet Wace, at the Battle of Hastings in 1066 Duke William of Normandy's minstrel performed the poem before the battle. This claim (made in his *Roman de Rou*, *c.*1160) and Pope Urban II's reference to Charlemagne and his knights at Clermont in 1095, indicate that the *Song of Roland* and perhaps other chansons about Charlemagne in the late 11th century already enjoyed wide currency as celebrations of Christian knights at war. Although no chansons survive from before the mid-12th century the poems were probably passed down orally and may have been developed 100 or even 200 years before they were written down.

CHARLEMAGNE AND MARSILIUN

The *Song of Roland* tells the story of the downfall and death of Charlemagne's favourite knight. The emperor was 36 when he led a short and largely unsuccessful campaign in Spain in AD778. In the poem, however, his army brought the whole of Muslim Spain under Christian control, save only the city of Saragossa; Charlemagne, moreover, was said to be 200 years old, a grizzled veteran of wars fought in God's name.

Marsiliun, the Muslim king of Saragossa, sent a message to Charlemagne saying that he would come to the French king's court at Aix for the festival of Michaelmas, would accept the Christian faith, and give Charlemagne hostages. His plan was to trick Charlemagne into returning to France, and he had no intention of honouring his promise: he would be happy to lose the hostages if it meant that Charlemagne was no longer threatening his city. Charlemagne accepted the offer.

THE TREACHERY OF GANELON

Charlemagne sent a message of acceptance through Roland's stepfather, Ganelon, who was jealous of Roland and plotted to bring about his downfall. Ganelon proposed a deal to Marsiliun: he would arrange for Roland and his friend Oliver to be in charge of the small rear section of Charlemagne's army, and Marsiliun could lie in wait for them in the mountains and defeat them. If he killed Roland, nothing would upset Charlemagne more.

Ganelon arranged it as he promised. Charlemagne was troubled by bad dreams, and was concerned that his beloved Roland would be vulnerable in the weak rear section of the army, so he made him promise to summon help with his horn if he needed it. The Muslim army attacked

◀ *Even the great must die. In this illustration from* The Mirror of History *by the 13th-century Dominican friar Vincent of Beauvais, the Battle of Roncesvalles rages while Roland's body is stretched out in death beside his sword.*

fiercely. Oliver urged Roland to blow the horn, but Roland refused, saying that a call for help would be shameful.

PASSAGES OF ARMS ON THE BATTLEFIELD

The poem presents the encounter between the armies as a series of individual combats between knights: in the first attack 11 Christian knights, including Roland, were victorious, while only one Muslim warrior, Margarit of Seville, triumphed. However, in the second attack, most of the Christian knights were laid low. Then Roland sounded his horn. Far ahead, beyond the Pyrenees in France, Charlemagne heard the call and ordered the front section of the army to mount and return to the pass.

But it was too late. On the battlefield only 60 Frankish knights were left alive. Oliver was mortally injured in one encounter, and having lost his sight, mistakenly attacked Roland with his great sword Halteclere. Roland identified himself and absolved Oliver, for he could see that he was dying. One by one the Christian knights died. Roland made sure

▼ This image of Roland sounding his horn to summon the help of Charlemagne and the rest of the army is from a 13th-century German edition of the poem.

that none of the Muslims could get their hands on his famous sword Durandel by arranging his body on top of it as he prepared for death. He died unconquered in spirit, asking God for forgiveness with his final breath.

AFTER THE BATTLE

Charlemagne and the Franks defeated the remaining Muslim forces. They marched home to France, carrying the bodies of Roland, Oliver and Archbishop Turpin, and buried them at Blaye, near Bordeaux. In Aix Charlemagne ordered the execution of the traitor Ganelon.

At the end of the poem, Charlemagne was called once more to holy war: the Archangel Gabriel visited the king in his bedchamber and demanded that he take his army to the aid of a certain King Vivien besieged by pagans in the city of Imphe. Charlemagne was deeply reluctant to agree to the angel's demands, and tore his beard, bemoaning his fate, but he knew that it was his duty to fight for Christianity and to turn back the infidels.

THE HISTORICAL BATTLE OF RONCESVALLES

We know nothing for sure about the Battle of Roncesvalles. Charlemagne certainly led a military campaign in Spain in 778, but the famous battle in the Pyrenees might never have taken place. If it did happen, it was probably a minor skirmish that was developed in legend and literature as a major chivalric event.

The earliest reference to Charlemagne's 778 campaign in Spain was broadly contemporary with the events, in the Royal Annals of his reign, but made no reference to a battle at Roncesvalles. However, when around a quarter of a century later the annals were revised, an account of an attack on the rear of his army in the Pyrenees was added.

Einhard's biography of Charlemagne, the *Vita Karoli Magni* (*Life of Charlemagne*), written in *c*.817–30, described the events as a minor defeat but named Hroudland, or Roland, as one of those killed. By *c*.840,

▲ *In northern Europe Roland became a symbol of the independence of cities from the nobility. Statues of the hero were raised in many squares – as here in Riga, Latvia.*

when a biography of Charlemagne's son Louis was written, the author not only mentioned the battle but also commented that the names of the men who died at Roncesvalles were so well known that they need not be mentioned; clearly the legend of the conflict and its aftermath was firmly established by this point.

If the battle did occur, we do not know whether Charlemagne was attacked by Basques or Muslims or by a combined army of both. In Spain, Charlemagne's troops had razed the city of Pamplona before heading northward through the Pyrenees, bound for France; perhaps the Basques wanted revenge for this act, and so launched a raid. Some accounts, on the other hand, suggested that Charlemagne had taken the emir of Barcelona hostage, and it may be that Spanish Muslims attacked the Frankish army in an attempt to avenge this act.

IN SEARCH OF GLORY
WILLIAM OF ORANGE, KNIGHT OF CHARLEMAGNE

One cycle of *chansons de geste* told of the heroic deeds of William of Orange, a knight in the service of the great Charlemagne. The poems celebrated in particular his battles against the Saracens in southern France.

THREE CYCLES OF CHANSONS

Chansons de geste were traditionally grouped in three cycles, according to a classification proposed by the trouvère Bertrand de Bar-sur-Aube in the first lines of his chanson *Girart de Vienne* in *c*.1180. The first cycle was the *Geste du roi*, songs principally about Charlemagne, including the *Song of Roland*. The second was the *Geste de Garin de Monglane*, a group of chansons mainly about William of Orange. The third cycle was the *Geste de Doon de Mayence*, about rebellions against the king's authority.

WILLIAM OF GELLONE

There were 24 chansons in the *Geste de Garin de Monglane* cycle, dating from the 12th–15th century. The cycle was named after the primarily legendary warrior Garin, and the hero of the poems was his great-grandson William – who was based on a combination of historical figures.

The main model was William (or Guihelm) of Gellone. As one of Charles Martel's grandsons, he was cousin to Charlemagne; under the king's patronage he was made count of Toulouse from AD790 to 811, and he took Charlemagne's son Louis the Pious into his household for his chivalric education. William was an obdurate opponent of the Muslim 'Saracens' of Spain on their incursions into southern France. In 793 he won a great victory over a Muslim army at the Roman city of Orange in southern France – this was celebrated in the 12th-century chanson *La Prise d'Orange* (*The Taking of Orange*) and his achievement won him his nickname as 'William of Orange'.

He fought the Saracens again at Villedaigne, and was defeated. This defeat, renamed the Battle of Aliscans and cast in heroic-elegiac light in the manner of the *Song of Roland*, became the subject of a whole series of treatments in the cycle of poems – including *La Chanson de Guillaume*, *Aliscans*, and *La Chevalerie Vivien* (see below).

Despite the upset at Villedaigne, William's manoeuvres drove the Islamic army to retreat to Spain; in the same campaign, however, another branch of the Saracen forces established a garrison at Narbonne. In 803 William campaigned in northern Spain and helped in the capture of Barcelona from the Muslims.

In 806, like many heroes of chivalric literature, he retired from life in the field to live as a monk in a monastery that he had founded at Gellone near Lodève. He made a gift to the monastery of a relic said

▲ *William of Orange and other paladins of Charlemagne were steadfast opponents of Islam in France and Spain. This illustration shows Turks and Moors regaining territory during the long struggle.*

to be a piece of Christ's cross, which Charlemagne had reputedly been given by the patriarch of Jerusalem and had passed on to William. He died in the monastery in 812 or 814, and was later sainted. The monastery became a major pilgrimage site for religious travellers bound for Santiago de Compostela.

WILLIAM OF PROVENCE

Another model for William was the 10th-century nobleman William I, Count of Provence, who decisively defeated Saracen raiders from Fraxinetum at the Battle of Tourtour in 973. The Saracens at Fraxinetum were pirate-raiders from

▲ *Louis I the Pious, son of Charlemagne, features often in the background to the chansons of Garin de Monglane.*

around the Mediterranean, who had been making inroads into southern France and northern Italy; the war of 973 began after the raiders took captive the abbot of the monastery of Cluny and demanded a ransom. William went on to take the Saracen base at Fraxinetum and drove the raiders right out of southern France. He was hailed as 'the Liberator' and 'Father of the Country'. Like William of Gellone, he subsequently retired from military life to become a monk.

THE BATTLE OF ALISCANS AND ITS AFTERMATH

In the poems William was celebrated as the paragon of feudal warriors, a loyal supporter of Louis the Pious. He took as his wife a Saracen sorceress, Orable, who converted to Christianity and accepted the name Guibourc.

The central episode in the William of Orange poems celebrated a chivalric defeat at the Battle of Aliscans (thought to be based on the Battle of Villedaigne, which was actually fought alongside the river Orbieux in south-western France but in the poem was relocated to an old Roman cemetery near Arles, farther east). The episode concerned William's beloved

nephew Vivien, who – like Roland – failed to summon his uncle's help in battle against a great Saracen army until it was too late; William rode on to the battlefield with a great army, but was himself defeated and then had to go home alone, with all his great knights cut down. This was described in *La Chanson de Guillaume* (*The Song of William*).

Another chanson, *Aliscans*, described how William had his revenge for this defeat, with the help of Guibourc's brother, a huge kitchen servant named Rainoart who fought with a wooden yoke used for bearing buckets of water. The chanson *La Chevalerie Vivien* explained Vivien's defeat by revealing that he had taken a vow never to retreat by even a single pace in battle, and had deliberately provoked an attack at Aliscans by killing an entire boatload of Saracen raiders. The battle was thought a fitting subject for chivalric literature for many years – the great 12–13th century German poet Wolfram von Eschenbach, author of *Parzival*, did his own version in the poem *Willehalm*.

YOUTHFUL EXPLOITS AND INHERITANCE TROUBLES

Two poems, *Les Enfances Guillaume* and *Les Enfances Vivien*, described the youthful exploits of the men who became these great knights. It was a convention to describe the youthful achievements of

knights either in a separate *enfances* poem or in a section of a longer work. Another chanson, *Les Narbonnais*, relates the *enfances* of all seven sons of William's father Aymeri of Narbonne. This chanson is interesting for casting light on the reality of land inheritance difficulties: Aymeri passed his land to his youngest son (rather than his oldest, as he would have done in reality) and the other six had either to conquer territories for themselves or to find paid employment at the court of the great Charlemagne. The poem ended with the six older sons riding in to drive off a besieging Saracen army at Narbonne.

AYMERI OF NARBONNE

One part of the cycle was based on the adventures of William's father, Aymeri of Narbonne. The poem *Aymeri de Narbonne* recounted how he captured Narbonne from the Saracens and was given feudal rights there as seigneur by Charlemagne. It also details his marriage to Ermenjart, sister of the king of the Lombards, and their many children – the fifth of his daughters was named as Blanchefleur and was said to be the wife of Charlemagne's son Louis the Pious.

▼ *Louis the Pious fought alongside William of Orange in one of his campaigns against Spanish Islam, leading an army to attack the city of Barcelona in 803.*

GERMAN KNIGHT AT COURT

SIEGFRIED AND THE *NIBELUNGENLIED*

The dragon-slaying warrior Siegfried, fearless hero of the German epic poem the *Nibelungenlied* (*Song of the Nibelungs*) of *c*.1200, was primarily based on a mythical character from German and Norse oral legend and folklore. In the *Nibelungenlied*, this ancient legend was overlaid with historical material, and the Siegfried of the poem is thought to have been based on famous figures from the era of the Frankish kings and earlier.

HISTORICAL BACKGROUND

The destruction of the Nibelungs (or Burgundians) described in the poem may be based on the defeat of the Burgundian kingdom by the Roman general Flavius

▼ *Siegfried's great reputation as a warrior, and his many heroic feats, including the slaying of a dragon, persuaded Princess Kriemhild to accept him as her suitor and, ultimately, her husband.*

Aetius and an army of mercenary Huns at Worms in AD436 when approximately 20,000 Burgundians were reputedly slaughtered. There are other relevant historical events; one is the marriage of Attila, King of the Huns, to Ildikó, a Burgundian princess, in the middle of the 5th century. Another possible influence for the tale is the feud that arose between the Merovingian queens Brunhilda and Fredegunde in the 6th century, which was so fierce that each woman persuaded her husband to go to war against the other.

One possible model for Siegfried was a Merovingian king of the Franks of around AD600. Another much earlier archetype could be Arminius, leader of the Germanic Cherusci tribe from the northern Rhine, who in AD9 fought in scale armour as he led a coalition of Germanic tribes to a famous victory over three Roman legions in the Battle of Teutoburg Forest, a victory whose fame rang down the ages.

▲ *Known as Etzel in the* Nibelungenlied, *Attila, King of the Huns from 434 to 453, is referred to as Atli in the Icelandic sagas.*

ANCIENT LEGENDS IN A COURTLY SETTING

The *Nibelungenlied* recast the Germanic-Norse folklore and historical elements within the setting of Christian knighthood and the conventions of courtly love, in much the same way that Welsh legends about King Arthur were reinvented for a courtly audience in the works of Chrétien de Troyes and others. However, although Siegfried, while he was courting Kriemhild, behaved in accordance with the courtly love conventions, the poem also displayed violent emotions and an emphasis on revenge that was more at home in older legends and folklore than in courtly love literature.

SIEGFRIED IN THE NIBELUNGENLIED

Siegfried, a German prince from Xanten on the lower Rhine, arrived at Worms to woo Kriemhild, the Burgundian princess and sister of King Gunther. Kriemhild, however, was resolved not to wed after she had a violent dream, which her mother interpreted as meaning that any man she married would meet a bloody end. A retainer of King Gunther, named Hagen, related Siegfried's many great feats including the killing of a dragon and his winning of a great treasure from brothers Schilbung and Nibelung. With King Gunther's permission, Siegfried led the Burgundian army in a war against the Danes and Saxons, and his heroism in battle helped to soften Kriemhild's feelings for him.

Then news arrived that a queen of wondrous beauty and martial strength named Brunhilde had offered to wed the knight who was capable of defeating her in conflict. King Gunther decided to send Siegfried, but used magic to make him invisible; while Siegfried performed acts of martial valour, Gunther would go through the motions and take the credit for Siegfried's victory. Siegfried's reward would be the hand of Lady Kriemhild in marriage. The plan worked: Brunhilde accepted Gunther as her husband, and Kriemhild wed Siegfried. But later, after a quarrel between the two wives, Kriemhild revealed the trick to Brunhilde.

Hagen then allied himself with Brunhilde to seek revenge and to protect Gunther's honour. From Kriemhild, he learned of Siegfried's only weak spot by pretending that he needed to know so that he could cover the great warrior in battle.

▲ *The water spirits of the Danube prophesy the defeat of Gunther's army to Hagen on his way to the court of Etzel.*

(After his slaughter of the dragon in his youth, Siegfried had bathed in the animal's blood and ever afterwards was invulnerable in battle – save in one tiny spot on his back, which without his knowing had been covered with a leaf from a linden tree while he was bathing.) Hagen put the knowledge to wicked use, and killed Siegfried by striking him with a spear in the vulnerable part of his back as he was leaning over a river during a hunting trip.

Siegfried was buried with great ceremony and Kriemhild, distraught with grief and brought low by mourning, lived on in Worms. She began to distribute the treasure of her dead husband, but Hagen stole it and hid it in the river Rhine.

The remainder of the poem described Kriemhild's violent revenge against the Burgundians who had murdered her husband and stolen her fortune. She married Etzel (based on Attila, King of the Huns), hoping he would help her get revenge. Some years later, at her insistence, Etzel invited King Gunther and Hagen to his court and in a mass battle Gunther was defeated and killed while Kriemhild herself killed Hagen with Siegfried's own sword. Kriemhild was then killed by the aged knight Hildebrand, who was horrified by the violence she had unleashed.

Hildebrand, whose name meant 'battle sword', was the brother in arms of Dietrich von Bern, an archetype of the just ruler and a legendary incarnation of the historical 5th-century King of the Ostrogoths, Theodoric the Great. According to the *Nibelungenlied*, Dietrich and Hildebrand were living in exile at Etzel's court at the time, and fought with great heroism in the battle between kings Etzel and Gunther and their retainers.

◀ *The grief of Kriemhild upon the death of her love Siegfried soon turned to vengeful fury in the* Nibelungenlied. *She achieved terrible revenge with the help of her second husband Etzel – Attila, King of the Huns.*

EL CID

THE LIFE AND LEGEND OF DON RODRIGO DIAZ DE VIVAR

Legends grew up about the chivalric feats of Spanish knight Don Rodrigo Diaz de Vivar even before he died in 1099. He was Spain's greatest general of the 11th century, who fought both for the Spanish crown and for the Moors or Saracens. In his own lifetime he was known as El Campeador ('the Champion') and El Cid (derived from the Arabic title *assid*, meaning 'lord'). The heroic legend and stirring historical facts of his life inspired many ballads and chronicles about El Cid, as well as the magnificent 12th-century poem, *Cantar de Mio Cid* (*Song of My Cid*).

BIRTH AND RISE TO FAME

Don Rodrigo was born at Bivar, near Burgos, in 1043 and had his chivalric education at the court of King Ferdinand I of Castile and Leon, where he rose to become commander of the royal army by the age of 22 under Ferdinand's eldest son, King Sancho II. However, when Sancho died in 1072 and was succeeded by his brother

▼ *In a celebrated incident the Cid, on behalf of the parliament of Castile, made King Alfonso VI swear that he had no part in the death of the Cid's brother Sancho II.*

Alfonso, Don Rodrigo lost the position to Count Garcia Ordonez, who became a great rival. Nevertheless he remained at court and married Alfonso's niece Jimena, and they had a son and two daughters.

After Don Rodrigo took Count Ordonez captive in 1079, King Alfonso cast him into exile in 1081. Don Rodrigo then entered the service of al-Mu'tamin, Moorish king of Saragossa in north-eastern Spain. He fought for al-Mu'tamin, and his successor al-Musta'in II, for almost ten years, winning many victories against fellow Moors and Spanish Christian kings.

PRINCE OF VALENCIA

After being briefly recalled by Alfonso, Don Rodrigo fought on his own account to take control of the Moorish kingdom of Valencia in 1090–94. He ruled the city, nominally under Alfonso VI but in reality in his own right, governing both Muslims and Christians. He turned the city mosque into a cathedral and appointed a French bishop named Jerome. As a statement of his princely status, he was able to wed his daughters, Cristina and Maria, to, respectively, Ramiro, Lord of Monzón and Ramón Berenguer II, Count of Barcelona.

▲ *El Cid was a Christian knight equally at home in the service of Islamic kings. Castile lost a great servant when it exiled him.*

However, Valencia was not a Christian city for long. Soon after the Cid's death in 1099, the city was besieged by Almoravids (a fresh wave of Muslims who had invaded Spain in 1086). King Alfonso VI tried to save the city, but decided he could not hold it, and the city was evacuated and burned. The Cid's body was taken for burial at the monastery of San Pedro near Burgos in Castile. The Almoravids took control of the ruins of Valencia and the rebuilt city remained Muslim until 1238.

THE CID'S FIRST VICTORY

Legends about Don Rodrigo told how he first achieved notice as a great knight by defending the honour of his father, Diego Laynez: with a single blow of his sword, he defeated the knight, Don Gomez, who

▶ *El Cid defeats Don Gomez at Callaforra, avenging an insult to his father Diego Laynez. This illustration is from a 1344 manuscript of the* Chronicle of Spain.

had slighted Diego. Gomez's daughter, Ximena, married the Cid because she was so enamoured of his strength and virtue.

The legend then described a number of campaigns against the Moors, fought in the service of 'King Ferrando' (Ferdinand I), and the declaration by Ferrando – who had heard the Moors call Rodrigo 'Çid' – that the warrior should be called 'El Cid'. Subsequently, Holy Roman Emperor Henry III, with the support of Pope Victor II, demanded tribute from Ferrando, who refused. In the ensuing war the Cid beat Remon, Count of Savoy, and a French army, then went to Rome to oversee the chastened pope signing a guarantee that a Holy Roman Emperor could never demand tribute from a Spanish king.

GREAT CHIVALRY

According to legend, following Ferrando's death, while in exile, the Cid performed countless feats of great chivalry and Christian love. In one tale he was riding to Santiago de Compostela to worship at the shrine of Spain's patron saint, St James, and he picked up a leper from the roadside and gave him a ride on his great horse

▼ *A statue in Burgos shows the Cid mounted on his trusty horse, Bavieca, and brandishing his magnificent sword, Tizona.*

Bavieca. Later at the inn, he shared his table and bed with the leper, trusting God to protect him from infection. In the night he woke to find the leper transformed into Lazarus – the dead man brought back to life by Christ in the Gospels. Lazarus predicted a glorious career for the knight.

Many episodes in the ballads and chronicles and the *Song of My Cid* described the Cid's military feats in battle against the Moors, emphasizing his tactical intelligence, his magnanimity in victory, his fairness in dividing the spoils of victory among his men, his piety in diverting riches to the support of churches and monasteries, and his personal physical prowess as a knight.

Like other knights of legend, he had a magnificent sword and horse, themselves celebrated in stories. According to the *Song of My Cid*, the Cid did not acquire his horse, Bavieca, until late in his career, when he captured it from a king of Seville who had tried to take Valencia. Bavieca was unquestioningly loyal and obedient, and by tradition never accepted another

rider after the Cid's death. When the horse died it was buried opposite the monastery of San Pedro. His sword was called Tizona.

LEGENDS OF THE CID'S DEATH

The legend of the Cid's death told that the great knight, forewarned in a dream by St Peter that he was to be called to heaven, instructed his leading comrades how to fight off an impending Moorish siege of Valencia and arranged for his body to lead into battle as if he were alive. In the battle that followed it was said that 70,000 angel knights came to the aid of the Cid's men, including one who carried a flaming sword and a bloody cross. The Christians drove their foes into the sea, where their blood turned the waves red.

Afterwards, the Cid's body was again strapped to his trusty Bavieca and led back to the monastery of San Pedro de Cardena. There it was placed on an ivory throne, with the sword Tizona in its hand, and reputedly sat there for ten years. A sweet smell arose from the body – an indication that the Cid was a saint.

DEFENDER OF JERUSALEM
LEGENDS ABOUT CRUSADER KNIGHT GODFREY OF BOUILLON

Fantastical legends grew up around the achievements of the knights who retook Jerusalem on the First Crusade (1096–99), notably Godfrey of Bouillon, one of the key figures of that episode. Godfrey, second son of Eustace, Count of Boulogne, was one of the first knights to scale the walls of the city in July 1099; he refused to be declared king, taking instead the title 'Defender of the Holy Sepulchre'.

Godfrey was the hero of a 14th-century romance narrative that reworked a cycle of 11th-century *chansons de geste*, known as the Crusade cycle, and combined them with the medieval legend of the 'Knight of the Swan', telling of a sleeping knight in a swan-drawn boat who appeared to defend a lady's honour on condition that she did not ask his name. In the Arthur tradition presented by Wolfram von Eschenbach in his *Parzival*, the Swan Knight was Sir Lohengrin, son of Sir Perceval, but in the Godfrey tradition the Swan Knight was the grandfather of the crusader knight.

▼ *Sir Percival's horse is killed, from the Queste del Saint Graal, c.1380-85. In some chansons the figure of Percival is said to be the grandson of Godfrey.*

THE SONG OF ANTIOCH
The reworked group of Crusade chansons (not named in the categorization of songs by trouvère Bertrand de Bar-sur-Aube) included the *Chanson d'Antioche* (*Song of Antioch*), which survives in a version dating from c.1180, and was based on an early poem believed to have been written during the First Crusade. This original poem was reputedly composed by Richard le Pèlerin ('Richard the Pilgrim'), a poet who travelled with the crusaders and is said to have begun the poem during the siege of Antioch. The chanson contained many hyperbolic descriptions and great lists of knights' names.

The late 12th-century version of the poem was written by Graindor de Douai, author of the other two reworked poems in the cycle – the *Chanson de Jérusalem* (*Song of Jerusalem*) and the *Chanson de Chétifs* (*Song of the Prisoners* – a reference to Christian knights held by Muslims in the Holy Land). All chansons featured Godfrey of Bouillon as a central figure.

The 14th century Godfrey of Bouillon narrative began with an account of the birth of the Swan Knight and proceeded to describe how that knight came to the

▲ *In the French version of the legend of Lohengrin, the Knight of the Swan was named Elias and married Beatrix of Bouillon, grandmother of Godfrey.*

rescue of the duchess of Bouillon by winning a duel against her persecutor, Regnier of Saxony. He then married the Duchess's

▼ *This 19th-century depiction of Godfrey, his brother Baldwin and their men crossing into Anatolia in 1097 captures the sense of exaltation among the crusaders.*

daughter and they had a daughter named Ida, but his wife asked his true name and so the Swan Knight had to leave – afterwards it emerged that the name was Elias. Then Sir Pons and Sir Gerart, kinsmen of Sir Elias, went on crusade to Jerusalem where they met Cornumarant, Muslim king of the city.

GODFREY THE CRUSADER

Many years afterwards, Ida's three sons – Eustace, Godfrey and Baldwin – went through their chivalric education and emerged as great knights. In Jerusalem, King Cornumarant's mother had a vision in which she saw Godfrey and his kin arriving in their full glory as crusaders – and also later knights' famous conflicts with Saladin at the time of the Third Crusade. As a result, Cornumarant made a voyage to Europe to visit Godfrey, and met a whole host of great figures of the Crusades on his travels: Robert Curthose; Tancred, Prince of Galilee; Bohemond of Antioch; Adhemar of Le Puy; Raymond of Toulouse and Hugh of Vermandois. Cornumarant's plan was to assassinate Godfrey of Bouillon and so make it impossible for his mother's troubling prophecy to come true, but faced with the knight in

▼ *Unstained amid carnage, Godfrey leads the way into the Holy City of Jerusalem.*

all his glory the travelling king was unable to do the deed. In fact his presence and mention of the city of Jerusalem had the unlooked-for result of planting the idea of making a crusade in Godfrey's mind.

The next stage of the narrative was the reworked *Chanson d'Antioche*. It described Pope Urban II's preaching of the crusade, the planning and preparations among the crusaders, their farewells to those staying behind, the journey to Constantinople and then the successful siege of Antioch, which lasted for eight months.

The narrative proceeded to describe the adventures of Christian *chétifs* ('prisoners') in the company of Corbaran, the deposed king of Antioch, on his return to his homeland. It included a section in which the prisoners performed the familiar knightly feat of killing a dragon, and then one of their number, Sir Arpin of Bourges, went to the aid of King Corbaran's son in various escapades; finally the captives were released and joined the other crusaders at the walls of Jerusalem.

▲ *In July 1099 Godfrey and the crusaders marched in procession around Jerusalem (in emulation of the Israelite leader Joshua at Jericho) believing the city would then fall.*

The crusader army, led by Godfrey, survived several assaults by the Saracens; in this version, Bohemond of Taranto was fighting with the crusaders rather than looking after his own interests, at Antioch (as the historical Bohemond was doing during the siege of Jerusalem). The narrative described how the crusaders tried repeatedly to take the Holy City without success before their prayers were answered and the city fell.

The story described how even in their moment of raucous triumph Godfrey and the other leaders of the crusader army remembered their proper humility and declined to be named king in Christ's city, but God sent them a sign indicating that Godfrey should be given the honour. After the capture of Jerusalem, the narrative ended with the death of Cornumarant.

GERMAN CRUSADER

EMPEROR FREDERICK I 'BARBAROSSA'

Frederick I, nicknamed 'Barbarossa' (meaning 'red beard'), was the Holy Roman Emperor from 1152 until his death in 1190. He went on two crusades, fighting with distinction alongside his uncle, Conrad III of Germany, on the Second Crusade (1145–49), and at the end of his life leading an army of 15,000 men on the Third Crusade (1189–92). He died attempting to cross the river Saleph in Cilicia (now part of Turkey) en route to the Holy Land.

THE SLEEPING KING

Frederick Barbarossa was hailed as one of the greatest of German rulers. His deeds were celebrated in the Latin chronicle *Gesta Friderici I Imperatoris* (*Deeds of the Emperor Frederick I*), written by the Cistercian monk and bishop Otto von Friesing. Legends swiftly grew up around Frederick's name, most notably to the

▼ *Because of his opposition to the papacy and efforts to impose authority in Germany Frederick was glorified in the 19th century as a symbol of German pride and unity.*

effect that he did not truly die, but can be found asleep in a cave in the Kyffhauser mountain in central Germany, and will ride forth to save Germany in her hour of greatest need.

According to this legend, his red beard has grown through the table before which he sits with his eyes half-closed. He stirs periodically to send a boy out to see if ravens are still flying around the mountain, for the prophecy has established that when the ravens stop flying Germany will desperately need his help.

AUTHORITY IN GERMANY

As Holy Roman Emperor, Frederick set out to restore the empire to the greatness it had enjoyed in the time of its founding father Charlemagne, and also in the 10th century under Otto I. At the start of his reign, he sent out an order for peace in Germany and gave a number of concessions to the princes of his territory to

▲ *Frederick became embroiled in a long power struggle in Italy with Pope Alexander III. Following defeat in the Battle of Legnano, he made peace with Alexander and his allies in the Treaty of Venice (1177).*

achieve this. He acted vigorously and effectively throughout his reign to defuse disputes and maintain his authority. He sought to emphasize his reign's continuity with that of Charlemagne, and organized a great celebration of the canonization of the former king of the Franks at Aachen in 1165.

CAMPAIGNS IN ITALY

Frederick led six expeditions into Italy to enforce his imperial rights there. On the first he was crowned Holy Roman Emperor by Pope Adrian IV (r. 1154–59), but he later fell out with the papacy and was excommunicated in 1160. On his fourth trip in 1167 he won a great military victory over a mighty papal army in the Battle of Monte Porzio near Tusculum (in modern Lazio, central Italy). Victory opened the way for Frederick to depose the pope, Alexander III (r. 1159–81), and appoint his own candidate, Paschal III, but an outbreak of plague in the imperial army ended the campaign and sent Frederick back to Germany.

THE EMPEROR WHO CHEATED DEATH

On the fifth Italian expedition, with an army of 8,000 knights, he suffered a heavy defeat fighting the pro-papal Lombard League at the Battle of Legnano. In the heat of the battle, Frederick's guard and standard bearer were killed and the emperor himself was thrown from his horse and left for dead. The army panicked and fled, and knights brought the news to Frederick's wife, Beatrice, in Pavia

▼ *A monument on the Kyffhauser mountain features this 6.5m (22ft) sandstone statue of Barbarossa apparently awaking from sleep, ready to come to Germany's aid.*

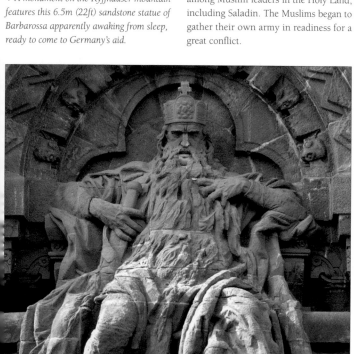

that her lord had been killed. For three days, his death was mourned, but he then appeared unannounced in Pavia, having recovered from his wound sufficiently to make his own way back home from the field of battle.

THE THIRD CRUSADE

Frederick made peace with the pope before embarking on the Third Crusade. He took the cross at Mainz Cathedral on 27 March 1188, and raised a vast German army, including 3,000 knights. They set out to follow the land rather than the sea route to the Holy Land since the army was too large to go by ship.

They travelled through Hungary and Serbia and reached Constantinople in 1189. They moved on into Anatolia and in May 1190 captured Iconium (now Konya in Turkey, at that time the capital of the Sultanate of Rum). The news of the army's approach caused consternation among Muslim leaders in the Holy Land, including Saladin. The Muslims began to gather their own army in readiness for a great conflict.

▲ *A 12th-century chronicle illustration shows Frederick, enthroned, with his two sons, Emperor Henry VI and Duke Frederick V of Swabia.*

However, on 10 June 1190 Frederick fell from his horse while crossing the river Saleph and died – either because the shock of the cold water gave him a heart attack or because he was impeded so badly by his armour that he drowned in the river, although the water was said to be only waist-deep. The death of their leader caused much of the army to panic and many abandoned the crusade and headed for home.

The command devolved on his son, Frederick of Swabia, who led the remnant of the army to Antioch. His aim was to bury his father in Jerusalem, but efforts to preserve the corpse using vinegar were not successful. Barbarossa's flesh was removed from his bones by boiling at Antioch, and buried there, while the bones were carried on by the army. Further reduced by fever, the army made its way to Tyre, where Frederick's bones were buried, and then to Acre. The crusade was carried on by Philip II of France and Richard I of England, who had travelled with their armies separately from Barbarossa.

THE ROMANCE OF COEUR DE LION

COLOURFUL LEGENDS ABOUT KING RICHARD I OF ENGLAND

The legend of King Richard I of England was growing even before his death in 1199, and was firmly established by c.1250, when the Anglo-Norman romance of *Richard Coeur de Lion* was written. Before the end of the 13th century this was expanded into an English poem that celebrated Richard as the perfect embodiment of chivalric virtue. At this time, the romance suggests, chivalry was thought to be epitomized by a taste for combating Saracens and a love of court poetry. The Richard of the legend was also marked by a superhuman bravery.

The romance gave Richard a marvellous origin, which was typical of literature of the period but curious perhaps given that Richard's true parents, King Henry II and Eleanor of Aquitaine, hardly needed improving upon. In the poem King Henry was said to have married the fairy daughter of the pagan king of Antioch, and they had three children: Richard, John and a daughter, Topias.

▼ *Richard and the Muslim general Saladin met in the course of the Third Crusade. An image from the English* Luttrell Psalter *(1340s) represents them jousting. Richard's face is hidden by his helmet. Both ride horses wearing elaborate caparisons.*

One day the mother fled, because her fairy nature meant that she could not sit piously through a church Communion service. She ran from the church, carrying Topias and John, but dropped John, whose leg was broken. Richard became king and in his very first act declared a tournament, at which much bravery was displayed. He chose the two most chivalrous performers, Sir Thomas Multon and Sir Fulk Doyly, to be his close companions. (In reality, as we have seen, Richard was not a keen tourneyer, but his reign was associated with the fighting of tournaments throughout England because he introduced a system of licensing for the holding of such events.)

A TASTE FOR SARACEN BLOOD

Later parts of the romance made much of Richard's enthusiasm for killing Saracens on crusade, and described how he not only struck the fiercest warriors down but also cooked them and ate their flesh with relish. They also described an imaginary duel between Richard and the great Saracen general Saladin.

Richard was warned in a dream sent from heaven that Saladin was planning an elaborate trick: with apparent generosity, Saladin had provided his adversary with

▲ *Philip II of France receives a messenger and takes the cross with Richard I prior to the Third Crusade.*

a fine horse to ride for the encounter in the lists, but in truth the horse was the son of the distinguished mare that Saladin himself was to ride. When the mare whinnied, Richard's horse would kneel in an attempt to drink its mother's milk, putting Richard at the mercy of the Saracen leader. Richard matched his opponent's cunning and took the precaution of filling his horse's ears with wax, so that when Saladin's mare whinnied it had no effect. He defeated Saladin in the encounter, but allowed him to escape with his life.

HOW RICHARD GOT THE NAME 'LIONHEART'

The 13th-century English *Coeur de Lion* gave a colourful account of how Richard came by his *nom de guerre*. It told how before the king ever went on crusade, when he was returning from a reconnaissance mission to the Holy Land, he was imprisoned by a certain King Modard of Germany. Richard proved a troublesome prisoner, for he killed Modard's son and made love to his daughter while in captivity, and in his rage Modard arranged for a starving lion to be released into the English king's cell.

Marked above all else by his bravery, Richard showed no fear as the lion came for him, its mouth wide open. With lightning speed, he reached down the creature's throat and tore its heart out. Then he broke out of his prison and marched into the great hall of the castle, where the king was sitting at dinner with his retainers and his fair daughter. Richard waved the bloody heart under the king's nose, then dipped it in some salt and ate it raw with apparent delight – and, as the poet noted, without bread. In awe of his captive, King Modard declared that he should be called 'Richard Lion Heart'.

▼ *Richard I's faithful minstrel Blondel hears his master's voice emanating from the dungeon of an Austrian castle where the king is held captive.*

▲ *Richard's legend emphasized his noble qualities. On his deathbed, he pardoned Bertrand de Gurdun, the young man who had fatally injured him.*

RICHARD AND BLONDEL

An often-repeated part of the legend was based on events after the crusade, during Richard's disastrous return to Europe when, after being shipwrecked near Venice, he was captured and jailed first by Duke Leopold of Austria, and then by Holy Roman Emperor Henry VI.

At the time when Richard was in Duke Leopold's dungeon, the romance said, no one at the English court knew what had become of him and Richard's favourite minstrel, Blondel, set out to search for his king. The poet wandered across all the countries of Europe and eventually arrived in Austria where he heard from a local that a great lord was imprisoned in Duke Leopold's castle. Suspecting that it might be Richard, he managed to get employment there as a musician. But he was not able to find out whether the prisoner was Richard. For many months he worked there without success, but one day he was in the garden and Richard, happening to look out of the window of his dungeon, saw him. Richard sang aloud the first verse

of a song they had composed together, and which nobody else knew, and Blondel, hearing the song, knew for sure that his lord was confined within. Shortly afterwards he left the castle and returned to England and reported to all where their king was imprisoned.

Blondel's legend grew up around the reputation of a French trouvère named Blondel of Nesle (a place near Amiens, northern France). Blondel, who reputedly got his name because he had long blond hair, was the composer of 25 songs. He was either Jean, Lord of Nesle, who like Richard fought on the Third Crusade; or his son, also Jean, who succeeded his father and fought on both the Fourth Crusade and the Albigensian Crusade. We do not know whether there was actually a connection between the historical 'Blondel' and King Richard.

A later version of the romance has a slightly different account of the Blondel legend. It suggested that the minstrel went around Europe while singing the first verse of the song that only he and Richard knew outside places where he suspected Richard might be incarcerated. Finally, when he hit upon the right place by chance, he heard Richard's voice replying from within, singing the second verse.

ADVENTURES IN LOVE AND ON CRUSADE

THE COURTLY REPUTATION OF BONIFACE OF MONTFERRAT

Boniface, Marquess of Montferrat in north-western Italy, presided over one of the most highly regarded courts of chivalry in Europe. His chivalric exploits were celebrated in song by his court poet and friend, the troubadour Raimbaut de Vaqueiras. Boniface fought against the Lombard League in Italy and Sicily, and led the Fourth Crusade in 1201–04.

Raimbaut declared that Boniface's knightly virtues were so great that they must have been bequeathed by the great figures of chivalric legend, an indication of the way in which the great figures of chivalry past and imagined were not only inspiring examples, but almost presiding deities of knighthood. Alexander the Great had given Boniface his generosity, while he had got his daring and bravery from Roland and the other 12 knights of Charlemagne. His courtesy and his charm

▼ *In the early part of the Fourth Crusade, the crusader army attacked and captured the city of Zara in Dalmatia (now Croatia).*

with the women of the court he must have got from Berart de Montdidier (who was the subject of a now lost epic poem).

PROTECTOR OF LADIES

Boniface's achievements as a young man in the 1170s, as described in Raimbaut's *Epic Letter*, were the very stuff of courtly chivalry. In one adventure, he rescued Saldina de Mar, a prominent young woman from Genoa, who had been seized by Albert of Malaspina and taken to his most inaccessible retreat. Boniface and Raimbaut rode in at suppertime and took possession of the young woman, then carried her off to her lover Ponset d'Aguilar, who was, according to the poem, expiring in his bed for love of the young lady.

The *Epic Letter* also described Boniface's rescue of the wealthy young woman Jacopina of Ventimiglia from her wicked uncle, Count Otto, who was plotting to take her money and dispatch her to Sardinia. On hearing the news that Count Otto was plotting against Jacopina, the

▲ *A near-contemporary Byzantine mosaic represents Boniface's crusader army capturing Constantinople in 1204. The mosaic is from a church in Ravenna, Italy.*

chivalrous Boniface sighed deeply, for he remembered the kiss that the lady had given him when she had asked him to protect her against her scheming uncle. He and Raimbaut, along with three other knights – Bertaldo, Guiot and Hugonet del Far – rode by night to her rescue and plucked her to safety from the quayside only moments before she was to be sent into exile.

CHIVALRIC ADVENTURES

According to the poem, they then had many adventures in her company as they rode across country, with enemy knights in pursuit. They had to go into hiding when knights rode out from Pisa to encounter them, for they were extravagantly outnumbered, and went without food or water for two days. Then they had a dramatic encounter with a group of 12 brigands at Belhestar Pass, during which Raimbaut was wounded in the neck but then was rescued by Bertaldo and Hugonet del Far.

That night, at last, they were welcomed into a comfortable home, and their host Sir Aicio was so entranced by the virtue, good looks and good standing of Boniface

▲ *In 1840 French romantic painter Eugène Delacroix painted this celebrated canvas of the crusaders' capture of Constantinople on the Fourth Crusade. The attack on the city was the culmination of centuries of ill-feeling between crusaders and Byzantines.*

that, according to the poem, he wanted to give his beautiful daughter, Aigleta, to the knight as a bride. However, Boniface did not wish to enter into this arrangement, although he did subsequently arrange a marriage for both Jacopina and Aigleta, and he ensured that Jacopina's inheritance was restored to her.

Raimbaut declared that with Boniface he had worked through many dramas of courtly love. His lord had arranged at least 100 marriages for ladies who would have otherwise pined away, tying them to the most noble barons, marquises and counts; and, Raimbaut claimed, he had never given in to the temptation to lie with a single one of those needy ladies.

PROWESS IN BATTLE

These adventures were recalled in the later part of the *Epic Letter*. The earlier sections praised Boniface's exceptional prowess as

a warrior and recalled the many exploits patron and poet had shared in the field – charging and unseating foes, jousting both on bridges and in river-fords, attacking castles and clambering over sheer walls, and braving many a danger.

In 1191–93 Boniface and Raimbaut fought in Italy, on the side of the Cremona League against the League of Milan. Then in 1194 they joined in Holy Roman

Emperor Henry VI's campaign to Sicily, where at the Battle of Messina, Raimbaut came to the rescue of Boniface, according to his writings, defending his lord with his shield against a storm of javelins, swords, daggers, knives and crossbow bolts. For this timely act of bravery, Boniface rewarded his loyal friend and court poet with a knighthood.

In the *Epic Letter* Raimbaut celebrated an incident in Italy in which Boniface, with only ten companions at his side, was pursued by 400 knights but did not take flight; instead he turned on his pursuers and struck them so hard that they were overcome with fear. The poem also praised Boniface's part in the Fourth Crusade, although this was not in truth a heroic endeavour – and diverted to the sacking of Constantinople, capital of the Byzantine Empire. Raimbaut summoned a vision of this event as a great chivalric encounter, the emperor of Constantinople fleeing from the crusader army, like a thief, with 'his heart down in his heels' and the Christian army as swift as hawks chasing herons, as fierce as wolves chasing sheep.

▼ *In 1201 Boniface was elected to lead the Fourth Crusade following the death of Count Theobald of Champagne, the original leader, from a mysterious malady.*

SCOTLAND'S GREATEST KNIGHT

SIR WILLIAM WALLACE

Sir William Wallace is celebrated as probably the greatest chivalric figure in Scottish history, heroic leader of resistance to the English invasion of Scotland, victor against all odds at the Battle of Stirling Bridge in 1297. His feats of chivalry inspired an oral tradition of tales about him that were collected together in the ballad *The Acts and Deeds of Sir William Wallace, Knight of Elderslie,* written in c.1470 by a poet called Henry the Minstrel or Blind Harry, and other works in the 16th century including the *History of William Wallace.*

Traditionally Wallace was said to have humble origins that were contrasted with the noble family of his contemporary

▼ *A bronze statue of William Wallace stands in a niche to the right of the gatehouse at Edinburgh Castle. It is matched by a statue of another great Scottish warrior, Robert the Bruce.*

Robert the Bruce. Modern research, however, suggests that Wallace's father was a minor noble, Ayrshire knight Sir David Wallace, a landholder as vassal to James Stewart, 5th High Steward of Scotland. The name 'knight of Elderslie' referred to Elderslie, near Paisley in Renfrewshire, which was once thought to be his place of birth, in c.1270.

GUERRILLA FIGHTER

Wallace first emerged as a guerrilla fighter combating the rule of King Edward I of England, who in 1296 sacked Berwick-upon-Tweed, defeated a Scottish army at the Battle of Dunbar, forced the Scottish king John Balliol to abdicate and, in an act of extreme provocation, removed the Scottish coronation stone, the Stone of Scone, to London.

In May 1297 Wallace led a company of 30 men in an attack on Lanark in which its English sheriff, William Heselrig, was killed. Wallace went on to attack and defeat a series of English garrisons that lay between the rivers Forth and Tay. Blind Harry's ballad invented a background story to add colour to these events. According to his version, Wallace's father and brother were killed after a fight with some English soldiers, and the attack on the sheriff of Lanark was an act of revenge for the Englishman's mistreatment of Wallace's young wife Marion.

Blind Harry also introduced a scene in which Edward I put 360 Scots barons to death at Ayr by sending them on horseback through a doorway, where a noose wrenched them from the saddle and hanged them. In Harry's account, these murders later provoked Wallace to kill the entire garrison by locking the gates and setting the city on fire. He then, according to Blind Harry, led his men to Selkirk Forest to hide, and subsequently – after a tip-off about English movements – they took refuge in the Highlands.

▲ *Sir William Wallace's story, as celebrated by the minstrel Blind Harry, was based more on legend than fact. Blind Harry's ballad was the basis for the 1995 historical movie* Braveheart.

THE BATTLE OF STIRLING BRIDGE

William Wallace's finest hour was on 11 September 1297 when, despite being vastly outnumbered, a Scottish army under his command defeated English forces under John de Warenne, Earl of Surrey, in the Battle of Stirling Bridge. The Scottish force took up position on flat ground to the north of a very narrow bridge across the river Forth and were able to pick off the vanguard of the English army after it had crossed the river, while the rest of the English army was stuck on the south side of the water – the bridge was so narrow that only two knights could cross at a time.

The weight of men made the bridge collapse, meaning that many Englishmen – hampered by weapons and armour – drowned in the river. According to Blind

Harry's version, the bridge was deliberately destroyed, brought down by a Scottish freedom fighter hiding beneath it. More than a hundred English knights were killed, including King Edward's treasurer in Scotland, Sir Hugh de Cressingham. The traditional accounts told that his skin was tanned and used to make belts and sporrans by the Scots, amid wild celebrations – including a new sword belt for William Wallace. After the battle Wallace was knighted, probably by Robert the Bruce himself, and was declared guardian of Scotland and leader of its armies.

THE BATTLE OF FALKIRK

In the aftermath of the battle Wallace raided Northumberland and Cumberland – Scotland was almost entirely clear of English forces at this point. Yet in the following summer Edward I invaded and defeated Wallace at the Battle of Falkirk on 22 July 1298, when the English king's cavalry and archers were far too much for Wallace's spearmen. One account of the battle reports that after the defeat, in flight from the battlefield, Wallace gained some consolation by overcoming and killing the

▼ *This 67m (220ft) sandstone Victorian Gothic monument near Stirling celebrates the career of Sir William Wallace and in particular his victory at Stirling Bridge.*

English knight Sir Brian de Jay, who was master of the English Templars. However, Wallace's reputation was ruined by the defeat and shortly afterwards he resigned as guardian of Scotland.

ESCAPE TO FRANCE?

Wallace disappeared from public view until his capture near Glasgow by the English on 5 August 1305. He may have carried on the battle against the English as a guerrilla fighter. According to tradition, however, he escaped to France – reputedly

▲ *A highly idealized and sentimental Victorian view of the trial of William Wallace at Westminster.*

he hid in the hold of a ship belonging to the pirate Richard Longoville, who was known as the 'Red Reiver' because of the red sails on his ships. Once at sea, Wallace was said to have burst from the hold, overpowered Longoville and forced him to carry Wallace and his men to France. He was also said to have travelled to Rome to ask the pope for aid against the English.

A TERRIBLE DEATH

After his capture Wallace was taken to London, where he was tried for treason – reputedly wearing a garland of oak leaves to signify that he was 'king of the outlaws'. He denied that he could have committed treason since he did not accept Edward I as his king, and was loyal only to King John Balliol of Scotland. After the trial, which inevitably found him guilty, Wallace was stripped naked and dragged by his heels through London to Smithfield, where he was hanged, drawn and quartered. His severed head was displayed on London Bridge and the four parts of his body put up in Aberdeen, Berwick, Newcastle and Stirling.

DEFENDER OF FRENCH CHIVALRY
MARSHAL DE BOUCICAUT

Jean le Meingre, known as Boucicaut, was a leading French knight of the 14th and 15th centuries, a major figure of the Hundred Years War, who also fought on crusades against the pagan Lithuanians in Prussia and against the Moors in Spain. He was famed for his skill in the saddle and defeated many of the greatest English knights of the day in the lists during the celebrated Jousts of St Inglevert in 1390. He also founded a chivalric order devoted to maintaining and defending the ideals of courtly love.

Boucicaut's feats were celebrated in a biography *Le livre des faits du Jean le Meingre, dit Boucicaut* (*An account of the deeds of Jean le Meingre, also known as Boucicaut*). The romanticized account combined real events with conventional stages in the life of a hero. It was written in 1408, while its subject was still alive, indicating the status he had achieved as an exemplar of chivalry.

▲ *Marshal de Boucicaut's final acts of chivalry were performed on the battlefield at Agincourt on 25 October 1415. He spent his last years as an English prisoner.*

LIFE AS A SQUIRE AND FIRST MILITARY ENCOUNTERS

Boucicaut began his chivalric education as a page at the court of King Charles VI of France. He had his first taste of military action at the age of just 12, when he rode out on campaign in the company of Louis II, Duke of Bourbon, in Normandy. He was knighted by the duke at the age of 16 in November 1382 and the next day fought in the Battle of Roosebeke in the County of Flanders (now in Belgium). He distinguished himself as the Duke of Bourbon's army defeated a Flemish force led by Philip van Artevelde.

Boucicaut's romanticized biography states that he was well in advance of other young people in his skill at the chivalric

pastimes, and that he grew up at a distance from others, with a natural reserve and haughtiness that his biographer deemed appropriate for a knight.

Two years later, in 1384, Boucicaut served alongside the knights of the Teutonic Order on their crusade against the pagan Lithuanians. Reputedly he was hungry to find opportunities to prove himself as a knight, and frustrated by a lack of warfare in France. Subsequently, he fought against the Moors in Spain, and afterwards travelled widely, as far as the Holy Land.

THE JOUSTS AT ST INGLEVERT

In 1390 Boucicaut and two other knights, Reginald de Roye and the Lord de Sempy, issued a challenge to fight all comers in a tournament at St Inglevert, near Boulogne, northern France. A year's truce was in place in the long war between England and France, and the challenge had the backing of King Charles VI of France, who made a grant of 6,000 francs to the defenders.

The French knights pledged that they would hold the lists for 30 days from 20 May. The challengers had to indicate on the day before they intended to fight whether they were to compete *à outrance* ('to the uttermost', with a sharpened lance) or *à plaisance* (in a joust of peace, 'for the pleasure', with a blunted lance). They were to do this by touching either a shield of war or a shield of peace put up by the defenders on a spruce tree beside the lists and giving their name, country and the name of their family to the nearby herald. Letters publicizing the challenge were sent far and wide, and as many as 100 knights and squires came from England, with around 40 from other countries.

There were 39 jousts in all, held on the 21–24 May, most fought *à outrance* but none resulting in death or serious injuries. The chronicle report of the event said that the jousting was of a very high standard, with several knights being knocked from their horses, many more losing helmets,

▼ *Boucicaut was a loyal servant of his country and the French king Charles VI, seen here at court receiving English envoys.*

and a large number of lances broken. King Charles VI reportedly attended the event incognito. There was no more jousting after 24 May although the three French knights 'held the lists' as promised in their challenge until 20 June. They were afterwards received as heroes in France.

MARSHAL OF FRANCE

On Christmas Day 1391, principally because of his great service as a crusader against heathens in Prussia and Livonia, Boucicaut was made Marshal of France by King Charles VI in a ceremony at the Cathedral of St Martin in Tours. In 1396 Boucicaut then took part in the Crusade of Nicopolis, as part of an army from France, the Holy Roman Empire, Hungary, Poland, England and other countries against the Ottoman Empire. This campaign ended in a major defeat at the Battle of Nicopolis in which the French general Jean de Vienne was killed and several knights, including Boucicaut, were taken prisoner. He was later ransomed.

THE ENTERPRISE OF THE GREEN SHIELD OF THE WHITE LADY

Back in Europe, in 1399 Boucicaut founded the chivalric order of the *Emprise de l'Escu Vert à la Dame Blanche*

▲ *Boucicaut was one of the three illustrious French knights who jousted against all challengers at St Inglevert in May 1390.*

('Enterprise of the Green Shield of the White Lady'). It had 12 knights as members, sworn for a period of five years to protect women who suffered oppression, particularly widows. Like the other main chivalric orders, the Green Shield of the White Lady had strong associations with tourneying – the order's members pledged to provide opponents in the lists for those who were required by a vow to a lady to perform a specific deed in a tournament but who could not find any competitors.

In 1401 King Charles VI appointed Boucicaut as the governor of Genoa, which had come under French control in 1396. Boucicaut had some success in conflicts against Venice and Cyprus, but the appointment proved short-lived, for the Genoese rid themselves of French control in 1409, while Boucicaut himself was absent on other business.

DEFEAT AT AGINCOURT

Boucicaut fought in the Battle of Agincourt in 1415, where he commanded the French vanguard. Following the English victory he was taken prisoner, and he died in Yorkshire in 1421 after spending his final years in captivity. His body was returned to France and buried in Tours.

THE EAGLE OF BRITTANY

BERTRAND DU GUESCLIN

Breton knight Bertrand du Guesclin, one of the great war captains of his age and a principal commander on the French side in the Hundred Years War, was another warrior celebrated in near-contemporary chivalric biographies. Known as a skilled general, who used guerrilla tactics to great effect against the English army, du Guesclin was famed above all for his impressive feats of arms. He was hailed as 'the Eagle of Brittany'.

Du Guesclin achieved legendary status in his lifetime, and was celebrated shortly after his death in 1380 in the *Chronique de Bertrand du Guesclin* (*Chronicle of Bertrand du Guesclin*), a poem written by Cuvelier. He rose from relatively humble origins among the minor nobility of Brittany to become the Constable of France between

▼ *Du Guesclin's chivalric qualities earned him his elevation to the rarefied position of Constable of France by Charles V in 1370.*

1370 and 1380, and the biographical poem emphasized the point that through deeds of arms it was feasible for squires to attain greatness from humble beginnings.

POOR PROSPECTS

Cuvelier's account emphasized that early in life the future knight's prospects looked poor. His parents were put off by his unattractive, swarthy looks and his aggressive manner, and although he was their eldest son (of ten children) they treated him like a mere servant. However, a passing nun predicted great things for the young man and caused the parents to think again. Then he ran away from home and lived for a while as a leader of warring gangs of village boys.

THE UNKNOWN KNIGHT

We know little of du Guesclin's early career. Cuvelier made up a story that he distinguished himself, aged 17, as an

▲ *Bertrand du Guesclin rose to high office, but was renowned for his simple warrior qualities – generosity and great energy.*

unknown knight at a tournament in 1337 at Rennes. The story recounted how du Guesclin arrived on a carthorse at the tournament, at which his father was competing. With such inadequate equipment, the young man was laughed out of the lists, but he managed to borrow armour and a horse from one of his cousins. He entered the tournament lists with the visor of his helmet closed, so that no one could recognize him, and defeated 12 knights, knocking every one of them from their horses. When his own father challenged him (not knowing who he was) du Guesclin refused to fight. He then jousted on until a Norman knight rode up to him and raised his visor with the tip of his lance: all were astounded at the disclosure, and his father was delighted to see the young man's true identity.

In the 1340s du Guesclin appears to have fought as a 'robber knight' from a base in Paimpont forest, near Rennes, harassing English forces. One story recounted how he took the castle of Grand Fougeray with a clever ruse: he disguised some of his companions as woodcutters, and sent them to the castle gates carrying stacks of wood. The English garrison let them in, then the 'woodcutters' flung down their wood and so blocked the gates open, allowing support troops to enter and take the castle.

KNIGHTING AND EARLY SUCCESSES

In fact du Guesclin was not a squire who leaped to glory – he was already 34 years old when he was knighted on the battle-field while serving under Marshal Arnoul d'Audrehem. He received the honour after distinguishing himself in a minor engage-ment in 1354 while repelling a raid by the English knight Sir Hugh Calveley. In 1356–57 he defended Rennes during a siege set by Henry of Grosmont, 1st Duke of Lancaster (one of the founder members of the Order of the Garter). Although du Guesclin was eventually forced to pay 100,000 crowns to the English army, the

▼ *It was a dark day for France when the 'Eagle of Brittany' succumbed to dysentery on campaign in the Languedoc. The castle that he captured in his last military action is visible in the background.*

▲ *Du Guesclin (left) lowers his lance to avoid fighting his father in the celebrated – and apocryphal – story of how he entered the lists as an unknown knight and defeated no fewer than 12 established knights.*

staunch resistance went a long way to restoring French spirits after the utter humiliation of the Battle of Poitiers.

In 1364 du Guesclin won a resounding victory over the army of King Charles II of Navarre at the Battle of Cocherel. The conflict was part of a disputed claim over the Duchy of Burgundy, and du Guesclin's triumph forced Charles II to abandon his claim to the duchy and make peace with King Charles V of France.

TWO DEFEATS, TWO RANSOMS

However, later that same year du Guesclin suffered a major defeat at the Battle of Auray, which was part of the Breton War of Succession between John de Montfort (supported by the English) and Charles de Blois (supported by the French). Du Guesclin was captured and subsequently ransomed for 40,000 gold francs by the king. Then in 1367 he was fighting in Spain in support of Henry of Trastamara against King Pedro of Castile when he was defeated by Edward the Black Prince in the Battle of Najera (Navarette) and again

captured. On this occasion du Guesclin was allowed to name his own ransom – and set a seemingly unpayable amount, reputedly 100,000 francs. Such was his reputation, and his value to the French cause, that the money was raised by the king and du Guesclin was returned to France.

COMMANDER OF FRANCE

The Hundred Years War against England was renewed in 1369 and du Guesclin retook Poitou and Saintonge from English control. He achieved his country's highest military honour when he was made Constable of France in 1370. He went on to regain large areas of France from the English during the 1370s, using the tactic of avoiding pitched battles until the French were in a sufficiently advantageous position to win.

Bertrand du Guesclin died in 1380 due to dysentery while on campaign in the Languedoc. His life ended, appropriately enough, in a military success – he had just taken the castle of Châteauneuf de Randon from its English garrison. Accounts of his death tell how the captain of the garrison brought the keys and laid them on du Guesclin's body. Such was his stature that he was buried in the tomb of the French kings in the Saint-Denis Basilica, Paris.

HERO IN THE LISTS

JACQUES DE LALAING

The 15th-century knight Jacques de Lalaing was one of the greatest tourneyers of his day. He achieved such renown during his life that he became the subject of two contemporary biographies: the *Chronique de Jacques de Lalaing* (*Chronicle of Jacques de Lalaing*) and the *Livre des faits de Jacques de Lalaing* (*Book Recording the Deeds of Jacques de Lalaing*).

Jacques was born to a noble family from Wallonia (Belgium), and received his chivalric education as an associate of the Duke of Cleves at the court of Burgundy. He won notice in his teens and early 20s in the tiltyard. In 1443, according to the biographies, he excelled during a daring raid carried out by the Duke of Burgundy on the city of Luxembourg. The raiding party used ladders to scale the city walls at night and were at large in the streets before dawn. The city's residents burst from their houses fully armed and heavily armoured but Jacques accomplished many astonishing feats of chivalry with sword and lance, which added to his reputation.

FAME AT NANCY

In 1445, the biographies continue, Jacques amazed onlookers with his performance in a tournament at Nancy held in the presence of the kings of France, Aragon and Sicily. He won four jousts on the first day, even beating an experienced knight from the Auvergne whom he hit so hard on the helmet with his lance that sparks flew and the knight was knocked unconscious.

Jacques was treated as a hero that night and received many gifts from admirers. On the next day he defeated no fewer than eight more knights, but through all this he showed humility and noble bearing.

It was the normal practice in these chivalrous biographies for chroniclers to praise the achievement of their subjects very highly, and exaggerate them, sometimes combining actual events from the life history with exemplary events from a

typical knight's life. However, in the case of Jacques de Lalaing, although many of the events described were extraordinary we know that they were true. The principal author of the *Livre des faits de Jacques de Lalaing* was Jean le Fèvre de St Remy, who served as herald to the Order of the Golden Fleece. His balanced account of Jacques's life does not gloss over the times when the knight almost met his match.

'FEATS OF ARMS'

In the same year, 1445, Jacques embarked upon his 'feats of arms' – prearranged encounters with other knights fought in full armour with weapons of war but according to agreed rules – either a fixed

▲ *In the tournament at Nancy, Jacques struck one opponent from his saddle so hard that he landed a full 7m (24ft) away.*

number of courses on horseback and on foot, or until one of the combatants was knocked to the ground. The first meeting was in Antwerp with Jean de Boniface, an Italian knight who was on a tour seeking opportunities to prove his chivalric worth. The agreed terms were for jousting until one of the knights broke six lances, then fighting on foot using first spears, then poleaxes, swords or daggers. The fight would end when one knight surrendered, or touched the ground with his hand, knee or any part of his body.

Before the contest commenced, Jacques was knighted by the Duke of Burgundy. As was appropriate Jacques then proved himself worthy of the honour: he disarmed de Boniface by knocking the poleaxe out of his hands, then forced him backwards with his own weapon. The Duke of Burgundy, who was refereeing, brought the contest to an end.

IN CASTILE AND SCOTLAND

In 1446–47 Jacques went on tour seeking glory, in the course of which he defeated a champion in Castile. In 1449 with his uncle Simon de Lalaing and a Breton squire named Herve de Meriadec, Jacques fought in a 'combat of six' against three Scottish knights at Stirling, before the king of Scotland. In fierce combat Jacques and his compatriots acquitted themselves well.

Later that year in Bruges he defeated an English squire, Thomas Que, when he came as close to defeat as he ever would after his hand was badly cut by the spike of the English squire's poleaxe. Yet, in great pain and with blood flowing, Jacques fought on and threw Que to the ground.

▼ *In a long career in the lists Jacques saw off many challengers, but neither he or nor any knight could withstand siege cannon, one of which ended his life at Poucques.*

▲ *In many of Jacques's 'feats of arms', jousting was followed by fighting on foot.*

'PASSAGE OF THE FOUNTAIN OF WEEPING'

Jacques then announced a challenge to all-comers to defeat him in a passage of arms. He was to erect a pavilion on the first day of every month from 1 November 1449 to 30 September 1450 and accept challenges to fight, either on horseback with lances, or on foot, either with poleaxes or with swords. The pavilion was hung with three shields, representing the three types of combat: challengers approached the pavilion and touched the appropriate shield. It was next to a fountain with a statue of a weeping woman and Jacques's challenge was called the 'Passage of the Fountain of Weeping'. He remained undefeated throughout the entire year, fighting 11 knights and squires. He entered some of the conflicts without armour on his right leg, and in one he fought without an armoured gauntlet on his right hand.

Afterwards Jacques made a pilgrimage to Rome. When he returned to the court of Burgundy he received a hero's welcome. In 1451 he was admitted to the chivalric brotherhood of the Order of the Golden Fleece, founded by Philip the Good, Duke of Burgundy, in 1430.

Jacques was killed by cannon fire while fighting for the duke of Burgundy at the siege of Poucques on 3 July 1453 during a campaign against Ghent. Jacques was just 32 years old at the time of his death, which was given added poignancy by the sense that – as with 'the English Achilles', Sir John Talbot, killed by gunfire at Castillion just two weeks later on 17 July 1453 – modern weaponry had dispatched a great knight, one who understood the traditional ways of chivalry and fought according to them.

THE 'ENGLISH ACHILLES'

SIR JOHN TALBOT

John Talbot, 1st Earl of Shrewsbury, was probably the most daring English commander of the Hundred Years War, so feared by the French for the ferocity of his lightning campaigns in 1427–53 that he was called the 'English Achilles' in reference to the Greek warrior who vanquished Hector before the walls of Troy. Talbot was a prolific knight who won no fewer than 40 battles and minor encounters in France, where his speciality was in surprising the enemy and conducting very aggressive attacks. In a manner typical of the age in which he lived, he combined ruthlessness on the battlefield, and a liking for making trouble off it, with a deep respect for the chivalric tradition and a staunch Christian faith.

NO LOVER OF PEACE

Sir John was a soldier from his youth, and according to some accounts fought aged around 16 in the royal army at the Battle

▼ *King Henry VI of England, proclaimed as King of France following the death of the French king, Charles VI, invests Sir John Talbot as Constable of France in 1436.*

> **SIR JOHN TALBOT**
> **Born**: 1384
> **Died**: 17 July 1453
> **Knighted**: unknown; made a Knight of the Order of the Garter c.1424
> **Famous for**: the ferocity and speed of attacks on French campaigns
> **Greatest achievement**: routing the French forces at Ry, 1436 – despite commanding a far inferior force

of Shrewsbury in 1403 between King Henry IV of England and a rebel force under 'Hotspur' – Sir Henry Percy. Certainly by the following year he was serving the king in the wars against Welsh rebels, and he fought in Wales for five years until 1409.

In 1414–19 Talbot was Lieutenant of Ireland, and by this stage had already gained a reputation for ferocious raiding tactics, which he used against Gaelic chieftains. One local chronicler noted of him that 'from the time of King Herod there has never been a more wicked soldier here'. In Ireland and back in England he

was a troublemaker, quarrelling fiercely with rival lords, and at one stage being thrown into the Tower of London.

KNIGHT OF THE GARTER

Talbot served Henry V briefly in France then after the king's death in 1422 was made a Knight of the Garter in 1424 by Henry VI. In 1427 he began a long period of military service in France, during which he truly made his name.

But his start was not propitious: in 1428–29 he took part in the siege of Orléans, and was unable to prevent its relief by Joan of Arc, then in June 1429 he was captured at Patay and held in prison for four years. He was released only after the French knight keeping him captive was himself captured by the English.

FAMOUS VICTORIES IN FRANCE

Thereafter Talbot went from strength to strength. In 1434–35 he defended Paris against the French army, then in autumn 1435 he withdrew to Rouen to defend Normandy. Probably his most famous hour came in January 1436 when, with only a small force at his disposal and with Rouen under threat, he launched a surprise attack that completely wrong-footed a much larger French army at Ry. In 1436 he was appointed Constable of France. Another of his celebrated feats was the retaking of Pontoise in February 1437 when his army attacked across the winter ice at dawn on Ash Wednesday, and totally surprised a garrison that was still in recovery after the celebrations of Shrove Tuesday (Mardi Gras).

In 1439 Talbot won another victory with a small force against a 6,000-strong army under Constable Richemont. His swift manoeuvres were often an attempt to bring the enemy to battle. In 1441, for example, he chased a French army back and forth four times across the rivers Oise and Seine trying to force a pitched battle.

LAST OF THE GREAT KNIGHTS?

The way in which he met his end on 17 July 1453 enhanced his reputation. He was leading an attempt to relieve the town of Castillion, which was under French siege, and in characteristic fashion attempted to catch the French off guard with a swift attack. However, the French army was entrenched in a strong defensive position and had substantial artillery at its disposal. The English attack came to nothing and Talbot was shot when he attempted to rally his men. He was celebrated thereafter as one of a dying breed of great knights, and his death seemed to symbolize the collision between an old way of making war and the sheer destructive force of artillery guns.

For all that he was a troublesome man and could be utterly ruthless, Talbot had many notable chivalric qualities. Throughout his long career he was extremely loyal to the royal house of Lancaster, and as a military general he was admired for his spirited raiding and his bravery in battle. He had a genuine inter-

▲ *Talbot died at Castillon in 1453. The attack he launched there, in the face of the French artillery, was rash – and resulted in his death. Following this defeat England lost nearly all its French possessions.*

est in the traditions of chivalry, and he compiled a collection of poems and handbooks that he gave to Margaret of Anjou when she married King Henry VI of England in 1445. He was a Knight of the Garter from 1424 to 1445, and quarrelled with fellow knight Sir John Falstoff whom

▼ The adventures imagined for questing knights could be quite exotic. In an image from a 'book of romances' given to Sir John by Margaret of Anjou c.1445, knights encounter some rather puny elephants.

he accused of having disgraced the order when he fled from the field of battle at Patay. Talbot established a collection of ornaments with Garter decorations for use on St George's Day at the Church of the Sepulchre in Rouen. He went on pilgrimage to Rome in 1450.

Initially Talbot was buried at Castillion, where the French expressed their admiration for his chivalric life by building a chapel in his honour. (It was destroyed during the French Revolution, but a memorial continues to mark the place where he died.) On his death a French chronicler hailed him as one who had been a thorn in the side of the French for many years. Sir John had an enduring reputation for chivalry in England and is a significant character in Shakespeare's play *King Henry VI Part 2* (c.1590–91).

CHAPTER TWENTY-ONE

KNIGHTLY LOVERS AT COURT

The French churchman and courtier Andreas Capellanus (meaning 'chaplain') attempted to codify the rules of engagement between knights and their ladies at court in *De Amore* (*About Love* or *The Art of Courtly Love*), written in *c.*1190. It was traditionally believed that the book described 'courtly love' as practised at the court of Eleanor of Aquitaine at Poitiers in *c.*1170, and was written for her daughter Marie de Champagne, but modern historians have cast doubt on this. Andreas argued that true love could not exist between a husband and a wife since it must be secret, difficult if not impossible to act on, and unconsummated. In this form it ennobled both the lover and the beloved and inspired the lover to great deeds of chivalry. The social system and romantic conventions in *De Amore* had been developed throughout the 12th century by the troubadours of Provence. One pioneer was Eleanor's grandfather William IX of Aquitaine, said to be a fine knight, a composer of songs, a deceiver of women and one of the world's most courtly men. The rarefied society of the knights and ladies who accepted the conventions of courtly love was at odds with the simple military ethos of the knights of Charlemagne as celebrated in *chansons de geste*. While Charlemagne's noble paladins expressed themselves primarily through physical deeds, religious ardour and plain emotions, the primary concerns for those committed to courtly love were affairs of the heart and distinctions of status.

▲ *Knights in romantic tales would fight in single combat for the right to woo a lady.*

◄ *Sir Lancelot steals his first kiss with Queen Guinevere. Their affair was typical of courtly love, pursued in secret and in defiance of marriage vows, but unlike many romantic attachments it was consummated, with tragic results.*

GAMES OF LOVE

HOW KNIGHTS PROVED THEIR DEVOTION

The interactions between ladies and their knights, in gardens or at tournaments, or even when knights departed on quests to prove their love, often resembled games. They were played for a high stake – the lady's love.

The 13th-century French poet and author of romances Jean Renart produced a striking vignette of highly refined courtly love in his narrative poem *Le Lai de l'Ombre* (*The Lay of the Shadow*) in c.1220. The poem concerns an educated knight, skilful in chivalric pastimes such as chess and hawking, who courted a married lady.

▼ *Jean de Saintré kneels before the lady, the Dame de Belles-Cousines, who is giving him an education in courtly love. Jean is a fictional knight, hero of a book (c.1450) by the Provençal author Antoine de la Sale.*

In the manner of courtly love, he had been captivated by her beauty from afar, and having been struck by love, he could apply himself to nothing, and dreamt longingly of his lady.

The poem presented the encounter between the two lovers almost like a chess match, with each attempting to outwit the other within the rules of the game of love, exhibiting detachment from their feelings. The knight approached his lady in a garden by a well, determined to win her over, and she welcomed him. Her first counter-argument to his statement of love was two-pronged: since he was courteous it was impossible that he should be without a true love already, and because he was so skilful in love he was no doubt an old hand at deluding ladies with stories of false devotion. He replied by saying that

her welcome showed that she was pleased to see him, but she responded that her friendliness was only social politeness.

She criticized him for being like many knights in misinterpreting social politeness as the sign of passion. He should not have aimed so high as to attempt to win her, she said. In reply he likened himself to Sir Tristan, describing how that knight had set sail without a mast, trusting in good fortune to bring him to Iseult. She replied and pointed out that she had a husband already who was a paragon of gallantry and chivalry.

The knight said that he was plunged in suffering and implied that it was her Christian duty to relieve it, likening her relieving his pangs of love to going on a crusade. He said he was ready to die for love of her. This gambit seemed to plunge her into deep thought.

Then he slipped a ring from her finger and put his own ring in its place, before quickly departing. Noticing too late what he had done, she recalled him. She said to him that if he loved her he would take it back because all lovers were bound by convention to do their lady's bidding. At this point it seemed that she had caught him. Then he looked down to where her face was reflected in the waters of the well and said he would give the ring to the one person he loved best after his lady; he then cast it on to her reflection saying that since she would not accept his gift or his love he would give it to her shadow. She was charmed by the courtesy of this gesture and accepted his offer of love.

COURTS OF LOVE

The intricate arguments in *Le Lai de l'Ombre* suggested that a third party might sometimes have been needed to judge the victor in the games of courtly love. Indeed, Andreas Capellanus's *De Amore* contained a number of judgements passed by great ladies on lovers at 'courts of love'. These

▲ *Skilful chess playing was one of the prescribed qualities of an educated knight who would make a suitable courtly suitor.*

courts were, in theory, like courts of law, but with ladies as their judges making their decisions according to the rules of courtly love.

The ladies mentioned by Andreas as judges included Eleanor of Aquitaine, Marie de Champagne and Ermengarde, Viscountess of Narbonne. In the 19th century, when the term 'courtly love' was first used, historians suggested that these courts of love actually sat and handed down judgements, but modern historians have been unable to find evidence that the courts existed beyond the references to them in poems. The latest thinking is that the courts mentioned in the poems were a poetic image for the meetings held by ladies, knights and poets at which they enjoyed poetry and debated the niceties of courtly love.

WILLIAM IX OF AQUITAINE

Troubadour poet William of Aquitaine was a man of extremely colourful character and behaviour who was twice excommunicated, yet he was also one of the leaders of the crusade of 1101. Duke of Aquitaine and Gascony, and Count of Poitou, William was the first known troubadour

poet, writing poems concerned with love in the vernacular Provençal language. Eleven of his poems survive under the name Count of Poitou. He was outspoken, and happy to court controversy. One of his poems described a convent in which the nuns should be selected for their beauty – or their ability as whores.

The first time he was excommunicated, for failure to pay Church taxes, he confronted the bishop of Poitiers at sword point, but did not persuade him to withdraw the anathema. The second time he was excommunicated was for kidnapping the Viscountess Dangereuse, the wife of his vassal Aimery I of Rochefoucauld (although she appeared to have been willingly taken). William installed her in his castle despite the fact that he was himself married. His wife retired to a monastery at Fontevrault, and the viscountess lived openly with William – he even carried her image on his shield.

As a knight he was less than exemplary: he was reckless in battle and lost many encounters while on the 1101 crusade. He subsequently fought in Spain, again without much success. His enduring fame rests more on his poetry and on the influence he had over his granddaughter, Eleanor of Aquitaine, who became one of the great courtly patrons.

▼ *In the 13th-century French poem of courtly love, the* Roman de la Rose (Romance of the Rose)*, the garden is the arena for romance. The poem was composed in two halves: the first, by Guillaume de Lorris in c.1230; and the second, by Jean de Meung, in c.1280.*

IN A LADY'S SERVICE

A KNIGHT'S DUTIES IN LOVE

Knights believed that the love they felt for a lady was a spur to acts of great chivalry. As love of Christ and faith in God had driven knights of the First Crusade to overcome seemingly impossible odds and regain possession of Jerusalem, so more secular-minded chivalric successors from the mid-12th century onwards drew inspiration from the lady they admired at court.

A SPUR TO ACTS OF DARING

In c.1130 in his *History of the Kings of Britain*, Geoffrey of Monmouth noted during a description of a bohort or peaceful tournament held at the court of King Arthur, that 'the ladies refused to grant their love to any warlike man who had not proven his bravery three times in battle'. He added that, as a result, in order to win the love of fair ladies the knights of the Round Table were 'ever more daring'.

LADY BECOMES LORD

French troubadour Bernart de Ventadorn (c.1130–90) compared the ties between a lover and his lady to those of the feudal relationship between a knight and his suzerain (feudal superior). This became a common image in the poems of courtly love. As the knight conventionally went through a long training, first as page, then as squire and finally as knight, so a lover would have to emerge from the ranks of hopeful admirers to be accepted as a devoted suitor and, in cases of high achievement, might finally become the lady's lover.

The knight offered service to the lady, as in a feudal relationship, and she offered protection to the knight, just as a feudal lord would. From this idea developed the custom of knights wearing a lady's 'favour' – usually a scarf or cloth – in tournaments or during a campaign. From the lady's love, or at least her interest, the knight drew strength.

To win the love of his lady the knight had to impress her. All his chivalric traits – bravery, courtesy, generosity, prowess and loyalty – were used to this end in order to generate his worth in her eyes.

A DISTANT TARGET

Within the conventions of courtly love some knights declared their love for and devotion to ladies they had not even met. Just hearing tales of a lady's beauty and the perfection of her bearing and manners was enough in some cases to convince a knight to dedicate himself to her service. Even if she were close at hand, the lady was often elevated far above the knight who devoted himself to her. She could prove a very hard mistress to please – in many cases the greatest deeds of devotion were not enough to win her favour.

OBEDIENCE EVEN UNTO SHAME

The knight had also to be obedient to his lady. In chivalric literature knights were sometimes ordered by their lady to do

◀ *For honour, and to win the admiration of his lady, a knight throws himself lustily into the jousting at a country* pas d'armes.

what must almost have been unthinkable – to fight deliberately badly at tournaments and bring shame on themselves. In the Old French romance *Perlesvaus* (*c*.1210) Sir Gawain was told by his lady to identify himself among the other identically armoured knights in the lists by losing repeatedly. He was obedient. When a knight approached to fight, Gawain fled on horseback and spent the rest of the tournament hiding behind King Arthur. (In a colourful image the romance said that Gawain was clinging as closely to Arthur as a magpie clings to a bush when it is trying to escape falcons that are intent on seizing it.)

Gawain lost a great deal of honour in the escapade, for Arthur was greatly ashamed of his knight and the other knights commented openly that Gawain did not serve his great reputation. But he was sustained by the knowledge that he had done it out of motives of the purest chivalry – to prove that his love for his lady was stronger even than his concern for his standing at court.

JOURNEYS OF DEVOTION

It was a duty for newly made knights to seek opportunities to prove themselves worthy of their new condition. This was

▼ *As part of his adventures in* Chrétien de Troyes's Knight of the Cart, *Sir Lancelot beheads Sir Meleagant, who had abducted Guinevere, and presents the head to her.*

one reason why knights were often made at the start of a campaign or just prior to a battle, because the knighting was a spur to acts of chivalry. In the same way, within the conventions of courtly love, a knight who had just won a lady's attention or love was expected to find ways of proving himself worthy of her. This often involved embarking on a career of knight errantry, travelling away from the lady and seeking adventures to win her love.

▲ *A devoted knight returns at the end of a quest in this romantic painting from 1921 by Sir Frank Bernard Dicksee.*

THE CHURCH AND COURTLY LOVE

The Catholic Church condemned the conventions and culture of courtly love. The official Church position was that marriage was a sacrament of the Christian Church and that within it sex was acceptable only as a means of procreation – ideally, Christians of the period were expected to be celibate. The poets of courtly love, on the other hand, praised romantic love, often between knights and married ladies, emphasized the power of sexual attraction and implied that acts of adultery were understandable when passions ran so high. One response of the Church in the 12th century was to begin to promote the cult of the Virgin Mary, Mother of Christ, as a focus for some of the passionate devotion that was otherwise directed along secular channels in love affairs and courtly love attachments.

KNIGHTS ERRANT
TOURS OF CHIVALRY

A familiar figure in the medieval romances, a knight errant was a knight who embarked on a long journey of adventures, often to prove his worth to his chosen lady, in order to win or justify her love. The journey generally involved marvellous adventures such as encounters with giants or rogue knights.

THE FIRST KNIGHT ERRANT

The first knight known as a knight errant in chivalric literature was Sir Gawain in the late 14th-century English poem *Sir Gawain and the Green Knight*. Challenged to attend the Green Knight's chapel after a year had passed, Sir Gawain embarked on a long journey with many adventures. When he reached the castle of Sir Bercilak (who turned out to be the Green Knight), he was greeted as a 'knyght erraunt'.

▼ *The slaying of a dragon was one among the many feats of strength performed by Sir Yvain, with his companion the Lion.*

However, many knights undertook a life of adventures of the kind we now call 'knight errantry' long before the Gawain poem was written. The convention had its roots both in the extravagant adventures of folklore – such as the Welsh legends which contain the earliest accounts of Arthurian knights – and in the tourneying trips embarked upon by knights as early as the 11th or 12th centuries. On these tours knights would travel to different tournaments seeking sport, renown and wealth through taking ransoms.

A FRANKISH KNIGHT AT THE CROSSROADS

An anecdote told of a Frankish knight during the First Crusade indicates that when knights embarked upon these trips seeking adventures they expected contests on their travels as well as at more formal tournaments. The story, told by Anna Comnena, daughter of Byzantine emperor Alexius Comnenus, tells of a Frankish

▲ *A lady attends to her knight as he prepares to embark on the quest to which she has commanded him.*

knight who sat on the imperial throne of Byzantium in the presence of her father, and was reprimanded for his lack of respect. He responded with defiant pride, declaring himself a noble Frank, saying that back in the French countryside there was a well-known place for issuing and answering challenges to combat to prove one's worth as a knight. The spot was at a crossroads near an old shrine and any knight could wait there, ready to fight, until another warrior came who was brave enough to compete and determine who was the most chivalrous. The knight in Anna Comnena's story said he was so famous that, although he had often waited there, no one had ever challenged him.

THE KNIGHT WITH THE LION

For some knights the voyage as a knight errant became an end in itself, and undermined the relationship with the lady. The Arthurian knight Sir Yvain, for example, stayed away so long on his journey of adventures that he clean forgot his lady at court – his wife, Lady Laudine – and for a while she banned him from returning.

Sir Yvain was based on Owain, an Arthurian knight in Welsh legend, where he was married to the sister of Iseult and in some versions was said to be the son of a goddess named Modron (a version of the witch Morgan le Fay). His story was given prominence by French poet Chrétien de Troyes in his poem *Yvain, the Knight of the Lion* (*c*.1170). In this account, Sir Yvain travelled into a magical forest to challenge a knight called Sir Esclados, who had defeated and humiliated Yvain's cousin, Sir Calogrenant. Sir Yvain killed Sir Esclados, then won the love of his widow, Lady Laudine, whom he married.

Back at court, Sir Gawain persuaded Sir Yvain to embark on a voyage of adventures and Lady Laudine allowed him to go on condition that he return within a year. When he forgot about her and she banned him from returning, Sir Yvain went mad with grief but at last recovered sufficiently to attempt to win her love back. He saved a lion from a serpent, and it became his companion, travelling with him as a symbol of his chivalric virtue: he became known as the 'Knight of the Lion'. Finally, impressed by his achievement, Lady Laudine permitted Sir Yvain to return.

As we saw in Chapter Five, this story was used as the basis for the staging of an Arthurian tournament held at Le Hem, Picardy, in 1278 by the lords of Bazentin and Longueval, when Robert II, Count of Artois, appeared as Sir Yvain with a live lion in his company. The stories of knight errantry were frequently the inspiration for theatrical enactments at tournaments, and there were many other examples of travelling knights in the Arthurian tales, notably in the story of Sir Lancelot.

SIR AMADIS OF GAUL

Another celebrated knight errant in the Arthurian tradition was the Portuguese hero Sir Amadis of Gaul, whose tale of wandering adventures dated from the

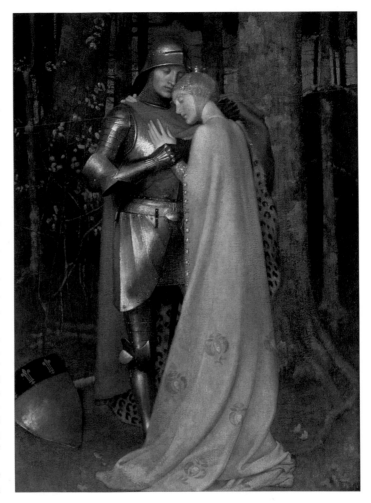

early 14th century. It was published in 1508 and became a great bestseller in Spain and Portugal in the 16th century.

Sir Amadis was said to be the son of Queen Elisena of England and King Períon of Gaul, and was abandoned on a barge in England. He had a chivalric upbringing from a knight named Sir Gandales in Scotland, then was knighted by King Períon and went through many adventures in an enchanted land. His lady, Oriana, became jealous of him and sent a letter denouncing him, which plunged him into madness from which he recovered only when Oriana's maid was sent to save him.

▲ *The forest – and in particular areas near water – was the haunt of female spirits. Warriors often encountered temptations of love on their trips of knight errantry.*

After fighting in support of Lady Oriana's father, King Lisuarte, he travelled for ten years as the 'Knight of the Green Sword' and ventured as far away as Constantinople where he defeated a great giant. Throughout his adventures Sir Amadis showed himself courteous and sensitive, and devoutly Christian, as well as unbeatable in battle and unafraid to spill blood.

THE GLORIES OF CHIVALRIC LOVE

ULRICH VON LICHTENSTEIN, JAUFRÉ RUDEL, LORD OF BLAYE AND SIR WILLIAM MARMION

The knights errant described in courtly romances had many imitators in the medieval era. The 13th-century Austrian knight and Minnesänger Ulrich von Lichtenstein described how he embarked on a long journey of adventure and fought in many tournaments to prove his love to his lady. The reputed feats of 12th-century French knight and troubadour Jaufré Rudel, Lord of Blaye, and those of the 14th-century English knight Sir William Marmion make intriguing comparisons.

JOURNEY IN A LADY'S SERVICE

Ulrich von Lichtenstein was a leading noble from the Duchy of Styria (now southern Austria), who served Margrave Heinrich of Istria as page and squire and was knighted in 1222 (in his early 20s) by Duke Leopold VI of Austria. He was also a notable poet, and portrayed himself as a chivalric knight and courtly lover par excellence in his 1255 poem *Frauendienst* (*Service of the Lady*).

According to the poem, Ulrich travelled from Venice to Vienna in 1226 disguised as the Roman goddess of love, Venus, to win honour for his lady. Every knight he met he challenged to a joust in his lady's name. In the course of his travels he broke no fewer than 307 lances and was undefeated in a single joust. But his lady remained unimpressed, and demanded further deeds to prove his devotion. He then planned a second quest in honour of a different lady, and disguised as King Arthur, but he never managed to embark on this quest.

In his poem he declared that a knight who, with courage in his heart, won the praise of his lady thereby also won great honour. He also declared that the knight should banish fear entirely, because the smallest trace of cowardice would make him unworthy of his lady's attentions, and he should also be willing to die rather than fail in order to win her acclaim.

JAUFRÉ RUDEL AND LOVE FROM AFAR

Jaufré Rudel, Lord of Blaye (near modern Bordeaux in western France), was a knight and troubadour of great renown in the mid-12th century about whom a colourful fictionalized biography was created.

In his poems he specialized in the convention of knights loving from afar ladies they may never have met. One of the few references to him outside his surviving songs – in a poem by the 12th-century troubadour Marcabru – suggests that he was *oltra mar* ('beyond the sea' – that is, on crusade). Rudel probably died while travelling on the Second Crusade, which took place between 1145 and 1149.

The legend of his life told that he took the cross and went on crusade because he was inflamed with a desire to glimpse and honour Countess Hodierna of Tripoli, whose beauty and dignity were praised lavishly by travel-weary pilgrims coming back from the Holy Land. He declared her to be his *amour de loin* ('distant love') and pledged his devotion to her before he departed; but during the voyage he fell terribly ill and when he reached Tripoli he was close to death. The countess, hearing of his devotion and his serious illness, descended from her castle to see him, and held the knight in her arms. In that instant he died in an ecstasy of fulfilled desire blended with a deep sense of his own unworthiness.

◄ *Knights could not really have jousted in the rounded area represented in this illustration from the 15th century. The knight on the left wears a fine heraldic swan on the top of his helmet.*

THE EXAMPLE OF SIR WILLIAM MARMION

In the 14th-century border wars fought between England and Scotland, Sir William Marmion rode to almost certain death to satisfy his lady's desire for renown. In *c.*1320 the Scots had the upper hand in the border conflict, and the castle of Norham in Northumberland was the scene of almost constant fighting between its English garrison and Scottish raiders. Around this time Sir William Marmion was feasting at Lincoln when his lady sent him a gilt-crested war helmet with the message that he should seek out the most dangerous place in the land to win her acclaim by wearing it in battle. He took counsel with his fellow knights at the feast and all agreed the best place to go would be Norham, so he travelled there with the splendid helmet in his possession.

Only four days after his arrival, a great raiding party numbering 160 brave-hearted warriors marched to the castle. The castle constable, Sir Thomas de Gray, called on Sir William and persuaded him that this was his chance to attain glory: 'Sir knight,' he declared, 'you have come to make your helmet famous ... Climb on your horse, behold your enemies, use your glittering spurs to launch a charge into their midst.' The constable said that he would prepare to fight but would hold back until Sir William had had his chance to prove his worth.

▼ *By 1823, when JMW Turner painted this view of Norham Castle in Northumberland, the scene of Sir William Marmion's heroics was a romantic ruin.*

▲ *A knight takes leave of his noble wife. His exploits on campaign or his adventures win honour both for himself and for his lady.*

Then, wearing magnificent armour that shone with gold and silver, and with his bright helmet sparkling in the sunlight, Sir William rode out alone to take on the raiders. He put up a noble fight, but was so outnumbered that he was injured in the face, dragged from his horse and was at risk of death. At this point Sir Thomas and the knights of the garrison rode out and drove all the raiders back in disarray; they helped Sir William remount and at his side they chased the raiders far into the countryside. William Marmion's chivalric feat is told in the chronicle *Scalacronica* written in *c.*1355 by Sir Thomas Gray, son of the Sir Thomas in the narrative.

ORLANDO IN LOVE
THE ROMANCES OF ITALY

A new cycle of romance epics in 15th- and 16th-century Italy cast a fresh light on the adventures of Roland, Oliver and other paragons of chivalry at the court of Charlemagne. Matteo Maria Boiardo's poem *Orlando Innamorato* (*Orlando in Love*) and Lodovico Ariosto's *Orlando Furioso* (*Orlando Maddened*) combined the military feats of Charlemagne's knights with narratives of courtly love that were developed in the Arthurian romances.

LOVE SEEN THROUGH A KNIGHT'S EYES

Matteo Maria Boiardo was a knight and a lyric poet. He served as captain of Modena in 1480–82 and of Reggio in 1487–94. He wrote a highly personal collection of love poems, describing his passion for Antonia Caprara and published in 1499 as *Amorum libri tres* (*Three Books on Love*). His

▼ *Orlando learns the terrible news that Angelica has eloped with the Saracen knight Medoro to Cathay (China). The scene is from Lodovico Ariosto's* Orlando Furioso.

Orlando Innamorato was the first poem to combine elements from the Carolingian and Arthurian romances. Boiardo also added classical influences, for he was a poet during the Italian Renaissance and translated many classical works by authors including Herodotus, Xenophon and Apuleius.

Boiardo's epic, which was left unfinished at his death, described the quests of Orlando (Roland) and many other knights to win the love of the beautiful pagan princess Angelica, daughter of Galafrone, the king of Cathay (China), and her love for Orlando's cousin Ranaldo. (Ranaldo was previously encountered in the *Doon de Mayence* cycle of *chansons de geste* as the hero Renaud de Montauban.) These quests, which included a full complement of bruising encounters, amid celebrations of great icons of the chivalric tradition such as the horse Bayard, with magical spells and exotic characters, were set against the background of Charlemagne in Paris coming under attack from a great Moorish army. In *Orlando Innamorato* the

virtues of religious faith, military honour and love of one's country are celebrated above all others.

LOVESTRUCK AT THE TOURNAMENT

Orlando Innamorato began with an account of a great tournament held in Paris by Charlemagne. The beautiful Angelica and her brother and champion Argalia arrived, declaring that whoever could defeat Argalia could have the hand in marriage of Angelica.

Orlando fell in love with Angelica at first sight, despite the fact that the beautiful Lady Alda (in this version of events, his wife) was at his side. Argalia proved to be invincible since he wore magic armour; he and his sister had really come to lay low the great champions of Charlemagne in preparation for an invasion by an army of Moors led by Agramante, Emperor of Africa. Argalia was also drawn by the fame of the Frankish knights: he wanted above all to capture Orlando's famous sword (here known as Durindan) and Ranaldo's horse Bayard.

After the first two jousts, in which Argalia triumphed, he and Angelica withdrew into a magical forest called the Forest of Arden. The leading knights of the court followed. Ranaldo drank from a magical stream whose waters made a knight hate his lady: thereafter he loathed Angelica. She, on the other hand, drank water from a stream that made those who did so fall in love, and seeing Ranaldo asleep nearby she fell in love with him. He woke, saw her, looked on her with hatred and rode away. She fell asleep on the ground.

Orlando found Angelica and was watching her when he was challenged by a passing knight – a typical event in the romances and tales of knight errantry, and one that made them popular as themes for enactment at tournaments of the age of chivalry. The knight, named Feraguto,

▲ *Sir Roger, a knight in* Orlando Furioso, *rescues Lady Angelica while mounted on a hippogriff – a legendary creature that is half horse and half griffin.*

fought with Orlando until they were interrupted by Feraguto's sister Fiordespina, who told him he had to return to Spain to defend his homeland against attack by an Asian king.

FIGHT IN AN ENCHANTED GLADE
Many more adventures followed. Orlando spent a period in an enchanted garden where he forgot his love of Angelica, his loyalty to Charlemagne and even his own love of honour, but he escaped and then at Angelica's castle at Albraca (believed to be Bukhara in Uzbekistan) he fought a Tartar emperor, Agricane, who was

another rival for Angelica's love. Their epic battle, in a magical forest, went on all day and through the night by moonlight until dawn. When finally Orlando prevailed, his rival declared his desire to become a Christian and begged to be baptized. Orlando consented to his wish and baptized him at a fountain in the wood.

ORLANDO DRIVEN TO MADNESS
The wanderings of Ranaldo, Orlando and Angelica eventually led them back to France, where Charlemagne was still being besieged by a pagan army. The poem was left unfinished at Boiardo's death but a continuation was written by Lodovico Ariosto in his poem *Orlando Furioso*, published in 1516.

Ariosto was a knight and courtier who, after briefly serving as commander of the

citadel of Canossa, was in the service of Cardinal Ippolito d'Este and later became governor of the province of Garfagnana in the Apennines. His poem was also set against the backdrop of a war between Christians commanded by Charlemagne, and Saracens led by Agramante near Paris. Ariosto's poem described how Orlando was driven into madness and despair by his unrequited love for Angelica, while a pagan champion named Ruggiero (who was a descendant of the ancient paragon of chivalry, Hector of Troy) devoted himself to the Christian maiden Bradamante. She was Ranaldo's sister and rode in white armour as the 'Virgin Knight'. The plot involving them was a tribute to the poet's patrons, the Este family, who were traditionally said to be descended from these two lovers.

WHEN A CHRISTIAN LOVED A PAGAN

IF KNIGHTS OF ONE FAITH LOVED LADIES OF ANOTHER

Tales of love between Christians and pagans, such as that between the pagan warrior Ruggiero and the Christian maiden Bradamante in *Orlando Furioso*, were a common theme in the courtly romances. Another great Italian epic poem, *Jerusalem Delivered* by Torquato Tasso, cast the historical figure of Tancred de Hauteville, who was a hero of the First Crusade, as the central figure of a romance, and invented a love affair for him with a Muslim warrior maiden named Clorinda. Such difficult inter-faith romances allowed for enchanting adventures in exotic locations as well as celebration of the ultimate triumph of the 'true faith' – it was an essential conclusion, as in *Orlando Furioso*, for the pagan to renounce his or her faith and seek baptism in Christianity.

A TALE TOLD BY CRUSADERS

A very popular version of this narrative was *Floire et Blancheflor*, a 12th-century French metrical romance that told of the undying love between Floire, warrior son of a Saracen king, and Blancheflor, the daughter of a Christian countess. The story is believed to have come originally from a Greco-Byzantine source, and was perhaps brought back to Europe from the Holy Land by crusader knights returning from a campaign.

The oldest known version of the tale was a French one of *c.*1160, and after 1200 it appeared for about 150 years in a variety of vernacular versions across Europe. An English romance version, *Floris and Blanchefleur*, of *c.*1250, was extremely well received. In the 14th century Giovanni Boccaccio told a version of the same story in his *Decameron* (*c.*1350).

PILGRIMS UNDER ATTACK

The original French version began with a Frankish knight travelling on the well-worn pilgrim path to the shrine of St James at Santiago de Compostela in northwest Spain. In his company was his daughter, recently widowed, and pregnant by her dead husband. The Frankish knight was killed in an attack by Fenix, King of Muslim Spain, and the daughter was taken into captivity. At Fenix's court – supposedly at Naples – the daughter gave birth, on Palm Sunday, to a girl, Blanchefleur, while on the same day Fenix's wife gave birth to a son, Floris.

The two children were raised together and when the time was ripe they fell in love. Fenix, wanting to prevent his son from marrying a Christian, sent Lady Blanchefleur away to Cairo (called Babylon in the poem), telling his son that his love

◄ *Cherubs look joyfully on as Tancred baptizes the Muslim maiden, Clorinda, in the climax of* Jerusalem Delivered.

▲ *For veteran crusaders and pilgrims, stories of Christianity and Islam at odds in love were an intriguing recasting of the war of the faiths fought out in the Holy Land.*

was dead. Sir Floris's grief was so extravagant that King Fenix, fearing his son might die, told him the truth. Sir Floris immediately travelled to Cairo to find her.

He found her incarcerated in a 'tower of maidens' kept for the pleasure of the emir, or ruler, of Cairo. Each year the emir selected a new virgin from the tower to be his wife, and killed the previous one. Floris played chess against the tower watchman, and managed to get himself smuggled into the tower by hiding inside a basket of flowers. There he encountered Lady Blanchefleur, and the couple were blissfully reunited. However, the emir grew suspicious and, visiting the tower, he caught Floris and Lady Blanchefleur together. His impulse was to kill them, but he restrained himself and asked his advisers, who were impressed by the intense love that the couple had for each other and asked that he spare them.

Floris was knighted by the emir, upon which he married Lady Blanchefleur; meanwhile, Blanchefleur's friend Lady Claris married the emir, who repented of the wickedness he had formerly shown and promised to kill no more brides. Shortly afterwards, the news arrived that

Sir Floris's father King Fenix had died, and Floris and Lady Blanchefleur therefore returned to Spain. Sir Floris converted to Christianity and ruled justly with his Christian bride. He even persuaded the people of his kingdom to convert to Christianity as well.

The English version of the story emphasized the chastity of the lovers. When discovered by the emir they told him that they had not consummated their love and he tested their claim by making Lady Blanchefleur bathe her hands in magical water that would discolour if she were not a virgin. She passed the test and as a result, in honour of their chaste self-control, the emir set them both free.

AUCASSIN AND NICOLETTE
Another popular tale of love across the religious divide was that of *Aucassin et Nicolette*, an early-13th-century French *chantefable* (a story intended for singing at court, proceeding through alternating segments of sung verses and recited sections of prose). It told of the love between Aucassin (a Christian knight and the son of the count of Beaucaire) and a Saracen maiden in captivity, Nicolette. It is thought to have been based on the same Greco-Byzantine original as *Floire et Blancheflor*.

Nicolette, daughter of the king of Carthage, was stolen as a young girl by slave traders and ended up as a servant of Sir Garin, Count of Beaucaire, near Arles in Provence. Sir Garin's son Sir Aucassin saw the slave girl and began to fantasize about her. He had been a very promising knight, a strong young man of great prowess, but now he began to abandon the military arts of war and just drifted about, dreaming of Nicolette.

The situation became so bad that when the town was besieged, Sir Aucassin refused to help his father in the fight, declaring that he wanted only to ponder on his love for Nicolette. Then his father was furious and sent Nicolette away, although he did not tell Sir Aucassin. Eventually Sir Aucassin said he would fight for the defence of his city if he could

▲ *The forest, the place where Aucassin and Nicolette (and other lovers of romance) were reunited, is presented as a place untouched by the laws of the world.*

see Nicolette one more time. His father agreed, without admitting that he had sent her away, and Sir Aucassin spearheaded the garrison of the town to a great victory over the besieging army.

Then Sir Garin admitted what he had done to Nicolette. Sir Aucassin was overcome with distress. He went for a ride in the magical forest nearby, and discovered Nicolette there. They were together for a while, but later travelled to a distant land, and became separated again. Nicolette returned to her father in Carthage and Aucassin travelled sadly home.

The final stage of the drama began when Nicolette set forth from her home disguised as a minstrel, with her face darkened by berry juice, determined to track her lord down. She came to France and performed a song before Sir Aucassin, who did not recognize her. The song, about a lady called Nicolette, moved Sir Aucassin to tears, and he offered the minstrel a vast amount of money to travel to Carthage in order to persuade the lady to return. Then, seeing that her beloved lord was still deeply devoted to her, Lady Nicolette revealed her true identity and the lovers were joyfully reunited.

INTO THE OTHERWORLD

KNIGHTS AND THEIR FAIRY LOVERS

It was a common theme in courtly romances for knights to enter into a mysterious 'Otherworld', where they could became lovers of fairy noblewomen. They could generally come and go from this Otherworld without harm, although there was often an element of danger attached to their dealings with ladies and lords of that often menacing world.

LANVAL AND HIS LADY

In the intriguing 12th-century lay, or narrative song, *Lanval*, a knight of King Arthur had been reduced to poverty because the king was failing to support him, but he found a lover and a patroness in the fairy world. The poem was one of 12 Anglo-Norman lays written by a woman poet known to history as Marie de France (see box). The poems explored and glorified the themes of courtly love.

The song of *Lanval* described how one day Sir Lanval was wandering in the meadow near King Arthur's court when he was waylaid by two lovely fairy maidens – one was carrying water in a golden bowl, while the other held a towel. They took him to the fabulously wealthy home of their beautiful mistress. This Otherworld home was an elegant pavilion, topped with a golden eagle, and was found nearby as if beyond an invisible barrier in the meadow. The lady became Sir Lanval's lover and said she would appear

MARIE DE FRANCE

The author of the lay *Lanval* is known as Marie de France on the basis of a line in the epilogue to a collection of fables she wrote. Marie, whose poems were known in the 12th century, is the oldest known woman poet in French literature. Her delightful and very well-composed songs were almost certainly an influence on the work of later trouvères. Marie may have been Marie de Champagne, daughter of Eleanor of Aquitaine, but since there is some evidence that her poems were written in England, it is more likely that she was Marie, the Abbess of Shaftesbury, half-sister of King Henry II of England, or Marie the Countess of Boulogne, daughter of King Stephen of England, or Marie de Meulan, daughter of a great French lord, who was married to Hugh Talbot. She dedicated the lays to 'a noble king', thought to be Henry II or his son, Henry the Young King.

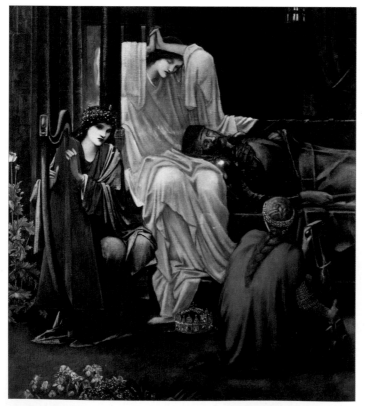

to him whenever he wished and make him as rich as he could want on one condition: that he must not tell another person of her existence. If he did, she would abandon him forever.

Sir Lanval happily accepted her terms. He enjoyed the comfort of eating and dressing well, and of being able to exhibit the chivalric virtue of *largesse* at court. He became known for his generosity: he would ransom prisoners, pay for jugglers and *jongleurs* and feed those without a patron of their own. His lady was happy

◀ *The Isle of Avalon, where Arthur is said to lie asleep, ready to come to the aid of England in her hour of greatest need, is part of the Otherworld realm. Ladies of that land attend him in his deathly sleep.*

for him to do as he pleased, as long as he did not break the one condition of their relationship – its secrecy.

However, one day Queen Guinevere approached Sir Lanval and attempted to seduce him. He rejected her advances, and she declared that he clearly did not like women. He retaliated rashly, declaring that he had a lady of his own who was fairer by far than Queen Guinevere.

Guinevere then accused Sir Lanval of trying to seduce her and denounced him for saying that a chambermaid was more beautiful than she was. Sir Lanval was called before the king in a full court with jury to answer for his actions. The jury declared that if Lanval could produce his mistress and prove that she was more beautiful than Guinevere he should go free. Lanval's heart sank as he realized that he had broken the terms of his agreement with his fairy mistress and that he could never expect her to help him again.

However, at the final moment the fairy mistress appeared before the court to prove that her knight had spoken the truth. She explained that even though he

▼ *In 'La Belle Dame Sans Merci', English poet John Keats wrote of a beautiful fairy lady who captivated a knight-at-arms and robbed him of all his energy and purpose.*

had broken their agreement, she did not want harm to come to him. All present, even King Arthur, were captivated by the beauty of this fairy lady, and they agreed that she was more beautiful even than Queen Guinevere.

As the lady was leaving, Sir Lanval leapt on the back of her white horse and rode away with her into the mists of magic. The poet said that Sir Lanval was never seen again, for she carried him off to the Isle of Avalon, the fabled final resting place of King Arthur himself.

Encounters with fairy women and the Otherworld were common in the Celtic folklore that fed into both the Arthurian romance tradition and into the Breton lays. The story of Sir Lanval, for example, may have had a common folkloric source with the story of Sir Yvain (as described in Chrétien de Troyes's *Yvain, the Knight of the Lion*), for Yvain also met a lady associated with water, and broke a promise to her.

SIR GUINGAMOR

Another Breton lay told the story of Sir Guingamor, with many similar themes to that of Sir Lanval (it was once thought to be another work of Marie de France, but modern historians think this unlikely). In

▲ *Knights who had encounters with ladies of the fairy realm risked losing control of their destiny. Here King Arthur himself lies in a daze before the queen of the fairies.*

this story, the knight was approached by the Queen of Brittany, who tried to seduce him, but he resisted her advances and so she taunted him, daring him to go on the hunt for the white boar – a task that had already cost the lives of ten knights. Like any good knight, Sir Guingamor could not resist the challenge to his prowess and his reputation, and departed on the quest with the king's horse and dogs.

While on the hunt he found a green marble palace and beyond it a beautiful maiden bathing in a pool. She promised him help if he stayed as her lover for three days; he did so and afterwards was able to catch the boar. His fairy lover allowed him to return to his home but warned him that he could not eat anything while there. When he returned to Brittany he found that three centuries had passed. Forgetting his instruction not to eat, he bit into a wild apple, and immediately became extremely weak. He was led back to the Otherworld and installed in the green marble palace by two beautiful maidens.

CHAPTER TWENTY-TWO

SAINTS AND OUTLAWS

The ideal of knighthood as represented in the image of the *miles Christi*, soldier of Christ, called for a saintly devotion to duty in protecting and defending the weak. The ideal found expression in the rule of life proposed for members of religious brotherhoods such as the Knights Templar, which called for taking vows of poverty and chastity, as well in the chivalric literature in the image of the saintly Sir Galahad, the purest of King Arthur's knights. In 1128 the Council of Troyes approved the rule for the Knights Templar that had been submitted by the order's co-founder, French knight Hugues de Payens. The Council's preamble, probably written by monastic reformer Bernard of Clairvaux, contrasted the new order of knighthood with secular knights, who were roundly condemned for failing to carry out their God-given duties, which were 'to defend poor men, widows, orphans and the Church'; far from doing this, the Council said, these knights were in competition among themselves to 'rape, despoil and murder'. The celebration of violence for religious ends embodied in the image of the soldier of Christ was supported by a vision of saints as chivalric warriors. Yet many knights did not live up to the ideal, and chivalric legends and romance also celebrated knights such as Robert le Diable, Guy of Warwick or Fulk Fitzwarin who fought from beyond the law, but were praised for their martial prowess and energy alongside the perfection of chivalry expressed in warrior saints such as St George.

▲ *Crusader knights fight in a battle.*

◄ *Medieval Christians interpreted the story of St George slaying the dragon as the victory of Christian chivalry over bestial sin and false religions.*

THE IDEAL CHRISTIAN KNIGHT

ST GEORGE

St George was venerated as an exemplar of Christian chivalry in the Middle Ages. His image as the perfect holy warrior partly had its origins in the celebration of his deeds by the Eastern Orthodox Church, where he was shown as a soldier in iconography from the 7th century onwards. Crusaders would have seen and been influenced by this iconography.

George was a Christian martyr of the 3rd century, who was traditionally said to have met his end in Lydda (now Lod in Israel). We know nothing for sure about his life, but his story was developed by the 6th century and was known in western Europe by at least the 8th century. The knights who returned from the First Crusade greatly popularized his name and his chivalrous deeds.

MARTYRED BY DIOCLETIAN

According to his hagiography, he was the son of an officer in the Roman army from Cappadocia (an ancient region now part of Turkey) and a mother from Lydda, who

▼ *When George refused to persecute Christians, and declared his own faith in Christ, the Roman authorities executed him before the walls of Nicodemia.*

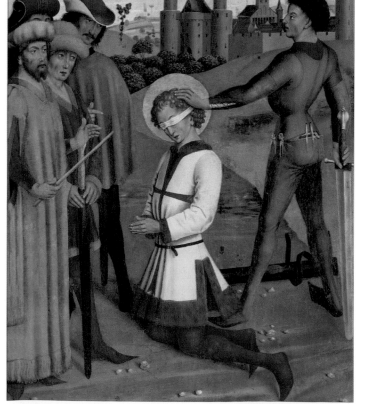

were both Christians. George was a superb soldier and rose through the ranks to become a member of the personal bodyguard of Emperor Diocletian.

In 303, according to the story, the emperor ordered a wave of persecution of Christians, but George revealed himself to be a Christian and refused to take part. He was savagely tortured. One of his terrible punishments was being tied to a wheel of swords. Finally he was beheaded at Nicodemia on 23 April 303. So nobly did he die, dedicating his soul to Christ, that his example convinced the Empress Alexandra and a pagan priest named Athanasius to turn to Christianity, for which they too were executed – in one account more than 1,000 Roman soldiers also converted and were put to death. George's body was taken to his mother's birthplace, Lydda, for burial.

A church built there during the reign of the first Christian emperor, Constantine I, was supposedly dedicated to George and housed his remains. It became a significant pilgrimage site. This building was destroyed in 1010, then the crusaders rebuilt it and dedicated it to St George. During the Third Crusade the army of the great Islamic general Saladin destroyed the holy building once more. It was finally rebuilt a second time in the 19th century.

GEORGE AND THE DRAGON

The celebrated story of St George and the dragon was originally told in the East, and was brought back to the West with the returning crusaders. In Europe it was recast within the conventions of medieval chivalric life – George was represented on a white charger, and killing the dragon with a lance like any knight at a tournament or in a crusader battle charge. The story was part of the very popular *Legenda Sanctorum* (Saints' Readings) – better known as *Legenda Aurea* (*Golden Legend*) – a collection of saints' lives written in *c.*1260 by Jacobus de Voragine, the archbishop of Genoa, which ensured its widespread dissemination.

The story told that the citizens of 'Silene' (perhaps Cyrene in Libya) or, in some sources, of George's hometown Lydda, were terrorized by a dragon that had taken up residence at the spring (or lake) where they drew their water. In order to get water, they had to entice the dragon away from the spring by offering animals and a young virgin, chosen by lots from the townspeople.

One day the victim chosen by chance was the princess, and although the king offered all his wealth in return for his daughter's life, the people refused to draw the lots again. She was sent out to the dragon but George arrived on his charger just as she was about to be given up to the beast. The princess tried to send him away, but George remained and made the sign of the cross before himself, as any good Christian warrior would before combat.

▲ *George represents the Church and all the knights who support it as he rescues innocence in the form of the princess. This fresco of c.1350 is from Verona, Italy.*

▼ *George's cult was strong in the Eastern Orthodox Church. An artist of the Novgorod School painted this icon in c.1150.*

Then George charged at the dragon with couched lance and wounded the beast severely. He called for the princess to throw him her girdle and he put this around the dragon's neck. The dragon came meekly along behind them to the town, where the people, upon seeing it, were very frightened; but George killed it as they watched. The citizens were so grateful to their saviour that they turned their backs on the pagan faith and converted to Christianity. In all the medieval romance accounts, St George's lance was called Ascalon after the city of Ashkelon (now in Israel), which was the scene of the concluding triumphant conflict of the First Crusade, when – fresh from their capture of Jerusalem – the crusaders defeated a relief army that had been sent by Fatimids of Egypt, in the Battle of Ascalon on 12 August 1099.

The dragon-slaying story is ancient and may have had its origin among the Indo-European tribes who spread out from the central Asian steppes to places as diverse as India, Greece and western Europe. It is found in myths from the ancient Near East (told by the Hittites), ancient India and ancient Greece.

PATRON SAINT

By the 14th century, St George was effectively the patron saint of knighthood. In 1348 King Edward III of England designated St George as the patron of his new knightly brotherhood, the Order of the Garter, and during Edward's reign George became recognized as the patron saint of England, replacing St Edmund in the role. During the reign of King Henry V of England (1413–22), St George's Day (23 April) was celebrated as a national holiday. George is also the patron of a very wide range of other countries including Greece, Montenegro, Georgia, Russia and Palestine, and of cities including Beirut and Moscow.

PATRON SAINTS AT WAR
SAINTS AS CHIVALRIC WARRIORS

◄ *St James the Greater (far left) is the patron saint of Spain. Here he is shown with St Jude and St Simon the Zealot. All three were among Christ's twelve apostles.*

At the Battle of Antioch in June 1098 the crusaders reported that they saw St George, St Demetrius and St Maurice fighting alongside them. (St Demetrius and St Maurice were, like George, both martyrs killed during the persecution of Christians in the Roman Empire.) The conflict at Antioch came at a time of heightened religious perceptions. Just before the clash, a monk named Peter Bartholomew claimed to have had a vision of St Andrew, reporting that the Holy Lance used to pierce Christ's side on the Cross was buried in Antioch, and after a search, the Lance was supposedly found. St Andrew then appeared once more and urged the crusaders to fast for five days in order to ensure victory.

The Battle of Antioch was quickly won and the saints, particularly St George,

became associated with the success of the First Crusade. While fighting in Palestine during the Third Crusade of 1189–92 King Richard I of England put the English army under the protection of St George. About the same time, the banner of St George (the red cross on a white background) became the accepted garb for English soldiers.

ST ANDREW AND SCOTTISH TRADITIONS
St Andrew had become established as the patron saint of Scotland in around the 10th century. In the Bible, Andrew was a fisherman on the Sea of Galilee and the brother of Simon Peter, the first pope; he was martyred on a diagonally shaped cross (of the kind shown on the flag of Scotland; known as a saltire in heraldry) at his own

request, because he declared himself unworthy to be crucified on a cross that was identical to the kind used to kill his Lord. According to Scottish legend, St Andrew's relics had been brought with God's guidance from Constantinople to the town of St Andrews in Scotland. A story told that a Pictish king named Ongus (probably Oengus mac Fergus of the Picts, 729–761) had seen a cloud in the shape of St Andrew's cross when fighting the English, and declared that the saint was overseeing the battle and leading the Scottish warriors on to victory.

LEGENDS OF ST GEORGE
There was a well-established tradition of legends and romance stories that presented the saints as chivalric warriors. The English prose romance *The Famous History of the Seven Champions of Christendom* (1596) celebrated the legendary achievements of the patron saints of England, Wales, Ireland, Scotland, Italy, France and

▼ *Weak from hunger but strong in their faith, the crusaders defeated a large army at Antioch. They attributed the unlikely victory to the saints who fought with them.*

▲ *St Andrew, patron saint of Scotland, had many martial associations. According to St John's Gospel, St Andrew was originally a disciple of John the Baptist.*

Spain. It was written towards the close of the age of chivalry by English romance author Richard Johnson, who drew on a centuries-old popular tradition of tales about saints fighting as brave knights against great armies full of heathens and riding to the rescue of courtly maidens.

Johnson's romance claimed that St George was the son of the High Steward of England and was born after his mother dreamed that she was about to give birth to a dragon. He came into the world with a red cross on his hand and an image of a dragon on his chest.

Like many a knight of romance before him, he was raised by a fairy lady in the wilderness of the woods. When George came of age, the lady presented him with his chivalric equipment: a suit of armour made of steel from Libya that reflected the light of heaven, a horse named Bayard (like that of the Carolingian hero Renaud of Montauban) and a sword named Ascalon, supposedly made by the ancient Greek Cyclops.

The lady then showed George an enchanted castle in the forest where she had imprisoned the other patron saints of Europe: St Denis of France, St James of

Spain, St Anthony of Italy, St Andrew of Scotland, St Patrick of Ireland, and St David of Wales. St George turned against the lady and imprisoned her in rock. Then he set the saints free and they embarked upon a series of adventures.

St George himself travelled to Egypt, where he killed a silver-scaled dragon and so saved King Ptolemy's daughter Lady Sabra, who was its next intended victim. Lady Sabra fell in love with St George, which enraged her suitor, King Almidor of Morocco.

King Almidor plotted against St George and sent him to the sultan of Persia with a letter. Without realizing, George was carrying his own death warrant, for the letter said he should be put to death as an enemy of Islam. He was thrown in jail, but on the day of his execution overawed his captor in the style of Richard I: two lions were sent into his cell and he plunged his hands into the animals' chests and tore their hearts out. He was spared execution, but imprisoned for seven years.

▼ *According to one tradition, St George went on to marry the princess he had saved from the dragon.*

UNDONE BY SORCERY

Finally George escaped and was reunited with the other seven patron saints. He sent the other six saints to Persia to defeat the sultan and his Saracen army. They did so in a five-day battle, but then they all fell victim to the tricks of a sorcerer who summoned up a glittering pavilion and a harem of beautiful maidens to entice the saints. The six champions, although saints, fell victim to this temptation and followed the maidens into the pavilion.

At this point St George arrived and he alone of all the saints was able to see through the sorcerer's spell. He pulled down the pavilion and set the other six champions free from enchantment for a second time. A final battle against the pagan forces of Persia followed, which ended in the death of 200,000 enemies of the Christian faith.

St George then enacted the pattern of the Crusades: a religious war led to political gains. He became ruler of Persia and parcelled out the lands he had gained among the other patron saints. Afterwards, all seven patron saints marched home to Europe. They made many converts to Christianity on their journey back.

HOLY WARRIOR

NORMAN KNIGHT ROBERT GUISCARD

The Norman knight and adventurer Robert Guiscard won a great name as a holy warrior in the mid-11th century, fighting on behalf of the papacy in Italy and Sicily against the Byzantine Greeks and Saracens. So great was his reputation that he was celebrated by the Italian poet Dante Alighieri in *La Divina Commedia* (*The Divine Comedy*) of *c*.1310–14, as one of the greatest Christian warriors, and was granted the right to abide in the 'Heaven of Mars', a place reserved for those who had achieved feats of undying fame in the service of the faith (see box).

◄ *Byzantine Emperor Alexius II Comnenus 1169–83 (r. 1180–83), son of Emperor John Comnenus and Empress Irene, depicted in a mosaic in Hagia Sophia.*

SOLDIER OF FORTUNE

Robert was the sixth son of Norman lord Tancred of Hauteville, and came to Italy in 1047 to seek his fortune. His older brothers William Iron-Arm, Drogo and Humphrey were already established in south-eastern Italy, where they fought for the Lombard princes against the Greeks of the Byzantine Empire. According to the traditional tale Robert left Normandy with just five knights and thirty footsoldiers in his company. Initially when he reached Italy he received no help from his older brothers and made his own way as leader of a robber gang, stealing from travellers and the Byzantine postal couriers and even pillaging monasteries.

STRONG BUT WILY

We know from an account by Byzantine princess Anna Comnena (1083–1153) that Robert was a man who had an exceptionally imposing physical presence. She wrote that he was taller than all his peers, broad-shouldered, red-faced with flaxen hair and with a powerful shout that was capable of making men flee. His eyes, she reported, burned with an indomitable spirit: he would be second to no one. (At the end of his career, Robert was a fierce

▲ *Pope Gregory VII relied on Guiscard and on Norman military might in his struggle against Holy Roman Emperor Henry IV.*

opponent of Anna Comnena's father, the Byzantine emperor Alexius Comnenus.)

Robert was also cunning – the name Guiscard was a form of the Old French *viscart*, meaning 'wily' or 'clever as a fox'. His feats were celebrated in *The Deeds of Robert Guiscard*, written by Norman chronicler William of Apulia in 1096–99.

FIERCE IN BATTLE

Robert first made his name fighting against the papal army at the Battle of Civitate in southern Italy, 1053, at a time when the papacy was trying to drive the Normans out of Italy. According to William of Apulia's account, Robert was knocked from his horse and remounted in the heat of battle no fewer than three times. Given the weight of the armour he would have worn and the chaos of the battlefield, this was an extraordinarily difficult feat and would have demanded enormous strength and fortitude.

ALLY OF THE PAPACY

Subsequently the papacy made allies of the Normans and in 1059 Pope Nicholas II (r. 1059–61) invested Guiscard as duke of Apulia, Calabria and Sicily. Guiscard pronounced himself to be a feudal vassal of the pope in these lands, but it would

▲ *Guiscard was one of the leaders of the Norman army that defeated the forces of Pope Leo IX at the Battle of Civitate.*

take a series of conquests over the following 20 years to make these titles a reality: Calabria was mostly held by the Byzantine Greeks, while Sicily was largely in Muslim hands.

Guiscard and his brother Roger took the Byzantine bases in Calabria at Cariati, Rossano, Geraco and Reggio in 1059–60. Then they returned to their base in Apulia to drive back a Byzantine army before invading Sicily. They gradually acquired control of the island.

Back on mainland Italy, in 1068–71 Guiscard besieged Bari, the capital of the Byzantine Empire in Italy. His victory there on 16 April 1071 drove the Byzantines out of southern Italy entirely. Then in 1072 he captured Palermo, making him master of Sicily as well.

THE LORD OF SOUTHERN ITALY

Guiscard made it his business to consolidate all these victories and the areas he had seized. He faced a number of revolts by Norman lords whom he had installed as vassals in his conquered lands, but put them all down in succession in 1073. His power had grown to such an extent that Pope Gregory VII excommunicated him for aggression against papal territories, but by the end of the 1070s they had been

reconciled. Guiscard controlled all of southern Italy save the independent Norman principality of Capua and the city of Naples.

ATTACK ON THE BYZANTINE EMPIRE

Beginning in 1081, Guiscard (although now aged 64) set out to make himself master of the Byzantine Empire. That year he occupied Corfu and then defeated the Byzantine emperor, Alexius, in the Battle of Dyrrhachium near Durazzo in October. The clash between Guiscard and Alexius, revered as among the greatest warriors of their day, soon achieved legendary status.

He might well have succeeded in achieving his ambition of becoming Byzantine emperor, but after taking Durazzo, with the way to Constantinople

open to him, he was recalled to Italy to save Pope Gregory VII. The pope was besieged in Castel Sant'Angelo in Rome by Holy Roman Emperor Henry IV, who had formed an alliance with Alexius.

Guiscard succeeded in lifting the siege and took the pope to safety. He resumed his Byzantine campaigns in 1084. He captured Corfu but he died of fever, along with 500 of his countrymen, on the Ionian island of Kefalonia on 17 July 1085.

After his death Guiscard was celebrated for having saved the ecclesiastical reforms of Pope Gregory VII in the face of the opposition of Henry IV, and as the founder of the Norman kingdom in Italy. He was typical of the younger son who was forced by the feudal system to make his own way in life, and achieved greatness by chivalric endeavour and strength of purpose.

WARRIORS OF THE FAITH IN THE HEAVEN OF MARS

The Heaven of Mars was the fifth of nine heavens encountered by the poet Dante, as described in perhaps the greatest of all works of medieval literature, *La Divina Commedia* (*The Divine Comedy*). The heaven was said to be for martyrs, confessors and soldiers. Biblical warriors Joshua and Judas Maccabeus also appeared to the poet in this heaven,

▼ *Beatrice leads the poet Dante through heaven in* The Divine Comedy. *The pair (left) view the eight holy warriors (right).*

among 'warriors of the faith', as did Charlemagne; Roland; William of Orange, another knight of Charlemagne, celebrated in romance; Renard, a Saracen knight reputedly converted by William; and the famous crusader Godfrey of Bouillon. Dante also praised Guiscard in the section of the poem dealing with Hell, where he described a devastated landscape with spirits reaching as far as the horizon as the image of what Robert Guiscard's enemies would look like after he had dealt with them using the full force of his martial vigour.

OUTLAW KNIGHTS

HEREWARD THE WAKE AND EDRIC OF SHREWSBURY

Alongside stories about the chivalric achievements of saints and biblical warriors, of the paladins of Charlemagne, of King Arthur's followers and of crusader knights, there was a medieval tradition of romance tales about outlaw knights. In England this tradition had its roots in popular narratives about Saxon and British warriors who fought the Norman invasion in the 11th century.

Prominent among these Saxon and British opponents of the Normans were Hereward and Edric. Hereward was a nobleman from Lincolnshire who led resistance to King William I of England from a base at Ely, deep in the treacherous fens, but finally succumbed to the power of the Norman war machine. He was the subject of a vigorous popular tradition, notably celebrated in the 15th-century *Gesta Herewardi* (*Deeds of Hereward*) by 'Ingulph of Crowland', Benedictine abbot at Croyland Abbey, Lincolnshire.

LINCOLNSHIRE LANDOWNER

Hereward appeared in the historical record as a landowner in Lincolnshire listed in the Domesday Survey. The *Anglo-Saxon Chronicle* named him as the leader of an

▼ *The Hereward tradition celebrated fierce native resistance to the Normans. His byname is believed to mean 'the Watchful'.*

▲ *Some accounts claim that Hereward was the son of Leofric, Earl of Mercia, and his wife Godiva, who famously rode naked in the streets of Coventry to persuade her husband to lift a toll imposed on his tenants.*

assault in 1070 on Peterborough Abbey, launched to protest the appointment of a Norman abbot named Turold. Afterwards, the *Chronicle* states, he retreated to Ely, and withstood Norman attacks for a year, then escaped when the rebel stronghold fell.

COURTLY ADVENTURES

The legends cast Hereward as a figure from courtly romance. They told that he was a wild character, who caused so much trouble to his noble father that he was banished from his estate. He then went on a series of romance adventures: tracking and killing a bear in Scotland; rescuing a lady from a giant in Cornwall; fighting in Ireland; then being shipwrecked in Flanders, where after a brief imprisonment he met his wife, Lady Tulfrida, and found a marvellous horse named Swallow.

A KNIGHT IN FLANDERS

It is likely that these adventures had some historical foundation: Hereward appears to have rebelled against King Edward the Confessor, unhappy at the monarch's close connections with the Normans, and was banished from England. In exile he found employment as a mercenary knight in the service of Baldwin V, Count of Flanders. He would have learned chivalry during this sojourn in Flanders.

According to the legend, Hereward returned to England in 1068 only to discover that his father's lands had been seized by the Normans, who had also killed his younger brother and stuck the dead man's decapitated head above the gateway to the family home. In that moment, Hereward dedicated his life to fighting the Normans. He killed the men responsible for his brother's death and gathered rebels around him at Ely. There on an island amid the marshes of fenland, they were besieged by the might of the Norman army, which was led by King William himself.

▶ *William defeats the Anglo-Saxon King Harold, and Norman rule begins in England, in this illumination, c.1280–1300.*

ASSAULT ON ELY

The Normans first tried to attack head-on, building a wooden causeway for their troops across the marshlands. But the causeway collapsed into the mud and many knights lost their lives and valuable equipment in the marshland. Then the Normans tried to bring the rebels down with magic: William employed a witch, who promised to cast a spell that would disarm the Saxons.

Hereward was determined to find out what the Normans were planning, and visited the besiegers' camp disguised as a wandering potter. There he heard the witch discussing her plans. He was not well disguised, however, and was almost discovered, and after getting into a fight in the kitchens he escaped. Just before he disappeared back into the safety of the fenland, he humiliated one of the finest Norman knights by disarming him and

sending him back to his companions with the news that they had missed the opportunity to capture Hereward himself.

Hereward and the rebels set a fire in the marshland that foiled the Normans' next attack. The blaze scattered the besiegers in all directions and the witch broke her neck in the ensuing panic. Eventually the Normans succeeded in reaching their island after the monks of the abbey of Ely showed the attackers a safe way across the marshes, but Hereward and his men, forewarned, took to their boats and vanished into the mists.

One version of the legend suggested that because of his great skill as a warrior Hereward was pardoned by William, and his lands were restored, but another suggested that he was finally tracked down and killed by the Normans.

WILD EDRIC

Another staunch opposer of William I was celebrated in legend as 'Wild Edric'. Edric was a Mercian aristocrat, believed to have been Earl of Shrewsbury, known by a

Latin name, Edric Sylvaticus ('Edric of the Woods') – because he primarily waged guerrilla warfare from the wilderness of the forests. Edric fought the Normans on the English–Welsh borders in c.1067–70. The *Anglo-Saxon Chronicle* reported that with a group of Welsh allies he attacked the Norman garrison at Hereford in 1067. He was also said to have been defeated by King William at Shrewsbury in 1069. In common with many of the local thegns, he had his land seized by force and then simply given to Norman lords; it was handed to either Ranulph de Mortimer or William fitzOsbern.

In the tales of Wild Edric he was said to have become lost while out hunting in the forests and to have taken a fairy bride. Like many other knights, he was deprived of his Otherworldly lady by failing to keep to an agreement – in this case not to speak of her origins. In Shropshire, Edric was celebrated as a warrior-leader in time of need, said to live in local lead-mines and be ready to ride forth at some future date when his country needed him sorely.

THE WILD HUNT

Both Hereward and Edric were said to ride in the Wild Hunt, a stampede of hunters, horses and dogs thought to be fairies or spirits of the dead, which was seen hurtling through the forests or sometimes the sky. Seeing the Wild Hunt was said to presage a disaster. In various traditions across Europe, the great figures of chivalry were said to be seen riding at the head of the Hunt: they included Charlemagne, with Roland carrying his standard; King Arthur; and Dietrich of Berne, the Germanic hero-king based on the 6th-century King Thedoric the Great of the Ostrogoths. Another leader of the Hunt was 'Herne the Hunter' who, according to the legend, was a huntsman in Windsor Park who had saved King Richard II's life then went mad and killed himself.

THE SCOURGE OF THE VIKINGS

SIR GUY OF WARWICK

Hero of English and French romances from the 13th to the 17th centuries, the legendary Guy of Warwick was celebrated as a native English opponent of Viking invaders, a knight errant, a vanquisher of fantastic monsters and paragon of Christian chivalry who rode to the Holy Land and defeated countless Saracens before finally retiring as a religious hermit. His story, probably written for the Norman earls of Warwick, is a good example of the 'ancestral romances' that were produced to glorify the origins of noble houses in the Middle Ages.

The oldest version of Sir Guy's story was probably in a 12th-century French tale. It was then reworked in English and Anglo-Norman versions. The oldest surviving manuscript is the 13th-century Anglo-Norman work *Gui de Warewic*; the oldest English version dates to *c.*1300. The central event in Guy's legend was the defeat in single combat of a mighty Danish warrior named Colbrand, a victory that was said to have saved King Athelstan of England when his capital Winchester was besieged by a Viking army led by kings Anlaf and Gonelaph. This may have had a historical foundation in the invasion of

▼ *The popularity of the Guy of Warwick tales derives in large part from their hero's successes in fighting Danish invaders.*

southern England by Danish troops in 993, although Winchester was actually saved from capture following payment of a bribe rather than victory by any English champion in single combat.

PARAGON OF CHIVALRY

The versions of Guy of Warwick's romance that survive probably contain additions by monastic scribes, for they include a wealth of religious elements. The legend of Guy remained extremely popular for centuries. In the 16th century his reputation as a great Christian knight was so high that he was included in contemporary lists of the 'Nine Worthies'.

According to the legend of his life, Guy was the son of the steward in the service of the earl of Warwick, and he was in love with the earl's daughter, Lady Felice. He was raised to knighthood, and to prove himself worthy of her love embarked on a career of knight errantry. He fought in numerous tournaments in France and Germany; then he freed the daughter of the emperor of Germany after she had been kidnapped; killed a dragon; he then went to Constantinople and fought against great armies of Saracens. He defeated the Saracens' champion Coldran in single combat, then killed the king of Tyre and the sultan of Constantinople. On his return to Warwick he was greeted as a

▲ *King Athelstan kneels before the warrior-turned-mendicant Guy. Athelstan was the first king to rule all of England.*

great Christian knight, a humbler of the enemies of the Christian faith, and Lady Felice finally agreed to become his wife.

PENITENT KNIGHT

However, almost immediately after the wedding, Sir Guy had a vision of Christ, who told him to undertake a penitential journey. Therefore Sir Guy embarked on a pilgrimage to the Holy Land. Perhaps mindful of the fate of Lady Laudine, wife of the Arthurian knight Sir Yvain, who was forgotten by his knight while he was away on a journey of knight errantry, Lady Felice gave Sir Guy a ring to wear, saying that each time he looked on it he should remember her. He wore the ring during his pilgrimage, on which he had many more extraordinary adventures, including conflicts with great giants.

Returning to Warwick once more, he defeated the Dun Cow, a vast cow that was terrorizing the countryside, as well as a boar in Windsor Park and a serpent in Northumberland. After these exploits, he

▲ *The lords and earls of Warwick are commemorated in this chronicle roll, written c.1477–85 by John Rous, priest at the chapel established at Guy's Cliffe.*

fought the Danish champion, Colbrand, who was holding Winchester under siege. The events were said to have taken place in 9th-century England, during the reign of King Athelstan. According to local Winchester tradition the battle against Colbrand took place by the walls of the Benedictine Abbey of Hyde, just outside

THE ANCESTRAL ROMANCE

Sir Guy's legends are examples of the 'ancestral romance': stories that celebrate the establishment of a noble house, or a branch of a family – in this case the earls of Warwick. These poems turn into legendary form the family's past elevation to greatness – as in this legend through the rise by way of martial exploits from humble origins to being fit to enter the established nobility as an equal of Lady Felice. Another of this type of ancestral romance is the Lusignan legend that built family history on the folklore about the water-spirit Melusine.

the city walls. (Hyde Abbey was demolished by Henry VIII in the mid-16th century Dissolution of the Monasteries.)

LIFE AS A HERMIT

Guy's victory over Colbrand won him King Athelstan's devotion. Afterwards, the knight returned to Warwick, but in disguise in order to hide himself away in a hermitage, to spend his last days in prayer and penitence after a life of violence in which he had spilled a great deal of blood. Each day he attended the house of his wife, Lady Felice, disguised in rags, in order to beg for alms. Finally as the appointed day of his death drew near, and he came to know for certain that he was to be called from his life on earth, he sent Lady Felice the ring so that at last she knew what had happened to her husband. She joined him at his hermitage and they were united for the last few days of Sir Guy's life.

GUY'S CLIFFE

The memory of Sir Guy was proudly celebrated in Warwick. Local legend claimed to have established the scene of his later hermitage to be a cliff in rocks above the River Avon just outside the town – a place afterwards called Guy's Cliffe. In 1394 a tower was added to Warwick Castle and

named in his honour, and supposed relics of his life, including his sword and pot, were collected there. A chantry (chapel) was established at Guy's Cliffe, complete with a statue of Guy, in 1423 by Richard de Beauchamp, 13th Earl of Warwick. A country house was built on the site in the 18th century, but it is now a ruin.

▼ *Christ commanded Guy to make penance for his many acts of violence by travelling to the Holy Land. This image is from the Athelstan Psalter (c.950) from Winchester.*

ROBBER KNIGHTS

EUSTACE THE MONK AND ROBERT LE DIABLE

◄ *The tale of Norman knight Robert the Devil – perhaps based on the life of Duke Robert II of Normandy – was popular in later centuries. This scene is from an 1831 opera about Robert by Giacomo Meyerbeer.*

while he was there. It also stated that he became a Benedictine monk in France before embarking on his life of crime and mercenary exploits, and he only left the religious life in order to avenge the death of his father.

The romance told a number of stories in which Eustace put his powers of black magic to the service of his pleasure or in order to enact his revenge. One such tale recounts the time when, after an abbot of a monastery refused to feed him, Eustace brought a pig's carcass to life in the shape of a hideous old woman and made her fly around the refectory driving the monks mad with fear and leaving the way clear for Eustace to seat himself at the high table and enjoy the food on offer.

Some knights of legend and romance were celebrated as anti-heroes for their wicked deeds pursued with great energy. One such story was that of Eustace the Monk, which told of an outlaw knight who was versed in black magic, switched sides at his convenience and accumulated a fortune as a naval mercenary. Similar tales were told in the legend of Robert the Devil, but in his case the wickedness had a purpose, for it led him eventually to take heed of his conscience and he ended his life a glowing example of Christian penitence and religious chivalry.

EUSTACE THE MONK

The romance of Eustace the Monk was written in the mid-13th century by a poet from Picardy. It was based on the exploits of a nobleman's son from Boulogne. According to the historical record, this Eustace was the seneschal of Renaud de

Dammartin, Count of Boulogne, but in around 1204 Eustace was accused of being dishonest, declared an outlaw and had his lands confiscated.

He fled into the deep forest, then became a naval mercenary in the English Channel. He worked for King John of England in 1205–12, commanding a fleet of 30 ships and leading raids along the Normandy coast. With the king's backing he seized the Channel Island of Sark as his base. In 1212, however, he switched sides and began to raid English ports. In 1215 he supported the revolt by rebel barons against King John's rule and he lost his life in 1217 when, while carrying supplies by sea to the rebels in England, he was intercepted by an English fleet and decapitated.

The romance of Eustace followed the facts of this life story quite closely, adding that early in life Eustace had travelled to Toledo in Spain and studied black magic

▼ *The romance of the wicked knight Robert the Devil was still very popular in the 16th century. This is the title page to* The Terrible and Marvellous Life of Robert the Devil, *published in 1563.*

THE WICKEDNESS OF ROBERT THE DEVIL

The legend of Robert the Devil told the story of a French knight, the son of the Devil, cursed to only use his strength in battle for immoral ends. He sought forgiveness and found salvation by riding out as an unknown knight to save Europe three times from Saracen attack. His name and story were connected to those of King William I of England's father Robert II, Duke of Normandy, also known as 'Robert the Devil'.

Duke Robert II of Normandy won a reputation for wickedness, and the nickname 'the Devil', by poisoning his own elder brother Richard in order to win power for himself in Normandy. Both Robert's children – William and Adelaide of Normandy – were illegitimate; they were the offspring of Robert's mistress, Herleva of Falaise.

Towards the end of his life, Robert made William his heir in Normandy and departed on pilgrimage to the Holy Land. According to the account in the *Gesta Normanorum Ducum* (*Deeds of the Norman Dukes*), written by a monk named William of Jumièges in *c.*1060, Robert succeeded in reaching Jerusalem but died on the return journey at Nicaea (modern Iznik, Turkey) in July 1035.

The oldest known version of the legend of Robert the Devil was written in Latin by a Dominican friar named Stephen of Bourbon in *c.*1250. It was rewritten as a 13th-century French metrical romance and was also the subject of a 14th-century miracle play. In the late 15th century, it achieved great popularity as a printed romance, first in French and later in English and Spanish.

THE DEVIL'S CHILD

According to the legend, Robert's mother was unable to have a child and turned to the Devil to help her become pregnant. From his earliest youth Robert was a chivalric prodigy, superb in the saddle, unbeatable in the lists, feared by knights who saw him at large in the countryside.

But because of his father, he was incapable of putting his strength to good use. He was so troubled by his wickedness that he went to the pope to ask for help, and the pope sent him to a hermit who possessed such extraordinary saintliness that he had won dominion even over the evil works of the devil. The hermit told Robert to put himself through a demanding series of penances designed to defeat his self-will. He had to take a vow of silence, get food from the mouth of a dog and endeavour to bring about situations in which he would be ridiculed and humiliated. Robert gladly did these things and at last found peace in his soul.

▼ *Nicaea, where Duke Robert II died, was an important city from classical times, and in 1097 was the scene of the first major action of the First Crusade.*

THE UNKNOWN KNIGHT

However, at this point the city of Rome came under threat from a great Saracen army and memories of Robert's fierceness in battle were still fresh enough to make men call upon him to come to the aid of the Christian city. At first he did not want to go back to life in the saddle, but an angel of God descended to convince him that it was necessary. He rode out as an unidentified knight, without heraldic device on his shield or helmet, and three times he single-handedly drove off the besieging Saracen army.

Finally Robert had succeeded in saving his soul. In variant endings of the legend he was either rewarded with the hand in marriage of the Holy Roman Emperor's fair daughter, or he retired to a hermitage, where he lived out his last days in peace and great holiness.

KNIGHTS OF THE FOREST

FULK FITZWARIN AND ROBIN HOOD

Some knights of legend and romance fought as outlaws because they had been wrongly dispossessed, and were only trying to regain their rightful inheritance. One such outlaw was the Shropshire knight turned forest raider Fulk Fitzwarin.

THE HISTORICAL FULK FITZWARINS

The deeds of Fulk Fitzwarin were celebrated in an English verse romance that is now lost but which was summarized in French, Latin and English versions that do survive. The romance accounts were based on the life of a landowner of that name who lost his property at Whittington, Shropshire, following a lawsuit in 1200. He then spent three years as an outlaw in the forests before being granted a royal pardon in 1203. Then he lived as a knight until 1215, when he joined the barons' revolt against King John. In this period he lost his property again, but regained it after John's death in 1216 and then he spent his remaining years on his estate until he died in the mid-1250s. This life history may combine those of two knights called Fulk Fitzwarin, father and son.

The romance described how Fulk had been raised at the royal court at Windsor Castle following the death of his father, and in this period had quarrelled violently with the future King John over a game of chess. John was losing, it was said, so he turned the board over, scattering the pieces, and hit Fulk in the mouth; Fulk simply hit him back, so John ran to his father King Henry to complain, but Henry told his son off for telling tales. John did not forget this childhood humiliation.

FOREST OUTLAW

In 1200 John got his revenge by dispossessing Fulk of his lands at Whittington and giving them to a rival lord. Fulk swore that he would not serve such a king and with his brothers took to the forests of

▲ *Far from the safety of court or castle, hunting with a few retainers, kings and great lords were vulnerable to attack. King John was ambushed by Fulk Fitzwarin.*

Shropshire. There he made his living by robbing King John's wagon trains and his soldiers. In true romance style, he next had an overseas adventure, spending a period as a pirate in the English Channel, rescuing the daughter of the king of Orkney and saving the duke of Carthage from a dragon.

On his return to England he and his brothers heard that King John was holding court at Windsor Castle and travelled to Windsor Forest. One day when King John rode out hunting, Fulk disguised himself as a charcoal burner and led the king into a trap, where his brothers and supporters were waiting. They surrounded the royal party and made the king promise to become Fulk Fitzwarin's friend once more. But John was dishonest, and as

soon as he had been released he sent Sir James de Normandy out with an armed force to capture Fulk.

IN SIR JAMES'S ARMOUR

In the forest, Fulk was warned that the knight and his men were coming, and he laid another trap. He captured Sir James and then exchanged suits of armour and horses with him. Fulk rode into the castle at Windsor, pretending to be Sir James, and presented the real Sir James to the king as 'the prisoner Fulk Fitzwarin'. Fulk got away with the trick and rode off on a fresh horse provided by King John, before the king had lifted the visor of the prisoner's helmet and discovered that his leading knight had been humiliated by the forest outlaw.

Subsequently there was another great battle in the forest during which Fulk was injured and his brother William was taken captive. Fulk escaped on a horse with the Earl of Chester, rode hard to the coast and managed to make his escape to Spain. He enjoyed further adventures, this time on the Barbary Coast of Africa, before he returned to England to free his brother from the Tower of London. Subsequently he captured King John once more while the king was out hunting, and finally he was able to force him to make peace. Fulk was no longer an outlaw and his castle and lands were restored to him.

ROBIN HOOD

Another great figure of English legend and folklore, Robin Hood, made his living as an outlaw in the forests and was often celebrated as a scourge of King John. In the earliest ballads Robin was just a humble yeoman, but from the 16th century, when his stories were printed, he was presented like Fulk Fitzwarin as a noble knight deprived of his rightful lands. Some versions of the tale also identified him as a crusader knight who returned from his service in the Holy Land to discover that

▲ *Emerging from the forest, Robin and other outlaws have the danger and force that were associated with the teeming natural world, outside the order of a town.*

▼ *One great figure of chivalry hosts another, as Robin Hood and his merry men entertain Richard Coeur de Lion in the forest. Robin lost some of his original menace when he was transformed in legend from an anarchic robber to a supporter of the crusader king.*

his lands had been seized by the corrupt officials of the usurping King John.

There was probably never a single historical figure on which the legends of Robin Hood are based, for the name first appeared in the 13th century as a general one for outlaws. By the following century, popular rhymes were celebrating the feats of a particular legendary outlaw of this name. The tradition of Robin Hood was based on the deeds of actual outlaws such as Hereward the Wake, Eustace the Monk and Fulk Fitzwarin.

In the 15th and 16th centuries Robin Hood was incorporated into May Day festivities, with people dressing as characters from the ballads, a practice that was popular at the court of King Henry VIII. In the early ballads the events were said to take place in the reign of King Edward (without specifying exactly which one), but in the 16th century the stories were relocated to the 1190s, when King John's corruption blighted the lives of the people of England.

PART SIX

DECLINE AND LEGACY OF KNIGHTHOOD

The 14th-century English poet Geoffrey Chaucer, in the Prologue to The Canterbury Tales, drew a portrait of 'a true and perfect gentle knight'. Chaucer served as a squire for that great royal patron of chivalry, King Edward III of England, and fought in 1359–60 in France, where he was captured close to Rheims and had to be ransomed as a prisoner. Chaucer emphasized key qualities of the chivalric code in his knight, who from the first day that he rode out as a knight had 'loved chivalrie, trouthe and honour, fredom and curtesie'. He had, the poet wrote, ridden far and wide 'in his lords werre' (in service of his lord), both in Christendom and 'hethynesse' (heathen lands). He jousted three times 'for oure feith' (in support of Christianity) in 'Tramyssene' (Tlemcen, Algeria) and each time killed his opponent. He was a distinguished knight, who remained humble and modest – and had 'no vileynye ne sayde' (never spoken rudely) to anyone. But Chaucer's knight was soon to face new and well-nigh insurmountable challenges. Beginning in the 14th century, the increasing use of artillery guns and the rise of professional soldiers changed the face of warfare and made the knight outmoded on the field of battle; these developments were coupled with the effects of long-term social changes that brought an end to the feudal societies in which knights had emerged and prospered.

▲ *Richard II of England became known for arrogance and an arbitrary style of government, which in retrospect can be seen to have undermined some of the central principles of chivalry.*

▶ *Geoffrey Chaucer reading the 'Legend of Custance' to Edward III and his Court, at the Palace of Sheen, on the anniversary of the Black Prince's 45th birthday.*

CHAPTER TWENTY-THREE

THE END OF AN ERA

The Battle of Crécy in 1346 saw the first appearance on a battlefield of a new weapon that was severely to undermine the power of the mounted knight – the artillery gun. As the French advanced, their Genoese crossbowmen unleashed an assault on the English, who fought back with their longbowmen and a volley of fire from cannon. The Genoese fled, but the French continued their advance. Italian chronicler Giovanni Villani reported that at the battle's end 'the entire plain was strewn with men brought low by arrows and cannon balls'. Crécy was still a high point in the age of chivalry but the social, political and military changes that were to make chivalry outmoded can be traced back to this date.

Social and political conditions were becoming significantly different from those that had brought knighthood into being – the feudal system was eroding, and the nature of war was altering as kings needed armies for long-distance campaigns. Knights were becoming a minority in armies, and were generally fighting for a fee rather than as a feudal duty to their lord. The rise of the bowmen, the use of infantry and the appearance of artillery made knights less effective as a fighting force. At the same time, the ideal of an international chivalric brotherhood had been deflated as the Crusades petered out in disillusionment and failure. Knights were increasingly grouped in secular brotherhoods, devoted to the service of an earthly rather than heavenly sovereign. These changes played out over the following 250 years, with the result that by the 17th century knights had become something of an anachronism.

▲ *Cannon are depicted in a scene from a siege in 1400.*

◀ *The cannon at the Battle of Crécy marked a change in the character of warfare.*

THE CHANGING FACE OF WARFARE

THE RISE OF INFANTRY AND THE LONGBOW

Changes in military tactics and the evolving nature of warfare reduced the importance of knights riding into battle as cavalry. The increasing use of disciplined infantry lines, and the effectiveness of bowmen against a cavalry charge, increasingly meant that knights were no longer masters of the field of battle in their traditional role.

ARCHERS VERSUS KNIGHTS

It was once proudly declared by English historians that their country's famous victories over much larger French armies in the Hundred Years War were built on the heroic achievement of yeoman archers. However, this traditional view is now seen as rather outmoded and partisan. The more modern view, while arguing that the longbowmen were not decisive in battle, nevertheless accepts that they played a crucial role – the archers blunted the force

▼ *The Battle of Agincourt began with an exchange of arrows and crossbow bolts before the French cavalry made the first charge. The English archers then unleashed a storm of arrows, driving the French knights back into their own footsoldiers.*

of the charge made by the enemy knights, who were then turned back by the lines of infantry. These infantry lines played the decisive role. They included knights who had dismounted to fight on foot.

THE POWER OF THE LONGBOW

It is easy to see why the longbowmen played such an important part. The arrows unleashed by English bowmen in the army of King Edward III at Crécy in 1346,

▲ *Crossbowmen operate their powerful weapons during a siege of Wartburg Castle, Germany, in the early 14th century.*

or that of Henry V at Agincourt in 1415, could knock knights out of the saddle and rip into a horse's flank, sending the beast crashing to the ground and spilling the rider on to the mud. The archers used yew bows of 1.5–1.8m (5–6ft) in length, strung with hemp. Ordinary arrows were of aspen wood with a conventional tip, but the archers also used heavier ash-and-oak arrows capable of piercing a knight's armour – these were 83cm (33in) long with a very narrow 'bodkin' point. The archers sometimes used arrows with 5cm (2in)-wide barbed heads designed to dig into the side of the enemy horse.

The archers' extraordinary effectiveness in battle derived principally from their ability to fire as many as 15 arrows a minute, one every four seconds, to create a volley. They used a high trajectory so that the arrows rained down on the enemy from above in a deadly storm. They also drove sharp angled stakes into the ground, pointing at the enemy, and stood among them as they fired. As the remnants of the

▲ *In the armies of Europe, mounted and unmounted crossbowmen, often mixed with javeliners and archers, occupied a central position in battle formations.*

enemy cavalry charge came upon them, they withdrew backwards, still firing, and the enemy horses and their riders impaled themselves on the stakes.

THE DEVELOPMENT OF THE CROSSBOW

Bowmen in medieval armies used the crossbow as well as the longbow. The crossbow had a bigger range and better penetrative effect against armour than the longbow. The weapons came into widespread use in Europe as early as the 10th and 11th centuries when crossbows were frequently used in sieges by specialist mercenaries from Genoa (northern Italy) or Gascony (south-west France).

The first crossbows were made mainly of yew wood and horn, and fired a bolt, or 'quarrel', around 30cm (12in) long with a pointed steel head. They had a range of about 275m (900ft) but were difficult to load, and as the weapons were made more powerful they were usually fitted with a windlass to bend the bow. Crossbow bolts were very effective against chain mail – and, as discussed earlier, the desire to provide some protection against the bolt was

▶ *Duelling with hand-axes at tournaments gave knights the necessary practice in fighting on foot.*

one of the key incentives for those who sought to improve knights' armour. In the 15th century even more powerful steel crossbows were developed, with a range of up to 450m (1,500ft). They used a square-headed bolt that was strong enough to crack plate armour.

VULNERABLE TO CHANGE

Knights were not well equipped to cope with changes in military technology. As a class they were conservative – while knights dismounted to fight on foot with the infantry, no member of the chivalric class would have considered becoming an archer. Bows were the weapons of the lower classes: crossbows were initially the weapons of specialist Italian mercenaries, while the archers who won great victories for English armies were peasants. Moreover, the bow was considered to be an unchivalric weapon because it encouraged fighting from a safe distance rather than in a face-to-face trial involving strength and prowess. Knights considered that using a bow was a sign of cowardice. The early 12th-century *chanson de geste* about the Burgundian chief Girart de Roussillon declares: 'May curses descend upon the first man who fought as an archer, for through fear he did not dare enter the fray.'

THE DECLINE OF KNIGHTHOOD

Military changes did not suddenly do away with knights in an instant. Both longbowmen and crossbowmen were a long-term problem for knights, dating back almost to the first years of chivalry. As early as 1139, Pope Innocent II had condemned 'the deadly art, which God hates, of crossbowmen and archers, must not be used against Christian knights on pain of anathema'; the effect of longbowmen was demonstrated in King Edward I of England's campaigns in Wales in the late 13th century, but knights continued to be an effective force long after that. The changes in military technology, the tactics of warfare, and the subsequent undermining of the role of knights, were slow and gradual – over centuries. In addition, these military evolutions are difficult to separate from the parallel social, political and cultural changes that were also contributing to the decline of the knight.

THE CANNON AND THE MUSKET

THE FIRST GUNS IN BATTLE

One key aspect of the military changes that undermined the importance of knights in battle was the introduction of the gun. Many of the early guns were difficult and dangerous to use, and they were often inaccurate, but they could be deadly even against full plate armour. Their introduction changed the balance of power on the battlefield, serving to weaken the strength of mounted knights and the use of cavalry as an offensive force.

THE ORIGINS OF GUNS

Gunpowder was probably invented in China, although some scholars argue that Arabs or even the peoples of ancient India were the first to develop the substance. One of the earliest guns was invented by Arabs in 1304: it was a tube of bamboo strengthened with iron, that fired an arrow using the explosive power of an early form of gunpowder called black powder. Gunpowder came to Europe in the mid-13th century – the English Franciscan philosopher Roger Bacon (c.1214–94) described its military uses – but guns of any sort were not widely used in battle until the 14th century.

▼ *John of Gaunt, Duke of Lancaster, used cannon during an assault on the town of Brest, France, in 1373.*

▲ *Firing produced a strong recoil, which was absorbed into the ground at the rear of the gun and through the wooden support.*

EARLY USE OF CANNON

Cannon were wheeled guns that fired iron balls or stones. The earliest reference to their manufacture is from 1326, when the city of Florence acquired two of the guns for defence. The first use of cannon in open battle was at Crécy in 1346.

There was a very wide range of heavy guns, with a wonderful variety of names including veuglaires, vasili, sclopi, pots-de-fer, crapaudines and serpentines. Very heavy cannon called bombards were developed in c.1380. Like many early guns they were inefficient and dangerous.

A later example of the bombard was Mons Meg, made for King James II of Scotland in 1449. It could fire shots weighing 180kg (396lb), and was one of the biggest types of bombard ever made.

Because heavy guns of this sort were so difficult to move about, they were mostly deployed in sieges, where they could have devastating effects on both stone and human flesh. They only came into serious use towards the close of the Hundred Years War (1337–1453). However, there are surprisingly few reports of knights being killed by cannon fire – one victim was Jacques de Lalaing, a knight from Wallonia, Belgium, who was killed in this way at the siege of Poucques in 1453 while serving the Duke of Burgundy in putting down a revolt by the people of Ghent. (De Lalaing's exploits were recorded by the celebrated Burgundian chronicler and herald Jean Le Fevre, a veteran of Agincourt, where he fought on the English side, and a member of the Order of the Golden Fleece.)

▲ *Gunners were vulnerable to attack while operating these early hand-held guns, which were very difficult to load, light and control.*

GUNS IN ISLAMIC ARMIES

The development of firearms and heavy artillery proceeded apace in the armies of Islam. The Moors in Spain used a form of cannon for defending the cities of Seville (1248) and Niebia (1262) under siege. Moorish artillery experts served in the armies of the kings of Spain in the mid-14th century. At the siege of Algeciras in 1342, Moorish defenders used cannon to great effect against the Christian besiegers. (The earls of Derby and Salisbury took part in this siege and may well have helped promote the cannon in England.)

The Ottoman Turks were on the receiving end of cannon fire when they were repelled by Byzantine guns during the siege of Constantinople in 1396. They had their revenge when they used 68 Hungarian cannon including 13 huge guns, each with a bore of more than 90cm (35in) and firing projectiles weighing 320kg (700lb), in their capture of Constantinople in 1453.

HAND-HELD GUNS

The first hand-held guns were developed in the 13th century. Called hand *gonnes*, or hand cannon, they were used in Islamic armies fighting the Mongols in *c.*1260 and appear to have been in use in Europe in 1281 when Italian *scopettieri* ('carriers of guns') were listed as fighting alongside crossbowmen. Early hand-operated guns of the 13th and 14th centuries looked like small cannon attached to wooden poles. The infantryman held the barrel under his arm and ignited the powder – hoping that the whole thing did not explode in his face. The early hand-guns were slow to load and difficult to aim, but if a gunner scored a direct hit he could kill a fully armoured knight outright.

More accurate hand-guns such as the arquebus, or hackbut, were developed in the 15th and 16th centuries. They used round balls as missiles, which could kill a knight in plate armour at short range, but at long range would only dent his armour. (New plate armour of this period was tested by firing an arquebus at its breast-plate and the dent from the ball would be made into a feature of the suit by surrounding it with engraving.) The arquebus was replaced by the matchlock musket in the late 16th century. This gun was as much as 2m (7ft) long and fired 4.5kg (10lb) shot, but could not be used in wet weather. During the 17th century the musket became the main weapon used by infantrymen, replacing the pike.

THE RISE OF GUNS

Knights despised gunners as much as they did bowmen, and in the early days Church authorities denounced them as the work of the devil. In practical terms guns had disadvantages: they were slow to load, of limited accuracy, the larger ones were difficult to transport and manoeuvre and, most of all, in bad weather they often could not be fired at all. But their advantages were that their missiles were more effective than arrows against plate armour, the guns were relatively cheap to produce and use in large numbers, and they could

be fired by troops with little or no training – in stark contrast to the longbow, which was so difficult to use properly that the archers needed to be members of an elite force, trained from childhood and even given a special diet.

CANNON AND NEW DEFENCES

The use of cannon in battle and sieges led to the development of new types of fortifications that were better able to withstand bombardment with cannonballs. The traditional medieval ring-shaped or square fortifications with perpendicular stone walls proved to be very vulnerable to cannon. In the mid-1400s in Italy the trace italienne, or star-shaped fort, was developed: this was a low-lying fortification, made from brick and earth since these materials, unlike stone, would not shatter when hit by a cannonball. It was designed in a star shape to give defenders the opportunity to provide covering fire from several different angles.

The first trace italienne fortifications were designed by the Florentine architect Antonio di Pietro Averlino (1400–69), also known as Filarete, in his *Trattato di architettura* ('Treatise on Architecture') of 1465. That great Renaissance man Michelangelo then put the theory into practice when he designed the earthwork fortifications for Florence. The style soon became widely popular, and was found outside Italy from the 1530s onwards.

▼ *The earliest cannon had to be moved into position by hand; the first wheeled gun carriages were developed in the 1400s.*

PAID TO FIGHT

THE RISE OF PROFESSIONAL SOLDIERS

The knight's military role was also undermined by the use of professional soldiers in armies. Beginning in the late 13th century, rulers in Europe had to force knighthood on wealthy landowners whose birth and wealth made them eligible to become a knight. This was a startling change from the situation in the previous two centuries, when achieving a knighthood was the crowning glory of many a life.

In England in 1292, for example, those gentlemen with an annual income of £40 per year or more were required to accept knighthood and its obligations. A principal reason why this kind of law was necessary is that the cost of equipping oneself as a knight, always high, had risen to such a level that many were unwilling to meet it. The recently developed plate armour was made by Italian and German specialists and was extremely expensive. Heavier armour meant that stronger horses needed to be bred: these, too, were very expensive, and a knight needed to take several with him on campaign because the horse, as we have seen, was a favourite target for the archers and was often killed beneath its rider during battle.

THE USE OF MERCENARIES

There was already a substantial history of paid soldiers and of mercenaries serving in armies. Mercenaries were skilled professionals who hired themselves out to the highest payer – such as the Genoese crossbowmen who were working in this way as early as the 11th century. From the time of King Henry I of England (r. 1100–35) onwards, there were some paid soldiers in otherwise feudal armies. Kings would accept *scutage* (payment) in lieu of feudal military service, and then use the money to pay soldiers.

The oldest surviving military contract in England is from 1213: Lord Robert of Berkeley agreed to provide military service, in company of ten knights, to meet a debt to King John of 500 marks. King Philip IV of France (r. 1285–1314) had a considerable proportion of his army in paid service, including cavalry known as gendarmes (from the French: *gens d'armes,* meaning 'men at arms').

The Hundred Years War (1337–1453) saw many paid soldiers in service on both sides. They were generally infantry or bowmen rather than knights, although King Charles VII of France had 1,500 cavalry serving for fixed pay. In this period Swiss mercenary infantrymen won a wide reputation for their discipline and effectiveness fighting with halberds (long spears with axe-like heads), with which they were able to haul a knight down from his horse. These men were available for hire, and their wearing of uniforms and marching to military music were widely influential. Under the influence of the Swiss, the first state infantry regiments were formed in France in the 1450s. This was part of a general movement in the 15th century towards the establishment of professional standing armies.

CONDOTTIERI

The same period saw the heyday of Italian mercenary bands of knights hired by competing Italian city-states. The leaders of these mercenary bands were called *condottieri,* from the Italian *condotta* for the 'contract' by which they tied themselves

▼ *Condottiere Guidoriccio da Fogliano was commander of the mercenary army of Siena, Italy in 1328, and he is commemorated in the famous fresco believed to be by Simone Martini.*

SIR JOHN HAWKWOOD

Leading *condottiere* Sir John Hawkwood came from humble origins as the son of a tanner in Essex, England. He achieved fame fighting in the army of King Edward III of England during the Hundred Years War, and was reputedly knighted for his battlefield prowess by the king or the Black Prince. In 1363, during a break in English–French

hostilities, he entered the White Company of Italian *condottieri* in the service of Pisa and was elected their captain within a year. He used his own force of longbowmen, and equipped his knights with lighter armour that made his troops more mobile. In *condottieri* fashion, by 1369 he was fighting for a new paymaster, Perugia, against papal troops and within a few years was fighting for the pope against Florence. He became immensely wealthy, with estates near Florence. Chivalry was a foreign concept to him: he would threaten his employers with desertion in order to get more money out of them. He died in Florence in 1394.

◄ *Sir John Hawkwood was known as 'Giovanni Acuto' in Italy. He married Donnina, illegitimate daughter of his then paymaster the Duke of Milan, in 1377.*

to a particular city or nobleman. The bands consisted principally of armoured knights fighting with traditional medieval weapons. The *condottieri* were famous for their ruthlessness and lack of chivalry: they would negotiate hard, driving their fee as high as they could, and were not above switching sides (even in the middle of a battle) if offered more money.

The first of these mercenary bands were non-Italians. The knights of the Catalan Company formed in 1303 had originally been in the service of King Peter III of Aragon, the Grand Company of *c.*1350 principally contained Hungarians and Germans. The English knight Sir John Hawkwood (see box) led the White Company in the wars of northern Italy for much of the second half of the 14th century.

► *Erasmo of Narni was a leading Italian mercenary knight in the late 14th century. His fame was such that the armour in which he fought was preserved for posterity, and Donatello immortalized him in stone.*

In the 15th century the *condottieri* were mostly made up of Italians, and were often noblemen fallen on hard times. Knights in these bands could make a great deal of money in a short period. Towards the close of the century, the *condottieri* bands were mostly overwhelmed by the heavy

artillery of the army of King Charles VIII of France, who invaded northern Italy to enforce his rather threadbare claim to the kingdom of Naples.

Probably the most famous *condottiere* was Erasmo di Narni, better known by his nickname Gattamelata ('Honeyed Cat'). He served Florence, Venice and the papacy and eventually became dictator of Padua in 1457. His renown was such that an equestrian statue of him by Donatello was erected in 1445–50, the first such statue since the days of the Roman Empire.

Another celebrated *condottiere* of the 16th century was Giovanni de' Medici (known as Giovanni delle Bande Nere – 'Giovanni of the Black Bands') who led a company of highly skilled Italian mercenaries during the Italian Wars. He initially fought for Pope Leo X in 1516–21 before switching sides in 1522 and joining the forces of Francis I of France. He then briefly went into the service of the Holy Roman Emperor, Charles V, before returning to French service. Giovanni was fighting in the army of Francis I when he was severely wounded at the Battle of Pavia in 1525. He died in 1526 after injuries sustained while fighting in the League of Cognac war. His name probably came from the black bands of mourning on his banner after the death of Pope Leo X in 1521.

THE LAST DAYS OF CHIVALRY
KNIGHTHOOD AS RANK AND TITLE

By the 15th and 16th centuries both the feudal system and the chivalric tradition had undergone profound changes. The age of chivalry was coming to an end.

DECLINE OF FEUDALISM

The rise of towns in the late Middle Ages had undermined the relationship between a feudal lord and his bonded vassals, replacing it with the one between the king and his subjects or between an elected representative body and a citizen. Because of the increasing importance of merchants, and the trade that made them rich, money was becoming more important than land.

Military changes, as we have seen, played their part in a decline of feudalism. The mounted warrior lost status on the battlefield. The supreme symbol of feudal power, the castle, lost its image of impregnability with the advent of more and more effective siege weaponry and guns. Military architects began to build low-lying fortifications from earth and brick such as the trace italienne in place of traditional defences.

▲ King from the age of 10, Richard II of England became known for arrogance and arbitrary government that encouraged plotting and factions at court and undermined the workings of chivalry.

CHIVALRIC SHIFT

At the same time there were changes in the philosophical, religious and cultural tradition of chivalry, which had grown up around knighthood and come to sustain it. Despite the erosion of the feudal system, knighthood retained its romance, but it began to function in a different context.

The rise of national feeling had profound effects. The religious brotherhoods of chivalry, in which knights' primary duty was religious, through swearing loyalty to Christ and the brotherhood, were replaced by secular brotherhoods of chivalry such as England's Order of the Garter or the Order of the Star in France, in which knights swore loyalty to their king. The traditional chivalric ideal of an international elite of knights, all equal in their brotherhood, was replaced by bodies of

knights tied to the service of their sovereign, conscious of national difference. Increasingly, distinctions of rank were made among knights, who once had been members of an equal brotherhood in which a humble warrior could be knighted on the battlefield for his prowess and become the equal of a prince.

Another contributing change was religious. The rise of Protestantism was associated with patriotism and national feeling and contributed to the undermining of the ideal of the international Christian brotherhood of knights. The humanistic philosophy of the Renaissance ran counter to the religious ardour that had sustained chivalry and driven knights to the Holy Land in the service of Christ.

PAGEANTS

Tournaments had once fulfilled a necessary role as martial training grounds, and provided an arena in which a man of relatively humble birth such as William

▼ Baldassare Castiglione (1478–1529), author of The Courtier, *ushered in a new concern with courtly etiquette among the nobility. When in Rome, he befriended the artist Raphael, who painted this portrait.*

Marshal could win sufficient honour to raise himself to the level of the upper nobility and of royalty. In the transformed world of the 15th and 16th centuries, tournaments were lavish affairs dominated by demonstrations of etiquette as much as prowess. Fighting became less important.

In the 13th and 14th centuries, lesser noblemen held their own tournaments, but the extravagant events of the next two centuries emphasized the pre-eminence of a prince or his near equivalents among the nobility. Tournaments increasingly became pageants, laid on by royal patrons, in order to demonstrate their own magnificence before their leading subjects. Chivalry stopped being a way of life and became an entertainment.

During this period, the chivalric romance that had embodied and sustained the philosophy of chivalry began to fade as a living literary form. Authors under the growing influence of Renaissance ideas turned to classical models. Tournaments abandoned the model of King Arthur and his knights and based their pageants on the warriors of the classical world.

COURTESY AND THE GENTLEMAN

The handbooks on chivalry that had once been so popular gave way to handbooks on courtesy. These books taught not how to be a knight but how to be a gentleman. An early example was *Il Cortegiano* (*The*

Courtier), written between 1513 and 1518 by the Italian courtier and diplomat Baldassare Castiglione. Presented in the form of discussions by courtiers at the Court of Urbino in 1507, the book considers how to act gracefully, with seeming effortlessness; the modesty and qualities that should mark a lady at court; how a courtier should avoid flattery in dealings with his prince; and what forms humour and honourable love should take.

◄ *Edward III confers the Order of the Garter on Edward the Black Prince. The creation of secular bodies of knights was at odds with the spirit of devotion that inspired the members of religious brotherhoods such as the Knights Templar and Hospitaller.*

The idealism of chivalric literature was notably absent in *The Courtier* and similar books on courtesy, which placed more emphasis on presentation, appearance and reputation than on virtues such as humility and bravery, so important in chivalry. In addition, the passion of courtly love was banished; a courtier was expected to show his prince the adoration and committed service that a knight showed his lady.

The gentleman replaced the knight as an ideal. He was a figure of society rather than a warrior. The key to being a gentleman was 'gentle birth': usually it was sufficient to show this status going back for three generations. The knight was a mounted warrior in origin with public status, but the gentleman had no such necessary function. By the end of the 16th century, the word 'knight' had become a title, and indication of social rank.

▼ *Flemish-born artist Marcus Gheeraerts the Elder engraved the procession of the Knights of the Garter in 1576, capturing the spirit of exclusiveness and refinement that was beginning to inform the brotherhood.*

THE ENDURING ROMANCE OF KNIGHTHOOD

REVIVALS OF CHIVALRY

Knighthood retained its romance throughout the long erosion of the feudal system and the decline of chivalric life. In the 16th and 17th centuries, and even later, princes and noblemen looked back with great enthusiasm on the glories of the age of chivalry. Occasionally, even into the 19th century, wealthy lords attempted to revive tournaments and other displays of knighthood.

TUDOR TOURNAMENTS

In England the monarchs of the late Tudor era were already looking back on the golden age of chivalry. Knighthood held a powerful appeal for them – particularly for King Henry VIII, who was a keen patron of and participant in tournaments. Henry designed some of his own armour for competing in tournaments and had an armoury established at Greenwich, near

▼ *At the Field of the Cloth of Gold in 1520, kings Francis I and Henry VIII erected grand temporary buildings and tournament lists that made the area resemble a city.*

London. He established tiltyards for holding tournaments at Greenwich, adjacent to Whitehall Palace (in Westminster) and at Hampton Court Palace (now part of south-west London).

Henry was matched in his devotion to tournaments by King Francis I of France, and their diplomatic meeting near Calais on 7–24 June 1520 was celebrated with an extraordinarily lavish show of the arts of chivalry. In line with the 15th-century *pas d'armes* ('passage of arms') that the kings were emulating, the event was extravagantly stage-managed.

The two kings and their retinues, numbering 5,000, camped in an array of tents and pavilions decorated with cloth of gold (a fabric made with gold thread and silk) – and for this reason the event became popularly known as the Field of the Cloth of Gold. Henry's camp took the form of a temporary palace – mainly built of canvas and painted cloth over timber frames – measuring 10,000sq m (108,000sq ft). Outside Henry's tent was a gilded fountain spouting claret, spiced wine and water.

Each king had a company of seven knights, supplemented by those who had arrived in response to proclamation of the event and who chose to fight on one side or the other. The kings jousted one against the other, and against the opposing team's knights. Upwards of 300 spears were broken, and one French knight was killed. After the jousting there was a form of tournament, but the knights fought in pairs rather than in an old-fashioned mêlée. There were also contests in archery and the two kings reputedly wrestled for a few throws. The kings and the knights dressed in great splendour in an attempt to revive the glories of the age of chivalry.

ACCESSION DAY TILTS

Henry's daughter, Elizabeth, continued the chivalric revival. On 17 November each year from 1570 until 1590 she celebrated the anniversary of her accession to the throne in 1558 with an 'Accession Day Tilt' at Whitehall Palace. The events were part of a deliberate official mythologizing of Elizabeth as a reigning goddess, and

▲ *Elizabeth I of England shared her father's enthusiasm for the age of chivalry and carried on his revival of tournament events.*

aimed also to replace some of the colour and popular entertainment of Catholic feast days, held no more under the Protestant Elizabeth. Her champion, Henry Lee, was one of her favourites, and he rode in her name in the tiltyard established by Henry VIII in the royal palace at Whitehall while the queen and her ladies, situated in a raised palace window, looked down on the chivalric exploits beneath them like ladies at one of the medieval tournaments.

Even in the beginning of the Stuart era in the early 17th century, the enthusiasm for the age of chivalry endured, and King James I's son Henry, Prince of Wales, was a keen jouster. But he died aged just 18 of typhoid fever in 1612. Thereafter, courtly interest in the chivalric tradition in England was focused on the court masques of Ben Jonson and Inigo Jones.

THE CARROUSEL

Events fashioned like tournaments continued to be held in continental Europe. The jousting and tourneying shrank to near disappearing point, while centre stage was given to displays of horsemanship in events called 'carrousels'. The knights in these extravaganzas often wore imitation

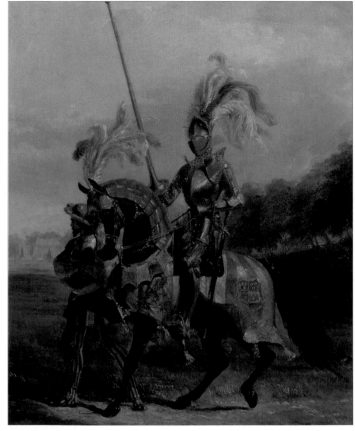

armour. The purpose was to make a show of the magnificence of the sponsor of the event. In time, these gave way to military parades, which fulfilled the same purpose.

INTO THE VICTORIAN ERA

Grand revivals of chivalric tournaments occurred as late as 1839, when the 13th Earl of Eglington held a tournament with jousting at Eglington Castle in Ayrshire. A great crowd of noble guests, enthused by the 19th-century revival of interest in chivalry and medieval life, wore medieval costumes and watched as knights paid homage to Lady Georgiana Sheridan, the Duke of Somerset's wife, in her guise as the event's 'Queen of Beauty'. However, the event was effectively rained off by a Scottish storm that made a mud bath of

▲ *Archibald Montgomerie, 13th Earl of Eglington, had an authentic-looking suit of armour made for his tournament of 1839.*

the lists. Two years in the planning, the event cost no less than £40,000 – the knightly way of life never did come cheap.

THE IDEAL KNIGHT

Right through to the 21st century, the knight has kept much of his lustre as a composite of nobleman and warrior, an idealized expression of personal honour, respectful devotion and religious fervour. His continued appeal is due as much to the knight's role in chivalric literature, with its enduringly popular narratives and affecting elegiac tone, as it is to his historical achievements.

THE LEGACY OF CRUSADING

AND THE MODERN ERA

On 7 October 1571 in the naval battle of Lepanto in the Ionian Sea, the ships of the Christian 'Holy League' commanded by Don John of Austria inflicted a heavy defeat on the fleet of the Ottoman Empire. The Holy League was an alliance of the papal states, Spain, Venice, Genoa, the Duchy of Savoy and the Knights of Malta (as the Knights Hospitaller were by then known). The league was formed by Pope Pius V (ruled 1566–72) to try to wrest control of the Mediterranean from the Ottomans – seemingly all-powerful in the region – after Sultan Selim II (reigned 1566–74) had invaded Cyprus in 1570.

The victory was celebrated as a great triumph for Christendom. The day of the battle, 7 October, was named the feast day of *Santa Maria della Vittoria* (Saint Mary of Victory) by the Catholic Church; in his

▲ *Religious or national war? Pope Sixtus V gave King Philip II of Spain's war against Queen Elizabeth I of England in 1588 the status of a crusade in support of true faith.*

▼ *No longer an invincible force? Christian ships drive the Ottoman fleet to destruction at the celebrated Battle of Lepanto, 1571.*

novel *Don Quixote* (first published 1605), Spanish author Cervantes wrote that Lepanto 'revealed to all the nations of the world the error under which they had been labouring in believing that the Turks were invincible at sea'. For all that, the

victory proved to have little or no long-term strategic effect, for Selim went on to conquer Cyprus in 1571 and in 1574 he drove the Spanish out of Tunisia, where they had made conquests at the start of the century. Nevertheless, Lepanto was important in that it gave a great boost to Christian morale in their long struggle against the Ottomans, which already by that date stretched back more than 200 years to the crusade of 1366, led by Venice, against Sultan Murad I.

The crusading spirit thus remained resolutely alive through the 16th century, and even survived well into the 17th. As late as the 1680s, Pope Innocent XI (ruled 1676–89) formed a new Holy League after the Ottomans besieged Vienna in 1683. The new League included the Holy Roman Empire, Poland, Muscovite Russia and the Venetian Republic and its campaign, culminating in a great victory at the second Battle of Mohacs (Hungary) in 1687, had definite crusading overtones.

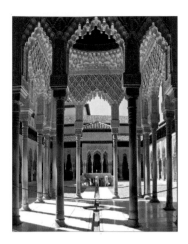

▲ *The beautiful Alhambra palace and fort was the residence of the Granada's Moorish kings in Spain. Via the Islamic courts of Spain, classical learning passed to Christian Europe and helped power the Renaissance.*

AUTHORITY TO CALL WARS

Historians generally identify Lepanto as the last major encounter with the Ottomans explicitly preached and financed (through taxes and the sale of indulgences) as a crusade. Yet all authorities agree that it is impossible to pinpoint a single end date for the era of the crusades. Crusading died gradually away, as the authority for calling and organizing wars passed from the pope and the Catholic Church to kings, princes and other heads of state.

The Protestant Reformation played an important part in this process. Beginning in the 16th century, the Reformation split the Church and undermined crusading. Protestants did not accept the basic premises of crusading – that the pope had the authority to call a war or that Jerusalem needed liberating. German theologian Martin Luther declared that there was no call to free Jerusalem from Muslim control – what did the city contain but an empty tomb?

Protestants, in fact, became the object of crusades. In 1588 Spanish forces were offered crusading privileges to fight in the Spanish Armada against Queen Elizabeth I of England – the crusade in this instance being the war waged by Catholic Spain against Protestant England. In this atmosphere, Francis Bacon, the Elizabethan-Jacobean philosopher and statesman was scathing of crusades and crusaders, writing that the wars were 'the rendezvous of cracked brains that wore their feather in their head instead of their hat'.

EFFECTS OF THE CRUSADES

It is clear that the crusades formed a highly significant period in the long and bloody history of the Holy Land. They contributed to the region's legacy of religiously motivated violence, a legacy whose effects are still tragically felt today. They also have a powerful resonance in the long history of distrust and hatred between some Christians and some Muslims.

Certain historians argue that the crusades decisively changed the course of history in the East. According to this argument, crusader attacks on the Byzantine Empire and, in particular, the capture and sacking of Constantinople in 1203 by the armies of the Fourth Crusade, weakened the empire to such an extent that it was

▼ *As in many crusading conflicts before, the Christian victors at Lepanto attributed their triumph to the intervention of the saints, in this case saints Peter and Paul, in battle.*

unable to resist the later onslaught of the Mamluks of Egypt and the Ottoman Turks – far from strengthening the position of Christianity in the East, the crusades catastrophically undermined it.

Others hold that this argument, which characterizes the Mamluks and Turks as a tide from the East that might have been stopped and driven back by a stronger Constantinople, is mistaken. These historians point out that the Byzantine Empire would probably have been too weak to withstand the Mamluks and Ottomans even without the events of 1203 and that crusader activity resulted in enduring Christian possessions in the East (such as Cyprus) that proved to be important bases for the struggle against the Ottomans.

In Europe, meanwhile, the crusades had a significant effect. Crusading endeavours brought both the Iberian Peninsula and the Baltic region within Christendom, in the first place by reconquering land from the Moors and, in the second, by defeating pagan tribes. The crusades also contributed significantly to the growth in wealth and power of the maritime republics of what is now Italy – cities such as Venice and Genoa, whose merchants carried armies and pilgrims to the East and grew rich on the trade in exotic goods, such as spices, sugar and oranges, that they carried back to Europe from the Holy Land and ports in the Byzantine achievements and endeavours were swept away by the Mamluks in the 13th century. The one truly enduring legacy was cultural, in focusing the attention of Christian Europe on the Holy Land, in encouraging the demonization of non-Christians and in contributing to the creation of a legacy of religious violence in the region.

CONTACT BETWEEN WEST AND EAST

One important side effect of the crusades, evidenced by the success of the trade carried on by Venetian, Genoan and other ships, was the establishment of increased contact between Europe and the East. Many now familiar foodstuffs – including spices (such as pepper, ginger, cloves and cinnamon) and fruits (such as dates, figs and oranges), as well as rice, almonds and cane sugar, according to some accounts – first came to Europe as a result of this trade. Returning traders, pilgrims and crusaders also introduced to European homes glass mirrors of the kind used in Constantinople and rugs and carpets like those found in the castles of Outremer.

Empire. It is no accident that it was in the city-states of Italy, made wealthy by trade, that the European Renaissance began.

By comparison, the crusades had a less permanent effect in the Holy Land and region. While the remains of buildings erected by crusaders, military brotherhoods and settlers of Outremer can still be seen in places, by and large their other

▲ *Venice grew rich on goods from the East – including the loot brought back after the sacking of Constantinople by the soldiers of the Fourth Crusade in 1204.*

▼ *Latterday crusade? A 19th-century painting imagines Christopher Columbus's landfall in the Americas as the coming of a Christian army driven by faith.*

▲ *The Monument to the Discoveries in Lisbon celebrates Henry the Navigator and other Portuguese who contributed to the explorations of the 15th–16th centuries.*

Some accounts claim that the game of chess, which originated in India and spread to the Persian Empire, was popularized in Europe by crusaders, travellers and traders returning from Outremer. Contact between Europeans and Arabs was made not only in the Byzantine Empire and the Holy Land but also in the Iberian Peninsula – itself, as we have seen, a crusade venue.

ANCIENT WISDOM

Contact with Arabs and Moors was, moreover, the route by which a great deal of classical philosophy and science made its way into Europe, where it powered the Renaissance of the 14th–17th centuries. Prior to the crusading era, when Muslim Arabs overran the lands of the Middle East in the 7th and 8th centuries, they found manuscripts and books from the days of ancient Greece and Rome; they were careful to preserve this knowledge, translating many volumes from Greek into Arabic.

Europeans came into contact with this knowledge in the Iberian Peninsula and via the Greek scholars of the Byzantine Empire; many of these Greeks fled to Europe to escape the Ottoman conquest of Constantinople in 1453. One of these was the theologian and collector Cardinal Basilius Bessarion (1403–72), who had been Latin Patriarch of Constantinople: he brought a priceless collection of books to Italy and gave them to the republic of Venice. They today form the core part of the well-known Library of St Mark's.

CASTLES AND CITIES

The crusades also had an effect on the military and sacred architecture of Europe. The monastic military brotherhoods, such as the Knights Hospitaller and the Knights Templar, were great builders. The Templars, as we have seen, built a great number of churches, many round in form as a homage to the *Templum Solomonis* (Temple of Solomon) in Jerusalem, their original headquarters. The brotherhoods also developed the concentric design in castles – the fortress had two sets of walls, a taller set within, around the 'inner bailey', and a lower outer set, around the 'outer bailey'.

We know that the future King Edward I of England was profoundly impressed by Krak des Chevaliers, the Knights' Hospitaller concentric castle near Homs in Syria, which he inspected while travelling on the Ninth Crusade (1271–72) and later, in association with his builder Master

James of St Georges, used the design in his Welsh fortresses, such as Beaumaris Castle in North Wales.

The crusade era also saw the rise of cities. Just as the maritime cities of Italy thrived, so throughout Europe the spread of towns and cities was driven by trade. In addition, kings such as Richard I of England sold off rights of self-government to municipal boroughs as a way of raising money for their wars. Some historians also suggest that the repeated failures of the crusading armies served to undermine feudalism and contributed to its decline as a form of social organization.

CRUSADING'S NEW FRONTIER

In the 15th and 16th centuries, the exploration of Africa and the Americas was in part informed and inspired by crusading ideology. Portuguese explorations of Africa and the Atlantic, organized and financed by Prince Henry the Navigator, were explicitly driven by crusading ideals – Henry was intrigued by the story of Prester John (the legendary Christian king, believed by many of Henry's contemporaries to reside in the East or in Africa and to be preparing a great war against Islam), and one reason for Henry's exploration of Africa was to seek help in the conquest of Muslim powers in the Holy Land.

The adventurer Christopher Columbus was sponsored in his voyages to the West Indies and central and southern America by Ferdinand and Isabella of Spain, who approved his exploration in 1492 immediately after their conquest of Granada. Columbus later declared that the wealth discovered in central America could fund a new crusade to the Holy Land. The Conquistadores who swept into Mexico and Guatemala, were driven by a desire for gold and land, but also by a fervour for religious conversion informed by the Reconquista. The energy, spirit of adventure and religious devotion that had sustained centuries of crusading fed into these voyages of discovery across the great oceans and thus made an enduring mark in the countries of the 'New World'.

INDEX

Abbasids 47, 53, 198, 199, 200, 26
Achilles 389, 392, 393
Acre 9, 96, 97, 100, 138, 153, 156, 165, 171, 174, 177, 191, 251, 260, 261, 264, 265, 303, 376
Council of Acre 192–3, 293
fall 266, 267, 268, 286, 296, 299
massacre 226–7
siege 222–3, 224–5, 293, 298
Adhemar, Bishop of Le Puy 120, 121, 131, 137, 143, 145, 148, 152, 157, 166, 285
Adrian I, Pope 26
Adrian IV, Pope 436
Aeneas 389, 392, 393
al-Afdal Shahanshah 56, 152, 155, 161
Afghanistan 47
Ager Sanguinis (Field of Blood) 180–1, 182
Agincourt 444, 445, 492, 494
Alain de Brittany 37
Alberic of Besançon 394
Albert of Aix 140
Albigensian crusade 213, 237, 244, 307, 314–15, 316, 317, 439
Alcantara, Order of 301
Alcuin 28
Aleppo 190, 191, 193, 196
Alexander III, Pope 261, 300, 301, 303, 437
Alexander of Bernay 395
Alexander the Great 14, 10, 22, 344, 389, 390, 391, 394–5, 440
Alexandria 268, 269, 271
alexandrines 395
Alexis II Comnenus 476
Alexius I Comnenus 116–17, 119, 122, 128, 130, 132–3, 140, 147, 150, 152, 153, 154, 155, 172, 173, 176, 177
siege of Nicaea 134, 135
Alfonso IX of Castile 307
Alfonso VI of Castile 432
Alfonso VI of Léon 309
Alfonso VIII of Castile 244, 310
Alfonso X of Castile 336, 351
Alfonso X of Castile and Léon 47
Alfonso XI of Castile 105, 334
Alfred the Great 34–5, 38, 45, 398

Aljubarrota 66
alliances 84–5
Almohads 237, 244, 310
Amadis of Gaul 459
Amalric I of Jerusalem 168, 198, 199, 201, 202, 204, 223, 293
Anacletus II, Pope 370
Anatolia 46, 48, 116, 127, 128, 129, 134, 136
march across 140–1
Andreas Capellanus 453, 454–5
Aneirin 402
Anglo-Saxon Chronicle 65, 82, 478, 479
Anglo-Saxons 28, 34–5, 37, 44, 64, 83, 95, 98, 418
Anglo-Scots border 70–1, 103, 104–5, 370, 461
Anna Comnena 90, 128, 129, 130, 140, 150, 164, 458, 476
Antioch 48, 138, 140, 141, 143, 152, 153, 261
Bohemond of Taranto 150–1
capture of 146–7, 474
defeat of Kerbógha 148–9
Nur ed-Din 198–9
siege 56, 144–5, 155, 172
archery 60, 95, 492–3
Ariosto, Lodovico 462, 463
Aristotle 43
Arius 24
Arminius 430
armour 60–1, 63, 92–3, 94–5, 137, 184–5, 357
tournaments 378–9
Arnulf of Choques 55, 160–1, 166
Arsuf 153, 177, 260
Battle of Arsuf 9, 211, 229
Arthur 11, 12, 13, 15, 328, 344, 345, 352, 354, 363, 384, 401, 409, 410, 430, 467
historical origins 402–3
Nine Worthies 391, 397
Sir Galahad 416–17
Sir Gawain 418–19
Sir Kay 406–7
Sir Lancelot 414–15
Sir Mordred 420–1
artillery 15, 491, 494–5
Artuqids 180
Ascalon 138, 155, 161
Ascalon 138, 165, 177, 292
Assassins (hashhashin) 231, 293
Assyrians 22, 91
Athelstan 480, 481
Attila 430, 431
Aucassin and Nicolette 465
Audley, Sir James 338, 340, 357
d'Audrehem, Arnoul 447
Augsburg 33
Avars 27, 31, 91
Aviz, Order of 301
Aymeri of Narbonne 427
Ayyubids 248, 250, 253, 258, 260, 283

Bacon, Francis 503
Bacon, Roger 494
Baghdad 46, 47, 53, 196, 198, 199
Balak 182
Balderic of Dol 118, 119, 122
Baldwin I of Jerusalem (Baldwin of Boulogne) 139, 141, 158, 160, 163, 166, 167, 172, 175, 176, 177, 183
Baldwin II of Jerusalem (Baldwin of Le Bourg) 151, 156, 166, 172, 173, 182, 183, 290, 294
Baldwin III of Jerusalem 109, 183, 191, 192, 198, 294
Baldwin IV of Jerusalem 169, 201, 202, 295
Baldwin of Flanders, 238, 239
Baldwin V of Jerusalem 202
Baldwin VI of Jerusalem 169
Balian of Ibelin 202, 203, 204, 205
Ballard, William 84
Balliol, John 336, 442, 443
Baltic crusades 206, 237, 244, 320–1
Banda (Sash), Order of 334, 354, 355, 380–1
banners 99
Bannockburn 67, 91, 104, 105
battles 89, 94–5
Ager Sanguinis (Field of Blood) 180–1, 182
Agincourt 444, 445, 492, 494
al-Mansourah 258–9, 260, 292
Aljubarrota 66
Arsuf 9, 211, 229
Ascalon 138, 155, 161
Bannockburn 67, 91, 104, 105
Bouvines 89, 95, 99
chivalric display 98–9
code of chivalry 108–9
Crécy 67, 103, 340, 353, 355, 356, 357, 491, 492, 494
Cresson 94, 283, 292, 293, 294
Dorylaeum 136–7, 138, 140, 150, 151, 172, 184, 185
Falkirk 336, 443
Halidon Hill 352, 353
Harenc 145
Harran 173
Hastings 37, 90, 93, 95, 98, 107, 424
Horns of Hattin 8, 55, 165, 175, 179, 202–3, 204, 205, 214, 215, 224, 225, 227, 228, 229, 248, 292–3, 301
Jaffa 232–3
Kosovo, Second 277
La Forbie 253, 255, 258, 260
Las Navas de Tolosa 94, 244, 300, 310–11, 317
Lepanto 9–10, 502, 503
Manzikert 47, 48, 16
Montgisard 201
Muret 317
Mount Badon 402
Nicopolis 274, 275
Otterburn 70

▲ A medieval tournament.

Poitiers 95, 99, 103, 106, 338, 340, 353, 356, 447
Rio Salado 312–13
Roncesvalles 27, 31, 98, 341, 424, 425
Stirling Bridge 442–3
Tannenberg 298
Teba 312
Tours 21, 23, 25
Varna 277
Baudricort, Robert de 373
Bavaria 57
Bayard 13, 337, 428, 429, 462
Baybars, Rukn al-Zahir 175, 253, 255, 258–9, 260–1, 264–5, 266, 287, 294, 298
Bayezid I 274, 275
Beaumanoir, Philippe de 346
Beaumaris Castle 81
Becket, Thomas à 61, 261
Bedivere 406, 418, 420, 421
Bedouins 53
Beirut 152, 153, 165, 167, 177, 267
Belgrade 280–1
Belisarius 23
Belvoir 175
Benoit de Saint-Maure 392–3
Bernard of Clairvaux 57, 186–7, 194, 195, 290–1, 295, 416
Bernard of Tremblay 109
Bernart de Ventadorn 456
Béroul 404
Bertran de Born 96
Bertrand de Bar-sur-Aube 434
Bertrand de Gurdun 439
Bethlehem 9, 10, 156, 250, 251
Béziers 316
Biblical world 344, 389, 390–1
Black Prince 11–12, 102, 103, 106, 109, 334, 341, 352, 355, 356–7, 447, 497
Crécy 11, 12, 67
Order of the Garter 68, 354, 367, 499
Poitiers 99
Sir John Chandos 338, 340, 341, 356, 357
Blanche of Castile 252, 260, 261, 262–3

▼ Pembroke Castle, Wales.

Blanche of Lancaster 85
Blind Harry 442–3
Blois, Charles de 447
Blondel 439
blood brothers 350–1
Boccaccio, Giovanni 393, 464
Bodel, Jean 345, 392
Bogomils 315
Bohemia 324–5
Bohemond of Taranto 8, 41, 118,
127, 130–1, 132, 133, 134, 135,
136, 137, 140, 141, 144, 145,
146, 148, 154, 155, 164, 172,
173, 435
Prince of Antioch 150–1, 152, 153,
160, 166
bohorts 87, 363
Boiardo, Matteo Maria 462, 463
Bolingbroke, Henry see Henry IV
Bonet, Honoré 106, 346
Boniface I, Pope 24
Boniface of Montferrat 239, 240, 243,
339, 440–1
de Boniface, Jean 448–9
Bonnivet, Guillaume de 349
booty 107
Bors 411, 414, 417, 420, 421
Boucicaut, Jean le Meingre 276, 323,
384, 444–5
Bouvines 89, 95, 99
Bramborough, Sir Robert 373
Braveheart 442
Brutus 389
Burne Jones, Edward 412
Byzantine Empire 8, 46, 47, 48–9, 51,
116–17, 124, 127, 130, 132, 134,
144, 145, 150, 151, 167, 171,
172, 176, 503
Fourth Crusade 240–1, 242–3, 503
Ottomans 276–7, 278–9, 495
recovery 267
Second Crusade 188, 189, 194,
195, 196
Third Crusade 218–19
Byzantium 23, 27, 322, 476

Caesarea 138, 139, 153, 168, 170,
171, 177, 260
Cairo 9, 47, 157, 198, 199
Calatrava, Order of 300, 301
Callisthenes 394
Calveley, Sir Hugh 447
Camelot 401, 403, 407, 410, 415,
419, 421
cannibalism 144, 147, 152, 155
cannon 15, 449, 491, 494, 495
Canute 35, 36
caravans 169, 170, 175, 202
Carcassonne 316, 318
carrousels 501
Castiglione, Baldassare 498, 499
castles 75, 78, 79 80–1, 336
sieges 100–1, 351
cataphracts 23
Cathars 206, 213, 307, 314–15,
316–17, 318–19
Catholicism 42, 501
Catholic expansion 212–13
cavalry 14, 21, 196, 492
development 22–3, 32, 91
discipline 94
Franks 30–1

Caxton, William 72
Celestine III, Pope 234, 235, 298,
301, 320, 321
chain mail 90, 92, 378
challenges to arms 363
Chandos, Sir John 14, 107, 338, 339,
340–1, 356, 357
chansons 13, 28, 83, 328, 344, 345,
426, 428–9, 453
Chanson de Roland 29, 98,99,
341, 342, 343, 344, 345, 423,
424–5
Godfrey of Bouillon 434–5
Voeux du Paon 391
charging 90, 94
chariots 22
Charlemagne 13, 21, 23, 24, 32, 34,
35, 38, 44, 45, 49, 64, 65, 98,
99, 110, 217
cavalry 30–1
Chanson de Roland 29, 98, 99,
341, 342, 343, 344, 345,
423, 424–5
chansons de geste 426, 428–9
Divina Commedia 477
Holy Roman Empire 26–7, 436
Nine Worthies 391
paragon of chivalry 28–9
Charles II of France
Charles II of Navarre 447
Charles III the Simple 33, 36
Charles IV Holy Roman Emperor 346
Charles IV of France 353
Charles Martel 14, 21, 24, 25, 26, 47,
390, 426
Charles of Anjou 266, 267, 327
Charles of Hungary 190, 380
Charles the Bald 25, 32, 33
Charles the Bold 351, 367
Charles V Holy Roman Emperor 349,
497
Charles V of France 106, 341, 363,
446, 447
Charles VI of France 444, 445, 450
Charles VII of France 79, 496
Charles VIII of France 348, 497
Chaucer, Geoffrey 60, 63, 72, 393,
486
chess 83, 455
chevauchée 102, 103, 357
Childeric III 26
Children's Crusades 246–7, 261
chivalry 11–12, 14–15, 122, 328, 333
battlefield chivalry 108–9
chivalric display 98–9
chivalric expression 334–5
chivalric handbooks 59, 63, 68,
72–3
chivalric orders 300-1, 354–5,
380–1
chivalric shift 498
chivalric symbolism 68–9
chivalric virtues 334
chivalric weddings 85, 364, 367
combat 347
knights errant 458–9, 460–1
meanings 335
reality 343
revivals 500–1
timeline 330–1
Chrétien de Troyes 14, 85, 328, 345,
403, 410, 411, 412, 415, 418, 430,

457, 459
Érec et Enide 408–9
Sir Kay 406–7
Christ 14, 44, 54, 55, 57, 143, 165
Second Coming 43, 119, 121, 125,
218
Christianity 8, 13, 14, 39, 44–5, 50,
52, 53, 160–1, 328, 346, 399, 412
Christian warriors 334–5, 342–3,
346, 423, 471, 498
courtly love 457
Eastern Church 48–9, 51
Great Schism 272, 273, 327
knighting 64, 68
tournaments 364, 370–1
Christine de Pizan 398
Church see Christianity
Cicero 43
Cilicia 167, 172
Clanvowe, Sir John 350
classical world 344, 345, 389, 392–3,
394–5, 396–7, 398–9, 499
Clement V, Pope 286, 296, 297
Clermont 8, 45, 115, 118–19, 120,
122, 123, 124, 125, 131
Clisson, Olivier 351
Clovis I 24, 44
coats of arms 92, 378
heraldic disputes 383
Columbus, Christopher 504, 505
Combat of the Thirty 373
condottieri 496–7
Conrad III of Germany 8, 187, 188–9,
190, 192, 193, 194, 216, 436
Conrad of Montferrat 214–15, 216,
222, 223, 224, 231, 238
Constantine III of Cilicia 87
Constantine the Great 48, 52, 54–5
Constantinople 8, 9, 46, 48, 49, 51,
117, 122, 124, 125, 127, 134, 172,
176, 177, 189, 267
Fourth Crusade 240–1, 242–3, 503
Ottomans 276, 277, 278–9, 495
People's Crusade 128–9
Prince's Crusade 130, 131, 132–3
Corineus 389
corsairs 272, 273, 286
Council of Acre 192–3, 293
Council of Troyes 11
County of Edessa 141, 163, 166, 167,
172–3, 179
County of Tripoli 163, 166–7, 179,
264
courage 333, 334, 338
courtesy 60–1, 73, 333, 370, 499
courtly love 73, 85, 345, 453
Christians and pagans 464–5
fairy lovers 468–9
games of love 454–5
courtly virtues 339
Crécy 67, 103, 340, 353, 355, 356,
357, 491, 492, 494
Cressingham, Sir Hugh de 289
Cresson 94, 283, 292, 293, 294
crests 378
cross, taking the 57, 110, 120–1, 122,
186–7, 214, 216
crossbows 92, 493
crusades 8–11, 92, 93, 94, 100, 103,
105, 107, 390–1, 491
ancient wisdom 505
architecture 505

contact between East and West
504–5
Crusade of 1101 176–7
Crusade of 1212 310–11
Crusade of 1239–41 252–3
Crusade of 1366 274–5
Crusade of 1390 273
Crusade of 1443 276–7
Crusade of Nicopolis 445
crusader pilgrims 56–7
crusading leagues 268
crusading privileges 309, 245
effects 503–5
exploration 505
Great Schism 272, 273, 327
resonance 15
timeline of first crusades 112–13
timeline of later crusades 208–9
weapons and tactics of the enemy
184–5
Cuchullain 418, 419
Culhwch and Olwen 403, 405, 406,
408, 418, 421
Cuvelier 446
Cyprus 235, 252, 265, 286, 287, 303

Dafydd ap Gruffyd 336, 337
daggers 91
Daimbert of Pisa 166
Damascus 8, 47, 53, 167, 177, 192,
182
Nur ed-Din 196, 197
siege of Damascus 193, 194, 293
Damietta 9, 248–9, 256, 257, 258,
259, 293
Danishmends 46, 134–5, 136, 151,
166, 172
Dante 476, 477
Dares the Phrygian 392
David 24, 389, 390, 399, 417
David II of Scotland 353
David, King 42, 52, 165
debonnaireté 370
defenders of the faith 44–5
Delacroix, Eugène 441
Dicksee, Sir Frank Bernard 457
Dictys of Crete 392
Diego Laynez 432–3
diplomacy 44
discipline 94, 109
Dobrzyn, Order of 305, 323
Donatello 497
Dorylaeum 136–7, 138, 140, 150,
151, 172, 184, 185
Douglas, James, 2nd Earl 70
Douglas, Sir James 'Black Douglas' 67,

▼ King Arthur's homecoming.

▲ *Lancelot and Guinevere.*

104–5, 312, 352
Douglas, Sir William 373
Dracul, Vlad 279

Duarte of Portugal 377
dubbing 64–5
Dubois, Pierre 296
Duqaq, Sultan 145, 155
Durandel 13, 99, 425
Dürer, Albrecht 372

Edessa 8, 116, 123, 191
  capture by Imad ed-Din Zengi
  182–3, 186
Edgar the Atheling 145
Edmund Ironside 351
Edric 478, 479
Edward I 9, 79, 80, 81, 82, 85, 100,
  104, 174, 255, 261, 263, 267, 303,
  336–7, 367, 390, 402, 442,
  443, 493
  Ninth Crusade 264–5, 505
  tournaments 364, 368, 378
Edward II 63, 105, 352, 364, 367
Edward III 67, 68, 79, 85, 102, 103,
  105, 108, 109, 341, 352–3, 382,
  486, 492, 497
  Order of the Garter 11–12, 352,
  354–5, 381, 499
  tournaments 340, 352, 365, 367,
  368
Edward IV 84
Edward of Woodstock see Black
  Prince
Eglington, Earl of 501
Egypt 9, 138, 152–3, 155, 156, 157,
  161, 198, 199, 240, 251, 287
  Fifth Crusade 248–9, 293
  Mamluks 253, 255, 260, 266
  Seventh Crusade 256, 257, 258–9
Eighth Crusade 336
  Louis IX of France 9, 10, 260–1
Einhard 27, 28, 425
El Cid, Rodrigo Diaz de Vivar 13,
  84–5, 309, 432–3
Eleanor of Aquitaine 15, 96, 97, 187,
  190, 191, 192, 195, 262, 374, 393,
  411, 438, 453, 455
Eleanor of Castile 85, 337
Elizabeth I 419, 500–1
Emicho of Leisingen 125, 130
England 122, 131, 145, 195
Enrico Dandolo, Doge of Venice 238,
  239, 242, 243, 244
Ephesus 116

Equestrian Order of the Holy
  Sepulchre 285
equipment 31
  sieges 100–1
  symbolism 69
Erec and Enid 85, 408–9
ergotism 125,
Eugenius III, Pope 8, 186, 188, 194,
  291
Eugenius IV, Pope 276
European crusades 188, 206, 244,
  307
Eustace of Boulogne 434
Eustace the Monk 482, 485
Evesham 79, 336
Excalibur 13, 99, 403, 406, 421

Falkirk 336, 443
Fatimids 8, 46, 47, 53, 56, 152–3,
  155, 161, 198, 200
Ferdinand and Isabella 213, 307, 312
Ferdinand I 432, 433
Ferdinand III of Castile and Leon 301,
  312
feudalism 25, 38, 75, 76, 168–9, 170,
  498, 505
fiefdoms 25, 75, 76
Field of the Cloth of Gold 364, 500
Fifth Crusade 9, 237, 245, 248–9,
  258, 293
fighting on foot 95
Filarete (Antonio Di Pietro Averlino)
  495
First Crusade 8, 39, 51, 52, 53, 56,
  61, 79, 110, 115, 179, 195, 206,
  307, 361, 423, 434, 435
  Battle of Dorylaeum 136–7
  capture of Jerusalem 158–9, 160–1
  first-hand accounts 140
  march across Anatolia 140–1
  march on Jerusalem 152–3, 156–7
  motives of crusaders 122–3
  People's Crusade 124–5, 127,
  128–9, 134, 147, 164
  Princes' Crusade 127, 130–1,
  132–3
  routes of the First Crusade 164
  siege of Antioch 56, 144–5
  siege of Nicaea 134–5
  taking Antioch 146–7, 148–9
Fisher King 410, 413, 414, 416, 417
Fitzsimon, Sir Richard 356
Fitzwarin, Fulk 376, 471, 484–5
Flanders 124, 131
Floris and Blancheflour 398, 464–5
Fourth Crusade 9, 235, 237, 339,
  439, 440, 441
  Constantinople 240–1, 242–3, 503
  Innocent III 238, 239, 240, 250
  route of the Fourth crusade 212
France 57, 122, 123, 124, 125, 131,
  160, 189, 195, 256, 260, 261
Francis I of France 69, 201, 343, 349,
  364, 497, 500
Francis of Assisi 248
Franks 21, 22, 23, 24–5, 44–5
  cavalry 30–1, 360, 361
Frederick I Barbarossa, Holy Roman
  Emperor 8, 211, 216–17, 218–19,
  436–7
Frederick II, Holy Roman Emperor 9,
  10, 57, 83, 237, 248, 249, 250–1,

252, 298, 323
Frederick of Swabia 187, 188,
  189, 192
Frederick V of Swabia 437
Froissart, Jean 14, 66, 67, 70, 82,
  92, 98, 102, 109, 333, 339, 340,
  349, 356
Fulcher of Chartres 115, 118, 119,
  120, 132, 133, 136, 137, 140, 153,
  159, 163, 180, 182
Fulk of Jerusalem 182, 183, 191, 192

Gabriel of Montgomery 372–3
Galahad 13, 335, 342, 401, 403, 411,
  412, 413, 414, 416–17, 418, 471
Garter, Order of 11–12, 68, 70, 335,
  340, 354–5, 356, 367, 498, 499
  St George 381, 473
Gaston III of Foix-Béarn 82
Gattamelata (Erasmo di Narni) 497
Gawain 406, 407, 410, 415, 418–19,
  421, 457, 458
Genoa 131, 171, 177, 240, 273,
  503, 504
gentlemen 203, 499
Geoffrey of Malaterra 361, 370
Geoffrey of Monmouth 235, 363, 389,
  396–7, 403, 406, 407, 411, 415,
  418, 420, 421, 456
Geoffroi de Charny 59, 68, 73
Geraint 408, 409
Gerard of Rideford 94
Germany 56, 57, 124, 125
Gesta Francorum 8, 118–19, 120,
  136, 137, 140, 148, 154, 158, 159,
  160, 161
al-Ghafiqi, Abdul Rahman 21
Gheeraerts, Marcus, the Elder 499
Ghibellines 326, 327
Gideon 42, 390, 391
Giovanni da Capistrano 280, 281
Giovanni da Legnano 346
Giovanni delle Bande Nere 497
Giovanni di Tommaso Angelo 397
Glastonbury 337, 402
Gnosticism 315
Godfrey of Bouillon 8, 41, 127, 130,
  132–3, 134, 135, 136, 137, 145,
  151, 153, 154, 155, 157, 158,
  164, 384, 391, 434–5, 477
  Equestrian Order of the Holy
  Sepulchre 285
  Kingdom of Jerusalem 138–9, 160,
  161, 166, 168, 170, 172, 183
Golden Fleece, Order of 355, 359,
  380, 448, 449, 494
Gothic cavalry 23
Grafton, Richard 357
Grail 334, 401, 410, 411, 412, 413,
  414, 416–17, 419, 420, 421
Graindor de Douai 434
Great Schism 49, 272, 273, 327
Greece 360, 390, 392, 393, 394, 398
Greek fire 397
Green Shield of the White Lady,
  Order of 445
Gregory IX, Pope 237, 251, 252, 302,
  318, 323
Gregory of Tours 24
Gregory VII, Pope 50–1, 244, 476,
  477
Gregory VIII, Pope 8, 205, 214, 217,

300
Gregory X, Pope 263, 266
Grosmont, Henry 447
Guelphs 326
du Guesclin, Bertrand 14, 16, 66–7,
  106, 107, 340, 341, 351, 370,
  446–7
Guibert de Nogent 118, 119, 120–1,
  122, 124, 147, 152
Guidoricchio da Fogliano 496
Guinevere 337, 338, 368–9, 401,
  403, 406, 407, 408, 414–15, 416,
  419, 420, 453, 457
Guingamor 467
Guiscard, Robert 50, 51, 476–7
guns 491, 494–5
Guthrum 34, 35
Guy of Lusignan 165, 202, 203, 222,
  223, 231, 374, 468
Guy of Warwick 384, 471, 480–1

Hacker, Arthur 411
Haifa 177, 267
Halidon Hill 352, 353
Harcourt, Sir Godfrey 67
Harenc 145
Harran 173
Hastings 37, 90, 93, 95, 98, 107, 424
hawking 39, 60, 63, 82–3
Hawkwood, Sir John 497
Hector 15, 384, 391, 392, 397
Hédouville, Louis de 409
helmets 90, 93, 378
Hengest 418
Henry I 61, 371, 496
Henry I of Jerusalem 223
Henry II 14, 61, 96, 97, 100, 195,
  216, 262, 295, 303, 364, 371, 372,
  374, 375, 392, 402, 415, 438
Henry II of France 372–3
Henry III 79, 84, 264, 265, 336,
  372, 375
Henry III Holy Roman Emperor 433
Henry IV 70–1, 322, 323, 351,
  381, 450
Henry IV Holy Roman Emperor 50–1,
  133, 138, 476
Henry IV of France 364
Henry of Trastamara 447
Henry the Navigator 505
Henry V 101, 351, 450, 473, 492
Henry VI 450, 451
Henry VI Holy Roman Emperor 106,
  234, 235, 415, 437, 439, 441
Henry VIII 302, 303, 349, 364, 367,
  379, 485, 500
heraldry 63, 84, 382–3
heralds 340, 364–5, 383
heretics 206, 244, 280, 307, 324
Hereward the Wake 478–9, 485
Heselrig, William 442
hetairoi 22
Holland, Sir Thomas 102
Holy Lance 140, 143, 148, 149, 151,
  155, 160, 161
Holy Roman Empire 26–7
Holy Sepulchre 52, 53, 56, 138, 153,
  160–1, 165, 170, 205, 285
holy war 41, 42, 118–19
  Christianity 44–5
  jihad 179, 180, 184, 185, 196,
  201, 203, 312

Last Judgement 43, 121
  theories of just and holy wars 43
Homer 392, 393
Homildon Hill 70, 71
Honorius III, Pope 237, 248 250,
  299, 317
honour 342–3
Horns of Hattin 8, 55, 165, 175, 179,
  202–3, 204, 205, 214, 215, 224,
  225, 227, 228, 229, 248,
  292–3, 301
horses 13, 22, 23, 60, 61, 69, 90–1,
  337, 377, 379, 397, 428, 429,
  433, 496
Hue de Tabarie 68–9
Hugh III of Jerusalem 265
Hugh of Vermandois 127, 130, 132,
  137, 138, 152, 155, 176
Hugues de Payens 177, 290, 291, 471
humility 333, 338, 342
Humphrey III of Toron 69
Hundred Years War 95, 109, 335,
  343, 445, 450, 492, 494
  Bertrand du Guesclin 14, 16,
    66–7, 106, 107, 340, 341, 351,
    370, 446–7
  chevauchée 102–3
  mercenaries 496
  private quarrels 347
  Sir John Chandos 339, 340–1
Hungary 124, 130, 276
  Ottomans 280–1
Huns 27, 430, 431
hunting 39, 60, 63, 82
Hunyadi, Janos 276, 277, 280, 281
Huon of Bordeaux 428, 429
Hus, Jan 324
Hussites 280, 307, 324–5

Iconium 219
Iftikhar al-Daula 156–7, 161
Ilghazi 179, 180–1, 182, 185
Imad ed-Din Zengi 179, 196
infantry 95, 492
Innocent II, Pope 370, 371, 493
Innocent III, Pope 9, 11, 94, 235,
  237, 244–5, 298, 290, 291, 326–7
  Albigensian Crusade 314, 315,
    316, 317
  Baltic crusades 320, 321, 322
  crusader privileges and indulgences
    245
  crusading taxes 245
  Fifth Crusade 245, 248
  Fourth Crusade 238, 239, 240, 250
Innocent IV, Pope 263
Iran 47
Iraq 47
Isabella 105, 352
Isabella of Jerusalem 223, 231, 238
Islam 46–7
  Sufism 197, 203
Italy 122, 131
  papal crusades 326–7

Jacques de Longuyon 391
Jacques de Mailles 348
Jacques de Vitry 342
Jaffa 157, 165, 228, 229, 232–3, 250,
  260, 261
Jaffa 232–3
Jakelin de Mailly 283, 292

James I 501
Jay, Sir Brian de 289
Jean d'Arras 468
Jean de Villemur 351
Jean Le Bel 353
Jeremiah 41
Jerusalem 8, 9, 10, 41, 48, 68, 79, 97,
  105, 108, 109, 117, 164–5, 206,
  390, 391, 434–5
  Arab city 53
  Church of the Holy Sepulchre 52,
    53
  Dome of the Rock 53, 205, 250
  Fifth Crusade 248, 293
  First Crusade 132, 134, 136, 143,
    144, 150, 151, 152–3, 154, 155,
    156-7, 158–9, 160–1
  hospital of St John 284
  King of Jerusalem 168, 169, 170
  Last Judgement 43, 121
  pilgrimage 54, 56, 57, 125, 131
  recapture by Saladin 204–5
  Richard I the Lionheart 230–1,
    232, 233
  Roman city 52
  Sixth Crusade 237, 251, 252, 253
  Temple Mount 250, 251
  Urban II's speech 119, 120
Jews 52, 53, 158, 171
  persecution of 125, 130, 138, 187,
    221, 261
jihad 179, 180, 184, 185, 196, 201,
  203, 312
John 339, 375, 484–5, 496
John I of Portugal 359
John II of Alençon 79
John II of France 73, 106, 107, 353,
  355, 356, 357
John Lord of Joinville 256, 257
John of Bohemia 11, 12, 356
John of Gaunt 75, 85, 272–3, 351
John of Ibelin 251, 252, 367, 401
John XXII, Pope 371
jongleurs 344
Jonson, Ben 501
Josephus 390
Joshua 42, 157, 390, 391, 477
jousting 361, 362–3, 370, 373, 379
  Joust of St Inglevert 70, 322, 363,
    444–5
Joyeuse 99
Judaism 390–1
Judas Maccabeus 41, 42, 52, 344,
  384, 390–1, 477
Julius Caesar 384, 391, 396–7
Justinian I 23

al-Kamil, Sultan 9, 248, 249, 250,
  258, 293
Kay 406–7, 410, 411, 418, 421
Keats, John 467
Kerbogha, Sultan of Mosul 143, 146,
  147, 148–9, 150, 151, 153, 155
Khalil, Sultan 266, 267
Khwarismians 9, 253, 255
Kilij Arslan 134–5, 136, 137, 155,
  176 182
Kilij Arslan II 190, 197
King Peter's Crusade 268–9, 270–1
Kingdom of Heaven 489
Kingdom of Jerusalem 9, 11, 55, 116,
  123, 163, 165, 166, 179, 195, 200,

201, 202, 203, 234, 235, 293
  Godfrey of Bouillon 138–9, 160,
    161, 166, 168, 170, 172,
    183, 269
  Saladin 8, 200, 201, 202, 203
  Sixth Crusade 252–3
Kings' Crusade 187
kiss of peace 350, 351
knighting 63, 64–5
  after bravery 66–7
  before battle 66, 67
  retreat and preparation 68
knights 11–13, 16, 59, 121,
  122–3, 328
  decline of knighthood 486, 488–9,
    491, 493
  domestic life 75, 76–7
  ideal knight 501
  knights errant 458–9, 460–1
  knights of the shire 78–9
  protectors of the weak 79, 471
  qualities 14, 73, 333, 334–5,
    338–9
  role in government 78–9
  sale of knighthoods 39
  service 13–14
  skills 73
  social origins 38–9, 382
  timeline of legendary knights
    386–7
Knights Hospitaller 10–11, 86–7, 99,
  109, 167, 169, 192, 197, 203, 227,
  228, 252, 253, 261, 264, 266,
  267, 276, 283, 295, 297, 300,
  354, 380
  Battle of Arsuf 229
  crusading leagues 268
  foundation 284–5
  King Peter's Crusade 269, 270
  Krak des Chevaliers 174–5, 505
  Malta 11, 288, 289
  Rhodes 11, 286–7, 296
Knights of Christ 299, 301
Knights of Our Lady of Mountjoie
  301
Knights of St Lazarus 11, 283, 304
Knights of St Thomas Acon 11, 283,
  302–3
Knights Templar 10–11, 79, 86–7, 99,
  109, 165, 169, 177, 192, 201, 203,
  223, 227, 228, 253, 256, 267,
  283, 300, 301, 342, 363, 380,
  375, 417, 471
  America 296, 297
  Ascalon 292
  banking 295
  castles 294–5, 505
  Cathars 319
  churches 295
  downfall 286, 296–7
  foundation 290–1
  Horns of Hattin 292–3
  al-Mansourah 292
  negotiation and diplomacy 293
  rivalry with Hospitallers 293
  siege of Acre 293
Kosovo, Second Battle of 277
Krak des Chevaliers 81, 163, 167,
  173, 174–5, 248, 264, 505
Kurds 199

La Forbie 253, 255, 258, 260
de La Sale, Antoine 454
ladies 60, 61, 62, 73
  games of love 454–5
  service 456–7
  tournaments 368–9
Lalaing, Jacques de 334, 448–9, 494
Lancelot 14, 69, 72, 338, 398, 401,
  403, 407, 413, 414–15, 416, 417,
  418, 419, 453, 457
lances 13, 31, 90
Laneham, Robert 419
Langton, Stephen 374
Lanval 466–7
largesse 73, 338–9, 357, 370
Last Judgement 43, 121
'Latins' and 'Greeks' 44, 48–9, 241
Le Fevre, Jean 494
Lee, Henry 501
Leo IX, Pope 477
Leo X, Pope 497
Leopold of Austria 106, 225, 234,
  439
Lepanto 9–10, 502, 503
Leybourne, Sir Roger 372
Liebniz, Gottfried 72
Limoges 108–9
Lindsay, Sir David 347
lists 364, 365, 372, 377
Lithuania 323
Livonia 320, 321
Livonian Brothers of the Sword 305,
  321
Llewellyn ap Gruffyd 336
Llull, Ramon 59, 63, 72, 76, 77, 296,
  334, 338
Lombards 26, 27, 28
longbows 92, 491, 492–3
Longespee, Sir William 378
Longoville, Richard 289
Lothair I 25
Lothair II of Germany 370
Louis of Bourbon 444
Louis IX of France 206, 255, 258,
  262–3, 264, 266, 318, 319, 336
  Eighth Crusade 9, 10, 260–1
  Seventh Crusade 256–7, 258–9
Louis of Bourbon 273
Louis the German 32
Louis the Pious 32, 64, 425, 426, 427
Louis VII of France 8, 96, 186,
  187, 188, 189, 190–1, 192, 193,
  194, 195
Louis XI of France 351
loyalty 333, 334, 338, 350
luxuries 170

▼ *Medieval heraldic devices.*

▲ *The keep of Saladin's castle.*

Maarat al-Numan 147, 152, 155
Mabinogion 406, 409
Macedonian cavalry 14, 22
maces 91
Madoc ap Llewellyn 100
Magna Carta 375
Magyars, 32, 33, 45, 78
Mahdia 272, 273
Malory, Sir Thomas 72, 338, 369, 403, 406, 412, 416, 418, 419, 421
Malta 11, 284, 288, 289
Mamluks 253, 255, 260, 265, 266, 269, 503
Manny, Sir Walter 343
manors 75, 76–7, 80–1
al-Mansourah 258–9, 260, 292
Manuel I Comnenus 188, 189, 190, 191, 194, 195, 196, 199, 240
Manzikert 47, 48, 16
Margaret of Anjou 451
Margat 175, 266
Marguerite of Flanders 85
Marie de Champagne 14, 411, 415, 453, 455
Marie de France 405, 466, 467
Marienburg 299, 323
Markward of Anweiler 237, 244, 326–7
Marmion, Sir William 461
marriages 84–5
Marshal, Sir William 83, 334, 367, 374–5, 384, 498–9
Martini, Simone 496
Master James of St Georges 80, 81
Maugis 428, 429
Maximilian I 379
Mehmed II the Conqueror 277, 278–9, 280, 281, 286, 287
mêlées 361, 362, 363, 370, 372, 376, 377, 379
Melisende of Jerusalem 182–3, 191, 192
Melusine 468–9
mercenaries 496–7
Mercers, Worshipful Company of 303
Merlin 403, 406, 416
mesure 338, 339
Meyerbeer, Giacomo 482
Michelangelo 495
military orders 10–11, 86–7, 169, 283
mining castle walls 101, 350, 351
minnesänger 344
minstrels 83, 344, 419, 424
Model Parliament 79
de Molay, Jacques 291, 293, 296–7

Mongols 260, 262–3, 265, 266, 268
Montagu, Sir William 372
Montesa, Order of 297, 301
Montfort 298
de Montfort, John 447
de Montfort, Simon 79, 336, 372
Montgisard 201
Montreal 168–9, 175, 248
Montségur 318, 319
Moors 206, 503
    Reconquista 212–13, 300, 301, 308–9, 311, 312–13
Mordred 402, 403, 406, 415, 418, 419, 420–1
de Morville, Sir Hugh 415
Mortimer, Roger 352, 367
Mount Badon 402
Muhammad 46, 47, 52, 53
de Munteny, Sir Arnulf 372
Muret 317
music 61, 63, 83
Muslim empires 46–7, 48
Muslim forces 28–9, 31, 94, 97, 98, 99, 425, 426–7, 432, 433, 437, 495
Muslim world 79, 80, 85, 92, 96, 423
al-Musta'in II 432
al-Mu'tamin 432

Navas de Tolosa, Las 94, 244, 300, 310–11, 317
Nazareth 9, 250, 251
Nennius 402
Neville, Sir William 350
Nibelungenlied 430–1
Nicaea 46, 116, 128, 129
    siege 134–5, 136, 138, 154, 172
Nicopolis 274, 275
Nine Worthies 42, 391, 392, 396, 397
Ninth Crusade 9, 255, 261, 264–5, 336, 505
Normans 12, 23, 36–7, 45, 50, 90, 93, 95, 98,116, 130–1, 136, 150, 185
    castle-building 100
Notker of St Gall 29
Nur ed-Din 179, 190, 191, 193, 195, 196–7, 198–9, 200, 201, 293

Odo of Bayeux 131
Ogier the Dane 428
Old Testament 41, 42
Ordonez, Count 432
Oriflamme 73
Orlando 462–3, 464
Orpheus and Eurydice 398–9
Orthodox Church 141, 169, 240
Ostrogoths 29, 431
Otranto 287
Otterburn 70
Otto I of the Germans 33, 436
Otto IV Holy Roman Emperor 89, 95, 99
Otto von Friesing 436
Ottomans 255, 273, 274–5, 502, 503
    attack on Malta 11, 289
    attack on Rhodes 11, 287, 288–9
    Belgrade 280–1
    Mehmed II 277, 278–9, 280, 281, 286, 287
Oultrejordain 168, 248
Our Lady of Bethlehem, Order of 305

outlaws 471, 478–9, 482–3, 484–5
Outremer 163, 166–7, 194, 195, 237, 252, 255, 264, 265, 266–7, 299, 504
    Baybars 260–1
    government 168–9
    life in the crusader states 170–1
Ovid 398, 411
Owain Glyndwr 100

pagans 188, 206, 237, 244, 298, 299, 307, 320–1, 503
pageantry 366–7, 498–9
pages 16, 60–1
paladins 344, 345, 423, 426
Palestine 8, 9, 47, 164–5
Palomides 359, 369
papacy 50–1, 272, 371
    authority to call wars 503
    crusades in Italy 326–7
    papal indulgences 51, 115, 121, 245
Paris 263
Paris, Gaston 345
Parisot, Jean 289
Parthian cavalry 14, 23
Partonope and Melior 469
pas d'armes 363, 404, 408, 409
Paschal I, Pope 25
Paschal II, Pope 10, 176, 284, 285
Paschal III, Pope 437
Patriarch of Jerusalem 169
Paulicians 315
Peace of God 121, 122
Pedro of Castile 447
Peele, George 336
Pelagius 9, 10, 237, 248, 249, 250, 258, 293
penance 55
People's Crusade 124–5, 127, 128–9, 134, 147, 164
Pépin 24–5
Pépin III 24
Pépin the Short 26
Perceval 14, 334, 335, 342, 410–11, 412–13, 416, 417
Percy, Sir Henry 'Hotspur' 70–1, 450
Peter Bartholomew 148, 149, 160
Peter Desiderius 391
Peter I of Cyprus 268–9, 270–1
Peter II of Aragon 368
Peter III of Aragon 497
Peter the Hermit 124–5, 127, 128, 129, 145, 157, 172
Petrarch 269
Philip I of France 118, 130, 138, 173
Philip II of France 8, 9, 97, 211, 216, 220, 221, 222, 223, 224, 225, 226, 234, 238, 247, 302, 437, 438
Philip II of Spain 372
Philip IV of France 89, 95, 99, 296–7, 496
Philip of Alsace 376
Philip of Flanders 15, 411
Philip of Ibelin 266, 271
Philip the Bold 85
Philip the Good 355, 359, 363, 364, 367, 380
Philippa of Hainault 353, 368
Pied Piper of Hamelin 247
Pierre d'Alvernhe 345
pilgrimage 52, 53, 54–5, 56–7, 79,

97, 165, 195
    German pilgrimage of 1064 56, 57
pillaging 102–3
Pippo Spano 106, 107
Poitiers 95, 99, 103, 106, 338, 340, 353, 356, 447
Portugal 188, 297, 300, 301
Prester John 186, 187, 505
Princes' Crusade 127, 130–1, 132–3
Principality of Antioch 116, 123, 155, 163, 166, 167, 180, 196
Protestantism 498, 501, 503
Prussian Cavaliers of Christ 305
Prussian crusades 299, 322–3
Publius Papinius Statius 393

Qalawun, Sultan 266, 267
Que, Thomas 449
quintain 60

Radulph of Caen 44, 152, 155, 172, 173, 185
Radwan 145, 150
Raimbaut de Vaqeiras 339, 440–1
Ramiro of Monzon 432
Ramón Berenguer II 432
ransoms 106
Raphael 498
Raymond du Puy 192, 285
Raymond IV of Toulouse 115, 127, 131, 133, 135, 136, 137, 140, 144, 145, 152, 153, 155, 157, 158, 160–1, 164, 166–7, 176, 187, 192
Raymond of Antioch 186, 190, 191, 194, 196
Raymond of Tripoli 202, 203, 292–3
Raymond VI of Toulouse 314, 316, 317
Reconquista 212–13, 300–1, 308–9, 311, 312–13, 505
Reformation 503
relics 55, 263
Remigius of Reims 24
Remon of Savoy 433
Renaissance 498, 499, 504, 505
Renart, Jean 454
Renaud of Montauban 13, 337, 428–9
René d'Anjou 364, 404
Reynald of Châtillon 168–9, 175, 197, 202, 203, 227
Rhineland 125, 138
Rhodes 11, 276, 284, 286–7, 296
Richard Earl of Cornwall 252–3
Richard I of Normandy 36
Richard I the Lionheart 9, 68, 96–7, 211, 220–1, 222, 223, 224, 225, 235, 238, 239, 302, 336, 339, 342, 355, 375, 383, 384, 390, 415, 437, 438–9, 467, 505
    Battle of Arsuf 229
    death 234
    Jerusalem 230–1, 232, 233
    march to Jaffa 228
    massacre at Acre 226–7
    and Saladin 230, 232, 233
    tournaments 370, 371, 438
Richard II 70, 75, 341, 351, 381, 498
Richard II of Normandy 36, 37, 38
Richard III 84
Richard le Pèlerin 434
Richard of Devizes 97
Rio Salado 312–13